The Population Debate

The Development of Conflicting Theories up to 1900

E. P. Hutchinson
University of Pennsylvania

HOUGHTON MIFFLIN COMPANY · BOSTON
New York · Atlanta · Geneva, Ill. · Dallas · Palo Alto

Under the editorship of
Ernest Q. Campbell

In memory of
Louise Forbes Hutchinson

Population study or demography in its present development is strongly oriented toward the present rather than the past, toward observation and empirical data rather than theory; but I believe that today's student of population can profit from better acquaintance with his predecessors, the problems of their day as they saw them, and the conclusions to which they came. In some fundamental respects today's national and world problems of population are indeed very different from those of past centuries; but certain elemental aspects of man's numbers in relation to his resources persist or recur over time, and an historical viewpoint can give a broader perspective of our contemporary concerns.

Furthermore, the roots of modern population thought run deep into the past. Concern with population numbers is as old as human history and, as Marshall said, the subject has attracted the attention of thoughtful men in all ages of the world. The earlier writers are our intellectual ancestors, and without indulging in ancestor worship we can credit them with laying the foundations on which modern population theory is built. As can be shown more fully later, they were an exceedingly varied group whose minds converged on the subject of population from many different starting points, and they differed widely in background and ability; but if they had a common quality it was that they were thoughtful men with concern for the problems of their day. If some of them appear to disadvantage from the perspective of our modern knowledge, it may be because they lacked sound information rather than because of any inferiority of their mental endowment. It is true that some of them had ideas to promote or purposes to serve, quite capable of grasping at any plausible argument; and the scarcity of restraining fact left them free to produce conjectures and theories that have only curiosity value today. The majority, however, had very good minds indeed, and the scarcity of solid information stimulated them to think the harder, so that in intellectual quality their writings do not suffer by comparison with later works.

A problem in tracing the development of population thought is that the early writers were both numerous and prolific, and their writings seem almost innumerable. There is the remark quoted but very properly disregarded by E. A. J. Johnson that no one under sixty years of age should presume to write on the history of economic thought. The same might be said of population thought, which runs throughout economic literature and elsewhere. Mackenroth, for example, author of the principal modern German work on population theory, stated frankly that he does not pretend to have read everything, for to do so would be impossible. It would also be unprofitable, for in population literature as well as in the economic world there is something the classical economists discovered and named, a point of diminishing returns beyond which additional work brings less and less reward.

In the present volume I have chosen to deal with only selected aspects of the pre-twentieth-century population literature. What is treated here may be called formal population theory, in contrast to the broader range of population thought in general. That is to say, the treatment is of the explicit theories and implicit but evident assumptions about population, not of the more general question of what views prevailed throughout a given society and period. And although official views and government policies on population are important elements in the total body of population thought, they are not included except as reflected in the private writings of persons in official positions. In other words, only the published literature is covered here, not documentary and archival sources.

Within the body of more or less formal population theory, treatment is further limited to a central theoretical development, the theories concerning the socio-economic consequences of a large and growing number of people. Theories about the influence of stationary, declining, or scanty numbers are not included, nor are theories about the influence upon population of socio-economic and other factors. What remains, however, is still by far the most considerable body of organized population theory, which was central to the long-continued debate over the significance of population numbers.

A choice also had to be made, with some reluctance, between several alternative approaches. A theory or idea can be seen in any of several different contexts, each of which adds another dimension to our understanding of the theory and its development. We can look upon a particular contribution as the product of its author, and seek to understand it in relation to the work of which it is a part, the author's total body of writings, and his personal characteristics and life experience. Or the contribution can be related to its contemporary setting of time and place. And finally, it can be viewed as an element in a stream of continuing intellectual development. It is quite true, as Oncken and probably many others have said, that to understand a social theory one needs to know the conditions of the time and the situation of the author. Nevertheless, since only one can be followed, it is the third, the longitudinal approach, that has been chosen here, to follow the development of certain ideas and the progressing analysis of the socio-economic consequences of population size and growth. But to provide some suggestion of the other dimensions, brief biographical sketches of the principal authors are assembled in the appendix, some note is made of authors' views outside the range of those directly cited, two periods are dealt with in some additional detail (eighteenth-century Sweden, nineteenth-century United States), and there are numerous if only brief references to contemporary concerns and prevailing ideas. On the latter point, as Eversley has said, population studies afford a wealth of material for the student of ideas; but it is equally true that social, economic, and intellectual history give a wealth of information to the student of population seeking to understand the population literature of another period.

Next, a word about the liberal use of quotations. It seemed best to let each author speak for himself, where a reasonably concise statement could be found or where it was important to give the author's exact words, for many expressed themselves in forceful and effective prose. Especially in the older writings, the original text carries some of the flavor of the times and the earnestness of the writer. But in every period there were those who had their own distinctive styles of writing, such as Marshall, Cannan, Steuart, and many others, and this individuality of expression is worth retaining.

Also, I hope the quotations will give the reader more feeling of direct contact with the original writers; and this seems to me important. As Robbins said in explanation of his own liberal use of quotations in a work on Torrens, with the incisive sort of remark for which he had a notable talent, "it is a vice of books about books that the original author tends to get lost in the commentary." Quotations are some protection against this vice; and they also serve a good purpose if they persuade readers to go to the original works and see for themselves. That can be rewarding. Occasional quotations are only a very small sample of a whole work and cannot do justice to the wealth of ideas that many contain. And apart from the additional ideas that may be found, there is an added scholarly reading pleasure to be derived from the varied styles of writing, such as the vigor and inventiveness of Elizabethan prose, the formality and explicitness of a German text, the quaintness of style from another century, or the personal manner of writing with which Steuart and others seem to speak directly to the reader. In addition to their writings, a number of the writers themselves merit closer acquaintance. Making up a highly varied group in background and experience, some were colorful personalities, others were distinguished in ability and accomplishment; and knowledge of their lives adds to our appreciation of their thoughts on population. They include, for example, Petty, the self-made man and "genius of all trades," de Saxe, whose life reads more like romantic fiction than biography,

Graunt, who in spite of few advantages in early life discovered a new world of knowledge and explored it with the eager curiosity of a pioneer, Winkelblech and Dumont, whose personal tragedies centered about their writings, and many others, each in his own way worth knowing.

There are also perhaps small but nevertheless satisfying discoveries and rewards to be found by the student who goes exploring by himself in the earlier population literature. For example, there is the other and less known side of Malthus, the political economist, which compares very favorably with the more famous Malthus, the author of the *Essay*. Or one can discover for himself that in population thought Steuart went much further than his fellow Scotsman and contemporary by whom he was completely eclipsed. Still other discoveries can be made, of works and authors that have been overlooked, of ideas that have been forgotten, of writers from another century whose thoughts are still meaningful.

To return to the quotations, I would encourage readers to give them attention, not to skip them as the hurried reader often does. To encourage attention to the quotations, they are not regularly summarized in the text that follows them, although comment is often added. Attention should also be called to the footnotes, which are sometimes used to supply supplementary material that falls outside the direct line of thought of the text.

Further on the subject of footnotes: in the case of works available in more than one edition, bibliographical references are to the first edition unless otherwise stated. If another edition has been used, that is regularly noted in the first reference to the work. If a work has appeared in a number of editions, references are often given not only by page but also by chapter and section for convenience in locating the passage in other editions.

Another matter to be mentioned here is that this account of certain theories does not go beyond the end of the nineteenth century. Reasons for this are given at some length in the first paragraphs of the final chapter. To bring the account up to the present would have been quite another undertaking; and moreover, it has been done perhaps as well as can be done in the United Nations report, *Determinants and Consequences of Population Trends*. It can be noted also that the twentieth-century developments that have most drastically altered the world population situation are technological changes affecting the determinants rather than the consequences of population trends; and the population theories dealt with here concern only the consequences. Or, to use Malthusian terms instead of those of the United Nations report, it is the population checks of disease and perhaps famine that have been notably reduced by modern advances. In this connection it can be pointed out that some of the Malthusian writers, as described later, were confident that if some checks are weakened or eliminated in the progress of society, other checks arise, and if modern technology has suppressed some checks, it seems to be creating numerous others, in the form of "the pill" and other efficient contraceptive devices, "the bomb," radioactive fallout, air pollution, etc. But while these potential checks may be determinants of future trends, they do not alter the socio-economic consequences of the trends. The consequences depend upon the nature of the social and economic system, which is slow to change in its fundamentals; and the theories dealt with in the following chapters, to repeat, are about the consequences of population size and growth.

In addition to ending at the twentieth century, this account stops with the material that has been collected to date. With interruptions, collection has gone on since 1940 and additional material is still being discovered; but my patient publishers have gently supported my own growing conviction that not enough is to be gained by delaying publication longer. Although some national literatures, especially the Italian, are much less fully covered than others, and doubtless some works have not been discovered, the main outlines of the theoretical development should be evident from the present material.

Thanks are due for help from many sources. Generous support from the John Simon Guggenheim Memorial Foundation is gratefully acknowledged. A fellowship grant from the Foundation in 1941–1942 gave opportunity for concentrated work on the history of population theories, and a second fellowship in 1956–1957 permitted special study of Swedish materials and the completion of portions of the manuscript.

I also wish to acknowledge my indebtedness to a number of libraries for generously giving access to their collections and for the uniform helpfulness of their staffs. These include the Library of Congress, the Swedish Royal Library (Kungliga Biblioteket), the Library of the British Museum, the libraries of the University of Pennsylvania and the University of California, Harvard University libraries (Widener, Houghton, Baker Memorial, and the Law School Library), the New York Public Library, and others.

I am also indebted to the many graduate students who took my course on population theory over the years, for classroom discussion has been helpful in exploring many topics and bringing out new aspects of the material. Dow M. Drukker, student and faithful assistant, was most helpful with the bibliographical work and the biographical notes. A large debt of gratitude is owed to the late Edwin B. Wilson of Harvard University who gave the original stimulus to this project and who for the nearly forty years I knew him was an unfailing source of sound advice and inspiration. And especially deeply felt is the obligation to my late wife, to whom this volume is dedicated, who through all the years of our marriage provided the help and encouragement and created the home environment that made this work a pleasure and the years spent on it seem short.

E. P. H.

Contents

1 · Introduction: A Population Dilemma   1

  1 · Fluctuation in Population Thought   1
  2 · Influences Affecting Population Thought   3
  3 · Sources and Evidence   5
  4 · A Dilemma of Population Theory   6

2 · Early Population Thought   8

  1 · Classical Period   8
  2 · Early Modern Period   14
  3 · Tudor England   20
  4 · Summary: Population Thought before 1600   26

*3 · The Rise of Population Theory in the Seventeenth
Century*   28

  1 · France   28
  2 · Central Europe   30
  3 · England before the Restoration   33
  4 · England after the Restoration   45
  5 · Population Theory at the End of the Seventeenth Century   66

*4 · Swedish Population Theory in the Eighteenth
Century*   69

  1 · The Dominant Opinion on Population   69
  2 · Some Variations on the Dominant Theme   75
  3 · Some Specific Effects of Population Size   80
  4 · Some Optimistic Assumptions   86
  5 · Traces of Pessimistic Thought   89
  6 · Final Comment   92

5 · Summary of the Optimistic Position before 1800   94

  1 · The Central Theme   94
  2 · Some Optimistic Assumptions   98

3 · Some Qualifications   103
4 · A New Element in Population Thought   106
5 · Summary   108

6 · *The Development of Pessimistic Doctrine before Malthus*   110

1 · The Power of Increase   111
2 · The Limitation of Numbers by the Means of Subsistence   115
3 · The Tendency of Population to Approach the Subsistence
    Limit   117
4 · The Concept of Checks on Population Growth   122
5 · The Concept of Overpopulation and its Consequences   125
6 · Ideas about Personal Responsibility and Restraint   132
7 · Synthesis: The Pessimistic Train of Thought   136

7 · *The Theory of Population and Distribution before 1800*   140

1 · Population and the Wage Level   140
2 · Rent and Prices   145
3 · Some Interrelations   148
4 · Summary   151

8 · *Production Theory and the Malthusian Controversy*   153

1 · The Malthusian Theory   154
2 · The Principle of Diminishing Returns   158
3 · 1815–1819: Gray to James Mill   164
4 · 1820–1829: Godwin to Say   166
5 · 1830–1839: Sadler to Eisdell   176
6 · 1840–1849: List to Roscher   183
7 · Later Theories: Bastiat to Marshall   187
8 · Summary and Comment   198

9 · *Population and Distribution in Classical Economics*   203

1 · Rent   204
2 · Prices   214

3 · Profits   219
4 · Wages   222
5 · Summary: John Stuart Mill   242
6 · Later Theories of Distribution   245
7 · Summary: Population and Distribution   252
8 · Summary: Population and the Standard of Living   255

10 · *Population Theory in Nineteenth-Century American Political Economy*   258

   1 · The First Decades: Baldwin, Raymond, Everett, Cardozo, and Others   260
   2 · 1830–1839   283
   3 · 1840–1849   292
   4 · 1850–1869   294
   5 · 1870 and Later   302
   6 · Some Features of American Population Theory   313

11 · *Other Population Theories of the Nineteenth Century: General Theories*   320

   1 · The First Two Decades   321
   2 · 1820–1829: Godwin, Ravenstone, and Others   337
   3 · 1830–1839: Sadler to Moreton   342
   4 · 1840–1849: Alison, Doubleday, and Others   347
   5 · 1850–1859   351
   6 · Later Theories of Population   356
   7 · Comment   362

12 · *Other Population Theories of the Nineteenth Century: Some Common Themes*   365

   1 · Another Viewpoint   365
   2 · Factors Affecting Fertility and Population Size   370
   3 · Explanations of the Status Differential   373
   4 · Progress and Population   374
   5 · Comment   378

13 · A Partial Solution   380

1 · One Further Step   381
2 · An Early Formulation of the Optimum Concept   385
3 · Later Development of the Concept   387
4 · The Place of the Concept   391

14 · In Retrospect: Foundations of Twentieth-Century Population Theory   394

1 · The Economic Question of Production   395
2 · The Economic Question of Distribution   398
3 · The Habits of the People   401
4 · Final Appraisal   404

Biographical Notes   409
Author Index   456
Subject Index   461

1
Introduction:
A Population Dilemma

People are the material out of which nations and societies are made, and concern over the number of people runs through history, from the early and undifferentiated writings of ancient times to the more elaborate and specialized formulations found in political economy, modern economics, and sociology. In the course of time, with shifting emphasis and point of view, a very wide range of roles has been attributed to population numbers and their change. At one extreme, a large and growing population has been looked upon as the only solid foundation of national strength and wealth, a necessary condition or even a cause of technological progress, the impelling force that has raised man from his primitive state and pushed him forward on the road to civilization. An equally considerable body of theory and speculation, however, asserts that the multiplication of mankind has had the contrary effect of forcing whole nations down into poverty and misery, generating crime and vice of all descriptions, and letting loose the scourges of war, famine, and disease. In the chapters that follow these two opposite conceptions are traced through the history of thought, and the development of theory and analysis of the significance of number of people is described.

1 · Fluctuation in Population Thought

Writers on the subject seem always to have had a population problem to worry about, but quite different problems have been seen by different writers and at different times. At times the problem has been thought to be too few people, at others, too many; and population growth has been regarded alternately as highly desirable or as harmful to the general welfare. Recent decades illustrate the variability of opinion about population numbers. During the 1920's there was a revival of Malthusian fears of overpopulation. The continuing growth of world population was regarded as cause for concern, and several books appearing at that time pointed out the eventual if not immediate danger of an overcrowded world.[1] Less than a decade later, however, a reversal of opinion began to appear. Because of local conditions fear of depopulation had long been prevalent in France, but now the same fear appeared in Germany and in other countries. Quite abruptly the problem of population numbers was redefined[2] from one of overpopulation to the opposite extreme of depopulation and race suicide.

The fluctuations in population views did not end there. A second postwar period, during which birth rates remained far above the lows of the preceding decade, brought new assertions that the population problem for the world as a whole and for the long run is too many rather than too few people. Concern over the depletion of resources and a continued increase in population led to a return of the older Malthusian view of the problem of population numbers.[3]

It is not a question here whether one or the other direction of population thought is more sound, for both views contain elements of truth and both are subject to criticism. Commenting on the fears of depopulation current in the 1930's, a well-known student of population remarked, "The whole history of population thought shows that populations adjust to conditions more promptly than do writers on population."[4] Populations do indeed adjust to changing conditions, but looking back, one might suspect that here was a too-rapid revision of opinion to fit what proved to be temporary fluctuations of fertility and population growth rates. Without trying to predict the future course of Western population or world population, it is worth noting that from an historical point of view reversals of opinion such as those recently observed are neither unique nor even unusual. Similar changes of opinion, although usually less abrupt, have occurred many times before; and the increase of numbers has been regarded with alternate alarm and approval.

In England, for example, several complete cycles of opinion on population can be traced. The losses suffered during the Black Death of the fourteenth century and succeeding epidemics were felt for some time afterward, and the shortage of people and laborers was recognized. Again in the sixteenth century there were apprehensions of a decline in numbers.

[1] E. M. East, *Mankind at the Crossroads,* New York: Scribners, 1923; E. A. Ross, *Standing Room Only,* New York: Century, 1927; G. H. Knibbs, *The Shadow of the World's Future,* London: Benn, 1928.

[2] Friedrich Burgdörfer, *Volk ohne Jugend,* Berlin: Vowinckel, 1932; Enid Charles, *The Twilight of Parenthood,* London: Watts, 1934; Gunnar and Alva Myrdal, *Kris i befolkningsfrågan,* Stockholm: Bonniers, 1934.

[3] William Vogt, *Road to Survival,* New York: Sloane, 1948; Fairfield Osborn, *Our Plundered Planet,* Boston: Littie, Brown, 1948; Fairfield Osborn, *The Limits of the Earth,* Boston: Little, Brown, 1953; J. C. Hertzler, *The Crisis in World Population,* Lincoln, Neb.: University of Nebraska Press, 1956.

[4] Norman E. Himes, *Medical History of Contraception,* Baltimore: Williams and Wilkins, 1936, p. 417.

Roscher mentions a "great dread of depopulation under the first two Tudors," but adds, "On the other hand, a great dread of overpopulation prevailed among English political economists at the end of the sixteenth and the beginning of the seventeenth century."[5] Marshall also points out

> . . . a regular ebb and flow of the opinion that the State should encourage the growth of numbers. It was in full flow in England under the first two Tudors, but in the course of the sixteenth century it slackened and turned. . . .[6]

Many writers of the Elizabethan period expressed the view that population numbers tended to grow too large;[7] and the belief that England was overpopulated is thought to have stimulated the colonizing activity of the time, including the establishment of the settlements in North America.[8] Later this position was reversed under the influence of the mercantilist economic theories which, if not as centrally concerned with population as is generally believed, nevertheless favored a large and growing population. About a century later, toward the end of the eighteenth century, the weight of opinion as represented by Malthus and his predecessors again began to turn and to focus on the dangers of overpopulation. Movements in the prevailing views on the subject of population numbers, although of a somewhat different character, are shown by Spengler[9] to have occurred in France, and similar changes of opinion probably could be demonstrated for other countries as well.

2 · Influences Affecting Population Thought

Whether a larger or a smaller population is regarded as desirable at a given time appears to depend quite as much upon the prevailing point of view and the social and political problems of the day as it does upon the known or assumed trend of population. It follows that the reversals of opinion that have occurred from time to time can be due to altered condi-

[5] Wilhelm Roscher, *Principles of Political Economy,* translated by J. J. Lalor from the 13th edition (1877) of *System der Volkswirtschaft* (1854), Chicago: Callaghan, 1922, footnote to section 254, p. 343.

[6] Alfred Marshall, *Principles of Economics,* 2nd ed. London: Macmillan, 1891, Book IV, Ch. 4, section 1, p. 230.

[7] For an account of population thought in the Elizabethan period, see Chapter 2, section 3, below.

[8] See, for example, Charles E. Stangeland, *Pre-Malthusian Doctrines of Population,* New York: Columbia University Press, 1904, pp. 110–117; and George L. Beer, *Origins of the British Colonial System, 1578–1660,* New York: Macmillan, 1908, Ch. 2. For doubts about Beer's conclusions, see Mildred Campbell, "Of people either too few or too many," pp. 169–201 in *Conflict in Stuart England. Essays in honour of Wallace Notestein,* edited by William Aiken and Basil Henning, London: Cape, 1960.

[9] J. J. Spengler, *France Faces Depopulation,* Durham, N.C.: Duke University Press, 1938.

tions and the emphasizing of other considerations rather than to changes in the trend of population numbers. The Malthusian theory, for example, would have been just as valid or invalid a century before its actual formulation, but students of the subject have shown it was by no means accidental that his theory appeared and attracted attention when it did. The theory was in fact a natural development of the contemporary intellectual currents,[10] and presented a point of view that is explainable in terms of the economic and social realities of the time. In general, some socio-economic and political situations predispose opinion in favor of population growth, while others exert the opposite influence. A declining standard of living or widespread unemployment quite naturally suggests that there is a surplus of people to be provided for or of workers to be employed. An aggressive or suspicious nation, on the other hand, might well take the opposite point of view and encourage the increase of its people, irrespective of the immediate economic situation. Similarly, nationalist philosophies, whether economic or political, tend to favor population growth, while the restriction of numbers is associated more with societies in which the welfare of the individual takes precedence.

Over time there may also be changes in the general orientation of social thought, causing shifts in the prevailing opinions on questions of population numbers. Ethical or religious views have sometimes dominated social thought. At other times political and economic considerations have held sway. As Cannan said, for example,

> The ancient Greek philosophers regarded population from a point of view which was quite different from that of the modern economist. They were interested in what are called political rather than economic questions, and their politics were the politics of small city states.[11]

Later, during the Middle Ages in Europe, views on population matters were largely based on religious or theological premises. More recently the orientation has been predominantly economic, but with a growing intermixture of social or humanitarian considerations.

There is of course no necessary uniformity of thought within a given environmental or ideological context, for different conclusions can be reached from the same starting point. For example, purely political premises can lead to quite different conclusions, depending upon the conditions. The Greek ideal was a stable population; but at other times it may have seemed most advantageous for the state to have an increasing, or perhaps even a smaller, number of citizens. Similarly, a predominantly religious orientation does not in all instances lead to the same views on population. It is not unnatural for religious groups, especially those in a

[10] See Chapter 6 below.
[11] Edwin Cannan, *Wealth,* London: King and Son, 1914, p. 54.

minority position, to identify the promotion of their faith with the propagation of the faithful. Whatever the reasoning involved, injunctions to "be fruitful and multiply" are found in many sacred writings, reenforced by the family institutions and by the laws and mores regulating population control practices. Opposite influences on population numbers are the equally widespread ideals of continence and chastity, various marital taboos, and religious celibacy. Nevertheless, even though the prevailing ideological orientation of a society does not necessarily determine the effective attitude toward population, a change from a predominantly religious to a secular point of view or from concern with national strength to individual welfare, may bring with it altered views on questions of population.

3 · Sources and Evidence

Population has only recently come to be regarded as a subject for separate study in its own right, but concern with population questions seems to be as old as organized human society; and the history of population thought can be traced from quite early times down to the present.[12] Whether a large and growing population was regarded as desirable or undesirable cannot always be determined, but sometimes can be inferred from governmental policies and measures affecting population. More explicit information is provided by the writings of social and political theorists.

There is less information about why a given size or trend in population number has been considered beneficial or harmful. The reasons for official policies are not always known or explained; and even the explanations offered may not reveal the true reasons in full. The desirability of population growth has sometimes been considered so obvious and so generally accepted that explanations appeared to be unnecessary. For the most part only the social and political theorists have attempted to analyze the significance of population and it is upon their writings that an account of the development of population thought must depend.

These two sources, governmental policies and individual writings on

[12] See Stangeland, *op. cit.*, for a detailed survey of the history of population thought up to the end of the eighteenth century. Other surveys of the subject are Rene Gonnard, *Histoire des doctrines de la population*, Paris: Nouvelle Librairie Nationale, 1923; and Francesco Nitti, *Population and the Social System*, New York: Scribners, 1894. There are also a number of more specialized or limited summaries of population theory, including James Bonar, *Theories of Population from Raleigh to Arthur Young*, London: Allen and Unwin, 1931; Robert von Mohl, *Die Geschichte und Literatur der Staatswissenschaft*, Erlangen: Enke, 1855–1858, Vol. III, Ch. 16; J. J. Spengler, *French Predecessors of Malthus*, Durham, N.C.: Duke University Press, 1942 (French edition, *Économie et population, les doctrines françaises avant 1800*, Presses Universitaires de France, 1954); and Johann E. Wappäus, *Allgemeine Bevölkerungsstatistik*, Leipzig: Hinrichs, 1858. Considerable material may also be found in histories of economic thought, such as those of Cannan, Gide, Haney, Johnson, Roscher, Spann, and Whittaker.

population, cannot be assumed to give altogether reliable evidence of the prevailing direction of population thought. Differences of opinion have doubtless always existed. And there may well be some selection of the views that are preserved in writing or that find expression in official action. The position taken by a government in matters affecting population does not necessarily agree with the views of its people, and in fact may be designed to counteract their behavior. Then, too, laws that are designed to affect population may serve other purposes as well. The Roman caducary legislation restricting the testamentary freedom of the unmarried or child-less may have served as well to produce revenue; and considerations of political or national advantage may lie behind attempts to regulate the reproduction of particular groups or to increase the population in strategic areas. Individual writers do not necessarily represent the prevailing thought of their times, nor are the opinions of all classes of society recorded and preserved with equal completeness. One is well advised to watch for specious reasoning in discussions of population questions. Some aspects of population policy have been and still are highly controversial, and the firm believer in numerical strength or in the exclusion of foreigners, for example, can always offer plausible arguments in support of his belief.

In spite of the limited sources and their shortcomings, a considerable body of population theory has developed over the course of time. But it must be recognized that the development has been largely incidental to other matters. With the exception of one rather short period, population questions have never been topics of primary interest in themselves, and their treatment has been for the most part incidental to other matters. Recommendations concerning population policy have been directed as a rule toward non-demographic objectives, such as reenforcing the military strength of the state, contributing to political stability, providing an ample labor supply, or easing the burden of poor relief. In such instances, how-ever, it is tacitly assumed that population in some way contributes to the desired end. In other words, there are implicit assumptions or hypotheses about the significance of population or population change; and the develop-ment of these assumptions and hypotheses is traced in succeeding chapters.

4 · A Dilemma of Population Theory

The fundamental question from the point of view of population theory is not whether a given size or trend of numbers is considered desirable or undesirable, but why. And at this level of theory a population dilemma has long existed, for two equally plausible and substantial bodies of theory and analysis point to divergent conclusions about the significance of population.

The contradiction between the two bodies of thought is not without basis, because in both fact and theory there are two natural and opposite aspects of the quantitative problem of population. A direct connection between the strength of a nation and the number of its people must have been apparent from the very beginnings of human society. Equally apparent is the contrary fact that the supply of the necessities of life is limited. At any given time one aspect of the problem commands more attention than the other, but both aspects presumably were recognized long before the beginning of recorded thought on population.

The two opposite aspects of the problem of population numbers are related in turn to man's dual role. People are both producers and consumers, so it is understandable that at times population growth should have been regarded primarily as an addition to manpower and productive capacity, at other times as an increase in the number of mouths to be fed.

A further reason for the long persistence of the contradictory theories is the lack of clear evidence of what influence population size and change have had on societies in the past. Past experience as well as contemporary observation can therefore be variously interpreted, and there has been ample opportunity for divergent assumptions and theories about the significance of population. The evolution of these theories is traced in the chapters that follow, to show the gradual restatement of the problem, the introduction of additional factors into the analysis, and, finally, the founding of the modern but still probably incomplete formulation.

2

Early Population Thought

1 · Classical Period

The history of formal, recorded population thought begins with Greece of the classical period, for there is little record of the direction of opinion in earlier times or in other ancient societies. What evidence there is indicates that a numerous population was generally regarded as a source of national power and military strength. National policy supported by social pressure and religious precepts sought to promote high fertility. Early sacred writings were often quite specific in stating the advantages, even the obligations, of having a large number of children, the promised benefits to be realized both during life and in the hereafter.

A direct identification of numbers with national strength is found in the Old Testament: "In the multitude of people is the king's glory; but in the want of people is the destruction of the prince."[1] There is, however, a suggestion of the opposite point of view in Genesis, where the explanation of the separation of Lot and Abraham is that "the land was not able to bear them, that they might dwell together: for their substance was great, so that they could not dwell together."[2] Even at that time it can scarcely have been a new observation that a limited area can support only a limited number of people.

Scattered indications of how people regarded population in ancient times are found in other sources. From Herodotus, for example, comes the report that among the Persians:

> Next to prowess in arms, it is regarded as the greatest proof of manly excellence to be the father of many sons. Every year the king sends rich gifts to the man who can show the largest number: for they hold that number is strength.[3]

[1] Proverbs 14:28. The New Revised Version reads, "In a multitude of people is the glory of a king, but without people a prince is ruined."

[2] Genesis 13:6. The next verse continues, "And there was a strife between the herdsmen of Abram's cattle and the herdsmen of Lot's cattle."

[3] Herodotus, *The History,* Rawlinson translation, London: Dent, 1910, Book I, Ch. 136.

The ancient writings of India are said to show "profound appreciation of the problem of Food and Population." According to an account of these writings they recognized the advantage of having a large population in time of war and saw no need to fear overpopulation. But at the same time they recognized the problem of sufficient food supply, suggested how the problem might be met by cultivation of waste land and other means, emphasized the duty of caring for dependents, and countenanced such measures as the denial of remarriage to widows that did in effect limit natural increase.[4]

The record of population thought in ancient Greece includes occasional references to population in the writings of the political theorists and some information on the population policies of the city states. The theoretical writings and the practical policies represent a consistent point of view: The objective in all cases was the welfare and security of the state, and population questions were discussed only as they related to this objective. As a result the position taken on population and its increase was dictated largely by the immediate situation, so that, instead of conforming to any uniform pattern of demographic objectives, the population thought and practice of the period covered a considerable range, varying with local political problems and institutions, the external situation of the state, and the current economic conditions.

Sparta and Athens differed widely in population policy, as in other respects. In Sparta the state absorbed many of the usual functions of the family, leaving little to the family beyond reproduction and even here the state tried to induce a maximum of fertility. Political disabilities, penalties, and restrictions of privilege were placed on bachelors, while special rewards and exemptions were given to the fathers of large families. Aristotle, in reference to the laws of Lycurgus for the encouragement of population growth in Sparta, reported that ". . . he who had three children should be excused the night watch, and that he who had four should pay no taxes."[5] Plutarch, in his life of Lycurgus, described the indignities suffered by unmarried men in Sparta. Athens also seems to have sought to promote the marriage and childbearing of its citizens, as a matter of practical politics. According to Dinarchus,[6] only fathers of legitimate children could hold the military command at Athens or appear as orators before the people. In addition there were laws against celibacy. But on the whole, in spite of some pressure of law and custom, marriage remained largely a matter of free choice for the Athenian citizen.

The desirability of population growth came to be questioned in Greece

[4] Khushal Talaksi Shah, *Ancient Foundations of Economics in India*, Bombay: Vora, 1954, p. 80.

[5] Aristotle, *Politics*, Book II, Ch. 9.

[6] Cited by George Ensor in *An Inquiry concerning the Population of Nations*, London, 1818, p. 2.

after the Pelopponesian War, and the altered economic and political situation of the peninsula may have been responsible. Earlier, the problem
created by population growth in an area of limited resources could be met
by active maritime trade and by an outflow of migrants to newly established colonies.[7] The Greeks of the postwar period, however, faced a
quite different political and economic situation.[8] The former outlets of
trade and migration were closing or already closed by the filling up of the
desirable colonial lands, trade rivals had appeared, Asia Minor was increasingly dominated by the Persians, and the western Mediterranean was
being blocked off by the expansion of Carthage and Rome. Referring to
this period, Mitford wrote:

> The modern reader . . . will then scarcely observe without wonder,
> that while Xenophon is anxious to increase the number of foreign resi-
> dents and slaves, the increase of Athenian citizens, the only secure and
> effective strength of a state, appears totally out of his consideration. But
> from all the remaining writers of the age, we may gather, that the spirit
> of every Grecian government, whether oligarchy or democracy, was gen-
> erally adverse to the increase of citizens. For every citizen, having an
> interest in a certain public capital, increase of citizens was increase of
> partners, which would diminish every old proprietor's share. . . . The
> combined considerations, therefore, of the means of subsistence and
> gratification, with the means of defense, would decide the degree of
> population to be desired in a Grecian republic. But unless danger was
> pressing, the general disposition was always adverse to an increase. The
> rich disliked it, . . . because there was a poor-law in Athens. The poor
> objected to it, in apprehension of its diminishing their chance of advantage
> from sacrifices, from treats to their wards, from pay from attendance on the
> tribunals. . . . Altogether, the idea of a common interest in a common
> stock, a fundamental principle of every Grecian republic, not only made
> the aversion to any increase of citizens popular, but gave the ablest poli-
> ticians . . . to imagine a necessity for limiting the number of citizens, and to
> a very scanty proportion.[9]

This attitude probably applied more directly to the admission of foreigners to citizenship than to the less apparent growth of numbers through
natural increase, but it nevertheless carried over to the latter, for the
political writers of the time were quite explicit in their advocacy of keeping the number of citizens of the state within specified limits.[10] In this

---

[7] See, for example, Gustave Glotz, *Ancient Greece at Work,* New York: Knopf,
1926, esp. Ch. 4.

[8] See, among others, Gaston Bouthoul, "Les différents aspects de l'équilibre
démographique," *Revue Internationale de Sociologie,* 46:119–129, March–April 1938.

[9] William Mitford, *The History of Greece,* London: Cadell & Davies, 1808, Vol.
III, pp. 16–17.

[10] These limits were customarily specified in terms of citizens rather than population in the modern sense. Although the precise use of the term "citizen" is not in all

respect they stood almost alone, for few later writers on population before modern times have clearly seen more than one side of the dilemma of population numbers.

Aristotle mentioned two earlier writers who believed that a constant population is desirable, saying that ". . . Phidon the Corinthian, one of the oldest legislators, thought the families and the number of the citizens should continue the same. . . ."[11] There was also Hippodamus who planned a state to contain 10,000 citizens divided into three classes.[12]

In his *Laws,* Plato (427–347 B.C.) outlined an ideal state that was to keep a close watch on the number of its citizens, so there should be neither too few nor too many. In fixing the proper size of state he recognized that

> . . . a sufficient quantity of the mass of people cannot be correctly stated otherwise than with reference to the land and cities of neighboring nations. As regards the land, how much of it is sufficient to feed how many temperate people — for of more there is no need — but as regards the number, how many would be able to defend themselves not altogether without resources against bordering tribes . . .[13]

The appropriate number of citizens was set at 5040, and the population was to be held constant at this figure, either by encouragement of procreation or by application of certain unspecified checks. If numbers should fall off despite measures favourable to increase, strangers might be admitted to citizenship as a last resort.[14] If numbers increased above the appointed level despite controls, emigration to colonies was suggested.[15]

Plato believed it essential to exercise quite close control of the number of citizens in a state, but for fuller understanding of his views on population we need to know his reasons for stipulating the constant population of 5040 citizens. Since he gave little explanation, his reasons can only be inferred. As regards the number 5040, he evidently considered it of some importance for it is mentioned no less than four times in *The Laws.* The only explanation he offers for his choice is that

> In our opinion, nothing can be more right than the selection of the number 5040, which may be divided by all numbers from one to twelve with the single exception of eleven, and that admits of a very easy correction; for if, turning to the dividend, we deduct two families, the defect in the division is cured.[16]

cases clear, it is nevertheless apparent, as Beloch (*Die Bevölkerung der Greichisch-Römischen Welt,* Leipzig, 1886) and others have indicated, that the citizens were only a rather small fraction of the total population.

[11] *Politics,* Book II, Ch. 6.　　　　[12] *Ibid.,* Book II, Ch. 8.
[13] *The Laws,* Book V, Ch. 8.　　　　[14] *Ibid.,* Book V, Ch. 10.
[15] *Ibid.,* Book IV, Ch. 3; Book V, Ch. 10.
[16] *The Dialogues of Plato,* Vol. IV, *The Laws,* Jowett translation, Oxford University Press, 1931 impression of 1871 edition, Book VI, p. 153. Jowett comments (*Ibid.,* Vol. II, *The Republic,* pp. cxxx–cxxxv) that there was some element of nu-

Plato must have had further reason for choosing this as the right number, however, for a number half as large or twice as large would have been as readily divisible. He presumably regarded this number of citizens as neither too small nor too large, sufficient for the defense of the state but not too large for efficient government and maintenance within a moderate-sized area. Certainly he saw both sides of the problem of population size, for an awareness of both is indicated in the first passage quoted from *The Laws* above.[17]

It would be more informative to know Plato's reasons for stipulating a constant number of citizens, but they also remained unstated. A constant population would naturally recommend itself as a way to avoid the opposite dangers of too many and too few people; and Plato may have regarded the advantages of stability of numbers as too obvious to call for explanations.

There is room for conjecture about Plato's reasons for a constant number of citizens. Malthus, for example, was able to see in the stipulation of a constant population a substantiation of his own views. He wrote that ". . . it is evident that Plato fully saw the tendency of population to increase beyond the means of substance."[18] Stangeland rejects this interpretation, inferring that

> In constructing his ideal state, Plato realized that with the practical communism involved in that state and the consequent removal of individual responsibility for offspring, control of population by the state would be the only adequate means of avoiding the disasters of excessive numbers.[19]

This seems to be an over-elaborate interpretation, or a reading into the original of later ideas. Plato emphasized the equal division of all property among the citizens and the subsequent preservation of each holding intact, with the prohibition of either alienation or addition to holdings and with one son inheriting the entire holding.[20] In view of this, it is entirely possible that the purpose of the stationary population in Plato's planned

merology in the choice of this particular number, and that "The number 5040, which is the number of the citizens in the Laws, is expressly based by him on utilitarian grounds, namely, the convenience of the number for division; it is also made up of the first seven digits multiplied by one another. . . . There is nothing surprising in the circumstance that those who were seeking for order in nature and had found order in number, should have imagined one to give law to the other. Plato believes in a power of number far beyond what he could see realized in the world around him. . . ."

[17] Plato's awareness that the population of a given area is limited by the capacity of the land to provide food is indicated more clearly in another connection, where he says that emigration is necessary when "the masses have become in the cities more numerous than according to the quantity of food to be got from the land" (*The Laws,* Book IV, Ch. 3).

[18] Thomas Robert Malthus, *An Essay on the Principle of Population,* 2nd and later editions, Book I, Ch. 13.

[19] Stangeland, *op. cit.,* p. 25.

[20] *The Laws,* Book V, Ch. 10.

state was simply to aid in maintaining the equal division of property. This equality was a basic principle of Plato's state, and a decrease or increase in the number of citizens would have upset the equality.

Aristotle (384–322 B.C.) was more explicit in his treatment of the political problem of population numbers in his ideal state. Like Plato, he saw need for a stationary population, but he went beyond his predecessor and supported his position with definite reasons. Without fixing a precise optimum number, he seems to have believed that the number of citizens in a state should be maintained between certain limits. He criticized Plato for not providing for a more rigid control of the number of children and citizens:

> It is absurd to render property equal, and not to provide for the in-creasing number of citizens. . . . it is more necessary than even to regulate property, to take care that the increase of the people should not exceed a certain number; and in determining that, to take into con-sideration those children who will die, and also those women who will be barren; and to neglect this, as is done in several cities, is *to bring certain poverty on the citizens, and poverty is the cause of sedition and evil.*[21] [italics added]

Aristotle made a similar point in his discussion of the laws of Lycurgus for the encouragement of population growth, in which he commented it was "evident . . . that if the people increased there must many of them be very poor."[22]

Aristotle's position was therefore basically the same as Plato's. They were in agreement that population numbers are an important political problem, that careful control of marriage and reproduction is essential, and that a stable population is in the best interests of the state. Plato proposed means of checking either increase or decrease from the appointed population figure. Aristotle did not specify an ideal population size. While recognizing both the possibility of increase and of decrease, he apparently looked upon an increase as the more immediate problem. He further ex-plained that an undue increase of numbers, at least under certain forms of government, brings with it "certain poverty," and that this in turn creates internal disorder. This explanation is of particular significance as the first direct reason for what has been called the pessimistic position with refer-ence to population increase, and contains the nucleus of much of the later theoretical development.

The political point of view taken by the Greeks in matters of population numbers was carried on in Roman population thought, but whereas the Greeks thought in terms of their small city states, the Roman political con-

---

[21] *Politics*, Book II, Ch. 6.
[22] *Ibid.*, Book II, Ch. 9.

ception was the empire or world state. In its early days Rome, like Greece, may have had an abundant and growing population. Unlike Greece, however, the Roman solution to the problem of supporting their growing population, with limited resources, was not foreign trade and emigration but war and territorial expansion. This was in effect, a double solution, for both the territorial gains and the military losses during the long period of almost continuous warfare relieved any pressure of population. But in the course of time, the solution was carried on to an overcorrection. With an expanding area of conquests, the continued drain of wartime losses, and a lowered fertility, the natural increase of the Roman population was checked, perhaps as early as the end of the Punic Wars, and a decline of numbers eventually set in.

The effect of these changes in the demographic situation of Rome was not so much to change as to activate or to reenforce the prevailing attitudes toward population numbers. The Roman institutions had been from the earliest time favorable to population growth. But with the expanding military effort of the republic and later the evident decline of fertility, these institutions came to be supplemented by the series of so-called caducary laws that culminated in the Augustan legislation. Whatever the private preferences and practices of the Roman people may have been, the public and official Roman attitude remained consistently in favor of population growth. Under the circumstances of first a small state surrounded by menacing neighbors, then growing demands for manpower made by a succession of wars and an expanding empire with a stationary or declining population, it could hardly have been otherwise. The opposite aspect of the problem, that there could be too many people, never presented itself to the Romans.

Consistent with the Roman character, the Roman view of population, as revealed by legislation and by occasional references to the subject, was entirely utilitarian and without theoretical elaboration. In the welfare of the state was to be found the welfare of the individual, and an increase of numbers was desirable not because of any expected betterment in the social and economic position of the citizens but because of the consequent strengthening of the state. In a numerous citizenry was military strength, and in an increase of the number of citizens was a corresponding increase in the number of potential soldiers.

2 · Early Modern Period

The ten centuries or more from the decline of classical civilization to the close of the Middle Ages contributed little to the literature of population thought. The practical problems of population size and subsistence cannot have diminished, but if there was discussion of these problems little has survived in the written record. In the occasional references to population during this period the earlier political formulation of the problem of population numbers was replaced by considerations of religious principle and morality, and the tentatively analytic treatment that had begun with the Greek political theorists disappeared almost completely.[23] The situation was described by Spengler:

> The medieval writers were not dominated by reasons of state and race, and they did not concern themselves with population theory as such, but they did comment upon certain moral matters related to population growth. In general, they looked upon population growth as a sign of God's favor, and subscribed to doctrines and practices conducive to such growth; for they held human life to be sacred, and marriage to be a sacrament, and they inferred from Holy Scripture that large families are good for the individual and the community, and in accord with the divine plan.[24]

A reawakening of population thought began in early modern times, for the problems of the growing states, the new intellectual currents, and the revival of classical learning again called attention to questions of population. The few surviving discussions of the subject afford us only a fragmentary record of the thought of their time, but they indicate a returning secular emphasis and a reappearance of population regarded as a political problem. Dominating this new and scanty population literature was the common-sense level identification of numbers with strength, but there was also an occasional reflection of ancient Greek thought and its conclusion that the desirable number of citizens is limited.

It is hazardous to make claims of priority in a subject such as population thought, which deals with matters of general observation and to which many different trains of thought may lead, but the Arab historian and social scientist Ibn Khaldun (1332–1406) can be considered a pioneer among the post-classical and early modern writers who concerned themselves with questions of population. Member of a non-European society that had maintained some tradition of scholarship and contact with classical learning through the Dark Ages, he had an advantage over his European contemporaries, and his treatment of population was advanced for its time.

An entire chapter of this *Prolegomena*[25] (c. 1380) was devoted to a

[23] For surveys of early Christian and medieval thought on matters relating to population see W. E. H. Lecky, *History of European Morals,* Ch. 4, 5; and Stangeland, *op. cit.,* Ch. II, part 2, pp. 55–87.

[24] Joseph J. Spengler, *French Predecessors of Malthus,* Durham, N.C.: Duke University Press, 1942, pp. 4–5.

[25] Ibn Khaldun, *An Arab Philosophy of History; Selections from the Prolegomena of Ibn Khaldun,* translated and arranged by Charles Issawi, London: John Murray, 1950, Ch. 5. See also Muhsin Mahdi, *Ibn Khaldun's Philosophy of History,* London: Allen and Unwin, 1957.

broad treatment of population. It described how states pass through a population cycle, from high fertility and low mortality in their youth to declining fertility and higher mortality in their later stages, and how states can promote the fertility of their subjects through wise and lenient government. But most important in the present connection is the account of the significance of population size. Differences between districts or towns in income and commercial prosperity, Ibn Khaldun stated, are attributable to differences in the number of people. This, he explained, is because a single individual is unable to provide for his own wants except by cooperating with other people in a society.[26] From this he drew the more general conclusion that ". . . the standard of living and wealth of a society will depend on the number of its members."[27] Especially noteworthy here is the fact that Ibn Khaldun went beyond the conventional statement of the political and military advantages of a large population and emphasized its economic significance. In so doing he introduced a new range of considerations into the discussion of population.

Francesco Patrizzi, or Franciscus Patricius, of Siena (1412–1494), is regarded by both Stangeland and Gonnard[28] as the first contributor to what became the body of modern population thought. His *De Institutione Reipublicae* (published 1518) contained views on population that were particularly well balanced even by later standards. While accepting the general proposition that a large population is desirable, he also recognized the possibility of people becoming too numerous. He may have adopted the latter idea from Plato and Aristotle, but there is no doubt of his introducing an important reservation when he added to the general statement of the desirability of an abundant population the qualification that abundant population is desirable only if there are sufficient means to support the people.

Several references to the subject of population numbers are contained in the works of Niccolo Machiavelli (1469–1527). In his *Discourses on the First Decad of Livy* (1512–1517), which he began to write before *The Prince* but did not publish until later, he said of the founding of a city that ". . . it is better to build in a fertile country where plenty of all things will make the inhabitants increase . . . ,"[29] implying that the number of people tends to increase in a condition of plenty and that this increase is desirable. Elsewhere in the *Discourses,* however, he stated that an overabundant population would be reduced by poverty and disease; and in this he anticipated the later concept of positive checks to population growth:

26 *Ibid.,* p. 92.
27 *Ibid.,* p. 95.
28 Stangeland, *op. cit.,* p. 90; Gonnard, *op. cit.,* pp. 90–91. Stangeland is in error in placing Patrizzi in the sixteenth century, perhaps confusing him with a later writer of the same name or being misled by the posthumous publication of his work.
29 *Discourses,* Book I, Ch. 1.

. . . when every province of the world so teems with inhabitants that they can neither subsist where they are nor remove elsewhere, every region being equally crowded and over-peopled, and when human craft and wickedness have reached their highest pitch, it must needs come about that the world will purge itself in one or another of these three ways (floods, plagues, or famines).[30]

In his most famous work, *The Prince* (1513), Machiavelli spoke of great wealth and a large number of men as being a ruler's sources of strength.[31] The consequences of population growth are mentioned again in his *History of Florence,* undertaken in 1520 and uncompleted at his death in 1527, which began with the frequently quoted sentence:

The people that inhabit the Northern regions beyond the rivers Rhine and Danube, living in a healthful and prolific climate, often increase in such numbers that some of them are obliged to abandon their paternal lands and to seek new countries for their habitation . . .,

and continued with the statement that the Roman empire was destroyed by the hordes thus set in motion.

These scattered references indicate that although Machiavelli made only passing mention of population he nevertheless recognized some of its political implications and recommended it to the attention of the wise ruler.

Concern that the number of people might become too large appeared from time to time in the sixteenth century, especially in Germany and England where local conditions led to this view. Roscher[32] and Stangeland[33] mention that the early German writers, Ulrich von Hutten (1488–1523) and Sebastian von Wörd (1500–1545?), believed there was danger of a population becoming too dense; and it was not until the time of the Thirty Years War (1618–1648) that a definite consensus favoring population growth appeared in Germany. Fear of overpopulation in England in the late Tudor period has already been mentioned,[34] and is described more fully in the following section. It was not until mercantilist political and economic theories became more influential in seventeenth-century England that opinion swung toward a more optimistic appraisal of population growth.

Although local conditions in Germany and England during the sixteenth and early seventeenth centuries may have tended to emphasize the possibility of overpopulation, the opposite view of the political desirability of a numerous and growing population found supporters elsewhere. The most notable of these were Bodin in France and Botero in Italy.

Jean Bodin (1530–1596), the French royal attorney, member of the Estates General, and political theorist, argued for a large population in his

[30] *Ibid.,* Book II, Ch. 5.   [31] *The Prince,* Ch. 10.
[32] Roscher, *Geschichte,* Ch. II, pp. 43–48.   [33] Stangeland, *op. cit.,* pp. 96–97.
[34] See p. 3 above.

Six livres de la république (1576). In principle he conceded that inequalities of wealth are a cause of discord and sedition, but he disagreed strongly with the recommendations of Plato, Aristotle, and More that the number of citizens should be limited. A large population, Bodin argued, is not in itself a cause of poverty; and having an ample number of citizens tends to give political stability rather than instability. In his own words,

> . . . they erre much which doubt of scarcitie by the multitude of children and citizens, when as no cities are more rich nor more famous in arts and disciplines than those which abound most with citizens. It is indeed lesse to feare that by reason of so great a multitude of citizens there will be deuisions, for there is nothing that doth keepe a citie more free from mutinies and factions than the multitude of citizens. . . .[35]

A large middle class, being situated between the poorer classes and the nobility, also has a stabilizing influence. Legislation designed to promote the increase of population, such as the Roman caducary laws, was recommended. Conversely, the artificial restriction of numbers through infanticide or abortion was unthinkable. It is of further interest that long before the development of regular governmental statistics, Bodin listed at some length the advantages of taking a census of the people.[36]

In an earlier, less known work, in which he sought to explain why prices were so high in France, Bodin gave as one reason the abundance of gold and silver, which in turn he attributed to prosperity and an ample supply of goods. Concerning the latter he wrote:

> Another reason for the many benefits that have come to us during the past six or seven score years is the large population that has multiplied in this kingdom since the civil wars of the houses of Orleans and Burgundy.[37]

Elsewhere he noted that the price of food is high in towns to which quantities of people and money have been attracted.[38]

By far the most important work in the history of population thought up to its time was the treatise *Delle Cause della Grandezza delle Città,* by Giovanni Botero (1540–1617), first published in 1588, and later appended to Botero's principal work, *Della Ragion di Stato* (1589). A member of the Jesuit order who became secretary to the Cardinals Borromeo and later an employee of the ruler of Savoy, Botero gave a broad discussion of population questions in his treatise, and anticipated by over two hundred

[35] *The Six Bookes of a Commonweale,* translated by Richard Knolles, London, 1606, Book V, Ch. 2, p. 571.

[36] *Ibid.,* Book VI, Ch. 1.

[37] Jean Bodin, *La Response de Jean Bodin au Paradoxe de Monsieur de Malestroit, touchant l'enchérissement de toutes choses et le moyen d'y remédier,* edited by Henri Hauser, Paris: Colin, 1932, p. 13.

[38] *Ibid.,* p. 31.

years many of the essential elements in the better known population theory of another member of the clergy, the Englishman, Malthus.

According to Botero, population numbers depend upon the operation of two opposing factors, the power of reproduction, on one side, and nutritive power or the means of subsistence, on the other. If there are no checks upon natural increase, the human species will multiply indefinitely; but in fact it can increase only up to the limit of the food supply.[39] As this limit is approached, further growth is restrained by inability to marry or by emigration, but also, it is implied, by a whole chain of causes such as crime, cannibalism, and war.

Although convinced that there is an eventual limit to the numbers of mankind, Botero was nevertheless in favor of a large and expanding population, for in this lay the immediate strength and security of a state. His treatise, for example, began with the definitions:

> A Citie is called an Assembly of Men, brought together to live happily: and, Greatnesse of a Citie is tearmed not the spaciousnesse of situation, or compasse of Walls; but the multitude of Inhabitants, and their power.[40]

Later he considered whether the planting of colonies strengthens or weakens a state. In a chapter dealing with the question he wrote:

> What shall wee say of Colonies? Whether were they a furtherance to Romes Greatnesse, or no? That they availed to the augmentation of Power, there is no question. But, whether they multiplyed thereby the number of Inhabitants, is a matter disputable. Yet, according to my understanding, they were a great help thereto: For, although it will seeme to some, that by the drawing out of men, to be transferred into Colonies, the Citie rather fell into diminution, than encreased; yet, perhaps, the contrarie may happen: because, as Plants cannot so well flourish or prosper in an Impebed where they have beene set, as in an open place, transplanted; so men propagate not so successfully, immured in the Circuit of a Citie. . . .[41]

The urban-rural differential in the rate of natural increase is evidently not a new observation.

Finally, how is one to resolve the dilemma of population numbers, seeing both the advantages of numerical strength and the consequences of a too numerous population? Botero answers:

> The ancient Founders of Cities, considering, that Lawes and Civill Discipline can difficultly be observed, where there are infinite numbers of

---

[39] Botero wrote: "But if it (population) proceed no further, it behoveth us to say, it is wrought by the defect of nutriment, and sustentation" (*The Causes of the Greatness of Cities,* London, 1635, Book III, p. 166).

[40] *Ibid.,* Book I, Ch. 1.

[41] *Ibid.,* Book II, Ch. 2.

people breeding confusion, limited the numbers of Citizens, beyond which proportion, they judged Order and forme could not be maintained. . . . Such were Licurgus, Solon, Aristotle. But the Romans imagining, that power consisteth for the most part, in the multitude of people; assayed by all means to encrease and people their Countrey. . . . If the World would be governed by Reason, and every man willingly rest content with that, which justly belongs to him, then would, assuredly, the judgment of the ancient law-makers be worthy to be embraced. But experience, which sheweth us, that by the Corruption of Humane Nature, Force prevaileth above Reason, and Armes in all points yield unto Lawes; teacheth us also that the judgment of the Romans deserves to be preferred before the opinion of the Grecians. . . .[42]

In effect this says that the policy that would theoretically be right in a utopian state of society does not meet the hard realities of the world as it actually is; and this is no less true in the twentieth century than it was in Botero's Italy of the sixteenth century.

3 · Tudor England

It has already been noted that population thought in England went through a complete cycle during the Tudor period,[43] from fear of under-population in the early years to conviction that the nation was overcrowded in the latter part of Elizabeth's reign. The period is therefore of particular interest in the history of population thought, and the record of opinion on population questions had grown more ample, so that the trend of thought can be followed.

The original Tudor-period attitude toward population, if not derived from earlier experience of the uncertainties of life, must have been fixed by the fresh memories of the Black Death of the mid-fourteenth century and the subsequent visitations of the same or other plagues during the remainder of the fourteenth and into the fifteenth century.[44] But whatever the reasons, it was believed that the kingdom suffered from lack of people; and linked with this belief was concern over enclosures, the conversion of land from agriculture to grazing, and a decrease in the number of rural holdings.

---

[42] *Ibid.,* Book III, Introduction.

[43] From the accession of Henry VII in 1485 to the death of Elizabeth in 1603.

[44] For estimates of population losses in the Black Death, and accounts of the later epidemics, see, for example: Anna M. Campbell, *The Black Death and Men of Learning,* New York: Columbia University Press, 1931; Charles Creighton, *A History of Epidemics in Britain,* Cambridge, 1891; Francis A. Gasquet, *The Black Death in 1348 and 1349,* 2nd ed., London, 1908; J. F. C. Hecker, *The Epidemics of the Middle Ages,* translated by Babington, London: Woodfall, 1844; Ada E. Levett, *The Black Death on the Estates of the See of Winchester.* Oxford: Clarendon Press, 1916; Charles F. Mullett, *The Bubonic Plague and England,* Lexington, Ky.: University of Kentucky Press, 1956; Josiah Russell, *British Medieval Population,* Albuquerque, N.M.: University of New Mexico Press, 1948.

Witness of this is an act from early in the reign of Henry VII, entitled "An act agaynst pullyng doun of tounes" (4 Henry VII, Ch. 19), which required owners of land and dwellings to "kepe susteigne and maynteyn houses and bildinges upon the seid ground and lond, convenient and necessarie for mayntenying and upholding of the seid tillage and husbondrie." In the explanatory preamble the reasons for the act were strongly stated, as follows:

> The Kyng, our sovereign Lord, havyng a singuler plesure above all thinges to avoide such enormitees and myschefes as be hurtfull and prejudiciall to the comen wele of this his londe an his subgettis of the same, remembreth that amonge all othre thinges great inconvenyences daily doth encreace by desolacion and pulling down and wilfull waste of houses and Townes within this his realme, and leyeng to pasture londes which custumeably have ben used in tilthe, whereby ydilnes grounde and begynnyng of all myschefes daily doo encreace, for where in somme Townes two hundred persones were occupied and lived by their laufull labours, nowe ben there occupied two or three herdemen and the residue fall in ydelnes, the husbondrie whiche is one of the grettest commodities of this realme is gretly decaied, churches destroied, the service of God withdrawen, the bodies there buried not praied for, the patrone and Curates wronged, the defence of this land agayn oure ennemyes outwarde febled and impaired. . . .[45]

That the problem and the concern over it continued long after is indicated by the instructions to the enclosure commissioners appointed in 1548, who were directed to look into the enforcement of the act and were informed of the importance of their task with the words,

> Ye shal do the King the greatest service that can be devised. For hereby his people and subjects (in the multitude of whom his honour and safty consisteth) shal be encreased; and ye shal shew your selves good members of the body and the commonwealth of the realm. . . .[46]

[45] R. H. Tawney and Eileen Power, *Tudor Economic Documents,* 3 vol., London: Longmans, Green, 1924, Vol. I, pp. 4–5.

[46] *Ibid.,* p. 42. A number of other documents included by Tawney and Power in their collection indicate continuing concern over enclosures and the decay of holdings. That concern is described as follows in an account of the Protectorate under Somerset during the minority of Edward VI, son of Henry VIII:

> "Of all the social grievances of the sixteenth century, enclosure was easily the most conspicuous. The statute books were full of legislation to check it. And the social reformers were unanimous in denunciation of it. . . . The preachers stormed against it in the pulpit. . . . Generally speaking the social reformers looked to the government to correct the evil and it is only fair to say of early Tudor governments that they worked hard at it. Nevertheless enclosures went on apace. Basically they proceeded from an understandable desire upon the part of the landowning classes to reorganize the contemporary patterns of cultivating the soil so as to yield a larger net return. Their rents were largely fixed by custom, their expenses, in response to the general rise of prices, were more than double. The soil, lacking adequate fertilization, was

Meanwhile, another point of view had been expressed in an important work of early in the century, the *Utopia* of Sir Thomas More (1478–1535). A contemporary of Machiavelli, More may have preceded him in his treatment of the population problem of a planned state, for the *Utopia* (1516), although not published until after *The Prince* (1513), is thought to have been written some years before publication. Not typical of the population thought of its period, More's work took a more theoretical view, followed closely in the Greek pattern, and proposed a policy of regulation of numbers. Each town in Utopia was to keep the number of its inhabitants approximately constant, and family size was also to be controlled as follows:

> No family may have less than ten, and more than sixteen persons in it; but there can be no determined number for the children under age. This rule is easily observed by removing some of the children of a more fruitful couple to any other family that does not abound so much in them. By the same rule they supply cities that do not increase so fast from others that breed faster; and if there is any increase over the whole island then they draw a number of their citizens out of the several towns, and send them over to the neighboring continent. . . .[47]

These colonists might later be drawn back if a deficit of numbers should develop in the mother country. On the taking of land to provide for surplus numbers, the statement is made:

> . . . they account it a very just cause of war for a nation to hinder others from possessing a part of that soil of which they make no use but which is suffered to lie idle and uncultivated; since every man has by the law of nature a right to such a waste portion of the earth as is necessary for his subsistence.[48]

This is an early modern statement of a "natural right" to equal distribution of natural resources, an argument that probably was not new even when More made it, and that reappears more prominently later, both as a justification of wars of conquest and in condemnation of restrictions upon international migration.

The more conventional view of the population question at that time is found in a work that appeared anonymously in 1549. Now attributed to John Hales (?–1571), an active member of the enclosures commission of 1548, *A compendious or briefe examination of certain ordinary complaints*

---

showing a steadily diminishing yield. The obvious alternative was the conversion of arable into pasture land and the raising of wool instead of corn. But this could only be achieved by a wholesale displacement of the tillers of the soil." (Conyers Read, *Mr. Secretary Cecil and Queen Elizabeth,* London: Jonathan Cape, 1955, pp. 48–49.)

[47] *Utopia,* Book II.

[48] *Ibid.*

was concerned with matters other than population, but did indicate that its author assumed without question that an increase of numbers is desirable.[49]

Evidence of differences of opinion on population and a persistence of the earlier Tudor-period attitude well on into the last quarter of the sixteenth century is contained in the famous *Chronicles* (1578) of Raphaell Holinshed (?–1580?). Noting that there were those who believed the nation was overpopulated, he gave a vigorous rebuttal in a chapter entitled "Of prouision made for the poor":

> Some also doo grudge at the great increase of people in these daies, thinking a necessarie brood of cattell farre better than a superfluous augmentation of mankind. . . . But if it should come to passe that any forren inuasion should be made, which the Lord God forbid for his mercies sake! then should these men find that a wall of men is farre better than stackes of corne and bags of monie, and complaine of the want when it is too late to seeke remedie.[50]

This attitude is quite understandable in view of the national problems of the time. Until near the end of the 1580's Britain felt increasingly threatened by dangers from without and within, dangers that did not subside until the defeat of the Spanish Armada.

Consistent with the view that an ample population was needed for national defense, Holinshed returned in a later chapter of the *Chronicles* to the earlier complaint that rural people were being displaced from the land and that the population was being reduced thereby.

> Where in times past, manie large and wealthie occupiers were dwelling within the compasse of some one parke, and thereby great plentie of corne and cattell seene, and to be had among them, beside a more copious procreation of humane issue whereby the realme was alwaiss better furnished with able men to serue the prince in his affaires: now there is almost nothing kept but a sort of wild and sauage beasts, cherished for pleasure and delight; and yet some owners still desirous to inlarge those grounds, as either for the breed and feeding of cattell, doo not let dailie to take in more, . . . affirming that we haue alreadie too great store of people in England; and that youth by marrieng too soone doo nothing profit the countrie, but fill it full of beggars, to the hurt and vtter vndooing (they saie) of the common wealth.
>
> Certes if it be not one curse of the Lord, to haue our countries conuerted in such sort from the furniture of mankind, into the walks and shrowds of wild beasts, I know not what is anie. . . . If a man may pres-

[49] (John Hales), *A compendious or briefe examination of certain ordinary complaints,* by W. S., gentleman, London, 1581. Also published under the title, *A discourse of the common weal of this realm of England.* Attributed by some to William Stafford.

[50] Raphaell Holinshed, *Chronicles of England, Scotland and Ireland,* reprint of the 1586 edition, London: Taylor, 1807, Second Book, Ch. X, p. 308.

entlie giue a ghesse at the vniuersalitie of this euill by contemplation of the circumstances, he shall saie at the last, that the twentith part of the realme is imploied upon deere and conies alreadie, which seemeth verie much if it be not dulie considered of.

. . . It is an easie matter to prooue that England was neuer lesse furnished with people than at this present; for if the old records of euerie manour be sought, and search made to find what tenements are fallen, either downe, or into the lords hands, or brought and united togither by other men: it will soone appeere, that in some one manour seuenteen, eighteene, or twentie houses are shrunke. I know what I saie by mine owne experience; notwithstanding that some one cotage be here and there erected of late, which is of little purpose. Of cities and towns either vtterlie decaied, or more than a quarter or halfe diminished, though some one be a little increased here and there; of townes pulled downe for sheepe-walks, and no more but the lordships now standing in them, beside those that William Rufus pulled downe in his time; I could saie somewhat. . . .[51]

In later Elizabethan times the tide of opinion turned and overpopulation came to be regarded not as the hypothetical and easily remedied eventuality of the *Utopia* but a present reality. The decline of the Spanish threat after 1588 and England's strengthened position made it easier to look at the population question from a domestic point of view. A "wall of men" no longer seemed as necessary as it had a decade or so earlier, and the prevailing poverty and distress were taken as evidence of too many people in the nation. It was evident to the contemporary observer that the necessary and good things of life were in limited supply. The productive arts were stationary or only slowly advancing; and if there were shortages, the more logical conclusion was that the number of consumers was too high than that production was too low.

This altered view of population was expressed by Richard Hakluyt (1552?–1616) in *A discourse concerning western planting*, a strong plea for colonization that appeared in 1584 and is said to have won the Queen's "favour and patronage" for its author.[52] As part of his argument for colonizing efforts, Hakluyt forcefully described the evil consequences of having too many people:

Truthe it is, that throughe our longe peace and seldome sicknes (twoo singuler blessinges of Almightie God) wee are growen more populous than ever heretofore: so that nowe there are of every arte and science so many, that they can hardly lyve one by another; yea many thousandes of idle persons are within this realme, which, havinge no way to be sett on worke, be either mutinous and seeke alteration in the state, or at leaste, very bur-

[51] *Ibid.*, Ch. XIX, pp. 344–345.
[52] G. M. Trevelyan, *English Social history*, London: Longmans, Green, 1942, p. 193.

densome to the commonwealthe, and often fall to pilferinge and thevinge and other lewdnes, whereby all the prisons of the lande are daily pestred and stuffed full of them, where either they pitifully pyne awaye, or els at lengthe are miserably hanged, even xx[ti] at a clappe oute of some one jayle.[53]

It is especially noteworthy here that Hakluyt saw a direct connection between surplus population, misery, and crime; or rather, that he attributed the misery and crime to a demographic cause, overpopulation, rather than to economic and social causes. At any rate, this served his argument, for he went on to say that the surplus of people could be put to good use in the plantations (i.e., the colonies).

Reading further, however, we find that he was not altogether consistent in his argument about population numbers, for he wrote:

And to answer some objections; where fooles for the swarminge of beggars alleage that the realme is too populous, Salomon saieth, that the power and strengthe of a prince consisteth in the multitude of the people.[54]

and added that the realm could be much more populous than it was and still provide enough food for its people if they were industrious enough.

The pessimistic attitude toward population numbers and their increase carried over into the Stuart period in the next century, and will be considered further in the next chapter.[55] In fact, there was no break in the continuity of population thought from late Tudor to early Stuart times; and prominent spokesmen for the Elizabethan point of view, such as Raleigh and Bacon, published their comments on population questions in the second and third decades of the new century.

Although it is population thought and theory rather than policies that concern us here, it is worth noting that the Elizabethan views of population and related matters also appear in various official measures. The interrelated problems of poverty, unemployment, and (it was thought) overpopulation were the great and continuing problems of the nation, and a variety of means were employed for solving them. The well-known Elizabethan poor law, the foundation of the system of poor relief for almost two centuries, came into operation in 1601. Colonial ventures were stimulated and supported for reasons of population as well as for other reasons. And consistent with practice of the time, the church and state did not hesitate to deal firmly with the private citizen in matters thought important for the

[53] Richard Hakluyt, *A Discourse concerning Western Planting* (1584), reprinted in *Documentary History of the State of Maine,* Cambridge: Wilson and Son, 1877, Vol. II, Ch. 4, p. 37.
[54] *Ibid.,* p. 43.
[55] See Chapter 3, section 3, below.

public good. According to a description of controls on marriage, for example:

> ... they who could not maintain a wife, might not marry; for a License they could not have, the Bishops taking care enough with their Officers that the poor might not have lawful favor of a License, lest their Hospitality might be charged, or impaired by their maintenance, and their publike denouncing the bands of Marriage the first time; the Parish for the like cause hindred it the second, if any cause were; & usually none were permitted marriage till the man were thirty five at least, and the woman thirty. . . .[56]

It would be too much to assume that these and other measures affecting population were purely or primarily population measures, for other purposes were no doubt served, but considerations of population were at least present.

4 · Summary: Population Thought before 1600

As seen from our day, the early population literature reviewed above seems to consist of a number of quite isolated contributions. In actual fact, however, there may have been a greater continuity of thought than now appears, for many contributions may have been lost and there are many gaps in the record. Plato and Aristotle, for example, evidently drew from the work of predecessors whose writings have not survived, and Ibn Khaldun, to cite another example, gives evidence of participation in a tradition of learning and may well have had predecessors and followers not known to Western scholars.

Although analysis of the significance of population and population growth remained rudimentary up to the end of the sixteenth century and did not begin its real development until well into the next century, some lines of thought can be traced in this early period and some forerunners of later developments can be recognized. Predominating was the common-sense recognition that population is labor force, military manpower, and national strength. This simple identification of numbers with strength runs throughout the history of population thought from earliest times to the present day. It is true of this early period as a whole that population was treated as a real and practical problem, and that the prevailing views on population questions were very responsive to changing conditions within each society. If there was war or the threat of war, numerical strength seemed desirable, whereas shortages of life's necessities suggested that there would be more for everyone if there were fewer consumers.

In spite of this practical orientation, however, traces of theory can be

[56] Charls G. Cock, *English Law or, a Summary Survey of the Household of God on Earth — together with an Essay on Christian Government,* London: 1651, p. 49.

found running through early writings on population. The theoretical element is best seen in the series of utopian writings of the political and social philosophers who dealt with the anticipated problems of a planned or ideal state, and it is especially the legacy of classical thought, from Plato, Aristotle and perhaps Ibn Khaldun to Machiavelli and More.

Quite a range of viewpoints was represented in both the theoretical and practical treatments of the question of population numbers. Aside from the obvious military considerations, there is the theoretically somewhat more sophisticated political viewpoint illustrated by the classical Greek writers and by Machiavelli and Bodin. Religious or theological viewpoints, not reviewed above, were dominant at times, and especially significant as a precursor of the seventeenth-century and later development was the appearance of economic considerations in the work of Ibn Khaldun, Machiavelli, Bodin, and Hakluyt.

The early formulation of several themes that later became prominent in the analysis of the significance of population numbers is also worth noting. The possibility of overpopulation was recognized in classical Greek times and by Machiavelli and others, and it was regarded as a reality in late Tudor times in England. The theory that population growth can or does lead to general poverty was quite explicitly stated by Aristotle, Machiavelli, and Hakluyt; but Bodin asserted that increased numbers would bring greater prosperity. A corollary effect attributed to undue population growth was political unrest. This was mentioned by Aristotle and Hakluyt, with Bodin again disagreeing in his belief that larger numbers gave greater stability. Lesser themes touched on here and there were crime, migration, and war as consequences of population growth and the poverty it was thought to create. Finally, both Machiavelli and Botero used the concept of checks to population growth long before Malthus.

Thus, although early population thought had not advanced far in the analysis of the significance of population size and growth, it had taken a few steps forward. At some times and to some observers, populousness appeared desirable; at other times and to other observers, it seemed all too evident that the number of people could become too great; and a few observers went beyond a simple statement of opinion to discuss the effects or significance of population size. On several points these tentative analyses foreshadowed some of the principal developments in later population theory.

3

The Rise of Population Theory
in the Seventeenth Century

In the history of population thought, the seventeenth century, especially its latter half, is notable for two developments. One is the growing dominance of the belief that a large and growing population is desirable; and from the middle of this century into the early 1700's was the period par excellence of populationist theory and policy. Attributed to the rising influence of mercantilism, the populationist views of the time also may have been strengthened by the frequent visitations of epidemic disease and by the colonial rivalries and wars that quite effectively removed any remaining fear of overpopulation.[1] The other notable development during this century was the rise of "political arithmetick," the lineal ancestor of modern demography, and with it a progressively more searching analysis of the significance of the population variable in human affairs. Out of this analysis came what we may call population theory, still quite rudimentary it is true, but nevertheless an advance over the observations and ideas about population that predominated in the early part of the century and before. Since this development was largely English, this chapter gives only brief notes on the treatment of population in other European countries and traces in some detail the course of English thought and theory.

1 · France

Near the end of the sixteenth century, in an edict of Henry IV dated April 8, 1599, concerning the draining of marshes, there was made the often-repeated statement that "The strength and wealth of kings and princes depends on the wealth and number of their subjects."[2] This might have been taken as the text for much of the discussion of population in France

---

[1] In England the plague was more or less continually present, but reached its greatest prevalence in 1603 (the worst plague year following the Black Death), again in 1625, and in 1665 (Mullett, *The Bubonic Plague and England*). Among the many wars of this period were the Thirty Years War, which devastated Central Europe in the first half of the century, the period of civil war in England ending with the Stuart Restoration in 1660, and the wars of Louis XIV, which involved all of Europe in the latter part of the century.

[2] Gonnard, *Histoire des doctrines de la population,* p. 110.

in the succeeding hundred years, and the same view came to prevail elsewhere.

In spite of the prestige of Bodin's *Six livres de la république* there were few immediate successors among Bodin's countrymen who carried on his treatment of the problem of population numbers. Seventeenth-century France was in fact more distinguished for its practical measures relating to population, notably for the populationist policies chiefly associated with Colbert, and for the pioneer enumerations, than for theoretical developments of the sort found in contemporary England and to a lesser extent in Germany.

Only three writers need be mentioned to illustrate seventeenth-century French thought on the question of population numbers:[3] Antoine de Montchrétien (1575–1621), Fénelon (1651–1715), and Vauban (1633–1707). Taking much the same position with regard to population numbers as did Bodin, Montchrétien said that of the many resources of France, "the greatest is the inexhaustible abundance of her men."[4] This he later qualified somewhat with the statement, "The wealth of a state does not depend simply on its area or on the number of its people," but also on the proper utilization of its land and inhabitants.[5] And the effective utilization of the nation's manpower was of the greatest importance, because, as he said, it is necessary to work in order to eat but also to eat in order to work.[6]

A number of references to population were contained in *Les Aventures de Télémaque* (1699), written by Fénelon (François de Salignac de la Motte) for the instruction of his pupil, the young Duke of Burgundy. The book is of particular interest for its presentation of ideas thought suitable for a future ruler of France. The central theme concerning population was that a large number of people was desirable because it provided the real foundation and strength of a nation:

> The number of people and the abundance of food constitute the real strength and wealth of a kingdom. The more the people multiply themselves the more they multiply the fruits of the earth by their labor.[7]

Also suggested was the reassuring thought that the people also benefited themselves by having many children: "The more children the workers have, the richer they are, if the prince does not impoverish them, for their children begin to help them from earliest childhood."[8] Furthermore, there was

[3] For surveys of French population thought in the seventeenth century, see Spengler, *French Predecessors of Malthus,* Ch. 1; and Gonnard, *op. cit.,* Ch. 2, 4.

[4] Montchrétien, *Traicté de l'oeconomie politique* (1615), Paris: Plon and Nourrit, 1889, p. 24.

[5] *Ibid.,* p. 31.

[6] *Ibid.,* p. 45: "Il faut travailler pour se nourrir et se nourrir pour travailler."

[7] Fénelon, *Les aventures de Télémaque,* Paris: Hachette, 1927, Book 17, pp. 462–463. Similarly Book 10, p. 128: "The king, who cannot be king without subjects and who is great only because of them, weakens himself gradually by weakening the people from whom he draws his wealth and power."

[8] *Ibid.,* Book 10, p. 114.

no need for the ruler to concern himself about the increase of his people; with a little restraint in taxation and a little encouragement of marriage, the wise ruler would soon see his people grow to countless numbers.[9] And if the people remained hard working, the larger numbers would be a source of greater wellbeing, for

> "The more children you have the wealthier you will be, provided that you see to it that they are industrious; for *the earth is inexhaustible and increases its fertility in proportion to the number of its inhabitants who cultivate it.*[10] (italics added)

The latter part of this sentence is especially important, for it is a clear statement of the fundamental optimistic position. It asserts to use more modern terms, that per capita production does not diminish as population and labor supply increase.

Finally, considering a remote possibility, Fénelon added, "If, in the long course of time, land should be lacking, colonies would be established.[11] This allows for any possible surplus of population. The total impression is, therefore, one of unqualified optimism regarding population growth, a belief that it can bring only beneficial effects.

The *Dixme Royale* of Vauban (Sebastien Le Prestre de Vauban) can be considered to represent late seventeenth-century thought even though it was not published until 1707, the year of its author's death, for it had been written ten or more years before. In this Vauban proposed a new form of taxation, a "royal tithe." In the preface of this work appears the much-quoted statement:

> . . . the grandeur of kings is measured by the number of their subjects; for therein is their welfare, their happiness, their wealth, their strength, their fortune, and all the consideration that they have in the world. . . . They could not take too much pains for the preservation and augmentation of this people that should be so dear to them.[12]

Actually Vauban took a much broader view of population than this indicates, for he recognized that a numerous population was not in itself the only prerequisite for national greatness, and that the happiness and prosperity of the people were essential to the good of the state.

2 · Central Europe

Jakob Bornitz (or Bornitius) was an early advocate of an expanding population among seventeenth-century German writers. A jurist and a writer on political and fiscal matters, he published his *Partitionum Po-*

[9] *Ibid.*
[10] *Ibid.*, Book 14, p. 367.
[11] *Ibid.*, Book 10, p. 122.
[12] Vauban, *Dixme Royale*, reprinted in Eugene Daire, Ed., *Économistes-financiers du XVIII siècle*, Paris: Guillaumin, 1843, p. 46.

liticarum in 1608. Confident that population growth was desirable, he gave particular attention to means by which a state could increase the number of its inhabitants and proposed the encouragement of immigration, various rewards to parents, and some penalties for the unmarried and childless.[13] Similar views on population were expressed by Hermann Latherus von Husum (1583–1640), whose *De Censu* appeared ten years later,[14] and Christophe Besold (1577–1638), whose principal works were the *Politicorum libri duo* (1618) and *Discursus politicus de incrementis imperiorum* (1623).[15] Besold, a jurist with varied experience in government service and a professor of law at several universities, improved on his immediate predecessors in discussing questions of population policy. Like them, he believed that population could and should be increased by inducements to immigration and judicious promotion of fertility. But he also believed that the number of people would increase of itself if production flourished, and that the attainable size of population depended among other things upon the supply of natural resources.

A considerable contribution to the discussion of population questions was made by Johann Joachim Becher (1635?–1685?), a famous Austrian chemist whose varied career included medicine and government service. His *Politische Discurs*[16] was published in 1668, and the *Psychosophia oder Seelen-Weisheit* in 1678. The former, as indicated by its subtitle, dealt specifically with the weighty question of how to make a city or state populous and prosperous. Becher began by asserting that an ample population is a necessary condition for civil society,[17] "for just as one swallow does not make a summer, so one man does not make a society." Further, he suggested there is a practical reason for wanting a large number of people: "The more populous a city is the more powerful it is." Every effort should therefore be made to secure a large population, especially since underpopulated nations are unable to defend themselves.[18]

Although Becher believed that population growth benefitted a nation and was led to some curious conclusions by this conviction,[19] he was well aware of certain limitations on population growth. Populousness alone was

---

[13] Wilhelm Roscher, *Geschichte der National-Oekonomik in Deutschland,* 1874 edition, Munich: Oldenbourg, Ch. 10, pp. 183–195.

[14] Stangeland, *Pre-Malthusian Doctrines of Population,* pp. 99–100; Gonnard, *op. cit.,* pp. 116–117.

[15] Roscher, *op. cit.,* Ch. 10, pp. 195–205; Stangeland, *op. cit.,* pp. 100–101.

[16] Becher, *Politische Discurs von den eigentlichen Ursachen des Auf- und Abnehmens der Städte, Länder und Republiken; in Specie, wie ein Land Volckreich und Nahrhaft zu machen.* The edition used here is the third, published in Frankfurt, 1688.

[17] *Ibid.,* Introduction; also, Part II, Ch. 2, p. 110.

[18] *Ibid.,* p. 2.

[19] He wrote, for example, that the reason for imposing the death penalty for murder and theft was that the former reduced populousness and the latter took away subsistence (*Ibid.,* p. 106).

not enough, he wrote, if the means of subsistence were lacking; and without ample subsistence, there could not be large numbers of people. Also, the potential size and growth rate of a population would be less with monopoly and concentration of wealth.[20]

The *De Jure Naturae et Gentium* (1672), of the celebrated German jurist, Samuel von Pufendorf (1632–1694), contained only passing references to population numbers, but the views expressed there were moderate and enlightened by contemporary standards. In accord with the prevailing thought of the time, it was considered desirable for a nation to be well peopled, but this was not to be attained by oppressive legislation or restrictions on personal liberty. In particular, the citizens should not be forbidden to emigrate if they so desired, nor should they be urged into marriage by the threat of penalties for non-marriage. Prudence should be exercised in marriage, and as for the bearing of children, Pufendorf declared, with a liberalism extraordinary for his time, that ". . . he who becomes the parent of a few children satisfies the law of nature as well as he who becomes the parent of many, and he whose wife bears him none at all has no cause to fear sin."[21]

Moderate views on population policy were also set forth in the *Institutiones Politicae* (1674) of Johann Heinrich Böcler (1611–1672). An ample population was indeed desirable, he suggested, and might be secured by judicious encouragement of immigration and wise regulation of the internal economy; but the number of people should not be allowed to increase beyond "the strength of the land." If this did occur, the surplus could be removed by emigration.[22]

A less qualified approval of numerical strength was expressed by Hermann Conring (1606–1681), in his *Examen Rerum Publicarum Totius Orbis* (1677). At one time or another professor of "natural philosophy," medicine, and law in German universities and a writer on many subjects, Conring conceded that numbers might become too great in extreme cases; but emphasized the military advantages of populousness and recommended various measures for achieving it.[23]

More moderate views on population policy were expressed in the *Christenstaat* (1685) of Ludwig von Seckendorf (1626–1692), a German statesman and scholar. In general he agreed with the popular opinion that a nation benefited from having a large number of people, but he was careful to qualify this position, saying for example: "There can not be too many industrious common people, provided that the authorities are diligent in the promotion of their livelihood and that the people exercise frugality

[20] *Ibid.*, pp. 2, 110.

[21] Samuel von Pufendorf, *De Jure Naturae et Gentium,* translated by C. H. and W. A. Oldfather, Oxford: Clarendon Press, 1934, Book VI, Ch. 1, p. 841.

[22] Roscher, *Geschichte,* 1874 edition, Ch. 14, p. 263; Stangeland, *op. cit.,* pp. 190–191.

[23] Strangeland, *op. cit.,* pp. 191–194.

and moderation."[24] Again with a significant qualification of the conventional statement, he gave the opinion that the greatest treasure of a nation was its numbers of well-nourished people.[25]

Many other references to the importance of populousness can be found from this period, but these German and Austrian writers, from Bornitz to von Seckendorf, best represent thought on population in Central Europe during the seventeenth century. Included among them were distinguished jurists, statesmen, scientists, and scholars, and they were all active participants in the intellectual life of their day. Having international experience and interests, they all concerned themselves with the problems of their country, but they viewed these problems from quite diverse points of view. Some saw them from a philosophical or historical perspective, some were influenced by nationalist sentiments, and others had a strongly ethical and religious orientation. Being principally concerned with other matters, their treatment of population questions was largely incidental and not in any degree analytical. Their reasoning in favor of populousness went little if any beyond the common-sense notion of "strength in numbers." Further explanation may well have appeared superfluous.

It is not surprising that these men all regarded numerical strength with approval. Several, such as Bornitz and von Seckendorf, had personally suffered from the Thirty Years War, and the others knew the war's aftermath at first hand. At a more theoretical level, they were all exposed to the full weight of mercantilist or cameralist doctrine that large numbers of people benefited a state. It is therefore more notable that many of the endorsements of populousness were qualified. Most of them recognized a necessary relation between population and "the strength of the land"; they more often than not recognized that the wellbeing of the people as well as their number was to be considered; and they expressed the enlightened view that population policies should not be dictated by national interests alone but also should respect individual rights. Fundamentally, their interest in population concerned questions of policy. While these writers did not analyze the implications of population numbers beyond the simple doctrine of numerical strength, they did qualify the doctrine of "strength in numbers" with good sense and principle. Thus they are in an intermediate position between the earlier pessimism and the excesses of the *Volksvermehrung* or populationist theories that followed.

3 · England before the Restoration

The assumption made during the late Tudor period that England was overburdened with people carried over into the new century, and skepti-

---

[24] Ludwig von Seckendorf, *Christenstaat,* Leipzig, 1716, Book II, Ch. 3, section 5.
[25] *Ibid.,* Book II, Ch. 13, section 1: ". . . auf der Menge wohl genährte Leute der grösseste Schatz des Landes besteht."

cism about the desirability of large numbers of people and the ability of the land to support them appeared in the works of two prominent Elizabethans, Raleigh and Bacon, who lived on into the Stuart period. This pessimistic view of population numbers was revealed in part by Sir Walter Raleigh (1552–1618) in his *History of the World.* Explaining why it was best that man was not immortal, he wrote, ". . . such is the infinite wisdom of God, as he foresaw that the earth could not have contained mankind; or else, that millions of souls must have been ungenerated. . . ."[26] Later in the same work he again expressed his conviction that the number of people, if they increased without limit, would exceed the capacity of the earth to support them: ". . . we know the multitude such, as if by wars or pestilence they were not sometimes taken off by many thousands, the earth with all the industry of man could not give them food."[27]

Population growth was mentioned again as a source of trouble, now as a cause of war, in Raleigh's *Discourse of War in General,* published in 1650:

> . . . the very progression of our kind hath with it a strong incentive even of those daily wars which afflict the whole earth. . . . the want of room upon the earth, which pincheth the whole nation, begets the remediless war. . . .

And further, on the same topic:

> . . . when any country is overlaid by the multitude which live upon it, there is a natural necessity compelling it to disburden itself and lay the load upon others, by right or wrong, for (to omit the danger of pestilence, often visiting them which live in throngs) there is no misery that urgeth men so violently unto desperate courses and contempt of death as the torments and threats of famine: wherefore the war that is grounded upon general, remediless necessity may be termed the general and remediless, or necessary war.

This is reminiscent of More's statement of a natural right to relieve overpopulation by force if necessary, and of Machiavelli's interpretation of the barbarian invasions as due to the pressure of growing numbers. The statement is notable also for its tracing of some consequences of overpopulation, whether based on observation or on an analytical line of thought — one, the danger of pestilence among crowds of people, and the other, a sequence of effects leading from overpopulation to famine and "desperate courses."

In following the evolution of the pessimistic theory of population that reached its full development almost two centuries later, it is worth noting that Raleigh either expressed or implied two fundamental elements of this

[26] Sir Walter Raleigh, *History of the World,* 1614, Book I, Ch. 4.
[27] *Ibid.,* Book I, Ch. 8, Section 9, subsection 5.

theory, first, the concept that food supply limits human numbers, and, second, the concept of checks upon population growth.

A number of references to population, some implying the undesirability of population increase, are found in the essays of Sir Francis Bacon[28] (1561–1626). In his "Essay of the True Greatness of Kingdoms and Estates"[29] he stated with some emphasis that the character and quality of the citizens is more important to the state than their number, for

> Walled towns, stored arsenals and armories, goodly races of horse, chariots of war, elephants, ordnance, artillery, and the like; all this is but a sheep in a lion's skin, except the breed and disposition of the people be stout and warlike. Nay, number (itself) in armies importeth not much, where the people is of weak courage; for, (as Virgil saith) "It never troubles a wolf how many the sheep be."

In the "Essay of Seditions and Troubles,"[30] he gave the seemingly sound advice, "Generally it is to be foreseen (i.e., seen to in advance) that the population of a kingdom, especially if it be not mown down by wars, do not exceed the stock of the kingdom which should maintain them." Individual self-interest might also call for a limitation of numbers, for contained in the "Essay of Marriage and Single Life" (1612) is the somewhat cynical aphorism, "He that hath wife and children hath given hostages to fortune; for they are impediments to great enterprises, either of virtue or of mischief." This may have been a paraphrase, if not an earlier version, of the old saying, "He travels the fastest who travels alone."

Finally, in the same vein as Raleigh and Machiavelli before him, Bacon wrote in the "Essay of Vicissitude of Things" (1625):

> . . . when there be great shoals of people which go on to populate, without foreseeing means of life and sustentation, it is of necessity that once in an age or two they discharge a portion of their people upon other nations; which the ancient northern people were wont to do by lot; casting lots what part should stay at home, and what should seek their fortunes.

Although these scattered comments do not fully reveal Bacon's views on population, they do indicate views similar to Raleigh's and, especially, a recognition that population size is limited by "the stock of the kingdom," and an underlying doubt about the desirability of population growth.

The argument that colonies, in addition to their other advantages, could serve as an outlet for England's surplus population was well presented in

[28] Because of the many editions of Bacon's works, reference is given to the *Essays* by title only. The editions used here were those publishd by William Bell, London, 1835; Houghton Mifflin, Boston, 1900(?); and Macmillan, London, 1920.

[29] First published in the 1612 edition of the *Essays*.

[30] First published in the final edition (1625) of the *Essays*.

forceful Elizabethan prose in *A Good Speed to Virginia*[31] (1609), by Robert Gray. Of particular interest here because of its account of English population conditions and their consequences, the tract spoke regretfully of earlier times, ". . . those times when our Country was not pestered with multitude, nor ouercharged with swarmes of people." In those happy days, he said:

> . . . this kingdome was not so populous as now it is, Civell warres at home, and forreine wars abroad, did cut off the ouer-spreading branches of our people. Our country then yielded unto all that were in it a sur-plussage of all necessities: it yielded preferment in due correspondencie, for al degrees & sorts of men. The commons of our Country lay frie and open for the poore Commons to inioy, for there was roome enough in the land for euery man, so that no man needed to encroach or inclose from another, whereby it is manifest that in those dayes we had no great need to follow strange reports, or to seeke wilde aduentures, for seeing we had not only sufficiencie, but an ouerflowing measure proportioned to euerie man; Religion and pietie taught us, that seeing our lot was falled unto us in a faire ground, and that we had a goodly heritage, rather to be content with our own than either politikely or ambitiously to undertake uncouth enterprises, unto which necessitie did no way urge us.

In contrast is the present overpopulated and unhappy state of the nation:

> But nowe God hath prospered us with the blessing of the wombe, and with the blessings of the breasts, the sword deuoureth not abroad, neither is there any feare in our streetes at home; so that we are now for multitude as the thousands of Manatles. . . . And therefore we may iustly say, as the children of Israel say here to Ioshua, we are a great people, and the lande is too narrow for us. . . .
>
> There is nothing more daungerous for the estate of common-wealths, then when the people do increase to a greater multitude and number than may iustly paralell with the largenesse of the place and countrey: for hereupon comes oppression, and diuerse kind of wrongs, mutinies, sedition, commotion, & rebellion, scarcitie, dearth, pouertie, and sundrie sorts of calamities, which either breed the conuersion, or euersion, of cities and common-wealths. For euen as blood though it be the best humour in the body, yet if it abound in greater quantitie than the state of the body will beare, both indanger the bodie, & oftentimes destroys it: so although the honour of the king be in the multitude of people, Pro. 14: 28, yet when this multitude of people increaseth to ouer great a number, the common-wealth stands subiect to many perilious inconueniences, for which cause many nations perceyuing their people to increase aboue a due and proportionable number, they have sent their ouerflowing multitudes abroad into other countreyes and prouiences, to the ende they might preserue their owne in greater peace and prosperitie. . . .

[31] Robert Gray, *A Good Speed to Virginia,* London, 1609. Also available in a reprint, New York: Scholars' Facsimiles & Reprints, 1937 (pages not numbered).

Our multitudes like too much bloud in the body, do infect our countrey with plague and pouertie, our land hath brought forth, but it hath not
milke sufficient in the breast thereof to nourish all those children which it
hath brought forth, it affordeth neither employment nor preferment for
those that depend upon it: And hereupon it is, that many seruiceable men
giue themselves to lewd courses, as to robbing by the high way, theft, &
cosoning, sharking upon the land, piracie upon the sea, and so are cut
off by shamefull and untimely death: others liue prophanely, riotously,
and idely, to the great dishonour of Almightie God, the detriment of the
commonwealth.

It is well to remember that the author's purpose was to promote the
settlement of Virginia, not to write a treatise on population, and that he
may have purposely overstated a plausible argument for colonies. The
passages quoted are not inconsistent with other contemporary discussions of
colonization and overpopulation, however, and they do rest on the theory
that overpopulation can lead to civil unrest, famine, poverty, crime, and
other evil consequences. The conclusion of this part of Gray's argument
was, of course, that these evils might be reduced by drawing off the surplus
people to colonies such as Virginia.

The question of plantations, or colonies, again led to discussion of the
dangers and consequences of an overabundant population in *The Antient
Law-Merchant*[32] (1622) of Gerard Malynes (1586–1641), an authority
on monetary and mercantile affairs and a writer on economic questions. In
a chapter, "Of Plantations of People, and new Discoueries," Malynes wrote,
in the now familiar vein:

> When the Common-wealth of the Empire of the Romans grew to be
> very populous, and men (idle) would haue stirred more commotions;
> Then the Plantation of Collonies of people in other Countries was most
> necessarie to be practiced, and means also to set the people on worke, or
> to employ them in the wars, to gouerne the quieter at home. . . . For
> vnlesse the three Impostumes[33] of the world, namely, Warres, Famine,
> and Pestilence, doe purge that great Bodie; all Kingdomes and Countries
> become very populous, and men can hardly liue in quiet, or without
> danger. Merchants therefore seeking to discouer new Countries, are much
> to be commended and cherished.[34]

Having thus stated the case against populousness and for the removal of
surplus numbers to colonies where they could be of better service to their
country, Malynes proceeded to recognize the other side of the matter:

> . . . let us obserue that in all popular gouernments, be it an Aristocracie,
> or Democracie, the means to make countries populous is thought reason-
> able, which in Monarchies is held to be dangerous. The concourse of people

[32] Gerard Malynes, *Consvetvdo, vel Lex Mercatoria, or, The Antient Law-
Merchant, London,* 1622. The edition used here was published in London in 1636.
[33] Literally, "abcesses."
[34] Malynes, *op. cit.,* Ch. 46, p. 164.

causeth the greater consumption of all things, and the revenues are great by Impositions, and it giueth life to Trafficke and Commerce.[35]

Although brief, Malynes's treatment of population is of some note in the development of English population thought. Malynes, himself of middle-class origin, was a forerunner and early spokesman for the rising merchant class that was to become more and more influential in national affairs and whose representatives were to make large contributions to economic and population theory in the latter part of the same century. Malynes concurred with his contemporaries and immediate predecessors in believing that unless population growth was checked by wars and other causes, it would lead to various effects harmful for the nation, and that colonies could be of service by drawing off some surplus inhabitants. But unlike others of his time, he also mentioned certain possible advantages of populousness, and it is especially noteworthy that the advantages he mentioned were of an economic order. The belief that numbers of people increased consumption and tax revenues and stimulated trade, quite new with Malynes, was to become much more widely accepted years later.

There was little reference to population in the controversy between Malynes and Edward Misselden (1608–1654) over commercial and economic policy. Misselden, a merchant and writer on economic subjects, maintained in his *Circle of Commerce* (1623) that England suffered from an unfavorable balance of trade, and recommended, in mercantilist fashion, that the remedy was to import less and export more. Regarding population he wrote only that "If the people of this Kingdome were numbered from Dan to Bersheba, I am persuaded, there were neuer more people, neuer lesse employment; neuer more Idlenes, neuer so much Excesse."[36]

Malynes replied with *The Center of the Circle of Commerce*[37] (1623), in which he took little notice of population numbers, but maintained, in equally good mecantilist fashion, that the nation needed plenty of money and that the root of the problem was the undervaluation of English money.

A later work, extolling the benefits to be derived from foreign commerce, was *A Treasure of Traffike, or a Discourse of Forraigne Trade* (1641), by Lewes Roberts (1596–1640), identified on the title page as a merchant. It was trade, he maintained, that gave strength and wealth to the nation. The number of workmen, he noted, "affords the abundance of the things wrought," but he added cautiously, "Now the over great number of work-men in all manufactories, would of it selfe be not onely improfitable to commerce, but also hurtfull if they were not also as good, skilfull, and as cunning. . . ."[38]

---

[35] *Ibid.*, p. 165.
[36] Edward Misselden, *Circle of Commerce*, London, 1623, pp. 133–134.
[37] Gerard Malynes, *The Center of the Circle of Commerce*, London, 1623.
[38] Lewes Roberts, *A Treasure of Traffike, or a Discourse of Forraigne Trade*, London, 1641, p. 13.

The colonial argument as it related to population was restated in an anonymous tract, *The Planters Plea*[39] (1630). New countries were assumed to have the virtue of forcing men to "labour, frugality, simplicity, and justice"; old countries were unfavorably contrasted because of their ". . . idlenesse, riot, wantonnesse, fraud, and violence, the fruits of well-peopled Countryes, and of the abundance and superfluities of long settled States."[40] In further account of the consequences of an excessive number of people, it was said that without

> . . . Warres, Pestilences and Famines, which unlesse they had wasted the people of these parts of the world, wee should ere this, have devoured one another; Yet it cannot be denyed, but the neare thronging of people together in these full Countreyes, have often occasioned amongst us ciuill Warres, Famines, and Plagues. And it is as true that God hath made advantage of some of these Warres, especially which have laid many fruitful Countreyes wast, to exercise men in these very labours which employ new Planters; by which he hath reduced them to some degrees of that frugality, industry, and justice, which had beene disused and forgotten through long continued peace and plenty.[41]

This of course led to the familiar conclusion that colonies could be used for "disburthening of full states of unnecessary multitudes."

To this conventional treatment the author added a section of questions and answers, in which he sought to remove any remaining doubts about the desirability of colonies. Among others, he anticipated this possible objection: "But the idelnesse or unprofitable labours of our people arise not from our numbers, but from our ill Government. . . ."[42] This may have been even then, as certainly it was in later times, a telling argument against those who attributed the ills of society to overpopulation; but the author replied with a show of reasonableness that good government could remove some but not all difficulties, and that there was little possibility of finding employment for all who needed work.

One more tract on the subject of colonies deserves mention for its ideas on the economic significance of population size. This was *Virginia: more especially the South Part thereof, Richly and Truly Valued*[43] (1650), by Edward Williams. A quite original argument in favor of colonies was given:

[39] Anon., *The Planters Plea, or the Grounds of Plantations Examined*, London, 1630. Reprinted in *Peter Force Tracts*, Washington: Peter Force, 1838, Vol. II, No. 3. E. A. J. Johnson attributes this to John White.

[40] *Ibid.*, p. 3.

[41] *Ibid.*, p. 5.

[42] *Ibid.*, p. 11.

[43] Edward Williams, *Virginia: more especially the South Part thereof, Richly and Truly Valued*, 2nd ed., London, 1650; also reprinted in *Peter Force Tracts*, Washington: Peter Force, 1844, Vol. III, No. 11.

It will be a generous and moving incouragement to all industrious and publick spirits, to imploy those parts with which God and nature hath blessed them in the discovery of such happy inventions as may drive on hopefull designs with a lesser number of hands then is usually assigned to them, which issues of the brain are legitimate and geniall to beginning Plantations, where the greatest want is that of people: but for our own or other popular (populous?) Kingdoms where we are commonly overprest with a greater multitude of labourers then imployers, by much lesse acceptable, since our indigent people look upon such Engins meerly as Monoppolies to engrosse their livelihood.[44]

Further on, in comparing the potentialities of Virginia with those of China, Williams wrote:

And if an invincible sloth doth not possesse us in Virginia, (wee meane the South) why should not wee rayse an equall or greater profit upon as fertile and convenient a soile? especially if we consider the populousnesse of the place, has so raysed the price of Land there, which we have heere gratis, where number of inhabitants doe so little take from our abundance, that they adde to our wealth, security and plenty, and the sole meanes to increase and improve upon Staples.[45]

In addition to familiar arguments this contains two new ideas that reappeared and received more emphasis later, first, the influence of population numbers on invention, and, second, the fact that populousness has "raysed the price of Land" in a densely settled country such as China.

Other writings that contained some discussion of population size and policy were those dealing with imaginary and ideal states, the "utopias." This type of work was most likely to appear in troubled times, but it recommended itself at any time as a means of discussing political matters with minimum great risk of the author's being penalized for criticism of the existing order.[46]

Several famous utopias appeared in England between 1600 and 1660, each containing some reference to population. Bacon's New Atlantis (written before 1617, published in 1627) described the careful regulation of marriage, but with emphasis on morality rather than on high fertility. There was only an indirect reference to population numbers in the re-

[44] Ibid., p. 6.
[45] Ibid., p. 28.
[46] For accounts of utopian literature, see, for example: Charles M. Andrews, Ed., Famous Utopias, New York: Tudor Publishing Co., 1901, introduction; Glenn Negley and J. M. Patrick, The Quest for Utopia, New York: Schuman, 1952; Frederic R. White, Famous Utopias of the Renaissance, Chicago: Packard, 1946; and Raymond Ruyer, L'utopie et les utopies, Paris: Presses Universitaires, 1950.
For an account of population thought in the utopias, see Hélène Bergues, "La population vue par les utopistes," Population, 6(2):261–286, April–June 1951.

mark that ". . . the king is debtor to no man, but for propagation of his subjects."[47] In view of Bacon's comments elsewhere on population matters, it is surprising that his *New Atlantis* made no provision for the regulation of numbers or for emigration. Perhaps he believed that the very advanced science and technology attributed to his imaginary state would solve the problem of subsistence.

Although not an English work, the *Civitas Solis* (1623) or *City of the Sun,* by the Italian monk, Tommaso Campanella (1568–1639), deserves mention here, for it was presumably known in England and may have had some influence on English utopian thought. It prescribed a very authoritarian regulation of marriage and procreation, but the purpose was eugenic and there was no stated policy regarding the number of inhabitants.

Two notable English utopias of mid-century were the *Leviathan* (1651) of Thomas Hobbes (1588–1679) and *The Commonwealth of Oceana* (1656) by James Harrington (1611–1677). The former gave no more attention to population than to recognize the more or less obvious dependence of the number of people on the food supply and to state that the continued growth of population would lead to emigration and, eventually, to war. In Hobbes' words:

> The multitude of poor, and yet strong people still increasing, they are to be transplanted into countries not sufficiently inhabited. . . . And when all the world is overcharged with inhabitants, then the last remedy of all is war; which provideth for every man, by victory, or death.[48]

This was less optimistic than the treatment of population in the proposals for emigration to colonies for it forecast an eventually overcrowded earth and was thus closer to the pessimistic views found in the early part of the century.

The last of the famous utopian works of this period was the *Oceana,* written by James Harrington and addressed to the Lord Protector of the Commonwealth. Openly critical of *Leviathan,* it differed from that work in being outspoken in favor of populousness. The people of a nation were referred to with eloquence by the Lord Archon as ". . . her treasure, the staffe by which she is sustained and comforted . . .";[49] and in the same connection he exclaimed, indignantly, "How brutish, and more than brutish, is that Common-wealth which preferreth the Earth before the fruits of her

---

[47] It is mentioned that a ceremonial feast was given in New Atlantis to "any man that shall live to see thirty persons descended of his body, alive together, and all above three years old"; but women were not so honored, and it is not clear that the purpose was to encourage high fertility.

[48] *Leviathan,* Part II, Ch. 30; in *The English Works of Thomas Hobbes,* edited by Molesworth, London: Bohn, 1841, Vol. III, p. 335.

[49] James Harrington, *The Common-wealth of Oceana,* London 1656, p. 108. See notes on Harrington and his work in James Bonar, *Theories of Population,* New York; Greenberg, 1931, Ch. II.

Womb?"[50] Taxation in Oceana was adjusted to encourage high fertility, with complete exemption granted fathers of ten children, half exemption for those with five children, and double tax burdens imposed on men married for three years or above twenty-five years of age who had no lawfully begotten children.[51] No explanation was given for these tax differentials, but their purpose seems obvious, especially in view of the comment about "people being the Riches of the Common-wealth." Another caducary provision was ". . . for as much as the Common-wealth Demandeth as well the Fruits of a man's body as of his mind, he that hath not been married shall not be Capable of these Magistracies. . . ."[52]

A later work by Harrington, *The Prerogative of Popular Government,* commented further on Oceana and replied to criticisms. Speaking of the populousness of his favorite model, Rome, he raised the question,

> That such a Populousness is that without which there can be no great Commonwealth, both Reason and good Authors are clear; but whether it ought to begin in the Country, or in the City, is a scruple I have not known them make.

The growth of the city, he reasoned, would stimulate the growth of the rural areas, for:

> . . . the more mouths there be in a City, the more meat of necessity must be vented by the Country, and so there will be more Corn, more Cattel, and better Markets; (and this will produce) more Laborers, more Husbandmen, and richer Farmers. . . .
> The Country then growing more populous, and better stock'd with Cattel, which also increases Manure for the Land, must proportionably increase in fruitfulness.

On the other hand,

> . . . a populous Country makes a populous City by weaning; for when the People increase so much, that the dug of Earth can do no more, the overplus must seek som other way of Livelihood: which is either Arms . . . or Merchandize and Manufacture, for which end it being necessary that they lay their Heads and their Stock together, this makes populous Citys.[53]

In other words, the growth of population beyond the food supply would stimulate the city to greater economic activity and thereby further increase the number of its inhabitants.

Hobbes, rather than Harrington, represented majority opinion among

[50] Harrington, *Oceana,* p. 108. The immediate object of this remark was mercenary marriage.
[51] *Ibid.,* p. 77.
[52] *Ibid.,* p. 79.
[53] The 1700 edition of Harrington's works, edited by John Toland, pp. 300, 301.

the writers who touched on population questions during the 1650's. Cock, whose description of the Elizabethan controls on marriage has already been quoted,[54] attributed the distress in England under the Stuarts to the imprudent relaxation of these controls. In contrast to the late marriage typical in the Tudor period, he said that under the Stuarts:

> . . . they coupled at fourteen, fifteen, sixteen, seventeen, eighteen a great age; this has bred multitudes of poor, weak and tender poor; and so for want of due provision roguish lazy poor; for many statutes are, but all to small purpose. . . .[55]

In his *Essay of Christian Government,* Cock returned to the question of population policy, saying there is ". . . no Nation, if not plagued with War or Diseases, but naturally it will grow over-numerous."[56] To this he added the advice:

> . . . if the Princes will in the use of the wisdom God hath given them to Rule by, Rule well and Safely, they must once every seven years number the people; if the Accidents, I must so call them, of Plague, War, Famine &c. hath not done it; and either by opening a fit way publikely known of easing their Counties burthen, by settling them in an other County: or if all Counties be full, by transporting them into another Country avoid this danger.
>
> This Act of Numeration well used, will take off the jealousie to what end such matters tend, and the well and carefully providing for the Colonies will encourage Adventurers; This will enlarge a Nation indefinitely; and if well carried on, will by just means so settle Christian interest, that great, if not universal, will be the propagation of the Gospel.[57]

This is one of the very earliest English proposals for a census of population.

A comment on the populousness of the time was contained in the tract, *Bread for the Poor* (1653) by Adam Moore. The numbers of poor were attributed to "The many peacefull yeers of our Dread Caesars Protection, begetting such multitudes of souls in the Tribes of our Israel, as former ages never saw."[58] The solution Moore proposed was the cultivation of waste lands instead of emigration to colonies.

In 1660 English population thought was on the eve of a period of great development, and it is therefore worth reviewing. The view taken of popu-

---

[54] See page 26.

[55] Part II of Cock's *English Law,* London, 1651, p. 49. This was written at a time when criticism of the Stuart reign was a means to favor.

[56] *Ibid.,* p. 148.

[57] *Ibid.*

[58] Adam Moore, Gent., *Bread for the Poor, and Advancement of the English Nation by Enclosure of Wastes and Common Grounds,* London, 1653, p. 3.

lation numbers and increase during the earlier years of the century was predominantly pessimistic. Almost everyone writing on the subject believed that England was overburdened with "great shoals of people," and their thinking was colored by this belief. Not as a hypothetical future development but as a present fact, population growth was believed responsible for poverty and distress, which could in turn lead to a long chain of other consequences. As Robert Gray wrote, "There is nothing more daungerous for the estate of common-wealths, then when the people do increase to a greater multitude and number than may justly paralell with the largenesse of the place." Among the many consequences he and others enumerated were epidemics of disease, internal discord and unrest, crime, and external wars. These and other ills of the nation were attributed to an overabundance of "the blessings of the womb." The thought that the ills of the nation might be due to misgovernment was either rejected or judiciously left unexpressed. Plagues, famines, and wars were by inference mixed evils, for they were a "purge for that great Bodie," the state, and a natural means of preventing or reducing overabundant numbers of people and the consequences thereof. There was a certain amount of looking back to supposedly happier days when the land was not so overcrowded, when wars and other causes "did cut off the over-spreading branches of our people." And if the natural checks to population growth were not sufficient, then there was the quite new and attractive possibility of sending the surplus to colonies — colonizing ventures were recommended as a means of converting the domestic liability of surplus people into an overseas asset. Except for Harrington's dissenting opinion, this was the most optimistic view taken of the problem of population numbers.

We may also note several themes that were to be more strongly developed later. As in definitive statements of the pessimistic theory by the classical economists in the early nineteenth century, there was expressed awareness that population was limited by "the stock of the kingdom," and the concept of checks to the increase of numbers was well developed. The tentative tracing of economic effects of population growth, including effects on the consumption of commodities, on tax revenues, on the price of land, on invention, and on business activity was especially significant in view of the evolution of analysis of the problem that followed in the late seventeenth century.

It should be added that population questions occupied very little space in the works mentioned above. The writers were concerned with other, more important matters, such as the welfare of their country, colonies, or the art of government. Population questions were touched on only as they related to these other topics, for population had not yet attracted attention as a subject in its own right.

4 · England after the Restoration

The Restoration period in England was one of vigorous development in the treatment of population, as in other fields, for pioneers in new directions of inquiry actively explored and developed new approaches to the social and political problems of the time. Two developments were especially important in the history of population thought, one, the foundation of modern population study in the empirical and statistical "political arithmetick" of Graunt and Petty, the other, the advancement of economic analysis by Petty, Child, Temple, and others, the precursors of the later political economists.

Two important works appeared in 1662. The first was *Natural and Political Observations upon the Bills of Mortality*[59] by John Graunt, a businessman who became a statistician and social scientist by avocation. In the introduction to this work, the pioneer demographic study, Graunt set forth as his purpose to show, among others things:

> That the greatest plagues of the City are equally, and quickly repaired from the Country: That the wasting of Males by Wars and Colonies do not prejudice the due proportion between them and Females: That the Opinions of Plagues accompanying the Entrance of Kings is false, and seditious: That London, the Metropolis of England, is perhaps a Head too big for the Body, and possibly too strong: That this Head grows three times as fast as the Body unto which it belongs, that is, It doubles its People in a third part of the time. . . .[60]

He believed the more rapid growth of the city must be due to migration from other parts of the country. One reason for this was probably that the city was less healthful because of its "Fumes, Steams, and Stenches," and also because of its greater assembly of people. On the latter he wrote:

> I considered, whether a City, as it becomes more populous, doth not, for that very cause, become more unhealthfull, I inclined to believe, that London now is more unhealthfull, then heretofore, partly for that it is

[59] *Natural and Political Observations mentioned in a following Index, and made upon the Bills of Mortality,* by John Graunt, Citizen of London, London, 1662; also reprinted in C. H. Hull, Ed., *Economic Writings of Sir William Petty,* Cambridge: University Press, 1899, Vol. 2; also published with an introduction by Walter F. Willcox, Baltimore: Johns Hopkins Press, 1939. For notes on the controversy over whether Petty was author or part-author, see introductory notes in the two reprinted editions cited above, as well as the following: Marquis of Lansdowne, *The Petty Papers,* London: Constable, 1927, Vol. 2, Ch. XXVII, and *The Petty-Southwell Correspondence, 1676–1687,* London: Constable, 1928, p. xxiii; Major Greenwood, "Graunt and Petty," *Journal of the Royal Statistical Society,* 1928, Vol. 91, Part I, pp. 79–85; E. Strauss, *Sir William Petty,* London: Bodley Head, 1954, p. 188.

[60] Graunt, *op. cit.* (1662 edition), "The Epistle Dedicatory."

more populous, but chiefly, because I have heard, that 60 years ago few Sea-Coals were burnt in London, which now are universally used.[61]

Furthermore, the fertility rate in London was less than that in the rest of the country. This he attributed to greater immorality and greater intemperance in feeding in the city; but he reflected further:

> Add to this, that the minds of men in London are more thoughtfull and full of business then in the Country, where their work is corporal Labour, and Exercizes. All which promote Breedings, whereas Anxieties of the minds hinder it.[62]

It was estimated that London's population doubled in sixty-four years. Graunt concluded from this that, contrary to some opinions, the Creation could not have been earlier than the 5610 years previous estimated from the Scriptures.[63]

Many other aspects of population were discussed by Graunt, with the wide-ranging curiosity of an explorer in a new world, but he occupied himself with discovering and describing and had little to say of the significance of population size. In spite of his doubts about the desirability of the concentration of people in London, he did assume that a large national population was desirable:

> Now forasmuch as Princes are not only Powerfull but Rich, according to the number of their People (Hands being the Father, as Lands are the Mother, and Womb of Wealth) it is no wonder why states by encouraging Marriage, and hindering Licentiousness, advance their own Interest, as well as preserve the Laws of God from contempt, and Violation.[64]

There appeared in the same year *A Treatise of Taxes and Contributions* (1662) by Sir William Petty (1623–1687), a friend of Graunt, a self-made man of many abilities, and one of the founders of the Royal Society. In the *Treatise* Petty agreed with Graunt that a large population was to be desired, but, significantly, he based his opinion not on the political or military advantages but on the wealth-producing capacity of a large population and the greater economy of government. It was, he said, an error to assume ". . . that the greatness and glory of a Prince lyeth rather in the extent of his Territory, than in the number, art, and industry of his people, well united and governed."[65] Returning to the subject, later he added:

> Fewness of People, is real poverty; and a Nation wherein are Eight Millions of people, are more than twice as rich as the same scope of

[61] *Ibid.*, Ch. XII, section 13, p. 70.
[62] *Ibid.*, Ch. VII, sections 7 and 8, p. 46.
[63] *Ibid.*, Ch. XI, sections 12 and 13, p. 63.
[64] *Ibid.*, Ch. 8, section 14, pp. 51–52.
[65] *The Economic Writings of Sir William Petty,* edited by C. H. Hull, Cambridge: University Press, 1899, Vol. I, Ch. 2, p. 22.

Land wherein are but Four; For the same Governours which are the great charge, may serve near as well, for the greater, as the lesser number.

Secondly, If the people be so few, as that they can live . . . with little labour, such as in Grazing, &c. they become wholly without Art.[66]

There are several important ideas here: that density rather than the size of population is the important factor; that populousness has a civilizing effect; and that the per capita cost of government falls as the number of people governed increases. Although it was still early in the reign of Charles II, concern with the cost of government was timely.

Further on, applying his theory of the wealth-producing effect of numbers in a way which anticipated some of the Volksvermehrung writers of the next century, Petty wrote:

> Here we are to remember in consequence of our opinion (That Labour is the Father, and active principle of Wealth, as Lands are the Mother) that the State by killing, mutilating, or imprisoning their members, do withall punish themselves; wherefore such punishments ought (as much as possible) to be avoided and commuted for pecuniary mulcts (i.e., fines), which will encrease labour and publick wealth.[67]

These and other ideas on population were repeated and developed in Petty's other works. He was a prolific writer with a particular interest in population matters, his works on the subject including *Political Arithmetick* (probably completed in 1676 or 1677, published in 1690), *Essay in Political Arithmetick, concerning the Growth of the City of London* (1682), *Observations upon the Dublin Bills of Mortality* (1681), *Five Essays in Political Arithmetick* (1687) and a number of others.[68] In *Political Arithmetick* he summarized the first chapter with the words, "A small Territory, and even a Few People, may by Situation, Trade, and Policy, be made equivalent to a greater . . .,"[69] but otherwise he quite consistently maintained the desirability of populousness and brought forward many reasons to support his belief. A recurrent argument, already noted above in the *Treatise,* was that there would be economic savings and efficiencies with a large and especially with a densely settled population. Expanding on the brief statement in the *Treatise,* he wrote in *Political Arithmetick.*

> I further add, that the charge of the Government, Civil, Military, and Ecclesiastical, would be more cheap, safe, and effectual in this condition of closer co-habitation than otherwise; as not only reason, but the ex-

[66] *Ibid.,* Ch. 3, p. 34.

[67] *Ibid.,* p. 68.

[68] There are many editions of Petty's works. Two collections have been used here, the Hull edition, referred to above, and *Several Essays in Political Arithmetick,* 4th ed., London, 1755.

[69] Petty *Economic Writings,* Vol. I, p. 268; *Several Essays,* p. 125.

ample of the United Provinces (i.e., of the Netherlands) doth demonstrate.[70]

Elsewhere in the same work he emphasized the practical advantages of having a given number of people concentrated in a small area rather than dispersed over a larger area;

> The charge of the cure of their Souls, and the Ministry would be far greater in one case than in the other; as also of mutual defence in case of Invasion, and even of Thieves and Robbers; Moreover the charge of the administration of Justice would be much easier, where Witnesses and Parties may be easily Summoned, Attendance less expensive, when Mens Actions would be better known, when wrongs and injuries could not be covered, as in thin peopled places they are.[71]

Another advantage of people living close together was

> . . . when England shall be thicker peopled, . . . the very same People shall then spend more, than when they lived more sordidly and inurbanely, and further asunder, and more out of the sight, observation, and emulation of each other; every Man desiring to put on better Apparel when he appears in Company, than when he has no occasion to be seen.[72]

The *Essay concerning the Growth of the City of London* considered at some length the consequences that might follow if (an "extravagant Proposal") the city should become seven times larger and include over four and a half million people. A city of that size, he was confident, could readily be supplied with all necessities, justice could be administered with speed and ease, the tax revenue would be large, transportation costs would be lower, and the arts and useful learning would be advanced. Fertility, he believed, would not be less in a large city, but there was the danger that the plague, more destructive in such a great population center, would raise deaths above births and lessen the population of the whole kingdom.[73] Of particular interest in this recital of advantages and disadvantages was the following:

> . . . in so vast a City Manufactures will beget one another, and each Manufacture will be divided into as many Parts as possible, whereby the Work of each Artisan will be simple and easy: As for Example; in the making of a Watch, if one Man shall make the Wheels, another the Spring, another shall engrave the Dial-plate, and another shall make the Cases, then the Watch will be better and cheaper, than if the whole work be put upon any one Man. And we also see that in Towns, and in the Streets of a great Town, where all the Inhabitants are almost of one

[70] Petty, *Economic Writings*, Vol. I, p. 290.
[71] *Ibid.*, p. 255.
[72] *Ibid.*, p. 290.
[73] Petty, *Several Essays*, pp. 25–32.

Trade, the Commodity peculiar to those Places is made better and cheaper than elsewhere.[74]

Also, shipping charges would be reduced on the larger volume of product. This is one of the earliest, perhaps the first enunciation of the theory that a large population permits division of labor.

Another economic aspect of population destined to become important in the later development of population theory was its influence on the rental value of land. In *Political Arithmetick* Petty wrote:

> . . . if a Man would know what any Land is worth, the true and natural Question must be, How many Men will it Feed? How many Men are there to be fed? But to speak more practically, Land of the same Quantity and Quality in England is generally worth 4 or 5 times as much as in Ireland, and but ¼ or ⅓ of what it is worth in Holland; because England is 4 or 5 times better peopled than Ireland, and but ¼ so well as Holland. And moreover, where the Rent of Land is advanced by reason of Multitude of People, there the Number of Years Purchase, for which the Inheritance may be sold, is also advanced. . . .[75]

That is to say, both the rent and the price of land are greater in more fully peopled nations.

A recurrent topic in Petty's studies of population was the balance between births and deaths, or the rate of growth, expressed in the then conventional terms of the period required to double the population.[76] It was only in projecting the process of doubling and redoubling far into the future that Petty was brought to any but optimistic conclusions about the effects of population growth. In the *Essay concerning the Growth of the City of London* he wrote:

> That if the People double in 360 years, that the present 320 Millions computed by some learned Men . . . to be now upon the Face of the Earth, will within the next 2000 Years, so increase, as to given one Head for every two Acres of Land in the habitable Part of the Earth. And then, according to the Prediction of the Scriptures, there must be Wars and great Slaughter, &c.[77]

This immediately followed a reference to Sir Matthew Hale's *Primitive Origination of Mankind,*[78] and the pessimistic note, so unusual for Petty,

[74] *Ibid.,* pp. 28–29.

[75] *Ibid.,* p. 148; or *Economic Writings,* Vol. I, p. 286.

[76] Petty calculated that London doubled its population every 40 years, England every 260 years. Projecting the two rates, he found that the population of London would equal that of the whole country by 1840, an inconsistency that has disturbed later computers of growth curves. Confident of his material, however, Petty concluded that the growth of the city must stop before 1840 (in *Essay concerning the Growth of the City of London*).

[77] Petty, *Several Essays,* p. 16; *Economic Writings,* Vol. II, p. 463–464.

[78] See below, p. 55.

may have come from that work. Also, Petty was speaking here theoretically rather than in his characteristically practical vein. With the same wide-ranging curiosity about all aspects of population that we saw in Graunt, Petty remained fundamentally practical and empirical in his point of view. He estimated the money value of a person to the state,[79] he was especially attracted to the question of population growth, past and future, he sought to trace and demonstrate the national interest as it was affected by the number of people, and his evaluations were predominantly in economic terms.

Although Graunt's and Petty's contemporaries and immediate successors did not share their special interest in population, the progress of population thought did not stop with them. Further contributions were made in discussions of national problems and especially in the developing economic literature of the time. A tract that appeared soon after Petty's *Treatise,* written by Samuel Fortrey (1622–1681), entitled *England's Interest and Improvement* (1663),[80] included measures for increasing the number of people among other recommendations for advancing the national interest. Wealth and populousness were the principal sources of national greatness and power, it asserted, and from this it followed that "The greatest thing therefore that any Prince can aim at, is to make his dominions rich and populous. . . . People and plenty are commonly the begetters the one of the other, if rightly ordered."[81] There might be those who doubted the wisdom of such a policy, saying,

> . . . it doth not appear that people are wanting, but rather that we have already too many, if we consider the number of poor people that are found in every place; and it might be prudence, first, to employ these, before we endeavour to multiply more.[82]

Fortrey believed, however, that with suitable encouragement of manufacturing and other employments population and wealth could both be increased.

Another brief note on the economic significance of population numbers appeared in *England's Treasure by Forraign Trade*[83] (1664), written by the mercantilist writer, Thomas Mun (1571–1641). Addressing himself to his son in "love and service of our Country," Mun considered the typically mercantilist question of how the kingdom might be enriched and its

[79] This Petty estimated to be £80; see *Political Arithmetick,* Ch. I; *Economic Writings,* Vol. I, p. 267; *Several Essays,* p. 123. Elsewhere he gave both higher and lower estimates.

[80] In John R. McCulloch, *A Select Collection of Early English Tracts on Commerce,* London, 1856. There is also a reprint (Cambridge: University Press, 1954).

[81] *Ibid.,* p. 219.

[82] *Ibid.,* pp. 224–225.

[83] Thomas Mun, *England's Treasure by Forraign Trade,* 1664; also reprinted (Oxford: Blackwell, 1949). Said to have been written about 1630.

treasure increased. The answer, he believed, lay in foreign trade; of population he remarked only that in the multitude of people lay "the greatest strength and riches of King and Kingdom," adding that ". . . where the people are many, and the arts good, there the traffique must be great, and the Countrey rich."[84]

A tract bearing added weight because of the prestige of its author was *A New Discourse of Trade*[85] (1668) by Sir Josiah Child (1630–1699), member of Parliament, governor of the East India Company, and leading representative of the merchant class. In the preface Child listed a dozen proverbial and "vulgar" errors he proposed to refute in his discourse, of which the following related to population:

> We have people enough, and more than we can employ.
> The admission of strangers is to call in others to eat the bread out of our own mouths.
> Our plantations depopulate, and consequently impoverish England.

It was in the chapter "Concerning Plantations" that his views on population were most fully set forth. Here he presented and defended a series of propositions that included the following:

> . . . that lands (though excellent) without hands proportionable, will not enrich any kingdom.
> That whatever tends to the depopulating of a Kingdom, tends to the impoverishment of it.
> That most Nations in the civilized Parts of the World, are more or less rich or poor, proportionately to the paucity or plenty of their people, and not to the sterility or fruitfulness of their Lands.
> I do not agree, that our People in England, are in any considerable measure abated, by reason of our foreign Plantations, but propose to prove the contrary.[86]

The first proposition, Child supposed, "would readily be asserted to by all judicious persons," and therefore could be taken as a matter of fact that required no proof. The second followed on the first, and in addition, "the substance and design of all my foregoing discourse" bore on this point. The third followed from the preceding two propositions, and "the whole World is a witness to the truth of it." The fourth was controversial, he recognized, but he maintained that the colonists were not qualitatively a serious loss to the mother country, and had the following to say of them:

> New-England, as every one knows, was originally inhabited, and has since successively been replenished, by a sort of people called Puritans, who could not conform to the ecclesiastical Laws of England. . . .

[84] *Ibid.*, p. 12.
[85] The edition used here is the 4th, published in London, 1740(?).
[86] *Ibid.*, pp. 191–192.

Virginia and Barbados were first peopled by a sort of loose vagrant people, vicious and destitute of means to live at home, (being either unfit for labour, or such as could find none to employ themselves about, or had so misbehaved themselves, by whoring, thieving, or other debauchery, that none would set them on work . . . and these, I say, were such, as had there been no English foreign Plantation in the World, could probably never have lived at home to do service to their Country, but must have come to be hanged, or starved, or died untimely of some of those miserable diseases, that proceed from want and vice; or else have sold themselves for soldiers, to be knocked on the head, or starved. . . .[87]

Neither did Child fear emigration as a quantitative loss, because:

. . . if that evacuation be grown to an excess (which I believe it never did barely on the account of the Plantations) that decrease would procure its own remedy; for much want of people would procure greater Wages, and greater Wages, if our Laws gave encouragement, would procure us a supply of People, without the charge of breeding them. . . .[88]

That is, a shortage of people would raise wages, which in turn would attract migrants.

A Treatise[89] (1671) by Roger Coke (d. 1696), author of several works on political subjects, began with a series of propositions or maxims, of which the following related to population:

1. The Law against Naturalization, before the Crown of England had the accession of the American Plantations, did exclude great numbers of People from subjection to the Crown, inhabiting and trading in England: and so it still doth.

2. Great numbers of People, is a mean, to improve Trade. This is evident in the nature of Man, in that every man, is in need of being supplied by another.

3. Lesser numbers of People, diminish Trade.

4. Greater numbers of People, encrease Strength.

5. Lesser numbers of People, diminish Strength.

10. The peopling the American Plantations, subject to the Crown of England, hath caused lesser numbers of People in England.

11. (same as above, for Ireland)

26. Men are necessary to improve Trade.

29. Men are necessary means to Trade.[90]

[87] *Ibid.,* pp. 196–198.
[88] *Ibid.,* p. 201.
[89] Roger Coke, *A Treatise wherein is demonstrated that the church and state of England are in equal danger with the trade of it,* London, 1671.
[90] *Ibid.,* p. 1.

Unlike Child, Coke believed that plantations or colonies were prejudicial to the mother country, but like Child, he looked at this and other questions of population from an economic viewpoint. This aspect appeared especially in his explanation of the second axiom:

> Greater numbers of people improve Trade. This is necessary in the nature of man, in that every man is in need of another to supply his necessities; whereby Trade is increased; but though every mans necessities must generally be supplied by another, yet so great a Providence is over industrious men, that scarce any man (not sick, aged, or impotent) but by industry might earn more than would supply his necessities; and so much as any man gets by being truly industrious above what supplies his necessities, is so much beneficial to himself & family, & also an enriching to the place.[91]

Coke's thought is not entirely clear here, but he seems to suggest that although every man can produce more than enough for his own needs and thereby enrich himself and the nation with the surplus, still, he is dependent upon others for some necessities, which he must obtain through trade. Therefore, the more people, the more surplus or wealth, and the more trade.

Later works by Coke were *England's Improvements* (1675) and *Reflections upon the East-Indy and Royal African Companies* (1695). The first presented and explained a number of propositions or theorems. In these Coke sought to demonstrate the desirability of admitting foreigners and permitting them to trade freely as means of developing England's population and economic strength. Concerning population numbers, he accepted the common belief that "The Glory, Majesty, and Grandeur of every Prince, consists not in the greatness of their Territories, but in the number of their Subjects, and good government of them. . . ."[92] An increase in the number of people, it was said, would increase trade[93] and, among other good effects, would enhance the value of land. As Coke explained, "Wheresoever therefore that Lands are plentiful in Proportion to the People, there the Lands are Cheap. And wheresoever the people are plentiful in Proportion to the Lands, they are Dear."[94] Foreign commerce would also be stimulated, as would be England's "navigation," or seafaring industry.

In the small tract entitled *Reflections upon the East-Indy and Royal African Companies . . .* (1695), Coke considered the value of encouraging the immigration of foreigners. In a chapter "On the State of the Nation in

[91] *Ibid.,* pp. 2–3.
[92] Roger Coke, *England's Improvements . . . and how the Navigation of England may be Increased,* London, 1675, pp. 5–6.
[93] *Ibid.,* p. 3.
[94] *Ibid.,* p. 4.

reference to the Law against Foreigners enjoying the Liberties of the Natives of England," he introduced the subject with the following statement:

> The Glory and Majesty of every Kingdom and Country is founded in the Number of People, and the well Ordering and Governing of them: So that as the Loss of any of the Subjects, is a Diminution of the Grandeur and Strength of that Country, so is the Addition of more Subjects, an Encrease of Both; and therefore it is not the greatness of the Extent of a Country, which makes it formidable, but the Number, and well Governing of the People. . . .[95]

Riches and trade also depended upon the number of people, he believed, and he pointed out, somewhat as Petty did, that ". . . wherever People are thin, or few, they are poor, lazy, rude, and of little use to the Publick. . . ."[96]

The economic treatment of population was developed somewhat further by Sir William Temple (1628–1699), statesman and author. In his essay, *Of Popular Discontents*,[97] he took the conventional position that "the strength and wealth of any country consist chiefly in the numbers and riches of the inhabitants,"[98] and even suggested that rewards be given for large families and that special taxes be levied on the unmarried. In his *Essay upon the Advancement of Trade in Ireland* (1673) he went much further, advancing the ingenious hypothesis that:

> The true and national ground of trade and riches is, number of people in proportion to the compass of ground they inhabit: this makes all things necessary to life dear, and that forces men to industry and parsimony. These customs, which grow first from necessity, come with time to be habitual with a country; and where-ever they are so, that place must grow great in traffic and riches, if not disturbed by some accidents or revolutions, as of wars, or plagues, or famines, by which the people come to be either scattered or destroyed.[99]

This argument was repeated almost word for word in *Observations upon the United Provinces of the Netherlands* (1672), with further deductions on the effects of a high population density:

> I conceive the true and original ground of trade to be, great multitude of people crowded into small compass of land, whereby all things necessary to Life become dear, and all men, who have possessions, are induced to parsimony; but those, who have none, are forced to industry

---

[95] Roger Coke, *Reflections upon the East-Indy and Royal African Companies* . . ., London, 1695, p. 14.

[96] *Ibid.*, p. 15.

[97] Jonathan Swift, who was Temple's secretary for a number of years and prepared a posthumous edition of some of his works, stated that this essay was written many years before the author's death.

[98] Sir William Temple, *Works,* London, 1770; Vol. III, section II of the *Essay.*

[99] *Ibid.*, Vol. III, pp. 6–7.

and labour, or else to want. Bodies, that are vigorous, fall to labour; such, as are not, supply that deficit by some sort of inventions or ingenuity. These customs arise first from necessity, but increase by imitation, and grow in time to be habitual in a country; and wherever they are so, if it lies upon the sea, they naturally break out into trade, both because whatever they want of their own . . . must be supplied from abroad; and because by the multitude of people, and smallness of country, land grows so dear, that the improvement of money that way is inconsiderable, and so turns to sea, where the greatness of the profit makes amends for the venture.[100]

With its purely economic orientation, this account of the advantages of a large population is especially important for the number of ideas it contains, especially the indication of a shift in emphasis from population size to population density and the imputation that population concentration has a stimulating effect on economic progress. If he was not the first to suggest these ideas, Temple at least stated and developed them more fully than had been done before.

After Graunt and Petty, the most important contribution to population thought in this period was made by Sir Matthew Hale (1609–1676), eminent jurist and authority on constitution and common law, a judge whose reputation for impartiality enabled him to serve under both Charleses and the Commonwealth, and, in his late years, lord chief justice of England. His views on population were set forth in two works, *A Discourse touching Provision for the Poor* (1673) and *The Primitive Origination of Mankind* (1677). Lacking the mercantile interests of his contemporaries, he did not treat population in economic terms, and, unlike them, his views had a pessimistic flavor reminiscent of the late Tudor and early Stuart periods. His skepticism about the desirability of populousness was expressed in the preface of the *Dicourse,* where he wrote that,

> . . . with us in England, for want of a due Regulation of Things, the more Populous we are, the Poorer we are; so that, that wherein the Strength and Wealth of a Kingdom consists, renders us the weaker and the poorer.[101]

The emphasis here is more on the "want of due regulation," it is true, than on the number of people. A later passage in the work was more explicit in attributing harmful effects to populousness:

> . . . it is most certain, that the Populousness of the Kingdom still increaseth . . . and consequently the Poor will be proportionably in-

[100] The 1814 edition of Temple's *Works,* Vol. I, Ch. 6. In the mercantilist literature of this time, the Dutch were the favorite example of how a dense population in a country of limited natural resources might be a stimulus to industriousness, ingenuity, and trade, and thereby bring national wealth.

[101] Sir Matthew Hale, *A Discourse touching Provision for the Poor,* London, 1673.

creased, so that we may reasonably suppose that in one seven Years, by the blessing of God, the very proceeds, that will be able and fit to work, of poor Families, will be more than double to what they are now, which will continually increase in a kind of Geometrical Progression. . . .[102]

Of particular note because of its connection with later controversy is this first use, as far as is known, of the term "geometrical progression" to describe the growth of population. It was observed earlier that the growth of population was conventionally expressed in terms of the period required for population to double, so the idea of a geometric progression of the number of people could easily arise.

The concept of geometric increase also appeared in Hale's *Primitive Origination of Mankind*. Assuming that only two children out of every family survived to maturity, that the average span of life of those living to maturity was sixty years, and that parents were on the average about twenty-five years of age at the birth of their children, he concluded that:

> . . . in the compass of about 34 years the number of two, namely the Father and Mother, is increased to the number of eight, namely, the Father and Mother, their two Children, and four Grand-Children; so that in 34 years they become increased in a quadruple proportion, and all coexisting: and although by that time we suppose the Father and Mother dye, yet in the like Period of thirty four Years by a Geometrical Proportion their Increase is multiplied proportionable to the Excess of their Number above Two.[103]

The ratio of increase, he noted, would be even greater if an earlier age of marriage or a longer span of life were assumed.

The reasoning here is somewhat faulty, in that no real increase is possible if each pair of parents has only two surviving children; or, to put it differently, the family lines entering through marriage are omitted from the calculation.

But faulty or not, this reasoning put Hale on a path of thought that Malthus was to tread long afterwards. Animals, birds, fishes, and lower creatures, Hale reflected, have a much greater capacity for multiplication than man, but nevertheless their numbers remain relatively stable from one season to the next. From this he inferred that in nature there are two opposing forces, or "Motions of Generations and Corruption," so balanced that numbers remain approximately constant. In his own words:

> In all this Consideration of the Reduction of Excesses and Increase of Animals and Insects, two things are observable in a special manner, namely

---

[102] *Ibid.*, Ch. 3.
[103] Sir Matthew Hale, *The Primitive Origination of Mankind*, London, 1677, Section II, Ch. 8, p. 205.

1. (that some species are stronger and prey on others)

2. That the vicissitudes of Generations and Corruption are by a kind of standing Law in Nature fixed in things, and the Motions and Qualities of Natural things are so ordered, to keep always that great Wheel (i.e., generations and corruption) in circulation; and therein the Accesses and Recesses of the Sun, the Influxes of the Heat thereof and of the other Heavenly Bodies, and the mutual and restless Agitation of those two great Engins in Nature, Heat and Cold, are the great instruments of keeping on foot the Rotation and Circle of Generations and Corruptions, especially of Animals and Vegetables of all sorts.

3. That yet these Motions of Generations and Corruptions, and of the conducibles thereunto, are so wisely and admirably ordered and contemperated, and so continually managed and ordered by the wise Providence of the Rector of all things, that things are kept in a certain due stay and equability; and though the Motions of Generations and Corruptions, and the Instruments and Engins thereof are in a continual course, neither the excess of Generation doth oppress and overcharge the World, nor the defect thereof, or prevalence of Corruptions doth put a Period to the species of things, nor work a total Dissolution in Nature.[104]

In the same manner, Hale believed, human numbers were kept in check by "Correctives of the Excess of Mankind," which he listed as follows:

1. Plagues and Epidemical Diseases
2. Famines
3. Wars and Internecions
4. Floods and Inundations
5. Conflagrations.

These were regarded as inevitable and necessary "prunings" of mankind. Of war Hale wrote:

> Wars seem to be in a manner a Natural Consequence of the overplenitude and redundancy of the Number of Men in the World: And so by a kind of congruity and consequence, morally necessary when the World grows too full of Inhabitants, that there is not room one by another; or that the common Supplies which the World should afford to Mankind begin to be too few, too strait, or narrow for the Numbers of Men; that natural propension of self-love, and natural principle of self-preservation will necessarily break out into Wars and Internecions, to make room for those that find themselves straitened or inconvenienced.[105]

Here, in substance, were the fundamentals of the pessimistic theory of population as later formulated: the power of increase in geometric progression, the concept of natural "prunings" or checks to population growth, and the conclusion that population growth would eventually bring its own

[104] *Ibid.*, Section II, Ch. 9., pp. 210–211.
[105] *Ibid.*, p. 215.

correction by leading to war and other evils that diminished the number of people.

Several other works that appeared in 1677 were lesser contributions to population thought but more typical of the thought of their time, for all assumed that a large number of people was desirable. One of these, by Andrew Yarranton (1616–1684?), entitled *England's Improvement by Sea and Land,* brought in the subject of population in recommending the establishment of linen manufacture in England. This would be a way to set the poor to work, Yarranton said, and it would attract

> . . . a multitude of People also, which is, and ever will be a great enrichment to the place where they are. . . . For where ever the Country is full of people, they are rich; and where thin, there the place is poor, and all Commodities cheap.[106]

An anonymous tract published the same year, *An humble address with some proposals for the future preventing of the decrease of the inhabitants of this realm,* was chiefly concerned with imprisonment for debt, but its argument was based on population considerations. It began with the statement that the nation could support and employ thousands more people than it did, and that

> . . . it is beyond all question, That the strength of the King, and Kingdome, both in peace, and war, consists in the multitude of it's inhabitants; and that the riches, and poverty of a Nation have their rise and origin from the number or poverty of them; and by the same causes a Nation is rendered either considerable or inconsiderable amongst it's Neighbors, as to Alliances, &c.[107]

Linking these first propositions with his main purpose, the author proceeded to describe how people were induced to emigrate by fear of imprisonment for debt, and proposed a sort of bankruptcy procedure whereby debtors who assigned all their estate to their creditors would be released from prison.

Another anonymous tract, entitled *England's Great Happiness,* presented the mercantilist case for a large population and the free admission of foreigners:

> . . . you cry up the Dutch to be brave people, rich, and full of Cities, that they swarm with people as Bee-hives with Bees; if a plague come, they are fill'd up presently and such like; yet they do all this by inviting all the World to come and live among them. You complain of Spain because their Inquisition is so high, they'l let no body live among them, and that's the main cause of their weakness and poverty. You find fault be-

[106] Andrew Yarranton, *England's Improvement by Sea and Land,* London, 1677, pp. 52–53.
[107] Anon., *An humble address . . .,* London, 1677, p. 1.

cause some of our people go to Ireland and the Plantations, and say we want people at home to fill our Cities and Countrie towns, and yet you'l allow none to come and fill up their rooms. Will not a multitude of people strengthen us as well as the want of them weaken Spain? sure it will. . . . Would not Foreigners living here consume our corn, cattle, cloth, coals, and all kinds of things we use? and would not that cause our lands to be better till'd, and our trades increas'd? would they not bring several new trades with them, or help to encrease those we have?[108]

This favorable attitude toward immigration, as seen before, was a natural corollary of the belief that more people meant greater national wealth and strength, and it was supported by mercantilist theory, for the migrants could bring needed skills with them and thereby increase national self-sufficiency, and help give a more favorable balance of trade.

Yet another anonymous tract, *Britannia Languens, or A Discourse of Trade* (1680)[109] presented the mercantilist view of population in even greater detail. It advanced the opinion that "People are therefore in truth the chiefest, most fundamental, and pretious commodity, out of which may be derived all sorts of Manufactures, Navigation, Riches, Conquests, and solid Dominion."[110] Too, population increase was believed desirable because of the stimulus it would give to economic development, for

> . . . suppose the people of England were trebled, 'tis plain that the Land must yield treble the produce in meer Victuals, else the people must starve; but these people will not starve . . . nor will they live needily or scarcely, if they can help it, and will therefore set themselves and others to the improving of all corners of Land in the Nation. . . . And as the people increase, so will the vallue of the Land.[111]

The last sentence is of particular interest as an indication that population growth affects the value of land.[112] The same influence was mentioned again in another connection: ". . . a Forreign Trade (if managed to the best advantage) will further advance the values of Lands, by necessitating a vast increase of people. . . ."[113] An effect on the wage level was also assumed:

> . . . plenty of people must also cause *cheapnesse of wages;* which will cause the cheapnesse of the Manufacture; in a scarcity of people wages must be dearer, which must cause the dearnesse of the Manufacture;

[108] *England's Great Happiness: or, A Dialogue between Content and Complaint,* by a real and hearty lover of his King and Countrey, London, 1677. Reprinted in McCulloch, *Early English Tracts on Commerce,* 1954 printing, pp. 263–264.

[109] Reprinted in McCulloch, *ibid.* This tract has been attributed to William Petyt but according to McCulloch, "we have no certain knowledge of the author."

[110] *Ibid.,* p. 458.

[111] *Ibid.,* p. 352.

[112] Also noted previously by Petty and Temple.

[113] Anon., *Britannia Languens,* p. 291.

But this populacy I speak of, must not be understood of those people which the *Extent of Territory* makes necessary for the meer tilling of the ground, keeping of Cattle, &c. . . . . The populacy I intend and which only can be serviceable to Manufacture, are those exuberant numbers which cannot find Imployment in husbandry, nor otherwise but in Trade. . . .[114]

This deserves particular notice for it introduced a relatively new idea of which much more was to be heard later, that plenty of people and workers meant lower wages and therefore low cost of production.[115]

Only passing mention was made of population in *A Discourse of Trade* (1690) by Nicholas Barbon (1640?–1698), doctor by training, member of Parliament, and actively interested in business and banking. Saying that it was to the advantage of a conqueror to preserve the population of conquered territory, he added:

To Burn the Towns, and Villages, and so force the People to remove, Is to lose the greatest share in Conquest; for the People are the Riches and the Strength of the Country, And it is not much more Advantage to a Prince, to have a Title to Lands in *Terra Incognita,* As to Countries without People.[116]

In Barbon's opinion, population was only one of several sources of strength, however, for the latter was also derived from "Ships, Excise, and Customs."[117]

The essays of the philosopher John Locke (1632–1704) contain little direct reference to population, although his thoughts on the subject are indicated here and there. *Some Considerations on the Consequences of the Lowering of Interest, and Raising the Value of Money* (1691) gives a supply and demand explanation of price determination:

All things, that are bought and sold, raise and fall their price, in proportion as there are more buyers or sellers. Where there are a great many sellers to a few buyers, there use what art you will, the thing to be sold will be cheap. On the other side, turn the tables, and raise up a great many buyers for a few sellers, and the same thing will immediately grow dear.[118]

[114] *Ibid.,* pp. 349–350.

[115] Child, previously quoted, had already noted the converse, that excessive emigration would raise wages.

[116] John Barbon, *A Discourse of Trade,* 1690; reprinted in J. H. Hollander, Ed., Baltimore: Johns Hopkins Press, 1905, p. 29.

[117] *Ibid.,* p. 31. Although not directly related to population, it is worth adding that Barbon distinguished two categories of wares, one that supplies "the Wants of the Body," the other "the Wants of the Mind." The former wants are few in number, the latter infinite (p. 14). Foreign trade and imports supply the latter; and domestic goods do not fill the same wants or have the same appeal. People desire novelties, not just necessities; and for this reason the restriction of imports leads to the decay of trade (p. 35).

[118] John Locke, *Works,* 12th ed., London: Rivington, 1824, Vol. IV, p. 39.

This is not explicitly applied to the price of labor, but wages are said to remain generally at the level of "bare subsistence."[119] Elsewhere in the same essay the author's views on population are revealed in part by the remark that it is harmful to hinder the coming of foreigners, because, among other reasons, "we lose their persons, increase of people being the increase both of strength and riches."[120]

> Locke

Locke's *Essays concerning the true Original, Extent, and End of Civil Government* expresses similar mercantilist opinions, first that "it is labour indeed that put the difference of value on every thing,"[121] and second, "Numbers of men are to be preferred to largeness of dominions."[122] Concerning the value of land in particular, he said that "It is labour then which puts the greatest part of the value upon land, without which it would scarcely be worth any thing: it is to that we owe the greatest part of all its useful production. . .,"[123] and further that "increase of people and stock, with the use of money" make land scarce, therefore valuable.[124]

More explicitly concerned with population was *A Discourse concerning the Having Many Children, in which the Prejudices against a Numerous Offspring are Removed* (1695), by Samuel Dugard (1645?–1697), member of the clergy and author of various publications on religious and other subjects. Evidently a man who practiced what he preached, for he was survived by ten children, Dugard presented various arguments for large families and a large population in the *Discourse,* which began by listing and then refuting reasons why people might prefer not to have many children. These reasons, quaintly expressed, but for the most part equally valid today, were:

> I. The Hinderance that Many Children are to Great Undertakings.
> II. A Free and Generous Way of Living being thereby maimed and cut short.
> III. The Afflictions that arise from Some, who in all probability, among so Many, will not prove well.
> IV. A man's Name sinking into Meanness by reason that where there are Many Children, there is not likelihood that a plentiful Provision can be made for them all.[125]

He also suggested some families might be influenced by the consideration, more true then than now, that where there is a plentiful issue, ". . . there are the more brought into a Miserable World, and larger Food is thereby afforded unto Death."[126]

Dugard proceeded to answer these objections in turn, and to establish

[119] *Ibid.,* p. 71.
[120] *Ibid.,* p. 63.
[121] *Ibid.,* p. 361.
[122] *Ibid.,* p. 362.
[123] *Ibid.,* p. 363.
[124] *Ibid.,* p. 364.
[125] Samuel Dugard, *A Discourse concerning the Having Many Children . . .,* London, 1695, pp. 6–7.
[126] *Ibid.,* p. 7.

the desirability of large numbers of children, employing, among others, the ingenious argument that

> The great difference between those who are called Rich, and those who are thought not so, is very often this, That *Servants* eat the Increases of the one, and *their own Children* the Increases of the other. . . .[127]

It was also in the national interest to have large families and a growing population, he believed, for

> . . . by the access of Number, Industry might be increased. The reason of so many wandring about, and begging their bread, to the shame of our Nation, is that overplenty which can tolerate such Droves to be so maintained. But were our own Inhabitants as many as our store of Provisions is great, there would in the main not be less of Necessaries and Conveniences but more of Labouriousness and Diligence; while many Heads would be at work to find out new Methods of Advantage, and Hands in all places employ'd for the every-way compleating them.[128]

Here again is the idea that the stimulus of necessity will spur men on to greater effort of body and mind.

In the same year that Dugard's *Discourse* was published there appeared a small volume written by John Cary, entitled *An Essay on the State of England*.[129] Cary presented his work to the reader with the disarming and ingenuous remark, ". . . what I have done hath not so much proceeded from an Itch of Writing, but purely from the Love I bear to my Native Country, whose Good and Welfare I delight in. . . ."[130] In explaining where the good and welfare of his country lay, Cary touched on population matters frequently and revealed his own ideas about the significance of population size and growth. In a sort of *histoire raisonnée,* he wrote:

> And as People increased so did Commerce, this caused many to go off from Husbandry to Manufacturers and other ways of living, for Convenience whereof they began Communities, this was the Original of Towns, which being found necessary for Trade, their Inhabitants were increased by expectation of Profit; this introduced Forreign Trade, or Traffick with Neighboring Nations; this Navigation. . . .[131]

This line of reasoning, that population growth sets in motion the process of development to a higher stage of economic and social organization, later became a very common argument for the optimistic theory of population.

[127] *Ibid.,* p. 17.
[128] *Ibid.,* p. 37.
[129] John Cary, *An Essay on the State of England in relation to its Trade, its Power and its Taxes,* Bristol and London, 1695.
[130] *Ibid.,* p. 178.
[131] *Ibid.,* p. 3.

Cary's conviction that a large population is beneficial to a nation also extended to the present time. Writing of Ireland, for example, he asserted that ". . . whatever hinders the Peopling, and consequently the cultivating and improving the Lands of Ireland, doth so far hinder the advancement of its true Interest," and referred to ". . . the strength and security of Ireland, which lies in a good Number of hardy People, enured to Labour. . . ."[132] Similarly, of the Dutch it was said that ". . . they find by Experience that as a Multitude of People brings Profit to the Government, so it creates Imployment to each other. . . ."[133]

Later in the same essay Cary attempted to trace the interrelations of several economic variables: ". . . you cannot fall Wages unless you fall Product, and if you fall Product you must necessarily fall Land."[134] The statement itself is open to question; but it shows an awareness of some connection between wages, the price of agricultural produce, and the value of land. The population variable did not enter into the equation, but Cary did not put major emphasis on population itself. England's interest, he believed, lay in developing its trade and manufactures.

Another writer who deserves mention in any account of late seventeenth-century English thought on population is Sir Charles Davenant or D'Avenant (1656–1714), holder of important official posts and author of numerous political and economic writings. Restatements of the current mercantilist views of population may be found in his principal works, which appeared in the last decade of the seventeenth century and in the early years of the eighteenth. The stimulating effect of a dense population was affirmed, somewhat after the manner of Temple, in *An Essay upon Ways and Means of Supplying the War* (1695). Here Davenant wrote:

> People are the real Strength and Riches of a Country. . . . 'Tis better that a People should want Country, than a Country should want People. Where there are but few Inhabitants, and a large Territory, there is nothing but Sloath and Poverty; but where great Numbers are confin'd to a narrow Compass of Ground, Necessity puts them upon Invention, Frugality and Industry. . . .[135]

Consistent with this was the following statement of the consequences of underpopulation:

> No Country can be truly accounted great and powerful by the Extent of its Territory, or Fertility of its Climate, but by the Multitude of its Inhabitants; and rich Soils not well peopled, have been ever a Prey to all Invaders.

[132] *Ibid.*, p. 93, 96.
[133] *Ibid.*, p. 124.
[134] *Ibid.*, p. 145.
[135] Sir Charles Davenant, *An Essay upon Ways and Means of Supplying the War*, London, 1695, p. 144.

> Where Countries are thinly Inhabited, the People always grow Proud,
> Lazy and Effeminate, Qualities which never fail to prepare a Nation for
> Foreign Subjection.[136]

Consistent with these views and with mercantilist theory, Davenant approved of the admission of foreigners.

Davenant later published a two volume collection of essays under the title, *Discourses on the Publick Revenues, and on the Trade of England* (1698). In the first discourse, *On the Uses of Political Arithmetic,* it was noted that "The wealth of all nations arises from the labour and industry of the people."[137] In another discourse, *Of the Plantation Trade,* this proposition used to demonstrate that the colonies could not have diminished the population of England, for the wealth of the nation had increased since the year 1600, and this increase of wealth could have come only from an increase in number of inhabitants.[138]

Up to this point Davenant appears completely optimistic in his population thought, convinced that people are the producers of wealth and that the increase of national wealth depends upon the growth of population. But somewhat more cautious views were expressed by Davenant in a work published in 1699, *An Essay upon the Probable Methods of making a People Gainers in the Ballance of Trade.*[139] In this essay national strength was said to depend upon not one but a number of factors: " 'Tis not extent of Territory that makes a Country Powerful, but Numbers of Men well employ'd, convenient Ports, a good Navy, and a Soil producing all sort of Commodities."[140] Later in the same work a further qualification was added:

> The Bodies of Men are without doubt the most valuable Treasure of a
> Country; and in their Sphere the ordinary People are as serviceable to
> the Commonwealth as the rich, if they are employ'd in honest Labour
> and useful Arts: And such being more in Number, do more contribute
> to increase the Nation's Wealth, than the higher Rank.
>
> But a Country may be Populous and yet Poor (as were the ancient
> Gauls and Scythians) so that Numbers, unless they are well employ'd,
> make the Body Politick big, but unweildy, strong but unactive, as to any
> Uses of good Government.
>
> Their's is a wrong Opinion, who think all Mouths profit a Country
> that consume its Product; And it may be more truly affirm'd, That he

136 *Ibid.,* p. 145.
137 Sir Charles Davenant, *Political and Commercial Works,* London, 1771, Vol. I, p. 138.
138 Sir Charles Davenant, *Discourses on the Publick Revenues, etc.,* London, 1698, Vol. II, Discourse III, pp. 195–196; or *Works,* 1771 edition, Vol. II, Discourse III, pp. 2–3.
139 The edition used here was the second, published in London, 1700.
140 *Ibid.,* p. 24; or *Works,* 1771 edition, Vol. II, pp. 192–193.

who does not some way serve the Common-wealth, either by being employ'd, or by employing Others, is not only a useless, but hurtful Member to it.[141]

Especially in contrast to Davenant's earlier treatment of the subject, this appears to be a declaration of intellectual independence from the more extreme mercantilist and populationist doctrine.

The prevailing views on population were restated in original phrasing in *Essays about the Poor, Manufactures, Trade, Plantations and Immorality* (1699)[142] by John Bellers (1654–1725), social reformer and prolific writer. His belief, in his own words, was that "Land, Cattel, Houses, Goods and Money are but the Carcas of Riches, they are dead without People; Men being the life and Soul of them."[143] People were also regarded as the economic substance of a nation, for ". . . nothing can be strictly said to inrich a Nation, but what increaseth its People, and with them, Supplies it with things that are lasting and necessary, more than they Spend,"[144] and labor together with land constituted the national wealth.[145]

Perhaps as a corollary of his belief in the economic value of people, perhaps in his role as reformer, Bellers argued against the death penalty, saying that it meant loss not only of the person executed but also of his posterity. Every "able man," he estimated, was worth £10 a year to the nation, or a total of £200 over a twenty-year period.

The final publication of the century that is of interest here is *Of Trade* (1697) by John Pollexfen (fl. 1697). This firmly stated the populationist case:

> Our moveable Riches had their Original, and must have their Increase from the Labour and Industry of our People, by digging out of the Bowels of the Earth, Manufacturing and making fit for use the Product thereof. . . . All which depends upon having many people. Therefore the obtaining more, and well imploying those we have, may deserve consideration in the first place.[146]

Pollexfen then went on to note, with a hint of wage theory, that because of idleness there was a scarcity of servants, which "hath advanced

[141] *Ibid.,* p. 34; or *Works,* 1771 edition, Vol. II, pp. 202–203.

[142] Reprinted in A. Ruth Fry, *John Bellers, Quaker, Economist, and Social Reformer,* London: Cassell, 1935.

[143] *Ibid.,* p. 63.

[144] *Ibid.,* p. 67.

[145] *Ibid.,* p. 69.

[146] (John Pollexfen), *Of Trade, by J. P. Esq., to which is annex'd The Argument of the Late Lord Chief Justice Pollexphen,* London, 1700, pp. 43–44. The 1700 edition appears to be a reprint of John Pollexfen's *A Discourse of Trade, Coyn, and Paper Credit . . .,* 1697. The Lord Chief Justice, Henry Pollexfen, was the brother of John Pollexfen. (See *Dictionary of National Biography,* Vol. XVI, p. 62.)

their Wages."[147] The prescription for curing this difficulty was "General Naturalization" in order to increase the number of working people.[148]

5 · Population Theory at the End of the Seventeenth Century

By the end of the seventeenth century the two sides of the population problem were already quite well stated, especially through the English contributions to the subject, and the modern formulation of the problem of population numbers was well on its way to development. The predominantly political or political-military consideration of the problem which had persisted since the earliest recorded population thought was giving way to economic considerations under the stimulus of expanding economic activity and the rising influence of people whose interests were mercantile and financial. Whereas most earlier writers on population had been clergymen, officials, or men of letters and learning, now there appeared businessmen and men of affairs. The national interest was still the context in which population questions were discussed, it is true, but new conceptions of the national interest were arising. At the level of practical politics were questions of the prosperity and employment of the people, political stability, promotion of internal trade, development of foreign commerce, and colonies: and in all these contexts population questions arose. Not unrelated were the dreams of an ideal state. As Bonar said, "Men were excited by the idea of a New World."[149] For some it lay tangibly across the wide Atlantic, for others it existed in a vision of Utopia or of an attainably greater and happier England or Germany or France of the future.

The treatment of population matters also was changing. There was less stating of intuitively perceived, overall relations between population numbers and socio-political conditions, and the discussion of population policy was becoming more analytical and dealt more with specific effects of population. The more factual and statistical approach of "political arithmetick" was establishing itself, and for the first time, in the works of Graunt, Petty, and Hale, population became a subject of attention in its own right.

Both the optimistic and the pessimistic positions became more clearly formulated during the century. On both sides there were those who recognized a necessary relation between population numbers and food supply, as well as the possibility of the former approaching the limit set by the latter. For the optimists, the possibility was theoretical and remote, however,

[147] Pollexfen, *op. cit.,* pp. 46–47.
[148] *Ibid.,* pp. 51–52.
[149] James Bonar, *Theories of Population,* p. 42.

and presumably there were ample means of relief, such as foreign trade or emigration, if the situation did arise. For the pessimists, overpopulation was more than a possibility, it was imminent, if not a present reality.

The pessimistic position was most fully developed in England during the first half of the century and later by Hale. From this viewpoint population growth was seen as an almost inevitable trend toward a surplus of numbers, unless checked by famine, disease, or war; and these checks, by implication, performed a necessary and even useful service. In varying forms, this view was expressed in particular by Raleigh, Gray, Malynes, Cock, and Hale. And if the checks to population growth did not intervene, and the population came to exceed "the stock of the kingdom," then the consequences included unemployment and poverty, crime, and civil unrest. Here the pessimists were speaking not theoretically nor of some future time. They believed that England was already overburdened with "the blessing of the womb," and to this they attributed many of the troubles of the time. In addition to internal troubles, war was cited as a consequence of overpopulation by Raleigh, Bacon, Hobbes, Petty, and Hale. Most notable was Hale's quite full statement of the basic elements of the pessimistic position, including the power of increase, the geometric progression of numbers, the concept of checks, and the consequences of overpopulation more than a century before its classical formulation by Malthus.

The optimistic belief that a large and growing number of inhabitants was beneficial to a state was generally accepted in continental Europe during most or all of the century and received its fullest statement in England after the Restoration of 1660. The basic article of faith, that people constitute the strength and wealth of the state, was repeated in endless variations. But this simple doctrine was qualified and elaborated. Many writers, without deviating from their optimism, pointed out that numbers of people alone are not enough: Montchrétien, for example, added that it was important to make good use of land and inhabitants; Seckendorf and Petty attached the condition that the people must be industrious to be useful to the state; Bacon emphasized that the quality of the people is more important than their numbers; Petty and Coke believe that good government is a necessary condition; Böcler and others cautioned that, whatever the advantages of a large population, it should not exceed "the strength of the land." Several mercantilist writers, such as Petty, Temple, and Davenant, expressed the belief that it is not so much the size of population as its density that contributes to national strength and wealth.

A particular contribution of the English mercantilist writers to population theory was their attempt to trace certain effects of population size and growth and to show in more detail how national strength and wealth are affected. Some conceded that numbers of people create shortages of food and other necessities, but they regarded this as good rather than harmful in the long run, for it provides a stimulus to greater effort and greater production. According to Temple and Davenant, it forces men to greater frugality and greater effort; the unknown author of *Britannia Languens* said it sets people to improving all corners of the land; and Dugard added that men would seek out "new Methods of Advantage." Temple, Davenant, and others believed that the pressure of necessity is a stimulus to invention.[150] Even more, it acts as a force for economic progress, leading to the greater development of agriculture, manufacturing, and trade, according to Cary, Malynes, Harrington, and Temple. Conversely, Petty and others characterized thinly populated countries as customarily backward and the people "without Art," and "poor, lazy, rude."

At a less theoretical level, Petty in particular sought to show precisely how a larger number of people benefits a nation. For one thing, it reduces the overhead cost per capita of various essential national services, such as government, the church, the administration of justice, and transportation. And the greater number of consumers and of workers permits a finer division of labor with greater efficiency and lower cost of production and with reduction of unit price to the consumer as the volume of production rises.

In view of later developments in population theory, it is interesting to note that the assumption essential to the optimistic position went almost unstated in the seventeenth century. Only Fénelon affirmed that per capita production does not diminish as the number of people increases, although the concept of what is now called constant or increasing returns was implicit in the entire optimistic argument.

As summarized above, the evolving economic analysis was largely concerned with the influence of population numbers on production. However, there were a few scattered observations concerning effects on distribution. Temple noted that "all things necessary to life" are dear if there are multitudes of people, and Yarrenton commented that with few people all commodities are cheap. Williams, Petty, Temple, Coke, and the author of *Britannia Languens* believed that populousness gives higher land value and higher rent, and according to Child, Pollexfen, and *Britannia Languens,* a shortage of people raises wages.

[150] Williams, however, argued the reverse, that a shortage of hands promoted invention, and that in more populous nations the people resisted new "Engins" as threats to their livelihood.

4

Swedish Population Theory
in the Eighteenth Century[1]

Because of the growing volume of publication on economics and population in the eighteenth century, the development of population theory from this time onward can be followed more readily by tracing separate ideas than by dealing with individual writers and publications. The following chapters therefore trace certain developments in population theory, first in the peripheral Swedish literature, then in the mainstream of European thought. The Swedish material is considered first because it is more closely linked in some respects with European thought of the preceding century, and it is described in greater detail because the Swedish sources are not widely available or well known in other countries.[2] The eighteenth-century Swedish material is interesting in its own right in the history of population study, for it comes from the period in which the oldest continuous series of official population data was established. At that time, only Sweden possessed reasonably reliable information about its people.

1 · The Dominant Opinion on Population

There was a high degree of unanimity of Swedish opinion on population throughout the eighteenth century. Emerging exhausted from a long period

[1] For a somewhat different coverage of the material in this chapter, see E. P. Hutchinson, "Swedish population thought in the eighteenth century," *Population Studies*, 13(1):81–102, July 1959.

[2] Several histories of Swedish economic thought during this period include some mention of views on population. Foremost is Eli Heckscher's great four-volume work, *Sveriges ekonomiska historia från Gustav Vasa*, Stockholm: Bonniers, 1935–1949. Volumes II:1 and II:2 cover the years 1720–1815. The first chapter (pp. 27–76) describes the demographic situation in Sweden; Chapter XII (pp. 812–890) in the latter volume is a survey of the economic thought. Also valuable are the following: J. W. Arnberg, *Anteckningar om frihetstidens politiska ekonomi*, Part I (all that was published), Uppsala, 1868; Georg Schauman, *Studier i frihetstidens nationalekonomiska literatur. Idéer och stömningar 1718–1740*, Helsingfors: Finska Litteratursällskapet, 1910; Karl Petander, *De nationalekonomiska åskådningarna i Sverige sådana de framträda i literaturen*, Stockholm: Nordstedt, 1912; and Karl Forsman, *Studier i det svenska 1700-talets ekonomiska literatur*, Svenska Litteratursällskapet i Finland, No. 312, Historiska och Litteraturhistoriska Studier, No. 23, Helsingfors, 1947.

of war, depleted in manpower, with the Baltic provinces lost, and no longer able to maintain its former position as one of the leading European powers, the nation turned its thoughts and energies toward internal reconstruction and economic development. Opinion differed as to how the national interest could best be advanced, some seeking a more favorable balance of trade, others seeking development of domestic industry, better use of natural resources, or advancement of agriculture; but it was agreed that a numerous population is a source of strength and benefit to the nation, that many of the nation's difficulties were due to a lack of people (*folkbrist*), and that efforts should be made to increase the population. There was no argument with regard to population policy in eighteenth-century Sweden.

More fundamental to the understanding of Swedish views on population are the reasons why a larger population was considered desirable. The Swedish writings of the period were not as a whole very analytical, but various reasons were given for the populationist views expressed. The underlying thought is revealed in part by comments on the importance of population numbers, recommended policies, the problem of emigration, and other questions related to population.

The old and familiar pattern of equating populousness with national strength was indeed present, and persisted on through the century. A quite striking aspect of eighteenth-century Swedish literature, however, was the very limited mention of the military aspect of population size. With an understandable revulsion against war as an instrument of national policy, the Swedish writers of this period gave little emphasis to the relation of population size to military strength except as it gave defensive strength. An early Swedish economist, who wrote only several years after the end of the wars of Carl XII, rejected war as a means of advancing the national interest and pointed out how England had prospered during the peaceful reign of Elizabeth.[3] A journal referred at mid-century to the "outmoded" idea that the kingdom is advanced by wars and conquest, and said that patriotic citizens now preferred peace and industry.[4] Most incisive was the remark of a later writer that many Swedes had died to extend the nation's boundaries, but that it would serve the nation as well to fill it with people.[5]

Instead of the military aspect, the writers of this period directed their attention toward the internal and economic advantages of a numerous population; and the changing terms in which the advantages of populousness were presented reflected the changing currents of thought on national problems and economic policy.

[3] Christopher Polhem, *Oeconomie och commercen uti Swerige* (Sweden's economy and commerce), Stockholm, 1720, p. 31.

[4] *Den Wälmenande Patrioten* (The well-meaning patriot), 1751, No. 1.

[5] Anders Chydenius, "Hvad kan vara orsaken, att sådanmyckenhet svenskt folk årligen flyttar utur landet?" (Essay on why so many Swedes emigrate), 1765, published in *Politiska Skrifter af Anders Chydenius* (Political Writings), edited by E. G. Palmén, Helsingfors, 1800, p. 3.

A first concern of the mercantilist writers in the period of peace and reconstruction following the death of Carl XII was with the industrial development of their country. In this they reflected the governmental policy, but they may also have influenced it. In their opinion a larger population would aid industrialization. This thought appeared in the works of Christopher Polhem (1661–1751), a pioneer Swedish writer on economic matters and one of the first of the so-called industrial mercantilists. Writing in the early postwar period, he took a rather conservative view of the question of population numbers, as is described more fully later,[6] but he conceded that there are some advantages of populousness. In an undated work, *Om manufacturers nytta* (On the advantage of manufactures), probably written in the early 1720's, he noted that among other advantages manufacturing provides additional means of subsistence. That in turn makes it possible for young people to marry in good season and add to the national population and subsistence, which constitute the real wealth of the nation and make it flourish.[7]

A similar emphasis on the need for industries appeared in the first major Swedish work on political economy, probably also the most influential, the *Arcana Oeconomiae et Commercii* (1730) by Anders Nordencrantz (1697–1772). The real treasure of a country, he asserted, is not its gold and silver but its industries, because they produce the commodities needed by man, and the more people and cattle there are, the more fruitful the land can be made.[8] The interdependence of industry and population was more strongly stated in an unsigned work of the following year, *Möjeligheten at i Swerige inrätta fabriquer och manufacturer* (1731). Its author, Edvard Carleson (1704–1767), said that

> A land's inhabitants are its true treasure, but if these inhabitants are not provided with work and industriousness (which is best done through manufactures and factories) they are like a treasure that is dead and buried underground.[9]

Except for this special attention to the needs of industry, and later of agriculture, the reasons given for desiring a large population were most often stated in terms of the contribution made by numbers of people to the

[6] See section 5 below.

[7] *Christopher Polhem's efterlämnade skrifter,* edited by Gösta Lindeberg, Lychnos-Bibliotek, Vol. 10:2, Uppsala, 1951, Vol. II, pp. 328–329. The term *manufacturer* refers to a manufacturing establishment of the handicraft stage of production, rather than a factory in the modern sense.

[8] Anders Nordencrantz (Bachmansson), *Arcana Oeconomiae et Commercii, eller handels och hushåldnings-wärkets hemligheter* (Secret principles of economics and trade), Stockholm, 1730, pp. 52, 173.

[9] (Edvard Carleson) (Carlsson), *Möjeligheten at i Swerige inrätta fabriquer och manufacturer* (Possibility of establishing factories and manufactures in Sweden), by E. C., Stockholm, 1731. Pages unnumbered; passage quoted is from the twenty-fifth page.

national wealth and economic strength. The conventional statement that large numbers give strength to a nation was often given an economic turn of thought, and quite divergent implications of population size were emphasized by different writers. Some of the views on population size are summarized below.

A typical statement of the significance of population size is found in the *Salus Patriae* (1741) of Erik Salander (1699–1764), an industrialist active in political affairs and author of several economic works. According to him, "What above all else gives a kingdom power and honor is a good supply of industrious people, well employed and with sufficient money in their hands."[10]

Writing a few years later, Christian König (1678–1762), an official who had spent a number of years in study abroad before entering government service, asserted that the basis of a land's well-being and prosperity is a large and growing population. He gave no further explanation of how population numbers produce these effects, but cited the works of Davenant, Graunt, and Petty, and went on to consider measures that would stimulate population growth.[11]

Some discussion of the significance of population size was contained in a treatise on economics published in 1747 by Anders Berch (1711–1774), holder of the first chair of economics in Sweden and an authoritative spokesman for contemporary mercantilism. According to Berch, a society may be considered fortunate if it includes many people, for their work assures their well-being. The strength or weakness of a nation depends upon the number of its inhabitants and their mode of employment, and populousness is the basis of economic strength.[12] This theme was more fully developed by Berch in his *Politiska Arithmetica* (1746), which began with the statement that "The principal foundation on which a nation's economy must be built, for the advancement of the public good, is the number of inhabitants." An ample population was said to be necessary if the people are to live in security from external threats, and is also necessary for internal well-being, because many industrious hands produce what is needed by man.[13]

[10] (Erik Salander), *Salus Patriae eller Sweriges wälfärd genom högstwårdande förbätringar wid the almänna närings-fång* (Sweden's welfare . . .), Stockholm, 1741, p. 62.

[11] Christian König, *Lärdoms-öfning* (Exercise of knowledge and experience), Stockholm, 1746, Vol. 4, p. 4.

[12] Anders Berch, *Inledning til almänna hushålningen, innefattande grunden til politie, economie och cameral wetenskaperne* (Introduction to general economy, including the foundation of politics, economics, and cameralism), Stockholm, 1747, pp. 25, 30.

[13] Anders Berch, *Sätt at igenom politiska arithmetica utröna länders och rikens hushåldning* (How to determine the management of kingdoms and lands by means of political arithmetic), p. 6. The edition used here was published in Vesterås, 1796.

The importance of population size was also emphasized by Johan Kryger (1707–1777), one of the most prolific writers on economic matters, active in the Academy, and head of the Statistical Commission (Tabellkommissionen) for several years before his death. In a weekly, *Den Wälmenande Patrioten,* which he published in 1751, it was stated that "The basis for a land's wealth and happiness consists unquestionably of a large number of industrious inhabitants. The more the better, for they are never too many."[14] And, "If a state owned all the treasures now found in the whole of Europe but was underpeopled . . . it would in time become poor and miserable."[15] Sweden's poverty, moreover, was said to be the result of a lack of people.

A rather similar account of the significance of population size was given later by Jacob Faggot (1699–1777), prominent member of a number of official commissions including the Statistical Commission, and leading member of the newly founded Royal Academy of Science. Describing a rural parish, he stated that "The strength of a country's economy consists of a numerous population and its employment." It is therefore good governmental policy, he believed, to look to the increase of both population and employment.[16]

The prevailing views were well stated in the first of an important series of articles in the Academy proceedings in 1754 to 1755 by Pehr Wargentin (1717–1785), an astronomer and mathematician who was secretary of the Academy, member of the Statistical Commission, and the leading Swedish demographer of his century. Writing of the desirability of having annul bills or lists of births and deaths, he began

> That a civil society's greatest strength consists of a quantity of good citizens is a saying that is now doubted by almost none . . . experience and a sounder knowledge of the art of government have now persuaded the majority that a numerous, obedient, and prosperous people gives to a careful government the most enduring strength. . . .

Population growth also contributes to wealth, he said, for ". . . agriculture, handicrafts, trade, and all industries that are to feed and provide the well-being of a population are carried on all the better the more working hands there are available. . . ."[17]

Wargentin also may have drafted the 1755 report of the Statistical Commission, whose members had expressed their personal opinions on popula-

[14] *Den Wälmenande Patrioten,* 1751, p. 147.
[15] *Ibid.*
[16] Jacob Faggot, "Beskrifning ofver Pernå Socken, belägen i Skärgården vid Finska Viken" (Description of Perna Parish . . .), *K. vet akad. handlingar,* 1750, Vol. XI(3), p. 264.
[17] Pehr Wargentin, "Anmärkningar om nyttan af årliga förtekningar på födda och döda i et land" (Remarks on the value of annual bills of births and deaths in a land), *K. vet. akad. handlingar,* 1754, Vol. 15(3), pp. 161–162.

tion elsewhere but whose collective report had at least semi-official status.[18] Commenting on what it considered to be the serious underpopulation of Sweden, the report added, ". . . a numerous populace is a land's greatest wealth and strength, and also an indispensable aid to the promotion and development of all elements of the rural and urban economy."[19] A Commission report in 1761, when E. O. Runeberg was a member, again stated that the strength nature bestows on a state depends upon a plentiful number of inhabitants.[20]

A more fully developed treatment of the need for and the role of a large population appeared in 1761 in the first part of an anonymous work attributed to Carl Leuhusen.[21] A quite original thinker, with a better than average knowledge of the foreign literature, and representing a liberal tendency in Swedish economic thought, Leuhusen began by stating, "A kingdom's wellbeing consists of the largest number of people possible, all of whom, through their labor, have sufficient means of livelihood, each in his own occupation." It is possible, he conceded, to imagine a country so heavily populated that it cannot support its people, as is perhaps the case in China, or from which migrants must go out to find work in other countries. Nevertheless, a large population is needed not only to carry on work, by which the people's comfort is increased, but also to protect themselves from attack. Without numbers of people the fields cannot be tilled, trades cannot be provided with workers, the mines are neglected, and so forth.[22]

The economic value of people and especially their contribution to production was emphasized in a work published in 1762 by Edvard Runeberg (elder brother of E. O. Runeberg, who was on the Statistical Commission), prominent economist and writer with a liberal turn of mind. Although he was writing of fiscal policy, with particular reference to the rate of exchange, he gave considerable attention to the economic role of population. If the quantity of goods is to be increased, then it is first necessary to increase the number of people, for it is not money but men that produce goods.[23] Presumably thinking particularly of Sweden, he stated as a principle that ". . . the increase of population in an underpeopled state is

[18] The members of the Statistical Commission in 1755 were E. Carleson, Faggot, Rudenschöld, and Wargentin.

[19] Aug. Hjelt, De första officiella relationerna om Svenska tabellverket, åren 1749–1757 (The first official reports on the Swedish statistical office, 1749–1757), Helsingfors, 1899, p. 6.

[20] Ibid., p. 24.

[21] Anon. (Carl Leuhusen), Tankar om de rätta och sanskyldig medel til Sweriges wälmåga (Thoughts on the proper and true means to Sweden's wellbeing), Part I, Stockholm, 1761.

[22] Ibid., p. 2.

[23] Edvard Runeberg, Tankar om penningars värden, eller afhandling om växelcoursen (Thoughts on the value of money, or a treatise on the rate of exchange), Stockholm, 1762, p. 47.

the right and natural means to its happiness, wellbeing, and power, when the other political conditions are appropriate."[24] He added that no other barometer of the rise and fall of the nation's strength equals the useful data provided by the Statistical Commission. However, it was deemed important that the people of a state be put to use, for this affects the relative strength, in trade and in war, of two equally populous states.[25]

The outstanding liberal and the most original thinker of the period was the clergyman and member of parliament, Anders Chydenius (1729–1803). In his contribution (1765) to the Academy's contest for the best essay on why so many people emigrated from Sweden, he wrote, "A land without inhabitants is a barren waste, a kingdom without subjects is a shadow that alarms only those who believe there are people there."[26]

Many other statements of the significance of population size could be cited for this period, but those noted above describe the prevailing opinion. The authors themselves were of diverse background and wrote for many different purposes, being conservative mercantilists and liberals, partisan supporters of the government and its opponents, industrialists and enthusiasts for agricultural development, but through all their writings ran a common conception of population as a prime productive factor, the source of national strength and prosperity.

2 · Some Variations on the Dominant Theme

There were many variations on the dominant theme, some of which have been seen above. König, as already noted, attached significance to the growth of population as well as to its size. Others, such as Carl Mennander (1712–1786), professor of theology, scientist, and archbishop in his later years, believed that population growth is necessary for advancement of the national economy.[27]

Many believed that the density of population is especially important, a view most prevalent in the latter half of the century when the analysis of the population factor had evolved somewhat further. Mennander, for example, wrote that the closer people live together the better they can unite their efforts to obtain the necessities and comforts of life. Living close together, they encourage each other to industriousness, thought, and discovery. If men had not congregated, there would not have been as many useful inventions, nor could the inventions have been as well developed or

[24] *Ibid.,* p. 54.
[25] *Ibid.,* pp. 54–55.
[26] Anders Chydenius, *Politiska skrifter*, p. 3.
[27] Carl Mennander, "Tal om folkhopens tillväxt, som grunden til rickets näringars upkomst" (Talk on population growth as basis for advancement of the kingdom's economy), *K. vet. akad. Praesid, tal,* Vol. 5(8), Stockholm, 1766, p. 4.

as widely available. Also, the inhabitants of a thinly peopled land cannot as well defend themselves.[28]

Johan Kryger especially emphasized the significance of population density. In one of his earliest works, *Tankar om Swenska fabriquerne* (1753), he compared Sweden and France and noted that the latter, with about one-third the area, had a much greater population. France was therefore much more highly cultivated; it was well provided with the necessities of life; communications between rural areas and cities were good; and the consequent good return to both city and rural dwellers was a stimulus to greater industriousness and greater thought.[29] The sparse rural population of Sweden, in contrast, was accustomed to engage in handicrafts for home consumption. If persuaded to work on a part-time basis for manufacturers, the workers expected high wages, did not work hard, and produced little, so that the price of the product was necessarily high. The consequences of underpopulation in Sweden were, therefore, high wages, high prices, and indolence of the workers.[30]

In a later address to the Academy Kryger returned to the subject, saying that if the entire population of Sweden and Finland could be concentrated in the south of Sweden there would undoubtedly be more food and greater general well-being.[31] Berch had expressed this idea some years before in his *Politiska Arithmetica* (1746). There Berch wrote that national wealth would be greater if all of Sweden's population were concentrated in Finland.[32] He cited Davenant in support of this opinion, and quoted with approval Temple's statement ". . . the true and original ground of trade (is) great multitude of people crowded into small compass of land, etc."[33]

The same thought was expressed elsewhere. In the 1761 report of the Statistical Commission, for example, it was stated that if two nations have the same area but one has twice the population, the latter will have twice the natural strength of the other and four times the economic strength. However, the report, did not go on to explain how the multiplication of economic strength occurs.[34] Another instance is found in a collection of essays published in 1763, in which Kryger wrote:

> Where the earth is fully tilled and the means of livelihood in a flourishing condition, it is there that there must be a large population. It follows

[28] *Ibid.*, pp. 5–7.
[29] J. F. Kryger, *Tankar om Swenske fabriquerne* (Thoughts about Swedish manufacturers), Stockholm, 1753, pp. 15–16.
[30] *Ibid.*, pp. 19–20, 25.
[31] J. F. Kryger, "Tal on folkbristens orsaker, verkan och hjelp" (Talk on the causes, effects, and relief of underpopulation), *K. vet. akad. Praesid. tal*, May 10, 1758; published separately, Stockholm, 1758, p. 26.
[32] Anders Berch, *Politiska arithmetica*, p. 16.
[33] From Temple's *Observations upon the United Provinces of the Netherlands;* quoted in full on p. 54.
[34] Hjelt, *op. cit.*, p. 25.

from this that of two nations, the one is most powerful and rich that, everything else being the same, supports the most inhabitants on the same area.[35]

Population density was also emphasized by the elder Runeberg. In an address before the Academy in 1760 he stated that, just as is true of nations, the regions within a nation that contain the most people relative to their area are the strongest.[36] He carried this thought further in a later publication, saying that national strength is proportional to population density, and introduced the term "natural strength" to denote the relation of population numbers to land area of a nation. The less populous of two nations may thus have the greater natural strength.[37]

Meanwhile E. O. Runeberg had described how population growth and increasing concentration of people lead to progressively greater returns. "It follows from man's nature that the more the population increases, the more there is increase of crowding, industriousness, and thought; and the greater these are the greater the supply of goods."[38] Furthermore,

> Many people produce a quantity of goods, a quantity of goods produces a lot of money, increases the wealth of the Treasury, and supports the state's administrative and defense organization. The closer people live together, the greater is private industriousness and the general well-being; but the further they are apart the weaker are economic activity, industries, and progress.[39]

And finally, "Many people concentrated in one place make a land more powerful than if they were spread widely about."[40] As Arnberg said, there was a mercantilist ideal of a dense population in a small area.[41]

According to another variant of the populationist theme, it is not so much the total number of people as the number of industrious and productive people that contributes to national strength and wealth. This was mentioned by Salander, as quoted above, and the same thought appeared in the writings of Estenberg,[42] the Runebergs, Christiernin, and others. According to E. O. Runeberg,

---

[35] J. F. Kryger, *Tankar wid lediga stunder* (Thoughts in leisure moments), Part II, Stockholm, 1763, No. 5, p. 173.

[36] Edvard Runeberg, "Tal om varors värden" (Talk on the value of goods), *K. vet. akad. Praesid. tal,* February 17, 1760, Vol. 3(15), Stockholm, 1760, p. 39.

[37] Edvard Runeberg, "Om Svea rikes folk-nummer och naturliga styrka" (Of Sweden's population size and natural strength), *K. vet. akad. handlingar,* 1764, Vol. 25(2), pp. 86–89.

[38] E. O. Runeberg, *Tankar om et rätt kammer och skatteläggnings wärk* (Thoughts of a wise exchequer and taxation policy), Stockholm, 1761, p. 18.

[39] *Ibid.,* p. 26.

[40] *Ibid.,* p. 29.

[41] J. W. Arnberg, *op. cit.,* p. 180.

[42] Carl Estenberg, *Förslag till en närings inrättande i Swerige* (Proposal for the establishment of an industry in Sweden), Stockholm, 1765, p. 2.

A quantity of money does not constitute the wealth of a state, for wealth consists of a quantity of goods; but these do not come without work, and without people there is no work. Therefore the wealth of a state depends on the working population, provided it is well employed.[43]

Edvard Runeberg in one of his later writings defined his concept of natural strength as consisting of a number of working people within a given area, and added that the ability of the state to feed and defend itself depends upon this factor.[44] Several years later Christiernin (1725–1799), then professor of jurisprudence, economics, and commerce, stated in an address before the Royal Academy of Uppsala that the power, well-being, and wealth of a state do not depend upon wide lands or a plentiful supply of money, but rather that

No community can therefore be considered powerful and rich if it does not have a numerous and industrious population, that through all sorts of flourishing industries produces a continuous and plentiful supply of all the things that serve as necessities, comforts, pleasures and ornaments, and for weapons and defense.[45]

There was also a belief that upon the quality of the population depends its value to the nation. Wargentin (as quoted above) believed that national strength is derived from a "numerous, obedient, and prosperous" population. Anders Duhre (c. 1680–1739), one of the early industrial mercantilist writers, stated as a principle of government that "Populousness alone is a land's greatest wealth," but added that the goodness of the people is also important. Goodness depends in part upon the inborn nature of the people, he noted, but it also depends upon their training; therefore the state can do much to strengthen itself through wise procedures.[46] König wrote that populousness is a necessary condition, but that the comfort and happiness of a society also depend upon the industriousness and skill of its members.[47]

Hindric Wrede (1696–1758), an army officer and public official with particular interest in economic affairs, in an address as head of the Academy accepted the common opinion that people are the wealth of a state, but attached the reservation that the people must be made productive. And if the ruler does not see to it that his subjects receive good upbring-

[43] E. O. Runeberg, *Tankar om et rätt kammar och skatteläggnings wärk*, p. 25.
[44] Edvard Runeberg, "Om folkhopens politiska fördelning eller skilnaderne i anseende til stånden" (Of the population's political distribution, or differences of class), *K. vet. akad. handlingar*, 1767, Vol. 28(3), p. 216.
[45] P. N. Christiernin, *Om handaslögdernas företräde för landtbruket* (The advantages of handicrafts to agriculture), *K. akad. i Uppsala*, November 23, 1770, Uppsala, 1771, pp. 13–14.
[46] Anders Duhre, *Sweriges högsta wälstånd, bygt uppå en oeconomisk grundval* (Sweden's greatest wellbeing, built upon an economic foundation), Stockholm, 1738, p. 11.
[47] König, *op. cit.*, p. 39.

ing and education so that they may become useful citizens, then populousness is not beneficial but harmful.[48]

Another aspect of population quality given considerable weight at the time was mentioned by Bengt Holmén in an anonymous tract published in 1765. According to this, Sweden did indeed suffer from underpopulation, but all attempts to increase the glory of God through increase of his people are of no avail if their upbringing is neglected, "for the great and fruitful mass of the godless is of no use."[49] A later writer, Hans Almgren, in a dissertation under Christiernin at Uppsala, stated that the happiness and strength of a state depend upon the number and skill of the workers and upon their strength of mind and body; but it was also his thesis that trade, especially foreign trade, advances the quantity and quality of the workers.[50]

Still other qualifications and reservations were introduced into the endorsements of populationist views. Berch[51] and the Runebergs,[52] as already noted, pointed out that the advantage derived from an ample population depends upon the use made of this resource. Samuel Hermelin (1744–1820), a widely travelled industrialist and cartographer, prominent in scientific and official activities, pointed out in an address before the Academy that although the strength of a kingdom depends upon the number of its people, it also depends upon how usefully their time and strength are employed, adding that a kingdom is weakened if the people are not put to good use.[53] Many others called attention to the same obvious point, cautioning that food and employment should be assured if efforts are made to increase the population. Duhre, Edvard Runeberg, and Wrede had mentioned that much depends upon how well the people are governed, and this was also touched on in the 1761 report of the Statistical Commission. A number of other writers also called attention to the need for good government if a nation is to derive fullest benefits from its demographic assets.

Overall, the Swedish literature appears a thoughtful, well-balanced treatment of the subject of population size. Although strongly convinced of the need for a large and expanding population, the Swedish writers as a group

[48] Hindric Wrede, "Om et borgerligit samhälles eller et land och rikes rätta styrka" (Of the true strength of a civil society, land, or kingdom), *K. vet. akad. Praesid. tal,* January 26, 1743; published separately, Stockholm, 1747, p. 26.

[49] Anon. (Bengt Holmen), *Grunden och hufwud-källan till rikets upkomst och bestånd* (Basis and principal source of the kingdom's origin and existence), Stockholm, 1765, p. 5.

[50] Hans Almgren, *Sveriges nytta af handelen och segelfarten på Ost-Indien* (Sweden's benefit from the India trade and seafaring), Uppsala, 1768, Introduction.

[51] Berch, *Inledning til almänna hushålningen,* p. 25.

[52] E. O. Runeberg, *Tankar om et rätt kammar och skatteläggnings wärk,* p. 25; Edward Runeberg, *Tankar om penningars värden,* p. 54.

[53] Samuel Hermelin, *Tal om näringarnes förhållande uti rikets sarskilda lands-orter* (Concerning economic conditions in different parts of the nation), *K. vet. akad. Praesid. tal,* August 4, 1773, Stockholm, 1774, p. 19.

were moderate in their views. One writer, Berch, raised the question of importing slaves in order to add to the population and labor force, but he did so cautiously and with reservations;[54] and the group as a whole avoided the exaggerations and excesses to which the populationist train of thought could lead.

3 · Some Specific Effects of Population Size

Prominent in the background of Swedish population thought of the period was the conviction that the nation suffered from *folkbrist*, the lack of people. This lack, as already noted, was thought to impede the industrial development of Sweden. Later, when dissatisfaction with the government's encouragement of industry grew and Physiocrat ideas were introduced from France, there was a parallel belief that Swedish agriculture was handicapped by underpopulation. This numerical weakness was sometimes stated in terms of a lack of workers rather than as a lack of people, but in any case the deficiency was presented as the great source of many or most of the nation's difficulties, weakening the nation's economy, depressing business activity, and leading to inefficiency or emigration of workers.

Contributing in some measure to the conviction of underpopulation was the belief that the population of Sweden had diminished. The influential utopian work of the preceding century, the *Atland* (1679–1702), by Olof Rudbeck (1630–1702), was a thinly disguised account of Sweden that told of the natural advantages and resources of the land, and the longevity and the fertility of the inhabitants, and it persuaded its readers of the populousness of olden times.[55] Among later writers, Johan Browallius (1707–1755), in a dissertation at Åbo in 1756, pointed to the great emigration from Sweden in earlier times as evidence of formerly greater population.[56] Edvard Runeberg believed that the population of Sweden once had been larger.[57] Mennander concluded that the population of ancient times could not have been as great because less land was cultivated then, but that it must have been as large or larger in the Middle Ages than in the eighteenth century. Land occupied in the Middle Ages was now abandoned, he pointed out, and people in those days were perhaps satisfied with less than

[54] See Karl Forsman, *Studier in det Svenska 1700-talets ekonomiska literatur* (Studies in the eighteenth-century Swedish economic literature), Svenska Litteratursällskapet i Finland, Historiska och Litteraturhistoriska Studier, No. 23, Helsingfors, 1947, pp. 218–219.

[55] Olof Rudbeck, *Atland eller Manheim*, 4 vol., Uppsala and Stockholm: Almquist and Wiksell, 1937–1950. See especially Vol. I, Ch. 4.

[56] Johan Browallius, *Tankar om Svenska folkbristen* (Thoughts on the Swedish underpopulation), under supervision of Professor Johan Kraftman, Åbo, 1756, p. 9.

[57] Edvard Runeberg, *Om Seva rikes folk-nummer* . . . , p. 102.

at the present time.[58] Another writer was convinced on theological or biblical grounds that the population had been reduced by deterioration of customs and morals, and that the population at present was much less than it had been before the flood.[59] Finally, in the last decade of the century, Elias Schröderheim (1747–1795), the governor of the province of Uppsala and former head of the Academy, gave an address before that body concerning the former population of Sweden. Like earlier students of the subject, he noted that some areas once cultivated were now abandoned, and presented estimates for the fourteenth and fifteenth centuries indicating a population as large or larger than that in 1792.[60]

A small minority of skeptical persons did express doubt about the tenuous estimates of a larger population in earlier times. Nordencrantz, writing anonymously, said that it was not certain the population was larger in the distant past but that it had certainly declined during the preceding period of war.[61]

With general agreement that there were too few people, there was much discussion of the advantages of populousness and the disadvantages of underpopulation. In addition to the general advantages of numerical strength described earlier, a number of specific effects were attributed to populousness and population growth, or were implied in accounts of the ill effects of underpopulation. Perhaps a survival of an older pattern of thought, there was some belief that it is desirable to have the workers numerous and poor. An early expression of this point of view appeared in the *Arcana* (1730) by Nordencrantz, where it was said, piously, that the poor people are of greater worth to a nation than silver and gold, and that it is not without purpose that God creates men of different condition.[62]

In the following decade a controversy about the consequences of luxury brought forth the comment that excessive consumption of food and drink is harmful because a few then consume what many could live on. It was pointed out that among the common people, overconsumption could best be prevented by allowing them to establish many households. This would obviously lead to more births, it would be easier to get servants, and

---

[58] Mennander, *Tal om folkhopens tilväxt* . . . , p. 12.

[59] (Magnus Orrelius), *Tankar om folkminskningen och sedernas förderf i Swerige* (Thoughts on the decrease of population and deterioration of customs in Sweden), Stockholm, 1767, Parts 1 and 2, and p. 46.

[60] Elias Schröderheim (Schröder), "Anmärkningar om Sveriges forna upodling och folkmängden" (Notes on Sweden's former cultivation and population), *K. vet. akad. Praesid. tal,* August 22, 1792, Vol. 11(15); published separately, Stockholm, 1793.

[61] Anon. (Anders Nordencrantz), *Owälduga tankar om Sweriges närwarande tillstånd i anseende til wälmåga och rikedom* (Impartial thoughts on Sweden's present condition with respect to wellbeing and wealth), Stockholm, 1761, p. 5.

[62] Anders Nordencrantz, *Arcana*, p. 52.

wages would be lower.[63] An anonymous writer later told how he had
introduced potatoes to a certain district a number of years before, and
upon inquiring later was told that the plants had been pulled up because
of fear that their productiveness would make the peasants unwilling to
work.[64] Another anonymous work said quite frankly that it is better for
a land to have so many workers that they are grateful for work than to
have so few that the employer is grateful to those who work for him;[65] and
it continued:

> When there are few and comfortable workers in a country, everything
> is expensive, trade stagnates, and the one contributes to the other. But
> when a country has many workers, they are glad to earn food and cloth-
> ing, and so prices become lower, trade increases, and one inhabitant pro-
> vides subsistence for another.[66]

The economics text by Berch, written about the same time, merely referred to the saying that the poor are the most useful members of a society,
and explained that they provide the majority of workers and producers.[67]
In 1752 Ungern Sternberg added that from a national viewpoint it is
undesirable for the workers to enjoy overabundance, because the prices of
goods are high or low according to whether the level of consumption of
the workers is high or low, and high prices inhibit exports.[68] Kryger developed the idea somewhat differently, writing that when there is a shortage
of workers wages go up, and, as is human nature, the workers then become indolent and less productive.[69] As Petander pointed out, this was
a train of thought from older mercantilism.[70] In Sweden it declined after
mid-century with the newer liberal trend of thought, and was disposed
of by Pehr von Asp (1745–1808), a diplomat of wide experience with
a particular interest in economics. Writing in 1800, he remarked that
no nation ever has to think of ways to make its people poor so that they
will do the necessary work, and that if a nation ever becomes so wealthy
that its people refuse to do the more unpleasant kinds of work, there are

[63] Olof Ehrenström, *Anmarkningar öfver det genswar som en obekant autor utgifvit* . . . (Comments on an unknown author's reply . . .), Stockholm, 1744(?), p. 5.
[64] Anon, *Wälmente tankar om hemmans klyfwande och sammanslående uti stora gårdar* . . . (Benevolent thoughts on the subdivision of holdings . . .), Stockholm, 1745(?), p. 31.
[65] Anon., *Et rikes nytta of många närings-lemmar* (A kingdom's benefit from many means of livelihood), Stockholm, 1746, p. 4.
[66] *Ibid.*, p. 5.
[67] Anders Berch, *Inledning til almänna hushålningen*, pp. 27–28.
[68] Mathias von Ungern Sternberg, "Tankar om Sveriges handel och allmänna hushållning" (Thoughts on Sweden's trade and general economy), *K. vet. akad. Praesid. tal*, January 25, 1752, Stockholm, 1752, p. 9.
[69] J. F. Kryger, *Tankar om Swenskå fabriquerne*, pp. 19–20, 25.
[70] Karl Petander, *De nationalekonomiska åskadningarna i Sverige* (Viewpoints of political economy in Sweden), Stockholm: Nordstedt, 1912, p. 47.

always plenty of workers willing to come in as immigrants from poorer countries.[71]

There was also a quite general belief that a large and growing population promotes economic development, and a number of different ways in which it might do so were suggested. For one thing, more people and more workers are needed for essential kinds of work. According to the monthly journal, *Hushålds-Råd,* published in 1734 to 1735 by Carl Carleson and largely devoted to economic questions, plenty of people were needed for the exploitation of Sweden's natural resources and for maintenance of the state.[72] A later journal, Kryger's *Wälmenande Patrioten* (1751), said, presumably of Sweden, that when a land has too few people relative to its size it cannot be properly cultivated, is covered with woods, and underdeveloped.[73] Leuhusen, among others, noted that in an underpopulated country the fields are not fully tilled, some trades are lacking, mines neglected and so on.[74] Faggot added that canals, roads, and other public undertakings can be constructed more readily if there are plenty of workers.[75]

For another thing, populousness was thought to stimulate business activity. With more people, more goods are produced,[76] and both internal trade and foreign commerce are increased. With particular reference to the growth of cities, Polhem wrote in 1726:

> The more people the more trade, the greater the profit for more tradesmen in staple cities. The larger and more populous the cities become, the larger the storehouses for them, and consequently the greater is security against crop failure and war that could otherwise put the whole kingdom in distress.[77]

With more people there could be a greater variety of handicrafts and manufactures, and more market towns.[78] Faggot and others noted that with

[71] Pehr von Asp, *Försök att utreda och på ett ställe sammanföra de första och allmänna grunderne i stats-hushållningsämnen, II, Fortsättning* (Attempt to investigate and to present in one place the first and general principles of economics, Part II, Continuation), Stockholm, 1800, pp. 50–51.

[72] Georg Schauman, *Studier in frihetstidens nationalekonomiska litteratur* (Studies in the literature of political economy in the Freedom Period), Helsingfors, 1910, pp. 140–157.

[73] Kryger, *Den Wälmenande Patrioten,* 1751, p. 34.

[74] Leuhusen, *op. cit.,* section 1, p. 2.

[75] (Jacob Faggot), *Systematiskt begrepp om almänna hushållningens brister och botemedel* (Systematic conception of national economic deficiencies and remedies), Stockholm, 1763, Part IV, pp. 30–43.

[76] Edvard Runeberg, *Om Svea rikes folk-nummer,* pp. 84, 85; Anders Schönberg, "Utkast om grunderna i allmänhet til näringars upkomst och förfall, uti borgerliga samhällen" (Outline of general causes of the rise and decline of industries . . .), *K. vet. akad. Intrades tal,* July 1, 1767, Vol. 2(9), p. 78.

[77] Christopher Polhem, *Åtskillige allmänne hushålds förslag* (Various general economic proposals), Stockholm, 1726, p. 23.

[78] Thomas Plomgren, "Tankar om handelen i gemen" (Thoughts on trade in general), *K. vet. akad. handlingar,* 1740, Vol. 1(2), p. 340.

a numerous population prices of goods would be low unless money was scarce, and so Swedish goods could undersell those from other countries.[79]

A number of other effects of population size were mentioned. Faggot earlier had said that the crown's revenue bears a direct relation to the number of citizens.[80] In an undated work, *Om manufacturers nytta* (Of the advantage of manufactures), Polhem, like Petty in England, pointed out that the more people and means of livelihood in a nation, the less each has to bear of the common burden, by which he presumably meant taxes and other obligations to the state.[81]

Another thought was that there is or can be more productiveness and greater efficiency of production if the population is large. It was an old idea, as described above, that the more workers there are, and the more competition among them for work, the harder they work. Berch had quoted Temple in his *Politiska Arithmetica,* agreeing that greater numbers force people to greater economy and effort.[82] E. O. Runeberg believed there is more industriousness and thought,[83] Schönberg that there is more industriousness and carefulness in a propulous state.[84] Johan Liljencrantz (1730–1815), a student of Wargentin and Berch, and later a high official in the government, appears to have been quite alone in expressing doubts about whether an increase in population leads to greater competition among workers and greater industriousness on their part. He feared that habits of indolence, once acquired, persist, and that people become satisfied with a minimal standard of living.[85]

Other effects in the direction of greater efficiencies of production were suggested. According to Edvard Runeberg,

> The more industrious workers a state contains the greater results must the people's work produce, including enlightenment in science and handicrafts, together with industrial strength, internal and external trade, in defense, in wealth to pay debts, etc.[86]

Mennander inferred that without concentrations of population there would not be as many useful inventions, and they would not be as well developed

[79] Jacob Faggot, *Systematiskt begrepp,* p. 30 ff.

[80] Jacob Faggot, *Svenska landtbrukets hinder och hjälp* (Swedish agriculture's impediments and aid), Stockholm, 1746, p. 51.

[81] *Christopher Polhelm's efterlämnade skrifter,* edited by Gösta Lindeberg, Lychnos-Bibliotek, Vol. 10:2, Uppsala, 1951, Vol. II, p. 329; and *Åtskillige allmänne hushålds förslag,* Stockholm, 1726, p. 17.

[82] Berch, *Politiska arithmetica,* p. 16.

[83] E. O. Runeberg, *Tankar,* pp. 18, 26.

[84] Anders Schönberg, *op. cit.,* pp. 78, 80.

[85] Johan Liljencrantz (Westerman), "Om Svenska näringarnes undervigt emot de utländske, förmedelst en trögare arbets-drift" (Of the weakness of Swedish industries relative to the foreign, by reason of less energetic work), *K. vet. akad. Intrades tal,* February 24, 1768, Vol. 2(10), p. 12.

[86] Edvard Runeberg, *Om Svea rikes folk-nummer,* p. 85.

nor as widely available.[87] Kryger, in the *Wälmenande Patrioten,* described how numbers of people favor the division of labor and specialization of employment, which adds to worker productivity and reduces the wage cost of goods.[88] At least one writer regarded an ample population as a necessary condition for a society.[89]

Although the supposed effects of a larger population on production received the greatest emphasis, some attention was given to the influence of population size on prices and wages. This subject was touched on in an anonymous work published in 1746. With few workers, it was said, wages are high; with more workers, their wages are lower, as are the prices of the goods they produce.[90] Berch dismissed the objection that populousness may make necessities expensive and so raise the cost of living, saying that high prices can be prevented by a plentiful supply of commodities, and that additional hands provide a greater supply. He also believed there are other ways in which the tendency to higher prices can be counteracted. The high prices themselves stimulate people to greater effort; and high prices, after all, increase the income of the general public.[91]

Edvard Runeberg further analyzed the interrelation of population, prices, and wages in *Tankar om penningars värden* (1762). If population grows and the rate of return or profit remains constant, the price of goods falls and the value of money rises. Conversely, a decrease of population diminishes production, raises prices, and depresses the value of money.[92] The level of prices can therefore be changed by variation in either population or the supply of money, or by a combination of both.[93] Faggot urged that it is good national policy to have an abundance of people and a shortage of money, for this keeps prices low and permits underselling of foreign competitors.[94] At the end of the century Pehr von Asp summed up his views on the relation of prices and population by saying that a plentiful food supply produces a low cost of living, which in turn usually stimulates population growth, which lowers the price of manufactured goods unless the supply of money is large.[95]

As already indicated, wage theory did not go much beyond a simple supply and demand formulation, in which the level of wages was inversely related to the number of workers. Thus one of the supposed advantages of a large population was that it would keep wages and prices low. Otherwise, not much attention was given to wages in treatments of the economic significance of population size. A few scattered comments can be noted to show this direction of thought.

[87] Carl Mennander, *Tal,* pp. 5–6.
[88] Kryger, *op. cit.,* No. 36, p. 279.
[89] Christian König, *op. cit.,* p. 39.
[90] Anon., *Et rikes nytta,* pp. 4–5.
[91] Anders Berch, *Inledning til almänna hushålningen,* pp. 38–39.
[92] Edvard Runeberg, *Tankar om penningars värden,* p. 51.
[93] *Ibid.,* p. 72.
[94] Jacob Faggot, *Systematiskt begrepp,* p. 30 ff.
[95] Pehr von Asp, *op. cit.,* Part V, p. 57.

Ehrenström's description of the wage effect of an increasing number of people has been noted.[96] Conversely, as another writer of the time indicated, restrictions on marriage and the number of households mean fewer workers and higher wages,[97] and the same idea was expressed by Kryger in several of his works.[98] Although disagreeing on some points, other writers accepted this view of an inverse relation between numbers and wages.

Analysis of the effects of a larger number of people did not include the question of rent. A hint was contained, however, in E. O. Runeberg's treatment of rent. Here he wrote that because fertile land produces more than less fertile land, some have concluded that rent depends upon fertility. The truth of the matter, however, is that more people settle on good than on poor land; and if they do not, no advantage is derived from the greater fertility.[99]

4 · Some Optimistic Assumptions

The general conviction that a large and growing population is beneficial was based on certain optimistic assumptions, for the most part unstated. One was that there is no need to fear that with larger numbers of people some will be unable to find employment. In a work published anonymously in 1731, Salander assured his readers that

> The more people the more work and business, and the more wealth and happiness. For the Creator has never stipulated how many people each land shall have, but rather says: Grow and multiply yourselves; and further, Man shall feed himself by the sweat of his brow.[100]

Another writer similarly asserted, "It is foolishness to believe that a kingdom can have too many inhabitants, or more than can be usefully employed, for one person's work creates steady employment for another."[101] Others agreed that a larger population would not create new economic problems, but rather would help solve the nation's old ones.

Another article of faith in the Swedish optimistic thought was that the nation possessed ample natural resources. Whether or not it can be traced to the influence of Rudbeck's *Atland,* as Forsman suggests,[102] there was a general belief among eighteenth-century Swedish writers that, despite the

[96] Olof Ehrenström, *op. cit.,* p. 5.

[97] Anon., *Et rikes nytta,* 1746, p. 4.

[98] Kryger, *Den Wälmenande Patrioten,* 1751, p. 279; and *Tankar om Swenske fabriquerne,* 1753, p. 26.

[99] E. O. Runeberg, *op. cit.,* p. 56.

[100] (Erik Salander), *Gensagor och uplysinger öfwer systematiske nödhielps-tankarnes grund-satzer* . . . Objections and information about the fundamentals of poor relief . . .), Stockholm, 1731, p. 79.

[101] Herman Dahlbom, *Förslager til Sweriges handels hefrämjande* (Proposals for the advancement of Sweden's trade), Stockholm, 1761, p. 111.

[102] Karl Forsman, *op. cit.,* p. 115.

northern climate, the land was naturally fruitful, resources could be much further exploited, and scientific studies could add greatly to the national well-being. Influenced by Linnaeus, the Academy in its early years gave much attention to the exploration of the nation's plant and mineral resources, and took a lively interest in the introduction and use of new plant species, such as the potato, the tobacco plant, and mulberry trees for domestic silk culture. Writing in the early 1720's, Polhem expressed the belief that "God has given every land in the world its own resources to support its inhabitants, otherwise the command to increase and fill the earth would have been in vain." Sweden, he conceded, is a cold, northern land, but nevertheless is sufficiently fruitful to support its people, even more fruitful than the rich and pleasant lands to the east and south.[103]

In the next decade Duhre expressed confidence that Sweden could feed more than twice as many people if agriculture became more efficient and if all arable land was brought into use.[104] Mennander in 1743 estimated the population of Sweden at 3,000,000 and believed that the land could support ten times as many people.[105] A few years later, in 1747, an anonymous tract on agriculture asserted that subsistence was so plentiful, even in the most remote future the earth could not become overfilled with people, no matter how much population growth was encouraged. It was further asserted that there was no land which could not be made more fruitful.[106]

This optimism about the capacity of the land continued in the second half of the century. Wargentin wrote in 1755 that no country was known which could not support more people, adding "Nor is it yet fully demonstrated that a land can have so many inhabitants that under a good government it cannot support itself through hard work, enterprise, and moderation." Quite the opposite: the more people, the greater the demand and the greater opportunity for men to earn their bread. At any rate, he said, it would take many centuries of continuing peace and prosperity before all lands on the earth became as populous as China was already.[107]

Kryger estimated that the earth could support twenty times as many people.[108] Europe would be much more prosperous, he believed, with twice as great a population, even if all trade with other parts of the world was cut off, for the land and sea are inexhaustible, the mountains contain untold treasures, of which only the smallest part has been found, and skills

[103] Christopher Polhem, *Svärjes sanskyliga velstånd* (Sweden's real wellbeing), reprinted in *Efterlämnade skrifter*, Vol. II, p. 191.

[104] Anders Duhre, *op. cit.*, p. 16.

[105] Carl Mennander, "Jämförelse emellan lantbrukarnas antal i Sverige och landets rymd och vidd" (Comparison between the number of farmers and the land area of Sweden), *K. vet. akad. handlingar*, 1743, Vol. 4(3), pp. 227–232.

[106] Anon., *Wälment förestallning om landsens bruk* (Well intended advice concerning the use of land), Stockholm, 1747, pp. 6, 9.

[107] Pehr Wargentin, "Anmärkningar," *K. vet. akad. handlingar*, 1755, Part III, Vol. 16(1), p. 8.

[108] J. F. Kryger, *Tal om folkbristens orsaker . . .*, p. 4.

and handicrafts can be developed far beyond their present level.[109] A wise Providence has seen to it that the earth always suffices for its inhabitants, and that man's numbers can never be increased beyond the food supply.[110]

This confidence of ample resources to provide for any foreseeable increase of mankind persisted to the end of the century. In 1795, for instance, an anonymous work attributed to Johan Gottmarck agreed with the "oft-repeated remark" that Sweden could support many times its present population. There is no lack of natural resources, the author went on to say, nor is there lack of the knowledge and skill to produce all that is needed. Furthermore, Sweden is as well able as any other land in the world to provide for its inhabitants and their increase.[111] Essentially the same opinion was expressed by von Asp.[112] Most Swedish writers of this period welcomed the prospect of population growth, saw no cause for concern, and anticipated no lack of food or resources.

Implicit in much of the discussion, although seldom expressed, was the assumption that per capita returns remain constant or increase as the number of people grows. This thought is implied in the *Arcana* (1730) of Nordencrantz, where it was said that "the more people and cattle the more fruitful can the land be made."[113] Similar comments are found elsewhere in his works; for example, in an anonymous tract published in 1761, he wrote that "The more populous a land is and the more wisely the people are employed, the better they are provided with the necessities of life."[114] He added that when population increases, food becomes more plentiful rather than more scarce. An anonymous tract, similarly optimistic, that appeared in 1745, presented arguments for ending the restrictions on the subdivision of farms, stating ". . . it is known that all land, of whatever sort, is more or less productive, according to whether more or fewer skilled people till it."[115]

Especially important as an indication of current thought was Wargentin's reply to an address by Kryger[116] on the causes and consequences of underpopulation. Although he was in a position to know the current opinions, both Swedish and foreign, he no doubt expressed his own ideas as he commented, "The old in-rooted belief that more mouths will more rapidly

---

[109] J. F. Kryger, *Tankar wid lediga stunder,* Part I, Stockholm, 1761, pp. 218, 220.
[110] *Ibid.,* p. 220.
[111] Anon. (Johan Gottmarck), *Sweriges moraliska, politiska, och oeconomiska tilstånd* . . . (Sweden's moral, political, and economic condition . . .), Stockholm, 1795, pp. 5, 32–33.
[112] Pehr von Asp, *op. cit.,* 1801, Vol. II, Part 13, p. 328.
[113] Anders Nordencrantz, *Arcana,* p. 173.
[114] Anon. (Anders Nordencrantz), *Owälduga tankar,* pp. 4, 5. See also his *Tankar om krig i gemen och Sweriges krig i synnerhet* . . . (Thoughts of war in general and Sweden's war in particular . . .), Stockholm, 1767.
[115] Anon., *Wälmente tankar,* p. 13.
[116] J. F. Kryger, *Tal om folkbristens orsaker.* . . .

empty the storehouse does not readily give way to another that agrees with thought and experience: that more hands still more rapidly fill the storehouse."[117] He added that an industrious farmer, fisherman, or other worker can produce more than he consumes, that the means of subsistence increase more rapidly than the number of workers in a society, and that the workers never become too numerous where the government knows how to make good use of them.[118]

The assumption of constant or increasing returns is also found in the writings of the Runebergs. E. O. Runeberg believed that as population density rises, men are forced to more mental and physical activity, which increases the supply of goods.[119] His brother Edvard gave the most explicit statement of constant or increasing returns, writing:

> We take it for granted here that the produce of the soil increases in the same proportion as the number of hands working on the land increases; and if this assumption is somewhat in error, it is more apt to be that the produce increases in a greater proportion than that it increases in a lesser proportion.[120]

It is only the increase of labor supply that possesses this quality, he added, for an increase of capital with a constant number of workers does not increase returns proportionately.[121] In a later work he reaffirmed his belief that per capita returns remain at least constant as population doubles in any given period, such as every twenty-five years.[122]

With these few exceptions, the basic assumption of proportional or increasing returns remained largely tacit; together with the assumption that resources were ample, however, it was fundamental to the prevailing optimistic thought on population.

5 · Traces of Pessimistic Thought

In spite of the dominance of optimistic opinion and the concern over underpopulation and emigration, a few traces of pessimism can be found in eighteenth-century Sweden. The Malthusian theory did not gain foothold in Sweden until the nineteenth century and was without or almost without Swedish anticipators. But there was the much older conservative view, widely prevalent in Europe of an earlier day and no doubt based on hard experience, that although a large population may give national strength, the

---

[117] Pehr Wargentin, in published copy of Kryger's address, Stockholm, 1758, p. 40.
[118] *Ibid.,* pp. 40–41.
[119] E. O. Runeberg, *Tankar,* p. 18.
[120] Edvard Runeberg, *Tankar om penningars värden* . . ., 1762, p. 43; also restated pp. 48–49.
[121] *Ibid.,* p. 43.
[122] Edvard Runeberg, *Om Svea rikes folk-nummer,* p. 109.

supply of food and other necessities is limited, and an increase in the number of people means a smaller average share for each. The few hints of pessimism found in Swedish writings of the eighteenth century perhaps were survivals of this older empirical point of view rather than anticipations of a new, more theoretical view of population.

The old ambivalence toward population, especially the realization that populousness brings with it some risk, was found in the writings of Polhem, the first Swedish economic writer. In the earliest of his works noted here, he wrote, "A land to which nature has given greater fertility of people than of soil has greater lack of subsistence than lands with greater plenty of the fruits of the soil than of people."[123] He then pointed out with some concern that no nation had produced more people than Sweden, which had almost filled the world with its migrants and colonists, but that now the way out is no longer open and the government would not make war in order to reduce a surplus population.[124]

A decade later, Carleson described the inhabitants of a nation as its treasure, but a treasure dead and buried if not provided with work and industriousness.[125] A similar reservation was made in an economic journal, a weekly published anonymously by Lars Salvius in 1738. Cast in the form of a conversation between Fru Svea (Sweden), Economics, and other characters, the journal contained in its first issue the sober remark by Fru Svea that large numbers of people are indeed a kingdom's principal strength, but that if they consume all that is provided for them they will fall into the greatest misery.[126]

The possibility of overpopulation was also touched on in Berch's *Politiska Arithmetica*. Here it was said that there may be too many people in a nation, in spite of Solomon's saying that people are a king's glory. The disadvantages of too large a population were not as apparent to the writer as those of too small a population, but he regarded as evidence of God's wisdom the fact that men do not live forever, otherwise the earth would become overcrowded.[127] In the case of Sweden, Berch went on to say, the population could conceivably be so large as to do harm rather than good; but he did not explain what the harmful effects would be, and closed the subject by quoting Aristotle to the effect that the inhabitants of a state should be neither too few nor too many.[128]

According to an anonymous tract of 1747, a large population in a nation without sufficient resources and wealth is burdensome, and the people live

[123] Christopher Polhem, *Oeconomie och commercen uti Swerige*, p. 31.
[124] *Ibid.*
[125] Edvard Carleson, *op. cit.*, p. 25 (quoted in section 1 above).
[126] Anon. (Lars Salvius), *Tankar öfwer den swenska oeconomien* (Thoughts on the Swedish economy), Stockholm, 1738, p. 2 of the first issue.
[127] Note the similarity of this to Raleigh's *History of the World*, Book I, Ch. 4.
[128] Anders Berch, *Politiska arithmetica*, pp. 8–11.

in misery. This statement was followed by the sensible comment that the soundest development is equal growth of population and the means of supporting it.[129] Ungern Sternberg stated the need for a balance between people and land for the case of a single farm or household, writing that "Many residents and plenty of people in a household that has plenty of land that can be made fruitful are most necessary; but many residents in a household without such land that can be tilled are harmful."[130] In the latter case there are perhaps twenty consumers for what would scarcely suffice for four to six, there are too many hands for the work a few could do, laziness appears as a consequence, and the nation loses labor that is needed elsewhere.[131]

In an exchange of pamphlets in a controversy in 1761, Abraham Sahlstedt (1717–1776), political economist and civil servant, expressed an unusual skepticism about the desirability of population growth in Sweden. All authorities, he noted, were agreed that the well-being of a state depends upon plenty of people and goods. He reasoned, however, that the recent increase of the number of people in Sweden must consist of young children, and that although they might eventually add to the national strength, they now were consumers rather than producers. Therefore, if there was already misery in Sweden, the growth of population would increase rather than decrease it. The problem was made more serious, Sahlstedt believed, because many people in search of personal comfort take employment as domestic servants and thereby decrease the number of productive workers. For these reasons he was skeptical whether the increase of population in Sweden was evidence of a greater national well-being.[132]

A few other elements and traces of pessimistic opinion can be found in the literature. Several writers stated that an increase in the food supply would be followed by an increase of population,[133] but this thought was not carried to any pessimistic conclusions. Belief in the existence of an eventual limit to population numbers was expressed in the latter part of the century by the Swedish writer Wadström, who wrote in *An Essay on Colonization* (1794) that every government should look for unoccupied land against the time ". . . when their population and manufactures shall

[129] Anon., *Wälment föreställning om landsens bruk*, 1747, p. 5.
[130] Mathias von Ungern Sternberg, *op. cit.*, p. 6.
[131] *Ibid.*
[132] (Abraham Sahlstedt), *Anmärkningar öfwer Tankar om Sweriges närwarande tilstånd, i anseende til rikedom ock wälmåga* (Comments on [Scheffer's] "Thoughts on Sweden's present condition with regard to wealth and well-being"), Stockholm, 1761, p. 4.
[133] For example, C. F. Scheffer wrote, in the anonymous tract to which Sahlstedt replied (see preceding footnote), that "as soon as the food supply in a land increases the population also increases to the same extent"; and similarly in von Asp's *Försök, Fortsättning*, 1800, p. 57.

exceed the proportion which they ought to have to the land they already occupy, when finally improved. That proportion certainly has a limit . . .,"[134] and von Asp,[135] writing in 1801, when he may have been influenced by Malthus, thought it was unwise to give relief to the poor without demanding work in return.[136]

However, as a whole, the Swedish population literature of the eighteenth century can be said to have contained only scattered traces of pessimistic thought. It is true that separate elements of the pessimistic position were stated by one or another Swedish writer, but the ideas so expressed do not appear to have penetrated deeply into the body of Swedish opinion on population. Instead they remained isolated examples of doubt about the desirability of population growth, and were never combined into a body of pessimistic theory, in contrast to the contemporary developments in population theory elsewhere. During this same period or even earlier, a few writers in other nations were taking much the same basic ideas and consolidating them into formulations of pessimistic theory that were the precursors of Malthus' more famous work.[137] And in the final years of the century, Malthus himself synthesized the various elements of pessimistic thought into his theory of population.[138]

6 · Final Comment

There are a number of other elements in Swedish thinking on population during the eighteenth century that might be mentioned. These include concern over emigration, discussion of the effects of luxury or overconsump-

---

[134] C. B. Wadström, *An Essay on Colonization, particularly applied to the West Coast of Africa,* London, 1794, p. 62.

[135] Pehr von Asp, *Försök, Ytterligare fortsättning,* Stockholm, 1801, p. 28.

[136] It is quite possible that a somewhat different distribution of views on the population question in eighteenth-century Sweden existed outside the range of the published literature that is dealt with here. A study by Nils Wohlin on Swedish policy on the subdivision of farms into smaller holdings (*Den svenska jordstyckningspolitiken in de 18:de och 19:de århundradena,* Stockholm: Nordstedt, 1912, esp. p. 461) indicates that concern over the continuing population growth was expressed by some government officials who no doubt saw the matter at first hand and as an actual administrative problem rather than a theoretical point of interest. And a more recent article (Gustav Utterström, "Labour policy and population thought in eighteenth century Sweden," *Scandinavian Economic History Review,* 10(2): 262–279, 1962) reports that Malthusian opinions were expressed by representatives of the nobility in debate on governmental policy affecting farm labor.

[137] Concerning the principal predecessors of Malthus, see Ch. 6 below, especially the last section.

[138] For an outline of Malthus' theory, see Ch. 8, section 1, below. It is a challenging question why the train of thought followed by Malthus and his predecessors arose in certain minds in certain times and countries, and not in others. Heckscher (*op. cit.,* I:886–887, 890) stated that mercantilist influence remained predominant in Sweden until into the nineteenth cenutry; but even if we accept this broad generalization, presumably much more needs to be considered to explain why Malthus had no Swedish predecessors of the sort found elsewhere.

tion, the liberal reaction against restrictions interfering with population growth that was part of the larger liberal reaction against the old pattern of political and economic controls,[139] and the development of the pioneering system for the collection of population data that grew out of interest in population questions. Although each of these is interesting in itself and as part of the total thinking about population, none are included in this account, which deals only with the significance attributed to population size and growth in the literature of the period.

Several characteristics of this body of Swedish writings can be restated by way of final comment. One is the almost complete dominance of the optimistic view that a large and growing population was desirable, together with the corresponding absence of fear that greater numbers would create shortages of work or resources. It is also noteworthy that there was little mention of the military advantage of populousness except for defense, and attention was given almost exclusively to the economic significance of population size. The few expressions of pessimistic thought did not constitute a definite reaction against the prevailing optimism; rather, most of these appear to have been remnants of the older, conservative view that the supply of food and other necessities is limited.

Analysis of the social and economic implications of the number of people was not carried very far, and several reasons for this can be suggested. For one (as will be shown more fully in the following chapter), the optimistic argument as it existed in the eighteenth century was a relatively simple one that did not lead to much theoretical or analytical elaboration. The real analytical development in the eighteenth and especially the nineteenth centuries was in the pessimistic argument, and that side of the population dilemma was not appreciated by the Swedish writers of the period. Another factor may have been the high degree of unanimity of the Swedish writers; presumably more controversy over the population question would have brought out more intensive inquiry into the interactions set in motion by demographic changes. Perhaps another is the brief flowering of Swedish political and economic thought in the so-called Freedom Period (1718–1772), an interlude of weakened royal authority, more popular government, and relaxed censorship. Less tangible but perhaps as influential may have been the utilitarian and non-theoretical Swedish turn of mind, and the fact that from the establishment of the official statistical system in 1749 onward, Sweden possessed more information about the number and condition of its people than did any other nation.

[139] The Act of June 30, 1747, for example, adopted after considerable debate, relaxed the long-standing restrictions on the subdivision of farms.

5

Summary of the Optimistic
Position before 1800

As shown earlier, the principal elements in the optimistic position had
already taken form by the end of the seventeenth century. During the
eighteenth century there was a greatly expanded volume of publication
referring to population, and the optimistic position was perhaps more fully
stated, although little that was essentially new was added. With only a few
exceptions the desirability of a large and growing population was accepted,
and inquiry was generally directed to finding out what conditions interfered with population growth, and to considering policies and measures to
promote increase. This chapter is therefore limited to a summary of the
optimistic position as it existed in the eighteenth century, without a full
review of the very considerable literature on the subject,[1] in only enough
detail to indicate the principal lines of argument. The Swedish literature,
covered in the preceding chapter, is not included here.

1 · The Central Theme

The central theme of the optimists in the eighteenth century as in the
seventeenth was that populousness gives national strength, or, conversely,
that a sparsely inhabited country is necessarily poor and weak. The military
aspect was sometimes emphasized, although less than in earlier times; and
it was combined more often than formerly with mention of the economic
strength also derived from large numbers of people. For example, Theodor
Lau (1670–1740) devoted the first chapter of his *Aufrichtige Vorschlag*
(1719) to a discussion of population, in which he maintained that:

---

[1] For further references to the population literature of this period, see the general
works on population theory listed in Chapter 1, section 3, above. The following may
also be useful: Anita Fage, "Les doctrines de population des Encyclopédistes," *Population*, 1951, Vol. 6(4), pp. 609–624; E. A. J. Johnson, *Predecessors of Adam
Smith*, New York: Prentice-Hall, 1937; and A. Sauvy, "Some lesser known French
demographers of the eighteenth century," *Population Studies*, 1951, Vol. 5(1), pp.
3–22 (also published as an appendix to the French edition of Spengler's *French
Predecessors of Malthus*).

I. The power and wealth of a state are rooted in the number of people.

II. The power, because where there are many people, many troops can easily be levied and formidable armies be put in the field.

III. The wealth, because many people lead to much trade, and commerce.[2]

The military point of view on population numbers also appeared, as one might expect, in an essay by the French field-marshal, Maurice de Saxe (1696–1750). The essay, *Reflections upon the Propagation of the Human Species,* was appended to the author's *Reveries and Memoires upon the Art of War*[3] (1757) and was introduced with the frank remark, "After having treated of a science, which furnishes us with means for the destruction of the human race, I am now going, on the other hand, to propose methods towards facilitating the propagation of it."[4] De Saxe then went on to recommend populationist policies with the ominous advice:

> The legislator who would form a system upon propagation, by the prudent establishment of such laws as were likely to contribute the most to that end, would lay the foundation of a monarchy, that could not fail to become one day formidable to the whole world.[5]

There was no suggestion that population growth might bring other, less desirable consequences.[6]

The greater security from invasion of well-peopled nations was mentioned by a number of writers, including Charles Castel, Abbé de Saint-Pierre (1658–1743), in his *Annales politiques*[7] (1757), and Joseph von Sonnenfels (1733–1781) in the *Grundsätze der Policey, Handlung, und Finanz*[8] (1765). An obvious consideration, this thought has already been observed in the contemporary Swedish literature, and can be found repeated in many sources.

A more sophisticated reason for wanting a large population, one that gained ground rapidly during the later mercantilist period, was that national wealth would be increased, human hands being the creators of all riches. This economic view of population, often combined with the older identification of numbers with national strength, had appeared among the English writers of the late seventeenth century, and was widely accepted

[2] Theodor Lau, *Aufrichtiger Vorschlag von glüklicher, vortheilhafftiger, beständiger Einrichtung der Intraden und Einkünfte der Souverainen und ihrer Unterthanen,* Frankfurt am Main, 1719, Vol. 1, Ch. 1, p. 5.

[3] Maurice de Saxe, *Reveries or Memoires upon the Art of War,* London, 1757.

[4] *Ibid.,* p. 189.

[5] *Ibid.,* p. 192.

[6] The military or strength-giving aspect of population also appears prominently in the Spanish work by Geronimo Uztariz (1670–1732), *Théorica y practica de comercio y marina,* 1724 (English translation, *The Theory and Practice of Commerce and Maritime Affairs,* London, 1751, p. 52 ff.

[7] Abbé de Saint-Pierre, *Annales politiques,* London, 1757, p. 18.

[8] Joseph von Sonnenfels, *Grundsätze,* 5th ed., Vienna, 1787, Ch. 2, section 28.

after 1700. In Germany this argument for populousness was presented by Lau, Darjes, Sonnenfels, and many others. It appeared prominently in the French literature of the period, as in *L'ami des hommes*[9] (1756–1758) by Mirabeau (1715–1789), and in the writings of Plumard de Dangeul[10] (fl. 1754), François de Forbonnais[11] (1722–1800), and Jacques Necker[12] (1732–1804). In England it pervaded much of the eighteenth-century discussion favoring population growth. Postlethwayt, who believed that "The real riches of a state are its superior degree of independence of other states,"[13] thought a large population desirable because it gives internal self-sufficiency and provides a surplus of goods for export.[14] Erasmus Philips (d. 1743) wrote, "It is certain that the Riches of a Nation consists of numbers of Industrious Inhabitants, who by their Labour and Application, furnish their Neighbors with Materials either for Use or Pleasure. . . ."[15] Others saw in populousness a source of wealth, and a basis for both internal trade and foreign commerce.

Although a majority believed that a large population is a means to national well-being, some thought that the relation lies in the opposite direction and that general well-being is a cause of populousness. In Germany, for example, Gottfried Achenwall (1719–1772) believed that a state benefits from a numerous population, but at the same time he recognized that a flourishing economy is the surest way to secure an increase of numbers and that national policy should be directed toward the former rather than the latter objective.[16] The anonymous author of *The*

[9] Victor de Riquetti, Marquis de Mirabeau, *L'ami des hommes, ou traité de la population,* Avignon, 1756–1758.

[10] (Plumard de Dangeul), *Remarks on the Advantages and Disadvantages of France and of Great Britain . . . ,* London, 1754; according to the translator's notes, from the 2nd edition. Title of the French original, *Remarques sur les avantages et les désavantages de la France et de la Grande Bretagne, par John Nickolls,* Paris, 1753. The author writes in Part V, p. 178 of the English edition, "It is in proportion to the number of men which a State possesses, that it can be esteemed powerful. It is in proportion to the number of its men, that its lands can be better cultivated; that the hands employed in its manufactures, and the arms which defend it, are more numerous; that the taxes and charges bear the lighter upon every one." The latter point also had been made by Petty.

[11] See, for example, *Principes économiques,* 1767, reprinted in *Mélanges d'économie politique,* edited by Eugene Daire and G. de Molinari, Paris: Guillaumin, 1847, Vol. 1, p. 176.

[12] Jacques Necker, *Sur la legislation et le commerce des grains,* Paris, 1775, p. 21.

[13] Malachy Postlethwayt, *Britain's Commercial Interest Explained and Improved,* London, 1757, Vol. 2, p. 368.

[14] *Ibid.,* p. 376. Further thoughts on population are contained in Postlethwayt's *Universal Dictionary of Trade and Commerce* (1751), which was in large part a translation of the French work by Jacques Savary des Brulons, *Dictionnaire Universal de Commerce.* Much of Postlethwayt's article, "Population," however, appears to have been taken from Davenant.

[15] Erasmus Philips, *An Appeal to Common Sense, London,* 1720, p. 18.

[16] Gottfried Achenwall, *Die Staatsklugheit nach ihren ersten Grundsätzen,* Göttingen, 1761, p. 178.

Politician's Dictionary (1775) stated quite bluntly that little thought need be given to population numbers, which take care of themselves if economic conditions are favorable, saying:

> Tell me of a kingdom, state, or prince, that has many millions of sub-jects; this decides nothing; tell me of some that is immensely rich, no other enquiry is requisite; he must have men. No fear can be more vain than that of an industrious wealthy kingdom wanting subjects. Let this nation continue to encourage and honour agriculture, manufactures and commerce; to be rich in the possession of great wealth from a vast stock of industry; let her see to these points, and she need not be concerned about the number of her people. Population will take care of itself. If you think you have not people enough, make more, which is as easily done as to manufacture a statue. Provide new employment, and new hands will inevitably follow.[17]

A variation was sometimes introduced, that it is not a large population in itself but rather a high density of settlement that has beneficial effects. This idea had been advanced earlier by Sir William Temple, and was adopted by a number of writers in the eighteenth century. It is found, for example, in the writings of Goudar, Darjes, and the Abbé de Saint-Pierre. According to the last:

> The strength of a state does not depend on the extent of its territory, but on the number of its inhabitants, to the extent that they are more concentrated together, more industrious, more disciplined in war, more diligent in the arts, and more usefully employed than other peoples.
> It may even be said that, the number of inhabitants being the same, a state smaller in area by three-fourths would be three times more strong and powerful than the same number of people spread over an area three times as great.[18]

This was so, he said, because of the better capacity of a populous state for defense and offense in war and the greater ease of communication and trade. Daniel Defoe (1661–1731) spoke of the economic advantages of the large concentration of people in London, which he believed gave more stimulus to trade than if the same number of people had been divided among ten cities.[19] Similarly, significance was attributed to population density in *The Elements of Commerce and Theory of Taxes* (1755)[20] of Josiah Tucker (1713–1799), in *Recherches et considérations sur la popu-*

[17] Anon., *The Politician's Dictionary, or a Summary of Political Knowledge*, London, 1775, p. 158.

[18] Abbé de Saint-Pierre, *op. cit.,* p. 18.

[19] Daniel Defoe, *The Complete English Tradesman*, Vol. 2, Ch. 34; reprinted in *Novels and Miscellaneous Works*, Oxford, 1841.

[20] Reprinted in *Josiah Tucker, a Selection of his Economic and Political Writings*, R. L. Schuyler, ed. New York: Columbia University Press, 1951.

lation de la France (1778)[21] of Moheau (1735–1820), and in a number of other works. Goudar (1720–1791) gave a somewhat different emphasis by saying that the important thing for national strength is density of population relative to that of other states.[22]

With or without these variations on the main theme, the general conviction remained that a large population is desirable. Some believed that population size is the all-important determiner of national well-being. Sonnenfels wrote, for example,

> I consider the enlargement of the society through the encouragement of population growth to be the basic principle of government . . . and the test of every measure undertaken for the advancement of the common good to be, is it favourable or unfavorable to population?[23]

For the most part, however, the treatment of the population factor was quite moderate and well-balanced, with number of people being regarded as one among several significant variables rather than all-important.

2 · Some Optimistic Assumptions

In addition to the central belief in the value of population, the optimistic position also included assumptions that gave assurance that large numbers or continued multiplication of people bring no serious consequences. A necessary assumption, one already observed in Sweden, was that land and other resources are adequate for present and future demand. At the end of the preceding century Fénelon had written that "the earth is inexhaustible"; and confidence in the future supply of necessities continued on into the eighteenth century. For example, Nicholas Baudeau (1730–1792), in a work published in 1771, expressed his belief that the productiveness of nature and the industriousness of man are without known limits, that production can increase indefinitely, and that in consequence population numbers and well-being can go on advancing together.[24] The best known statement of this belief was made near the end of the century by William Godwin (1756–1836), who wrote,

> Three fourths of the habitable globe is now uncultivated. The parts already cultivated are capable of immeasurable improvement. Myriads of

[21] Republished, Paris: Geunther, 1912; René Gonnard, editor. See especially Book I, Ch. 1.
[22] Ange Goudar, *Les intérêts de la France mal entendus*, 3 vol., Amsterdam, 1756, Vol. 1, p. 291–293.
[23] Sonnenfels, *op. cit.*, Ch. 2, section 26.
[24] Nicholas Baudeau, *Première introduction à la philosophie économique*, 1771; reprinted in *Collection des économistes et des reformateurs de la France*, Auguste Dubois, Ed., Paris: Geunther, 1910, p. 13.

centuries of still increasing population may pass away, and the earth be still found sufficient for the subsistence of its inhabitants.[25]

Another assumption essential to the optimistic position, and of particular interest in view of later developments, was that total production would increase at least in proportion to population or labor supply. This was the assumption, seldom stated but often implied, of constant or increasing per capita returns and no immediate limit on the expansion of production.

A few indications of this underlying assumption can be found. Fénelon, as noted earlier, had written that the products of the soil remain proportioned to the number of producers. William Wood (1679–1765), in the introduction of his *Survey of Trade* (1718), was not so explicit but expressed confidence that Providence has made it possible for every industrious man to earn more than enough for his own needs.[26] Jacob von Bielfeld (1716–1770), who had strong populationist views, gave particular attention to measures for increasing population and dismissed the problem of providing for the larger number of people with the remark,

> Experience proves that the proportion between the quantity of labor employed in agriculture and the quantity of produce always advances in equal progression, and that the increase of grain could be pushed excessively far if there were more hands to till the soil.[27]

Others, neither invoking nor assuming a general law of constant or increasing returns, cited various ways in which larger numbers of people expand production. In the seventeenth century, Temple, Dugard, Davenant, and the author of *Britannia Languens* believed that populousness stimulates men to greater effort. The same thought was expressed in many ways and by a number of writers during the eighteenth century. George Berkeley (1685–1753) considered ways of promoting industriousness in his *Essays toward Preventing the Ruin of Great Britain* (1721), and wrote that "The number of people is both means and motives to industry. It should therefore be of great use to encourage propagation. . . ."[28] The subject was more fully treated by Sir James Steuart (1712–1780), who cannot be classed with the optimists. In *An Inquiry into the Principles of Political Oeconomy* (1767), the leading work in political economy before *The*

[25] William Godwin, *Enquiry concerning Political Justice* (1793) 2nd ed., London, 1796, p. 510. The passage quoted here remained in the 4th ed., 1842, Vol. II, Book VIII, Ch. 8.

[26] William Wood, *A Survey of Trade*, London, 1718, p. 1.

[27] Jacob von Bielfeld, *Institutiones politiques*, The Hague, 1760, Vol II, Ch. 14, section 11. In addition to the usual measures to promote increase he advocated the abolition of divorce, the prohibition of emigration, and the repression of murder, suicide, and duelling.

[28] George Berkeley, *Works*, Oxford: Clarendon Press, 1871, Vol. 3, p. 198.

Wealth of Nations, Steuart devoted a chapter to the "causes and consequences of a country's being fully peopled," and raised the question,

> Is multiplication the efficient cause of agriculture, or is agriculture that
> of multiplication? I answer, that multiplication is the efficient cause of
> agriculture, though I allow, that, in the infancy of society, the spon-
> taneous fruits of the earth, which are free to all, are the efficient cause of
> a multiplication, which may rise to the exact proportion of them. . . .[29]

He believed, in other words, that the growth of demand urges on the husbandman, and therefore, ". . . procreation . . . must be considered as the first, or at least the most palpable political cause of setting mankind to work. . . ."[30]

An alternative theory was given by Butel-Dumont (1725–1788), who maintained that the union of efforts leads to proportionately greater returns, saying, by way of illustration, that one hundred men together have much more than one hundred times the strength of a single man. Furthermore, as a group increases in size, there is more competition, more stimulus to effort, and a greater and greater expansion of production.[31] Moheau cited the greater efficiency of dense concentrations of population.[32]

Josiah Tucker assumed that increase of the number of inhabitants of a country leads to increased production as a result of improvement of land, better fertilization, and more intensive cultivation.[33] Conversely, he believed that

> Where a country is thinly peopled, it is impossible to promote a brisk
> and general circulation of Industry and Labour, by reason of the Distance
> and Diffusion of the People from each other, and the Consequence of
> that, their Want of Rivalship and Emulation. . . .[34]

In addition, a thinly peopled country also suffers from weakness and poverty, and from the more absolute and despotic treatment of "vassals" by their landlords.[35]

The assumption that population growth increases production was sometimes extended to represent populousness as a stimulus to business activity and economic development. This idea was found in Petty's writings, and Temple described how the pressure of necessity urges men to "industry and

[29] Sir James Steuart, *An Inquiry into the Principles of Political Oeconomy,* London, 1767, Vol. I, p. 114.
[30] *Ibid.,* p. 116.
[31] Butel-Dumont, *Théorie du luxe,* London and Paris, 1771, Part I, Ch. 1, especially pp. 6, 18.
[32] Moheau, *op. cit.,* Book I, Ch. 1.
[33] Josiah Tucker, *Reflections on the expediency of a law for the naturalization of foreign protestants,* London, 1751–1752; reprinted in translation by Turgot, *Oeuvres,* Paris: Alcan, 1913, Vol. I, pp. 453–458.
[34] Josiah Tucker, *Elements of Commerce and Theory of Taxes,* p. 63.
[35] *Ibid.,* p. 64.

parsimony" and leads to the development of trade. In *Britannia Languens* populousness, or "populacy," was said to be "serviceable to manufactures," and Davenant held a similar opinion.

Parallel ideas were expressed by a number of writers in the eighteenth century, of whom only a few need be mentioned for illustration. Early in the century, Theodor Lau, as previously quoted, expressed the opinion that where there are many people there must be active trade and commerce. Jean-François Melon (1675–1738), in his *Essai politique sur le commerce* (1734), described an hypothetical case in which population growth led to manufacturing and the further development of agriculture.[36] An over-crowded people must turn to trade, he said, if they are unable to migrate.[37]

Defoe, in *A Plan of English Commerce* (1728), undertook to show how trade would strengthen England. It would also increase the population, he said, and he described at some length the good effects:

> As the Numbers of People increase, the Consumption of Provisions increases; as the Consumption increases, the Rate of Value will rise at Market; and as the Rate of Provisions rises, the Rents of Land rise; So the Gentlemen are with the first to feel the Benefit of Trade, by the Addition to their Estates. . . .
>
> As the Consumption of Provisions increase, more Lands are cultivated; waste Grounds are inclosed, Woods are grubb'd up, Forrests and common Lands are till'd, and improv'd; by this more Farmers are brought together, more Farm-houses and Cottages are built, and more Trades are called upon to supply the necessary Demands of Husbandry: In a Word, as Land is employ'd, the People increase of Course, and thus Trade sets all the Wheels of Improvement in Motion; for from the Original of Business to this Day it appears, that the Prosperity of a Nation rises and falls, just as Trade is supported or decay'd.[38]

Later in the same work Defoe considered the great trade and wealth that would come to the mother country as its colonies filled with people, writing with anticipation:

> The Colonies would be encreased in People beyond expressing; and consequently, not only the Consumption of Provisions would be encreased there, which is, as before the grand Fund of their Prosperity; but the Consumption of Manufactures, and all European Exportations to them, would be in Proportion encreased. . . .
>
> It would take up a Volume by it self, to lay open all the glorious

---

[36] Jean-François Melon, *Essai politique sur le commerce*, 1734; reprinted in *Écono-mistes-Financiers du XVIII siècle*, Eugene Daire, Ed., Paris: Guillaumin, 1843. See especially Ch. 1.

[37] *Ibid.*, Ch. 3.

[38] Daniel Defoe, *A Plan of English Commerce*, 1728, reprinted in the 1928 edition of his works, Oxford: Blackwell, Vol. 14, pp. 13, 14. Compare John Cary, *An Essay on the State of England;* see p. 62 above.

Schemes of Improvement in Trade, which would be the Consequence of such a Business, and particularly the Encrease of our Manufactures here, by the Demand of Goods from thence, when the Numbers of People in those Colonies should be thus encreas'd. . . .

Let them tell us, or but guess at for us, what a glorious Trade to *England* it would be to have those Colonies encreased with a Million of People, to be cloth'd, furnish'd, and supply'd with all their needful Things, Food excepted, only from us; and ty'd down for ever to us by that immortal, indissoluble Bond of Trade, *their Interest.*[39]

Ideas resembling those of Temple on some points were stated by William Bell (1731–1816) in a tract published in 1756, inquiring into the causes and consequences of populousness.[40] With regard to the consequences, he believed that increasing numbers stimulate the people of a nation to seek greater "ease and pleasure" and disposes them to turn to commerce.[41] In conclusion, he wrote:

From the whole of what has been suggested may be clearly seen a perfect harmony between the true interest of commerce, and the most effectual means of augmenting a people. For as in the first part of this enquiry it was shewn, That no Nation can in the end become as POPU-LOUS as it is capable of being, unless commerce and refinement are avoided, till the more necessary arts alone have well filled it with inhabitants; so it has in the next place appeared, that TRADE can no where be brought to so flourishing and permanent a state, as where it has from the first been cultivated by an exceedingly numerous people.[42]

Published shortly thereafter, the *Annales politiques* of the Abbé de Saint-Pierre supported the recommendation of populationist policy with the assertion that populousness favors the development of commerce, promotes the arts, and improves communications within a society.[43] Sonnenfels wrote that "the more people, the more needs and the more complex the internal economy."[44]

Developing out of the discussion of population size and growth as a stimulus to greater effort, emulation and competition, more intensive agriculture, trade, and manufactures, there emerged a concept of population as a civilizing factor that forces mankind to improve its methods of production, its economic system, and its form of social organization. This

[39] *Ibid.,* concluding chapter; quotations from pp. 269–271.
[40] William Bell, *A dissertation on the following subject: What causes principally contribute to render a nation populous? and what effect has the populousness of a nation on its trade,* Cambridge, 1756.
[41] *Ibid.,* pp. 31–32.
[42] *Ibid.,* p. 36. Bell believed that refinement and "imaginary wants" check population growth.
[43] Abbé de Saint-Pierre, *op. cit.,* p. 18 ff.
[44] Sonnenfels, *op. cit.,* Ch. 2, section 30.

ultimate development of the optimistic position remained for the most part latent in eighteenth-century discussion of population, however, and awaited the next century for full statement.[45]

The optimistic position was indeed carried to extremes by a few of its adherents, both in statements of the practically limitless capacity of the earth for more inhabitants and in their arguments for more people by any means and at all costs. There were the believers in the infinite perfectability of human society and in the boundless resources of the earth, to whose views Malthus was to take particular exception. There were also the somewhat fantastic extremes to which the populationist or *Volksvermehrung* views were carried by some of their more enthusiastic adherents.[46] However, the majority of those who accepted the optimistic position and who favored the further increase of numbers were careful to introduce certain reservations, realizing that population growth is most desirable under certain conditions and within certain limits. A number of qualifications were accordingly attached to the optimistic doctrine, even by some of its more vigorous proponents.

3 · Some Qualifications

Perhaps the most frequently applied qualification was that population increase is desirable only insofar as provision can be made for the additional people. Seckendorf had said that there can not be too many common people, provided that they are industrious and that provision is made for their food supply.[47] Christian Wolff (1679–1754), in his *Vernunftige Gedanken* (1721) on various political and social matters, said reasonably that in establishing a state one must have enough households to assure well-being and safety, and in the spirit of the title of his work added that

[45] One exception is the preface of an anonymous work published in 1782 and attributed to J. C. Adelung, in which it was explicitly stated that population and culture advance together in geometric progression (*Versuch einer Geschichte der Culture des menschlichen Geschlechts*, Leipzig, 1782).

[46] Darjes, for example, is quoted as saying that even beggars are an asset to a nation for they contribute some revenue to the government (Roscher, *Geschichte*, Ch. 19). According to Justi (*Grundsätze der Policey-Wissenschaft*, Göttingen, 1759, Book I, Part II, Ch. 4, section 85), "it must be taken as a fundamental law that a country can never have too many people." Bielfeld likewise said that overpopulation is impossible, and that the punishment of murderers is justified on grounds that it reduces the population, if for no other reason, because of the weakening of the state (Roscher, *Geschichte*, p. 426). On the same grounds, however, Ludwig von Hess (1719–1784) recommended the abolition of the death penalty, and included in a long list of recommendations for the protection and increase of population the very original suggestion that large dogs should not be allowed free on the streets lest they frighten pregnant women (von Mohl, *Die Geschichte und Literatur der Staatswissenschaft*, p. 472).

[47] Seckendorf, *Christenstaat*, Book II, Ch. 3, section 5.

the people should be "not too many and not too few." He explained that there are too many people if they are unable to find subsistence, too few if the land can support more or if the people are unable to defend themselves against external enemies. But governmental policy should not be directed only toward the increase of population; it should also seek to develop the supply of necessities, because "Needy subjects and many beggars are of little advantage to a land."[48]

Although Johann Süssmilch (1707–1767) supported the Volksverme-hrung theory in his celebrated *Göttliche Ordnung* (1741), he nevertheless introduced a slight qualification into his statement of the desirability of a large population, writing that the largest possible ". . . number of subjects, proportioned to the food supply, is the basis of happiness, of power and of safety, as well as of wealth."[49] Sonnenfels, who believed the principal objective of political science is to increase population, admitted that limits on population size are set by the nature of a state and its physical situation. There are states that are by nature destined to be small, though this does not mean they should not try to become as populous as their resources permit.[50]

Another modification occasionally introduced was that it is not numbers alone but also the composition or quality of the population that is important, just as Bacon had said that a large army does not necessarily give strength, for courage may be lacking. Similarly, Sir James Caldwell (1734–1781) pointed out in discussion of Irish affairs that ". . . populousness alone is not always sufficient for national Defense; a considerable Number of the People must be so employed as to be peculiarly fitted for military Operations."[51] Another parallel to Bacon's thought is the suggestion by Bielfeld that "One should not believe that it is the number of inhabitants alone that makes a state formidable. It is the quality and not the quantity of subjects which gives it strength."[52] The same thought was expressed by Adam Ferguson (1723–1818), who had especially moderate views on the subject of population:

> To increase the numbers of mankind, may be admitted as a great and important object; but to extend the limits of any particular state is not, perhaps, the way to obtain it. . . .

[48] Christian Wolff, *Vernunftige Gedanken von den Gesellschtlichen Leben der Menschen* (1st ed., 1721), 4th ed., Frankfurt and Leipzig, 1736, Part II, Ch. 3, section 274, pp. 209–210.

[49] Johann Süssmilch, *Die Göttliche Ordnung in den Veränderungen des menschlichen Geschlechts aus der Geburt, dem Tode, und der Fortpflanzung desselben,* Berlin, 1761 edition, Ch. 10, section 205.

[50] Sonnenfels, *op. cit.,* Ch. 2, sections 26, 27.

[51] Sir James Caldwell, "An Enquiry how far the Restrictions laid upon the Trade of Ireland . . . . are a Benefit or Disadvantage . . . ," in *Debates Relative to the Affairs of Ireland, in the Years 1763 and 1764,* London, 1766, Vol. II, p. 746.

[52] Bielfeld, *op. cit.,* Vol. II, Ch. 4, section 4.

The measure of enlargement to be wished for in any particular state, is often to be taken from the condition of its neighbors. . . .

Notwithstanding the advantage of numbers, and superior resources of war, the strength of a nation is derived from the character, not from the wealth, nor from the multitude of its people.[53]

A somewhat similar opinion is found in *An Essay upon Money and Coins* (1757–1758), written by Joseph Harris (1701–1764), in which it was said that the strength of a state is not to be measured by its area and population, but that strength depends upon a number of factors, such as the fertility of the soil, the form of government, and the skill and industriousness of its people.[54] *The Politician's Dictionary* (1775) asserted, "No nation is rich or powerful by means of mere numbers of people; it is the industrious alone that constitute a kingdom's strength."[55]

Sometimes the emphasis was shifted from the total population to the employable segment of the population and its mode of employment. As early as 1615 Montchrétien had asserted that the wealth of a state does not depend upon land and people but upon the use made of them.[56] In England a number of years later, John Cary had made the sensible remark in *A Discourse on Trade* (1696) that ". . . (although) People are the Wealth of a Nation, yet it can only be so, where we find Imployment for them, otherwise they must be a Burthen to it. . . ."[57] The same idea was frequently expressed by writers on population in the eighteenth century. To quote only one, Arthur Young (1741–1820), who carried his skepticism to a point where he became more pessimist than optimist in his views on population:

Of all the subjects of political economy, I know not one that has given rise to such a cloud of errors as this of population. It seems, for some centuries, to have been considered as the only sure test of national prosperity. The politicians of those times, and the majority of them in the present, have been of the opinion, that, to enumerate the people, was the only step necessary to be taken, in order to ascertain the degree in which a country was flourishing. Two-and-twenty years ago, in my "Tour through the North of England, 1769", I entered my caveat against such a doctrine, and presumed to assert, "that no nation is rich or powerful by means of mere numbers of people; it is the industrious alone that constitute a kingdom's strength."[58]

[53] Adam Ferguson, *An Essay on the History of Civil Society* (1st ed., 1767), 6th ed., London, 1793, Part I, section 9, pp. 97, 99, 101.

[54] Joseph Harris, *An Essay upon Money and Coins,* London, 1757–1758; reprinted in McCulloch, *A Select Collection of Scarce and Valuable Tracts on Money,* London, 1856, p. 363 (Part I, Ch. 5, of the *Essay*).

[55] Anon., *The Politician's Dictionary,* p. 130.

[56] Montchrétien, *Traicté de l'oeconomie politique,* p. 31.

[57] John Cary, *A Discourse on Trade,* 2nd ed., London, 1714, p. 48.

[58] Arthur Young, *Travels in France during the years 1787, 1788 and 1789* (1st ed., 1792), 2nd ed., London, 1794, Part II, Ch. 5.

The sentence Young quotes from his earlier work is identical with the excerpt given above from the anonymous *Politician's Dictionary*.

4 · A New Element in Population Thought

While the optimistic doctrine was being modified and even somewhat weakened from within by these amendments and qualifications, a new element or point of view was emerging: a growing liberal or social orientation. Neither inherently optimistic nor pessimistic, its effect was to weaken the optimistic theoretical position somewhat more, for it gave greater emphasis to considerations of individual well-being that accorded better with pessimistic doctrine, and it brought a corresponding diminution in emphasis on the political element, or perhaps more strictly speaking the mercantilist and national aspect of population.

Goldsmith's *Vicar of Wakefield* (1766) could introduce himself to the reader by saying, with honest conviction, "I was ever of the opinion, that the honest man who married and brought up a large family, did more service than he who continued single and only talked of population." Gradually, however, there developed a disposition to regard procreation less as a service and duty of the citizen to the state and more as a matter of personal decision and responsibility. Associated with this was the quite new emphasis on the responsibility of the state for the welfare of its citizens, and a belief that a government best serves its own interests by promoting individual welfare.

The liberal turn of thought is quite evident in Wolff's *Vernünftige Gedanken* (1721). Convinced of the need for a large population, he believed this objective could be attained by ensuring that men are able to support their families, by good treatment of foreigners, and by leniency of government, as well as by more usual measures. And the people should not be oppressed either in religion or in financial respects, for if they see that other nations are happier, they will emigrate and take their wealth with them.[59]

Consideration of the people as a means to encourage population growth was recommended by other writers. According to Postlethwayt, "A nation will be more or less populous according as it's inhabitants are more or less able to subsist by their labour, and as their property is more or less secure."[60] Butel-Dumont wrote that the well-being of a state depends upon the happiness of its citizens.[61] Baudeau, after stating his agreement with Mirabeau and Physiocrat doctrines, was more concerned with the liberty, happiness, and well-being of the people than with their numbers,[62] and there are numerous other examples of similar views from this period.

[59] Wolff, *op. cit.*, esp. pp. 210, 212, 565–570.
[60] Postlethwayt, *Britain's Interest*, p. 376.
[61] Butel-Dumont, *op. cit.*, Ch. 4, pp. 72–104.
[62] Baudeau, *op. cit.*, esp. pp. 107, 109.

In some cases an attempt was made to reconcile the newer and the older theory, with the argument that the most populous states are also the ones that provide the greatest happiness for their people. Hume in his *Essay of the Populousness of Ancient Nations* (1752) spoke of "the general rule that the happiness of any society and its populousness are necessarily attendants." Du Buat-Nançay (1732–1787) discussed the matter at length in his *Éléments de la politique* (1773) and reasoned that to limit reproduction is to deprive many beings of life and to decrease the total of happiness; that "The interest of all individuals is always, at least in some respects, the interest of the society"; and that it is in the best interests of both individual and society to have as many people as possible.[63] Necker also defended the old doctrine, writing that the total amount of happiness in a nation is greater with a larger and poorer population,[64] but in a later work he expressed the more liberal thought that a government seeking to enlarge the population should do so by improving the lot of its people, and avoid burdensome taxation and severity that would drive them to other countries.[65] William Paley (1734–1805), the English theologian and moral philosopher, was predominantly optimistic in his outlook on the question of population size and quite explicit in his statement of the relation of happiness to populousness. In his influential *Principles of Moral and Political Philosophy* (1785) he stated that the fundamental objective of all rational politics is "to produce the greatest quantity of happiness in a given tract of land," and then went on to state that in all but extreme cases ". . . the quantity of happiness produced in any given district, so far depends upon the number of inhabitants, that . . . the collective happiness will be nearly in the exact proportion of the numbers."[66] From this he drew the corollary conclusion that ". . . the decay of population is the greatest evil that a state can suffer; and the improvement of it, the object which ought, in all countries, to be aimed at, in preference to every other political purpose whatsoever."[67] Finally, to mention only one other expression of this point of view, the *Grundlehre der Staatswissenschaft* (1792) of Heinrich Jung (1740–1817) also took the position that a well-peopled state can best insure the happiness of its members.[68]

However, these attempts at reconciliation of the two objectives of populousness and individual welfare were not entirely convincing, and

[63] Louis G. du Buat-Nançay, *Éléments de la politique ou recherche des vrais principes de l'économie sociale,* 6 vol. in 3, London, 1773, Vol. I, Book II, Ch. 9–13, incl., pp. 144–187.

[64] Jacques Necker, *Sur la legislation et le commerce des grains,* pp. 32–33.

[65] Jacques Necker, *De l'administration des finances de la France,* Paris, 1784, pp. 213–214.

[66] William Paley, *The Principles of Moral and Political Philosophy,* 2 vol., Dublin, 1785, Vol. II, Book VI, Ch. 11, p. 368.

[67] *Ibid.,* p. 369.

[68] Cited by Stangeland, *Pre-Malthusian Doctrines of Population,* p. 315.

there were inevitably those with a skeptical or pessimistic turn of thought who maintained that the two were inconsistent with each other. Ferguson implied this is his *Essay on the History of Civil Society* (1767), in which he said that the primary object of government should be the well-being of the people, not their multiplication. In his own words:

> . . . the happiness of men, in all cases alike, consists in the blessings of a candid, and active, and strenuous mind. And if we consider the state of society merely as that into which mankind are led by their propensities, as a state to be valued from its effect in preserving the species, in ripening their talents, and exciting their virtues, we need not enlarge our communities, in order to enjoy these advantages.[69]

Voltaire, in characteristic manner, wrote that "The main point is not to have a surplus of men, but to make those that we have as little unhappy as is possible," and again, ". . . what difference does it make whether there are many or few men on the earth? The essential thing is that this poor species shall be as little uphappy as is possible."[70] Further exploration of the relation between continued population growth and individual welfare came later, but was largely the work of the pessimistic school.

5 · Summary

The so-called optimistic doctrine or school of thought is not to be regarded as a thoroughly integrated theoretical system. Rather, it was an underlying philosophy of population, which was variously stated and which appeared in a variety of manifestations. Still, it is possible to identify the principal elements of the optimistic view of population size and growth as developed up to the end of the eighteenth century.

The central and traditional proposition, repeated endlessly, was that a large population is the source of national strength and security. In most cases the statement of this proposition was quite general. In some instances the military advantages of a numerous citizenry were emphasized.

An alternative emphasis was upon population as a source of national wealth. According to still other variations, it is not the size alone but rather the density of population or the number of workers that confers the advantages of power and wealth.

The economic formulation of the optimistic position took more and more the form of a theory of production, based on the assumption that the ratio of total product to total population remains constant or improves as population increases. Two types of reasoning were advanced to support this thesis. According to one, the resources of the earth are inexhaustible

---

[69] Ferguson, *op. cit.*, p. 87.
[70] Voltaire, *Dictionnaire philosophique,* "Population," conclusions of section 2 and 3.

or, alternatively, the returns of labor maintain a constant or increasing proportion to the input of labor. According to the second type of reasoning, the growth of population promotes the efficiency of production, as by stimulating competition and effort, facilitates communication, and induces a more intensive and more efficient agriculture. This argument was extended to assert that the pressure of meeting the needs of a growing population induces economic progress and leads to a higher form of economic organization, through the development of trade and manufactures.

At the same time an increasing number of modifications and reservations were being attached to the optimistic doctrine. One significant reservation, essentially a denial of the principle of constant returns, was that further increase is desirable only insofar as the additional people can be provided with land or employment. In some instances the emphasis was shifted from total numbers to the quality or composition of the population.

An important development was the appearance of a new point of view of population, in addition to the older political and national viewpoint and the newer economic orientation. This new liberal or social element in population thought brought with it greater emphasis on the welfare of the individual and less on the interests of the state. Efforts were made to reconcile this social objective with the traditional quantitative objective, but in its full development the new approach was to lead to a rejection of the optimistic position.

The optimistic doctrine of the desirability of a large and growing population was thus weakened internally by progressive modifications as well as by the rise of a new and discordant point of view. At the same time, it was attacked externally by those who denied its basic premises, in other words, by the numerous precursors of Malthus.

6

The Development of Pessimistic
Doctrine before Malthus

In spite of the ascendancy of the optimistic doctrine of population in the eighteenth century, there were some dissenters. Old ideas were waning, new intellectual currents were stirring, and a few writers were moved by skepticism or independence to doubt the prevailing populationist theory and policy. Others, perhaps more numerous, were brought to the same conclusion by observing unemployment, poverty, and shortages which suggested that numbers of people were more burden than benefit to the society. It was a time of change, both in the way men lived and in the way they thought, a time of cultural as well as political revolution. Mercantilist influence was being supplanted by the new economic philosophy represented by Adam Smith; the cultural revolution of which the Industrial Revolution was only a part was continuing and accelerating; and both distress and political idealism in France and other countries led to questioning of the prevailing social order. There was also, one can infer, a gradual change in man's thinking about himself and his place in the world, a growing feeling that he need not resign himself to his fate and accept the will of God with pious resignation, but rather that he was in some measure the master of his own destiny and therefore had responsibilities toward himself and his fellow men. With these and other stirrings of change, there was an undercurrent of concern over problems of the contemporary economic and social order, and a search for diagnoses and cures for the ills of society.

The attention to questions of population was set in this context of inquiry and questioning, and, whether based on theoretical grounds or on observation and experience, several lines of thought eventually led to conclusions quite contrary to the optimistic doctrine of population during the eighteenth century. Several of these ideas, not all of which are necessarily pessimistic in themselves but which were eventually consolidated into the pessimistic doctrine of population, are outlined below.

1 · The Power of Increase

In the absence of direct information on the true state of population, for regular census enumerations were not to be initiated until the following century, various theories were current in the eighteenth century about the trend of population numbers. Largely because of exaggerated ideas of the populousness of antiquity, some believed that the population of Europe had declined greatly since Roman times and that the downward trend was perhaps continuing. Others believed that although numbers might vary locally, the population of the world as a whole remained constant. A few others, relying more on observation, called attention to the great reproductive power and capacity for multiplication of the human species.

Late in the sixteenth century, Botero, in many respects the first real precursor of Malthus, had written that "The powers of generation are the same now as one thousand year ago, and, if they had no impediment, the propagation of man would grow without limit and the growth of cities would never stop."[1] In the following century, the English contemporaries Graunt, Petty, and Hale, as noted earlier, had the concept of a geometric increase of mankind. Graunt, in *Natural and Political Observations upon the Bills of Mortality* (1662), estimated the increase of mankind after the creation, using a period of doubling of sixty-four years. Petty made a somewhat similar calculation for the descendants of Noah. Hale specifically applied the term "geometric proportion" to the increase of population and assumed a doubling of numbers in each generation of about twenty-eight years, a period that, he believed, might be shortened under some conditions. Toward the end of the century Gregory King (1648–1712) in his *Natural and Political Observations and Conclusions upon the State and Condition of England* (1696) spoke of a doubling of the English population in a period of six hundred years.[2]

Many estimates of the time required for doubling the population were made in the eighteenth century. Maurice de Saxe, in *Reflections upon the Propagation of the Human Species* (1757), assumed an average of two daughters per mother in a hypothetical computation, which gave a geometric increase of population, doubling in each generation, which he took to be thirty years in length. If three daughters instead of two were produced in each family, the period of doubling would be even less.[3]

[1] Cited by Bonar, *Theories of Population*, p. 16.
[2] Published in the second and later editions of George Chalmers, *An Estimate of the Comparative Strength of Great Britain and of the Losses of her Trade from every War since the Revolution*, London, 1802, p. 417.
[3] de Saxe, *Reveries or Memoires upon the Art of War*, pp. 194–195. It is interesting to note that like later demographers he based his computation of the rate of reproduction on the female sex.

Süssmilch, in *Göttliche Ordnung,* pointed out that there was considerable variation in the rate of growth. Under certain conditions population would double in ninety-six years, under different assumptions it might take as little as forty-two years.[4]

Hume set a lower figure in his essay, *Of The Populousness of Ancient Nations* (1752), saying, "Almost every man who thinks he can maintain a family will have one; and the human species, at this rate of propagation, would more than double every generation."[5] Robert Wallace (1694–1771), who was engaged in a controversy with Hume, calculated the possible rate of increase in *A Dissertation on the Numbers of Mankind in Ancient and Modern Times* (1753). He assumed that all who reach maturity marry and that there are six children of each marriage, of whom four survive to adult life. The period of doubling so obtained was thirty-three and one-third years.[6] At this rate, he noted, the population of the earth could increase to billions in a relatively short time. Gonnard mentions the Italian economist Gherado d'Arco (1739–1791), who believed that the number of people more than doubled in a generation.[7]

More empirically, the American colonists were often cited in evidence of man's capacity for increase and their period of doubling was reported to be twenty-five years or less. Adam Smith (1723–1790) in *The Wealth of Nations* (1776) stated that the population of the American colonies doubled every twenty or twenty-five years.[8] Thomas Short (1690?–1772) in his *Comparative history of the increase and decrease of mankind in England and several countries abroad* (1767) quoted American authority for the statement that the colonists were doubling their numbers in as little as twenty or twenty-five years.[9] Short also republished in the appendix of his work several letters, signed with the pseudonym Publicola, which had recently appeared in a London newspaper. In one of these letters the period of doubling in North America was reported to be twenty-five years.[10] And somewhat later Joseph Townsend wrote, in *A dissertation on the poor laws* (1786), that "The population of North America doubles every five and twenty years; but in some provinces every fifteen years."[11]

[4] Süssmilch, *Die Gottliche Ordnung,* Part I, Ch. 8.

[5] David Hume, *Essays Moral, Political and Literary,* New York: Longmans, Green, 1898, Essay II, p. 384.

[6] Robert Wallace, *A Dissertation on the Numbers of Mankind in Ancient and Modern Times,* Edinburgh, 1753, p. 3.

[7] Gonnard, *Histoire des doctrines de la population,* p. 249.

[8] Adam Smith, *An inquiry into the nature and causes of the wealth of nations,* Book III, Ch. 4.

[9] Thomas Short, *Comparative history . . . ,* London, 1767, preface, p. iii.

[10] *Ibid.,* Appendix, Letter II, p. 165.

[11] In *A select collection of scarce and valuable economic tracts,* edited by McCulloch, London, 1859, Vol. 7, p. 420 ff. The same statement is found in Townsend's *Journey through Spain,* Vol. 2, p. 362.

Benjamin Franklin was the American writer best known in Europe at that time, and he was most often cited as the source of the twenty-five-year figure; but his basis for the estimate has not been found and perhaps it was only a reasonable estimate. Another American, a contemporary of Franklin who also estimated the period of doubling, was the Reverend Ezra Stiles (1727–1795), a noted New England clergyman who later became president of Yale (1778–1795); and it was to him that Thomas Short referred. As Stiles wrote in a sermon or address delivered in 1760 and published the following year, "New England has advanced 120 years in rapid increase, the term of doubling being 20, or according to Dr. Franklin 25 years," and "Tho' the period of doubling for the whole colony is 25 years . . . yet the period is different for different parts of the colony. While on the sea-coast it is above 25 years, yet within land it is 20 and 15."[12]

In more theoretical terms, Paley referred to the provision of nature for an "indefinite multiplication," and expressed the opinion that the human race could double in the space of twenty years under favorable conditions[13] and that the food supply was capable of indefinite increase.

Like a number of other elements of the classical pessimistic doctrine, the concept of geometric increase in population appeared in *Riflessione sulla*

[12] Ezra Stiles, *A discourse on the Christian Union, the substance of which was delivered before the Reverend Convention of the Congregational Clergy in the Colony of Rhode Island; assembled at Bristol, April 23, 1760*, Boston, 1761, pp. 108–109. Actually, Stiles' views on the period of doubling of the New England population were part of a broader population theory concerning a natural cycle in the growth of nations. As he explained his theory, "In new settled countries the transplanted colonies, by an established Law of Nature, in a good climate, do increase to a certain *patrial* maturity, when they begin to decline. At the beginning of this increase the period of doubling is very short, and the augmentation rapid — afterwards the period of doubling is extended till it gradually ceases, and is succeeded with a diminution, slow at first, but rapid at last. The period of *patrial maturity,* as well as of *patrial doubling* doubtless in some measure corresponds to the nature of the climate: — the former in our climate may have been about 1000 or 1200 years; the latter 20 to 25 years. The period of rapid patrial doubling in 25 years may reach its akme in one third of the term requisite to the final akme of increase. The ratio of patrial doubling continues equable for 3 or 400 years, when in consequence of another law of nature, this ratio begins at once to be greatly extended" (p. 103). New England already having experienced 120 years of rapid growth, doubling in numbers every 20 or 25 years, it followed according to the theory that "Above 160 years of rapid increase yet remain, by which time thro' the blessing of heaven we may become many Millions. After this we may continue to increase in extended periods of doubling for 7 or 800 years, till we shall have reached the summit of the patrial increase in 11 or 1200 years, from the first settlement of America . . ." (pp. 109–110). Finally, Stiles projected the trend forward at twenty-five-year intervals of doubling to obtain an estimate of four million in 1835, and added the comment that "With pleasure we anticipate the rapid settlement of new towns and provinces around us, and filling them up with millions of inhabitants to the distance of 100 years forward, look over this wide spread wilderness, see it blossom like the rose, and behold it planted with churches . . ." (pp. 120–123).

[13] Paley, *The Principles of Moral and Political Philosophy*, Book VI, Ch. 11, p. 148.

Popolazione delle Nazioni per rapporto all'Economia Nazionale (1790), written by Giammaria Ortès (1713–1790) and published only eight years before Malthus' *Essay*. According to Ortès, population is capable of growing in a geometric progression, doubling every thirty years.[14]

The question of population increase was mentioned in passing by Joseph Townsend (1739–1816) in his *Journey through Spain in the Years 1786 and 1787* (1791), in which he gave the following estimate:

> If we suppose, in a good climate, with plenty of food and healthy habitations, the number of children in each family on the average to be four, and the mean age to which they shall arrive to be fifty years; if the men marry at the age of twenty-one, and the women at nineteen, then one couple, at the end of thirty-three years, would leave twelve descendants. In fifty-nine years there would be twenty-four persons . . . ,[15]

and so on. As evidence of the capacity for increase, he then referred to a case of five persons being cast away on an island in 1590, whose descendants had increased to 12,000 when they were finally discovered. He cited further the Biblical account of the estimated seventy Israelites who entered Egypt and whose male descendants aged twenty and over numbered 603,550 some four hundred thirty years later. He computed the time of doubling at twenty-seven years.

Others discussed man's great potentiality for multiplication without using the concept of geometric increase. Bernard de Mandeville (1670?–1733), for example, wrote in *The Fable of the Bees* (1706) that man's generative powers are such that his numbers would soon grow to excess were it not for various retarding influences, saying:

> . . . in populous Nations we see, that War, wild Beasts, Hanging, Drowning, and a hundred Casualties together, with Sickness and all its Attendants, are hardly a Match for one invisible Faculty of ours, which is the Instinct Men have to preserve their species.[16]

and further, that "Our Species alone would have overstock'd the Earth, if there had been no wars. . . ."[17] Richard Cantillon (1685?–1734), author of the *Essai sur la nature du commerce en general* (written 1730–1734) wrote that "Men multiply like mice in a barn, provided that they have an unlimited supply of the means of subsistence."[18] This statement is better

[14] For an analysis of Ortès' work, see John R. McCulloch, *The Literature of Political Economy*, London, 1938 ed., pp. 264–265.

[15] Joseph Townsend, *Journey through Spain in the Years 1786 and 1787*, London, 1791, Vol. II, p. 360.

[16] Bernard de Mandeville, *The Fable of the Bees*, 1729 ed., London, Part II, Fifth Dialogue, p. 284.

[17] *Ibid.*, p. 295.

[18] Richard Cantillon, *Essai sur la nature du commerce en general*, edited by Henry Higs, London: Macmillan, 1931, p. 82.

known through Mirabeau's repetition of it in *L'ami des hommes*.[19] John Brückner (1726–1804), in his *Théorie du système animal* (1767), spoke of the enormous powers of multiplication of animal species, and pointed out that the same was true for man.[20] Theodore Mann (1755–1809), whom Strangeland lists as a true predecessor of Malthus, spoke of population as naturally increasing in an indefinite progression.[21] Similar but as a rule less explicitly stated views appear in a number of other sources.

2 · The Limitation of Numbers by the Means of Subsistence

Just as frequently expressed during the eighteenth century was the opinion that the food supply limits the number of people. In a sense this was no more than a statement of obvious fact, with neither optimist nor pessimist implications unless combined with assumptions about the supply of land and other resources or about the trend of per capita returns. If the optimistic assumption of constant returns or better was made, then the limitation was only theoretical. However, for some writers the statement of a limitation on human numbers was a denial of the optimistic doctrine of population.

The idea of a naturally imposed limit on the number of people in an area has already been seen in earlier writings on population, especially those of Raleigh, Bacon, Botero, Besold, Becher, and Hobbes; it was in fact inherent in most early statements of pessimistic views. During the eighteenth century it was mentioned by so many political and economic writers that only a few of the more notable statements of this principle of limitation can be noted here.

Early in the century William Derham (1657–1735), in a work that gave considerable attention to population, *Physico-Theology* (1713), developed the concept of a balance being maintained in the numbers of the lower animals, saying that the world could maintain only such a number as could find subsistence.[22] This was also said to be true for man himself.

In France, Goudar stated as a general principle that the number of men depends upon the means of subsistence.[23] The idea also appears in a

---

[19] Mirabeau, *Lami des hommes*, Vol. I, Ch. 2, p. 31: "Les hommes multiplient comme les rats dans une grange, s'ils ont les moyens de subsister. C'est une axiome que je n'ai pas inventé. . . ."

[20] John Brückner, *A Philosophical Survey of the Animal Creation* (translation of *Théorie du système animal*, 1767), London, 1768, section 5.

[21] Cited by Strangeland, *Pre-Malthusian Doctrines of Population*, pp. 321–324.

[22] William Derham, *Physico-Theology, or a Demonstration of the Being and Attributes of God from his Works of Creation*, 1798 ed., London, Vol. I, Book IV, Ch. 10. The passage in question is quoted later in this chapter.

[23] Goudar, *Les intérêts de la France mal entendus*, Vol. I, p. 294.

work by Benjamin Franklin (1706–1790), the first American writer to be noted here. In *Observations concerning the Increase of Mankind, Peopling of Countries* . . . (1751) Franklin wrote that laws for the encouragement of marriage

> . . . may hasten the filling of a country that has been thinned by war or pestilence, or that has otherwise vacant territory; but cannot increase a people beyond the means provided for their subsistence.[24]

Or, in his summary, "There is in short, no bound to the prolific nature of plants or animals, but what is made by their crowding and intefering with each other's means of subsistence. . . ."[25] Applied to immigration, this led him to the conclusion that

> The importation of foreigners into a country that has as many inhabitants as the present employments and provisions for subsistence will bear, will be in the end no increase of people; unless the new comers have more industry and frugality than the natives, and then they will provide more subsistence, and increase in the country; but they will gradually eat the natives out. Nor is it necessary to bring in foreigners to fill up any occasional vacancy in a country; for such vacancy (if the laws are good) will soon be filled by natural generation. . . .[26]

Shortly after that, William Bell expressed the opinion that the principal obstacle to the natural increase of mankind is "the great difficulty men experience in procuring support for themselves."[27] As an optimist, however, Bell believed that this only stimulates the people of a nation to seek additional means of support.[28] Sonnenfels, as previously noted, believed that the nature and physical condition of a nation set limits on its population. Adam Ferguson implied that the increase of mankind is limited by what he called "the necessary of life" which is a variable factor, low for some peoples and higher for others.[29]

The principle of limitation of man's numbers by food supply received its fullest and most explicit statement in Steuart's *Inquiry into the Principles of Political Oeconomy* (1767). He stated that the number of animals must be ". . . in proportion to the quantity of food produced by the earth, *regularly throughout the year,* for their subsistence,"[30] and added that this is also true for man. After further discussion of the subject, he summarized:

[24] Benjamin Franklin, *Observations concerning the Increase of Mankind, Peopling of Countries* . . . , reprinted as extra number 63 of *Magazine of History,* 1918, p. 15. Also reprinted in McCulloch's *Literature of Political Economy,* and elsewhere.

[25] *Ibid.,* p. 22.

[26] *Ibid.,* p. 21.

[27] William Bell, *A dissertation on the following subject* . . . , p. 3.

[28] *Ibid.,* pp. 31–32.

[29] Ferguson, *An Essay on the History of Civil Society,* Part III, section 4, p. 238.

[30] Steuart, *An Inquiry into the Principles of Political Oeconomy,* Book I, ch. 3, p. 18.

From what has been said, we may conclude, that the numbers of mankind must depend upon the quantity of food produced by the earth for
their nourishment; from which, as a corollary, may be drawn,

That mankind have been, as to numbers, and must ever be, in proportion to the food produced; and that the food produced will be in the compound proportion of the fertility of the climate, and the industry of the
inhabitants.[31]

Adam Smith, Steuart's contemporary and fellow Scotsman, gave less
attention to population than did Steuart; but several references to the limitation on population growth are to be found in his works. In his *Essay on
Colonies,* written on the outbreak of the American revolution, he said that
". . . the populousness of every country must be in proportion to the degree
of its improvement and cultivation."[32] In *The Wealth of Nations* Smith
again referred to the subject:

> Every species of animals naturally multiplies in proportion to their
> means of subsistence, and no species can ever multiply beyond it. But in
> civilized society it is only among the inferior ranks of people that the
> scantiness of subsistence can set limits to the further multiplication of the
> human species; and it can do so in no other way than by destroying a
> great part of the children which their marriages produce.[33]

A further note was added by Moheau, who recorded his agreement with
Franklin that there is a limit to the number of people the earth can nourish,
but pointed out that this is a world limit and that the population of a
nation is not necessarily restricted in this manner.[34]

However it was stated, the concept of a population limit was quite
widely accepted during the eighteenth century; but the significance attached
to it depended on the accompanying assumptions. For those who took a
gloomy view of the supply of resources and the future trend of production, the concept of a limit was a premise that led to pessimistic conclusions.

3 · The Tendency of Population to Approach the Subsistence Limit

In addition to those who stated the obvious fact of an ultimate dependence of population numbers upon the means of subsistence, there were
some who went further and maintained that population actually does approach the subsistence limit. There was no mistaking the pessimistic

[31] *Ibid.,* Book I, Ch. 4, p. 24.
[32] Adam Smith, *Essay on Colonies,* republished in *Government of Dependencies,*
Universal Classics Library, Washington and London: Dunne, 1901, p. 16.
[33] Adam Smith, *The Wealth of Nations,* Book I, Ch. 8.
[34] Moheau, *Recherches et considérations sur la population de la France,* Book I,
Ch. 13, pp. 190–191.

implications of this assumption, and it was in effect another step in the pessimistic sequence of thought.

The belief that population numbers naturally grow toward the limiting value was expressed frequently by the French political economists of this period. Melon, whose *Essai politique sur le commerce* was published in 1734, talked about the growth of population to a point at which the land is insufficient and at which the people have to turn to trade, emigration, or invasion of other countries; but he was on the whole optimistic in supposing that greater need could also lead to progress in agriculture and industry.[35] The tendency of population numbers to approach the limit was more clearly stated by Cantillon:

> . . . we could multiply all sorts of animals in such numbers as we wish to maintain even to infinity if we could find lands to infinity to nourish them; and the multiplication of animals has no other bounds than the greater or less means allotted for their subsistence. It is not to be doubted that if all land were devoted to the simple sustenance of Man the race would increase up to the number that the land would support.[36]

Mirabeau, according to Gonnard the principal French precursor of Malthus,[37] apparently believed that populations actually were at or close to the subsistence limit. Early in *L'ami des hommes,* he wrote, "The measure of the means of subsistence is that of the population."[38] The meaning of this sentence is not clear, but Gonnard interprets it not as the truism that subsistence sets the limit but rather that there actually are as many people as can be supported. This interpretation is supported by several of Mirabeau's later statements, such as:

> Superfluous consumption is a crime against society on the order of murder and homicide. . . .[39]
>
> In general and as a rule, it is neither wars nor epidemics that depopulate a state; but if you put one more horse in the state, all other things remaining the same, you are certain to kill at least four men there.[40]

The assumption here, apparently, is that a horse consumes as much food as four men. Similarly, the explanation given by Mirabeau for the supposed decrease of population in England is that ". . . England has become rich, that wealth increases consumption and therefore decreases the population by that much."[41] And finally, ". . . increase the means of subsistence and you increase the number of men. . . ."[42] Taken together, these reveal a very literal acceptance of a fixed subsistence limit and of population grown to its fullest extent.

[35] Melon, *Essai politique sur le commerce,* Ch. 1, 3.
[36] Cantillon, *op. cit.,* Ch. 15, p. 67.
[37] Gonnard, *Histoire des doctrines de la population,* pp. 160–165.
[38] Mirabeau, *L'ami des hommes,* Vol. I, Ch. 2, p. 20.
[39] Mirabeau, *op. cit.,* Vol. I, Ch. 2, p. 24.   [40] *Ibid.,* p. 33.
[41] *Ibid.,* p. 44.   [42] *Ibid.,* p. 45.

The works[43] of François Quesnay (1694–1774) reveal a skeptical view of population. In a series of unsigned articles on *Despotisme de la Chine*,[44] he gave a direct denial of the optimistic doctrine, writing that in Europe

> . . . it is believed that a large population is the source of wealth; taking the effect for the cause, for everywhere the population exceeds the wealth; it is wealth that multiplies wealth and population; but the propagation of men always goes beyond wealth.[45]

Later in the same series of articles Quesnay wrote

> . . . propagation has no limits except those of the means of subsistence, and that it always tends to exceed the latter: everywhere there are men living in poverty. One might perhaps say that there are also accumulations of wealth everywhere, and that it is the inequality of the distribution of property that gives to some an abundance and that denies the necessities of life to others; also that the population of a kingdom would not exceed the wealth of the nation if this were more equally distributed. . . .[46]

While admitting that this might be true in exceptional cases, he maintained that widespread poverty could not be attributed to maldistribution of wealth, but only to an excess of population as compared to the resources of a country.[47]

The tendency of population to increase up to the limit of subsistence was also stated by Claude Auxiron (1728–1778) in the *Principes de tout gouvernement*[48] (1766) and by François de Forbonnais in his *Principes économiques*[49] (1767) and other works. François de Chastelleux (1734–1788), expressing the same view as Mirabeau's and using the same phrasing, wrote in *De la félicité publique* (1772) that "The means of subsistence

---

[43] Quesnay, *Oeuvres économiques et philosophiques*, Oncken ed., Paris, 1888.

[44] *Ibid.;* originally published in *Ephemerides du citoyen*, March–June, 1767.

[45] *Ibid.*, Ch. 1, section 3, p. 579. Oncken quotes this passage, which he takes to be Malthusian in tone, and infers that some of Malthus' ideas on population must have come from the Physiocrats (August Oncken, *Geschichte der Nationalökonomie, I, Die Zeit vor Adam Smith*, Leipzig: Hirschfeld, 1902, Book II, Ch. 1, p. 380). The dependence of population on wealth was also stated by Quesnay in his article, "Hommes," in the *Encyclopedia*. The article is republished with notes by Etienne Bauer, *Revue des Doctrines Économiques et Sociales*, 1908, 1:6–84.

[46] *Ibid.*, p. 635.

[47] Useful accounts of the views of Quesnay and the other Physiocrats are given in Henry Higgs, *The Physiocrats*, London: Macmillan, 1897; Oncken, *op. cit.*, Book II, Ch. 1; and the following works by Georges Weulersse: *La mouvement physiocratique en France, 1756–1770*, Paris: Alcan, 1910; *Les physiocrates*, Paris: Dein, 1931; *La physiocratie sous les ministères de Turgot et de Necker (1774–1781)*, Paris: Presses Universitaires, 1950; and *La physiocratie à la fin du règne de Louis XV (1770–1774)*, Paris: Presses Universitaires, 1959.

[48] Claude F. J. Auxiron, *Principes de tout gouvernement*, 2 vol., Paris, 1766, pp. 301, 302.

[49] Republished in *Melanges d'économie politique*, edited by Daire and Molinari, Paris: Guillaumin, 1847, Vol. I.

are the measure of the population. If the quantity of subsistence diminishes the number of men must diminish in the same proportion."[50] This implies a population that is actually at its upper limit. The same implication is present in the statement of Etienne de Condillac (1714–1780) that population must decrease in proportion as per capita consumption increases.[51] It appears again later in a memorandum by Theodore Mann[52] in 1781, and in *L'économic politique moderne*[53] (1786) by Jean de Herrenschwand (1715–1796). According to the latter, ". . . the human species cannot multiply except in proportion to its food supply, no matter how great its fertility."[54] It was his belief that the general principle held true at all stages of economic development, the hunting, the pastoral, and several agricultural stages, although the maximum figure was different in each case.

Perhaps because of conditions in France in the eighteenth century, the tendency of population to press on the means of subsistence was most evident to the French writers, but it also was mentioned by several English writers of the period. The fullest statement of the tendency was made by Steuart in his *Political Oeconomy* (1767), where he wrote:

> . . . the generative faculty resembles a spring loaded with a weight, which always exerts itself, in proportion to the diminution of resistance: when food has remained some time without augmentation or diminution, generation will carry numbers as high as possible; if then food come to be diminished, the spring is overpowered; the force of it becomes less than nothing, inhabitants will diminish, at least, in proportion to the overcharge. If, upon the other hand, food be increased, the spring which stood at 0, will begin to exert itself in proportion as the resistance diminishes; people will begin to be better fed; they will multiply, and, in proportion as they increase in numbers, the food will become scarce again.[55]

Steuart returned to the subject several times in this work, and made the final comment that "I have shewn, I think, more than once, that multiplication never can stop but for want of food."[56] If so, he had at the same time made a strong case against the optimistic doctrine and had given strong support to the pessimists.

The same conviction, that population expands to the fullest extent permitted by the food supply, can be detected in Adam Smith's *Wealth of*

[50] François de Chastelleux, *De la felicité publique*, Amsterdam, 1772, Vol. II, Ch. 7, p. 140.
[51] Etienne de Condillac, *Le commerce et le gouvernement*, Paris, 1795 edition, Part I, Ch. 25, pp. 172–173.
[52] Cited by Stangeland, *op. cit.*, pp. 321–324.
[53] Jean de Herrenschwand, *De l'économie politique moderne. Discours fondamental sur la population*, London, 1786.
[54] *Ibid.*, p. 4.
[55] Steuart, *op. cit.*, Book I, Ch. 3, p. 20.
[56] *Ibid.*, Ch. 14, p. 94.

Nations[57] (1776), in Paley's *Principles of Moral and Political Philosophy*[58] (1785), and in Townsend's *Dissertation of the Poor Laws* (1786) and *Journey through Spain*[59] (1791). Paley wrote that

> Wherever the commerce between the sexes is regulated by marriage, and a provision for that mode of subsistence, to which each class of the community is accustomed, can be procured with ease and certainty, there the numbers of the people will increase; and the rapidity, as well as the extent of the increase will be proportioned to the degree in which these causes exist.[60]

According to Townsend, "It is the quantity of food which regulates the numbers of the human species";[61] and he expressed this belief many times in his writings.

The rejoinder to this line of thought and its pessimistic implications took various forms, as we have already seen, such as optimistic assertions that resources are ample, that per capita returns remain stable or even advance as population grows, or that the limit on population size is remote. Another optimistic answer was that although population does tend to approach the subsistence limit, the ultimate effect is beneficial. An example of this reasoning is found in *An Estimate of the Comparative Strength of Britain* (1782) by George Chalmers (1742–1825). Reviewing the controversy over whether the population had increased or decreased, he wrote:

> It is instinct, then, which is the cause of procreation; but it is food which keeps population full and accumulates numbers. We behold the force of the first principle in the vast numbers of animals, either of the fish of the sea, the fowls of the air, or the beasts of the field, which are yearly produced: we perceive the essential consequence of the last from the multitudes that annually perish for want. Experience has shewn to what an immense extent the domestic animals may be multiplied, by providing proportional subsistence. In the same manner man has been found to exist and to multiply in exact proportion to the standard of his means of subsistence, and to the measure of his comforts.[62]

Chalmers proceeded from this, however, to the optimistic conclusion that "wants promote industry; industry gains food; and food increases numbers."[63] He believed that in this was demonstrated "the energetic principle

[57] See especially Book I, Ch. 8, of *The Wealth of Nations*. See further reference to Smith in the section on wage theory, Chapter 7, section 1, below.

[58] Paley, *op. cit.*, Vol. II, Book VI, Ch. 11.

[59] Townsend, *Dissertation*, Section VIII; and *Journey through Spain*, especially pp. 360–364.

[60] Paley, *op. cit.*, p. 373.

[61] Townsend, *Dissertation*, p. 418.

[62] George Chalmers, *An Estimate of the Comparative Strength of Britain during the Present and four Preceding Reigns, and of the Losses of her Trade from every War since the Revolution*, London, 1782, p. 123.

[63] *Ibid.*, p. 124. Chalmers cites Steuart in support of this view, although Steuart's thinking on population as a whole was much less hopeful.

of population exerting its active powers of production," and said that this principle led to barter, husbandry, manufacture, and commerce.

Another line of optimistic counter-argument, more effective by modern judgment, did not come until later. This was the contention, supported by census data and by observation, that population numbers do not necessarily go on expanding until the subsistence limit is reached.[64]

In another part of the world, according to Dittmer, "The Emperor Chien Lung anticipated Malthus by five years when he called upon all classes of his subjects to 'economize the gifts of heaven, lest, ere long, the people exceed the means of subsistence.' "[65]

From these excerpts it is clear that the concept of a restricted food supply and a tendency for population to multiply up to the subsistence limit was quite widely diffused in the pre-Malthusian period. This being so, there were inevitably some who were sufficiently skeptical of the optimistic doctrine to carry their thinking on the subject to other conclusions.

4 · The Concept of Checks on Population Growth

The subject of checks on population growth was a matter of interest to both those who believed in and those who doubted the desirability of a large and growing number of people, and almost every writer on population included some mention of impediments to increase. A great deal of thought was given to discovering what interfered with population growth, and there were long accounts of checks from the obvious to the ingenious. In addition to such obvious factors as disease, war, and famine, attention was given to impediments to marriage, religious and other celibacy, suicide and duelling, military service, improper care of children, lack of medical care, economic factors such as poverty and unemployment, burdensome taxation and other governmental measures that might affect population, luxury and waste, urbanization, immorality, and many other things. Claude Herbert (1700–1758) classified the obstacles to population as physical, political, and moral.[66] Herrenschwand dichotomized the checks into the physical, which operate when population attains the subsistence limit, and the moral, which operate before population reaches that limit.[67]

[64] See Chapter 7, section 3, below, for notes on the beginnings of this new line of thought.

[65] C. G. Dittmer, "Density of population and the standard of living in North China," *Publications of the American Sociological Society,* 1925, Vol. XIX, pp. 196–199. For further information on Malthusian ideas in China, see Jean Chesneaux, "Un prémalthusien chinois: Hong-Lian-Ki," *Population,* 15(1): 89–95, Jan.–March 1960; Leo Silberman, "Hung Liang-Chi: A Chinese Malthus," *Population Studies,* 13(3): 257–265, March 1960; and Ping-ti Ho, *Studies on the population of China,* Cambridge: Harvard Press, 1959.

[66] Claude Herbert, *Essai sur la police générale des grains* (1st ed., London, 1753), reprinted, 1910, Paris: Geuthner, p. 107 ff.

[67] Herrenschwand, *op. cit.,* p. 5.

The populationist writers' objective was, of course, to discover and remove the checks to increase. The more skeptical or pessimistic also employed the concept of checks, but in a different manner and for different purposes. Among the pessimists two different usages of the concept may be distinguished. According to one, the various natural or induced checks to human increase retard or prevent numbers growing to excess; by implication the checks, although regrettable in themselves, are nevertheless useful in preventing the even worse consequences of overpopulation. According to the other usage, various checks come into operation as a consequence of imminent or actual overpopulation. Actually, the two different usages frequently occurred together and cannot be entirely separated; but as far as they can be separated, the treatment of checks in the first sense (as a preventive of overpopulation) is outlined in this section, and the latter usage is considered in the next section, on overpopulation and its consequences.

The idea that checks to population increase might serve a useful purpose was found earlier in Raleigh's *History of the World,* in which he said that wars and pestilence keep numbers within the limits of subsistence.[68] In the same way Hale referred to plagues, famines, wars, floods, and conflagrations as being "correctives of the excess of mankind."[69] Charles Cock had written that there was "no Nation, if not plagued with War or Diseases, but naturally it will grow over-numerous";[70] and similar views have been seen expressed by Malynes and Hobbes, as previously quoted.

A similar attitude was taken by some writers in the eighteenth century. Mandeville in *The Fable of the Bees* (1706) spoke of the various checks as barely able to limit population growth.[71] His opinion of the checks as being necessary evils was revealed by remarks such as "I believe that Wars of all sorts, as well as Diseases, are natural means to hinder Mankind from encreasing too fast . . . ,"[72] and ". . . Nature produces no extraordinary Numbers of any Species, but she has contriv'd Means answerable to destroy them."[73]

Many checks are mentioned in *Göttliche Ordnug,* by Süssmilch, including epidemics, wars, famine, floods, castrations, religious celibacy, and the inability of soldiers to marry.[74] Although strongly in favor of population growth, he nevertheless considered the possibility that these checks might serve a purpose, and wrote that "War, plague and such scourges of the

[68] See earlier reference to Raleigh, Chapter 3 above.
[69] Hale, *Primitive Origination,* Section II, Ch. 9, p. 211.
[70] Cock, *English Law,* Part II, *Essay on Christian Government,* p. 148.
[71] Mandeville, *op. cit.,* Part II, Fifth Dialogue, pp. 284, 295.
[72] *Ibid.,* pp. 303–304. Among other hazards to life he mentioned "Diseases, Doctors, Apothecaries, and other Accidents, that take away Man's Life, and shorten his Days" (p. 297).
[73] *Ibid.,* pp. 288–289.
[74] Süssmilch, *op. cit.,* Part I, Ch. 9.

human race can nevertheless be judged on two bases. They might be means for the prevention of an excessive population. They could also be looked upon as punishments."[75] He preferred the latter view, especially since other means are presumably employed in the *göttliche Ordnung,* or divine order of things, to control numbers. Population increase, he believed, is brought to a stop when numbers attain their full size, the probable mechanism being a higher mortality, a lower birth rate, or later marriage.

Claude Herbert, although favorably disposed toward population growth, nevertheless wrote in his *Essai sur la police générale des grains* (1753) that "It is evident that their numbers would increase to infinity, were it not for physical, political, and moral obstacles."[76]

In the *Natural History* of Buffon (1707–1788), under the account of the hare, there is developed the concept of a balance being maintained in the numbers of animals through the action of the opposing forces of fecundity and of destruction, much as in Hale's earlier work. Parallel to the case for animals, it is said, man's numbers tend to be kept at a constant level by infanticide and celibacy as well as other checks that operate on the human species.[77]

An important work on population was the *Recherches sur la population* (1766) of Messance. Commenting first that the excess of births over deaths in the rural areas is needed to fill up the cities and to repair the losses due to war, epidemics, pestilence, and other causes, he continued:

> But as in the laws of Providence nothing occurs by chance, these scourges may have their utility; perhaps they maintain the balance between the number of inhabitants of the earth and the products determined for their subsistence, preventing the human species from multiplying too much and overburdening the surface of the earth, from which there might result misfortunes greater than those caused by wars, pestilences and epidemic diseases.[78]

A short time after Messance, Brückner expressed the same view of the ultimate usefulness of the preventives of overpopulation. First describing the enormous powers of multiplication of animal species, he discussed the consequences of their excessive increase,[79] and drew a parallel for the human race. In a later section,[80] he pointed out that although man may not be subject to the same checks as the animal species, he does sometimes

[75] *Ibid.,* section 204.
[76] Herbert, *op. cit.,* p. 107.
[77] Buffon, *Natural History* (1st ed. 1749–1767), translated by William Smellie, London, 1812, Vol. IV.
[78] Messance, *Recherches sur la population des généralités d'Auvergne* . . . , Paris, 1766, p. 2.
[79] Brückner, *op. cit.,* section 5.
[80] *Ibid.,* section 10.

attack his fellow men, and cannibalism and warfare operate directly as checks. Then he continued, almost paraphrasing Messance:

> Amongst other obstacles to an undue increase of the human species, we may consider famine and pestilence. These are terrible calamities; yet they are unavoidable, where men have too long enjoyed uninterrupted prosperity, and exceed the proper limits of population. It is for this reason also, that Providence frequently intermixes with the common blessings of life, the miseries of war. . . . War is doubtless terrible, but it by no means presents to our view, such a horrible spectacle as plague or famine.[81]

Progress in the arts and sciences, he believed, might banish war and plague as checks on human increase, but it would bring into operation other checks, such as luxury, effeminacy, sensuality, debauchery, "all impediments to a *detrimental increase* of the human species."[82] A similar opinion that checks are useful appeared in Arthur Young's *Travels in France:*

> Great cities have been called the graves of the human species: if they conduct easily to the grave, they become the best *euthanasia* of too much populousness. They are more apt to prevent increase than to destroy, which is precisely the effect wanted in such a country as France, where the division of property has unhappily nursed up a population, which she cannot feed. . . .[83]

In conclusion, it can be seen that a body of strongly pessimistic opinion, although it was still a minority opinion, had developed by the latter part of the eighteenth century. A prominent manifestation of this pessimistic opinion was the belief summarized above that the various checks to population growth, however evil they may be in themselves, are still lesser evils compared to the consequences of overpopulation.[84]

5 · The Concept of Overpopulation and its Consequences

One manifestation of pessimism concerning population checks was noted in the preceding section. There remains the central concept of the developing pessimistic doctrine, the concept of checks as consequences of overpopulation. Here was a direct denial of optimistic doctrine, the con-

[81] *Ibid.,* pp. 110–111.
[82] *Ibid.;* italics added.
[83] Young, *Travels in France,* Vol. I, p. 414.
[84] It was William Eden (1744–1814) who was somewhat skeptical of the alleged checks and who wrote that one could point to a number of things, such as civil liberty, emigration, or migration to the cities, as having a particular effect on population, but that so little is known of their real effects that one could as well maintain they had the opposite effect (*Letters to the Earl of Carlisle,* 3rd ed., to which is added a fifth letter on population . . . , London, 1780, pp. 181–184).

viction that there can be too many people and that the consequences are harmful.

By this time the concepts of overproduction and natural checks were already well established among natural scientists, and it is an interesting but unanswered question as to what extent the scientists influenced and in turn were influenced by those who wrote about population. Often they were the same people, for there was less specialization of knowledge in the eighteenth century than has since developed. Those who wrote of overproduction in nature might extend their remarks to the human species, or those who wrote of human overpopulation might draw parallels from the animal world. Such parallels were drawn by Hale, Buffon, Derham, Franklin, Brückner, and Steuart, and there were no doubt many others who had the same idea.

For example, Buffon, in connection with his remarks on the productiveness of the hare, referred to the barbarian invasions as due to a multiplication of numbers, much as Machiavelli had done. Derham devoted a chapter of his *Physico-Theology* to "The balance of animals, and the due proportion in which the world is stocked with them." There he wrote that

> The whole surface of our globe can afford room and support only to such a number of all sorts of creatures. And if by their doubling, trebling, or any other multiplication of their kind, they should increase to double or treble that number, they must starve or devour one another.[85]

And Franklin, as quoted earlier in this chapter, wrote of the crowding of plants and animals that acted as a "bound" to their increase.

Steuart and Brückner are quoted more particularly below. One other, especially noteworthy writer who pointed out the tendency of both animal and human populations to overproduce was the distinguished British naturalist, Erasmus Darwin, grandfather of Charles Darwin, author of *The Origin of Species*. In the elder Darwin's poetic work, *The temple of nature* (1803), the processes of overproduction and of natural checks among the lower forms of life are described, and the parallel for mankind is then drawn in the following lines:

> Human progenies, if unrestrain'd,
> By climate friended, and by food sustain'd,
> O'er seas and soils, prolific hordes! would spread,
> Ere long, and deluge their terraqueous bed:
> But war, and pestilence, disease and death,
> Sweep the superfluous myriads from the earth.[86]

[85] Derham, *op. cit.,* Vol. I, Book IV, Ch. 10, p. 257.
[86] Erasmus Darwin, *Temple of Nature,* Canto IV, lines 369–374. Of an earlier work by the same author, *Zoonomia,* it has been said that "No doubt it prompted Malthus's *Essay on Population* which appeared four years later . . ." (C. D. Darlington, *Darwin's place in history,* Oxford: Blackwell, 1959, p. 13). As it stands, how-

The concept of human overpopulation certainly was not new in the eighteenth century, for a number of references before 1700 to the consequences of having too large a population have been noted above. Machiavelli, for example, believed that when the world becomes overpopulated it must necessarily purge itself by means of floods, famines, and plagues.[87] Hakluyt associated crime and unrest with an overabundance of people. Other evils attributed to overpopulation were war (by Hobbes and Petty[88]), and increase of poverty (by Hale[89]).

With or without mention of its consequences, references to human overpopulation were much more numerous in the eighteenth century, especially in pre-revolutionary France. Cantillon regarded famines in China as a means by which numbers are forcibly restrained within the limits of the food supply.[90] Plumard de Dangeul, who was convinced of the advantages of a large population, nevertheless noted that "A country may doubtless contain more inhabitants than it can support, or employ with the products of its own growth. . . ."[91] And Buffon made an explicit statement of checks being brought into operation by excessive numbers: "When any part of the world is overcrowded with men, they either disperse or else destroy one another, and often establish customs and laws such as to give too great a check to this excess."[92] Two such customs he mentioned were celibacy and infanticide. Messance saw the consequences of overpopulation as being even worse than wars, pestilence, and epidemics.[93] In the following year, 1767, Quesnay stated that poverty is the consequence of a population too large in relation to the wealth of a nation, spoke of "the indigence made inevitable by the excess of population" in China, and added that "The excess of population in China sometimes forces the poor to commit acts of inhumanity that horrify one. . . ."[94]

Also in 1767, Steuart in England set forth in detail his views of the consequences of an overabundant population. In an early chapter of his *Political oeconomy,* he wrote concerning the control of numbers in nature that

> We see how beneficent, I might have said prodigal, nature is, in bestowing life by generation. Several kinds of animals, especially insects, multiply by thousands, and yet the species does not appear annually to

ever, this is an interesting but unproved statement, for the writer does not go beyond the assertion to present evidence; and the elder Darwin has not generally been included among the intellectual predecessors of Malthus.

[87] Machiavelli, *Discourses on the decad of Livy;* see p. 17.
[88] Petty, *Essay concerning the growth of the City of London;* see p. 49.
[89] Hale, *A discourse touching provision for the poor;* see p. 55.
[90] Cantillon, *op. cit.,* Ch. 15, p. 69.
[91] Plumard de Dangeul, *op. cit.,* p. 182.
[92] Buffon, *op. cit.,* Vol. IV, "The Hare."
[93] Messance, *op. cit.,* p. 2.
[94] Quesnay, *Despotisme de la Chine,* Ch. 1, section 3, p. 580; Ch. 7, p. 634.

increase. . . . It is therefore reasonable to conclude, that what destroys such vast quantities of those produced, must be, among other causes, the want of food.[95]

Then he continued, in more general terms:

Those who are supposed to be fed with the spontaneous fruits of the earth, cannot, from what has been said, multiply beyond that proportion; at the same time the generative faculty will work its natural effects in augmenting numbers. The consequence will be, that certain individuals must become worse fed, consequently weaker; consequently, if in that weakly state, nature should withhold a part of her usual plenty, the whole multitude will be affected by it; a disease may take place; and sweep off a far greater number than proportioned to the deficiency of the season. What results from this? That those who have escaped, finding food more plentiful, become vigorous and strong; generation gives life to additional numbers, food preserves it, until they rise up to the former standard.[96]

Explaining more particularly how this automatic regulation of numbers operates for mankind, he added a statement that quite fully anticipated nineteenth-century pessimistic thought on the subject:

. . . the generative faculty in man, and the care and love we have for our children, first prompt us to multiply, and then engage us to divide what we have with our little ones. Thus from dividing and subdividing it happens, that in every country where food is limited to a certain quantity, the inhabitants must be subsisted in a regular progression, descending down from plenty and ample subsistence, to the last periods of want, and even sometimes starving for hunger.[97]

This is perhaps the most deeply pessimistic statement concerning population that has been encountered up to this point. Steuart further noted that with a constant food supply any increase in fertility would be counterbalanced by a corresponding rise in mortality.[98]

Still a third, and important contribution to the pessimistic school of thought was the *Théorie du système animal* (1767) of John Brückner. According to Brückner, the animal species are capable of rapid multiplication, but ". . . the different species can only subsist in proportion to the extent of land they occupy, and whenever the number of individuals exceeds this proportion, they must decline and perish."[99] As regards man, he noted, there are those who believe that overpopulation is impossible:

But the truth is, that the consequences widely differ according to the state of the country where it (the increase of population) takes place.

[95] Steuart, *op. cit.,* Book I, Ch. 3, p. 19.
[96] Steuart, *op. cit.,* Book I, Ch. 3, pp. 19–20.
[97] *Ibid.,* p. 20.
[98] *Ibid.,* Book I, Ch. 13.
[99] Brückner, *op. cit.,* section 6, p. 83.

Amongst a free and enlightened people, who are secured by the situation of their country, or any other means, from all foreign invasion; where every tract of land may be improved, the human race cannot be too numerous — (but) there are others where it is pernicious. To introduce new inhabitants into those countries, is to introduce violence, rapine, and murder. . . .[100]

In other words, the consequences of population growth depend upon other circumstances. Under some conditions it may have no ill effects; under other conditions it may be disastrous. But as noted in the preceding section, Brückner believed that various checks postpone or prevent overpopulation and its consequences.

Several years later Chastelleux in his *De la felicité publique* (1772) mentioned the possibility of overpopulation, saying that a country which has too many inhabitants in proportion to subsistence is not strong.[101] The essay, *De l'homme* (1772), by Helvétius (1715–1771), presented an imaginary case in which population growth started a train of development leading to industrial and commercial advances but also led eventually to the impoverishment of the majority of the people, the development of vice and crime, and the decay of the mores. The alternative ways of reducing surplus population, as Helvétius saw it, were war and the exposure of children such as allegedly occurred in China.[102] His statement that "in all countries, the great multiplication of men was the unknown but necessary and remote cause of the loss of the mores (moeurs),"[103] and other comments, suggest that he believed the serious consequences of population growth are not hypothetical but real.

The possibility of and the consequences of overpopulation were also mentioned in *La politique naturelle* (1773) of Paul Thiry, Baron d'Holbach (1723–1789), in which China was again taken as the example, and the occurrence of famines was assumed to be the result of a surplus of people.[104] A wise government, he believed, should attempt to preserve a proper proportion between the population and its land and resources.

Writing several years later and considering the effects of population growth, Necker reflected that larger numbers of people would increase the competition between workers and depress their wages. Pursuing this train of thought, he added, in close paraphrase of Steuart,[105]

The growth of the population doubtless condemns the laboring class of citizens to privations; nature's provision of an impetuous attraction be-

[100] *Ibid.*, section 7, p. 86.
[101] Chastelleux, *op. cit.*, Vol. II, Ch. 7, p. 141.
[102] Claude Helvétius, *Works*, Paris: Mercure de France, 1909, section IV.
[103] *Ibid.*, p. 227.
[104] Holbach, *La politique naturelle*, London, 1773, Vol. II, Discourse VII, section 20.
[105] See p. 128.

tween the sexes, together with love for the fruits of their union, are the causes of the multiplication of men on the earth. These sentiments dominate the poor as well as the rich. . . . Every being prefers to share his food with wife and children rather than to live alone and have a more varied diet. It is thus that the population expands, and by expanding it inevitably increases the number in misery.[106]

Started thus on a pessimistic train of thought, Necker nevertheless maintained that the total amount of happiness continues to advance with population numbers; and, his underlying optimism triumphing over his analysis of the effect of population growth, he concluded the discussion with the final comment:

There is however a point at which the population will stop of itself, and that is when it comes to exceed the means of subsistence. Then there will be suffering and mortality, but this evil is the result of the abundance of good; it is a filled vase that runs over. This sort of misfortune is little known on the earth; the scourge of Heaven, the errors and destructive passions almost always check the natural growth of population.[107]

One of the few German works of this period to mention the possibility of overpopulation was the *Patriotische Phantasien*[108] (1775) of Justus Möser (1720–1794). Here it was said that population may increase too rapidly, especially if unwisely encouraged. The result of an excessively large population, it was said, is a high death rate, especially among young children, and crime and various types of immorality may also follow.[109] High infant mortality as a check on further increase when the subsistence limit is reached was also mentioned in Adam Smith's *Wealth of Nations* (1776).[110]

Overpopulation is mentioned and its harmful effects discussed in a memoire by Mann that appeared in 1780. According to Stangeland's summary, Mann believed that

Misery, discouragement, disease and vice are the usual lot of superabundant populations pressed into a narrow space, where labor furnishes insufficient resources and where the excessive number of hands establishes a low rate of wages.[111]

The concept of overpopulation and the belief that checks may act both as preventives of and as consequences of an excessive number of people

---

[106] Necker, *Sur la legislation,* pp. 30–31.
[107] *Ibid.,* p. 33.
[108] Justus Möser, *Patriotische Phantasien,* Berlin, 1775.
[109] *Ibid.,* see especially Vol. I, Ch. 42, and Vol. II, Ch. 35.
[110] Smith, *op. cit.,* Book I, Ch. 8; see also previous references in this chapter.
[111] Stangeland, *op. cit.,* pp. 322–323.

are found in a somewhat later work, *L'économie politique moderne* (1786) by Herrenschwand. According to him:

> The limits of the multiplication of the human race are of two sorts; physical and moral. They are physical when procreation has carried mankind to the full measure of all its possible food supply. They are moral when obstacles of any sort prevent procreation from carrying the numbers of mankind either to the full measure of all its actual food supply, or to the full measure of all its possible food supply.[112]

In the case of hunting peoples, Herrenschwand said, excess population results in malnutrition, disease, and famine, and these checks operate until numbers are reduced below the subsistence limit. In the case of pastoral peoples, local overpopulation is relieved by migration. Among agricultural peoples, migration may be resorted to, or relief found through trade. However, if not relieved, the ultimate consequences of overpopulation are famine and increased mortality from other causes.[113] Already noted is the belief current among pre-revolutionary French writers that their country was overpopulated.[114]

The belief that overpopulation existed on the Continent was strongly expressed in two English works published early in the decade in which Malthus wrote his *Essay.* These were Joseph Townsend's *Journey through Spain* (1791) and *Travels in France* (1792) by Arthur Young. Townsend, after discussing the high rates of increase of which mankind is capable, went on to state the consequences of an overnumerous population, saying that "In a fully peopled country, to say, that no one shall suffer want is absurd. Could you supply their wants, you would soon double their numbers. . . ."[115] Stangeland also quoted the same work:

> Their numbers must be limited because their food is so; and were they to establish a community of goods they must either cast lots who should emigrate, or they must all starve together; unless they chose rather to agree that two only in every family should marry, and when a cottage became vacant could find means to settle which of the expectants should unite to take possession of it.[116]

Young, in reporting his observation in France, concluded that both France and Spain were overpopulated, and spoke of poverty and unemployment as results of surplus numbers. Of France he wrote,

> Couples marry and procreate on the *idea,* not the *reality,* of a maintenance; they increase beyond the demand of towns and manufactures; and

[112] Herrenschwand, *op. cit.,* p. 5.
[113] *Ibid.,* pp. 33, 43 ff, 486.
[114] See also Paul Leroy-Beaulieu, *La question de la population,* Paris: Alcan, 1913, p. 33 ff.
[115] Townsend, *Journey,* p. 364.
[116] Stangeland, *op. cit.,* p. 343.

the consequence is, distress and numbers dying of disease, arising from the insufficient nourishment.[117]

This summary of accounts of overpopulation and its consequences could be extended, but it is enough to show that the concept of overpopulation was current well before Malthus wrote and that a considerable range of evils had been attributed to an excess of people. As in the fully developed nineteenth-century statement of pessimistic doctrine, population growth and overpopulation were described as forces capable of bringing an entire people to poverty and distress. Like the contemporary optimistic literature, this pessimistic body of thought rested largely on assertion, personal interpretation of obeservations, and assumptions that as a rule were not made explicit. Both the optimistic and the pessimistic thought of the eighteenth century were based on assumptions about production. The pessimists' assumptions, so far as they can be identified, were that the supply of land and other resources is limited, that there is a limit to the total amount of production, and that the per capita supply of the means of subsistence must fall as the number of people increases. Only a few pessimistic writers supplemented their conclusions by considering the effects of population growth on wages and the pattern of distribution.[118] But if not more solidly based than the long-established doctrine, the pessimistic position was more and more vigorously asserted by its supporters in the late eighteenth century, and these supporters included writers of considerable ability.[119]

6 · Ideas about Personal Responsibility and Restraint

Although they were relatively minor elements in eighteenth-century pessimistic thought, two opinions expressed by a few writers of this period may be noted, first, that parents have a responsibility not to produce more

[117] Young, *Travels in France,* Vol. I, p. 413.

[118] See Chapter 7.

[119] Published soon after Malthus' *Essay* but apparently written without knowledge of the work was *Reflections upon the evil Effects of an increasing Population* (Gloucester, 1800), by Edward Gardner. Believing that "The utility of an increasing population has . . . never yet been questioned" (p. 5) and that he had made a new discovery, Gardner denied that a large and growing population is a source of national advantage or that a dense population gives prosperity; he asserted that an increasing population is "one great source of national calamity" (p. 3). He conceded the possibility that "In some countries, where the territory is extensive and fruitful, and where the labour of man is amply repaid by the bounties of nature, population may be a national blessing," but he was convinced that "where the extent of soil is limited, and where no very strict attention is paid to its improvement, where artificial riches contribute to multiply the human species, without providing an ounce of bread for their subsistence, the increase of numbers must be the increase of misery" (p. 10). Under the latter conditions population growth was said to lead to decay of morals, "every civil evil," the development of vice in all classes of society (pp. 13–14), and an increased demand that brings higher prices for provisions (pp. 23–24).

children than they can care for, and second, that restraint in procreation should be exercised. The immediate impetus to this line of thought was most often the problem of poor relief. Several British predecessors of Malthus looked askance at the fertility of the poor and regarded poor relief as in some measure a subsidization of unwise childbearing.[120] A suggestion of this point of view is found in *Gulliver's Travels* (1726) by Jonathan Swift (1667–1745), where it is said that ". . . the Lilliputians think nothing can be more unjust than for people, in subservience to their own appetites, to bring children into the world, and leave the burden of supporting them on the public."[121]

It is evident from the *Observations on the Defects of the Poor Laws* (1752) by Thomas Alcock (1709–1798) that many were of the same opinion. He wrote that an effect of the high taxes for poor relief had been to ". . . put many Gentlemen and Parishes upon contriving all possible Methods of lessening their Number, particularly by discouraging and sometimes hindering poor Persons from marrying; when they appear likely to become chargeable . . . ,"[122] and that "When the Minister marries a Couple, tho' but a poor Couple, he rightly prays, 'that they may be fruitful in procreation of Children.' But many of the Parishioners pray for the very contrary."[123]

The tendency of poor relief to multiply the number of recipients without providing for their gainful employment was strongly stated in the anonymously published *Dissertation on the Poor Laws* (1786), by Joseph Townsend. In his *Journey through Spain* of several years later, Townsend repeated the same views, and concluded from his observations in Cadiz that the operation of the relief system there would soon put as many beggars in the streets as before the workhouse was established.[124] According to Arthur Young, "We have found, by long experience in England, that the more money is expended, even well and humanely expended, the more poor are created. . . ."[125] This concern over the multiplication of the poor can be expected to appear whenever relief rates are high.[126]

---

120 The idea that it was useful to have large numbers of poor was expressed less frequently by British writers, who were well aware of the cost of poor relief, than by the contemporary Swedish writers. Mandeville quoted with approval the remark that "The Poor have nothing to stir them up to labour, but their Wants, which it is Wisdom to relieve, but Folly to cure." He added that there is a lot of hard and dirty labor to be done, and that if the condition of the poor were improved, such labor was likely to go undone (*Fable of the Bees*, 6th Dialogue, pp. 424, 426).

121 Jonathan Swift, *Voyage to Lilliput*, Ch. 6.

122 Thomas Alcock, *Observations on the Defects of the Poor Laws*, London, 1752, p. 19.

123 *Ibid.*, p. 20.

124 Townsend, *Journey through Spain*, Vol. II, p. 364.

125 Young, *Travels in France*, Vol. I, p. 451.

126 Florez-Estrada describes a little-known Italian work, *Riforma degl' Instituti pii della citta de Modena* (1787) by Lodovico Ricci (1742–1799), a report on the

The idea of parental responsibility and of need for restraint in child-bearing is so general that it may have occurred to a number of people independently, provided they were of a sufficiently pessimistic turn of thought regarding population; so probably the idea cannot be traced to a single point of origin. Franklin was aware of the existence of deliberate restraint, and wrote in his *Observations:*

> In cities, where all trades, occupations and offices are full, many delay marrying, til they can see how to bear the charges of a family; which charges are greater in cities, as luxury is more common: many live single during life, and continue servants to families, journeymen to trades, &c, hence cities do not by natural generation supply themselves with inhabitants; the deaths are more than the births.
>
> In countries full settled, the case must be nearly the same; all lands being occupied and improved to the heighth; those who cannot get land must labour for others that have it; when labourers are plenty their wages will be low; by low wages a family is supported with difficulty; this difficulty deters many from marriage, who therefore long continue servants and single.[127]

Ortès, only a few years before Malthus, wrote that the difficulty of providing subsistence acts on mankind's reason to repress increase and to keep their number within appropriate limits.[128] The Marquis de Condorcet (1743–1794) conceded that population at some remote time might come to reach or even exceed the means of subsistence, but he was, nevertheless, convinced that this is no cause for alarm, provided that meanwhile there has been progress in the arts and sciences and an advance in the level of intelligence. The reason he gave for this optimism was that

> Men will know then that, if they have obligations towards beings not yet born, they do not consist in giving them existence but rather happiness; they will have for objective the general well-being of the human race or of the society in which they live; of the family to which they belong; and not the childish idea of burdening the earth with useless and unhappy beings. There might then be a limit to the possible supply of the means of subsistence, and therefore to the maximum size of population, without there resulting this premature destruction, so contrary to nature and to the prosperity of the society, of a portion of the beings that have entered the world.[129]

---

charitable institutions in the city of Modena that anticipated Malthus' views about the harmful effects of poor relief on a number of points (Alvaro Florez-Estrada, *Cours éclectique d'économie politique,* translated from the Spanish by L. Galibert, 3 vol., Paris, 1833, pp. 76–81). Ricci's report is republished in *Scrittori Classici Italiani di Economia Politica,* Vol. 48, Milan, 1804.

[127] Franklin, *op. cit.,* topics 3, 4.

[128] McCulloch, *The Literature of Political Economy,* pp. 264–265.

[129] Condorcet, *Esquisse d'un tableau historique des progrès de l'esprit humain* (1st ed., 1794) 4th ed., Paris, 1798, Tenth Epoch, p. 364.

Without actually using the term, this unmistakably refers to prudential restraint.

However, only the optimists believed that self-control and restraint in reproduction could eventually check population growth. The pessimists, perhaps more mindful of the multiplication of the poor, did not believe that the population problem they visualized would solve itself in that fashion. They saw no alternative to the poverty and misery they predicted if population expanded to the subsistence limit, and their distrust of the economic and demographic effects of poor relief led some to doubt the feasibility of the various egalitarian and utopian proposals current in the latter part of the eighteenth century. Wallace and Townsend in particular were skeptical of such proposals. According to Wallace's criticism of various utopian schemes:

> Under a perfect government the inconveniences of having a family would be so intirely removed, children would be so well taken care of, and every thing become so favourable to populousness, that though some sickly seasons or dreadful plagues in particular climates might cut off multitudes, yet in general, mankind would increase so prodigiously that the earth would at last be overstocked, and become unable to support its numerous inhabitants.[130]

The end result, as he saw it, was that the growth of numbers would bring the utopian society to war or to the adoption of unnatural customs.[131] He concluded that the proposals of More and others made attractive reading but that they were "airy systems" that were impractical because of the vices of mankind and the artificial stimulation of population growth.[132]

Townsend, an equally strong pessimist and equally skeptical of egalitarian proposals for the alleviation of want, disposed of the subject with the emphatic statement in his *Dissertation of the Poor Laws* (1786):

> It is the quantity of food which regulates the numbers of the human species. . . . As long as food is plenty they will continue to increase and multiply; and every man will have the ability to support his family, or to relieve his friends, in proportion to his activity and strength. The weak must depend upon the precarious bounty of the strong; and, sooner or later, the lazy will be left to suffer the natural consequences of their indolence. Should they introduce a community of goods, and at the same time leave every man at liberty to marry, they would at first increase their numbers, but not the sum total of their happiness, till by degrees, all being equally reduced to want and misery, the weakly would be the first to perish.[133]

---

130 Wallace, *Various prospects of Mankind, Nature, and Providence*, London, 1761, p. 114.

131 *Ibid.*, pp. 117–118.

132 *Ibid.*, p. 122 ff. Note Aristotle's somewhat similar doubts about Plato's *Republic* (see p. 13).

133 Townsend, *Dissertation on the Poor Laws*, p. 418.

He added that ". . . when the increase of people is unnatural and forced, when it arises only from a community of goods, it tends to poverty and weakness."[134] Reminiscent of Steuart's thought on the progression toward overpopulation and general want, this comment reveals attitudes toward proposals for human betterment and toward multiplication of the poor that were duplicated later and aroused more opposition in Malthus' *Essay*.

7 · Synthesis: The Pessimistic Train of Thought

The fame of Malthus' *Essay* has somewhat obscured the fact that the pessimistic doctrine of population was already well developed and well stated before he wrote. As the foregoing account was shown, the doctrine of the immediate or ultimate harmfulness of a population that is too large in relation to its means of subsistence was based on a series of frequently stated propositions. These included propositions about the great reproductive power of mankind, the limited means of subsistence, the tendency of reproduction to carry numbers to the subsistence limit or to a state of overpopulation, and the harmful effects of such an imbalance between population size and subsistence. Logical corollaries were a belief in the ultimately beneficial role of the various checks, the shift of emphasis from the older belief in childbearing as a patriotic duty to the newer belief in the responsibility of parents for the well-being of their children, misgivings about the fertility of the poor and the effects of poor relief, and to some extent the concept of restraint in childbearing.

The preceding sections have dealt with separate elements in the pessimistic view of population size. Many writers are seen to have anticipated Malthus; and it is also worth noting that a few not only preceded him on separate points but also combined them in the train of thought now attributed to him. Although each was mentioned in several connections above, several of these real forerunners of Malthus are noted again below and a summary is given of their formulations.

Perhaps the first of these forerunners was Botero,[135] who preceded Malthus by more than two hundred years. According to McCulloch, Botero's *Delle cause della grandessa delle città* (1588) gave evidence that he was "fully master of all that is really true in the theory of Malthus." In this work Botero maintained that although man's generative powers are such as to make possible great increase of numbers, population is in fact restricted to the limits set by the means of subsistence. As numbers approach the subsistence limit, further increase is checked by the greater struggle for existence with a resulting rise in mortality.

---

[134] *Ibid.*, p. 422.
[135] For further evaluations of Botero's contributions, see Bonar, *Theories of Population*, pp. 16–17; McCulloch, *The Literature of Political Economy*, p. 253; Stangeland, *op. cit.*, pp. 105–107.

The *Primitive Origination of Mankind* (1677) by Matthew Hale developed a somewhat similar line of reasoning. Mankind is capable of increasing in a "geometrical proportion," it was said, and of doubling in thirty-four years or less. The potential for multiplication of the lower animals is much greater, yet by the action of the opposing forces of "generations" and of "corruptions," their numbers remain relatively constant. In the same way man's numbers are in large measure controlled by correctives or checks, such as wars, plagues, and other causes of morality. Hale regarded war in particular as "a Natural Consequence of the over-plenitude and redundancy of the Number of Men in the World."

Robert Wallace perhaps should also be included in a list of forerunners of Malthus, for his *Dissertation on the Numbers of Mankind* (1753) and *Various Prospects of Mankind* (1761) present several pessimistic elements. These include a belief in man's ability to increase "so prodigiously that the earth would at last be overstocked," the concept of checks, and the conviction that population growth would nullify humanitarian schemes to alleviate want.

Hale's work was paralleled on many points by the *Théorie du Système Animal* (1767) of John Brückner. As Hale had done, Brückner pointed out that animal species possess great powers of multiplication but that their numbers are held in check by the limited means of subsistence. If the "law of multiplication" allowed numbers to rise too high, the surplus would be eliminated rapidly. In the same manner, he believed, a balance is maintained in the numbers of plants. In the case of man, an increase in numbers might be under some conditions both possible and desirable; but in the main the same condition of equilibrium is enforced in human populations. Wars and other checks prevent a detrimental increase of man's numbers, and if these checks are insufficient to prevent increase the calamities of famine and pestilence are unavoidable. If progress in the arts and sciences succeeds in banishing the more brutal checks, their place will be taken by various types of debauchery and vice.

Steuart deserves special mention among the forerunners of later pessimistic thought, for although his treatment of the population question was not cast in the form later adopted by Malthus, he gave the most extended analysis of the economic significance of population that had yet been attempted within the framework of political economy. Dissenting from the prevailing optimistic opinion, he regarded population as being limited in size by the food supply, believed that population naturally expands up to the limit imposed by subsistence, and was convinced that the inescapable consequence is misery and starvation for a majority of the people. Especially noteworthy is his explanation of an automatic mechanism pressing population toward the subsistence limit,[136] which reappeared in another

[136] See pp. 120, 128 above.

form in Townsend's writings[137] and which contained the substance of the later "iron law" or subsistence theory of wages. In these respects Steuart is more directly a predecessor of classical economics and its treatment of population than a forerunner of the Malthusian theory.

Many elements of the Malthusian doctrine are also found in the *Riflessione sulla populazione delle nazione per rapporto all'economia nazionale* (1790) of Giamarria Ortès. Considerable differences in emphasis can be noted, although Ortès had the concept of a geometric increase of mankind, of a tendency of numbers to press on the means of subsistence, and of the operation of checks to increase. He believed that as the subsistence limit is approached, men are faced with the alternatives of either poverty and its attendants or prudential restraint.

Joseph Townsend should be added to this list of formulators of the pessimistic train of thought and anticipators of Malthus. In his *Journey through Spain* (1791) he discussed at length man's capacity for rapid multiplication and advanced the opinion that in a fully peopled country some must necessarily suffer want. A more complete statement of the tendency toward and the consequences of overpopulation was contained in his anonymous published *Dissertation on the Poor Laws* (1786). Expressing ideas stated earlier by Steuart and putting them in the form of a sort of parable, he wrote:

In the progress of society, it will be found that some must want; and then the only question is this, Who is most worthy to suffer cold and hunger, the prodigal or the provident, the slothful or the diligent, the virtuous or the vicious? In the South Seas there is an island, which from the first discoverer is called Juan Fernandes. In this sequestered spot John Fernando placed a colony of goats consisting of one male attended by his female. This happy couple finding pasture in abundance, could readily obey the first commandment, to increase and multiply, till in process of time they had replenished the little island. In advancing to this point they were strangers to misery and want, and seemed to glory in their numbers; but from this unhappy moment they began to suffer hunger; yet continuing for a time to increase their numbers, had they been endued with reason, they must have apprehended the extremity of famine. In this situation the weakest first gave way, and plenty was again restored. Thus they fluctuated between happiness and misery, and either suffered want or rejoiced in abundance, according as their numbers were diminished or increased; never at a stay, yet nearly balancing at all times their quantity of food. This degree of equipoise was from time to time destroyed, either by epidemical diseases or by the arrival of some vessel in distress. On such occasions their numbers were considerably reduced; but to compensate for this alarm, and to comfort them for the loss of their companions, the survivors never failed to meet returning plenty.

[137] See below.

They were no longer in fear of famine; they ceased to regard each other with an evil eye; all had abundance, all were contented, all were happy. Thus, what might have been considered as misfortunes, proved a source of comfort; and to them at least, partial evil was universal good.

When the Spaniards found that the English privateers resorted to this island for provisions, they resolved on the total extirpation of the goats, and for this purpose they put on shore a greyhound dog and bitch. These in their turn increased and multiplied, in proportion to the quantity of food they met with; but in consequence, as the Spaniards had foreseen, the breed of goats diminished. Had they been totally destroyed, the dogs likewise must have perished. But as many of the goats retired to the craggy rocks, where the dogs could never follow them, descending only for short intervals to feed with fear and circumspection in the valleys, none but the most watchful, strong and active of the dogs could get a sufficiency of food. Thus a new kind of balance was established. The weakest of both species were among the first to pay the debt of nature: the most active and vigorous preserved their lives.[138]

Townsend then applied his parable to the case of the poor, saying that the giving of relief merely aggravates the problem it is designed to alleviate, for it does not increase production of the means of subsistence, it prevents the operation of natural checks on increase, and permits a continued high fertility of the recipients. Contained in this passage and its application is the full force of pessimistic thought as it had developed toward the end of the eighteenth century.[139]

[138] Townsend, *Dissertation on the Poor Laws,* pp. 416–418.

[139] A number of other writers have been credited as forerunners of Malthus, including Mann, Mirabeau, and Ricci. It is a curious fact that Brückner, Ortès, Mann, Townsend, Ricci, and Malthus were all members of the clergy, and their predominance in this group of pessimistic writers appears too great to be a coincidence. Townsend gives us a clue when he explains at the beginning of his *Dissertation* how distressing it is to see and hear of the miseries of the poor, and that the clergy have to do this in the course of their duties. He revealed his own thinking by adding that there was much abuse of charity by the lazy.

7

The Theory of Population
and Distribution before 1800

Up to this point discussion of the economic significance of population size has been almost entirely in terms of the influence on production. Underlying both optimistic and pessimistic thought as they developed up to the end of the eighteenth century were assumptions about the influence of population size and growth on total or per capita production, and a basic point of disagreement was whether production could or did in fact advance in proportion to population. The theory of distribution, dealing with the influence of population size on the share going to the worker in the form of wages, to the landowner in the form of rent, and so on, was largely a nineteenth-century development; but some steps in that direction were taken earlier, as summarized below.

1 · Population and the Wage Level

The mercantilists and early political economists believed that there is a relation between the supply of labor and the level of wages, and that a numerous population, by providing a plentiful supply of workers, tends to insure low wages. However, it was also recognized that the relation is not altogether simple and direct, for the wage level also appears to have some effect on the labor supply, either on a short-term basis by stimulating migration of workers, or on a long-term basis by affecting the natural increase of population. The *New Discourse of Trade* (1668) by Josiah Child, for example, includes an early statement that contains part of what was later to be known as the subsistence theory of wages. According to Child, "much want of people would procure greater and greater wages," which would in turn increase the labor supply by attracting immigrants.[1] Some years later, in 1680, the author of *Britannia Languens* expressed what was presumably both accepted and obvious in saying that "in a scarcity of people wages must be dearer."[2]

[1] Child, *New Discourse of Trade,* Ch. 10, p. 201.
[2] McCulloch, *A Select Collection of Early English Tracts on Commerce,* London, 1856, p. 349.

The relation between population and wages was mentioned more frequently in the eighteenth century. Sir Matthew Decker (1679–1749) in his anonymously published *Essay on the Causes of the Decline of Foreign Trade* (1744), writing of the shortage of sailors (which he attributed to the practice of pressing or conscription, that drove eligible people away), asked "would not the remaining Few double or treble their Wages?"[3] Later in the same work he traced the effects of a decline in foreign trade, among which he included a decrease in "the Stock of People." In his words:

> For as Employment lessens, the most Industrious, rather than starve here, will fly to other Countries where Trade can maintain them; so the Consumption of these being taken away, the Demand at Market must grow less, and of course Rents must fall; yet the Farmers Charges must grow greater; for the *fewer Hands, the higher Wages are.* . . .[4] [italics added]

In his *Observations* (1751), Franklin stated that "when labourers are plenty their wages will be low."[5] The same idea was expressed in France by Mirabeau and Turgot. In *L'ami des hommes* (1755) Mirabeau said that ". . . where there are more people obliged to work for a living, services necessarily become cheaper for all men."[6] Turgot (1727–1781), in the *Réflexions sur la formation et la distribution des richesses* (1766), expressed the same opinion, saying that competition between laborers keeps down wages.[7] The tendency, he believed, is for wages to be held at a minimum level: "In all kinds of work the wages of the laborer must be and actually are limited to what is necessary for his subsistence."[8]

A contemporary and countryman of Mirabeau and Turgot, the Abbé Jean Joseph d'Expilly (1719–1795), related the wage level to the price of necessities rather than to the supply of labor. In his *Dictionnaire* (1762–1770), the long article on population, which drew heavily from Plumard de Dangeul's *Remarques,* explained the relation of consumption, prices, and wages: "The employment of men increases with consumption; consumption with low prices, which depend on the cost of labor; the latter follows the price of the necessities of life. . . ."[9] Wages were also said to be affected by the industriousness and ability of the workers. No mention was made of how a change of population might affect the volume of demand.

---

[3] Anon. (Sir Matthew Decker), *An Essay on the Causes of the Decline of Foreign Trade,* London, 1744, p. 12. Also attributed to William Richardson. Reprinted in McCulloch's *Select Collection of Scarce and Valuable Tracts on Commerce.*

[4] *Ibid.,* Part II, p. 39.

[5] Franklin, *Observations,* topic 4.

[6] Mirabeau, *L'ami des hommes,* Vol. I, Ch. 7, pp. 188–189.

[7] Anne Robert Turgot, *Oeuvres,* Paris: Alcan, 1913, Vol. 2, p. 537 (section 6 of *Réflexions*).

[8] *Ibid.*

[9] Jean Joseph d'Expilly, *Dictionnaire geographique, historique et politique des Gaules et de la France,* 6 vol., Paris, 1762–1770; Vol. 5 (1768), p. 791.

Steuart believed that the population or labor supply and the wage level act on each other, the supply of labor affecting its price, but the price of labor in turn affecting the supply. In reply to an article by a Dr. Breckenridge in the *Danish Mercury* of March 1758 stating that the population of England would decline were it not for immigration from Scotland and Ireland, Steuart wrote that:

> . . . the importation of grown men into a country so far resembles the importation of slaves into our colonies, that the one and the other diminishes the price of labour, and thereby prevents marriage among certain classes of the natives. . . . Now were the Scots and Irish to come no more into England, the price of labour would rise; those who now cannot bring up children, might then be enabled to do it, and this would make the English multiply themselves. . . .[10]

In a later chapter dealing with the supply and demand for labor, Steuart wrote, "If there be found to be too many hands for the demand, work (i.e., wages) will fall too low for workmen to be able to live; or, if there be too few, work will rise, and manufactures will not be exported."[11] Expressed here is a theory of an interaction and automatic regulation of labor supply and wages that was incorporated later into nineteenth-century classical economics.

An inverse relation between labor supply and wages was asserted in an anonymous English work, *An essay on trade and commerce* that appeared in 1770.[12] The now conventional statement that competition between workers forces down wages appeared in Helvétius' essay *D l'homme* (1772) and in Necker's *Sur la legislation et le commerce des grains* (1775).[13] Arthur Young's *Political Arithmetic* (1774) described the regulation of population numbers by the wage level:

> The national wealth increased the demand for labour, which had always the effect of raising the price; but this rise encouraged the production of the commodity, that is, of man or labour, call it what you will, and the consequent increase of the commodity sinks the price.[14]

Thus the fluctuation of labor supply would in its turn affect the wage level. An apparent contradiction to this was the statement by Möser that ". . . a land in which labor is cheap has the fewest; and one in which it is dear has

[10] Steuart, *An Inquiry into the Principles of Political Oeconomy,* Book I, Ch. 15, p. 97. This will be recognized as an early statement of a theory later named after the American political economist, Walker.

[11] *Ibid.,* Book II, Ch. 10, p. 224.

[12] Anon. (J. Cunningham?), *An essay on trade and commerce,* by the author of *Considerations on Taxes* . . . , London, 1770. Here it was said (p. 18) that "a plenty of working hands tends in various ways to make labour cheap." See also pp. 19, 20.

[13] Necker, *Sur la legislation* . . . , Ch. 6, p. 29.

[14] Arthur Young, *Political Arithmetic, containing Observations on the State of Great Britain; and the Principles of her Policy in the Encouragement of Agriculture,* London, 1774, p. 61. See also pp. 66–67.

the most inhabitants. . . ."[15] This was not really inconsistent with other views, however, for what Möser had in mind was that low wages tend to reduce the number of laborers and high wages to expand the labor supply.

Adam Smith's treatment of the question of wage determination does not fit very well into any one of the later developed categories of wage theory. There is, he stated, a short-term regulation of wages through the operation of supply and demand, together with a long-term effect of the wage level on the supply of labor. Scarcity of hands leads to competition among the employers, who bid up wages. Liberal wages then operate to increase population, and enable the workers to provide more amply for their children, thereby lowering the level of mortality. High wages also increase the desirability of children, especially if they are employed at an early age. In illustration Smith reported that in America "A young widow with four or five children, who, among the middling or inferior ranks in Europe, would have so little chance for a second husband, is there frequently courted as a sort of fortune."[16] Further on he definitely stated that there is a tendency for population increase to keep wages down to the subsistence level:

> If the reward should at any time be less than what was requisite for this purpose (subsistence), the deficiency of hands would soon raise it; and if it should at any time be more, their excessive multiplication would soon lower it to this necessary rate.[17]

The actual monetary level of wages, it was noted, is of course affected by the price level. Elsewhere in the same chapter, however, a suggestion of the wage-fund theory of wage determination enters, with the statement that "The demand for those who live by wages, cannot increase but in proportion to the increase of the funds which are destined for the payment of wages,"[18] and the explanation that it is not the amount but the increase of national wealth that produces high wages. For this reason, Smith noted, the highest wages are not found in the richest nations but in those that are growing in wealth most rapidly.

Mann, as previously cited,[19] agreed with Smith and others in believing that wages are related inversely to the number of workers. Somewhat later, Herrenschwand advanced the theory that the determining factor for the wage level is the ratio of labor supply to capital. In his own words, "When a nation has fewer hands than capital wages are high. . . . When on the contrary a nation has more hands than capital wages are low. . . ."[20] On

---

[15] Möser, *Patriotische Phantasien*, Ch. 15, p. 103.
[16] Adam Smith, *Wealth of Nations*, Book I, Ch. 8.
[17] *Ibid.*
[18] *Ibid.*
[19] See p. 130.
[20] Herrenschwand, *De l'économie politique moderne*, p. 200.

this basis an increase in the number of laborers does not necessarily depress wages; it does so only if this increase exceeds the growth of capital.

There was thus some diversity of opinion on the mechanism of wage formation by the latter part of the century. For the most part, those who discussed the subject assumed a simple supply and demand mechanism over a short period of time and an inverse relation between the supply of labor and the price it could command. Over a longer period of time, wage level was thought to affect the labor supply by stimulating the migration of workers or by affecting their fertility and mortality. Some writers thought this process of interaction between population or labor supply and wages tended to give a stabilization of wages at a subsistence level just sufficient to maintain the workers and their families. According to alternative formulations, wages depend upon the ratio of population or labor to capital, or to a portion of capital used for the payment of wages. Even under these alternatives, however, an increase of labor supply could lower wages below the level that would otherwise prevail.

In spite of its implications for the significance of population size and growth, the wage question did not bring out a clear difference of opinion between the optimists and pessimists. For the former, who carried on a mercantilist heritage, it was by no means evident that low wages were a subject for concern. As has been seen in the account of Swedish and other mercantilist thought, low wages were often regarded as beneficial to a nation because they kept down costs of production and benefitted exports and the international balance of trade. There may also have been some thought that low wages kept the workers in a state of need advantageous to employers. According to a modern summary of mercantilist thought:

> . . . the Mercantilist did not perceive that the poverty of the majority was incompatible with the wealth of the whole; quite the contrary, he came to believe that the majority must be kept in poverty that the whole might be rich. At times he proposed that a high standard of comfort among the great body of the common people was destructive of national wealth; at others, that an effective means of enriching the nation was to multiply the population beyond the point where average prosperity would begin to decline. . . .[21]

Many examples of this point of view have been cited in previous chapters. It was indeed a rare and original thinker who asserted, as Defoe did in his *Complete English Tradesman,* (1725–27):

> As the people get greater wages, so they, I mean the same poorer part of the people, clothe better, and furnish better; and this increases the consumption of the very manufactures they make; and then that con-

[21] Edgar S. Furniss, *The Position of the Laborer in a System of Nationalism. A Study of the Labor Theories of the later English Mercantilists,* Boston: Houghton Mifflin, 1920, p. 8; see also Ch. 7.

sumption increases the quantity made; and this creates what we call inland trade, by which innumerable families are employed and the increase of the people maintained; and by which increase of trade and people the present growing prosperity of this nation is produced.[22]

This was a quite remarkable statement for the middle of the eighteenth century, for Defoe was writing in advance of his time.[23]

It should be added that Adam Smith took the same view of the desirability of high wages some fifty years later in his *Wealth of Nations* (1776). There, in discussing the question whether improvement of the laborers' condition is an advantage or a disadvantage to the nation, he stated firmly that it is an advantage: "No society can surely be flourishing and happy, of which the far greater part of the members are poor and miserable."[24] And, "The liberal reward of labour, therefore, as it is the effect of increasing wealth, so it is the cause of increasing population. To complain of it is to lament over the necessary effect and cause of the greatest publick prosperity."[25] Smith added that a liberal wage "increases the industry of the common people."[26]

But for the most part, the eighteenth-century discussion of the population question remained in the context of national interest as it had long been defined, rather than in the newer context of social or humanitarian concern with individual well-being; and therefore the argument provided for the pessimists in the developing wage theory was not vigorously exploited by them until the next century.

2 · Rent and Prices

The few pre-nineteenth-century writers on population who discussed the relation between population size or change and distribution gave most attention to the influence on wages, but also gave some thought to the probable effects on rent and commodity prices. The obvious assumption, under a simple supply and demand analysis such as was applied to the question of wage determination, was that both prices and the rental value of land increase with the number of people.

Several English mercantilist writers in the latter part of the seventeenth

[22] Defoe, *Complete English Tradesman*, Vol. I, Ch. 25, p. 252.

[23] More typical for the period is Mandeville's remark in *The Fable of the Bees* that there is a lot of unpleasant work to be done, and that the pressure of poverty is the only way to compel men to do it; or Arthur Young's comment that "every one but an ideòt (sic) knows, that the lower classes must be kept poor, or they will never be industrious. . . . they must be (like all mankind) in poverty, or they will not work" (*The Farmer's Tour through the East of England,* London, 1771, Vol. 4, p. 361).

[24] Adam Smith, *Wealth of Nations,* 1st ed., 1776, Book I, Ch. 8, p. 96.

[25] *Ibid.,* p. 99.

[26] *Ibid.,* p. 100.

century had pointed out the apparent relation of rent or the value of land to population size. Petty, who was a large landowner and therefore is assumed to have had an interest in as well as first-hand knowledge of the matter, wrote about the relation of population to the value of land in his *Political Arithmetick* (written 1676 or 1677). According to his account,

> If there were but one Man living in England, then the Benefit of the whole Territory could be but the Livelihood of that one Man: But if another Man were added, the Rent or Benefit of the same would be double, if two, triple; and so forward, until so many Men were planted in it, as the whole Territory could afford Food unto. . . .[27]

Petty went on to say,[28] that the value of land in different countries is proportional to the density of population. Similarly, the *Britannia Languens* (1680), published before Petty's work, noted that the value of land is advanced by an increase in the number of people.[29]

Analysis of the effect of population size and change on rent was not greatly advanced during the eighteenth century, for the treatment of economic and other aspects of population continued to be general, without detailed tracings of specific effects. Defoe, writing in 1728 on *A Plan of the English Commerce,* supported his contention that numbers of people are the wealth and strength of a nation by saying that "As the Numbers of People increase, the Consumption of Provisions increases, the Rate or Volume will rise at Market, and as the rate of Provisions rises, the Rents of land rise. . . ."[30] He returned to the subject in another work, where he pointed out that the large sums spent for the relief of the poor increase the consumption of food and manufactured goods, and added, much as before, "The consumption of provisions increases the rent and value of the lands; and this raises the gentlemen's estates, and that again increases the employment of people, and consequently the numbers of them. . . ."[31] Defoe thus attributed to increased consumption the power of starting an economic process that would add to rents, stimulate an increase in population, and thus, presumably, add further to the volume of demand.

The opposite case, a decrease of the number of people, was considered by Decker in the *Essay on the Causes of the Decline of Foreign Trade* (1744). He believed[32] that the lowered demand would reduce rents. Conversely, an increase in the number of people would add to demand and to the return from land.[33]

[27] Petty, *Political Arithmetick,* Ch. 4; Vol. I, p. 286, of the Hull edition of Petty's works; p. 148 of the 4th edition of *Several Essays in Political Arithmetick.*
[28] See p. 49 above.
[29] See quotation, p. 59 above.
[30] Defoe, *A Plan of the English Commerce,* Part I, Ch. 1, p. 13; fuller quotation, see p. 101 above.
[31] Defoe, *The Complete English Tradesman,* Vol. I, Ch. 25, p. 252.
[32] See p. 141 above.
[33] Decker, *Essay,* Part II, p. 65.

The influence of population growth on rents was noted by Turgot in his *Essai sur le commerce* (1753) and by Josiah Tucker in *Elements of Commerce and Theory of Taxes* (1755). Turgot believed that population growth is of particular advantage to landholders, because it enriches them through the greater demand for produce and the increased rental value of land. Tucker simply stated that the effect of population growth is to cause rents to increase. The observation that the multiplication of people adds to the income of landowners appeared in a pamphlet by Tucker, *Reflections on the Expediency of a Law for the Naturalization of Foreign Protestants* (1751–1752), translated by Turgot in 1755 and included in an edition of his works.[34]

What later proved to be the most significant contribution to rent theory during this period was made in 1777 by James Anderson (1739–1808) in *Observations on the Means of Exciting a Spirit of National Industry*.[35] Here Anderson traced the origin of rent to differences in the quality of lands, the superior fertility of some tracts enabling their owners to demand rent for their use. It was not until many years later that attention was called to the role of population growth in forcing the extension of cultivation to poorer lands by increasing demand.[36]

The influence of population change on the price of commodities received less attention. Temple had pointed out the obvious relation in the *Essay upon the Advancement of Trade in Ireland* (1673) by saying that a high density of population "makes all things necessary to life dear."[37] The author of *Britannia Languens* had reasoned another way and come to another conclusion, as far as manufactured goods were concerned. He thought that the prices of such goods depend upon the level of wages rather than on demand alone, and he therefore concluded that prices decrease as the number of people and laborers grows larger.[38]

Of the eighteenth-century writers who touched on the subject, Defoe reasoned that with more people the consumption and therefore the price of provisions advances.[39] The opposite conclusion was reached by Decker, who followed the author of *Britannia Languens* in believing that prices depend upon the wage cost of producing commodities. Consequently, he reasoned, a decrease in the number of people raises food prices by raising wages.[40]

The relation of population to prices thus remained doubtful at the theo-

[34] Turgot, *Oeuvres*, Vol. I, pp. 453–458; see especially section 9.
[35] James Anderson, *Observations on the Means of Exciting a Spirit of National Industry*, Edinburgh, 1777.
[36] See below, for further discussion of Anderson's work, in connection with the theory of diminishing returns.
[37] Temple, *Works*, 1770 edition, Vol. III, pp. 6–7.
[38] See p. 59 above.
[39] Defoe, *A Plan of the English Commerce*, Part I, Ch. 1, p. 13; quoted on p. 101 above.
[40] See quotation from Decker, p. 141 above.

retical level, for different assumptions that seemed equally reasonable led to different conclusions. Another approach to the problem unusual for its time, was taken by Messance, who apparently was not satisfied to depend upon current theory. Like later scholars, he wondered about the variation of the price of grain, and assembled what information he could find on the subject. In his *Recherches* (1766) he noted that the fall of grain prices in England at that time was attributed to a decrease in population, but he was skeptical of this explanation because, as his own data showed, in France the price of grain had fallen during a period of population growth. Neither could grain prices be linked with export control, for the exportation of grain from England had been permitted after 1689 but was prohibited in France. It was his conclusion that the fall of the price of grain was due to the period of peace in both countries and to the "bonne culture."[41] Although Messance did not summarize his results in these terms, the implication of his findings was that price determination is not a simple matter and that the trend of population is not the decisive factor.

3 · Some Interrelations

It is seen that the discussion of the influence of population size on wages, rents, and prices was found only in scattered comments up to the end of the eighteenth century. But if there was as yet no systematic treatment of the relation of population to distribution, still, there emerges from the scattered comments a growing recognition of the interrelation and interaction of the various factors. From a simple supply and demand analysis it seemed evident that the wage price of labor would vary inversely with the supply of labor or with population size. By a parellel line of reasoning it was inferred that the value or rent of land and the price of commodities would vary directly with the number of people or consumers. However, the possibility of other interrelations was seen by some writers. The price of commodities might depend upon the cost of production rather than upon the volume of demand, according to *Britannia Languens,* Decker, and Expilly, in which case the growth of population, by lowering wages, would presumably reduce prices rather than raise them; and wages in their turn might depend upon the cost of the workers' necessities, as pointed out by Expilly.

There was also some awareness that these relations did not go in one direction only, and that population might be affected by the economic variables at the same time it influenced them. Differences in wage level between one area and another would induce movements of people, and over a longer period of time the wage level could affect fertility and mortality, and thereby lead to an increase or decrease in the number of people.

[41] Messance, *Recherches*, pp. 181–182.

Another relation between population and economic factors that received much more attention in the next century but that was touched on in the eighteenth-century literature, was the relation between population size and the prevailing level of consumption or the general well-being of the people. It has been seen that the predecessors of Malthus were vigorously developing the concept of population size as the determiner of the level of well-being. But a few writers before 1800 suggested that the relation might be in the opposite direction, that is, that the prevailing and customary level of living[42] in a nation influences the number of people living there, and that population size, therefore, is not determined solely by the food supply.

The first clear statement of this idea that has been found was made by Cantillon. In the *Essai* (1734) he wrote:

> The Increase of Population can be carried furthest in the Countries where the people are content to live the most poorly and to consume the least produce of the soil. In Countries where all the Peasants and Labourers are accustomed to eat Meat and drink Wine, Beer, etc. so many Inhabitants cannot be supported.[43]

A trace of the same thought appears in William Bell's *Dissertation* (1756) which dealt with various population questions. Bell conceded that the great obstacle to the increase of mankind is "the great difficulty men experience in procuring support for themselves";[44] but he also expressed the opinion that the population of some countries is not greater because of the "manners and customs"[45] of the people, not because of any natural limit on population. It is not clear precisely what Bell had in mind here, but that he may have included per capita consumption when he wrote of manners and customs is suggested by his inclusion of "diminishing the number of their imaginary wants"[46] among measures for rendering a nation populous.

Mirabeau, in *L'ami des hommes,* remarked in similar fashion, "An abundant supply of money naturally diminishes the population, in proportion as it increases the consumption of every individual. . . ."[47] However, he was apparently thinking in terms of a population actually at the subsistence limit, where the bringing in of another horse or any superfluous consumption would take food away from some people.[48] Bell, on the other hand, was thinking of a population checking its growth before the subsistence limit was reached.

---

[42] The term *level of living* is used here to mean the actual average per capita consumption, *standard of living* to mean the desired level.

[43] Cantillon, *Essai,* p. 83.   [44] Bell, *Dissertation,* p. 3.

[45] *Ibid.,* p. 2.   [46] *Ibid.,* p. 8.

[47] Mirabeau, *L'ami des hommes,* Vol. II, Ch. 8.

[48] See reference to Mirabeau, p. 118 above.

This idea that different levels of living set different population limits reappeared in Ferguson's *Essay on the History of Civil Society* (1767). The limit to the increase of mankind, he wrote, is determined by the "necessary of life," and he explained that "The *necessary of life* is a vague and relative term: it is one thing in the opinion of the savage; another in that of the polished citizen: it has a reference to the fancy, and to the habits of living."[49] The maximum size of a population, therefore, is not set by the food supply alone but also depends upon a cultural variable, the consumption habits of the people.

This important principle was expressed again by Steuart in his *Inquiry* (1767), in language similar to that of Cantillon:

> The more frugal a people are, and the more they feed upon the plentiful productions of the earth, the more they may increase in number.
>
> Were the people of England to come more into the use of living upon bread, and give over consuming so much animal food, inhabitants would certainly increase, and many rich grass fields would be thrown into tillage. Were the French to give over eating so much bread, the Dutch so much fish, the Flemish so much garden stuff, and the Germans so much sourkraut, and all take to the English diet of pork, beef, and mutton, their respective numbers would soon decay, let them improve their grounds to the utmost. These are but reflections, by the by, which the reader may enlarge upon at pleasure.[50]

Among other writers who recognized the influence of this factor on population size were Condillac and Paley. Condillac wrote, in part, that ". . . men consume more or less according to whether they have greater or lesser needs: the consequence is that the population diminishes in proportion to the growth of needs. . . ."[51] In his judgment, a smaller population at a higher level of living was preferable to the largest possible population at the subsistence level.[52] This was far removed from the mercantilist ideal of population. Paley contributed a statement of a fundamental truth when he wrote in his *Principles of Moral and Political Philosophy* (1785) that:

> It is not enough that men's *natural* wants be supplied, that a provision adequate to the actual necessities of human life be attainable: habitual superfluities become real wants; opinion and fashion convert articles of ornament and luxury into necessities of life.[53]

[49] Ferguson, *Essay on the History of Civil Society*, p. 213 (or 6th ed., 1793, p. 238).

[50] Steuart, *op. cit.*, Book I, Ch. 18, p. 117. Or as Justi wrote, soon after Steuart, "the simpler the customs and mode of life of a people the greater their numbers" (Anaxagoras von Occident [J. H. G. von Justi], *Physicalische und politische Betrachtungen über die Erzeugung des Menschen und Bevölkerung der Länder,* Smirna [Leipzig?], 1769, p. 51).

[51] Condillac, *Le commerce et le gouvernement,* Part I, Ch. 25, pp. 172–173.

[52] *Ibid.,* p. 180.

[53] Paley, *Principles,* Vol. II, Book VI, Ch. 11, pp. 374–375.

This is as mature and definitive a statement of the relative and elastic nature of human wants as can be found in the later literature on the subject, but its relevance to the population problem was not emphasized until much later. Paley went on to say that even in the lower orders of society men will not marry unless they can have "their accustomed mode of life."[54] Concerning the dangers of luxury he wrote,

> When by introducing more superfluities into general reception, luxury has rendered the usual accommodations of life more expensive, artificial, and elaborate, the difficulty of maintaining a family conformably with the established mode of living becomes greater. . . ,

and then men will be less inclined to marry, for "men will not marry to sink their place or condition in society."[55] In so writing Paley set forth a strong argument against pessimistic thought.

4 · Summary

In the development of population theory the eighteenth century was an intermediate period between the earlier mercantilist optimism and nineteenth-century Malthusianism. At first glance, population theory and especially the analysis of the significance of population size does not appear to have advanced greatly during the century before Malthus. But actually the foundation of the older system of thought was being undermined, and the intellectual and theoretical foundation of much of the later development was being laid. Ideas grow and evolve, they do not appear full blown; the essentials of the Malthusian theory and many of the essentials of nineteenth-century population thought already were being stated and stated well.

Important for the development of population thought was the trend away from the older emphasis on the interests of the state, dominant in mercantilist thinking, and toward the newer social and humanitarian concern with the well-being of the individual. This trend, which was to proceed much further in the next century, was not directly concerned with population, but was a much broader intellectual and political movement. Nevertheless, it was perhaps responsible in part for turning the current of opinion from optimism to pessimism, for at least in its early stages it contributed more to the pessimistic body of thought. It may, incidentally, explain the prominence of members of the clergy among the predecessors of Malthus who looked with concern at the social problems of their day and who dissented from the opinion that the larger the population the better for the state and all its people.

Up to this point the significance of population size had been discussed

[54] *Ibid.*
[55] *Ibid.*, p. 378.

largely in terms of its influence on the volume of production, but a beginning was made on a theory of distribution. Most attention was given to the question of wage determination, and here the assumption of a supply and demand mechanism in which the population affects labor supply but not demand for labor led to the conclusion that wages vary inversely with population or labor supply. An extension of this analysis led to the early formulation of the subsistence theory of wages, according to which wages tend to stabilize at the minimum level required for the maintenance of the workers.

Supply and demand analysis was also applied to the question of rent and price determination. Here population was taken to represent the demand or consumption side, and rents and prices were assumed to vary in direct relation to the number of consumers. A few writers gave attention to interrelations among wages, rent, and prices; in effect they raised the question whether a change in the number of people affects the price of commodities, for example, from the demand or from the supply side. However, the eighteenth-century writers, like their successors, tended to regard an increase in population as either adding to production or to consumption, but not both.

As summarized up to this point, the developing theory of the relation between population and distribution gave strong support to the pessimistic view, for it explained how a large or growing number of people could lead to high rents, low wages, perhaps high commodity prices, and general poverty. Some implications of the new area of inquiry led in the opposite direction, although this was not fully realized at the time. A few writers in the eighteenth century reasoned that rents, prices, wages, and population could interact and that the relation between population size and the condition of the people is in the opposite direction from that assumed by the pessimists. They believed that the wage level and the customary level of living of a population determines its size, not vice versa; and both reason and observation convinced them that mankind checks its multiplication before the subsistence limit is reached. This line of reasoning, only tentatively stated in the eighteenth century, later provided one of the most effective counter-arguments against pessimistic theory.

8

Production Theory and the Malthusian Controversy

The half-century or so following publication of Malthus' *Essay* in 1798 was the period of most active development in the history of population thought. Much of the population literature of this period was controversial and polemic, and can be omitted or only briefly noted here. Nevertheless, considerable progress was made in the theory and analysis of the significance of population, and that developing theory and analysis concern us here. In tracing this development, two separate lines of inquiry can be distinguished, one following an old path concerned with the relation of population to production, the other treading newer ground, the relation of population to distribution. This distinction was clearly made in the nineteenth-century literature, and the two different lines of inquiry brought important new contributions to bear on the population question. The following chapters are therefore organized in terms of production and distribution theory rather than according to the older and no longer as useful division between optimistic and pessimistic thought.

Since this period is the most important one in the development of population thought, it is treated in somewhat greater detail than was the eighteenth century. The organization is by author, to give adequate attention to individual contributions, and, as far as this organization permits, the order is chronological. Summaries at the end of each chapter bring together the separate sequences of topics and ideas. The American population literature of the period is reviewed separately, for although it was largely patterned after European models, it came from a different economic and demographic environment and contained some distinctive points of view. A number of population theories that do not fit into the production or distribution frame of reference and thus fall outside the mainstream of development, but which contributed in other ways to understanding of the population question are summarized in later chapters.[1]

[1] Chapters 11 and 12.

1 · The Malthusian Theory

The Malthusian theory of population has been so much discussed that, to borrow a phrase from Gibbon, the subject has become familiar to the reader and difficult to the writer. A brief re-examination of Malthus' *Essay* is desirable here, however, for some supporters of Malthus, as well as some of his critics, may not be above suspicion of "relying on popular dogma instead of going to the original sources";[2] and two aspects of the theory need particular attention at this point. These are Malthus' thoughts on the relation of population to production and his imputation of certain consequences to population size or growth. Other aspects of his theory fall outside the scope of this account.

No evaluation is made here of Malthus' personal contribution to population thought. That is a controversial matter, and it is well known that the most divergent judgments are made of his originality and understanding of the problem. Some of his followers regarded the *Essay* as the greatest single contribution to population literature. Others regarded Malthus as no more than a plagiarist. Kautsky, for example, one of the severest critics, wrote that "It was as correct to name the new population theory after Malthus as to name America after Amerigo Vespucci. Both did no more than to spread the news of what others had discovered."[3] It seems fair to say that, viewed in relation to the background of earlier population literature, the *Essay* was not so much a sudden advance as it was a natural development and synthesis of current trends of thought.[4]

The thesis of the *Essay on the Principle of Population as it affects the Future Improvement of Society*,[5] published anonymously in 1798 as a rebuttal to the optimistic predictions of Godwin, Condorcet, and others, was that a major cause of human misery and the great obstacle to human progress is the tendency of population to grow too large relative to the means of subsistence. The thesis was expressed in the form of a sort of syllogism, with the following premises or propositions:

> That the increase of population is necessarily limited by the means of subsistence.

[2] Or as Bonar said in reference to Malthus, "When an author becomes an authority, he too often ceases to be read" (*Malthus and his Work,* 1885; 2nd ed., London: Allen and Unwin, 1924, p. 2).

[3] Karl Kautsky, *Der Einfluss der Volksvermehrung auf den Fortschritt der Gesellschaft,* Vienna, 1880, p. 23.

[4] See Chapter 6 above. A remark made by Max Lerner with reference to Adam Smith is fully as well applicable to Malthus: "No first rate mind whose ideas sum up an age and influence masses and movements to come is in any purist sense original" (Introduction to the Modern Library edition of *The Wealth of Nations*).

[5] Malthus, *Essay,* first edition, reprinted for the Royal Economics Society, London: Macmillan, 1926. References to the first edition are to this reprinting.

That population does invariably increase when the means of subsistence increases.[6]

That the superior power of population is repressed, and the actual population kept equal to the means of subsistence by misery and vice.[7]

Underlying Malthus' thesis were assumptions about the relation of population to production and about the consequences of population approaching the subsistence limit. Malthus' thinking on the relation of population to production was indicated in the third proposition and more fully set forth elsewhere in the *Essay*. The power of increase of population, he believed, is superior to that of the means of subsistence, so that population inevitably approaches the subsistence limit. This is to say, although Malthus did not express his thought in these terms, per capita production diminishes as the number of people increases. Support for this belief was provided by Malthus' interpretation of historical evidence and by the celebrated ratios. Some evidence for the ratios was afforded by known rates of population growth, as in the American colonies or states, and by the progress of agriculture; but in the main the ratios rested on an appeal to reason and common knowledge.

With this much established, Malthus proceeded to consider the consequences. The greater part of the *Essay,* especially the later editions, dealt with the checks on increase that allegedly are brought into operation by excessive reproduction and the consequent deficiency of the means of subsistence. Among primitive peoples ". . . misery is the check that represses the superior power of population, and keeps its effects equal to the means of subsistence."[8] In the next higher stage of society, the pastoral, similar checks operate. In the highest or civilized state, with the land being used for both pasturage and for agriculture, a much greater density of population can be supported, but checks nevertheless come into operation. As population increases, the so-called positive checks begin to operate. Of these Malthus wrote "The positive check to population, by which I mean, the check that represses an increase which is already begun, is confined chiefly, though not perhaps solely, to the lowest orders of society."[9] This type of check takes the form of food shortage, poverty, and misery.

The only alternative Malthus saw was the earlier operation of what he called the preventive check. In spite of the strength of the reproductive instinct in man, he wrote, "reason interrupts his career," and prudential considerations come to check increase. This preventive check might be

---

[6] Consciously or unconsciously, Malthus paraphrased a biblical passage in his second proposition, although he is not known to have appealed to biblical authority on this point. The passage is Ecclesiastes 5:11, "When goods increase, they increase who eat them."

[7] Malthus, *op. cit.,* Ch. 7, pp. 140–141.

[8] *Ibid.,* Ch. 3, p. 44.

[9] *Ibid.,* Ch. 5, p. 71.

called immoral restraint,[10] for "... this restraint almost necessarily, though not absolutely so, produces vice."[11] Malthus summarized:

> To these two great checks to population, in all long occupied countries, which I have called the preventive and the positive checks, may be added, vicious customs with respect to women, great cities, unwholesome manufactures, luxury, pestilence, and war. All these checks may be fairly resolved into misery and vice.[12]

He saw no other alternatives.

In 1803 Malthus published a much expanded second edition of the *Essay,* no longer anonymous, and gave a more detailed defense of the original thesis. The thesis was stated in the first chapters, and the remainder of the work mainly described the operation of the principle of population among ancient and primitive peoples as well as in each of the principal states of Europe.

A more detailed classification of the checks was given in the second and later editions. Two broad types of checks were recognized, ultimate and immediate.[13] Of these Malthus wrote:

> The ultimate check to population appears then to be a want of food, arising necessarily from the different ratios according to which population and food increase. But this ultimate check is never the immediate check, except in cases of actual famine.
>
> The immediate check may be stated to consist in all those customs, and all those diseases, which seem to be generated by a scarcity of the means of subsistence; and all those causes, independent of this scarcity, whether of a moral or physical nature, which tend prematurely to weaken and destroy the human frame.[14]

The immediate checks were in turn divided into two types, the preventive and the positive. Of the former, Malthus said "The preventive check, as far as it is voluntary, is peculiar to man, and arises from the distinctive superiority in his reasoning faculties which enables him to calculate distant consequences."[15] This restraint through forethought was said to produce vice in some instances. When not leading to this result it was "the least evil that can arise from the principle of population." When it took the form of restraint from marriage and was not followed by "irregular gratification" it could properly be called moral restraint.[16]

The theory stated by Malthus can be regarded as fundamentally a theory

[10] Malthus did not use this term, but it is useful in contrast to the different treatment of restraint in the later editions of the *Essay.*
[11] Malthus, *Essay,* first edition, Ch. 2, pp. 28–29.
[12] *Ibid.,* Ch. 5, pp. 99–100.
[13] These terms were not introduced until after the second edition.
[14] Later editions of the *Essay,* Ch. 2.
[15] *Ibid.*
[16] The second and later editions.

of the relation of population to production. Viewed in these terms, it depends upon several points: first, whether per capita production decreases as the number of people increases; second, whether population does in fact continue to increase if per capita production decreases; and third, whether the consequences of an increasing population and diminishing per capita production are those described by Malthus.[17]

Of these points, the first is the most crucial and perhaps the most vulnerable part of the theory. Malthus was convinced that population can and in actual fact does increase faster than production; but his interpretation of observations and his use of the ratios were not sufficient to prove the point or to convince the skeptical. It remained for Malthus' followers to reenforce the theory at this weakest spot.

The second point, concerned with the actual course of population, is less crucial for it depends in part upon the first, and Malthus had introduced preventive checks and moral restraint as alternatives to the positive checks. Although he admitted the possibility, he seems to have been doubtful whether restraint would be exercised to limit population, and to have believed on the basis of his survey of many nations that populations continue increasing to a point at which the level of living is depressed.

The third point depends to some extent upon the other two. To support his contention that excessive population is the great cause of human misery, Malthus supplemented his original *Essay* with long accounts of conditions in many nations. Some circularity of reasoning can be noted here, for the presence of human misery in many nations was taken both as evidence of an overabundance of people and as an indication of the consequences of overpopulation. Moreover, the evidence assembled by Malthus could be interpreted differently. As an early anonymous critic pointed out, the first two propositions could be accepted without the third following. Malthus, it seemed to him, had been drawn into ". . . the great error of all system-formers; and by confining his attention to one object solely, he has neglected the operation of all the other wheels in the great machine of society,"[18] and although vice and misery undeniably existed and had existed for a long time, they could be attributed to causes other than the principle of population.[19] In short, although Malthus' *Essay* was the fullest statement made of pessimistic thought up to that time, it was not a proof of the principle of population but rather an elaborate and in many respects plau-

[17] Although not directed specifically to these three points, this chapter deals primarily with the question of the trend of per capita production as population increases, Chapter 9 bears on the question of whether poverty and misery ensue, and Chapters 11 and 12 review nineteenth-century views on whether population does in fact go on increasing.

[18] Anon., *Remarks on a late publication entitled "An Essay on the Principle of Population, etc." by T. R. Malthus*, London, 1803, p. 4.

[19] *Ibid.*, p. 36.

sible structure of information and inference, which some would choose to accept and others to reject.

2 · The Principle of Diminishing Returns

The Malthusian theory was not immediately incorporated into economic thought. The French political economist, Jean-Baptiste Say (1767–1832), is said not to have known of Malthus[20] when he published his *Traité d'économie politique* in 1803, but in his comment on population he agreed with his British contemporary on several points.[21] In the following year Say's fellow countryman and political economist, Dutens (1765–1848), merely noted that population is limited by the food supply, and that food production beyond the needs of the agricultural population permits the growth of industry.[22] The German political economist, Julius von Soden (1754–1831), whose treatise on political economy appeared in 1810, similarly showed little or no Malthusian influence. Mildly optimistic concerning population, he was sure that population cannot naturally grow to a size harmful to national well-being because productive power increases with population growth. Unbounded population growth is out of the question, he believed, unless there is major disturbance of orderly economic activity.[23]

Already noted as one of the weakest but most essential elements in the Malthusian theory is the proposition that population tends to press on the means of subsistence. The ratios used to support this proposition were open to criticism, but during Malthus' lifetime a new development in economic theory strongly reenforced his theory at its weakest point. This was the principle of diminishing returns in agriculture.

As Cannan has said,[24] it was doubtless well known to prudent farmers that in practice it is not profitable to extend the cultivation or fertilizing of land beyond a certain point. Well before the time at which Malthus first wrote, the essence of the principle had been stated, although usually with

[20] Gonnard, *Histoire des doctrines de la population,* p. 301.

[21] Jean-Baptiste Say, *Traité d'économie politique,* 2 vol., Paris, 1803. See especially Vol. I, Ch. 46, pp. 385–403, which deals with the relation of production to population. Here it is stated that for all species, numbers are limited by the ability to obtain subsistence (p. 387); that foresight influences human reproduction (pp. 387–388), but nevertheless the attraction of the sexes is such that in every nation more are born than can be supported, so that infant mortality and other checks operate (p. 389 ff).

[22] J. Dutens, *Analyse raisonnée des principes fondamentaux de l'économie politique,* Paris, 1804, pp. 151, 161–162. Also in his later work, *Philosophie de l'économie politique,* 2 vol. Paris, 1835, Vol. II, pp. 125, 127.

[23] Julius von Soden, *Die Nazional-oekonomie,* 4 vol., Leipzig, 1810, Vol. 4, Book 4, pp. 114, 124.

[24] Cannan, *History of Theories* . . . , Ch. 5, section 4, p. 147; *Wealth,* 1st ed., Ch. 4, p. 62.

no direct reference to population. In 1766 the French engineer and economist, Auxiron, described an inevitable progression to poorer and poorer
soils as population increases, and pointed out that "the average amount of
labor expended by the farmers will rise as their numbers multiply." Some,
he said, will disagree with this statement and assert that the product remains proportional to the number of workers, but experience shows that
is not so.[25] And two years later Turgot wrote, still more explicitly:

> There is then a maximum of production which it is impossible to ex-
> ceed, and when this point is reached, advances (i.e., in the intensity of
> cultivation) produce nothing whatsoever.
>
> In this case the fertility of land is like a spring which one bends by
> loading it successively with equal weights. If the weight is light and the
> spring not very flexible, the action of the first weights might be almost
> nothing. When the weight becomes sufficient to overcome the initial re-
> sistance, the spring will be seen to bend perceptibly; but when it is bent
> to a certain point, it will give greater resistance, and a weight which would
> have made it bend an inch before will no longer make it bend by more
> than half a line. The effect will thus diminish gradually.

Similarly,

> Seed thrown on a naturally fertile but unprepared land would be an ad-
> vance almost entirely lost. If it were tilled once, the product would be
> greater; a second, a third tilling might not merely double or triple, but
> quadruple or decuple the product, which would thus increase in a much
> greater proportion than the advances, and that up to a certain point at
> which the product would be the greatest possible relative to the advances.
>
> Beyond this point, if the advances were increased, the product would
> still increase, but less and less until, the natural fertility of the land
> being exhausted and art unable to add anything more, further advances
> would add nothing to the product.[26]

There is no reference to any influence of population growth in extending the
intensity of cultivation; and as Cannan said, "There is, of course, no reason
to suppose that this passage had any influence on English political
economy."

The observation that returns might also diminish as cultivation becomes
more extensive was implied in a work that appeared a few years after
Turgot's. This was *Observations on the means of exciting a spirit of national industry* (1777) by a Scottish writer, James Anderson. In explaining
the origin of rent, Anderson pointed out that in every country "there are
various soils, which are endued with different degrees of fertility." If
demand pushes cultivation to the poorer soils, then the cost of production

[25] Auxiron, *Principes de tout gouvernement,* Vol. I, pp. 25, 302–303.
[26] Turgot, Sur le Memoire de Saint-Peravy, *Oeuvres,* pp. 644–645.

rises, or, in other words, the rate of return diminishes.[27] Here again there was no mention of the possible effect of population growth in forcing agriculture to a stage of diminishing returns, but the basic idea was there, ready for the role of population to be pointed out later.[28]

Although several other writers of the eighteenth century are credited with the concept,[29] the principle of diminishing returns did not become generally recognized and accepted until its almost simultaneous and apparently independent statement by the four English writers, Malthus, West, Ricardo, and Torrens. An explanation for this convergence of thought is found in the controversy over agricultural policy in England toward the latter part of the Napoleonic Period. At this time British agriculture was being encouraged, and the area under cultivation was greatly enlarged. According to the prevailing supply and demand theory of price formation, it was to be expected that the much-increased production would depress the price of grain. In fact the price remained high, and explanations were sought. Although the price was in part artificially maintained, and eventually further supported by the protectionist Corn Law of 1815, some observers saw the possibility that the price level was due to the greater cost of production on the poorer lands recently brought into cultivation.

Some idea of a tendency toward diminishing returns can be detected in the first edition of Malthus' *Essay*, in his discussion of the limits to the increase of agricultural production.[30] Malthus was more explicit in an essay published in 1814, *Observations on the Effects of the Corn Laws*, in which he gave the following explanation of the higher price of corn or grain in England:

> A part of it, and I should think, no inconsiderable part, is occasioned by the necessity of yearly cultivating and improving more poor land, to provide for the demands of an increasing population; which land must of

[27] Anderson, *Observations*, Edinburgh edition, 1777, postscript of letter XIII, p. 376.

[28] Although Anderson's words, as summarized here imply that increased production will require the use of poorer soils, he later expressed high optimism about the trend of returns from agriculture, writing that "The melioration of the soil must ever be proportional to the means that are made use of to augment its productiveness." Here he had in mind the application of labor and manure to land, and he believed that in the future it might be possible to feed a hundred people from one acre of land (James Anderson, *Recreations in Agriculture, Natural History, etc.*, 1803, Vol. 4, pp. 375, 376).

[29] Wermel (*The Evolution of the Classical Wage Theory*, New York: Columbia University Press, 1939, p. 91) credits Steuart; Spengler (*French Predecessors of Malthus*, p. 274) mentions Forbonnais.

[30] Cannan (*Theories of Production and Distribution*, p. 144). He also points out (p. 146) Malthus' statement in the second edition of the *Essay* that "ungrateful soils" must be used in a state of populousness whereas only the most fertile soils will be used by a smaller population, but that he carried the thought no further (*Essay*, 2nd ed., 1803, p. 472).

course require more labour and dressing, and expence of all kinds in its cultivation.[31]

It was natural for Malthus' thought to turn in this direction, and here for the first time the population factor is brought in as a cause of diminishing returns, or more strictly speaking, increasing cost of production.

Early in the following year Malthus returned to the subject in his essay entitled *An Inquiry into the Nature and Progress of Rent.* Here he stated that

> . . . the reason why the real price of corn is higher and continually rising in countries which are already rich, and still advancing in prosperity and population, is to be found in the necessity of resorting constantly to poorer land. . . .[32]

Because of the greater cost of production on these inferior lands, the price of corn would necessarily increase relative to wages.

David Ricardo (1772–1823) believed that the increase of population is the immediate rather than fundamental cause of an advancing price of corn. In a letter of October 23, 1814, to Malthus, presumably referring to the latter's views as expressed in the *Observations* of that year, Ricardo wrote:

> A rise in the price of raw produce may be occasioned by a gradual ac-
> cumulation of capital, which by creating new demands for labour may
> give a stimulus to population and consequently promote the cultivation
> or improvement of inferior lands; but this will not cause profits to rise but
> to fall, because not only will the ratio of wages rise, but more labourers
> will be employed without affording a proportional return of raw produce.
> The whole value of the wages paid will be greater compared with the
> whole value of the raw produce obtained.[33]

After reading Malthus' essay on rent the next year, Ricardo prepared and published *An Essay on the Influence of a low Price of Corn on the Profits of Stock*[34] (1815). This was primarily concerned with distribution, but although Ricardo's emphasis was still on the relation of population to wealth or capital rather than on changes of population, he nevertheless accepted the view that the growth of population is attended by a diminishing of returns to agriculture. Cannan summarizes Ricardo's position in this essay as follows:

[31] Malthus, *Observations on the Effects of the Corn Laws, and of a rise or fall in the price of Corn on the Agriculture and general Wealth of this Country,* reprinted by Johns Hopkins Press, 1932, p. 32 (p. 40 of the original).

[32] Malthus, *An Inquiry into the Nature and Progress of Rent, and the Principles by which it is Regulated,* London, 1815, p. 41.

[33] *Letters of David Ricardo to Thomas Robert Malthus, 1810–1823,* edited by James Bonar, Oxford: Clarendon Press, 1887, pp. 47–48.

[34] Second edition of the *Essay,* reprinted in *Economic Essays of Ricardo,* edited by E. C. K. Gonner, London: Bell, 1923. References are to this reprinting.

. . . (1) that increasing density of population tends to force recourse to inferior land and more expensive methods of cultivation, and thus to diminish the productiveness of agricultural industry; (2) that it would always actually force recourse to poorer land and more expensive cultivation, and thus actually diminish the productiveness of agricultural industry if there were no improvements in agriculture; and (3) that, as a general rule, or in the long run, in spite of the improvements which take place in agriculture, it does actually force recourse to poorer land and more expensive cultivation. . . .[35]

Of particular importance was Ricardo's statement of the ways in which costs of production would be increased, by the extension of cultivation to land of worse quality, by the use of land of equal quality but less favorable situated, or by the more intensive cultivation of land already in use. Ricardo subsequently restated these views with little modification in his *Principles of Political Economy and Taxation* (1817) and in an essay, *On Protection to Agriculture*[36] (1822).

Appearing somewhat before Ricardo's *Essay on the Influence of a low Price of Corn,* and apparently unknown to Ricardo when he wrote, was a tract by Edward West, *The Application of Capital to Land*[37] (1815). This contained a full statement of the principle of diminishing returns. To use West's own words:

> The principle is simply this, that in the progress of the improvement of cultivation the raising of rude produce becomes progressively more expensive, or in other words, the ratio of the net produce of land to its gross produce is continually diminishing.[38]

In the case of a new colony,

> . . . the first occupiers have their choice of the land, and of course cultivate the richest spots in the country: the next comers must take the second quality, which will return less to their labour, and so each successive additional set of cultivators must necessarily produce less than their predecessors.[39]

The same result follows the alternative procedure of applying the additional labor to the tracts of land already under cultivation. In a long established country,

> In the pastoral state, the only labour of the tribe is that of tending their cattle. . . . As population advances it is necessary to have recourse to agriculture; in this state somewhat more labour is necessary to support

---

[35] Cannan, *History of Theories,* Ch. 5, section 4, p. 165.
[36] See Ch. 2, p. 47 of the *Principles* (1891 edition, London: Bell); section 1, subsection 2 of *On Protection to Agriculture.*
[37] Reprinted by Johns Hopkins Press, 1903. This reprinting is used here.
[38] *Ibid.,* p. 1.
[39] *Ibid.,* p. 13.

even the same number of mouths; but yet it is at first small if compared with the quantity of produce. . . . As each cultivator is driven into a narrower compass by the pressure of population, he is obliged to till soils which are comparatively ungrateful and exhausted: the cattle are fed on artificial grasses; and expensive manures are brought from a distance to enable the land to yield successive crops, instead of being left, when exhausted, as in the earlier stages of improvement, to renovate itself.[40]

And,

The additional work bestowed upon land must be expended either in bringing fresh land into cultivation, or in cultivating more highly that already in tillage. In every country the gradations between the richest land and the poorer, must be innumerable. The richest land, or that most conveniently situated for a market, or, in a word, that which, on account of its situation and quality combined, produces the largest return to the expense bestowed on it, will of course be cultivated first, and when in the progress of improvement new land is brought into cultivation, recourse is necessarily had to poor land, or to that at least which is second in quality to what is already cultivated. It is clear that the additional work bestowed in this case will bring a less return than the work bestowed before. . . . That this diminution of the return of the soil to the additional expense bestowed on it takes place gradually, may also be proved by the same reasoning.[41]

In other words, returns diminish, regardless whether recourse is had to poorer land, to land less favorably situated, or to a more intensive cultivation of the land already in use. But this tendency might be partly or even more fully compensated, according to West, by the subdivision of labor or by improvements in production methods through the use of machinery.

In the same year, apparently without having read the recent essays by Malthus, West, and Ricardo, Robert Torrens (1780–1864) published *An Essay on the External Corn Trade,* in which he stated that the extension of cultivation reduces the productive power of labor and capital in agriculture by bringing inferior lands into use.[42]

From its formulation in this group of essays, the principle of diminishing returns came to be one of the fundamentals of classical economic theory. In relation to the population controversy, it was in effect a direct contradiction of the optimistic belief that per capita returns remain constant or advance with the growth of population. Conversely, it supported the Malthusian theory at one of its weakest points by providing an apparently scientific law that explained how population growth leads inexorably to the impoverishment of a people. Curiously enough, however, Malthus did

[40] *Ibid.*
[41] *Ibid.,* p. 14.
[42] Robert Torrens, *An Essay on the External Corn Trade,* London, 1815, pp. 73–74, 177.

not incorporate the principle into his theory of population, even though he contributed to its development. The principle was clearly stated some twenty years before his death, and two later editions of the *Essay* were prepared during his lifetime,[43] but even though some reference was made to diminishing returns in these last editions, the principle was never incorporated into the central argument. It remained for Malthus' followers, especially John Stuart Mill, to include it in the definitive statement of the Malthusian theory. As Cannan remarked, ". . . to imagine that the *Essay on the Principle of Population* was ever based on the law of diminishing returns is to confuse Malthusianism as expounded by J. S. Mill with Malthusianism as expounded by Malthus."[44]

3 · 1815–1819: Gray to James Mill

The relation of population to production was examined further in the continuing Malthusian controversy and in the growing literature of political economy. In the same year that the principle of diminishing returns was stated and restated, the optimistic side of the population controversy was strongly set forth by Simon Gray in *The Happiness of States* (1815). Gray's views on population as developed in this and subsequent publications[45] will be described later; only his views on production are noted here. The growth of the number of people, he believed, leads to greater production and greater wealth. An equilibrium is maintained between population and subsistence, for "consumption regulates the demand; and the demand regulates the supply."[46] Population determines the supply of the means of subsistence, not the opposite as Malthus believed:

> Population, whatever be the ratio of its increase, carries in itself the means of finding sufficient food. Its increase supplies it with an additional numbers of hands. Only about one out of every six or seven of the new persons . . . is wanted to cultivate in order to feed himself and the rest.[47]

Gray did not mention diminishing returns, and it is very likely that the principle had not yet been stated at the time he wrote.

In a later work, *Gray versus Malthus* (1818), a restatement and defense of his own *Happiness of States,* which Gray published under the pseudonym George Purves, Gray reaffirmed that population increase "carries in

[43] The 5th edition in 1817, and the 6th edition in 1826.

[44] Cannan, *History of Theories,* Ch. 5, section 3, p. 144.

[45] Simon Gray, *The Happiness of States,* London, 1815; *Gray versus Malthus: The Principles of Population and Production,* London, 1818; and "Remarks on the production of Wealth . . . in a letter to the Reverend T. R. Malthus," *The Pamphleteer,* 17(34): 385–416, 1820.

[46] Gray, *The Happiness of States,* Book VI, Ch. 2.

[47] *Ibid.,* Book VI, Ch. 3, p. 439.

itself the power of fully supplying its various wants," and that "the amount of population thus regulates the amount of subsistence."[48] He further gave what then was doubtless the best rebuttal to the principle of diminishing returns by pointing out that population does not in fact increase beyond the means of subsistence, and that there is ample unused land even in Europe.[49]

The year after Gray's first work a similarly optimistic theory of population was advanced by John Weyland (1774–1854) in *Principles of Population and Production* (1816). This contained the seemingly contradictory propositions that "population has a natural tendency to keep within the powers of the soil to afford it subsistence,"[50] and that the increase of numbers just beyond the point of plentiful supply gives a stimulus to progress in methods of production and in economic organization. As Weyland explained the latter proposition,

> During the alternate progress of population and subsistence in the earliest and most advanced stages of society, a *previous* increase of people is necessary to stimulate the community to a further production of food; and consequently to the healthy advancement of a country in the career of strength and prosperity. It results from this proposition that the incipient pressure of population against the *actual* means of subsistence, or, more correctly speaking, the excess of population *just beyond the plentiful supply of the people's want,* instead of being the cause of most of the miseries of human life, is in fact the cause of all public happiness, industry, and prosperity.[51]

The Malthusian theory was more favorably received by Malthus' fellow political economists. The principle of diminishing returns was soon firmly established in political economy, and the related population question came to be regarded as one of the major concerns of the new science. The majority of the political economists accepted the substance of the Malthusian theory, although they often did so with some modification or change of emphasis.

Two treatises on political economy appeared during the remainder of the decade, one written by Destutt de Tracy, the other by Ricardo. The less well known of these works, Destutt de Tracy's *Treatise on Political Economy*[52] (1817), accepted the Malthusian theory of population, but made the important distinction between the means of subsistence and the means of existence, of which the latter includes what is actually consumed

---

[48] Gray, *Gray versus Malthus,* p. 10.

[49] *Ibid.,* Book I, Ch. 5.

[50] John Weyland, *The Principles of Population and Production, as they are affected by the Progress of Society: with a View to Moral and Political Consequences,* London, 1816, p. 21.

[51] *Ibid.*

[52] Antoine Louis Destutt de Tracy, *A Treatise on Political Economy,* translated from the French, with foreword by Thomas Jefferson, Georgetown, 1817.

and may include some enjoyments. And, he wrote, it is to the supply of the latter rather than of the former that population adjusts itself.[53] The same distinction was made in his *Élemens d'idéologie*[54] (1801–1815). Ricardo, who was a friend and friendly critic of Malthus, early accepted the substance of the theory of population. As he wrote in his principal work, *On the Principles of Political Economy and Taxation* (1817):

> It is a truth which admits not a doubt, that the comforts and well-being of the poor cannot be permanently secured without some regard on their part, or some effort on the part of the legislature, to regulate the increase of their numbers, and to render less frequent among them early and improvident marriages.[55]

Accepting the conclusion that the growth of population hastens the onset of diminishing returns, Ricardo gave little further thought to production and turned his attention to the relations between population, capital, and the pattern of distribution. As in his essay of several years before, he did not assign to population the primary role Malthus had given it, but wrote in the *Principles* that:

> Mr. Malthus appears to me to be too much inclined to think that population is only increased by the previous provision of food,—"that it is food that creates its own demand,"—that it is by first providing food, that encouragement is given to marriage, instead of considering that the general progress of population is affected by the increase of capital, the consequent demand for labour, and the rise of wages; and that the production of food is but the effect of that demand.[56]

This reduced population change to a dependent variable, or rather, pointed out quite soundly that there are complex interrelations between population and economic variables, and that population increase has antecedents as well as consequences.

4 · 1820–1829: Godwin to Say

Several notable contributions to the population controversy and to economic literature appeared in 1820, including Godwin's reply to Malthus. Soon after the appearance of the *Essay* Godwin had issued a very moderate reply, *Thoughts occasioned by the perusal of Dr. Parr's spital sermon, etc.* (1801), in which he praised Malthus and his work, with the words "Of this

---

[53] *Ibid.*, pp. 124–125.

[54] *Élemens d'idéologie*, 2nd ed., Paris, 1818, Vol. IV, p. 277.

[55] *The Works and Correspondence of David Ricardo*, edited by Piero Sraffa, Vol. I, *On the Principles of Political Economy and Taxation*, Cambridge: University Press, 1951, Ch. 5, pp. 106–107. This is a reprinting of the third edition (1821), with notes of changes from the first and second edition.

[56] *Ibid.*, Ch. 32, p. 406.

book and the spirit in which it is written I can never speak but with un-feigned respect."[57] And of Malthus;

> This author has a claim, perhaps still higher, upon my respect. With the most unaffected simplicity of manner, and disdaining every parade of science, he appears to me to have made as unquestionable an addition to the theory of political economy, as any writer for a century past. The grand proportions and outline of his work will, I believe, be found not less conclusive and certain, than they are new. For myself, I cannot re-fuse to take some pride, in so far as by my writings I gave the occasion, and furnished an incentive, to the producing so valuable a treatise.[58]

The ratios Godwin regarded as "unassailable," but he mildly disagreed with Malthus' opinion that the only outlook is for vice and misery. He could not see that population growth had produced them in the past, nor did he "despair of the virtues of man."

Godwin's later life was less successful and less happy, and his final reply to Malthus, *On Population* (1820), was written in a quite different spirit. It was a bitter personal attack on Malthus and an attempt to demolish his theory of population by weight of evidence and argument. Godwin's argument will be reviewed later;[59] here it can be noted that he denied that a diminishing of returns actually occurs in the progress of population. He contended, "There is no principle respecting man and society more cer-tain, than that every man in a civilized state is endowed with the physical power of producing more than shall suffice for his own subsistence."[60] Whatever poverty existed in England he attributed to inequalities of dis-tribution rather than to any law of nature.

In the same year Malthus published his *Principles of Political Economy* (1820), which has been eclipsed by the fame of his *Essay* but which per-haps deserves to be regarded as his major work. Like Ricardo's *Political Economy,* this gave most attention to distribution, and it did not go beyond the *Essay* in discussing the relation of population to production. Worth noting, however, is the statement of the importance of the balance between production and consumption:

> . . . it has been stated by Adam Smith, and stated truly, that there is a balance very different from the balance of trade, which, according as it happens to be favourable or unfavourable, occasions the prosperity or

---

[57] William Godwin, *Thoughts occasioned by the perusal of Dr. Parr's spital ser-mon, preached at Christ Church, April 15, 1800; being a reply to the attacks of Dr. Parr, Mr. McIntosh, the author of an essay on population, and others,* London, 1801, p. 10. An interesting account of "the redoubtable Dr. Samuel Parr," his sermon, and Godwin's reply is given by Herschel Baker in his *William Hazlitt,* pp. 101–104.

[58] *Ibid.,* p. 56.

[59] See Ch. 11 below.

[60] William Godwin, *On Population. An Inquiry concerning the Power of Increase in the Numbers of Mankind,* London, 1820, p. 17.

decay of every nation: this is the balance of the annual produce and consumption. If in given periods the produce of a country exceeds its consumption, the means of increasing its capital will be provided, its population will soon increase, or the actual numbers will be better accommodated; and probably both. If the consumption in such periods fully equals the produce, no means of increasing the capital will be afforded, and the society will be nearly at a stand. If the consumption exceeds the produce, every succeeding period will see the society worse supplied, and its prosperity and population will be evidently on the decline.[61]

From this it presumably followed that undue population increase, by disturbing the balance, would adversely affect capital formation and prosperity.

In 1820 Torrens issued a second, enlarged edition of his essay of five years before. In this he stated the opposite tendencies of diminishing and increasing returns, or of increasing and diminishing cost of production:

> As an increasing population compels us on the one hand to resort to inferior soils, and thus raises the natural price of raw produce, so it leads on the other hand to more accurate division of employment, and to the use of improved machinery, and thus lowers the natural price of all wrought goods.[62]

Torrens pointed out that the one tendency might counteract the other, but at a given level of economic development the rate of profit depends upon "the quality of land under cultivation." Profits fall as poorer and poorer land is used, until population growth is checked by famine.[63]

Torrens' statement of opposing tendencies was of course not new, for West, as mentioned earlier, had pointed out the same thing in his *Application of Capital to Land*[64] (1815). A related comment with reference to the price of corn was later made by Ricardo in *On Protection to Agriculture* (1822):

> In the progress of society there are two opposing causes operating on the value of corn; one the increase of population, and the necessity of cultivating, at an increased charge, land of an inferior quality, which always occasions a rise in the value of corn; the other, improvements in agriculture, or the discovery of new and abundant foreign markets, which always tend to lower the value. Sometimes one predominates, sometimes the other, and the value of corn rises or falls accordingly.[65]

[61] Malthus, *Principles of Political Economy*, 1820; reprinted with Ricardo's notes as Vol. II of *Works and Correspondence of David Ricardo*, Ch. 1, section 2, pp. 16–17. Same wording in 2nd edition (1836).

[62] Torrens, *An Essay on the Influence of the external Corn Trade upon the Production and Distribution of National Wealth*, 2nd ed., London, 1820, p. 407.

[63] *Ibid.*

[64] See p. 163.

[65] Ricardo, *Economic Essays*, p. 282 (section 5, subsection 14, of essay).

The year after the new edition of his earlier work appeared, Torrens issued *An Essay on the Production of Wealth*[66] (1821). It referred to population only in connection with other topics; but with regard to the opposite tendencies of returns, which Torrens traced to population, he wrote:

> As population increases, and it becomes necessary to take in new soils, or to cultivate the old in a more expensive manner, it constantly requides an augmenting quantity of capital to raise the same quantity of produce; while, on the contrary, the advance of a country in wealth and population, by giving occasion to improvements in machinery, and to more perfect divisions of employment, enables the same number of hands, and consequently the same expenditure for food, to work up a greater quantity of material. From this conjoint operation of these causes, the value of raw produce is, in the progress of society, perpetually increasing with respect to manufactured goods; or to express the same thing in a different form, the value of manufactured goods is perpetually diminishing with respect to raw produce.[67]

He later drew a corollary from this, that

> . . . in all new settlements, the increasing value of raw produce must gradually check its exportation, and the falling value of wrought goods progressively prevent their importation; until at length the commercial intercourse between nations shall be confined to those peculiar articles, in the production of which the immutable circumstances of soil and climate give one country a permanent advantage over another.[68]

Another and pessimistic conclusion to which Torrens came was that

> . . . from the relative proportion, according to which population and capital have, in all old countries, been hitherto found to increase, the supply of labour has such a tendency to exceed the demand for it, that the labouring classes, even when there is no extraordinary stagnation or revulsion in the channels of industry, are commonly reduced to a degree of distress and temptation, for which, in the actual state of knowledge and of morals, there is no conceivable remedy except in a system of colonization, sufficiently extensive to relieve the mother country from superfluous numbers.[69]

---

[66] Torrens, *An Essay on the Production of Wealth,* London, 1821. In explaining why he believed there was still a contribution to be made to political economy, in spite of the outstanding work of Malthus and Ricardo, Torrens spoke of Ricardo as dealing in terms of reasoning and theory, Malthus as having a particular faculty for observation, and that the one was deficient in the other's quality. "If Mr. Ricardo generalises too much, Mr. Malthus generalises too little" (Introduction, p. iv).

[67] *Ibid.,* p. 144.

[68] *Ibid.,* p. 288–289.

[69] *Ibid.,* p. 232. An earlier parallel statement by Torrens appears in *The economists refuted, or an inquiry into the nature and extent of the advantages derived from trade,* London, 1808, p. 35. Emigration or colonization as a substitute for poor relief was recommended in his "A paper on the means of reducing the poor rates,"

Although on different grounds, this was nevertheless a Malthusian conclusion.

James Mill (1773–1836), like Ricardo, gave more attention to distribution analysis than to the relation of population to production, in his *Elements of Political Economy* (1821). There he treated the subject of political economy under four headings, production, distribution, exchange, and consumption. He made no direct mention of population as a variable in production, but accepted the principle of diminishing returns. In Mill's statement, however, capital is the immediate variable that determines the onset of diminishing returns, which may come either from extension of capital to land of the second degree of fertility, or from the application of a second "dose" of capital to land of the first degree of fertility.

Mill further emphasized the role of capital by presenting a variant of the Malthusian thesis according to which the critical variable is not population but the relative rates of increase of population and capital. In his own words:

> If it were the natural tendency of capital to increase faster than population, there would be no difficulty in preserving a prosperous condition of the people. If, on the other hand, it were the natural tendency of population to increase faster than capital, the difficulty would be very great. There would be a perpetual tendency in wages to fall. The fall of wages would produce a greater and a greater degree of poverty among the people, attended with its inevitable consequences, misery and vice. As poverty, and its consequent misery, increased, mortality would also increase. Of a numerous family born, a certain number only, from want of the means of well-being, would be reared. By whatever proportion the population tended to increase faster than capital, such a proportion of those who were born would die: the ratio of increase in capital and population would thence remain the same, and wages would cease to fall.
>
> That population has a tendency to increase faster, than, in most places, capital has actually increased, is proved, incontestably, by the condition of the population in almost all parts of the globe. In almost all countries the condition of the great body of the people is poor and miserable. This would have been impossible if capital had increased faster than population. In that case wages, of necessity, would have risen, and would have placed the labourer in a state of affluence, far above the miseries of want.[70]

This might almost have been Malthus writing, except for the substitution of the capital-population ratio. Mill then presented evidence of the potential for rapid population increase. With five children taken as the average

---

The Pamphleteer, London, 1817; and *A letter to Lord John Russell* . . . , London, 1837.

[70] James Mill, *Elements of Political Economy,* 2nd ed., London, 1824, Ch. 2, section 2, pp. 44–46.

number per family, mortality considered, population can double in a relatively brief interval. Actually, wrote Mill, it remains approximately constant in most countries because of poverty and prudence. Finally, he endeavored to demonstrate that capital as a rule increases less rapidly than population. To this he attributed the economic ills of society as well as to man's powers of reproduction.

In the same year a moderate and persuasive statement of the case against the Malthusian theory of population was made in *A Few Doubts as to the Correctness of some Opinions generally entertained on the Subject of Political Economy* (1821) by Piercy Ravenstone. The author, about whom little or nothing is known, argued that mankind does not in fact increase indefinitely to a condition of overpopulation and misery, that census data for the United States prove the rate of natural increase there is not as great as had been commonly believed, and that the theory of diminishing returns is not consistent with the known facts. On this last point Ravenstone contended that "The produce of the earth, as it is entirely dependent on the industry of man, so it is always commensurate with the amount of industry exerted."[71] In other words, there is no diminishing of the returns to labor. As numbers advance, division of labor is made possible, and the condition of men improves rather than deteriorates. In Ravenstone's words:

> It is accordingly with the numbers of a people that its comforts of every kind increase . . . and, when the will of nature is not counteracted by human regulations, plenty and abundance will always grow up in proportion to the growth of population. . . . Every addition to the numbers of people extends in more than a proportionate degree the limits of its means of subsistence.[72]

The tendency is therefore toward increasing rather than diminishing returns. Concerning the latter theory Ravenstone held the opinion that

> The doctrine of first, of second, of third qualities of soil, by which it has been attempted to prove, that corn must necessarily be dearer in a well-peopled country, than in one where population is less abundant, is entirely without foundation. . . . Those who have paid attention to this subject well know, that it is not the best soils which are the first cultivated, but those pieces of land which are most conveniently situated.[73]

It cannot be certain Ravenstone was the first to advance this argument against the principle of diminishing returns, but his statement of it is of interest since the idea is generally attributed to Carey, the American writer, who presented it a number of years later.[74] In 1823 Ensor stated his

[71] Ravenstone, *A Few Doubts* . . . , London, 1821, p. 149.
[72] *Ibid.*, pp. 174, 175.
[73] *Ibid.*, pp. 407–408.
[74] See Ch. 11 below for a further account of Ravenstone's views on population.

disagreement with Ricardo, writing that the best lands are probably the last to be cultivated, and that the first to be used are those easiest to cultivate.[75]

The *Cours d'économie politique* by Henri Storch, published in 1823, made little reference to population except for a chapter on health and population. There the views expressed had a mildly Malthusian tone: the number of people in a nation always adjusts itself to annual production; there is a continued tendency to increase, but mortality rises to check multiplication. The less conventional assertion was made in several places that an unequal distribution of wealth reduces the population of a nation.[76]

The Malthusian theory of population was accepted almost in its entirety in the early works of John McCulloch (1789–1864), whose views were most fully set forth in his *Principles of Political Economy* (1825). He did follow James Mill in emphasizing the ratio of population to capital rather than the absolute number or the multiplication of people, but conceded Malthus had demonstrated that

> . . . every increase in the numbers of a people, occasioned by artificial expedients, and which is not either preceded or accompanied by a corresponding increase of the means of subsistence, can be productive only of misery, or of increased mortality; that the difficulty never is to bring human beings into the world, but to feed, clothe, and educate them when there; that mankind do every where increase their numbers till their multiplication is restrained by the difficulty of providing subsistence, and the poverty of some part of society; and that, consequently, instead of attempting to strengthen the principle of increase, we should rather endeavour to strengthen the principles by which it is controlled and regulated.[77]

The essential question for McCulloch, however, was whether population increases more rapidly than capital. In the early settlement of a country the advances in industry and capital are able to keep pace with population, but in countries long settled a diminishing of returns sets in with the enforced use of poorer and poorer land. The power of population increase remains unimpaired even when returns diminish, and is sufficient to double numbers in a period as short as twenty-five years. In this case, McCulloch said, the two Malthusian alternatives are inescapable:

[75] George Ensor, *The poor and their relief*, 1823, p. 315.

[76] Henri Storch, *Cours d'économie politique*, 5 vol., Paris, 1823; Vol. III, Book II, Ch. 1, especially pp. 318, 324–325, 330. The *Cours* was prepared for the education of the Russian Grand Dukes Nicholas and Michael and was published with notes by J. B. Say.

[77] John R. McCulloch, *The Principles of Political Economy*, Edinburgh, 1825, Part II, section 5, p. 194; also 3rd ed., 1843, Part I, Ch. 8, pp. 220–221. (Wording of 3rd ed. quoted here.)

. . . it is obvious, that if the tendency to multiplication . . . were not checked by the prevalence of moral restraint, or of prudence and forethought, it would be checked by the prevalence of vice, misery and famine. There is no alternative.[78]

In these respects McCulloch's views remained essentially unchanged throughout the numerous editions of his work, but in the third (1843) and subsequent editions he shifted to a more optimistic conclusion about the population problem. In the preface of the third edition McCulloch announced his conversion to more optimistic views by expressing the opinion that

. . . the inferences drawn . . . from this principle (of population) are contradicted by the widest experience; that the too rapid increase of population is almost always prevented by the influence of principles which its increase brings into activity; that a vast improvement has taken place in the condition of the people of most countries, particularly of those in which population has increased with the greatest rapidity; and that . . . we are really indebted to the principle of increase for most part of our comforts and enjoyments, and for the continued progress of arts and industry.[79]

McCulloch had become convinced that moral restraint does in fact prevent overpopulation. There was, he wrote,

. . . the wise arrangement of Providence, that this change in the circumstances (diminishing returns) . . . never fails to bring along with it a corresponding change in the habits of the people, so that their numbers are proportioned to the greater difficulty experienced in procuring supplies of food, not by an increase of mortality, but by a diminution of births.[80]

Furthermore, the effect of the principle of population is on the whole beneficial rather than harmful, for

. . . the tendency to increase is not inconsistent with the improvement of society. . . . In point of fact, the principle of increase is not merely consistent with the continued improvement of the bulk of society, but is itself the greatest cause of this improvement. . . .[81]

McCulloch thus accepted many of Malthus' premises but drew different conclusions by putting greater faith in the effectiveness of prudential control, by believing that population increase is checked before it becomes harmful, and by considering the increase of numbers to be beneficial.

Regarding the principle of diminishing returns, with its implications for the influence of population growth on production, McCulloch's views also

[78] McCulloch, *Principles*, 3rd ed., p. 228. Similarly stated, 1st ed., pp. 207–208.
[79] *Ibid.*, 3rd ed., Preface, p. xiv.
[80] *Ibid.*, p. 227.
[81] *Ibid.*, p. 231.

became somewhat more optimistic in later editions of the *Principles*. In the first edition (1825) he wrote that as population grows and the demand for food increases,

> The productive energies of the earth itself gradually diminish, and we are compelled to resort to soils of a constantly decreasing degree of fertility; but the productive energies of the labour employed to extract produce from these soils, are as constantly augmented by the discoveries and inventions that are always being made. Two directly opposite and continually acting principles are thus set in motion. From the operation of fixed and permanent causes, the increasing sterility of the soil must, in the long-run, overmatch the increasing power of machinery and the improvements of agriculture. . . .[82]

In the third edition (1843), which marked McCulloch's conversion to somewhat greater optimism, this passage was changed to read,

> The productive energies of the earth gradually diminish, and we are compelled to resort to less fruitful soils; but the productive energies of the labour employed in their tillage are as constantly augmented by the discoveries and inventions that are always being made. Two directly opposite and continually acting principles are thus set in motion. From the operation of fixed and permanent causes, the increasing sterility of the soil is sure, in the long run to overmatch the improvements already made in machinery and agriculture, prices experiencing a corresponding rise, and profits a corresponding fall. Frequently, however, these improvements more than compensate, during lengthened periods, for the deterioration in the quality of the soils successively cultivated. . . .[83]

In this restatement the prospect of ultimate overpopulation and reduced returns is more remote, if not entirely removed.

The celebrated work of Johann von Thünen (1783–1850), *Der isolierte Staat*[84] (1826–1863), is known chiefly for its early statement of the concept of marginal productivity and its application to the theory of distribution.[85] The principle of diminishing returns, being fundamental to the concept of marginal productivity, was of course stated by von Thünen, who demonstrated that the ratio of added product to added input decreases as additional amounts of fertilizer are applied to land.[86]

The German treatise, *Staatswissenschaften* by Karl Pölitz (1772–1838), appeared in 1823. This did not deal in detail with the relation of population to production, but did note that the number of people in a nation is

---

[82] *Ibid.*, 1st ed., p. 383. This passage is quoted more fully in Chapter 9, section 2, below.

[83] *Ibid.*, 3rd ed., pp. 497–498.

[84] Johann von Thünen, *Der isolierte Staat in Beziehung auf Landwirtschaft und Nationalökonomie*, reprinted in *Samlung sozialwissenschaftlicher Meister*, No. 13, Jena; Fischer, 1930.

[85] See further references to von Thünen in Chapter 9.

[86] von Thünen, *op. cit.*, Book I, section 7b.

seldom too large in relation to its productive power,[87] that shortage of means of subsistence is usually due to mismanagement such as impediments put in the way of trade and business,[88] that a population contains both productive and unproductive elements,[89] and that it is unwise to stimulate population growth artificially because it interferes with natural population phenomena.[90]

A later French work, the *Économie politique*[91] (1829) of Joseph Droz (1773–1851), gave an intelligent and rather original treatment of population. Perhaps unconsciously stating the converse of an earlier remark by Ensor,[92] Droz noted sagely that

> When a state becomes more prosperous, people increase there. From this fact it has been concluded that to make a state prosper it is necessary to increase its people. This was to take the effect for the cause.[93]

Production, he wrote, is increased by a growth of population, but the increase is not proportionate unless the country is newly settled. In old countries population growth is attended by a decrease in per capita production.[94] Of the Malthusian theory, finally, Droz believed that it did not correspond to reality and that population does not grow in geometric progression.

The writings of the influential French economist, Jean-Baptiste Say spanned much of the period of the Malthusian controversey, from his *Traité d'économie politique* (1803) through the *Lettres à M. Malthus*[95] (published in 1820), to the *Cours complet d'économie politique* (1828–1830). The treatment of population in the *Traité,* as described earlier in this chapter, did not go beyond the conventional statements that a dense population permits division of labor,[96] that population has the power of infinite increase and will grow as fast or faster than the means of subsistence,[97] and that as a general rule the population of a nation is at the limit set by its production.[98] Say later differed from Malthus on a number of points, but more on economic than population questions, and his later works have a stronger Malthusian flavor regarding population. In a section

---

[87] Karl H. L. Pölitz, *Die Staatswissenschaften im Lichte unsrer Zeit,* 2nd edition, 5 vol., Leipzig, 1827–1828, Vol. II, p. 151.

[88] *Ibid.,* p. 154. [89] *Ibid.,* p. 114.

[90] *Ibid.,* p. 115.

[91] Joseph Droz, *Économie politique ou principes de la science des richesses,* Paris, 1829. The edition used here is the third, published in Brussels, 1837.

[92] See p. 335. [93] Droz, *op. cit.,* Ch. 6, p. 204.

[94] *Ibid.,* p. 206.

[95] J. B. Say, *Lettres à M. Malthus sur différens sujets d'économie politique . . . ,* Paris, 1820. An English translation of the letters appeared the same year in *The Pamphleteer,* Vol. 17, pp. 289–345, and a more precise translation by John Richter was published the following year under the title *Letters to Mr. Malthus, with Catechism of Political Economy,* London, 1821.

[96] Jean-Baptiste Say, *A Treatise on Political Economy,* translation of the 4th edition of the *Traité,* by C. R. Prinsep, Boston, 1821, Book I, Ch. 8, p. 50.

[97] *Ibid.,* Book II, Ch. 11, p. 137. [98] *Ibid.,* p. 138.

of the *Cours,* Say wrote that it is not war or famine and disease that check human increase, for these checks are not equal to the potential power of reproduction. The limit on the increase in numbers, for man as well as for other species, is set by space and food supply.[99] It is therefore futile to attempt to change the population of a country by direct measures; emigration produces no lasting change in numbers, and increase is impossible unless a greater supply of the means of subsistence can be provided.[100] There are, he noted, some who maintain agricultural production can be expanded to support a large population, but we cannot afford to put in more than one day of work to produce food sufficient to support a man for only one day. And while it is true that improvements in agriculture and industry increase productive capacity, it is not safe to assume that equal advances can continue indefinitely.

5 · 1830–1839: Sadler to Eisdell

A strongly anti-Malthusian position was taken by Thomas Sadler (1780–1835) in *The Law of Population* (1830), which asserted the contrary of most of Malthus' propositions. The theory of population he proposed as a substitute for Malthus' is described later; and only his views on the trend of production need be noted here. Subsistence depends upon population, he believed, rather than population upon subsistence, and he was convinced that returns increase rather than diminish. Sadler wrote, in explanation, that "The stimulus created by population preceding production, when thus universally felt, is not only the cause of the production of sufficiency, but of the diffusion of increasing plenty."[101] As a result, the food supply increases more rapidly than population in the course of human progress; and with a greater quantity of food come higher quality and a more dependable supply.

A more restrained, more telling argument against the Malthusian theory appeared the following year in *Introductory Lectures in Political Economy* (1831) by Richard Whately (1787–1863), newly appointed Archbishop of Dublin, formerly professor of political economy at Oxford. In the course of nine lectures given at that university, Whately made the strong point that the Malthusian theory runs counter to the fact that "all civilized countries have a greater proportionate amount of wealth, now, than formerly." As he said of Malthus' theory:

> On this theory, our own country, and almost every other in the civilized world, ought to possess scantier means of subsistence in proportion to the population, now, than some centuries ago. But we know that the reverse

[99] Say, *Cours*, Part VI, Ch. 1. The same view is expressed in the *Traité*, especially in Book II, Ch. 11.
[100] *Ibid.*, Part VI, Ch. 6.
[101] Michael T. Sadler, *The Law of Population*, London, 1830, p. 122.

is the fact; and that our population, though so greatly increased since the time, for instance, of Henry VIII, is yet better off, on the average, in point of food, clothing, and habitations, than then.[102]

Whately was no doubt on solid ground in believing that the Malthusian theory could be more successfully attacked on the basis of fact than of theory.

Published in the same year and taking a somewhat similar approach to the population question was *An Essay on the Distribution of Wealth*[103] (1831) by Richard Jones (1790–1855). Like Whately, Jones preferred to seek answers to the disputed questions of political economy and population in observation rather than theory, being convinced that "the experience of the past and present, can alone . . . afford any sure foundations for anticipations as to the future." Although he admired Malthus, whom he considered superior to Ricardo and second only to Adam Smith in laying the foundations of economic knowledge, Jones believed that Malthus' successors had carried many of his principles to erroneous conclusions.[104] His thoughts on the population controversy were only briefly outlined in the preface of his uncompleted work, but he was led by the English experience to doubt whether returns in agriculture did in fact diminish.[105] The rise of rent in England he attributed to better farming and greater production; he did not accept the Ricardian explanation that it was due to the use of poorer land.[106]

In the next year Thomas Chalmers (1780–1847), credited by Cannon with being the first eminent writer to attack the theory of diminishing returns in agriculture, published the work, *Political Economy in connexion with the Moral State and Moral Prospects of Society*[107] (1832). It is not historically true, he asserted, that the condition of the laboring class has deteriorated with the progress of population. Actually, the opposite has been true. Population growth may have stimulated the improvement of production methods, so that

[102] Richard Whately, *Introductory Lectures on Political Economy,* 2nd ed., London, 1832, p. 185.

[103] Richard Jones, *An Essay on the Distribution of Wealth and on the Sources of Taxation,* Part I, *Rent* (all that was published), London: Murray, 1831.

[104] *Ibid.,* p. vii. "The earliest distinct views of those laws which govern the revenues of the landed proprietors, and the wages of the laborers in the most advanced stages of civilization, will always be to be traced in his works on population, and on rent. . . . But Mr. Malthus has been singularly unfortunate in his successors; under their treatment, his works, instead of being made the foundations of a superstructure of useful truth, have been used to give the semblance of plausibility to a mass of error, ingenious and harmless in some of its parts, but as a whole, most delusive, and unfortunately most mischievous." When he wrote this, Jones cannot have foreseen that he himself was to be Malthus' successor in the chair of political economy at the East India College.

[105] *Ibid.,* p. xiii.

[106] *Ibid.,* pp. 277–286.

[107] Chalmers, *Political Economy,* Glasgow, 1832.

. . . as the fresh soils that had to be successively entered on became more intractable, the same amount of labour, by the intervention of tools and instruments of husbandry, may have become greatly more effective.[108]

Chalmers referred here to what had happened rather than to what might be expected to happen in the course of time. He conceded that agriculture could not be extended indefinitely to poorer and poorer soils without an eventual decrease in returns. He believed this possibility was remote[109] but conceivable in view of the power of population to multiply. As he said:

> The tendency of a progressive population to outstrip the progressive culture of the earth, may put mankind into a condition of straightness and difficulty—and that for many generations before the earth shall be wholly cultivated. . . . Certain it is, at all events, that the produce of the soil cannot be made to increase at the rate that population *would* increase. Neither mechanical invention nor more intensive manual labour is sufficient for this purpose.[110]

Like Malthus before him, Chalmers saw only one way to avoid the evils of overpopulation: ". . . the only way, we apprehend, of preventing this overflow, with all its consequent wretchedness and crime, is by the formation of a higher taste for comfort and decency among the peasantry themselves."[111] Fundamentally, then, Chalmers agreed with the Malthusian doctrine. The points on which he differed were his interpretation of the trend of production in the past and his doubts of the imminence of overpopulation.

Also in 1832 there appeared a work expressing almost unqualified optimism concerning the possibilities for expanding production as population grows. This was *An Inquiry into the Principle of Population* (1832) by Thomas Edmonds (1803–1889). Here it was asserted that the economic effects of population growth cannot be harmful. Whatever the tendency toward poorer land in agriculture, there has in fact been no diminution of returns because of improvements in methods, for application of additional capital has kept up the productivity of labor. The free entry of foreign grain has obviated the need to use poorer soils in England,[112] and employment opportunity has expanded with population growth. With unbounded optimism for the future, Edmonds assured his readers that "the powers of labour are unlimited," that there are inexhaustible possibilities of invention, and that there is no reason to assume the land can produce only one crop a year. At some future time it may be possible with greatly improved agricultural methods to get as many as twenty crops a week from one plot of land.[113]

---

[108] *Ibid.*, Ch. 1, section 7, p. 5.   [109] *Ibid.*, section 16, p. 17.
[110] *Ibid.*, section 18, p. 21.   [111] *Ibid.*, section 20, p. 23.
[112] Thomas Edmonds, *An Inquiry into the Principle of Population*, London, 1832, p. 45.
[113] *Ibid.*, p. 64.

A somewhat later work was the *Principles of Political Economy* by Scrope (1797–1876). While it is too unguarded in its statements to be highly convincing, the book contains a chapter on population and subsistence that presents a number of arguments against the principle of diminishing returns and the Malthusian theory. Considering the two theories to be closely linked, Scrope attacked them both. The doctrine of decreasing returns he regarded as pernicious and in "contravention to every known fact," for production is increased daily by advances in agriculture and in the useful arts.[114] There are vast amounts of unused land and resources, and the use of inferior soils in agriculture is not evidence of need but of advances in agricultural techniques.[115] The plants and animals man uses for food can multiply faster than man; the earth has the capacity to support "almost any conceivable . . . multiple of the number of human beings now existing on its surface."[116] It is the prudential check that would produce endless crime, vice, and misery,[117] and if want and famine now exist, they are due to "the folly or criminality of man," or to mismanagement of man's affairs rather than to a law of nature.[118]

The *Political Economy* of the Spanish economist Florez-Estrada (1765–1853) was published in 1833 in Paris. Apparently well read in the foreign literature on political economy, the author expressed his admiration for Malthus, whom he regarded as the leading economist after Adam Smith, and he accepted the Malthusian theory of population without major modification. In his first volume, concerned with production, he wrote that the division of labor must be incomplete in a nation that is only sparsely populated,[119] but on the other hand, capital cannot increase as fast as population.[120] As the number of people increases, it becomes necessary to cultivate inferior land, which raises the cost of production and makes the accumulation of capital more difficult.[121] Religious celibacy cannot be accused of affecting the population of a nation because the number of people always corresponds to the means of subsistence, but the abolition of religious celibacy would add to the population to the extent that it enlarged the proportion of workers.[122] Florez-Estrada wrote:

> The growth, wellbeing, and the civilization of a society, as well as the strength and power of a state, depend on the relation between population numbers and the means of subsistence, and in addition on the fair distribution of wealth.[123]

[114] G. Poulett Scrope, *Principles of Political Economy, deduced from the natural Laws of Social Welfare and applied to the present state of Britain,* London, 1833, pp. 265–266.

[115] *Ibid.,* p. 268.

[116] *Ibid.,* pp. 282, 284.

[117] *Ibid.,* p. 286.

[118] *Ibid.,* pp. 277–278, 293.

[119] Alvaro Florez-Estrada, *Cours électique d'économie politique,* translated by L. Galibert, 3 vol., Paris, 1833, Vol. I, pp. 154, 207.

[120] *Ibid.,* pp. 307–310.

[121] *Ibid.,* p. 319.

[122] *Ibid.,* pp. 323–324.

[123] *Ibid.,* p. 330.

The writings of the English economist, Nassau William Senior (1790–1864), include many references to the population question that was being actively discussed at the time.[124] Like McCulloch in his later years, Senior cannot be classed as a follower of Malthus, for although he accepted part of the Malthusian doctrine of population, his views diverged considerably on several points. In 1828 Senior delivered two lectures on population at Oxford in which he agreed with Malthus that population is capable of increasing to such an extent that general poverty and misery will be produced, but expressed assurance that a prosperous society would check its multiplication.[125]

Senior's views on economics and population were most fully set forth in the *Political Economy*[126] (1836). Of the basic propositions of economic science stated in that work, the following formed the foundation of his views on population and production:

> That the Population of the world, or, in other words, the number of persons inhabiting it, is limited only by moral or physical evils, or by fear of a deficiency of those articles of wealth which the habits of the individuals of each class of its inhabitants lead them to require.
>
> That the powers of Labour, and of other instruments which produce wealth, may be indefinitely increased by using their Products as the means of further Production.
>
> That, agricultural skill remaining the same, additional labour employed on the land within a given district produces in general a less proportionate return, or, in other words, that though, with every increase of the labour bestowed, the aggregate return is increased, the increase of the return is not in proportion to the increase of labour.[127]

Senior agreed with Malthus that the human race is capable of doubling its number in twenty-five years, but the plants and animals used by man for food are also capable of multiplying in a geometric ratio. However, population is limited by the diminishing of the returns to agriculture, and for this reason the food supply cannot keep pace with population. Population growth is subject to moral and physical checks, corresponding to Malthus' preventive and positive checks. Mankind is thus faced with the Malthusian alternatives, for ". . . the powers of population, if not restrained by prudence, must inevitably produce almost every form of moral and physical

---

[124] A useful account of Senior's writings and a review of his economic theories is Marian Bowley's *Nassau Senior and Classical Economics,* London: Allen & Unwin, 1937. See especially Part I, Ch. 3, and Part II, Ch. 2.

[125] Senior, *Two Lectures on Population,* London, 1831, p. 34.

[126] The first edition, *Outline of Political Economy,* was published in 1836 as part of the *Encyclopedia Metropolitana.* The edition used here is a reprint, published in London, 1850.

[127] *Ibid.,* p. 26.

evil."[128] It was Senior's belief that man would come to use the moral check to a greater and greater extent,[129] but he wrote that, at the time,

> . . . there are few portions of Europe, the inhabitants of which would not now be richer if their numbers were fewer, and would not be richer hereafter if they were now to retard the rate at which their population is increasing. No plan for social improvement can be complete unless it embrace the means both of increasing the production of wealth, and of preventing population from making a proportionate advance.[130]

Senior thus accepted much of the Malthusian thought of his time, although with some qualifications; but he also maintained some distinctively different opinions.

Particularly noteworthy here is Senior's statement of the two opposite influences that affect the productivity of labor. Contributing to the increase of production is the ability to use the products of labor to add to the means of production. And operating in the contrary direction is the tendency to diminishing returns in agriculture. The outcome is that "Additional labour when employed in manufactures is more, when employed in agriculture is less, efficient in proportion."[131] Further analyzing the difference between agriculture and manufactures in the trend of returns, Senior wrote:

> The advantage possessed by land in repaying increasing labour, though employed on the same materials, with a constantly increasing produce, is overbalanced by the diminishing proportion which the increase of the produce generally bears to the increase of the labour. And the disadvantage of manufactures in requiring for every increase of produce an increase of materials, is overbalanced by the constantly increasing facility with which the increased quantity of materials is worked up.[132]

Senior thus not only stated the opposite tendencies of returns in agriculture and industry with an increasing labor input, but also recognized the fundamental difference in the two cases, the one operating with a constant supply of its raw material (land), and other employing additional amounts of material as production increases. The same point was made some seventy-five years later by Wicksteed, who pointed out somewhat more directly the noncomparability of the two cases.[133]

Considerable originality was shown by George Ramsay (1800–1871) in

---

[128] *Ibid.*, p. 39.   [129] *Ibid.*, p. 42.
[130] *Ibid.*   [131] *Ibid.*, p. 81.
[132] *Ibid.*, p. 83.

[133] Philip Wicksteed, *The Commonsense of Political Economy*, reprint of the first (1910) edition, London: Routledge, 1933, Vol. II, Ch. 5, pp. 527–529. Here it is shown that in the case of the diminishing returns to more intensive agriculture, the amount of land remains constant while increasing doses of the other productive factors are applied. Returns would also diminish in industry, according to Wicksteed, if the labor input were doubled with no increase in machinery and equipment.

An Essay on the Distribution of Wealth (1836). Although largely concerned with distribution, there were some notes on population and production. Ramsay expressed admiration for Malthus and fully accepted his theory of population. He also accepted the principle of diminishing returns as it applied to all old countries, which led to the conclusions that agricultural production cannot keep up with population growth and that mankind cannot escape the Malthusian alternatives, the preventive or positive checks.[134]

The direction that returns actually took, however, was thought to vary at different stages of national development:

> In the early progress of states, when none but land of the first fertility need be cultivated, so great is the excess of man's production over his necessary consumption during the time, that it is probable his fellow-labourers may gain more by the addition made through his exertions to the national capital, than they lose from his competition. But in old countries the case is reversed. The gross produce is then so much diminished from the necessity of having recourse to inferior soils, that the subsistence of the men employed engrosses so large a proportion as to leave but little over.[135]

By implication, therefore, the significance of population growth depends upon the stage of development of the population and economy.

The *Familiar Letters*[136] (1832) by John Burn (1774?–1848) was an attempt to find a reasonable solution for unemployment and related problems with the aid of common sense and sound information instead of theoretical analysis. Reason told Burn that Malthus must be wrong and that a numerous population must be a source of advantage to a nation. Past experience in England had shown that production could advance as rapidly as population, and there was no reason to believe it could not continue to do so.[137] Concerning the ratios, he found that the geometric ratio gave absurd results if projected backward, and concluded from this test that the ratios were equally inapplicable to the future.[138] Finally, trusting to what data and information he could find, Burn came to the following conclusions about the connection between population and subsistence:

> That subsistence must ever keep pace with population, no man in his senses can doubt or dispute. That population must ever press on subsistence is equally clear. . . . Again: increase of population is said to be increase of competition with those already in existence; an egregious

[134] George Ramsay, *An Essay on the Distribution of Wealth,* Edinburgh, 1836, pp. 109, 111.

[135] *Ibid.,* p. 122.

[136] John Burn, *Familiar Letters on Population, Emigration, and Home Colonization,* 2nd ed., London, 1838.

[137] *Ibid.,* Letter II, pp. 6–10.

[138] *Ibid.,* Letter XXVII, pp. 182–188.

error: as if subsistence was stationary, and could not be increased by new cultivators. The new comers are competitors, it is true, for food, but with the existing population to take any of their share of it from them. On the contrary, they are competitors with the barren acres, not yet cultivated, nor needed before the birth of the parties, to get their additional subsistence thence. . . .[139]

And:

Population then as it increases, increases production. Does production, therefore, re-act, and increase population? No, it only supplies the existing wants. Its tendency is, in truth, to retard rather than accelerate population. The most prolific are not the full, but the scantily fed portion of the people, as experience shows to our daily observation.[140]

Although directed toward the problem of providing for the unemployed, Burn's remarks on population were given additional weight by his attempt to establish a factual basis for his proposals.[141]

A final work to be noted in the 1830's was the *Treatise on the Industry of Nations* (1839) by Joseph Eisdell, the first volume of which dealt with production and contained a chapter on population. Eisdell's thought included the old views that a numerous and dense population is useful to the state, that populousness promotes the division of labor, that a sparse population retards progress, and that the postponement of marriage leads to vice. It may be true, Eisdell wrote, that private restraint adds to private wealth, but it reduces national wealth by checking the labor supply and production.[142] Considerable attention was given to Sadler's theory of population, and the observed course of population and wealth was considered to disprove the Malthusian theory. Some assurance was also given that Providence would not allow the consequences predicted by Malthus.

6 · 1840–1849: List to Roscher

The Malthusian theory of population and its pessimistic implications were rejected by Friedrich List (1789–1846), one of the few leading economists to do so. In his principal work, *Das nationale System der politischen*

---

[139] *Ibid.*, p. 184.

[140] *Ibid.*, p. 186.

[141] Applying his observations and conclusions to contemporary problems, Burn strongly argued for settling the unemployed at home in agricultural settlements on waste land rather than encouraging their emigration to the colonies. If population growth increased production, the emigration of the surplus workers would decrease production and add to foreign competition. In the case of emigration, the emigrants would be lost as consumers as well as in other respects. And the argument that colonies would be helpful in time of war was fallacious, for the same people would be a surer resource and strength if near at hand.

[142] Joseph Eisdell, *Treatise on the Industry of Nations,* London, 1839, Vol. I, Ch. 18, p. 555.

Oekonomie[143] (1841), List maintained that each economic order has its own characteristic population capacity, which increases with the progress of economic development. Contrary to Malthus' view, population does not tend to increase more rapidly than the means of subsistence. Large tracts of land remain unexploited, and the productivity of agriculture on the land already under cultivation is being greatly expanded. There are in addition no visible limits to discoveries, inventions, and advances in techniques of production, so that the fear of overpopulation can be dismissed as groundless.[144] Population increase is desirable as a measure of national protection, for "In our day, a nation which does not grow must perish, seeing that all other nations are growing from day to day."[145] There are few if any historical periods in which this national argument did not carry considerable weight.

An outstanding example of the growing use of information in place of speculation on the population question was *Des systèmes de culture* (1846) by Hippolyte Passy (1793–1880). He found, especially for France and England, that progress in agricultural techniques had greatly changed the productiveness of land, and that lands formerly considered the poorest are now among the most productive.[146]

Passy also tested the pessimistic assumption that population growth leads to subdivision of holdings and to eventual misery. From information that he presented in some detail he found that the population increase had occurred in the cities and that there had been little increase in the number of people living in rural areas. At the same time there had been a growing prosperity of agriculture and of the rural population.[147]

John Stuart Mill (1806–1873) made a strong defense of the Malthusian theory of population in *Principles of Political Economy*[148] (1848), and gave the theory its definitive statement in classical economics. In later editions of the *Principles* he modified his position somewhat, but he continued to accept the essentials of the theory. Underlying Mill's thought on population and its relation to production was the principle of diminishing returns. Here Mill recognized the opposite tendencies of diminishing and

[143] The edition used here is the English translation by S. S. Lloyd, *The National System of Political Economy,* London: Longmans, Green, 1909.

[144] *Ibid.,* Ch. 11, especially p. 103.

[145] Quoted by Othmar Spann, *The History of Economics,* translation from the 19th German edition by Eden and Cedar Paul, New York: Norton, 1930. The reference is to List's *Kleinere Schriften,* F. Lenz, Ed., Vol. I, p. 521.

[146] Hippolyte Passy, *Des systèmes de culture et de leur influence sur l'économie sociale,* 2nd edition, Paris: Guillaumin, 1853, p. 54.

[147] *Ibid.,* pp. 204–210. Passy's work was cited at some length and referred to as a masterpiece by Leroy-Beaulieu (*Essai sur la répartition des richesses,* Paris, 1881, pp. 21, 81–82, 94).

[148] All page references to the *Principles* unless otherwise noted are to the 5th edition, London, 1865. Because of the many editions of the *Principles,* references are also given by book, chapter, and section to aid location.

increasing returns from land. Returns tend to decrease as poorer lands come into use, but improved methods have a counteracting influence. As he said,

> Whether agricultural produce increases in absolute as well as comparative cost of production, depends on the conflict of the two antagonist agencies, increase of population, and improvement of agricultural skill.[149]

The influence of population growth, according to Mill, is to further diminish the returns on agriculture, for the expansion of demand with a greater number of consumers operates to force poorer lands into cultivation.

Mill recognized that a certain size and density of population is desirable to provide a sufficiently extensive market to permit the division of labor. However:

> As population increases, and the power of the land to yield increased produce is strained harder and harder, any additional supply of material, as well as of food, must be obtained by a more than proportionally increased expenditure of labor.[150]

Furthermore, this stage of diminishing returns begins quite early.

> In all countries which have passed beyond a rather early stage in the progress of agriculture, every increase in the demand for food, occasioned by increased population, will always, unless there is a simultaneous improvement in production, diminish the share which on a fair division would fall to each individual.[151]

Mill did not commit himself definitely as to whether this stage was already reached in specific instances, saying only that

> Whether, at the present time or any other time, the produce of industry, proportionally to the labour employed, is increasing or diminishing, and the average condition of the people improving or deteriorating, depends upon whether population is advancing faster than improvement, or improvement than population. After a degree of density has been attained, sufficient to allow the principal benefits of combination of labour, all further increase tends in itself to mischief, as far as regards the average condition of the people. . . .[152]

The implication, however, was that diminishing returns had already set in generally. Like Malthus, Mill was convinced that

> The niggardliness of nature, not the injustice of society, is the cause of the penalty attached to over-population. An unjust distribution of

[149] *Ibid.*, Book IV, Ch. 2, section 3, p. 282.
[150] *Ibid.*, Book I, Ch. 12, section 3, p. 238; see also Book IV, Ch. 2, section 2, p. 281.
[151] *Ibid.*, Book I, Ch. 13, section 2, p. 245. The phrasing is changed from that of the first edition, which reads "a very early stage in the progress of agriculture."
[152] *Ibid.*, p. 246.

wealth does not even aggravate the evil, but, at most, causes it to be some-what earlier felt.[153]

The principal points on which Mill diverged from Malthus were his incorporation of the principle of diminishing returns into the Malthusian argument, and, not described above, his somewhat greater confidence in moral restraint as an effective rational check. With regard to the influence of population growth on production, Mill stated in unmistakable terms that the consequence of population growth is a diminishing of returns. The only exceptions to this rule that he recognized were in the case of countries that have not yet advanced in agriculture, or where advances in the methods of production are sufficient to counterbalance the tendency toward diminishing returns.

Brief but highly optimistic comments on the population question were contained in *De la propriété* (1848) of Louis Thiers (1797–1877). All property, he held, is the product of labor, and it is man who gives fertility and value to land. Population growth can create no problems, therefore, for ". . . if we can imagine a day when all of the globe will be inhabited, man will obtain, from the same surface, 10 times, 100 times, 1,000 times more than he raises now."[154]

Population questions were given considerable attention in the writings of Wilhelm Roscher (1817–1894), the leading German economist of his time; and although the topic was not specifically emphasized, some indication is given of his thought on the relation of population to production. In a work on colonies and emigration published in 1847–1848, he described the Malthusian consequences of overpopulation,[155] but noted that a dense population favors the division of labor in an "advancing" or developing nation and thereby contributes to its wealth and strength. Population growth, however, would have bad effects in a stationary or regressing nation.[156]

In his *System der Volkswirtschaft*[157] (1854) Roscher mentioned population size as one factor determining the extent of the market and therefore the feasibility of the division of labor. Population growth was also said to demand a wider extent of cultivation, or the use of less advantageously situated lands. In any case, the costs of production would tend to rise.[158] Opposite in effect, according to Roscher, is the fact that

> A dense population is not only a symptom of the existence of great productive forces carried to a high point of utilization; but is itself a pro-

---

[153] *Ibid.*, Book I, Ch. 13, section 2 (1st ed.): same in 5th ed., p. 245.

[154] Louis A. Thiers, *De la propriété*, Paris, 1848, pp. 131–132.

[155] Wilhelm Roscher, *Kolonien, Kolonialpolitik und Auswanderung*, 2nd ed., Leipzig and Heidelberg, 1856, pp. 36–37.

[156] *Ibid.*, p. 37.

[157] The edition used here is the translation by J. J. Lalor of the 13th (1877) ed., *Principles of Political Economy*, Chicago: Callaghan, 1882.

[158] *Ibid.*, Book III, Ch. 2, section 156.

ductive force, and of the utmost importance as a spur and as an auxiliary to the utilization of all other forces.[159]

Roscher then considered the two opposite conditions of underpopulation and overpopulation.[160]

7 · Later Theories: Bastiat to Marshall

The *Harmonies économiques* (1850) of Frederic Bastiat (1801–1850) remained uncompleted at his death. From his introduction it appears to have been his intention to deal further with the subject of population in a later part of the work, but the direction of his thinking on population is quite well indicated in the completed portion. And from the notes he left, an expanded second edition that included a chapter on population was prepared and published in 1851.[161] Man's needs can expand indefinitely, he wrote, but so can the means of supplying these needs.[162] Here he explained that he meant indefinite and not infinite. But man's desires grow faster than his ability to satisfy them, so there is some want and misery at every stage of civilization. This he believed serves a purpose, for it acts as a stimulus to mankind.[163]

Concerning the Malthusian problem, Bastiat believed the solution lay in something Malthus had overlooked, the greater productive efficiency of a denser population. As he wrote in explanation

> A greater density of population, then, is accompanied by a greater portion of *gratuitous utility*. That density imparts greater power to the machinery of exchange; it sets free and renders disposable a portion of human efforts; it is a cause of progress.[164]

And:

> The density of population not only enables us to reap more advantage from the machinery of exchange, it permits us to improve that machinery, and increase its power. Where the population is condensed, these improvements are advantageous, because they save us more efforts than they exact; but where the population is scattered and thin-spread, they exact more efforts than they save.[165]

This is not so much a denial of the tendency toward diminishing returns as an assertion that the net effect is for returns to increase, the downward tendency being more than cancelled by the opposite influence of the

---

[159] *Ibid.,* Book V, Ch. 3, section 253.   [160] See Chapter 13, section 2 below.
[161] Frederic Bastiat, *Harmonies économiques,* 1st ed., Brussels, 1850; 2nd ed., Paris, 1851.
[162] *Ibid.,* 1st ed., p. 76.   [163] *Ibid.,* p. 77.
[164] *Ibid.,* p. 116.   [165] *Ibid.,* Ch. 4, p. 117.

greater efficiency in production secured through a greater density of population.[166]

Roger de Fontenay, one of the editors of the posthumous edition of Bastiat's *Harmonies,* later published his own *Du revenu foncier* (1854), with the explanation that he was seeking to carry on Bastiat's uncompleted refutation of certain theories of Ricardo and Malthus. Asserting that differences in the productiveness of land are due to man rather than to differences in natural fertility of the soil,[167] he advanced as the real law of agricultural production that yield increases with greater input of capital and diminishing input of labor.[168] Concerning the allegedly opposite trends of returns in agriculture and manufacturing, Fontenay pointed out that industry contributes in many ways to increase agricultural production,[169] and that the data available to him showed that production had increased faster than population, that production per worker had increased, and that real wages had risen.[170]

A re-evaluation of the Malthusian theory in the light of both theory and actual observations was attempted in *Population and Capital*[171] (1854) by George Rickards (1812–1889). The volume consisted of ten lectures given at Oxford, of which all but the first dealt with the population question and sought to separate truth from error in Malthus' *Essay.* Rickards could not believe that population numbers tend to surpass subsistence, nor that the ills of society are attributable to that tendency, and he gave a number of the usual reasons in support of his views.[172] It is true, he wrote, that the mass of people in civilized countries is subject to poverty and misery, but the essential question is not whether these conditions are present, but rather, "Has their condition deteriorated or improved with the increase of their numbers?" The only possible answer is that there has been improvement in the condition of the people.

With regard to the principle of diminishing returns in agriculture, "Experience shows that extended cultivation is the effect of industrial enterprise,

---

[166] For an account of the sources used in preparing the chapter on population and for comment on Bastiat's views on population as presented in the second edition, see notes given by Roger de Fontenay, one of the editors.

[167] Roger de Fontenoy, *Du revenu foncier,* Paris, 1854, p. 42.

[168] *Ibid.,* Ch. III, especially p. 72.

[169] *Ibid.,* Ch. IV.

[170] *Ibid.,* Ch. V.

[171] George K. Rickards, *Population and Capital,* London, 1854.

[172] Among others: wealth accumulates faster than the number of people, and the means of existence advances relative to population (p. 48). Plants and animals can multiply much more rapidly than men. The twenty-five-year doubling of the American population is not a normal growth rate, and it should be viewed in relation to the prodigious growth of resources and production in the United States (pp. 73–74). Malthus compared the theoretical growth of population with the actual growth of subsistence, or compared population growth in new countries with the trend of production in old countries (*ibid.*). Population growth is a stimulus to industriousness and invention (pp. 155–156).

not of physical necessity — the work of increasing wealth, not of struggling poverty."[173] Experience also indicates, he believed, that the returns do not in fact diminish in agriculture. From this review he came to the conclusion that "The most populous nations . . . are populous, indeed, because they are wealthy; but they have become wealthy also by means of their populousness."[174] However, this is true only where "vicious institutions or abuse of the powers of government" have not given an unnatural stimulus to the multiplication of mankind.

A chapter on the "law of population" was included in the German *Grundzüge der National-Oekonomie* (1856) by Max Wirth (1822–1900). Although Wirth accepted much of the foundation of the Malthusian theory, he came to a different and more hopeful conclusion about the course and effects of population numbers. The problem, he insisted rightly enough, was much more complex than visualized by Malthus, who, he claimed, had traced the source of all human ills to one law and prescribed a single panacea.[175] The preventive controls, Wirth argued, are a product of self-control, and self-control is a product of civilization. The commandment to exercise self-control in reproduction is a difficult one to obey, "but it is necessary if we want to be happy."[176] The obstacles to family formation, however, can be the mainspring of civilization; and the growth of population, if it develops naturally from the conditions within a nation, can be advantageous and a necessary condition for the growth of production.[177]

A French political economy that appeared several years later, the *Traité*[178] by Courcelle-Seneuil (1813–1892), presented a quite highly developed socio-economic analysis and system based on principles from economics, population study, and knowledge of human behavior. Concerning the relation between population and production, it was said that the principle of diminishing returns makes the production of food and raw materials more difficult as population increases, but the contrary influences of inventions and other factors contribute to production. Which of these two processes is the stronger determines whether in a given case there is improvement or worsening of the condition of the people.[179] Like Wirth and others before him, the author believed that civilization brings greater use of the preventive controls, especially since in civilized society man's wants rise above the subsistence level.

Concerning population and production, Courcelle-Seneuil wrote, further:

[173] *Ibid.*, p. 139.
[174] *Ibid.*, p. 170.
[175] Max Wirth, *Grundzüge der National-Oeconomie,* Koln, 1856, Ch. 25, p. 448.
[176] *Ibid.*, p. 461.
[177] *Ibid.*, p. 475. These views remained substantially unchanged in the 5th (1881) ed., Vol. I, pp. 504–530.
[178] Jean Gustave Courcelle-Seneuil, *Traité théorique et practique d'économie politique,* 2 vol., Paris: Guillaumin, 1858.
[179] *Ibid.*, pp. 394–395.

There are two truths in particular that should never be lost to view: the first is that every additional person who comes into the world and does not there find what he needs for subsistence through an increase of total production or through a reduction in the share of some other person, is condemned to death. The second is that a lasting increase of population cannot be maintained except by a reduction of unproductive consumption if production is stationary, or by not increasing unproductive consumption if production is increasing.[180]

This presents the other side of the relation between population and production, with population size now dependent upon production and per capita consumption.[181]

Only a few more of the later writers of this period need be mentioned, for classical economics and its critics had little more to add to the discussion of population and production. Karl Marx (1818–1883) severely criticized both Malthus and his theory of population, but otherwise did not give much attention to the population variable in economic affairs. This may have been because of his skepticism about whether there is any general law of population. Every society, he believed, has its own pattern of population phenomena.

In *Das Kapital* (1867) the factor of population size was mentioned in connection with the division of labor:

Just as a certain number of simultaneously employed labourers are the material pre-requisites for division of labour in manufacture, so are the number and density of the population . . . a necessary condition for the division of labour in society. Nevertheless, this density is more or less relative. A relatively thinly populated country, with well developed means of communication, has a denser population than a more numerously populated country with badly-developed means of communication; and in this sense the Northern States of the American Union, for instance, are more thickly populated than India.[182]

The qualification introduced here, that effective population density depends upon communications as well as number of people, appears to be a reasonable refinement of the simpler and more usual concept.

The *Volkswirthschaftslehre* (1868) by Mangoldt, published the year after *Das Kapital,* expressed shrewd doubts about some commonly accepted generalizations. Early in the book its author posed the question of what leads to more successful productive effort in some nations than in others. It cannot be that a greater population gives an advantage, he reasoned, because the larger number of people adds to demand as well as to supply.

[180] *Ibid.,* p. 173.
[181] See a later chapter for further account of Courcelle-Seneuil's thought in this direction.
[182] Karl Marx, *Das Kapital,* translation by Moore and Aveling of the 3rd edition, New York: Modern Library, 1936, Ch. 13, section 4, p. 387.

The ratio of children to adults may be of some significance, however, for that affects the ratio of producers to consumers.[183] This also applies to the number and proportion of old people, and health conditions are also important.[184] Also to be reckoned with are the opposed drives, toward family and procreation, on one side, and toward foresight, on the other. Which predominates is not certain but depends upon the character of the people, economic conditions, and so on.[185]

In the same year an introductory English text in political economy, by James E. Thorold Rogers (1823–1890) was published, entitled *A Manual of Political Economy*[186] (1868) and designed for use in schools and colleges. Critical of the Malthusian theory, Rogers believed that there are strong motives for prudential restraint, and that although there may have been reason for alarm in Malthus' day, because of general poverty and poor harvests, there is no longer reason to fear population growth because food supplies have become more ample.[187]

In a chapter on rent, Rogers attacked the foundation of the Ricardian theory, asserting the assumption that the best lands are occupied first is "quite hypothetical and has absolutely no historical foundation."[188] Furthermore:

> There is not a shadow of evidence in support of the statement, that inferior lands have been occupied and cultivated as population increases. The increase of population has not preceded but followed this occupation and cultivation. It is not the pressure of population on the means of subsistence which has led men to cultivate inferior soils, but the fact that these soils being cultivated in another way, or taken into cultivation, an increased population became possible.[189]

That is to say, the prevailing theory that population growth leads to the occupation of progressively poorer land confuses cause with effect.

The extension of agriculture to poorer land or the more intensive use of better land were attributed by Rogers to advances in agriculture, stimulated by demand and by high wages.[190] The advances in agriculture were believed due not to pressure of a growing population but to "intelligent self-interest" on the part of the farmers, who try to increase production and lower costs.[191]

In the last part of his *Manual* Rogers considered emigration, and rejected it as a means for relieving overpopulation unless carried on in large

---

[183] Hans von Mangoldt, *Volkswirthschaftslehre,* Stuttgart, 1868, p. 37.

[184] *Ibid.,* p. 39.   [185] *Ibid.,* p. 399 ff.

[186] The edition of the *Manual* used here is the 2nd, Oxford: Clarendon Press, 1869.

[187] *Ibid.,* p. 74.   [188] *Ibid.,* p. 154.

[189] *Ibid.,* p. 155.   [190] *Ibid.,* p. 157.

[191] *Ibid.,* p. 158.

scale and systematically; but he believed that voluntary emigration had brought important results by developing remote areas.[192]

The changing position of the population question in political economy, at least in the English school, is illustrated in the works of John Cairnes (1823–1875). In his first lectures at Dublin in 1857,[193] the newly appointed professor expressed the opinion that the doctrine of population is "quite fundamental in the science of political economy." Malthus and others, he said, had answered most objections, and only a few remaining points would be dealt with in his lecture.[194] Cairnes then proceeded to defend the Malthusian theory against the critics who, he said, had misinterpreted it, and he stated his own thought:

> The material well-being of a community evidently depends on the proportion which exists between the quantity of necessaries and comforts in that community and the number of persons amongst whom these are to be divided, of which necessaries and comforts by far the most important item is food. All plans, therefore, for improving the condition of the masses of mankind, in order to be effectual, must be directed to an alteration in this proportion, and to be permanent, must aim at making this alteration permanent. Now, Malthus showed that the strength of the principle of population is such that, if allowed to operate unrestrained, no possible increase of food could keep pace with it. It consequently followed that, in order to [sic] the permanent improvement of the masses of mankind, the development of principles which should impose some restraint on the national tendency of the principle of population was indispensable; and that, however an increase in the productiveness of industry might for a time improve the condition of a community, yet this alone, if unaccompanied by the formation of habits of self-control and providence on the part of the people themselves, could not be relied upon as an ultimate safeguard against distress.[195]

[192] *Ibid.*, pp. 258–259. There is a certain interest in looking back at forecasts made in a previous century, to see how well they have been fulfilled. Rogers concluded his discussion of emigration in a somewhat philosophical and prophetic vein, writing that "The tide of empire may change, and the influence of Europe may, in a century or two, be lost in the vast and rapid progress of communities which, as yet, are in their infancy. But the course of this progress will be the gain of humanity" (p. 259). To this he added that it is impossible for Great Britain to control and defend her colonies in the long run, but that other ties will remain: "the possession of that social system which this country has developed in the course of its political and economical history, the extension on our part, and the inheritance on theirs, of those memories, laws, municipal institutions, and with them those liberties which our race has won, all which it is bound to commend to its so-called dependencies, are a tie which is not the less powerful, because it is seldom recognised as the real bond between Great Britain and her distant children. It is, however, just as strong in the United States as it is in the so-called colonies" (p. 260).

[193] The edition used here is *The Character and Logical Method of Political Economy*, Dublin, 1869. This contains six lectures, including "Of the Malthusian doctrine of population."

[194] *Ibid.*, pp. 105–106.

[195] *Ibid.*, pp. 113–114.

However academic its tone, this endorsement of Malthus must have taken on additional force in Dublin so soon after the great famine.

By the time Cairnes wrote his principal and final work, *Some Leading Principles of Political Economy* (1874), he no longer considered the population question central to political economy,[196] but he did include some reference to the influence of population size and change on production and distribution. The population controversy, he noted, was dying out because of "the gradual progress of sound reason getting the better of the strongest prepossessions," and also because Darwin had recently shown that all forms of life tend to increase faster than their subsistence.[197]

Because of the tendency toward diminishing returns, ". . . as population increases and larger demands are made upon the resources of the country, the cost of producing commodities tends constantly to rise."[198] This tendency may be counteracted by technological advances, "But, in point of fact, it has never been found in the history of any country, that such inventions have kept pace with the declining rate of return yielded by natural agents. . . ."[199] Cairnes also continued firm in his belief that ". . . the limitation of his numbers . . . is the circumstance on which, in the last resort, any improvement at all of a permanent kind in the labourer's condition turns."[200] In spite of this firm retention of the Malthusian point of view, the population factor was now more subordinate in Cairnes' political economy, reduced to the position of a secondary variable, called into play in the adjustment to changing economic conditions.

Karl Kautsky (1854–1938) in *Der Einfluss der Volksvermehrung auf den Fortschritt der Gesellschaft* (1880) was not as strongly anti-Malthusian as he later became, but he presented here a socialist-oriented criticism of the Malthusian theory instead of dealing with the subject indicated by the title. While admitting that overpopulation, although not the only reason for the condition of the poorer classes, would lead inevitably to general poverty, he believed the difficulty lay primarily in a maldistribution of population in relation to resources.[201] A decrease in population such as might have been considered desirable under the Malthusian theory would not operate to the advantage of the laboring classes, for the demand for the products of labor would be correspondingly diminished.[202] In effect, therefore, Kautsky rejected the common theory of the relation of population

---

[196] W. Stanley Jevons (1835–1882) had recently written his *Theory of Political Economy* (1871), in which he took the position that the Malthusian doctrine of population was not any part of economics, and considered population size to be a given factor rather than a variable (*The Theory*, Ch. 8).

[197] Cairnes, *Some Leading Principles of Political Economy*, New York: Harpers, 1874, p. 157.

[198] *Ibid.,* p. 119.

[199] *Ibid.*

[200] *Ibid.,* p. 280.

[201] Karl Kautsky, *Der Einfluss der Volksvermehrung . . .* , Ch. 1.

[202] *Ibid.,* pp. 53, 70 ff.

numbers to production and gave another diagnosis of the economic ills of society.

Only passing reference to the problem of production in relation to population growth was made in the *Essai sur la répartition des richesses*[203] (1881) of Paul Leroy-Beaulieu (1843–1916). It was his opinion that Malthus and others had been at fault in representing as imminent the dangers of overpopulation, when in fact they would not appear until far in the future. Three things had been overlooked by Malthus, he believed, the great resources of unused land, the check on fertility resulting from a rise in the standard of living, and the extent to which improvements in production were possible.

Yves Guyot (1843–1928), in *La science économique* (1881), made an optimistic appraisal of the effect of population growth on production. Knowing of the great industrial progress that had been made since Malthus' day, he could point out that Malthus had not foreseen the growth of industrial capacity and the great expansion of production.[204] And experience during the century, particularly in England and France, indicated that the means of subsistence could grow faster than population. It could even be said that population has an arithmetic growth and wealth a geometric growth.[205]

The Principles of Political Economy (1883) by Henry Sidgwick (1838–1900) marks the end of a period in the development of the theory of population and production and the beginning of the modern treatment of the subject. At the time Sidgwick wrote, the population controversy had long since died down, a majority opinion on the population question had formed in the field of political economy, and from the perspective of the last quarter of the century Sidgwick could attempt a final judgment on "the law of population" and its allied "law of diminishing returns."[206]

Sidgwick regarded part of the Malthusian theory as truism. The key proposition that population tends to increase beyond the means of subsistence and is prevented from further growth only by the preventive and positive checks, he wrote, is certainly not a truism; it cannot be proved and rests on inductive reasoning, but when the proposition is properly limited it can be considered "incontrovertible."[207]

It can hardly be disputed, Sidgwick wrote further, that by doubling and redoubling population can increase beyond the present ability to produce.

[203] Paul Leroy-Beaulieu, *Essai sur la répartition des richesses, et sur la tendance à une moindre inégalite des conditions,* Paris, 1881.

[204] Yves Guyot, *La science économique,* Paris, 1881, p. 187.

[205] *Ibid.,* p. 190.

[206] Henry Sidgwick, *The Principles of Political Economy,* London, 1883, Book I, Ch. 6.

[207] *Ibid.,* Book I, Ch. 6, section 3, pp. 148–149.

There is also the tendency toward diminishing returns. Concerning this Sidgwick made the following full statement:

> The Law of Diminishing Returns, then, affirms that the productiveness of labour does tend to diminish, as the number of labourers to a given unit of land increases, after a certain degree of density of population has been reached. The degree of density, it should be observed, varies with the development of the industrial arts, and the accumulation of capital: it tends to be removed continually further back by the progress of Invention, provided that through the accumulation of capital, the improvement of processes which Invention renders possible is actually realized. The necessity of thus limiting the scope of the law of diminishing returns to communities of a certain density, was conclusively shown by Carey, and is now generally recognized. In fact, in a thinly-peopled country we have to enunciate a Law of Increasing Returns; every additional labourer tends to make labour on the average more productive, since he enables the whole body of labourers to realize more fully the advantages of cooperation. And this tendency to increasing returns continues to apply, in all branches of industry except agriculture and mining, without any limit from density of population, except such as arises from sanitary considerations. The closer human beings live to one another, the greater tends to be the *quantum* of utility derived from a given *quantum* of labour in conveyance and communications; the greater, therefore, tends to be the development of cooperation by exchange; and as the scale on which each particular branch of manufacture may be profitably organized because thus proportionally larger, the production itself tends correspondingly to become more economical. . . .[208]

With regard to the existing status of returns in England and the most advanced European nations:

> There can be little doubt that in these the growth of population has passed the point at which the average efficiency of labour begins to be decreased by any addition to its quantity, other things remaining the same. . . .[209]

Sidgwick's conclusion was:

> (1) that actually the proportional returns to capital and labour in England are less than they would be if England were less densely populated; and (2) that they tend *ceteris paribus* to be decreased by any increase of population even if capital is increased proportionally.[210]

Future developments of invention or of foreign trade, Sidgwick continued, could permit still further growth of population without reduction of productiveness, but no law governing the interaction of the opposite

[208] *Ibid.*, pp. 150–151.
[209] *Ibid.*, p. 151.
[210] *Ibid.*, p. 153.

tendencies affecting returns can be stated. Nor is it possible to predict to what extent population growth will be checked by moral restraint. Consequently, he concluded, the future course of the condition of the people is not predictable.

The trend of economic thought toward an increasingly qualified acceptance of the Malthusian theory and toward a more cautious statement of the relation between population and production, evident in Sidgwick, was carried much farther by Alfred Marshall (1842–1924), successor of Ricardo and Mill as the ranking economist of his time, and the last writer to be considered here. In his *Principles of Economics*[211] (1890) Marshall accepted the law of diminishing returns in agriculture, writing explicitly:

> Although an improvement in the arts of agriculture may raise the rate of return which land generally affords to any given amount of capital and labour; and although the capital and labour already applied to any piece of land may have been so inadequate for the development of its full powers, that some further expenditure on it even with the existing arts of agriculture would give a more than proportionate return; yet these conditions are rare in an old country. And, except when they are present, the application of increased capital and labour to land will add a less than proportionate amount to the produce raised, unless there be meanwhile an increase in the skill of the individual cultivator. Further, whatever may be the future developments of the arts of agriculture, a continued increase in the application of capital and labour to land must ultimately result in a diminution of the extra produce which can be obtained by a given amount of capital and labour.[212]

Unlike his predecessors, however, Marshall did not attribute to population a very large influence on returns, either in production as a whole or in agriculture itself, for he recognized many forces and variables potentially affecting production. Not only is there an early stage of increasing returns, he saw, but also "In the absence of any special cause to the contrary, the growth of population and wealth will make the poorer soils gain on the richer,"[213] since the productivity of the poorer soils can be aided by the application of capital and labor. Beyond this:

> . . . the pressure of population on the means of subsistence may be restrained for a long time to come by the opening up of new fields of supply, by the cheapening of railway and steamship communication, and by the growth of organization and knowledge.[214]

With respect to all branches of production taken together and in the long run, the counteracting tendencies of returns may give a law of con-

[211] The edition of the *Principles* cited below is the second, published in 1891.

[212] *Ibid.*, p. 209. On a preceding page Marshall made the quotable remark, "This tendency to a Diminishing Return was the cause of Abraham's parting from Lot, and of most of the migrations of which history tells."

[213] *Ibid.*, p. 218.

[214] *Ibid.*, p. 224.

stant return[215] instead of a net increase or decrease. Here Marshall was inclined to believe that the net effect of an increase in the number of people is an increase of the efficiency of labor. Admitting that in the extreme a large increase in numbers could lead to unhealthful conditions and lowered returns in agriculture, he went on to conclude:

> All this and more may be granted, and yet it remains true that the collective efficiency of a people with a given average of individual strength and energy increases more than in proportion to their numbers. If they can for a time escape from the pressure of the Law of Diminishing Returns by importing as much food and other raw produce as they want on easy terms; if, as may be reasonably supposed, their wealth increases at least as fast as their numbers; if they avoid habits of life that would enfeeble them; then ever increase in their numbers is likely *for the time* to bring a more than proportional increase in their power of obtaining material goods. For it enables them to secure the many various economies of specialized skill and specialized machinery, of localized industries and production on a large scale; it enables them to have increased facilities of communication of all kinds; while the very closeness of their neighborhood diminishes the expense of time and effort involved in every sort of traffic between them, and gives them new opportunities of getting social enjoyments and the comforts and luxuries of culture in every form.[216]

To this statement, made with characteristic care and qualification, Marshall added with particular reference to his own nation and time that

> The accumulated wealth of civilized countries is at present growing faster than the population: and though it may be true that the wealth per head would increase somewhat faster if the population did not increase quite so fast; yet as a matter of fact an increase of population is likely to continue to be accompanied by a more than proportionate increase of the material aids to production. . . .[217]

In this passage Marshall had reference to the actual course of development as he saw it in the part of the world he knew best, not to the entire world, to a hypothetical case, or to an indefinitely long period of future population growth; and it is not surprising that his viewpoint was different from that of his less optimistic predecessors. He lived at a time of rising returns and growing population, when the Malthusian problem if not entirely lost to view had at least receded into the distance. Like all other writers on population, Marshall must have been influenced by the time and place in which he lived, and these were exceptionally favorable to an optimistic appraisal.

215 *Ibid.,* p. 376.
216 *Ibid.,* pp. 377–378.
217 *Ibid.,* p. 378.

8 · Summary and Comment

One of the first questions faced by the nineteenth-century writers who inquired into the socio-economic significance of population was the old and still unanswered question of the relation of population to production. According to one body of opinion, carried over from the preceding century, a rising number of people stimulates production and tends to raise the level of living; but according to another almost equally old and considerable body of opinion, population growth has quite the opposite effect. Prominent on the latter side was the Malthusian theory, which was in substance a general theory of population and production. Its pessimistic conclusion rested on the assumptions, more tacit than explicitly stated, that the supply of necessities is limited and difficult to increase, and that increase of the number of people weighs more heavily as an increase of consumers than of producers. These assumptions were open to question, and they were questioned; but the opposing optimistic position also rested on assumptions about production that were equally subject to doubt.

Such contrary opinions could persist only because neither theory nor empirical evidence gave a clear answer to the question of how population change affects production. Observations varied and could be variously interpreted, and at the theoretical level, where much of the debate was carried on, the net influence of the population variable was especially difficult to evaluate because the members of a population simultaneously play the opposite economic roles of producer and consumer. Therefore, an increase in the number of people can add to both supply and demand, and it was difficult for the writers on population to see both roles equally clearly. Few if any did. For those who were impressed with the limited supply of land and other resources and convinced of the difficulty of adding to production, population growth represented an increase in the number of mouths to be fed and a threat to the level of living. For those who saw the other side of the coin, however, population growth was seen as an increase in the number of hands that produce and a promise of greater well-being for all.

Both approaches contained elements of truth, but both tended to overlook or oversimplify the heart of the problem, whether population growth in adding to both producers and consumers brings a greater proportionate increase of supply or of demand. The question was in other words, how per capita returns or productivity are affected by population size; and rather surprisingly, the nineteenth-century population debate did not focus very sharply on this issue.[218]

---

[218] It has been said that Malthus never thought in terms of returns per head (Robbins, "The Optimum Theory of Population," p. 104 in *London Essays in Economics: in honor of Edwin Cannan,* London, Routledge, 1927), but the remark seems

The issue appeared to be resolved and the Malthusian thesis confirmed when the principle of diminishing returns was formulated in the second decade of the century. This stated as a natural law of production from the soil that, if the volume of production is increased beyond a certain point, the point of diminishing returns, the output per unit of labor and capital becomes less and less. Here, ready made, was strong support for the Malthusian theory, for the new principle explained how population growth, by adding to demand, tends to depress per capita production. Accepted by the majority of the political economists and achieving the status of a natural law, the principle of diminishing returns became one of the fundamentals of classical economics, and, with the companion principle of population, seemed for a time to have ended the population controversy in favor of the Malthusians.

In spite of the prestige of the new principle and its supporters, however, debate over the relation of population to production continued. It was carried on at two levels, one concerned with a question of fact and the other with a question of theory. The question of fact involved the actual course of population and well-being; and as the nineteenth century advanced it became increasingly clear that both population and general well-being were rising. This observation provided a telling answer to the gloomy predictions derived from the Malthusian theory and the principle of diminishing returns, and the answer was given by Gray, Ravenstone, McCulloch, Whately, Chalmers, Burn, List, Passy, and Guyot, among others. Say and several other writers, however, cautioned that past advances in productivity due to inventions, greater use of power and machinery, and other efficiencies in production do not prove that such progress will be able to keep pace with population growth in the future. When Malthus wrote, he unquestionably believed that a worsening of the condition of the bulk of the population because of excessive numbers was a present fact, not just a future or hypothetical possibility. It is understandable that those who lived in more prosperous and hopeful times later in the century took a different view of the population problem, but some of Malthus' successors, notably John Stuart Mill and Sidgwick, believed, in spite of the greater general well-being, that population had already passed the point of diminishing returns and that the condition of the people as a whole would be better if their numbers were smaller. The appeal to fact and observation, therefore, was not able to settle the question of the influence of population growth on per capita production, even though it may have raised some doubt about the inevitability of the Malthusian progression to poverty and misery.

---

more applicable to Malthus the author of the *Essay on Population* than to Malthus the political economist, the less well known but more substantial *alter ego*.

The question of theory, which received more attention than the question of fact, concerned the long-run effect population growth could be expected to have on production. The majority of the political economists accepted the principle of diminishing returns as the final answer to this question, but some of the writers reviewed earlier in this chapter restated the familiar optimistic assertion that population growth calls forth an equal or greater growth of production. These included Gray, Chalmers, Burn, and Wirth, and they pointed out a number of ways in which an advancing number of people may stimulate production. Others, such as Godwin, Ravenstone, Sadler, Edmonds, Scrope, and Ricardo, struck at the foundations of the prevailing production theory by attempting to disprove the principle of diminishing returns.

Although subject to such attacks from without, production theory and the role it attributed to population were more affected and modified by changes from within the main body of thought. Early in its development, the new principle was recognized as being more applicable to some types of production than to others. Further consideration limited its applicability to agriculture and to other industries, such as mining, that employ a fixed or closely limited source of production, and a tendency toward increasing returns with increasing production was recognized to exist in manufacturing. These opposite tendencies were described by West, and later by Torrens, Ricardo, Senior, John Stuart Mill, Courcelle-Seneuil, and many others. Ramsay and Sidgwick thought of increasing and diminishing returns as occurring at different stages in economic development, the former in new and developing nations, the latter in older nations. Senior was discerning enough to see the fundamental dissimilarity of the conditions under which the opposite trends of returns were assumed to occur in agriculture and manufacturing.

Because of the differing and opposing trends of returns, the net movement of returns with a change in the number of people could be seen to depend upon the relative size of different segments of the economy and upon the relative strength of their respective tendencies toward greater or smaller returns, rather than upon the direction of population change alone. Other lines of reasoning suggested by the developing production theory pointed to the same conclusion, that population is only one of a number of economic variables affecting productivity. In their increasingly detailed treatment of the subject the political economists recognized three principal agents of production: land, labor, and capital. Other natural resources might be included with land or classified separately. In addition, the level of per capita returns obviously was affected by a technological variable that included not only inventions but also improvements in the processes or organization of production. Since volume of production and per capita returns presumably depended upon all these factors, a growth in population and labor supply tending to bring on diminishing returns might not lead to that result if counterbalanced by advances in other factors such as capital or technology. Thus the effect was to reduce the population variable to a position of only one among several factors affecting productivity, and to counteract the exaggerated claims about the influence of population on production made by both the Malthusians and their opponents.

At this point the theoretical issue of the relation of population to productivity could be restated in overall terms of the balance between the tendencies toward increasing returns and diminishing returns at a given level of population size or growth, other variables affecting production assumed to remain the same, and a judgment could be formed even if the problem could not be explored fully at the theoretical level or answered empirically. To the majority of the economists of Malthus' generation it was the tendency toward diminishing returns that dominated, and this view may have been reenforced by a persisting conviction that production from the soil is the most basic industry. As late as mid-nineteenth century John Stuart Mill believed diminishing returns to be the dominant tendency beyond a quite early stage of economic development, and concluded that after the early stage all increase in number of people must lead to a lowering of per capita production, except as counterbalanced by improvements in the productive process.[219] It can be inferred, furthermore, that Mill was not hopeful that improvements could for long keep pace with population growth.

After Mill there was a gradual turning of the tide of opinion on the question of population and production, an ebbing of the fear of overpopulation. The tendency toward diminishing returns came to be regarded as less irresistible and inevitable than it had been thought. The place attributed to agriculture in the total economy waned as that of manufacturing grew. And there was decreasing assurance that population is a major variable affecting productivity. Those who were trained in the classical tradition and who by temperament looked at the theoretical long run rather than the immediate present retained an underlying Malthusian pessimism. Cairnes, for example, could write that

> The material well-being of a community evidently depends on the proportion which exists between the quantity of necessaries and comforts in that community and the number of persons amongst whom these are to be divided . . . ,"

and added the thoroughly Malthusian conclusion that the condition of the laborers cannot be improved permanently unless they limit their numbers. Sidgwick, also trained in the classical tradition, nevertheless grew somewhat

219 As Mill wrote, "The materials of manufactures being all drawn from the land, and many of them from agriculture, which supplies in particular the entire material of clothing; the general law of production from the land, the law of diminishing returns, must in the last resort be applicable to manufacturing as well as to agricultural history" (*Principles,* 5th ed., 1865, Vol. I, Book I, Ch. XII, section 3, p. 238).

ambivalent on the population question, doubting whether populousness would depress productiveness, and at the same time he expressed the opinion that returns would be greater in the most advanced nations if their numbers were smaller. And, finally, Marshall, more a forerunner of the coming century than a last representative of the nineteenth, went even further in emphasizing the multiplicity of factors affecting productivity and minimizing the economic role of population.

This trend, it should be noted in conclusion, did not go so far as to deny entirely the influence of population on production or to dismiss the population problem. The population variable was merely reduced to a position of one among several factors affecting productivity, in place of the exaggerated role attributed to it by both the Malthusians and their opponents. And the problem of overpopulation and its consequences was not entirely dismissed as a product of Malthus' imagination: it was changed from a present or imminent reality to a theoretical and rather remote eventuality.

9

Population and Distribution
in Classical Economics

As described in Chapter 7, the theory of distribution in relation to population remained quite rudimentary through the eighteenth century. Labor was regarded as the principal factor in production, and the discussion of distribution was largely devoted to the question of wage determination. The subsistence theory or "iron law" of wages that developed in the eighteenth century was carried over into the nineteenth, but in the theoretical system of classical economics that developed early in the new century the treatment of distribution was much expanded. Three principal productive factors were distinguished, land, labor, and capital. The theory of distribution accordingly dealt with the division of the total product into three main shares, rent for the landowner, wages for labor, and profit for capital.

Underlying the distribution theory of classical economics were the concept of supply and demand mechanism regulating the division of the product, the newly formulated theory of diminishing returns, some elements of the principle of population, and several lesser components. The population variable entered in two possible ways, as both demand and supply, for its fluctuations could be seen to affect not only the volume of consumption but also the labor supply. Most directly, a change in the population appeared to affect wages, but theoretically its effects could extend to rent and profits. Moreover, a change in any one of the three major shares of the total product would necessarily affect the portion going to the other two. Therefore, a change in the number of people, like a change in any other factor in the economic system, presumably would affect the whole system of distribution. Perhaps because the Malthusian controversy was active well through the first half of the nineteenth century, the political economists of the period gave considerable attention to population and were quite explicit in tracing its influence on distribution.

In order to follow the several elements in this theoretical development, theories of the influence of population on wages, rent, profits, and prices in classical economics are considered separately below. Most attention is given to the role of population in wage theory, for it was the wage theory of this period that bore most directly on the population controversy. The classical wage theory as it related to population, however, rested in part on assumptions about the influence of population on rent and profits, and one mechanism by which population change was thought to affect distribution was through its effects on prices. The relation of population to rent, profits, and prices is therefore described first. The separate elements are then brought together in a summary of the relation of population to distribution as set forth by John Stuart Mill, representative of mature classical economics and author of the definitive statement of classical distribution theory.

1 · Rent

The development of rent theory affected the whole treatment of distribution in classical economics, for it was incorporated into the analysis of wage, profits, and price determination, and at the same time it pointed out certain implications of population size and growth. Rent theory, as seen in Chapter 7, was not very sophisticated before the nineteenth century, and the analysis of the effects of population growth on rent did not go much beyond the commonsense conclusion that an increase in demand for food raises the value and rental price of land. There was one notable exception, however. One eighteenth-century writer, in advance of his time, gave an explanation of the origin of rent along the lines nineteenth-century economic theory was to take. This was James Anderson, who wrote, in his *Observations on the means of exciting a spirit of national industry* (1777):

> In every country there are various soils, which are endued with different degrees of fertility; and hence it must happen, that the farmer who cultivates the most fertile of these, can afford to bring his corn to market at a much lower price than others who cultivate poorer fields. But if the corn that grows on these fertile soils is not sufficient fully to satisfy the market alone, the price will naturally be raised in that market to such a height, as to indemnify others for the expence of cultivating poorer soils. The farmer, however, who cultivates the rich spots, will be able to sell his corn at the same rate in the market with those who occupy poorer fields; he will, therefore, receive much more than the intrinsic value for the corn he rears. Many persons will, therefore, be desirous of obtaining possession of these fertile fields, and will be content to give a certain premium for an exclusive privilege to cultivate them; which will be greater or smaller according to the more or less fertility of the soil. It is this premium which constitutes what we now call rent. . .[1]

[1] Anderson, *Observations*, Edinburgh edition of 1777, postscript of Letter XIII, p. 376.

There is no suggestion here that population growth may push agriculture toward the use of poorer soils and diminishing returns, but the basic idea was there to be pointed out later.

In the early 1800's rent was explained most often in supply and demand terms. For example, William Dawson, a Scottish writer and economist, explained the relation of population numbers to the level of rent and wages in these words:

> . . . the relative value of land and labour must vary as either of them is more or less plentiful, in proportion to the demand. When fertile land is in great plenty, and labourers scarce, and when the owners are anxious to increase their spare produce, to purchase manufactures and luxuries . . . the labourers not only obtain high wages, but the land-owners . . . find that it is to their interest to treat them well in every respect.
>
> . . . in a populous country, where the people live in a simple state, and cannot better their condition by emigration, it is evident, that, as they increase in numbers, land and food must become more scarce, and those who have no land must . . . as tenants, give a greater part of the produce for liberty to occupy land, or . . . (as) labourers a greater part of their time for food. They will be obliged to submit, as their numbers increase, to harder conditions of various kinds, for food, or for liberty to occupy land.[2]

The value of land, by this account, depends upon the supply relative to demand as determined by the number of people; and there is a similar supply and demand determination of the wage level.

Distribution theory in classical economics was especially the work of Ricardo, with contributions and exchange of ideas from Malthus and Torrens. Best known for its rent theory, Ricardo's distribution theory was based on the concept of different degrees of fertility of land and a diminishing of returns, but it also dealt with wage determination, profits, and prices.

Most fully set forth in the *Principles of Political Economy and Taxation* (1817), Ricardo's theory of distribution was outlined in his earlier writings. In the *Essay on the Influence of a low Price of Corn on the Profits of Stock* (1815) he dealt with the hypothetical case of a new country, and for the most part assumed equal advances of population and wealth. Under these conditions the rate of return in agriculture and of profits on capital used in agriculture presumably remain constant for a time,

> . . . because land equally fertile and equally well situated might be abundant, and, therefore, might be cultivated on the same advantageous terms, in proportion as the capital of the first and subsequent settlers augmented.[3]

[2] William Dawson, *An Inquiry into the Causes of the general Poverty and Dependence of Mankind,* Edinburgh, 1814, p. 8.

[3] Ricardo, *Economic Essays,* p. 226.

But if a growth of population makes it necessary to expand food production, cultivation has to be extended further and further afield, and even though ample amounts of land of equal fertility are available, the costs of transportation rise and capital requirements advance as a result. With such expansion of the area under cultivation, according to Ricardo, the returns on the land first used remain as before, but "the general profits of stock (i.e., capital) being regulated by the profits made on the least profitable employment of capital in agriculture," the return to capital decreases. The widened difference in net return between the better situated and the more distant land also raises rent and otherwise affects the pattern of distribution.[4] If population and capital continue to grow, more land must be cultivated and the process continues to raise rent on the most desirable land and lower the return to capital. These effects appear more strongly if cultivation is extended to land of poorer quality. As Ricardo wrote, ". . . by bringing successively land of a worse quality, or less favourably situated into cultivation, rent would rise on the land previously cultivated, and precisely in the same degree would profits fall. . . ."[5] The same result follows if additional capital is applied to land already in use rather than to the development of new land. In any case, although Ricardo did not especially stress the point, population growth could set in motion the development of more extensive or more intensive cultivation. However, in Ricardo's opinion, capital accumulation is the more fundamental dynamic process. It can stimulate population, lead to a diminishing of returns, and produce other changes affecting distribution.[6]

In the same year as Ricardo's *Essay,* Torrens published *An Essay on the External Corn Trade* (1815), which he later expanded and retitled *An Essay on the Influence of the External Corn Trade upon the Production and Distribution of National Wealth* (1820). In general, Torrens assigned a secondary role to population growth, and, like Ricardo, he ascribed to the process of capital formation the major role in determining wages and the growth of population. It was his view that

> . . . it is the accumulation of capital, and the consequent reduction in
> the rate of profits and interest, which enhance the wages of labour, give

[4] *Ibid.,* p. 228. See p. 207 for more detailed explanation of the process of rent determination, as given by Ricardo in his *Principles.*

[5] *Ibid.,* p. 229.

[6] Leslie mentions that Ricardo acknowledged his indebtedness to Malthus and West for his theory of rent, and quotes the following from Ricardo: "In all that I have said concerning the origin and progress of rent, I have briefly repeated and endeavoured to elucidate the principles which Mr. Malthus has so ably laid down, on the subject in his Inquiry into the Nature and Progress of Rent, a work abounding in original ideas." (Thomas Edward Cliffe Leslie, *Essays in Political and Moral Philosophy,* London, 1879, Essay XXVI, pp. 383–384. This essay was originally published in the *Fortnightly Review,* February 1, 1879.)

spur to population, and increase, in the home market, the demand for corn.[7]

Nevertheless, Torrens gave full recognition to population growth as a dynamic factor influencing wages, rents, and profits. He used two now familiar lines of reasoning in deducing the effects of an increase in the number of people on the distribution of the total product, one by leading to diminishing returns in agriculture, and the other through the effect on wages.

As Torrens explained, an increase in population can lead quite directly to diminishing returns in agriculture. In the absence of corn imports, the growth of population forces poorer lands into cultivation and thus raises the price of corn by increasing the cost of production. Rent is increased by the widening of the differential between the best and poorest lands under cultivation.[8]

Ricardo's theory of distribution was most fully set forth in his *Principles* (1817).[9] As in his *Essay* of 1815, he traced the ability of the landowner to demand rent for the use of land to gradations in the quality of land in use:

> It is only, then, because land is not unlimited in quantity and uniform in quality, and because in the progress of population, land of an inferior quality, or less advantageously situated, is called into cultivation, that rent is ever paid for the use of it. When in the progress of society, land of the second degree of fertility is taken into cultivation, rent immediately commences on that of the first quality, and the amount of that rent will depend on the difference in the quality of these two portions of land.
>
> When land of the third quality is taken into cultivation, rent immediately commences on the second, and it is regulated as before, by the difference in their productive powers. At the same time, the rent of the first quality will rise, for that must always be above the rent of the second, by the difference between the produce which they yield with a given quantity of capital and labour. With every step in the progress of population, which shall oblige a country to have recourse to land of a worse quality, to enable it to raise its supply of food, rent, on all the more fertile land, will rise.[10]

Ricardo explained further, however, that it is not population growth alone that leads to the use of different qualities of land and to the rise of rent.

[7] Torrens, *Essay*, 2nd ed., p. 52.

[8] *Ibid.*, pp. 214–215 and elsewhere. Much the same line of reasoning was developed by Torrens in *A letter to the Earl of Liverpool on the state of agriculture . . .*, London, 1816.

[9] The edition of the *Principles* used here is Sraffa's, which follows the text of the third edition but is based on a collation of the three editions that appeared during Ricardo's lifetime and notes differences among the three editions.

[10] *Ibid.*, p. 70.

Two factors at least are involved, for "The rise of rent is always the effect of the increasing wealth of the country, and of the difficulty of providing food for its augmented population."[11] He added that "Population regulates itself by the funds which are to employ it, and therefore always increases or diminishes with the increase or diminution of capital."[12] Population growth for Ricardo, therefore, was evidently only a link in the chain of cause and effect from capital growth to diminishing returns and higher rent.

The Ricardian theory of rent became firmly established as one of the fundamentals of political economy. Whether because of its derivation from the principle of diminishing returns, which had achieved the status of a natural law, or because of the prestige of its author and supporters, or because it provided a seemingly scientific explanation for the behavior of food prices during the period of the corn-law controversy, the new rent theory was accepted by most ranking political economists. Only an occasional writer proposed an alternative explanation for rent or ventured to question the underlying principle of diminishing returns.

Malthus' rent theory was set forth in *An Inquiry into the Nature and Progress of Rent* (1815), and his views of the influence of population size on distribution were most fully stated in the *Principles of Political Economy*[13] (1820), which incorporated the substance of the earlier work on rent. Writing as a political economist, he no longer attributed to population the dominant role he had given it in the *Essay,* but he included it among the major variables affecting rent, wages, profits, and prices.

Malthus and Ricardo were long-time correspondents who maintained a genuine friendship while disagreeing on a number of economic questions,[14] and Malthus freely asserted his own views on rent and distribution theory. According to Malthus it is basically the interaction of supply and demand that determines the pattern of distribution. With regard to rent, he noted four principal factors that can lead to higher rent:

[11] *Ibid.,* p. 77.
[12] *Ibid.,* p. 78.
[13] A condensed reprinting, with Ricardo's notes, is given in Volume II of Sraffa's edition of *The Works and Correspondence of David Ricardo.* References below are to the 1936 reprinting of the second edition of the *Principles* (1836), which presents Malthus' thought more fully at some points than the first edition.
[14] For the correspondence see the *Letters of David Ricardo to Thomas Robert Malthus, 1810–1823,* edited by James Bonar, Oxford, 1887. See also Sraffa's edition of the works and correspondence of Ricardo. Concerning the relations between Malthus and Ricardo, Keynes wrote, "Malthus and Ricardo were not hindered by the contrary qualities of their minds from conversing together in peace and amity all their days. The last sentence in Ricardo's last letter to Malthus before his death runs: 'And now, my dear Malthus, I have done. Like other disputants, after much discussion, we each retain our own opinions. These discussions, however, never influence our friendship; I should not like you more than I do if you agreed in opinion with me.' " (J. M. Keynes, *Essays in Biography,* New York: Horizon Press, 1951, p. 123.)

. . . 1st, Such an accumulation of capital compared with the means of employing it, as will lower the profits of stock; 2dly, such an increase of population as will lower the corn wages of labour; 3dly, such agricultural improvements, or such increase of exertions as will diminish the number of labourers necessary to produce a given effect; and 4thly, such an increase in the *price* of agricultural produce, from increased demand, as, while it probably raises the money price of labour, or occasions a fall in the value of money, is nevertheless accompanied by a diminution either temporary or permanent, of the money outgoings of the farmer, compared with his money returns.[15]

Although he agreed with Ricardo that an increase of demand that brings more land into cultivation can increase rent,[16] Malthus did not emphasize the diminishing of returns so much as the relation of rent to the net return on land. As he wrote, "It may be laid down then as a general truth, that rents naturally rise as the difference between the price of produce and the cost of the instruments of production increases."[17] Of the four conditions he listed as contributing to higher rent, the second and perhaps the fourth proceed from an increase of population. In one case, the net return on land rises because of lower wages; in the other, because of higher food prices relative to the cost of production. Although based on a somewhat different line of reasoning from the Ricardian rent theory, Malthus' analysis nevertheless led to the same conclusion that population growth tends to enlarge the landowner's share of the total product.

James Mill, whose *Elements of political economy* appeared in 1821, agreed with Ricardo and Torrens in emphasizing the role of capital and the ratio of capital to population. Like them, he also traced the origin of rent to the diminishing of returns on capital applied to land, whether applied to increase the extent or the intensity of cultivation. The trend toward diminishing returns and rising rent on the best lands would be strengthened, he agreed, if population growth brought poorer land into use.

The Ricardian explanation of rent and the influence of population growth in extending cultivation to less fertile land was stated in *Principles of Political Economy*[18] (1825), published anonymously by J. C. Ross, who noted in regard to population and distribution that "a scanty and scattered

[15] Malthus, *Principles,* Ch. 3, section 2, p. 158; also *Inquiry,* p. 22.

[16] Malthus, *Principles,* Ch. III, section 2, p. 148 ff.

[17] Malthus, *Inquiry,* p. 27.

[18] John McIniscon, a fisherman, *Principles of Political Economy and of Population: including an Examination of Mr. Malthus' Essay on those Subjects,* 2 vol., London, 1825. Reprinted in 1827 with enlarged preface and changed title: J. C. Ross, *An Examination of Opinions maintained in "The Essay on the Principles of Population" by Malthus; and in the "Elements of Political Economy" by Ricardo; with some Remarks in Reply to Sir James Graham's "Address to the Land-owners,"* 2 vol., London, 1827.

population invariably occasions cheapness of corn and lowness of rents."[19]

From the following year is the first volume of *Der isolierte Staat*[20] (1826–1863), a work by the German economist von Thünen. Von Thünen made full application of the analysis of distribution in terms of marginal productivity, an important development in distribution theory. The concept itself was a logical development from the theory of diminishing returns in agriculture. From the Ricardian theory, which traced rent to the differential advantage of rent-yielding land over the poorest land in cultivation, it was a natural extension to relate wage level and rate of profits to the marginal or least profitable uses of labor and capital. It has been seen that Malthus, Ricardo, and James Mill all used the marginal concept; and priority in its use has been attributed to a number of others.[21]

In *Der isolierte Staat* von Thünen applied the marginal concept to all three major shares in distribution. His distribution theory is described mainly in a later section on wages, but one may note here that the first part of the work dealt with the principle of diminishing returns and gave a quite conventional Ricardian statement of the origin of rent. Rent, von Thünen wrote, corresponds to the advantage in fertility or situation of a given plot of land over the poorest land that must be cultivated to supply the existing demand.[22] Population change did not figure prominently in his analysis of distribution except for wages, but by implication an increase in the number of people could shift the margin of cultivation, bring less fertile land into use, and increase rent on land above the marginal point.

[19] *Ibid.*, 1827 reprint, p. xxi.

[20] Johann von Thünen, *Der isolierte Staat in Beziehung auf Landwirtschaft u. Nationalökonomie.* The edition used here is Vol. XIII of the collection, *Samlung sozialwissenschaftlicher Meister,* Jena: Fischer, 1930. Some sources give the dates 1842–1850 for this work. According to biographical notes in *Allgemeine Deutsche Biographie,* the first volume was published in 1826, republished in 1842, and the final volume did not appear until 1863, after von Thünen's death.

[21] Wicksell gives priority to Anderson, followed by Malthus and West, then Ricardo (*Vorlesungen über Nationalökonomie,* Jena: Fischer, 1913, Part I, pp. 175–176). Whittaker (*A History of Economic Ideas,* New York: Longmans, Green, 1940, p. 592), Douglas (Paul H. Douglas, *The Theory of Wages,* New York: Macmillan, 1934, p. 34), and many others credit von Thünen as the first to advance the marginl productivity theory of wages. A claim to priority can also be made for John Rooke (1780–1856) the self-taught English writer on political economy and other subjects. In *An Inquiry into the principles of national wealth, illustrated by the political economy of the British Empire* (Edinburgh, 1824), Rooke gave attention to the last or marginal unit of labor (p. 12) and to "the last portion of additional produce raised from the soil by cultivation" (p. 57) in applying a concept of marginal cost. In a pamphlet published the following year, *Claim to the original publication of certain new principles in political economy* (London, 1825), a copy of an earlier letter to E. D. Davenport, he stated that he first applied the marginal analysis to rent determination in the fourth of a series of essays, written in November 1814 and published in *The Farmers' Journal* on February 20 and March 20, 1815. On the strength of this Rooke has been credited as a co-discoverer with Malthus, Ricardo, and Torrens of the doctrine of rent (Seligman, "On some neglected English economists," *Economic Journal,* 1903).

[22] von Thünen, *op. cit.,* Book I, section 25, p. 230.

Also published in 1826 was an influential German work, *Grundsätze der Volkswirthschaftslehre,* the first volume of the *Lehrbuch der politischen Oekonomie*[23] (1826–1837) by Karl Heinrich Rau (1792–1870). According to Rau rent corresponds to the surplus produced above the cost of production; it therefore depends upon the fertility of the soil and the amount of capital employed.[24] If greater demand makes it necessary to cultivate land of less favorable fertility or location, the differential is added to the rent of the better land.[25] If for the same reason more capital is applied to land, the return on capital decreases and the cost of the product advances.[26]

In Rau's analysis, population growth increases the demand for food but does not necessarily raise rent and prices. The actual effect depends upon how the greater demand is met. The cost of the product will advance if greater production is attained by (1) the use of poorer or more distant land, (2) the use of capital beyond the point of increasing cost, or (3) importation from distant regions. In these cases rent must rise.[27] Rau believed that as a general rule rent rises with the advance of population and national well-being, for greater demand generally has to be met at greater cost.[28]

Several years later an English work on political economy by Samuel Read[29] (fl. 1829) raised objections to the Ricardian rent theory. Read was an optimist who saw no necessary upper limit to production or population, and he naturally rejected a rent theory based on the assumption of a diminishing of returns. Instead, he asserted that the level of rent depends quite directly upon the number of people and, to a lesser extent, several other factors. In his words:

> . . . the highness or lowness of the rent of any portion of land will depend chiefly on the populousness or otherwise of the place, country, or neighborhood, where it is situated; that is to say, the rent of land will be high where it is thickly-peopled, and low where it is thinly-peopled, and the contrary.
>
> The riches or poverty of the population, and the fertility or barreness of the land, are also circumstances which add necessarily to the highness or lowness of rent.[30]

The location of land also affects its claim to rent, according to Read, who believed that Ricardo had given too little emphasis to this factor.[31]

---

[23] The edition of the *Grundsätze* used here is the third, published in Heidelberg in 1837.

[24] Rau, *Grundsätze*, pp. 222–223. [25] *Ibid.*, section 213, p. 226.

[26] *Ibid.*, section 215a, p. 230. [27] *Ibid.*, section 216a, pp. 233–234.

[28] *Ibid.*, p. 239.

[29] Samuel Read, *Political Economy, An Inquiry into the natural Grounds of Right to vendible Property, or Wealth,* Edinburgh, 1829.

[30] *Ibid.*, p. 297. [31] *Ibid.*

Another 1829 work on political economy, the *Économie politique*[32] by the French economist Joseph Dros (1771–1850), rejected the Ricardian rent theory but on grounds other than those given by Read. Dros did not deny the tendency to diminishing returns as population increases,[33] but regarded rent simply as payment for permission to use land. The amount of rent paid, he believed, depends upon the amount of produce that can be obtained from the land, which in turn depends upon the skill with which the land is used as well as its fertility.[34]

A detailed critique of rent theory was given in a work by Richard Jones (1790–1855), published in 1831, *An Essay on the Distribution of Wealth and on the Sources of Taxation*.[35] In the preface the author explained that he regarded the questions of political economy as questions of fact rather than of theory, for "the experience of the past and present, can alone . . . afford any sure foundation for anticipations as to the future."[36] Having that approach, Jones quite naturally preferred Malthus to Ricardo.[37]

Unfortunately, Jones's views on population and its relation to distribution were not included in the published part of his uncompleted work, except as he outlined his intentions in the preface. However, it can be inferred that he did not consider the number of people an important variable affecting the level of rent. He believed that voluntary restraint checks population growth,[38] and that the rise in rent that had occurred in England was due to better farming and greater production, not the use of poorer land.[39] Jones also was convinced that low wages, such as might arise from an overabundance of laborers, do not benefit the landowners but rather harm them by reducing the productiveness of the workers.[40]

Thomas Chalmers, as described in Chapter 8, denied that the returns to agriculture have in fact diminished, which naturally led him to reject the Ricardian explanation of rent. Rent, he asserted, corresponds to the excess of product over the cost of production, and it does not depend upon gradations in the quality of land.[41]

[32] Dros, *Économie politique;* the edition used here is the 3rd, published in Brussels, 1837.

[33] *Ibid.*, p. 206.　　　　　　　　　　[34] *Ibid.*, Book III, Ch. 2.

[35] Richard Jones, *An Essay on the Distribution of Wealth and on the Sources of Taxation, Part I, Rent* (all that was published), London, 1831.

[36] *Ibid.*, p. xxiv.

[37] The shrewd comparison of Ricardo and Malthus made by Torrens was quoted earlier (p. 169). There is also the comment made by Simon Patten that "Malthus was a much better observer than Ricardo, and the world he saw was much nearer the real England than that of Ricardo." Patten attributed some of the difference to Malthus being a country man, Ricardo a city man and associate of businessmen (Simon N. Patten, "Malthus and Ricardo," *Publications of the American Economic Association,* Vol. IV, No. 5, pp. 350–352, September 1889). See reference to Jones in Ch. 8 for his opinion of Malthus and his followers (p. 177).

[38] See Ch. 12 for Jones's views on population.

[39] Jones, *op. cit.*, pp. 277–286.　　　　　[40] *Ibid.*, pp. 290–291.

[41] Thomas Chalmers, *op. cit.*, Appendix, pp. 459–460.

Arguments against the Ricardian theory and for a different explanation of rent were given by the French economist Dutens in his *Philosophie de l'économie politique*[42] (1835). In his early work, published in 1804,[43] Dutens had touched on population in the account of distribution, but particularly with reference to wages. In the *Philosophie* he did not deny the tendency toward diminishing returns or the ability of population growth to bring poorer land into use, but maintained that rent depends upon the value of the product in excess of the cost of production.[44] It therefore corresponds, he said, to what the cultivator owes to the productive power of the land, over and above what is due to human effort and capital investment. Rent thus increases directly with the fertility of the soil, but is also affected by the growth of population, the advance of civilization, the location of the land, and the ease of transportation.[45] With particular reference to population, Dutens stated that the cost of production of wheat advances as population growth brings poorer land into use. Although advances in agriculture may lower prices temporarily, in the long run cost of production and prices advance with the number of people.[46]

A similar analysis of rent and its relation to population growth was contained in an English work on political economy, *An Essay on the Distribution of Wealth* (1836) by George Ramsay. The value of land and the rent it can command were linked to the price of food. As demand grows the price of food will rise, and some landowners will be willing to let others use their land in return for part of the profit, to avoid the trouble of tilling the land themselves. This, according to Ramsay, is the origin of rent, which arises as a result of high prices.[47]

Ramsay next considered the effect of different qualities of land. If the best quality of land is unlimited, there is no rent; nor is there unless the society has the institution of private property in land. The existence of land of second quality does not lead to rent, argued Ramsay, because rent will be paid even if all the land is of the same quality, provided it is all in use. In such a case, Ramsay reasoned, growth of population and demand will increase food prices and rent, and there is no limit to the increase unless population becomes stationary. If different qualities of land are available, a sufficient rise in prices makes it feasible to cultivate the poorer land. The result is a permanent advance in the price of food, which is regulated by the cost of production on the poorest land whose produce is needed to meet the demand; and the difference in cost from production on the better land will be demanded as rent.[48]

[42] J. Dutens, *Philosophie de l'économie politique,* 2 vol., Paris, 1835.
[43] Dutens, *Analyse raisonnée des principes fondamentaux de l'économie politique.*
[44] Dutens, *Philosophie,* Book II, Ch. 3, especially pp. 226–227, 244.
[45] *Ibid.,* p. 221.
[46] *Ibid.,* pp. 251–252.
[47] Ramsay, *An Essay on the Distribution of Wealth,* 1836, pp. 261–262.
[48] *Ibid.,* pp. 263–265.

Ramsay explained further that consumer preferences, as they affect demand and prices, affect rent. He illustrated by pointing out that a demand for meat can give rental value to pasture land that cannot be cultivated, and that if the demand for and the value of cattle rise high enough cultivated land will be turned into pasture.[49] He added the observation that rural overpopulation is a reason for high rents in Ireland, both because of competition for land and because low wages lead to high profits on land and therefore to high rent.[50]

Only brief mention need be made of a work on political economy that appeared a few years before John Stuart Mill's *Principles*. This was *The Logic of Political Economy*[51] (1844) by Thomas De Quincey (1785–1859), in which a fully Ricardian explanation of rent was given.

2 · Prices

The supposed influence of population growth on prices, especially the price of food, already has been indicated in part in the preceding section. Under the simple supply and demand explanation that persisted into the nineteenth century from earlier economic theory, the increase of demand produced by population growth was thought to force up prices. By an alternative line of reasoning, prices were traced to the cost of production. Here the law of diminishing returns in agriculture indicated that greater production to meet the needs of a larger population raises costs of production and food prices; and other possible effects of population growth could be traced from the same source.

As is known from the history of the corn-law controversy, the high price of food during the Napoleonic Wars attracted particular attention from the English economists, who had assumed before that time that an increase in production such as had occurred would tend to lower prices. In 1800 Malthus published an anonymous pamphlet[52] that explained the prevailing high prices in accordance with his *Essay* of two years before. The real cause of the high price of food, he asserted, is the increase in the number of people. According to his explanation, if there are fifty people and food for only forty, the price of food stabilizes at a level at which only

---

[49] *Ibid.*, pp. 273–274.

[50] *Ibid.*, p. 319.

[51] Thomas De Quincey, *The Logic of Political Economy*, Edinburgh and London, 1844.

[52] Anon. (Malthus), *An Investigation of the Cause of the present high Price of Provisions*, by the author of the *Essay on the Principle of Population*, London, 1800. Here Malthus explained his own position in terms that sound surprisingly modern more than a century and a half later, saying that he wrote "as a lover of truth, and a well-wisher of my country. I have no sort of connection whatever with any of these middle men or great farmers, who are now the objects of public indignation; and, as an individual with a small fixed income, I am certainly among that class of persons on whom the high price of provisions must fall the heaviest" (p. 4).

forty can buy. He repeated his earlier argument that giving poor relief without adding to the food supply forces up the price of food and increases the number of people who are at the margin of want.⟩

Little reference to the influence of population on distribution was made in the economic treatise published in 1806 by the German writer Sartorius (1765–1828), but it was noted that an increase in the number of people raises the price of commodities.[53]

The principal development affecting price theory, the formulation of the law of diminishing returns by Malthus, Ricardo, Torrens, and West, came in the middle of the next decade. Since this was described earlier,[54] it is enough to note that the high prices of agricultural produce were attributed to increased cost of production when cultivation is extended to poorer land. Malthus especially emphasized the agency of population growth, and wrote, as previously quoted, of the higher price of corn:

> A part of it, and I should think, no inconsiderable part, is occasioned by the necessity of yearly cultivating and improving more poor land, to provide for the demands of an increasing population; which land must of course require more labour and dressing, and expence (sic) of all kinds in its cultivation.[55]

Malthus' co-discoverers of the law of diminishing returns traced the same effect on food prices, but emphasized the role of capital accumulation in stimulating population growth.

At the same time, it was pointed out that returns, cost of production, and prices may follow an opposite course in manufacturing. Ricardo, for example, wrote in his *Principles:*

> The natural price of all commodities, excepting raw produce and labour, has a tendency to fall, in the progress of wealth and population; for though, on one hand, they are enhanced in real value, from the rise in the natural price of the raw materials, this is more than counterbalanced by the improvements in machinery, by the better division and distribution of labour, and by the increasing skill. . . .[56]

Torrens made the same point in his *Essay on the Influence of the External Corn Trade,*[57] stated even more fully in *An Essay on the Production of Wealth,* in which he concluded that "the value of manufactured goods is perpetually diminishing with respect to raw produce."[58]

The later treatment of the relation of population to prices remained for

[53] Georg F. C. Sartorius von Waltershausen, *Abhandlungen, Die Elemente des National-Reichtums,* Göttingen, 1806, p. 11.

[54] See Chapter 8, section 2, above.

[55] Malthus, *Observations on the Effects of the Corn Laws,* p. 32.

[56] Ricardo, *Principles,* Sraffa edition, pp. 93–94.

[57] Torrens, *Corn Trade,* pp. 374–375.

[58] *Wealth,* p. 144. For fuller quotation of this passage, see Chapter 8, section 4, above.

the most part in the pattern set by this earlier work. Of particular interest is the treatment of price determination in *The Population and Wealth of Nations* (1819) by Sir Egerton Brydges (1762–1837), who gave a quite original but not highly analytical treatment of population and political economy. Writing to express his disagreement with some portions of Say's *Traité d'économie politique,* Brydges stated that he differed from Ricardo on several points and that his own views were closer to those of Malthus. In part he linked prices to wages, for he believed that prices must rise if wages go too high; and he added that high prices decrease production and injure the workers by reducing the demand for their labor.[59] Later in the same work Brydges described price determination in clearly marginal terms:

> Price is the cost of producing the commodity under the least favourable circumstances of those to which it is necessary to have resort, for the purpose of producing the quantity in demand.
>
> The Price of Corn is the amount of that expenditure in labour and capital, which is indispensible in the least fertile of the soils, which are required to be brought into cultivation, to supply the subsistence adequate to the calls of the market.[60]

Brydges did not go on to point out the effect on prices of an increase in population and of "the quantity in demand," but the implication is clear. His explicit treatment of population was chiefly embodied in a vigorous attack on the Poor Laws. His one conclusion concerning population was the quite general one that ". . . a large Population is only good, when it keeps its proportion both to its means of subsistence; to the due distribution of its Riches; and the healthiest and most moral modes of employment."[61]

Malthus, in his *Principles of Political Economy* (1820), adhered to a quite strict supply and demand interpretation of price determination, saying that both the natural and market prices of commodities depend upon the relation of supply to demand and that this is also true of monopoly prices. He asserted that costs of production do not affect prices, except as they regulate the supply of commodities relative to the demand.[62]

McCulloch's *Principles of Political Economy* (1825) recognized several different cases with respect to price determination. In general, the effect of increased demand such as produced by population growth was believed to depend upon the condition of the supply. In the case of commodities whose supply is limited or controlled, prices were said to be regulated directly by the relation of demand to supply. If the supply is not limited, however, "no variation of demand, unaccompanied by a variation in the

[59] Sir Egerton Brydges, *The Population and Riches of Nations,* London, 1819, p. 18.
[60] *Ibid.,* pp. 21–22.
[61] *Ibid.,* pp. 241–242.
[62] Malthus, *Principles,* Ch. 2, section 3, pp. 69–73.

cost or real value . . . has any lasting influence over prices."[63]   In this case the cost of production determines price; and accordingly, an increase in the number of consumers and in demand raises prices only if the unit cost of production is greater for a larger than for a smaller supply.   It would therefore be consistent with McCulloch's analysis to conclude that population growth does not have a uniform effect on prices, but can raise the price of some commodities and lower the price of others.

The effect on prices of an increase in population and demand would be magnified if greater production could be achieved only at the cost of diminishing returns, or, conversely, with increasing costs of production. McCulloch dealt at some length with the contrary tendencies toward diminishing returns and more efficient production, and described their influence on the pattern of distribution.   Wages and profits were mentioned, but since McCulloch dealt especially with the effect on prices, the passage is quoted in full below:

> Had the inventive genius of man been limited in its powers, and had the various machines and implements used in agriculture, and the skill of the husbandman, at once attained to their utmost perfection, the rise in the price of raw produce, and the fall of profits consequent upon the increase of population, would have been much more apparent and obvious. When, in such a state of things, it became necessary to resort to poorer soils to raise an additional quantity of food, a corresponding increase of labour would plainly have been required—for, on this supposition, no improvement could take place in the powers of the labourer himself. Having already reached the perfection of his art, a greater degree of animal extertion could alone overcome fresh obstacles. More labour would, therefore, have been necessary to the production of a greater quantity of food; and it would have been necessary in the precise proportion in which the quantity of food was to be increased. So that it is plain, if the arts had continued in this stationary state, that the price of raw produce would have varied directly with every variation in the qualities of the soils successively brought under tillage.
>
> But the circumstances regulating the real and exchangeable value of raw produce in an improving society, are extremely different. Even there, it has, as has been shown, a constant tendency to rise; for, the rise of profits consequent upon every improvement, by occasioning a greater demand for labour, gives a fresh stimulus to population, and thus by increasing the demand for food, again inevitably forces the cultivation of poorer soils, and raises prices. But it is evident, that these effects of this great law of nature, from whose all-pervading influence the utmost efforts of human ingenuity can never enable man to escape, are rendered less palpable and obvious in consequence of improvements. After inferior soils are cultivated, more labourers are, no doubt, required to raise the same

[63] McCulloch, *Principles,* 1st ed., p. 255; 3rd ed. (1843), p. 316.

quantities of food; but, as the powers of the labourers are improved in the progress of society, a smaller number is required in proportion to the whole work to be performed, than if no such improvement had taken place. It is in this way that the natural tendency to an increase in the price of raw produce is counteracted in the progress of society. The productive energies of the earth itself gradually diminish, and we are compelled to resort to soils of a constantly decreasing degree of fertility; but the productive energies of the labourers employed to extract produce from these soils, are as constantly augmented by the discoveries and inventions that are always being made. Two directly opposite and continually acting principles are thus set in motion. From the operation of fixed and permanent causes, the increasing sterility of the soil must, in the longrun, overmatch the increasing power of machinery and the improvements of agriculture—and prices must experience a corresponding rise, and profits a corresponding fall. Occasionally, however, improvements in the latter more than compensate for the deterioration in the quality of the former, and a fall of prices and rise of profits take place, until the constant pressure of population again forces the cultivation of poorer lands.[64]

According to McCulloch, the diminishing of returns may be counteracted and its consequences averted for a time by progress in invention and efficient production; but in the long run the pressure of population growth and the resort to poorer soils must raise the price of food and alter the pattern of distribution. In later editions of the *Principles* he expressed more optimism that these consequences might be long postponed, although he conceded that production cannot be increased indefinitely without an eventual diminishing of returns.

The *Principles of Political Economy* by J. C. Ross appeared the same year as McCulloch's work of the same title. Giving a Ricardian explanation of rent, Ross related food prices to the cost of production at the margin of cultivation: "The price of corn, then, is regulated by the quantity of labour and capital bestowed on that quality of land which yields no greater return than is equivalent to the general rates of profit. . . ."[65] Elsewhere in the same work it was stated that it is not supply and demand but cost of production that determines prices.[66] A similar view was apparently taken by Dutens, for he reasoned that the growth of population forces up the price of food by requiring the cultivation of poorer land,[67] rather than pointing out the possible effect of population growth on the balance of supply and demand.

Senior's *Political Economy* (1836) gave some attention to the relation of population to prices. Like McCulloch, Senior believed an increase in population would have opposite effects on the prices of different types of

[64] McCulloch, *Principles,* 1st ed., pp. 381–383.
[65] Ross, *Principles of Political Economy,* 1827 reprint, p. 104.
[66] *Ibid.,* p. 236 ff.
[67] Dutens, *Philosophie,* Vol. I, p. 203.

commodities; but where McCulloch had traced the difference in effect to the conditions of supply, Senior considered the relative weight of raw materials and labor in the cost of production:

> So far as the price of any commodity is affected by the value of the raw materials of which it is formed, it has a tendency to rise; so far as the price consists of the remuneration to be had for the labour and abstinence of those employed in manufacturing it, it has a tendency to fall, with the increase of population.[68]

In other words, the wage and raw material components in cost of production and price are affected differently by population growth, and the net effect depends upon the relative weights of the two components.

Only one other writer need be mentioned to indicate the range of treatment of prices in the period before John Stuart Mill. This is De Quincey, who write of "that land which determines the price of wheat," by which he meant the last or poorest land in use; and he explained further that "the least advantageously grown must rule the price."[69]

The classical economists traced the influence of population size on food prices through several different chains of cause and effect. All agreed in concluding that population growth tends to raise prices, but they differed in the path of reasoning by which they came to this conclusion and in the factors they emphasized. In addition to the fundamental supply and demand concept of price determination, there was the alternative explanation in terms of diminishing returns, or its converse, increasing costs, as population growth requires increased production. An extension of the latter was the linking of prices to the coat of production on marginal land, the least efficient source of food whose produce is needed to satisfy the demand.

At the same time the analysis of price phenomena was further elaborated. It came to be recognized that increased production brings divergent trends in the unit costs of raw materials and manufactured goods. It was pointed out that population growth can also affect the cost of production by affecting wages, which are a larger fraction of the cost of production of some commodities than of others; and the effect on wages presumably would be such as to lower instead of raise the cost of production. There was, in fact, reason to suspect that the influence of population size and growth on prices, seeming unmistakable in both theory and commonsense appraisal, was more complex than had been supposed.

3 · Profits

The relation of population to the rate of profit or return on capital appeared less direct, and it received less attention than other aspects of distribution.

---

[68] Senior, *Political Economy,* 3rd ed., 1854, p. 119. This passage unchanged from the first edition.

[69] De Quincey, *op. cit.,* pp. 217, 218.

Profits were considered to depend most directly upon capital supply and demand, but several writers noted an indirect influence of population. Ricardo, in his *Essay on the Influence of a low Price of Corn on the Profits of Stock,* stated that profits may increase if population grows more rapidly than capital, for wages are then depressed.[70] In the same essay Ricardo suggested another link between population and profits. If population and capital advance equally, he reasoned, there is a diminishing of returns and a lowering of the marginal productivity of capital in agriculture. Here he wrote of "the general profits of stock (i.e., capital) being regulated by the profits made on the least profitable employment of capital in agriculture."[71] Continued growth of population and capital would further shift the marginal position, raise rents, and lower profits.

Torrens in his essay on the external corn trade listed three variables that affect the rate of profits, ". . . the quality of the soil under cultivation, . . . the degree of skill with which labour is applied, . . . and the quantity of the production of labour absorbed as wages."[72] Of these, the first and last may be affected by population size, according to the prevailing economic theory.

Malthus, as will be described more fully in the account of his wage theory, believed there tends to be an inverse relation between the rate of return on capital and the wage level, for, as he wrote, "An increase of capital tends to raise the wages of labour, and a fall of wages tends to raise the profits of stock."[73] He assumed that in the long run, however, both fall as a nation reaches full development of wealth and population. As a general rule, he wrote,

> . . . the varying rate of profits depends upon the causes which alter the proportion between the value of the advances necessary to production, and the value of the produce obtained.
>
> The two main causes which affect these proportions, are, the productiveness, or unproductiveness of the last capitals employed upon the land, by which a smaller, or a greater proportion of the value of the produce is capable of supporting the labourers employed. This may be called the *limiting* principle of profits. And, secondly, the varying value of the produce of the same quantity of labour occasioned by the accidental or ordinary state of the demand and supply, by which a greater or smaller proportion of that produce falls to the share of the labourers employed. This may be called the *regulating* principle of profits. . . .[74]

Over a limited period of time profits may either advance or decline, according to Malthus, for

[70] Ricardo, *Economic Essays,* Gonner edition, p. 226.
[71] *Ibid.,* p. 228.
[72] Torrens, *An Essay on the Influence of the External Corn Trade,* 2nd ed., pp. 384–405.
[73] Malthus, *Principles* (1936 reprint of 2nd ed.), Ch. 3, section 2, p. 158.
[74] *Ibid.,* Ch. 5, section 2, p. 271.

In the progressive cultivation of poor land, occasioned by the increase of capital and population, profits as far as they depend upon natural fertility, will regularly fall; but if at the same time improvements in agriculture are taking place, they may certainly be such as, for a considerable period, not only to prevent profits from falling, but to allow of a rise.[75]

He was convinced, however, that in the long run improvements cannot keep pace with population growth.[76] In view of this and the accepted theory of wages, he added, one might reason that perhaps

. . . the increase of population will lower wages, and, by thus diminishing the costs of production, will increase the profits of the capitalists and the encouragement to produce. Some temporary effect of this kind may no doubt take place, but it is evidently very strictly limited. The fall of real wages cannot go beyond a certain point without not only stopping the progress of the population but making it even retrograde; and before this point is reached, the increase of produce occasioned by the labour of the additional number of persons will have so lowered its value, and reduced profits, as to determine the capitalist to employ less labour.[77]

Eventually, Malthus believed, the advance of population and wealth must reduce the productiveness of labor on the last units of land taken into cultivation, and thus lower the rate of profits.

McCulloch, as seen, came to the same conclusion, that as growing population and demand lead to the use of less productive land, the rate of profits on capital must fall; but he added that the rate of profits may be maintained if increased efficiency of production counteracts the tendency toward diminishing returns.[78]

Malthus' conclusion about the eventual effect of population growth on profits was supported by von Thünen in *Der isolierte Staat*. The prevailing rate of return on capital, it was stated there, is set by the return on the last invested unit of capital.[79] Since an increase in population or labor force was believed capable of shifting the marginal position in the direction of lower returns, the effect on profits would follow.

A different analysis of population and profits was given by Ross in his work on political economy. Ross did not trace the relation of population to profits through diminishing returns and marginal productivity, and he came to somewhat different conclusions than did Malthus and von Thünen. In theory there would be a tendency for profits to fall if capital increases faster than population, according to Ross; but he doubted whether this could in fact continue, for in the long run the number of laborers is pre-

[75] *Ibid.*, Ch. 5, section 4, p. 282.
[76] *Ibid.*, Ch. 3, section 8, p. 195.
[77] *Ibid.*, Book II, Ch. 1, section 2, p. 312.
[78] McCulloch, *Principles,* 1st ed., p. 383; quoted in section 2 of this chapter.
[79] von Thünen, *op. cit.*, Book II, Part II, section 9, p. 498.

sumably proportional to the means for supporting them.[80] Also, as he pointed out,

> The desire of food is limited in every person by the narrow capacity of the human stomach; but the desire of conveniences and ornaments, of buildings, dress, furniture, equipage, the possession of rare and curious productions, artificial or natural, seems to have no limit.[81]

He concluded, therefore, that there is no limit to the amount of capital that can be used.

Population and profits are also related in another manner, according to Ross. Elsewhere he wrote that the rate of return on capital affects the trend of population: "Population regulates itself by the funds which employ it, and therefore always increases, or becomes stationary; or diminishes with the increase or diminution of the income of productively employed capital."[82] Not inconsistent with the other view, that change in the population or labor force of a nation may affect the rate of return on capital, this passage emphasized that in theory population and profits may interact in various ways, with neither altogether independent of the other.

4 · Wages

The term "wages" was given several different meanings in the economic writings of this period. First and perhaps most common, it was used to denote nominal or money wages. An alternative meaning was real wages or purchasing power; in a third usage, the term referred to the share of the total product going to the workers. It is not always clear in what sense the term was used, but in the discussion that follows, the second usage, real wages, is intended, unless another meaning is specifically indicated.

From their predecessors the early nineteenth-century political economists inherited a predominantly supply-and-demand explanation of wage determination, together with the assumption that in the long run the interaction of labor supply and demand tends to stabilize wages at or near the subsistence level, the amount just sufficient to provide the worker and his family with the bare necessities of life and to maintain the population. In this context of wage theory, population change was regarded as a mechanism for adjusting labor supply to the demand for labor, a mechanism that operates in such a way that wages are returned to the subsistence level if they move temporarily above or below that level. The effect of the population variable on wages was thought to be on the labor supply side, for wages presumably vary inversely with population size. In the development of wage theory in the

---

[80] Ross, *An Examination* . . . , p. 198.
[81] *Ibid.*, p. 199. Compare Barbon (1690), p. 60 above.
[82] *Ibid.*, p. 106.

nineteenth century, especially at the hands of the classical economists, other links between the population variable and wages were traced, and a number of factors other than population were brought into the analysis of wage determination. Without attempting to trace the development of wage theory as a whole during this period, the following account indicates the role attributed to population in wage theories of certain political economists during the first half of the nineteenth century.[83]

The *Traité* (1803) by Jean-Batiste Say included a quite conventional statement of the subsistence theory of wages and of the tendency of population to multiply up to the limit set by the food supply.[84] However, it was noted that the habits of the people greatly affect what they consider necessary, and one can infer from this that the wage level would be affected also.[85]

In 1804 another French economist, Dutens, presented both familiar and new ideas on wages in his *Analyse,* in which some mention was made of the population variable. The wage level depends first, Dutens wrote, upon the political status of the workers. If they are slaves, they receive only their subsistence, but if they are free they receive enough to support themselves and their families. This latter level of wages Dutens called the natural level, to distinguish it from the current level of wages, which might temporarily be above or below the natural level, according to the amount of competition for employment.[86]

Dutens also believed the wage level is affected by the growth or decline of national wealth,[87] but in the long run wages must remain close to the natural level because population growth expands the labor supply to meet any increase of demand.[88]

These views were restated by Dutens in a later work, the *Philosophie de l'économie politique* (1835), in which he repeated his definition of the natural wage and his belief that population change tends to adjust wages to that level.[89] He commented further in this later work that population

[83] Concerning wage theories of this period, see, for example, Edwin Cannan, *Theories of Production and distribution;* Carroll R. Daugherty, *Labor Problems in American Industry,* 4th ed., Boston: Houghton Mifflin, 1938, Ch. 4; Maurice H. Dobb, *Wages,* Cambridge: Cambridge University Press, 1928; Paul H. Douglas, *The Theory of Wages,* New York: Macmillan, 1934; John T. Dunlop, Ed., *The Theory of Wage Determination,* London: Macmillan, 1957; Richard A. Lester, *The Economics of Labor,* New York: Macmillan, 1941; K. W. Rothschild, *The Theory of Wages,* Oxford: Blackwell, 1954; and Michael T. Wermel, *The Evolution of the Classical Wage Theory,* New York: Columbia University Press, 1939.

[84] Say, *Traité,* 1803, Vol. II, Part 4, Ch. 9. Essentially the same views were expressed by Say in later editions of the *Traité* and in his published letters to Malthus.

[85] *Traité,* Vol. II, pp. 237–238.

[86] Dutens, *Analyse,* Ch. IX, pp. 58–59. Adam Smith had also written of a natural level of wages, but he defined it only in general terms, as "an ordinary or average rate" (*Wealth of Nations,* 1776, Book I, Ch. 7, p. 66).

[87] Dutens, *Analyse,* p. 63.

[88] *Ibid.,* p. 110.

[89] Dutens, *Philosophie,* Vol. I, p. 195.

growth forces up the price of food and consequently raises the monetary level of both natural and current wages.[90]

In 1814 the Scottish economist Dawson wrote that as a nation becomes more populous and its labor force increases, the workers are forced to accept harder conditions to obtain food and land.[91] On wages he wrote,

> Thus it appears, that the reward of labour, in a simple state of society, is regulated by the proportion that the quantity of fertile land, *which the owners wish to let,* and of food, *which they wish to exchange for labor,* bears to the number of people who have no land.[92]

This is still a supply and demand theory of wages in a sense, but with the difference that it depends upon the supply-demand balance of food and land on one side, and landless laborers on the other. The conclusion is the same as before: an increase in population tends to depress the real wages of labor.

A distinction between the natural wage level and the market price of labor was made in a work published the following year, Torrens' *Essay on the External Corn Trade,* best known for its early statement of diminishing returns in agriculture. As Torrens explained:

> The proper way of regarding labour, is, as a commodity in the market. It therefore has, as well as everything else, its market price and its natural price. The market price of labour is regulated by the proportion which, at any time, and any place, may exist between the demand and the supply; its natural price is governed by other laws, and consists, in such a quantity of the necessaries and comforts of life, as from the nature of the climate, and the habits of the country, are necessary to support the labourer, and to enable him to rear such a family as may preserve, in the market, an undiminished supply of labour.[93]

Most noteworthy here is the introduction of comforts and "the habits of the country" as factors affecting the natural wage level, in addition to the more usual elements of supply and demand and of maintenance of the labor supply.

As already seen, Ricardo's distribution theory emphasized the role of capital, considered population change especially in relation to capital change, and for the most part dealt with equal advances of population and wealth. In an early work, the *Essay on the Influence of a low Price of Corn on the Profits of Stock* (1815), Ricardo linked wages to the relative changes in population and capital before the onset of diminishing returns in agriculture, saying that wages are depressed if population grows more rapidly than the supply of capital. Here Ricardo seems to have been

[90] *Ibid.,* Vol. I, pp. 203–204.
[91] See earlier reference to Dawson, section 1, above.
[92] Dawson, *op. cit.,* p. 10.
[93] Torrens, *Essay on the External Corn Trade,* p. 62.

thinking in essentially supply and demand terms, with capital as the labor-demand function. Under the conditions of an ample supply of first quality land and no change in agricultural techniques, according to Ricardo, real wages remain constant if capital and population increase in equal proportion.[94] But with the onset of diminishing returns, a greater proportion of the product goes to the landowner, and the shares remaining for profits and wages are diminished.[95]

Considering more particularly the consequences of an altered proportion between capital and population, Ricardo classified societies as stationary, advancing, or retrograde, according to whether their supply of capital was constant, increasing, or decreasing, and wrote, concerning wages:

> The rise or fall of wages is common to all states of society, whether it be the stationary, the advancing, or the retrograde state. In the stationary state it is regulated wholly by the increase or falling off of the population. In the advancing state, it depends on whether the capital or the population advance at the more rapid course. In the retrograde state, it depends on whether population or capital decrease with the greater rapidity.[96]

In other words, according to Ricardo the wage level depends upon the ratio of population to capital. This again is essentially a supply and demand wage theory, in which population represents the supply factor and capital the demand factor.

This interpretation of Ricardo's wage theory is supported by his correspondence with Malthus. In a letter probably written in October of 1815 he said, referring to the relation of wages to profits, "till the population increases to the proportion which the increased capital can employ, wages will rise,"[97] indicating that he looked on capital as an employment-providing factor in production. In the same letter he definitely rejected a productivity theory of wages, writing that "Wages do not depend upon the quantity of a commodity which a day's labour will produce...."[98] In 1816, in another letter to Malthus, Ricardo stated explicitly that "wages depend on demand and supply of labour, and on the cost of the necessaries on which wages are expended."[99] The latter part of the statement indicates he was thinking here of money or nominal wages.

In his *Principles,* published two years after his *Essay,* Ricardo followed Torrens and others in distinguishing between the natural and the market rate of wages. These he defined thus:

[94] Ricardo, *Economic Essays,* p. 227.
[95] *Ibid.,* p. 228.
[96] *Ibid.,* p. 236.
[97] James Bonar, Ed., *Letters of David Ricardo to Thomas Robert Malthus, 1810–1823,* Oxford, 1887, Letter No. 37, p. 97.
[98] *Ibid.,* p. 97.
[99] *Ibid.,* Letter No. 49, October 5, 1816, p. 120.

The natural price of labour is that price which is necessary to enable the labourers, one with another, to subsist and to perpetuate their race, without either increase or diminution.[100]

The market price of labour is the price which is really paid for it, from the natural operation of the proportion of the supply to the demand.[101]

It was Ricardo's belief that the market price as a rule remains near the natural price of labor, and that population tends to vary so as to maintain this relation. In his words,

When . . . by the encouragement which high wages give to the increase of population, the number of labourers is increased, wages again fall to their natural price, and indeed from a re-action sometimes fall below it.[102]

Ricardo was speaking here of real wages. In his opinion the nominal or money rate of wages rises in the long run because food prices tend to rise.[103]

A number of original and reasonable thoughts on the relation of population size to distribution were contained in a less well known work that appeared in the same year as Ricardo's *Principles*. Written by John Barton, this was entitled *Condition of the Labouring Classes of Society*[104] (1817). Trusting observation in preference to theory, Barton questioned some of the accepted beliefs of political economy, such as that the demands for labor can grow only with increase in the funds supposedly used for the payment of wages, that the demand for labor ultimately regulates the supply of labor, and that increasing the demand for labor is the only means of raising wages. Past experience, he said, does not confirm these beliefs. On the first point, he distinguished between fixed and circulating capital, and wrote, "The demand for labour depends then on the increase of circulating and not of fixed capital."[105] And the ratio of circulating to fixed capital, he believed, diminishes as a nation advances in wealth and civilization.

Another topic Barton discussed was the adjustment of the labor supply to demand. He pointed out that the adjustment must be slow because an increase or decrease in births does not affect the labor force for at least fifteen or sixteen years, or as much as twenty-one years in the case of skilled labor. The lowering of death rates by high wages must also be slow to affect the labor supply, Barton reasoned, and he pointed out the very

[100] Ricardo, *Principles,* Sraffa ed., Ch. 5. p. 93.
[101] *Ibid.,* Ch. 5, p. 94.
[102] *Ibid.*
[103] *Ibid.,* p. 395; "With every increase of capital and population, food will generally rise, on account of its being more difficult to produce. The consequence of a rise of food will be a rise of wages. . . ."
[104] The edition used here is the one found in *A Reprint of Economic Tracts,* Baltimore: Johns Hopkins Press, 1934.
[105] *Ibid.,* p. 17.

real possibility that workers may choose to use higher wages to raise their level of living rather than to increase their numbers.[106]

The Population and Riches of Nations by Brydges appeared in 1819. Of the wage level he wrote in normative terms, that "(It) ought to be sufficient to afford not only subsistence, but even comfort according to the station of the receiver. But it ought not to go beyond this."[107] As described earlier, Brydges believed that high wages injure the workers by raising prices and reducing the demand for labor. He did not link population size with wage level.

Malthus' views on wages were principally set forth in his *Principles of Political Economy,* in which he explained the pattern of distribution in terms of supply and demand. Paralleling his treatment of the other shares of the product, Malthus stated that the wages of labor depend upon the supply and demand of necessities relative to the supply and demand of labor.[108] In doing this he combined elements of several earlier wage theories and introduced more variables into the equation for wage determination.

Nevertheless, Malthus believed that in the long run wages must be adjusted to the cost of production of labor: they must meet the cost of supporting the workers and of maintaining the labor supply. In his words,

> It is as the condition of the supply, that the prices of the necessaries of life have so important an influence on the price of labour. A certain portion of these necessaries is required to enable the labourer to maintain a stationary population, a greater portion to maintain an increasing one; and consequently, whatever may be the prices of the necessaries of life, the money wages of the labourer must be such as to enable him to purchase these portions, or the supply cannot take place in the quantity required.[109]

Malthus followed Torrens, Ricardo, and others in distinguishing between the market price and the natural price of labor, but introduced in his discussion of wage determination some further ideas that are worth quoting at length:

> The natural or necessary price of labour in any country I should define to be that price which, in the actual circumstances of the society, is necessary to occasion in average supply of labourers, sufficient to meet the effectual demand. And the market price I should define to be, the actual price in the market, which from temporary causes is sometimes above, and sometimes below, what is necessary to supply this demand.
>
> The condition of the labouring classes of society must evidently de-

---

[106] *Ibid.,* pp. 20–22.
[107] Sir Egerton Brydges, *The Population and Riches of Nations,* p. 18.
[108] Malthus, *Principles* (1936 reprint of 2nd ed.), Ch. 4, section 1, p. 217.
[109] *Ibid.,* Ch. 4, section 1, p. 218.

pend, partly upon the rate at which the funds for the maintenance of labour, and the demand for labour are increasing; and partly, on the habits of the people in respect to their food, clothing, and lodging.

If the habits of the people were to remain fixed, the power of marrying early, and of supporting a large family, would depend upon the rate at which the funds for the maintenance of labour and the demand for labour were increasing. And if these funds were to remain fixed, the comforts of the lower classes of society would depend upon their habits, or the amount of those necessaries and conveniences, without which they would not consent to keep up their numbers to the required point.

It rarely happens, however, that either of them remains fixed for any great length of time together. The rate at which the funds for the maintenance of labour increase is, we well know, liable, under varying circumstances, to great variation; and the habits of a people though not so liable, or so necessarily subject to change, can scarcely ever be considered as permanent. In general, their tendency is to change together. When the funds for the maintenance of labour are rapidly increasing, and the labourer commands a large portion of necessaries, it is to be expected that if he has the opportunity of exchanging his superfluous food for conveniences, and comforts, he will acquire a taste for these conveniences, and his habits will be formed accordingly. On the other hand, it generally happens that, when the funds for the maintenance of labour become nearly stationary, such habits, if they ever have existed, are found to give way; and, before the population comes to a stop, the standard of comfort is sensibly lowered.

Still, however, partly from physical, and partly from moral causes, the standard of comfort differs essentially in different countries, under the same rate of increase in their funds for the maintenance of labour. Adam Smith, in speaking of the inferior food of the people of Scotland, compared with that of their neighbours of the same rank in England, observes, "This difference in the mode of their subsistence is not the cause, but the effect, of the difference in their wages, though, by a strange misapprehension, I have frequently heard it represented as the cause." It must be allowed, however, that this correction of a common opinion is only partially just. The effect, in this case as in many others, certainly becomes in its turn a cause; and there is no doubt, that if the continuance of low wages for some time, should produce among the labourers of any country habits of marrying with the prospect only of a mere subsistence, such habits, by supplying the quantity of labour required at a low rate, would become a constantly operating cause of low wages.[110]

Malthus expresses here a supply and demand interpretation of wage level, similar to that of Ricardo and others, in which the amount of capital, or more particularly the wage fund, is the demand function and population or labor supply is the supply function. It is especially noteworthy here that

[110] *Ibid.,* Ch. 4, section 2, pp. 224–225.

population is not considered a completely independent variable as it was in the *Essay;* rather it is affected by underlying factors, "the habits of the people," that are capable of checking population growth and maintaining wages above the subsistence level.[111]

A wage fund element appeared in the paragraphs quoted, on the demand side of the equation; and it was stated more fully in a later section of the same work:

> What is essentially necessary to a rapid increase of population is a great and continued demand for labour; and this is proportioned to the rate of increase in the quantity and value of those funds, whether arising from capital or revenue, which are actually employed in the maintenance of labour.
>
> It has been generally considered, that the demand for labour is proportioned only to the circulating, not the fixed capital of a country. But in reality the demand for labour is not *proportioned* to the increase of capital in any shape; nor even, as I once thought, to the increase of the exchangeable value of the whole annual produce. It is proportioned only, as above stated, to the rate of increase in the quantity and value of those funds which are actually employed in the maintenance of labour.[112]

Like others who looked upon capital as providing employment for the workers, Malthus did not appear to have considered that the accumulation of capital may have the opposite effect, to the extent that capital can be substituted for labor.

The interaction of capital growth and population growth with respect to wage level was described further by Malthus in his account of the course of corn wages (i.e., real wages) over a period of about five centuries, since the time of Edward III:

> . . . though the funds for the maintenance of labour may be increasing fast, the population may be increasing faster, and the money wages of labour will not rise in proportion to the price of corn. To this cause I am strongly disposed to attribute the inadequate rise of the money wages of labour during the reigns of Henry VIII, Mary, Edward VI and Elizabeth. The state of things in the early part of the 16th century must have given a powerful stimulus to population; and considering the extraordinary high corn wages at this period, and that they could only fall very gradually, the stimulus must have continued to operate with considerable force during the greatest part of the century. In fact, depopulation was loudly complained of at the end of the 15th and beginning of

[111] Nevertheless, Malthus still held that the poor were largely responsible for their condition. Elsewhere in the *Principles* (Ch. 5, section 3, p. 279) he wrote, "It is quite obvious . . . that the knowledge and prudence of the poor themselves, are absolutely the *only* means by which any general and permanent improvement in their condition can be effected. They are really the arbiters of their own destiny. . . ."

[112] *Ibid.,* Ch. 4, section 3, p. 234.

the 16th centuries, and a redundancy of population was acknowledged at the end of the 16th. And it was this change in the state of the population, and not the discovery of the American mines, which occasioned so marked a fall in the corn wages of labour.[113]

In addition to the wage fund element within the broader supply and demand analysis, Malthus introduced the principle of diminishing returns into his discussion of wage formation. Unlike some earlier writers, he did not look upon the growth of population and demand as the sole cause of the extension of agriculture to poorer lands. As he said,

> If capital increases in some departments, and the additional quantity cannot be employed with the same profits as before, it will not remain idle, but will seek employment either in the same or in other departments of industry, although with inferior returns, and this will tend to push it upon less fertile soils.
>
> In the same manner, if population increases faster than the funds for the maintenance of labour, the labourers must content themelves with a smaller quatity of necessaries. The *value* of produce will consequently rise; the same quantity of corn will set more labour in motion, and land may be cultivated which could not have been cultivated before.[114]

The real wages of labor, or as he called them, the corn wages, Malthus believed, depend among other things upon how far the process of diminishing returns has been carried, for

> When the last land taken into cultivation in any country is fertile, and yet worked with some skill, there will be a large produce to divide between profits and wages, and it will depend upon the abundance of this produce and the manner in which it is divided, but chiefly on the former, whether the average corn wages are high or low.[115]

Concerning the outlook for real wages and profits in the long run, however, Malthus believed that

> An increase of capital tends to raise the wages of labour, and a fall of wages tends to raise the profits of stock; but these are only temporary effects. In the natural and regular progress of a country towards its full complement of capital and population, the rate of profits and the corn wages of labour permanently fall together. Practically, this is often effected by a rise in the money price of corn, accompanied by a rise, but not a proportionate rise, in the money wages of labour.[116]

The underlying assumption here, fundamental to the pessimistic position and accepted in the economic thought of the time, was that there is a

[113] *Ibid.,* Ch. 4, section 5, p. 256.
[114] *Ibid.,* Ch. 3, section 2, p. 158. See also p. 21 of Malthus' *Inquiry.*
[115] *Ibid.,* Ch. 4, section 1, p. 219.
[116] *Ibid.,* Ch. 3, section 2, p. 158.

naturally fixed upper limit to a nation's population and economic development. The optimistic concept of an ever-expanding economy did not enter into the classical economics of Malthus' day.

Malthus' wage theory is varied, and does not fit entirely into any single category of wage theory. Based on a supply and demand analysis, it considers both the supply and demand of labor and the supply and demand of the commodities necessary to the workers; the population variable, although not emphasized, enters at several points, either directly or by implication. Population enters most directly as the labor supply factor, but it also appears on the demand side, for Malthus related the labor demand to the ratio between population and capital or to that part of capital that is in the hypothetical wage fund. Population enters also into the supply-demand balance of necessities, for here it presumably affects not only the volume of demand but also the per capita supply if population increase has pushed production beyond the point of diminishing returns. Beyond this basic conception of the factors involved in wage determination, Malthus introduced certain other considerations, among them that factors other than population growth may lead to a diminishing of returns, that wages must at least equal the cost of production of the labor supply needed, and that the cost of production of the labor supply and therefore the level of wages depend upon "the habits of the people."

The discussion of wages in James Mill's *Elements of Political Economy* (1821) centered around the proposition that "the rate of wages depends on the proportion between Population, and Employment, in other words, Capital."[117] To quote from Mill's own summary,

> It thus appears, that, if population increases, without an increase of capital, wages fall; and that, if capital increases, without an increase of population, wages rise. It is evident, also, that if both increase, but one faster than the other, the effect will be the same as if the one had not increased at all, and the other had made an increase equal to the difference.[118]

> Universally, then, we may affirm, other things remaining the same, that if the ratio which capital and population bear to one another remains the same, wages will remain the same; if the ratio which capital bears to population increases, wages will rise; if the ratio which population bears to capital increases, wages will fall.[119]

From this mechanism of wage determination, together with the assumed rise or fall of mortality with increased poverty or prosperity, Mill came to

[117] James Mill, *Elements of Political Economy,* (2nd ed., 1824), Ch. 2, section 2, p. 41.
[118] *Ibid.,* p. 43.
[119] *Ibid.,* p. 44.

a theory of automatic adjustment of the rate of population growth to the rate of capital accumulation.[120]

Close agreement with Malthus' population and wage theories was expressed by Thomas Joplin (c. 1790–1847) in his *Outlines of a System of Political Economy* (1823). It is, therefore, enough to note his belief in natural regulation of wage level. Wages, he stated, are regulated by labor supply and demand, and the elasticity of the labor supply soon adjusts it to meet changes in demand.[121] If war, pestilence, or famine decrease the number of people, he explained, there is only a temporary rise in money wages because the higher wages increase the cost of commodities and thereby lead to a lower demand. The balance of foreign trade also becomes unfavorable if prices rise, and as a result prices eventually are forced to a lower level. Money wages must fall along with prices, but real wages may remain for a time above the original level until population growth has restored the original numbers.[122] This population adjustment would not be long delayed, Joplin was confident, for "Population keeps so close upon the means of subsistence, that an increased demand for labour is very soon supplied."[123]

Ranking with Malthus' *Principles* for its treatment of wage theory was McCulloch's work of the same title published five years later. Like many other political economists of the time, McCulloch distinguished between a "natural" level of wages and the market or actual wage. The former he defined thus:

> The natural or necessary rate of wages must, therefore, be determined by the cost of producing the food and other articles which enter into the consumption of the labourers. And though a rise in the market or current rate of wages is seldom exactly coincident with a rise in the price of necessaries, they can never, except in the rare case when the market rate of wages greatly exceeds the natural or necessary rate, be very far separated. However high the price of commodities may rise, the labourers must always receive a supply equivalent for their support: If they did not obtain this supply, they would be left destitute; and disease and death would continue to thin the population, until the reduced numbers bore such a proportion to the national capital as would enable them to obtain the means of subsistence.[124]

[120] As previously quoted, "By whatever proportion the population tended to increase faster than capital, such a proportion of those who were born would die; the ratio of increase in capital and population would thence remain the same . . ." (*Ibid.*, Ch. 2, section 2).

[121] Thomas Joplin, *Outlines of a System of Political Economy*, London, 1823, pp. 91–92.

[122] *Ibid.*, pp. 97–98.

[123] *Ibid.*, p. 99.

[124] McCulloch, *Principles*, 1st ed., pp. 335–336. See also *Treatise on Wages*, p. 94, for similar statement.

McCulloch explained further that he did not consider the natural level of wages fixed at the subsistence minimum, as was assumed in the "iron law" of wages, but rather that the natural level is sufficient to provide the workers with what habit makes necessary to them. This opinion was later restated in his *Treatise on the Circumstances which determine the Rate of Wages* (1851), in which he noted that the natural rate of wages is sufficient to provide subsistence for the workers and their families, and that it depends upon the cost of necessaries and on the "habits and customs" of the poor.[125] This fully agreed with Malthus' conception of the natural level of wages.

In one respect McCulloch's wage theory and that of the principal contemporary political economists resembled the older "iron law" of wages, for it assumed an automatic stabilization of the wage level through population increase or decrease. As described earlier, McCulloch thought a drop in wages below the natural level would bring a diminution of the labor supply and a subsequent return of wages to their former level. The opposite adjustment would occur if market wages long exceeded the natural price of labor. But McCulloch suggested an alternative mode of adjustment, for he believed that a longstanding disparity between the natural and market prices of labor might be eliminated by an upward or downward adjustment of the natural price rather than by a change in the market price of labor. That is to say, there might be an upward or downward revision of the consumption habits of the people.[126]

An upward or downward revision of the consumption habits of the people is likely to occur, McCulloch argued, because of the long period required for the labor supply to adjust to the demand. As he wrote in the first edition of the *Principles,*

> The natural or necessary rate of wages is not, therefore, a fixed or unvarying quantity; and though it be strictly true that the market rate of wages can never sink permanently below its contemporary natural rate, it is no less true that this natural rate has a tendency to rise when the market rate rises, and to fall when it falls. The reason is, that the number of labourers in the market is a given quantity, which can neither be speedily increased when wages rise, nor speedily diminished when they fall. When wages rise, a period of eighteen or twenty years must plainly elapse before the effect of the increased stimulus that the rise gives to the principle of population can be felt in the market. During all this period, therefore, the labourers have an increased command over the necessaries and conveniences of life:[127] In consequence their habits are improved;

[125] *Treatise on Wages,* pp. 25–26; also p. 31, where McCulloch quotes Adam Smith in support of this concept of the natural rate of wages.

[126] McCulloch, *Principles,* 1st ed., pp. 344–346; also, *Treatise on Taxation,* pp. 164, 381; and *Treatise on Wages,* pp. 33–34. Compare Malthus' *Principles,* pp. 224–225, quoted above.

[127] Except, it should be noted, that the laborer has to support an additional number of children from birth until they enter the labor force. (Footnote added.)

and as they learn to form more exalted notions with respect to what is required for their comfortable and decent support, the natural or necessary rate of wages is proportionally augmented. But, on the other hand, when the rate of wages declines either in consequence of an actual diminution of the capital of the country, or of a disproportionate increase of population, no corresponding immediate diminution can take place in the number of labourers, unless they have previously been subsisting on the smallest possible quantity of the cheapest species of food required to support mere animal existence. If the labourers have not been placed so very near the extreme limit of subsistence, their numbers will not be immediately reduced when wages fall, by an increase of mortality; but they will be gradually reduced, partly, as has been already shown, in that way, and partly by a diminished number of marriages and births:[128] And in most countries, unless the fall were both sudden and extensive, it would require some years to render the effects of increased mortality, in diminishing the supply of labour in the market, very sensibly felt; while the force of habit, and the universal ignorance of the people with respect to the circumstances which determine the rate of wages, would prevent any effectual check being given to the formation of matrimonial connections, and consequently to the rate at which fresh labourers had previously been coming into market, until the misery occasioned by the restricted demand on the one hand, and the undiminished supply on the other, had been very generally and widely felt.[129]

McCulloch repeated the argument concerning the lag in the adjustment of labor supply to demand in the *Treatise on Taxation* and the *Treatise on Wages.*[130]

In his discussion of wages, McCulloch dissented from the older and more widely accepted view that low wages are advantageous to the employer and to the society as a whole. As he wrote, in the first edition of the *Principles:*

It has . . . been often contended . . . that high wages, instead of encouraging industry, uniformly become a fruitful source of idleness and dissipation. Nothing, however, can be more entirely incorrect than these representations — more completely opposed both to principle and experience. . . . Whenever the wages of labour are so low, as to render it impossible for an ordinary increase of exertion to make any material and visible addition to their comforts and conveniences, the labourers invariably sink into a state of idleness, and of sluggish and stupid indifference. But the desire to rise in the world, and to improve our condition is too deeply seated in the human breast ever to be wholly eradicated. And as soon as labour is rendered more productive, as soon as an in-

---

[128] Here again the same long lag must follow before the supply of new workers entering the labor force each year is reduced, except as mortality may deplete the number. (Footnote added.)

[129] McCulloch, *Principles,* 1st ed., pp. 344–346. Repeated in the 3rd edition, pp. 392–393, with only minor changes in wording.

[130] McCulloch, *Treatise on Taxation,* p. 164; *Treatise on Wages,* pp. 33–35.

crease of industry brings a visible increase of comforts and enjoyments along with it, indolence uniformly gives place to exertion; a taste for the conveniences and enjoyments of life gradually diffuses itself; increased exertions are made to obtain them; and ultimately the workman considers it discreditable to be without them. . . . The experience of all ages and nations, proves that high wages are at once the keenest spur — the most powerful stimulus to unremitting and assiduous exertion, and the best means of attaching the people to the institutions under which they live.[131]

Remarkable in its time, even by modern standards this is a highly enlightened statement of the advantages of a high wage level to a society. In the *Treatise on Taxation* McCulloch further recommended high wages:

A population which consumes but few luxuries is always in a very perilous situation; being confined to necessaries, it can make few or no retrenchments in bad years, so that if dearth in such cases be not accompanied with all the horrors of famine, it must drive the poor in crowds to the workhouse. But a population which is habitually supplied with luxuries can, by relinquishing or diminishing their use, provide a resource in bad years, and can withstand their pressure with comparatively little difficulty.[132]

McCulloch returned to the subject in the *Treatise on Wages,* in which he asserted that "No country can be flourishing where wages are low; and none can be long depressed where they are high," and that the true interest of the capitalist or employer is not opposed to that of the worker because security and tranquillity are more important than high profits alone.[133]

Another aspect of wages McCulloch considered was the proportion of the total product they claim, as distinct from their actual amount in money or commodities. The proportion going to labor was seen to depend upon several factors, but especially on the ease or difficulty of production. McCulloch, who accepted the theory of diminishing returns and the Ricardian explanation of rent, believed that labor's portion of the total product is relatively small when only fertile soils are used, and that it increases as cultivation is extended to poorer and poorer soils, except as this is counteracted by inventions and other advances in the technology of production.

The *Principles of Political Economy* (1825) by J. C. Ross, who wrote under the pseudonym McIniscon, presented views that were for the most part generally accepted, but with some distinctive turns of thought. Like his contemporaries in political economy, Ross recognized both a "natural"

---

[131] McCulloch, *Principles,* 1st ed., pp. 352–353. Compare earlier statements of the same point of view by Defoe and Adam Smith, Chapter 7, section 1, above.

[132] McCulloch, *Treatise on Taxation,* p. 381.

[133] McCulloch, *Treatise on Wages,* pp. 47, 48–49.

price and a market price of labor.[134] He believed that if government does not interfere, market wages remain at or near the natural level and the return on capital is sufficient to permit wage payments that will provide the worker with ". . . the necessaries and enjoyments adapted to his station in life, sufficient for what he may deem the comfortable existence of himself, and a family of an average number."[135] This was Ross's concept of the natural wage level. Here he explained that in the natural state of society, by which he presumably meant in the absence of government interference, capital growth is sufficient to provide for the natural increase in the number of people.[136] But it may be inferred that Ross was by no means optimistic about the natural state of society being maintained, for he added the gloomy comment that the natural price of labor ". . . depends on the habits and customs of the people, and on the amount of the contributions levied on them for the support of idleness, priestcraft, kingcraft, and open tyranny."[137]

Population growth, said Ross, leaves wages unaffected, provided capital grows at a similar rate; but if it becomes more difficult to provide food for a growing population, then the natural price of labor must rise unless there are compensating advances in agricultural techniques.[138]

Quite conventionally, Ross attributed fluctuations in wages to variations in labor supply and demand and to varying prices of commodities,[139] but for the long run he linked wages to the relative rates of growth of population and capital. If the people of a nation are poor and miserable, he wrote, it is because capital has advanced less rapidly than population, and this condition in turn he attributed to ignorance and misgovernment: "Capital can be more easily destroyed than population."[140]

In 1826 there appeared two important German works that dealt in part with wage theory, the *Grundsätze der Volkswirthschaftslehre,* the first volume of Rau's *Lehrbuch,* and the first portion of von Thünen's *Der isolierte Staat.* Rau's treatment of wages was a systematic and conservative statement of the theory of wage determination before the use of the concept of marginal productivity. He began by dealing quite explicitly with the necessary or minimum level of wages. The wages of simple unskilled labor, he wrote, must be sufficient to meet the subsistence needs of the workers, and this depends not only upon the length of their working lifetime but also upon the age at which they enter the labor force. The total wages of laborers must therefore be sufficient to support the laboring class as a whole, including the families of the laborers. Otherwise the labor supply will diminish until the wage level rises.[141]

Rau explained further that the needs of the workers also depend upon

134 Ross, *op. cit.,* Ch. VII, p. 65.   135 *Ibid.,* p. 66.
136 *Ibid.,* p. 68.   137 *Ibid.,* p. 69.
138 *Ibid.,* p. 66.   139 *Ibid.,* p. 71.
140 *Ibid.,* pp. 80–81.
141 Rau, *Grundsätze,* 3rd ed., section 190, p. 194.

their customary mode of life, which is affected by the climate and natural conditions of the region, by the customary standard of living dependent in part upon the previous level of wages, and by the position of the various classes of laborers in the society.[142] The monetary wage level also is affected by the price of the most important foods and necessities.[143] In this connection Rau noted that population increase and the advancement of general well-being in a nation tend to raise the prices of plant and animal products because of the greater difficulty of producing more; but the prices of mineral products do not necessarily advance in the same manner.[144]

According to Rau, the supply of capital affects the level of wages. With an ample supply of capital, wages can be higher than they would be otherwise, but the high wages tend to limit themselves because they stimulate an increase in the labor supply.[145]

Rau's final comment on wages was that high wages permit better care and training of children. This gives a nation a larger population, and a better trained, more industrious, and more cultivated body of citizens.[146]

As described earlier, von Thünen applied marginal productivity analysis to rent, wage, and profit determination in terms of the contribution to the total product made by the last unit of land, labor, or capital. In the second part of *Der isolierte Staat* (1826–1863) von Thünen developed his wage theory. In the hypothetical case of an estate whose labor force is being expanded, more workers can be added until the amount contributed to the total product by the last worker is just equal to his wages. When the increment of returns is reduced to this level, no more workers can be employed unless wages are reduced. Assuming that this is done and that all the workers are of equal skill, the wages of all are reduced, not merely the wages of the last men to be hired.[147]

Von Thünen extended this illustration to a more general application, with the statement that labor's low wages are due to the early marriage and rapid increase of the laboring classes such that the supply of labor exceeds the demand. Like Malthus before him, von Thünen concluded that the workers themselves are responsible for their low wages.[148]

In a parallel way, the prevailing rate of return on capital was said to be set by the return on the last invested unit of capital.[149] From this it followed, according to von Thünen, that it is to the advantage of the workers if capital accumulates, for that raises the level of wages by diminishing the share of the product going to capital.[150]

[142] *Ibid.*, section 191, p. 196.　　[143] *Ibid.*, section 192, p. 197.
[144] *Ibid.*, section 185, p. 187.　　[145] *Ibid.*, section 199, p. 208.
[146] *Ibid.*, section 201, p. 211.
[147] von Thünen, *op. cit.*, Book II, Introduction, pp. 415–416. See also Book II, section 4, p. 464, and section 19, pp. 576–577.
[148] *Ibid.*, Book II, section 2, p. 441.
[149] *Ibid.*, Book II, section 9, p. 498.
[150] *Ibid.*, p. 499.

Von Thünen summarized his position with regard to wages as follows:

> If the population in the laboring classes increases while the amount
> of cultivated land and of capital remains constant, the additional laborers
> cannot be employed at the prevailing wage. This is for the reason that
> this wage takes the entire product of the last laborer to be employed, and
> every additional worker would produce a smaller product, so that the em-
> ployment of the additional laborers at the prevailing wage would result
> in loss to the entrepreneur. Only if these workers accept a lower wage
> could the entrepreneur employ them and undertake new work, whose
> value corresponds to the lowered wage.
>
> If the number of workers still increases in spite of the declining wage
> level, wages must fall lower and lower because the work performed be-
> comes less and less productive.
>
> Now if with a growing population labor is expended on progressively
> less profitable objects and on progressively poorer soil, where is the lower
> limit of wages?
>
> This limit is not reached until labor becomes so unproductive that its
> product becomes equal . . . to the subsistence level; for man cannot work
> for a wage less than what is necessary for his sustenance.[151]

Von Thünen's wage theory contains elements of supply and demand, of
subsistence, and of productivity theory. It may be regarded as a logical
synthesis and development of the contemporary wage theories. In the
present connection von Thünen's application of the concept of marginal
productivity is particularly significant because it provides a definite theoretical mechanism by which the growth of population and labor supply,
like any other change in the factors of production, shifts the marginal
position and alters the distribution of the product among landowner, labor,
and capitalist. In von Thünen's presentation, the population variable
affects wages directly in two ways, first, by increasing demand and pushing
production toward diminished returns, and second, by adding to the labor
supply. In both ways the marginal productivity of labor and thus the wage
level may be affected; but in von Thünen's static analysis these two con-
current or consecutive effects of population growth were not considered
together. This can also be said, of course, of the other contemporary
treatments of population and wage theory.

After the development of distribution theory by Ricardo, Malthus, von
Thünen, and others of their period, before John Stuart Mill, little was
added to the analysis of the relation of population and wages. Thus it is
sufficient to mention briefly only a few writers during this period, to indicate
current thought on wages and some of the more distinctive points of view.

The *Political Economy* (1829) of Samuel Read devoted a chapter to
the subject of wages and gave particular attention to the influence of non-

[151] *Ibid.,* Book II, section 19, pp. 579–580.

economic factors. According to Read, the natural level of wages depends in the first place upon the number of workers competing for employment, that is, upon the size of the population;[152] but the number of people is affected in turn by the political conditions under which they live. With regard to the tendency of population to increase up to the subsistence limit, he asserted

> . . . it is only where they are ill-governed, oppressed, and ignorant, that the inferior ranks of people multiply beyond the limits of a liberal subsistence. Under other circumstances they must necessarily . . . improve their condition, and habits, and modes of life, and acquire higher and higher wages in proportion as wealth and population increase.[153]

He added that:

> There is no necessity, however, in the nature of things, or in fact, that wealth, or population, or wages, should ever decrease or diminish, or even become stationary upon the earth; for as the produce of the earth (and still more wealth in general) may be continually and indefinitely augmented, it follows incontestably that both population and wages may be continually and indefinitely augmented also; because, let the augmentation of wealth be great or small, it is evidently possible that a part of it may go to support additional numbers, or inhabitants, and another part to augment the wages of labour; and to produce this result, it is only necessary that population should increase in a less degree than wealth, (which, as I have already demonstrated, is uniformly and invariably the case), and that the labourer should be placed under circumstances favourable to the development of his prudential habits, i.e. in a state of security under good government.[154]

Thus taking the view of the earlier population optimists that the ills of society are due to mismanagement rather than to inescapable natural causes, Read criticized Malthus' theory of population, and summarized his own position by asserting that the condition of the lower classes of society depends upon whether they are subject to good or bad government.[155]

The *Cours éclectique d'économie politique* by the Spanish economist Florez-Estrada, published in French translation in 1833, gave a fairly conventional account of distribution. Wages were said to fluctuate with variations in the ratio of the number of workers to the amount of capital with which to pay them,[156] and as a result, wages must fall if population grows more rapidly than capital.[157] However, a lower limit on wages is set by the price of commodities that are indispensable to the workers.[158] In the

---

[152] Read, *Political Economy*, p. 325.   [153] *Ibid.*, p. 326.
[154] *Ibid.*, p. 328.   [155] *Ibid.*, p. 330.
[156] Florez-Estrada, *Cours éclectique d'économie politique*, Vol. II, p. 102.
[157] *Ibid.*, Vol. II, p. 91.
[158] *Ibid.*, Vol. II, p. 94.

long run, wages must fall as the wealth and population of a nation increase, because it becomes progressively more difficult to obtain subsistence.[159] Nevertheless Florez-Estrada was confident that improvement in the mode of life of the working class would prevent excessive growth of population.[160]

Nassau William Senior set forth his views on wages in a series of lectures published in 1830[161] and in his later work, *Political Economy*. A supporter of the wage fund theory of wages, Senior wrote:

> . . . as the rate of wages depends in a great measure on the number of labourers, and the rate of profit on the amount of capital, both high wages and high profits have a tendency to produce their own diminution. High wages, by stimulating an increase of population, and therefore an increase of the number of labourers, and high profits, by occasioning an increase of capital . . . if the amount of capital employed in the payment of wages increases, the number of labourers remaining the same, profits will fall; and . . . if the number of labourers increases, the amount of capital and the productiveness of labour remaining the same, wages will fall; and . . . if they both increase in equal proportion, both will have a tendency to fall, in consequence of the larger proportion which they will each bear to the power of the natural agents whose services each require.[162]

The lower limit of wages, Senior added, is at the subsistence level. In a later section, Senior quite explicitly accepted the wage fund theory, writing that the rate of wages depends upon "the extent of the fund for the maintenance of labourers, compared with the number of labourers to be maintained."[163] He believed this to be axiomatic,[164] although there remains the question of the size of the hypothetical fund and what determines it. Senior was careful to specify that this fund is not the same as the wealth or capital of a nation, for these include much that cannot be consumed by the laborers. He later stated that the size of the fund depends in part upon the productivity of labor.[165]

Senior's wage theory was thus not merely a wage fund theory but contained elements of supply and demand and productivity. The level of wages might, therefore, be reduced through population growth, as that increases the labor supply relative to the demand for labor, reduces the ratio of the wage fund to the number of laborers, or diminishes the laborer's productivity by forcing him to use less efficient instruments of production. But it was Senior's opinion that in fact the wages of labor have advanced with the increase in population because of growing efficiency of production.

Also published in 1830 was *An Essay on the Distribution of Wealth*, by

[159] *Ibid.*, Vol. II, p. 107.
[160] *Ibid.*, Vol. II, p. 103.
[161] Senior, *Three Lectures on the Rate of Wages*, London, 1830.
[162] Senior, *Political Economy*, p. 140.
[163] *Ibid.*, p. 153.
[164] Senior, *Three Lectures*, Preface, pp. iii–iv.
[165] Senior, *Political Economy*, p. 174.

George Ramsay. In other respects quite original, this gave only a conventional, Malthusian treatment of population and wages. The immediate determinant of the wage level, Ramsay said, is supply and demand; and demand for labor is proportional to the amount of circulating capital. The latter increases more slowly than total capital, for the ratio of circulating to fixed capital tends to decrease in the progress of national wealth.[166]

Ramsay concluded ". . . the condition of the labourers, that is of the great majority of every nation, must in a great degree depend upon the *limitation of their numbers*."[167] Beyond this, wages were said to be somewhat affected by the number of hours of labor. At the upper limit, wages cannot exceed what the laborer produces.[168] Combined with the principle of diminishing returns, this led logically to the conclusion that continued population growth must eventually depress wages.

A final work considered here is *The Logic of Political Economy* (1844) by De Quincey. This set forth quite concisely that the wage level depends upon four factors: the increase or decrease of population, the increase or decrease of capital, fluctuations in the price of necessities, especially food, and, finally, "the traditional standard of living."[169] Of these, the next to the last concerned nominal rather than real wages. De Quincey saw clearly that these elements might reinforce or counteract each other; as for example, the depression of wages by population growth might be counteracted by growth of capital.[170] And he realized that the four elements are not independent of each other, that ". . . of the four great elements for determining wages, not one can be relied upon as an insulated or unconditional force; all are dependent upon each other, and each upon all."[171] This is true not only of wage determination but of distribution as a whole, and the various shares into which the total product is divided are themselves interdependent and also capable of reacting in various ways on labor, capital, and the other elements in production. Some but not all of these relations and interactions had been traced by the pioneering political economists of the first half of the nineteenth century.

In the context of population and wage theory, what the political economists had done was to adopt or develop several theoretical explanations of the process of wage determination: the theories of supply and demand, of the wage fund, of simple productivity, and of marginal productivity. These were alternative explanations, but it is worth noting that each led by a

[166] Ramsay, *op. cit.*, Part II, Ch. 2, p. 86.
[167] *Ibid.*, p. 97.
[168] *Ibid.*, pp. 105, 119.
[169] De Quincey, *The Logic of Political Economy*, p. 130.
[170] *Ibid.*, p. 135.
[171] *Ibid.*, p. 139. De Quincey's thoughts on the population question, which were anti-Malthusian, were further set forth in his "Notes from the pocket-book of a late opium-eater, No. 2, Malthus," *London Magazine*, October 1823, pp. 349–353; and "Answer of the opium-eater to Mr. Hazlitt's letter respecting Mr. Malthus," *ibid.*, December 1823, pp. 569–573.

somewhat different path to the same conclusion, that population growth is capable of forcing wages down to a physiologically or culturally determined minimum. The weight of economic authority was thus on the Malthusian side of the population controversy.[172]

5 · Summary: John Stuart Mill

In order to follow the elements of distribution theory, the preceding sections have dealt separately with the relation of population to rent, prices, profits, and wages as described by the political economists of the first half of the nineteenth century; but in fact these elements are closely interrelated and were often treated together by the writers of this time. To bring together these different parts of the discussion of distribution, John Stuart Mill's analysis of the relation of population to distribution as a whole is summarized below, followed by additional notes on some aspects of distribution theory.

In the *Principles* Mill set forth his own considered views on political economy rather than a summary of contemporary economic thought, but his work can be regarded as the authoritative statement of classical economics. A modern economist has written, very aptly:

> In this treatise Mill rounded out and summed up the classical system of which Ricardo had been the leading architect. Mill wrote with dignity, assurance, and authority. His mind was not beset by doubts concerning the true principles of political economy. 'The most important proposition in political economy,' he proclaimed, 'is the law of production from the land, that in any given state of agricultural skill and knowledge, by increasing the labour, the produce is not increased in an equal degree.' In Mill's world, diminishing returns defined the production function in agriculture, and thus set the stage within which economic progress could unfold. Population and technology were the dynamic factors in economic life, but population was considered the more potent variable.[173]

Mill's distribution theory in particular was based firmly on the principles of diminishing returns and population; and except for a somewhat more optimistic tone late in his lifetime, his adherence to these principles did not change from the first edition in 1848 to the seventh that appeared in 1871, two years before his death.

[172] The foregoing account of population and wage theory gives particular attention to the role of population in wage theory, and the population question was indeed much in the minds of the writers of this period; but it should be noted that many emphasized the role of capital and many recognized the influence of technology and other variables on wages and the entire pattern of distribution.

[173] Arthur F. Burns, *Economic Research and the Keynsian Thinking of our Times,* 26th Annual Report of the National Bureau of Economic Research, New York, 1946, p. 3.

In the second book of the *Principles* Mill dealt at length with wages, more briefly with profits and rent, and he set forth what he considered to be the principles determining these shares of the product. The rate of profits was traced to the productivity of invested capital in excess of the costs of production, especially labor cost; but the population variable did not enter directly into Mill's discussion at this point. The level of rent was traced in turn to the yield in excess of that on marginal or no-rent land: "The rent, therefore, which any land will yield, is the excess of its produce, beyond what would be returned to the same capital if employed on the worst land in cultivation."[174] Again, treatment of the population variable was postponed.

Wages, Mill stated firmly, are fundamentally determined by the action of supply and demand, and the wage fund is the demand function. In his words,

> Wages, then, depend mainly upon the demand and supply of labour; or, as it is often expressed, on the proportion between population and capital. By population is here meant the number only of the labouring class, or rather of those who work for hire; and by capital, only circulating capital, and not even the whole of that, but the part which is expended in the direct purchase of labour.[175]

Defending this explanation of wage determination, Mill maintained further that the wage level is not affected by the price of necessities, except as price affects labor supply and demand. According to his explanation,

> . . . dearness or cheapness of food, when of a permanent character, and capable of being calculated on before hand, may affect wages. In the first place, if the labourers have, as is often the case, no more than enough to keep them in working condition, and enable them barely to support the ordinary number of children, it follows that if food grows permanently dearer without a rise of wages, a greater number of the children will prematurely die; and thus wages will ultimately be higher, but only because the number of people will be smaller, than if food had remained cheap. But, secondly, even though wages were high enough to admit of food's become more costly without depriving the labourers and their families of necessaries; though they could bear, physically speaking, to be worse off, perhaps they would not consent to be so. They might have habits of comfort which were to them as necessaries, and sooner than forego which, they would put an additional restraint on their power of multiplication; so that wages would rise, not by increase of

[174] Mill, *Principles,* Book II, Ch. XVI, section 3, p. 520. Because of the number of editions of the *Principles,* references are given by book, chapter, and section as well as by page. Page references are to the 5th edition (1865); and the wording is unchanged from the first edition unless noted.

[175] *Ibid.,* Book II, Chapter XI, section 1, p. 420. The qualifying word *mainly,* in the first line of the quotation, was not used in the first edition.

deaths, but by diminution of births. In these cases, then, wages do adapt themselves to the price of food; though after an interval of almost a generation.[176]

Both alternatives involve an adjustment of population and labor supply to the higher prices, either voluntarily by limitation of reproduction, or involuntarily through mortality.

In the opposite situation, a permanent drop in prices, Mill believed, the alternatives are a permanent rise in "the standard of comfort regarded as indispensable," accompanied by a voluntary limitation of numbers, or an increase of population that ultimately returns real wages to their former level.[177] In this connection Mill affirmed his conviction that ". . . it is impossible that population should increase at its utmost rate without lowering wages,"[178] and he restated the Malthusian alternatives of the preventive or the positive checks to population.

Having set forth the principles governing distribution, Mill dealt in a later section of his work with the effects on rent, profits, and wages of changes in the three dynamic factors, population, capital, and the productive arts.[179] Considering first an increase in population alone, Mill identified two separate lines of economic consequences, one from the addition to the labor supply, the other from the addition to demand and the resultant impetus to diminishing returns. From the former would follow lowered real wages for labor and increased profits for the capitalist. From the latter, assuming no improvements in methods of production, would come higher food prices and rent.[180]

The second simple case considered by Mill was an increase in capital alone. This theoretically raises real wages and lowers profits. If the improved condition of the laborers leads to greater demand for food, secondary effects are diminishing returns and increasing costs of production in agriculture, higher rent, and still lower return on capital.[181]

The third case Mill considered was equal growth of population and capital.[182] In this case the dominant factor was said to be the advancing cost of producing food for the larger population. Food prices and rent

---

[176] *Ibid.*, Book II, Chapter XI, section 2, p. 424.

[177] *Ibid.*, Book II, Chapter XI, section 2, p. 426.

[178] *Ibid.*, Book II, Chapter XI, section 3, p. 430.

[179] *Ibid.*, Book IV, Chapter III.

[180] *Ibid.*, Book IV, Chapter III, section 1. Mill noted further that the rise in profits due to the increase in labor supply may be counteracted by the higher cost of production arising from the increase in demand, that the tendency toward lower wages may be opposed by the greater labor requirement of the additional production, and that the landowner is the only sure gainer.

[181] *Ibid.*, Book IV, Chapter III, section 2.

[182] *Ibid.*, Book IV, Chapter III, section 3. Unequal growth of population and capital was said to correspond to the first or second cases, according to which variable advanced the more rapidly.

would rise, money wages would increase but real wages remain constant, and the rate of profits would fall. The fall of profits, however, might be counteracted by improvement in methods of production, the third of the dynamic factors.

Finally, Mill assumed simultaneous advances in population, capital, and methods of production in agriculture, while the habits of the workers and thus their real wages remain fixed. Under this assumption, according to Mill, rent and money wages decline and profits increase, provided improvements in agriculture proceeded more rapidly than population growth. If, on the other hand, population advances more rapidly than improvements in agriculture, rent and money wages rise and profits fall unless there is a decline in the real wages of labor.[183] The more rapid advance in improvements Mill believed to be rare. Improvements in methods of production generally come gradually, he wrote, and "Population almost everywhere treads close on the heels of agricultural improvement, and effaces its effects as fast as they are produced."[184] It was Mill's conclusion that in the general progress of society the landlords profit most, the condition of the workers is not improved, and the rate of profits falls.[185]

Such was Mill's distribution theory as it related to population, and it represented mature classical economics on the subject. With a strong underlying Malthusianism, it presented population growth as a force that depresses wages and worsens the worker's condition. However, its pessimism is relieved in some measure by Mill's recognition of two possible counteracting forces, at least in the short run. One is technological progress. The other reflects the fact that Mill's system of distribution was not a rigid system of economic determinism, for he acknowledged the noneconomic factor of the habits of the people, and stated clearly that these habits can determine the wage level.[186]

6 · Later Theories of Distribution

A few theories of distribution after Mill remain to be mentioned. Since they were largely within the framework of classical economics, they are noted only briefly below except as they contained distinctive ideas on the relation of population to distribution.

The *Théorie de la richesse sociale* (1849) by Antoine Walras (1801–1866) stated that population grows rapidly in a prosperous society, that

[183] *Ibid.*, Book IV, Chapter III, section 5, p. 304.

[184] *Ibid.* The qualifying word "almost" was not used in the first edition.

[185] *Ibid.*, Book IV, Ch. III, section 5, p. 307.

[186] See especially Book II, Ch. XI, section 2; also Book IV, Ch. III, section 5, p. 304. It is also worth noting, although the topic has not been dealt with here, that Mill's population ideal was the stationary state, an interesting point of agreement between classical economics and classical Greek thought on population. On this point see Mill, *Principles,* Book IV, Ch. VI, especially section 2.

advancing civilization creates a greater variety of wants, and that the greater volume of demand from these two sources increases the price and the rental value of land.[187]

Several years later there appeared one of the few attacks on the Ricardian rent theory, by the German economist Johann Karl Rodbertus (1805–1875). In the third letter of his *Sociale Briefe* (1851) he gave a systematic refutation of the Ricardian theory, and advanced his own theory of rent as a substitute. In relation to population, he asserted that productiveness in agriculture has in fact increased,[188] and that if other factors remain constant a greater population leads to greater production, higher wages, a greater rate of profit on capital, and higher rent.[189] Concerning the economic significance of population he wrote,

> The more populous nations also as a rule are more wealthy, the less populous ones poorer. For the greater productivity of labor is of intellectual origin, and it appears as if the creative power of the human mind . . . grows with contact and cooperation.[190]

If food prices are sometimes higher in more populous nations, Rodbertus attributed it to greater wealth rather than to populousness itself.[191]

The influential *System der Volkswirtschaft* (1854) by Roscher rejected the wage fund theory and explained wage determination in terms of supply and demand.[192] An increase in the labor supply relative to demand tends to lower wages, it was said, but wages cannot fall below the cost of maintaining the labor supply. In a later edition of the *System* Roscher foreshadowed an important later development by recognizing both underpopulation and overpopulation, indicating that the significance of population size for a nation may be quite different at different stages of its growth.

Published in the same year, *Du revenu foncier* (1854), by the French economist Fontenay, cited objections to Ricardian rent theory, raised by various economists. The author's contention, based on the evidence he could assemble, was that returns in agriculture do not diminish as population increases, and that, in French experience, population, productivity, real wages, and rent had all advanced together.[193] Rent he defined as the difference between the cost of production and the value of the total product, and denied that it was a function of soil fertility in itself.[194]

[187] Antoine Auguste Walras, *Théorie de la richesse sociale,* Paris: Guillaumin, 1849, p. 74.
[188] Johann Karl Rodbertus, *Sociale Briefe,* Berlin, 1851, p. 6.
[189] *Ibid.,* pp. 136–139.
[190] *Ibid.,* p. 265.
[191] *Ibid.*
[192] Roscher explained further that various factors, such as the skill of the workers, affect the demand for labor and therefore the wages that are paid for it.
[193] Fontenay, *Du revenu foncier,* Ch. V.
[194] *Ibid.,* Ch. VIII.

A similar appeal to the growing body of economic data was made by another French economist, Baudrillart (1821–1892). His *Manuel d'économie politique* (1857) was in most respects a conventional presentation, but he expressed doubts about certain widely accepted generalizations of political economy. Baudrillart questioned whether the wage level is affected by the price of necessities,[195] presented arguments against the Ricardian rent theory,[196] and disagreed with the Malthusian theory of population.[197] Concerning the relation of population growth to food prices he pointed out that price data were available for the past fifty years in France, and that although the population had grown steadily the price of wheat had not advanced. This was said to be true also in other nations.[198]

A German work of a few years later, the *Nationalökonomie*[199] (1861) by Schäffle (1831–1903), gave a conventional account of rent, wages, and population, as did a later English work, the *Manual of Political Economy* (1863 or 1864) by Henry Fawcett (1833–1884). Giving a Ricardian account of rent and other elements of distribution and a Malthusian treatment of population, Fawcett included among the results of population growth an increase in food prices, higher rent, and lower wages unless counteracted by capital accumulation and improvements in agriculture.[200]

Some reservations about the widespread opinion that population growth tends to depress wages were expressed by the German economist Mangoldt, whose *Volkswirthschaftslehre* (1868) was mentioned earlier. Immigration, he believed, seldom forces down wages because the immigrants usually try to escape from the laboring class and become independent producers.[201] A natural increase in population, he continued, generally adds to the labor force, but the conclusion that this exerts a downward pressure on wages rests on the assumption that demand does not increase.[202] Mangoldt did not object to the iron law of wages if it was amended to place the level of stabilization at the customary level of expenditures of the workers.[203] But he believed that the law that describes the actual course of wages is that wages rise higher and higher as the customary needs of the workers advance.[204]

The English economist Rogers, whose *Manual of Political Economy* also appeared in 1868, saw no reason to fear an undue increase in the number

---

[195] Henri Baudrillart, *Manuel d'économie politique,* Paris: Guillaumin, 1857, p. 337.
[196] *Ibid.,* pp. 389–390.
[197] *Ibid.,* Part IV, Ch. VI.
[198] *Ibid.,* p. 394.
[199] Albert E. F. Schäffle, *Die Nationalökonomie, oder allgemeine Wirthschaftslehre,* Leipzig, 1861.
[200] Henry Fawcett, *Manual of Political Economy,* 2nd ed., Cambridge and London: Macmillan, 1865, pp. 86, 90, 147, 152, 159, and elsewhere.
[201] Mangoldt, *Volkswirthschaftslehre,* p. 398.
[202] *Ibid.,* p. 399.
[203] *Ibid.,* p. 402.
[204] *Ibid.,* p. 403.

of people, and although he gave considerable attention to the population question he apparently saw little relation between population and distribution. For example, he denied that population growth leads to the use of lands of poorer quality, and explained rent as the value of the produce of land above the cost of production.[205]

The beginning of a change in economic thought on population was marked by *The Theory of Political Economy* (1871) by Jevons. Here Jevons expressed the opinion that the Malthusian principle of population is not a part of economics, and on the whole he regarded population as a given factor in production rather than an economic variable. Thus the population variable did not enter into his analysis of distribution. Concerning wages, Jevons rejected the wage fund theory in favor of a productivity and residual theory. In his opinion wages depend upon the productivity of labor, with the laborers receiving the residue after deduction of rent, taxes, and interest.[206]

Cairnes, whose views on population in relation to production were reviewed in the preceding chapter, dealt less fully with the influence of population on distribution. Although living in a period when advances in technology and industry were much more apparent than in the first half of the century, Cairnes retained much of the older view that population growth leads to diminishing returns and higher prices of raw materials and food, and that the advances derived from improved production methods are swallowed up unless the laborers restrict their reproduction.

Cairnes believed that the interaction of population growth and technical progress tends to stabilize the price of grain in the long run:

> . . . an advance in the price of the staple food, after it attains a certain elevation, inevitably reacts on population, and, checking the demand, arrests the extension of cultivation, and by consequence, the advance of normal price. The progress of industrial invention comes no doubt in time to affect the course of agriculture, and then ensues a succession of cyclical movements which may be thus described. The cost of producing corn for a time falls: the condition of the labourer improves, and with the improvement in his condition he marries earlier, and brings up a larger family: population increases, and, the demand for food increasing with it, cultivation is extended to soils which, previous to the introduction of the better agricultural processes, could not have been profitably cultivated; at length the 'margin of cultivation' attains a range where the inferior quality of the natural agents brought into requisition just neutralizes the gain derived from the advance in agricultural skill. At this point the cost of producing the most costly portion of the nation's food is just where it was before improved processes had been introduced into agriculture; and the normal price of food attains its former eleva-

---

[205] Rogers, *Manual of Political Economy*, Ch. 12, esp. p. 162.
[206] Jevons, *The Theory of Political Economy*, 1871, Ch. VIII.

tion. The labourer's condition, unless so far as the standard of comfort has been raised in the interval, returns to its former level; and the high rates of subsistence once more react on and control population. Under the influence of a play of motives of this kind, the normal price of corn has in all long-settled countries been kept, as a permanent state of things, within the limit which it has reached at a comparatively early stage of their career. . . .[207]

Somewhat restated, this was typical classical economic theory with its system of automatic regulation through the agency of population adjustment.

Cairnes went on to say that the prices of meat and other articles of consumption tend to rise, in contrast to the stabilization of grain prices. Although stated in somewhat different terms, his final conclusion was that of the earlier classical economists: capital accumulation and improved production methods permit a higher level of living, but this can be secured and maintained only if population increase is restrained.[208]

Several works immediately preceding Sidgwick's *Principles* illustrate the changing attitude toward population, and the questioning of the basic assumptions and conclusions of political economy that had seemed so firmly established at the time John Stuart Mill wrote. *La science économique* (1881) by the French economist Yves Guyot expressed optimism concerning the ability of production to grow more rapidly than population, and rejected the Ricardian rent theory.[209] Leroy-Beaulieu's *Essai sur la répartition des richesses* (1881) similarly disagreed with both Malthus and Ricardo, more on factual than theoretical grounds. The iron law of wages, he asserted, never existed except in the imaginations of a few economists;[210] and the same was said of the wage fund.[211] According to Leroy-Beaulieu wages are affected by three classes of factors: the ratio of physical capital (capiteaux materiels) to population, the increase in worker productivity, and the advantage of one production factor over another under the laws and customs of a nation.[212]

A third work of the same period, similarly critical of political economy, was *The Dismal Science* (1882) by William Dillon. This singled out the basic principles of political economy for particular attack:

> Taken together, these three laws — the law that the rate of wages depends upon the proportion between capital and population, the Malthusian law of population, and the Ricardoan theory of rent — may be said to constitute the foundation of all the teachings of the Current English Economy as regards the causes which determine the distribution

[207] Cairnes, *Some leading Principles of Political Economy,* 1874, p. 125.
[208] *Ibid.,* esp. pp. 275–282.
[209] Guyot, *La science économique,* Book IV, Ch. 1, and Book V, Ch. 1.
[210] Leroy-Beaulieu, *Essai,* p. vii.
[211] *Ibid.,* p. 382.
[212] *Ibid.,* p. 384.

of wealth in our present social system. These laws have been the subject of discussion for more than half a century. They deal with subjects about which it is of supreme importance that the truth should be known. One would say, that if the subjects of wages, population, and rent are susceptible of scientific treatment at all, the truth with regard to them ought by this time to be determined with such a degree of definiteness and finality as to negative the possibility of rational controversy. Yet, what is the fact? We have briefly examined the state of recent and present authority, both in England and to some little extent in other countries, as bearing on the three great subjects just mentioned. As the result of our examination, we have found that so far is it from being the fact that "the period of controversy is passing away, and that of unanimity rapidly approaching," that, in truth, the "period of unanimity" never at any time seemed farther off than it seems to be at the present.[213]

Although largely concerned with the shortcomings of political economy, Dillon did offer some positive ideas of his own, for example, that the product of labor is the source of wages, and that the level of wages depends upon the laborers' standard of living.[214]

Sidgwick was not unaware of the limitations of classical economic theory, but in his *Principles* (1883) he conservatively restated much of the substance of classical theory. In his treatment of distribution, the population factor entered most prominently in the discussion of wages. Rejecting the wage fund theory, he related the wage level to the productivity of labor, but saw labor as the residual claimant who receives what is left of the product of his work after payment for the use of capital and land. This concept of wage determination led Sidgwick to the same conclusion as that of the earlier classical economists regarding the influence of population growth on wages, although by a somewhat different path of reasoning. The share of the product going to labor, he wrote,

> . . . tends to bear a smaller proportion to the total number of labourers as that number increases; supposing other things, including the amount of capital used in their aggregate industry, to remain the same. . . . In my view this result is due to the fact that if labourers increase in number, capital remaining stationary, the industrial demand for the aid of capital will tend to rise, and therefore the portion of the total produce paid for the use of a given amount of capital will tend to be greater; at the same time the proportion of total produce to the number of labourers will tend to be less, as the loss of efficiency of the capital-aided labour, due to the diminished returns from land, is likely to be greater than the gain in efficiency from the increased advantages of cooperation.[215]

[213] William Dillon, *The Dismal Science,* Dublin, 1882, p. 58.
[214] *Ibid.,* Ch. IV, esp. pp. 115, 122.
[215] Sidgwick, *Principles,* 1st ed., 1883, Book II, Ch. VIII, section 5, pp. 322–323 (also 3rd ed., 1901, p. 312).

The latter reason for lower wages, lower productivity in agriculture, Sidgwick traced to the law of diminishing returns, which he accepted fully.[216] An increase in the number of people thus was believed to reduce wages in two ways, first by decreasing the residue left for labor, and second by reducing the laborer's productivity.[217]

Further conforming to the classical view, Sidgwick believed that in European nations generally there was an automatic interaction of population change and wages:

> . . . it is evident that if general wages rise the force of the check (to population growth) will almost certainly be diminished, and a stimulus will be given to population of which the ultimate tendency will be to lower wages again. Similarly, if wages fall through any cause, the check will become more stringent; and so, other things remaining the same, wages will tend to rise again, when population has been thereby reduced.[218]

The reservation was introduced here that a considerable rise in wages may add to the productive powers of present and future laborers, and thus counteract the tendency of population growth to adjust wages downward.[219]

Although Sidgwick departed in some respects from the classical analysis and, as will be seen later, contributed to a new development in population thought, the classical conception of the role of population in distribution appears to have retained much of its vigor.

The trend of late nineteenth-century thought, however, was away from the Malthusian and classical view of population, as we have seen already in the case of production theory; and in distribution theory as well, population played a declining role. The change of opinion and the diminished role assigned to population were especially evident in the work of Alfred Marshall, the last writer to be considered here. In his *Principles of Economics* (1890) Marshall dealt with value or price determination and with distribution in terms that included supply and demand, but instead of basing his analysis on a few dominant laws or forces in the classical manner he gave a much more varied and eclectic explanation of economic processes. The result, although lacking the theoretical unity of the classical system, nevertheless was probably much closer to the realities of the labor market and the marketplace.

No very important role was left for population in Marshall's treatment of distribution, although it was not omitted entirely. Although he believed supply and demand determine the short-term market price of labor, for example,

---

[216] *Ibid.*, Book I, Ch. VI, section 3, p. 150.

[217] See later account of Sidgwick's belief that a stage of increasing returns precedes the onset of diminishing returns.

[218] Sidgwick, *op. cit.*, Book II, Ch. VIII, section 6, p. 325.

[219] *Ibid.*, p. 327.

he did not bring in population as a factor affecting the demand for the products of labor, nor as a factor affecting wages through the supply of labor, for that supply depends, other things remaining constant, upon the prospective earnings in any given occupation.[220] Presumably a continuing increase in the number of people would tend to diminish returns and lower wages, but it was by no means certain that these results would follow: ". . . the action of the Laws of Increasing and Diminishing Return appear pretty well balanced, sometimes the one, sometimes the other being the stronger."[221] Similarly, in his marginal treatment of wages and prices, population played little or no direct part. This followed quite logically from Marshall's premises, for if the trend of returns with increasing production is considered to be neither up nor down, then the influence of the population variable is neutral or indeterminate.

7 · Summary: Population and Distribution

In addition to population's role in production the political economists of the classical period explored a second broad range of economic effects of population, its influence on distribution of the product between the major claimants, landlord, capitalist, and laborer. As the preceding summary shows, distribution theory included among its basic principles much of the Malthusian theory of population, the law of diminishing returns, and the Ricardian explanation of rent; and all these pointed to the significance of population for the pattern of distribution in a society.

Although they disagreed among themselves, the writers of this period as a group did much to establish and organize the subject of population in relation to distribution. In particular they pointed out the dual economic role of population, described the system of factors and variables involved in distribution, adopted or developed alternative systems explaining the impact of population change on distribution, and traced the presumed effects on prices, wages, rent, and profits.

Population was seen to affect both the demand for subsistence and the supply, for people are both consumers and the necessary agents of production; but although it was apparent at the commonsense level, this duality of role was difficult to treat at the theoretical level. With John Stuart Mill the most notable exception, the writers of this period tended to emphasize only one aspect of population or to treat the two separately rather than to explore their net effect. Thus when wages were being considered, population change was generally viewed in terms of labor supply without allowance for its effect on demand, and the relation of population to prices was

---

[220] Marshall, *Principles of Economics,* 2nd ed., 1891, Vol. I, p. 612.
[221] *Ibid.,* p. 719.

seen largely in terms of demand for commodities except as the law of diminishing returns brought in the matter of productivity.

The classical analysis, even if not able to handle all the complexities of
the problem, nevertheless distinguished the elements involved in the production and distribution system. The system as visualized by the classical
economists included as the principal factor of production a fixed, or at
least limited land supply, and the variable factors, labor supply, capital,
and methods of production. The principal shares of the product were rent
to the landowner, wages to the laborer, and profits to the capitalist. Prices
were responsive to changes in these factors and in the volume of demand
as determined by the number of consumers and their per capita consumption.

The population variable entered into this system of economic factors in
more ways than one, and the effects of population change could be traced
in several different ways through the system. If a simple supply and demand analysis was used, population change could alter the supply-demand
balance of both labor and the means of subsistence, directly affecting wages
and prices. The latter effect would be reenforced by any tendency to a
diminishing of returns or an increase of cost as the volume of production
increased. Beyond this, secondary effects could be traced to other elements
in the system. Or, in place of supply and demand, interrelations could
be traced in other terms, such as productivity or costs of production.

Wage determination, for example, was variously explained in terms of
labor supply relative to demand, by the wage fund theory which was
basically a supply and demand theory, in terms of the productivity of labor,
by marginal productivity analysis, or as the residual share after payment for
the use of land and capital in production. However, all wage theories led to
the same conclusion, that population growth tends to depress wages. There
was of course ample opportunity for disagreement about the precise
effects of an increase in the number of people, but from Malthus and
Ricardo to Mill and Sidgwick, the weight of opinion in political economy
was that continued population growth must eventually if not immediately
lead to a worsening of the condition of the people. This conclusion, moreover, was reached by several different paths of reasoning: by any of the
alternative wage theories, by the law of diminishing returns that pointed to
lower productivity and higher prices, by the Ricardian rent theory according
to which increased agricultural production diverts a large share of the product to the landowner, and by the Malthusian conviction that temporary advances in wages and general well-being are automatically cancelled by
their stimulation of population growth.

A growing number of reservations, however, were attached to this general concept of the economic significance of population size. It had long
been recognized that there is a lower limit to the wage level, at the cost

of production of the needed labor force; and according to classical economic opinion this lower limit is not at the subsistence level but at the people's customary level of living (see section 8 below).

There was also a gradual redefinition of population as an economic variable. It is understandable, in view of the Malthusian controversy in the early part of the century, that many political economists and other writers gave particular attention to population. But most of those who dealt with the subject, especially in later years, recognized that it was only one of several variables and that the economic consequences of a population change depend upon other circumstances as well. Many emphasized the role of capital and the importance of the relative movements of capital and population, and for some writers capital was the fundamental variable controlling population change. Progress in the efficiency of production was also recognized as a dynamic factor in the economic system that could interact with other factors and affect the pattern of distribution. Its influence on the level of living was seen to be opposite that of population growth; and optimism concerning advances in production methods grew in the later classical period.

One result of these developments was that the place of the population variable in distribution theory was much reduced by the end of the nineteenth century. With more and more detailed examination of prices, wages, and other aspects of distribution, it had become increasingly apparent that distribution phenomena could not be explained adequately in terms of one or a few simple principles or forces, but that more complex explanations were needed. In Marshall's work this led to multiple-factor treatment of distribution that gave little weight to the population variable; and it was omitted entirely by some writers. Over the same period, furthermore, there was increasing doubt whether the trend of net returns with increasing production really is downward; and as a corollary the population variable appeared less decisive for the trend of returns. From Malthus near the beginning of the century to Marshall near the end, estimates of the influence of population on distribution had gone through nearly the full range from being the dominant factor to one of uncertain significance. However, the deflation of the population variable as an economic force was not quite as complete as may appear. Marshall and his contemporaries, like the writers of Malthus' time, were primarily concerned with understanding and solving the problems of their own day. If they did not see population as a present or imminent threat, it did not mean they had discarded it entirely as an economic force. For the majority of them the Malthusian danger probably still existed; but it was removed to a hypothetical case or to a remote future in which excess population might raise prices, force down wages, and depress the general level of living.

Another dimension in the form of another variable was also introduced into the treatment of population and distribution. This arose from the realization that the problem does not lie entirely within an economic context, but that the consumption pattern, wage level, and population size itself are affected by cultural factors, the "habits and customs" of the people. Since this development is of some significance in the history of population thought, it is considered separately below.

8 · Summary: Population and the Standard of Living

The conception of the economic consequences of population growth derived from eighteenth-century political economy and supported by nineteenth-century analysis of production and distribution was that of a natural, almost inevitable force that depresses per capita consumption or the level of living until checked by a rise in mortality or a decrease in fertility. A significant development in nineteenth-century population thought was a progressive softening and transformation of this older and pessimistic conception.

Prevailing opinion about the relation of population size and volume of production to the level of living might have been expressed by the following equation:

$$\text{level of living} \simeq \frac{\text{production}}{\text{population}}$$

This is of course an oversimplification, but the level of living was seen as a dependent variable affected directly by production and inversely by population. The assumption of an inverse relation between level of living and number of people is found throughout classical economics, in the works of Torrens, McCulloch, Senior, John Stuart Mill, and many others. A corollary expression of the same fundamental belief was the opinion that a change in the volume of production, from whatever cause, presents the alternatives of a change in the level of living if the population remains constant, a change in the number of people while the level of living remains constant, or smaller changes in both.[222]

This formulation could have been attacked on grounds that it took too static a view of production or that it looked upon population change as a change in the number of consumers but not producers. Within political economy, however, deviation from this strict formulation took the direction of a growing recognition that population is not an ultimate variable but

[222] Leroy-Beaulieu added another alternative, writing that a society may use increased power of production to work less, consume more, or increase its numbers. He added that it depends on national character which alternative is chosen, and that Germany and Belgium have principally increased their population, France its level of living and leisure (*Essai,* pp. 419–420).

is in some measure dependent upon the degree to which the preventive check is exercised, and that the prevailing level of living is not merely a dependent variable but may play a more active role by influencing reproductive behavior.

From Malthus to John Stuart Mill there was strong doubt about whether the people would make effective use of the preventive check; but even these fundamentally pessimistic writers altered their positions somewhat in their later works, and others expressed more confidence in voluntary control of reproduction. In political economy the change can be observed in connection with the concept of a "natural" level of wages. This concept, which was noted only incidentally in the section on wages above, was common in nineteenth-century wage theory, where it was assumed that population and labor supply tend to adjust in such a way as to stabilize wages at the natural level in the long run. But whereas the natural level formerly had been assumed to be at the subsistence minimum, it came to be put at a higher level sufficient to provide the customary comforts and conveniences of the people (Say, Torrens, Malthus, McCulloch, John Stuart Mill and others).

This concept of the natural wage in effect assumed a new determinant of population size and wages, the customary level of consumption, or the standard of living.[223] It was duly pointed out that the standard of living, and therefore the population attainable with a given amount of production, varies from one society to another, and of course the variation from one social class to another had long been observed in England and elsewhere. It was but another step to conclude that the most effective means of promoting the preventive check and limiting population growth is to raise the standard of living. Malthus himself stated this quite clearly and admirably as early as the second edition (1803) of his *Essay:*

> In most countries, among the lower classes of people, there appears to be something like a standard of wretchedness, a point below which, they will not continue to marry and propagate their species. This standard is different in different countries, and is formed by various concurring circumstances of soil, climate, government, degree of knowledge, and civilization, &c. The principal circumstances which contribute to raise it are, liberty, security of property, the spread of knowledge, and a taste for the conveniences and comforts of life. Those which contribute principally to lower it are despotism and ignorance. In an attempt to better the condition of the lower classes of society, our object should be to

[223] According to Rogers, "The customary food of a people, as it has its effect on the rate of wages, so it powerfully affects the growth of population" (*Manual*, p. 70). The same thought can be found in Steuart and in many other writings. Not long after Steuart, Paley (*Moral and Political Philosophy*, p. 375) had written that even in the lower orders of society men will not marry unless they can have "their accustomed mode of life."

raise this standard as high as possible, by cultivating a spirit of independence, a decent pride, and a taste for cleanliness and comfort among the poor.[224]

A number of later political economists came to the same conclusion, including Cairnes, who wrote,

> I am inclined to attach much more importance, as a means of controlling population, to the creation of modes of existence or habits of life in which the prudential faculties are called into energetic play, than to any amount of direct Malthusian teaching.[225]

Noteworthy here is the inversion of the old formulation relating population and consumption. In the new form:

$$\text{population} \simeq \frac{\text{production}}{\text{standard of living}}$$

That is to say, population becomes the dependent variable, and the customary per capita consumption or standard of living determines population size at a given level of production.[226] If only partly true, still the new formulation served to redress the balance of opinion that had swung too far in the opposite direction during the years of active Malthusian controversy. Actually, the old and new formulations may both be valid but apply to two different types of society. That is, the older formulation may be thought of as approximating the situation of the underdeveloped society with high fertility and low level of living, in which population size may be a crucial factor affecting the average condition of the people. The newer formulation presumably is more applicable to the society in which material well-being is high and fertility effectively controlled. No society can be homogeneous in this respect, however, and the proportion of families whose size is influenced by economic and related considerations must vary widely from one society to another.

[224] Malthus, *Essay,* 2nd ed., 1803, Book IV, Ch. VIII, p. 557. The passage remained unchanged except for punctuation to the last edition of the *Essay.*

[225] Cairnes, *Some leading Principles,* p. 293.

[226] This was stated as a "law of population" by Courcelle-Seneuil in the formula, $p = (r-i)/c$, where p is population, r is "revenue" or production, i is the amount removed by inequalities of distribution, and c is minimum per capita consumption. Thus for population to increase, as he pointed out, there must be an increase in r or a decrease in i or c (Courcelle-Seneuil, *Traité,* Vol. I, pp. 161–162).

10

Population Theory in Nineteenth-Century American Political Economy

Although American experience was often cited by European writers on economic and population questions, American population and economic thought lay outside the mainstream of development, and with only an exception or two had no influence on the central body of theory and generalization. Nevertheless, American thought in this subject area has a certain interest in its own right, like Swedish thought in the eighteenth century, for it arose in a setting very different from Europe in socio-economic conditions and established patterns of opinion, and therefore had some distinctive features of its own.

The English economist Leslie, in an account of political economy in the United States, observed that "With exceptions and qualifications . . . American political economy is in the main an importation from Europe, not an original development. . . ."[1] Political economy in fact was of European origin and development. Among the American writers of the period, some were of European birth and others were trained abroad, and the models they followed were from classical economics. But while some American writers remained fully loyal to the classical tradition and European precedents, others declared their intellectual independence on points on which their observations or convictions differed from Old World doctrine. This occurred especially in relation to rent and population, for the Ricardian and Malthusian theories did not agree with New World experience, which in many respects diverged widely from the European.

On population in particular, long established conviction in the United States ran counter to classical theory. Since earliest pioneer and colonial days, increase in the number of people had been considered necessary for greater security and prosperity. As Auld (1820–1867) later wrote about immigration,

[1] T. E. C. Leslie, "Political economy in the United States," *Fortnightly Review,* October 1880, 28:489. This article was also republished in Leslie's *Essay in Political Economy,* London: Longmans, Green, 1888.

It was early felt that wild luxuriance of nature needed hands to gather it, and that the ancient and boundless forests required something more than the natural increase of the first colonists to fill them during the first century, in order that they might become arable land.[2]

More direct evidence of this point of view is the preamble of the Declaration of Independence, which included in the enumeration of grievances against King George III the statement that

He has endeavored to prevent the population (i.e., populating or peopling) of these States; for that purpose obstructing the laws of naturalization of foreigners; refusing to pass others to encourage their migration hither, and raising the conditions of new appropriations of lands.

After independence was achieved, opinion within the United States continued to favor population increase. The new nation felt that it needed greater numbers of citizens to insure its survival.[3] Vacant lands, undeveloped resources, and optimism for the future gave little basis for the Malthusian doctrine of population.[4] The advantages of a growing number

[2] J. B. Auld, in J. D. B. DeBow, *The Industrial Resources, Statistics, etc., of the United States,* 3rd ed., New York: Appleton, 1854, vol. 3, p. 396.

[3] Niles' *Weekly Register,* for example, welcomed new arrivals with the words, "Come, and assist us to prepare by an increased population and strength, to resist any attempt that may be made to put down our dangerous example of successful rebellion" (*Register,* X, 373, August 3, 1816).

[4] Jarvis in 1872 mentioned the curious theory, quite the opposite of the Malthusian doctrine, that the white race could not long maintain itself in the United States without renewal from abroad. According to Jarvis:

"There is a belief held by a few in both Europe and America, that the climate of the United States is unfavorable to the Caucasian constitution. This is put forth distinctly by Mr. Clibborne, in a paper which he read before the British Association for the Advancement of Science at Cheltenham, in 1856, entitled 'The Tendency of the European Races to become extinct in the United States.' This was published in the volume of Transactions of the society for that year.

"The sum of Mr. Clibborne's idea is embraced in the following sentence: 'From the general unfitness of the climate to the European constitution, coupled with the occasional pestilential visitations which occur in the healthier localities, on the whole, on an average of three or four generations, extinction of the European races in North America would be almost certain, if the communication with Europe were entirely cut off.' Knox repeats this opinion in his English lectures on the races of men.

"The existence and rapid increase of the large population in the United States are held not to conflict with this theory, for these facts are explained by the supposition that our people are composed mostly of strangers from abroad and their children, whose families are extraordinarily fertile in the first generation in America, although they soon become sterile, and in course of a century or less, yield their places to new arrivals, as their predecessors had done for ages before them, and as their successors will do forever after them.

"Mr. Louis Schade, in his work published at Washington, in 1856, affirms this principle of American deterioration of human life, and says that the power of natural increase of those who were here eighty-two years ago is reduced to the annual rate of 1.38 percent, while all the rest of the growth of population

of people seemed obvious; and such opposition to immigration as developed during the nineteenth century was based on cultural and qualitative grounds rather than fear of excessive population numbers. Given this background of opinion and the conditions of a new country differing greatly from those in Europe, it is not surprising that the Malthusian doctrine was supported by few American writers.

Although ideas about population were rather widely diffused, especially concerning immigration and immigration policy, formal analysis of the significance of population was largely confined to the literature of political economy and public affairs. Since American writers were few in number and their treatment of population was for the most part general, separate discussion of theories of production and theories of distribution is not continued, and the principal writers are dealt with in chronological order of their first or principal publications. To avoid a second treatment of the American writers in Chapter 11, their general conceptions of population and their analyses of the socio-economic significance of population size are described here.

1 · The First Decades: Baldwin, Raymond, Everett, Cardozo, and Others

The size and growth rate of its population was a matter of general interest in the new nation, and much information was provided by the newly established decennial censuses. Newspapers and other periodicals published notes and articles about population for the general public, and more extensive summaries of census data were contained in manuals or compendia describing the geography, people, resources, and businesses of the United States. One of the earliest of these manuals was *A view of the United States of America* by Tench Coxe (1755–1824) published in 1794. Throughout the work, Coxe, a Philadelphia merchant and member of the Continental Congress in 1788, took for granted the desirability of an increasing population, and regarded immigration with full approval.[5] Another

---

within that period is due to new immigrants and their very fruitful families.

"Mr. Frederic Kapp, in an address read before the American Social Science Association and printed in their Journal for 1870, warmly supports this doctrine. . . ."

(Edward Jarvis, "Immigration," *Atlantic Monthly*, 29:454, April 1872.) It is not known, however, whether this theory influenced American population thought. Jarvis tested the theory to the best of his ability, and rejected it with the remark, "It is a noteworthy fact, that the rate of natural increase has diminished with the increase of foreigners" (p. 487).

For a more detailed account of this theory, see E. P. Hutchinson, "A forgotten theory of immigration," in *In the Trek of the Immigrants,* O. Fritiof Ander, Ed., Rock Island: Augustana College Library, 1964, pp. 49–57.

[5] Tench Coxe, *A view of the United States of America . . . ,* Philadelphia: William Hall and Wrigley & Berriman, 1794. See esp. pp. 42, 165, 227.

early compilation, *Economica, a Statistical Manual for the United States* by Samuel Blodget, was published in 1806 and contained information about population and immigration, as well as other matters. Population also received attention in the works of John Melish, a Scotsman who settled in Philadelphia and whose publications included *A Statistical Account of the United States* (1813), *A Geographical Description of the United States* (1816), and *A Statistical View of the United States, Containing a Geographical Description of the United States, and of Each State and Territory* (1822).[6] Similar works were Adam Seybert's *Statistical Annals of the United States of America* (1818), George Tucker's *Progress of the United States in Population and Wealth* (1843), and J. D. B. De Bow's *The Industrial Resources, Statistics, etc., of the United States* (1854).[6a]

These accounts of the United States contain numerous references to population, but they are almost entirely descriptive. As far as the authors' thoughts about population are revealed, they remain within the contemporary American pattern: natural resources are plentiful for the foreseeable future; an increase in the number of people is desirable; and the advantages of such an increase are considered self-evident. Further analysis of the significance of population numbers, except in elementary terms of labor force and military manpower, had to await the development of an American political economy.

Baldwin · The first American writer considered here is Loammi Baldwin (1780–1838), distinguished civil engineer, son of the engineer of the same name who is now best remembered as the discoverer of the Baldwin apple, and author of a seventy-five-page pamphlet entitled *Thoughts on the Study of Political Economy* (1809).[6b]

This work was not a treatise on political economy but rather a statement of the need for such a treatise and an outline of what it should contain. It began with a sentence or two that might have come from much earlier mercantilist writings:

> Population, industry, and credit, are the primary instruments of national strength and prosperity. In every nation, however refined or however remote from refinement, the number of its inhabitants is the best index of its power, and as the ratio of increase or decrease varies, national strength and happiness will fluctuate. Industry and population are so intimately blended in every question, which involves the accumulation of

[6] For a bibliography and an account of Melish's writings, see Marvin E. Wolfgang, "John Melish, an early American demographer," *The Pennsylvania Magazine of History and Biography*, 82(1):65–81, January 1958.

[6a] This is the third edition of De Bow. The title of the first two editions (1852–1853) was *The Industrial Resources . . . of the Southern and Western States*.

[6b] Loammi Baldwin, *Thoughts on the Study of Political Economy in connection with the Population, Industry, and Paper Currency of the United States*, Cambridge, Mass.: Hilliard and Metcalf, 1809.

enjoyments, that little satisfaction can result from treating them separately. Population gives a spur to industry; industry multiplies the products of labour. . . .[7]

There follows a fourteen-page section on population that merits Baldwin a place among the early students of population in the United States. The section presents information obtained from the two preceding censuses, states the need for more information, especially on the foreign-born, and discusses the rate of natural increase and how it may be estimated. Baldwin also recognized the high rate of internal migration and ventured the opinion that

So large a part of the United States remains unoccupied, that the population will not probably be stationary for many ages to come. For until the whole extent of country becomes peopled by many millions more than now inhabit it, this emigration from old to new settlements must, in the nature of things, continue.[8]

Baldwin was acquainted with Malthus' work, and while he believed there was no need to fear want in the United States, he wrote:

If, however, as is sometimes the case, persons marry without previously calculating whether their labour or incomes will be a certain source of support, they will not only bring distress upon themselves and their families, but incumber society with the maintenance of their children.[9]

After re-emphasizing the need for more census data, Baldwin concluded with a plea for a separate system of political economy for the United States:

In such circumstances, nothing can be applied here by copying from others; every thing relative to political economy must be original . . . we cannot be too cautious how we assume for correct maxims, those which are found in European works on political economy.[10]

This might well have been the motto for the American school of political economy, which did not develop until several decades later.

Raymond · The first text or treatise on political economy by an American was *Thoughts on Political Economy* by Daniel Raymond (1786–1849?), first published in Baltimore in 1820.[11] The work did not present a formal theory of population, but the population factor was mentioned in passing at a number of points, sufficient to indicate Raymond's estimate of its social and economic significance.

One basic economic role of population and labor is said to be in the production of wealth, for although the earth is the source of wealth, labor is what brings it forth.[12] National wealth, defined as "capacity for acquir-

[7] *Ibid.*, pp. 5–6.   [8] *Ibid.*, p. 15.
[9] *Ibid.*, p. 11.   [10] *Ibid.*, p. 67.
[11] Other editions, retitled *Elements of Political Economy* and not greatly changed from the first edition, appeared in 1823, 1836, and 1840.
[12] Raymond, *Thoughts on Political Economy*, Part I, Ch. 6, p. 111.

ing the necessaries and comforts of life," also is increased by greater density of population,[13] but it depends even more upon the industriousness of the people and other factors.

Raymond presumably was acquainted with the principle of diminishing returns as set forth by the English political economists; and on this fundamental element of economic doctrine he did not accept classical authority. Like later American dissenters on this point, he based his dissent not so much on theoretical grounds as on observation. As he wrote,

> According to our experience, the fruits of the earth are multiplied almost in proportion to the labour bestowed upon it; and were that labour increased a hundred fold, it is impossible to say, that the product might not be increased very nearly in the same proportion.[14]

He qualified this on the following page with the further explanation,

> I am far from supposing that the earth is capable of being made to increase its fruits with the same rapidity that the unrestrained powers of procreation are capable of multiplying the human species.[15]

However, he was confident that unless the laws of nature are interfered with, population does not multiply beyond the means of subsistence.

The influence of population size and change on distribution was not specifically treated by Raymond, and his thought is only partly indicated here. A supply and demand theory of wages is suggested at one point:

> If a country produces twice as great a quantity of food as another, it will also contain twice as great a population, and twice as many labourers, who will want employment, and therefore keep down the price of labour. . . .[16]

The labor supply factor played little part in Raymond's wage theory. Wages must be sufficient for subsistence, and it can be inferred that he considered that the subsistence needs of the workers claim the first share of the product.[17] Beyond this minimum the wage level, at least in agriculture, was thought to depend upon the relation of the worker to the land, that is to say, whether they are owners or landless employees,[18] and not upon the productivity of the workers.[19]

The population factor received no greater emphasis elsewhere in Raymond's theory of distribution. With regard to prices, he wrote, "The price of everything depends on the proportion which exists between the supply and demand,"[20] but he did not discuss the possible effect of variation in the

13 *Ibid.*, Part I, Ch. 2, p. 37.
14 *Ibid.*, Part II, Ch. 5, p. 312; also 2nd ed. (1823), Vol. II, p. 111.
15 *Ibid.*, 1st ed., p. 313.
16 *Ibid.*, 2nd ed. (1823), p. 88.
17 *Ibid.*, Vol. I, p. 193.
18 *Ibid.*, 1st ed., Part II, Ch. 4, p. 282.
19 *Ibid.*
20 *Ibid.*, 2nd and 3rd ed., Vol. I, p. 183.

number of people. The rental value of land and the division of the product between landowner and laborers were said to depend upon population density, the equality or inequality of the division of property, and the rate of growth of public wealth.[21]

Raymond's views on population were more fully revealed in other connections, especially in his brief treatment of the Malthusian theory.[22] Throughout his work it is evident that he accepted some of Malthus' basic propositions, but he came to different conclusions and was disposed to reject the Malthusian theory. He was convinced that "the power of procreation in the human species is vastly greater than the capacity of the earth to yield them food."[23] Further, he believed that population numbers tend to increase with the food supply, for he wrote that "If one country is more productive of food than another, it will also be more productive of men."[24] The same thought appears in his argument that labor-saving machinery leads to an increase in population and in human wants rather than to a decrease in the amount of work to be done. He wrote in part:

> If population remained always stationary . . . then the want of food would always remain stationary . . . but with the procreative powers of the human species, this can never be the case. As soon as the necessaries of life are furnished to those in being, a new, more numerous, and more hungry race springs up. . . . The only effect, therefore, of labour saving machinery, is to substitute one species of toil for another.[25]

Up to this point Raymond's population thought was in agreement with Malthus, but he differed from Malthus in attributing major importance to the degree of inequality in the division of property. According to Raymond, inequality of division is a cause of poverty, and it also affects population size. The latter effect was traced through the food supply. As he explained,

> . . . the abundance of food, and consequently, the increase of population, will always depend materially upon the proportion that exists between the quantity of labour employed in producing the necessaries, and the comforts of life.[26]

Increased demand for the comforts of life, he went on to say, decreases the proportion of labor expended in the production of necessities and thus checks population growth. In his words:

[21] *Ibid.*, pp. 187, 191–192.
[22] *Ibid.*, 1st ed., Part II, Ch. 3.
[23] *Ibid.;* see also earlier quotation from Part II, Ch. 5, p. 313.
[24] *Ibid.*, Part II, Ch. 4, p. 283.
[25] *Ibid.*, Part II, Ch. 5, pp. 311–312.
[26] *Ibid.*, Part II, Ch. 2, p. 235.

The restraints upon the increase of population, do not ordinarily arise from any incapacity in the earth, to produce food, or from any natural inability in man to procure it; but from a thousand artificial causes, which grow out of civil society. . . . There are very few people who starve in any country, or whose increase is repressed by the actual want of food; but there are multitudes in every country especially in all old countries, where property is very unequally divided, whose increase is repressed by their artificial wants, or want of those things, which, from habit, and the customs of the country, they have come to consider as essential to their happiness; and these are always in proportion to the unequal division of property. . . . Artificial wants produce their effect in restraining the increase of population, long before actual want begins to operate.[27]

This was the substance of Raymond's position on the Malthusian population problem, and he maintained it in later editions of *Political Economy*. Lack of food he recognized as the ultimate limiting factor, but the growth of artificial wants, he thought, is the operating check, " a wise provision of nature, to prevent the world from becoming too fully peopled."[28] Raymond seems to have realized, moreover, that this check would operate more on the upper than on the lower economic groups, for he noted that the level of artificial wants is very different for the different classes of a society.[29]

Mathew Carey · Carey (1760–1839) was the founder of a leading publishing firm in Philadephia, a businessman who made an avocation of political economy, a prolific writer of essays and pamphlets on many subjects, and throughout a zealous advocate of tariff protection against foreign goods. An immigrant from Ireland himself, he understandably gave immigration a prominent place in his discussion of national policy, but gave other population matters little attention in his writings; and his thought on the significance of the number of people was revealed only by several brief comments.

Most explicit on the subject of population was a statement in *The New Olive Branch* (1820), made with a quite typical show of practical good sense:

Some political economists have asserted that the strength of a nation consists in the number of its inhabitants. This, without qualification, is manifestly erroneous. A numerous population, in a state of wretchedness, is rather a symptom of debility than of strength. Such a population is ripe for treason and spoil. But a dense population, usefully and profitably employed, and in a state of comfort and prosperity, constitutes the

[27] *Ibid.*, Part II, Ch. 2, pp. 236–237.
[28] *Ibid.*, 3rd ed., Vol. II, p. 21.
[29] *Ibid.*, 1st ed., Part II, p. 238.

pride and glory of a statesman, and is the basis of the power and security of nations.[30]

Writing less theoretically in a later pamphlet, *Emigration from Ireland and Immigration into the United States* (1828), Carey gave demographic reasons for both the distress of the Irish in their homeland and their usefulness in the United States. For the former, he wrote of "The distressed situation of the Irish nation, particularly the working class, from the redundancy of population, and the want of adequate employment for them. . . ." For the latter, he noted that the deficiency of workers in the United States had raised wages. The conclusion, naturally, was that the immigration of the Irish should be encouraged, to the benefit of both immigrant and employer.

Tucker · Preceding Mathew Carey in his earliest writings was George Tucker (1775–1861), essayist and economist, and for many years professor of moral philosophy and political economy at the University of Virginia. His first major work was the *Essays on Various Subjects of Taste, Morals, and National Policy*[31] (1822). Published anonymously, this was a collection of essays said to have been written in 1813 and for the most part published soon after in *Port Folio* under the title of "Thoughts of a Hermit."[32] Three of the essays, "On the Future Destiny of the United States," "On Density of Population," and "On the Theory of Malthus," gave the most detailed discussion of population questions by an American writer up to that time.

The first of these essays began with the statement:

> The rapid increase of our population as well as its diffusion, furnish a subject of speculation that is interesting on account of their effects on the moral and political condition of the United States, and curious, because it presents a spectacle to which history affords no parallel.
>
> So far as we are acquainted with the annals of human society, in the old world, population, where it has increased at all, has always advanced by slow and imperceptible gradations: for being every where in proportion to the means of subsistence, which are at first scanty and precarious, it is only where men have learnt to increase these means by industry, by frugality, and above all by the invention of useful arts, that their numbers are capable of augmentation.[33]

Tucker then noted that the first censuses demonstrated that the population of the United States was doubling about every twenty-five years, gave his

---

[30] Mathew Carey, *The New Olive Branch*, Philadelphia: Carey and Son, 1820, p. 233. Reprinted in *Essays on Political Economy*, Philadelphia: Carey and Lea, 1822, p. 376.

[31] *Essays on Various Subjects, etc.*, by a citizen of Virginia, Georgetown, D.C., 1822.

[32] *Ibid.*, Preface.

[33] *Ibid.*, p. 1.

opinion that immigration could not greatly affect the period of doubling, and then turned to the question of the foreseeable consequences of rapid growth.

It was evident to Tucker that national strength would be greatly increased, but it was the more specific effects of growth that attracted his attention. The filling up of the states west of the Alleghenies, some had predicted, would lead to their separation from the eastern states, but Tucker dismissed this as unlikely. The Middle West, he believed, would become

> . . . the seat of extensive manufactures: for in no other way can the large redundancy of hands, beyond what are necessary to cultivate the soil, or are likely to hold it, find employment and subsistence. . . . This is the origin of manufactures, which are in proportion to the density of population; which again is in proportion to the fertility of the soil.[34]

In addition to these and other internal effects,[35] the consequences of the expansion of the American population would be felt in Europe. The expanding market for imported manufactures would immediately encourage the growth of the European population; but in the long run it might have the opposite effect, because

> . . . when in process of time our augmented population shall be more able to supply us with manufactures, and to consume the surplus productions of our agriculture, then the number of our foreign manufacturers, no longer able to obtain food from abroad in exchange for the products of their labour, must decrease, and feel in its full force all the mischief of an excessive population.[36]

The second essay, which first appeared in 1815,[37] went on to consider the influence of population density on "national wealth, advancement of literature and arts, and individual virtue and happiness." According to Tucker, a greater density favors national defense, permits division of labor, reduces transportation costs, and leads to "greater industry and emulation."[38] It may also give an impetus to higher civilization, for

> In a thin population few can have the leisure indispensable to proficiency in learning and science. . . . For the same reason, indeed, that there is less wealth in such a community, there is also less of juvenile instruction and of individual leisure. The elements of taste and genius abound, no doubt, in every soil, but they are matured and perfected only

[34] *Ibid.,* p. 19.
[35] Tucker noted, for example, that the large growth of the English-speaking population would be a stimulus to writers in that language (p. 20).
[36] *Ibid.,* pp. 22–23.
[37] *Port Folio,* series 3, vol. 6, 1815, pp. 164–175. Minor changes of wording are found in the 1822 edition.
[38] Tucker, *Essays,* pp. 68–72.

by the genial influence of the riches and applause which populous countries alone can give.[39]

The effect on the general well-being of the people, however, was less clear, for here Tucker saw both advantages and disadvantages in a dense population. As he wrote,

> Upon the whole it would seem that, if a denser population seems likely to produce peculiar vices and sufferings, it is also favourable to peculiar virtues and enjoyments. A diffusive population is also in some respects auspicious, and in other unfriendly, to morality and happiness.[40]

It is no doubt true, Tucker considered, that with a more dense population there tends to be a more unequal division of the materials that contribute to man's enjoyment; but

> ... still it does not follow that a country where the population is compact, without being redundant, may not be more favourable to happiness, than one whose numbers are scattered over an extensive surface. There may, perhaps, be a middle point between excessive thinness and closeness of population which is most propitious to human comfort and enjoyment; and possibly, that point to which it would naturally arrive, and where it would as naturally stop, if nature was not counteracted by our unwise intermeddling, might give us the golden mean.[41]

Tucker clearly had the concept of an optimum size or density of population, and believed that population might stabilize there naturally rather than continue increasing to the subsistence or Malthusian limit.

After considering both sides of the question of the relation of human happiness to population density, Tucker arrived at the following judgment:

> Without, however, indulging in visions, which may be as fallacious as they are agreeable, let us consider the world as it actually is, and ask in what stage of population is the greatest happiness probably found. If our pride or partiality leads us to the conclusion that man is happier in America than he is on the old continent, yet still this question recurs, would our happiness be increased or diminished by a yet further density of numbers?
>
> A greater facility in procuring the conveniences and elegancies of life could not, we may suppose, but be felt by our whole community. If this increase of the materials of enjoyment were the consequence of an increase of toil and care, the case would be different; but the gain, as has been shown, proceeds from the greater ingenuity and skill, and saving of labour, which a denser population produces. Thus, if the greater part of that irksome labour, which is now expended in wagoning our bulky commodities to market, or in the slovenly cultivation of our extensive

39 *Ibid.*, pp. 72–73 (*Port Folio*, pp. 167–168).
40 *Ibid.*, p. 78 (*Port Folio*, p. 170).
41 *Ibid.*, p. 81 (*Port Folio*, p. 173).

fields, was devoted to the fabrication of comfortable and ornamental apparel, of commodious houses, of elegant and convenient furniture, every one will say that our situation would be greatly improved.[42]

In support of this conclusion Tucker cited Hume's opinion that the happiness and virtue of the English people had advanced with their numbers.

In the third essay Tucker began by accepting as obvious the Malthusian principles that population always presses on subsistence and that nature has set a limit on the numbers of mankind, but he rejected the conclusion that the pressure of population leads to misery and vice. To support this position he gave the following arguments. First, vice and misery exist in the United States where there is no excess of population, and therefore must be due to some other cause. Second, there is shortage of subsistence in Norway, Sweden, and other countries, but not a greater amount of vice and misery. Third, where vice and misery are associated with overabundance of population, the latter can be attributed to "some misjudged regulation, or absurd institution, or prevalent error of opinion." Fourth, if society does not condemn improvident marriage and does attach odium to vices that check population, it must be that "the common sense of mankind" does not agree with Malthus. Fifth, if the generative faculty is in fact stronger than the growth of subsistence, why has mankind not been more stimulated to increase subsistence? Sixth, if the generative faculty is as great as supposed, how can a decrease in population in some nations be explained?[43]

This reasoning led Tucker to inquire whether there are not checks to further growth that increase spontaneously with population density. The answer, he believed, lies in the growth of cities as civilization advances. He considered cities "the most effective and the least objectionable check to redundancy," and their effect is to reduce fertility and increase the amount of disease.[44] Marriage comes later among civilized people, and this may produce vice; but fundamentally ". . . it is the want (i.e., lack) of the means of procuring luxuries, and of gratifying the artificial desires and wants of civilized life, which in this way arrests the further multiplication of the species."[45] In summary, Tucker presented his substitute for the Malthusian theory:

If the foregoing views be correct, the result seems to be, that mankind will rapidly multiply where subsistence is easily obtained, as in America: that as a country increases in density of numbers, and improves in civilization, checks to redundancy also increase, independent of the greater difficulty of subsistence, until they are sufficient to keep its popu-

[42] *Ibid.*, pp. 82–83 (*Port Folio*, pp. 173–174).
[43] *Ibid.*, pp. 308–314.
[44] *Ibid.*, pp. 315–316.
[45] *Ibid.*, pp. 318–319.

lation stationary: that although in the present state of society, these checks are often misery and vice, in some form or other, yet these evils are accompanied, and more than redeemed, by the benefits which civilization confers: that none of them, except disease, seem beyond the reach of human remedy, and if we could ever hope to see them abolished, then the virtuous self-control which their abolition necessarily implies, would exactly adapt the numbers of every community to its means of affording them comfortable subsistence.[46]

Expressed here is Tucker's anticipation of a natural and automatic stabilization of population at an optimum level through the influence of artificial wants and civilization rather than stabilization at a Malthusian equilibrium maintained by vice and misery.

Later works by Tucker, *The Laws of Wages, Profits, and Rent* (1837), *Progress of the United States in Population and Wealth* (1843), and *Political Economy for the People* (1859), restated and amplified the views contained in the *Essays*. The *Laws*[47] again described population growth as an active agent in pushing societies on toward higher stages of social and economic development,[48] but it went beyond Tucker's earlier work in tracing the influence of increased numbers of people on distribution and on the level of living. Largely on the basis of supply and demand, Tucker concluded that real wages fall, while rent and food prices rise with population growth.

Concerning wages, he wrote that when population has grown to a point at which all fertile land is occupied, further growth depresses real wages because a given amount of labor exchanges for less produce than before.[49] Here it is the increase in demand that adds to the value of produce, unless there is a counter improvement in production methods; but the greater demand may be met in part by resort to poorer soils,[50] in part by an increasing replacement of meat in the diet by plant products such as bread and potatoes.[51] The influence of population growth on real wages, however, may be counteracted by improved methods of production.[52]

In this connection Tucker expressed his disagreement with Ricardo's explanation that resorting to inferior soils depresses wages by raising the price of produce. Without explicitly stating a productivity theory of wage determination, Tucker reasoned that with the use of inferior soils the productivity of labor and the price of labor fall together.[53] He argued further that

> Raw produce does not rise (in price) because inferior soils are cultivated, but they are cultivated because raw produce has risen; and the effect

---

[46] *Ibid.*, pp. 329–330.
[47] *The Laws of Wages, Profits, and Rent,* Philadelphia: Carey and Hart, 1837.
[48] *Ibid.*, p. 16. [49] *Ibid.*, p. 20.
[50] *Ibid.*, p. 20. [51] *Ibid.*, p. 22.
[52] *Ibid.*, p. 25. [53] *Ibid.*, p. 34.

of their cultivation is to lessen or to arrest the rise rather than to produce it. This error runs through all the reasoning of the Ricardo school. They see that the increase of population is the remote cause of the rise of raw produce; but in tracing out the intermediate links, they mistake an effect for a proximate cause.[54]

Tucker also made the point that the worker's consumption is not a constant factor but rather, it can be shifted to cheaper means of subsistence by the pressure of competition. Tucker estimated that a given area of land provides twice as much subsistence in bread as in meat, six times as much in potatoes. Therefore,

> As population advances, and the means of subsistence become comparatively scarcer, a proportional number of the community must pass from one of these modes of subsistence to another; and if the lowest standard of comfort for the labouring class should be above either of these modes, and not yield to the pressure of increasing numbers, then population will become stationary.[55]

In his *Political Economy,* published more than twenty years later, Tucker maintained his earlier views on the interrelation of population growth, the cultivation of poorer soils, prices, and real wages.[56] Concerning wages he wrote that "When land is abundant, compared with population, the price of labor, from its relative scarcity, will . . . be naturally high, and that of land and its products, from their abundance, will be low."[57] It is interesting in this connection that he further deduced the growth of the population of the United States would bring an end to slavery by reducing wages to a point at which it was no longer profitable to keep slaves.[58]

Tucker's views on rent were most fully set forth in his *Laws.*[59] The level of rent was said to depend upon "the relation between the quantity of fertile land and the number who derive subsistence from it."[60] This was explained in terms of supply and demand for subsistence, with population as the demand factor. At the same time, population growth would further increase the share of the product going to the landowner by depressing wages. According to Tucker,

> . . . at whatever point the population becomes stationary, by reason of its having reached the limits of subsistence, the rate of wages will have gradually diminished from the whole amount produced by the labourer, deducting the profits of capital, to the quantity required for his necessary support; and the difference between this maximum and minimum price,

[54] *Ibid.,* pp. 35–36.
[55] *Ibid.,* p. 23.
[56] See especially pp. 54–56, 79, of *Political Economy for the People,* Philadelphia, 1859.
[57] *Ibid.,* p. 54.
[58] *Ibid.,* pp. 88–90.
[59] Tucker, *The Laws,* Ch. 8.
[60] *Ibid.,* p. 95.

is, in the progress of society, gradually transferred to the landlord by way of rent.[61]

Tucker thus agreed with the classical economists in identifying the landlord as the eventual beneficiary of population growth; but he differed in denying that graduations in the quality of soils have any agency in producing rent.[62] In his words:

> It thus appears that neither is a resort to soils of inferior fertility, to lands more distant from market, nor different results from successive outlays of capital on the same lands, necessary either to the existence of rent, or to its progressive increase, but that it is caused solely by the increase of population, together with the capacity which the same soil possesses of supporting a greater number by reason of their resorting to a more frugal mode of subsistence.[63]

The same views on rent were restated in the *Political Economy*.[64]

As for Tucker's later views on the Malthusian theory of population, his *Laws* and *Political Economy* indicate an increased acceptance of some elements of Malthus' thought, and a persistent underlying optimism about the population question, perhaps an intermingling of imported ideas and American points of view. He came to believe that an expanding population and labor supply exert pressure on subsistence and the level of living, and he was not optimistic about the immediate outlook for the exercise of restraint in reproduction.[65] But at the same time, he believed Malthus had somewhat overrated the tendency to increase and underrated the strength of the checks to population.[66] And he was hopeful that good laws, wise government, and popular education could reduce the number of poor by furthering industriousness and self-restraint.[67]

Everett · Many of the common arguments against the Malthusian theory were presented in *New Ideas on Population*[68] (1823) by the Ameri-

[61] *Ibid.*, p. 100.
[62] *Ibid.*
[63] *Ibid.*, p. 121.
[64] Tucker, *Political Economy*, esp. pp. 53–54.
[65] In the *Laws*, p. 23, Tucker wrote ". . . the past history of mankind instructs us that the restraints of prudence and decent pride have never yet been sufficient to arrest the multiplying propensity, though they may check its force: and we cannot reasonably expect them to keep the population within the limit of liberal subsistence, without a more improved and enlightened state of society than has yet existed."
[66] "While I readily admit the ability and value of Mr. Malthus's work, it has long appeared to me that he has somewhat overrated the multiplying propensity of mankind, which I do not think too strong, and has undervalued the checks to redundancy" (Tucker, *Political Economy*, p. 221).
[67] *Ibid.*, p. 223.
[68] Full title: *New Ideas on Population, with Remarks on the Theories of Malthus and Godwin*, Boston and London, 1823. The page references below are to the Boston edition.

can diplomat and magazine editor, Alexander Everett (1790–1847). Population growth was said to be a normal occurrence,[69] which acts as a stimulus to the evolution of societies to higher stages of social and economic organization.[70] Everett's main contention was that increasing population is a cause of abundance, not of scarcity.[71] According to his explanation,

> As long as the principal effect of the increase of population is to bring under cultivation additional tracts of land, the positive resources and wealth of the society will doubtless be augmented in the same proportion, but the means of subsistence will be neither more nor less abundant than they were before. . . . It is only when the population begins to increase upon the territory already appropriated, that it produces the effect of augmenting the supply of the provisions in proportion to the demand.[72]

That is to say, productivity increases with more intensive cultivation, not with expansion of the area under cultivation. And the natural consequence of a rise in productivity, according to Everett, is a proportional rise in wages, unless this is prevented by political and economic regulation of the distribution of the product.[73]

Without departing from his anti-Malthusian position, Everett recognized the existence of checks to population, among which he enumerated physical evil, private vice, vicious political institutions, and barbarism.[74] The checks, he believed, were less active in the United States, and he attributed the rapid growth of population to this rather than to immigration.[75]

Most original and promising was Everett's consideration of the "economical" effects of an increase in population, in the early chapters of his work. With an all too rare perception of both the producer and the consumer aspects of population, he wrote that "The economical effect of an increase of population, is an augmentation in the supply of labor and in the demand for its products,"[76] and made the just comment on Malthus that "He appears throughout his work to consider the increase of population, simply in its effect upon the consumption of the means of subsistence, without regarding its operation upon their supply."[77] But even though Everett focused attention on the problem central to the economic implications of population growth, the relation of the increased demand to the increased supply, he did not succeed in developing his answer beyond the common optimistic assertion that population growth facilitates the division of labor, leads to greater productive skill, and promotes various advances in techniques of production at different levels of economic organization.[78] This general

[69] *Ibid.*, p. 37: "The increase of population is to nature, what the natural growth of the body is to individuals."
[70] *Ibid.*, Ch. III.
[71] *Ibid.*, p. 120.
[72] *Ibid.*, p. 39.
[73] *Ibid.*, p. 111.
[74] *Ibid.*, p. 75.
[75] *Ibid.*, p. 84.
[76] *Ibid.*, Ch. II, p. 21.
[77] *Ibid.*
[78] *Ibid.*, Ch. II and III.

theme was developed through the remainder of the work, which is one of the most persuasive contemporary replies to Malthus.

A later and unsigned work by Everett, his *America*[79] (1827), that was an account of the Western Hemisphere nations, did not touch on the population question except to state certain arguments against Malthus in the concluding chapter. There Everett wrote

> One of the most remarkable features in the probable future as well as the past progress of our country, is the rapid and before unprecedented increase of population. . . . This circumstance is at once a proof and a principal co-operating cause of our extraordinary prosperity. . . . It remained for a writer of the present day to start the strange paradox . . . that an increase in the numbers of the people (excepting some peculiar cases) is a public misfortune, and that it is the business of a wise legislator to check population and not to encourage it. It is generally known, however, and Mr. Malthus is the first to admit, that labour is the only source of wealth. What then creates more wealth or capital? why of course more labour. And what furnishes an addition of labour? clearly the increase of population, which increases the number of labourers.[80]

He added that population growth leads to the division of labor, that it is "the great natural spring of the welfare of states,"[81] and that it adds to the productivity of labor by increasing the skill with which it is employed.[82]

McVickar · In 1825 John McVickar (1787–1868), clergyman and professor of moral philosophy at Columbia, republished McCulloch's article on political economy from the Encyclopedia Britannica, under the title *Outlines of Political Economy,* together with his own notes and comments. McVickar's notes included only brief references to population and did not develop his thought on the subject, but they did indicate both acceptance of Malthus and conviction that the United States benefited from the rapid growth of its population.

With regard to Malthus, McVickar endorsed McCulloch's statement that Malthus had demonstrated that population has a constant tendency to exceed the means of subsistence; and he wrote of the *Essay* that ". . . it is a work which has settled conclusively and finally the great operating principle which regulates the advance of national population."[83] McVickar then restated Malthus' principles of population, and within the same page referred to the rate of population growth as the surest criterion of national

[79] (Alexander Everett), *America: A general Survey of the Political Situation of the several Powers of the Western Hemisphere,* by a citizen of the United States, Philadelphia: Carey & Lea, 1827.

[80] *Ibid.,* pp. 338–339.

[81] *Ibid.,* p. 339.

[82] *Ibid.,* p. 340.

[83] McCulloch, *Outlines of Political Economy,* with notes by John McVickar, New York, 1825, pp. 145–146.

prosperity.[84] Here he presumably thought of population growth as the consequence of prosperity, but in later reference to the rapid growth of population in the United States he stated that "It is this rapidly increasing population which gives life to the productive industry of our country, and will long avert from us the evils of a permanently overloaded market."[85] This indicates concern over the possibility of overproduction in the United States, and, while not incompatible with McVickar's earlier remarks, leaves uncertain his full views on population.

Cardozo · J. N. Cardozo (1786–1873) was a South Carolina editor, economist, and advocate of free trade, who published his *Notes on Political Economy* (1826) to counteract what he considered erroneous ideas in McVickar's *Outlines of Political Economy*. Quite thoughtful and scholarly in tone, Cardozo's work was directed especially against the economic theories of Ricardo and Malthus. Although not emphasizing an American point of view, it nevertheless maintained its independence of European authority in political economy.

Most concerned with demonstrating inconsistencies and erroneous assumption in Ricardo's economics, which he believed was "destined to perish," Cardozo attacked the foundations of classical economics by questioning the principle of diminishing returns and the Ricardian rent theory, and while explaining his views on these subjects, revealed his own ideas on population. At one point he implied that population growth can raise the price of necessities, but he did not say this result necessarily follows.[86] The population variable was not mentioned in his explanation of the cause of higher rent, which he attributed to a deficiency of supply relative to demand.[87] More explicitly on rent and population, he wrote further:

> It follows that as population increases and fresh land must be cultivated to raise the additional food required, the rent paid for the use of land of decreasing fertility will be relatively less than that already in cultivation by the difference in its naturally productive power. The rent received for land of this comparative inferiority will then be in proportion to the surplus it can be made to yield, after the deduction of all the expenses of cultivation, including, of course, average profits and

[84] *Ibid.,* p. 146: "In judging of the prosperity of a country, the amount of population affords no criterion — but the rate of population the surest and best.

"The population of a country may be either progressive, stationary, or retrograde. In the first the mass of the people are comfortable and prosperous — in the second their lot is tolerable — but in the last it is wretched.

"The first or happiest state is prolonged by whatever delays the necessity of resorting to inferior soils for food — by improvements in agriculture at home, and free admission of corn from abroad."

[85] *Ibid.,* p. 169.

[86] J. N. Cardozo, *Notes on Political Economy,* Charleston, 1826, p. 33.

[87] *Ibid.,* p. 25.

wages, as in the instance of the land first cultivated. On every descent in the scale of fertility, the same principle will apply.[88]

Here, however, Cardozo stated his view that population growth does not lead to the use of inferior land, but rather that

> The increase of population . . . depends on the extent of the improvements in agriculture, and inferior land is laid down in tillage exactly in proportion as these improvements extend. This is the reverse of the new theory which connects the augmentation of population and produce with the increased difficulty instead of the increased facility of production.[89]

This conclusion was a major point of divergence from the currently accepted principles of political economy.

Cardozo restated and applied the above conclusion in his chapter on profits and wages. According to his analysis,

> The number of consumers is increased in proportion to the addition made to the means of subsistence, on the principle that as quantity augments, price is reduced and consumption enlarged. The labourers, in the ratio of their increase, are compelled to receive less wages, which enables the capitalist, with the same money amount, to employ an additional number of labourers, or an additional quantity of labour, which is the same thing, and which, as we see, has been already provided. Thus is capital made not more instrumental to the increase of population than population to the increase of capital — thus is the ratio of their increase precisely equal. Wages do not encroach on profits nor profits on wages. All that is necessary to the final results is, that science and skill should be able to overcome the difficulty of production on land of a decreasing fertility.
>
> The effect of an augmentation of the quantity of raw produce, from the diminished difficulty of production, must give such a stimulus to population as will reduce money wages. There is the cost of producing labourers as well as the cost of producing the labourer's subsistence. The cost of production with regard to the labourer, is the price of that food and those necessaries which are essential to the continuance of the race of labourers, and ensure a sufficient supply of them. And as the consequence of an addition to supply, is a decline in price, money wages must inevitably fall, on the same principle that raw or manufactured products are reduced in price from increased facility of production. But if the cultivator will be able to command an increased quantity of labour, in consequence of a fall in money wages, (labour being the most costly of the instruments of production,) it will further stimulate production on the land, promoted, as it must be, by additional skill and science. Raw produce must again augment in quantity, its price must again fall, and by

[88] *Ibid.*, p. 34.
[89] *Ibid.*, p. 35.

enabling the labourers to command more food and necessaries, induce them further to increase, which will again add to the supply of labour in the market. Thus the same series of effects is always recurring and never interrupted but by the folly of selfishness of those who are entrusted with power.[90]

With the assumption of equal growth of capital and population, and greater productivity, Cardozo concluded that money wages fall, while real wages and the condition of the workers improve. As for the eventual limit to this process,

> Whenever the entire globe is cultivated to the utmost extent of its capacity to produce, and the population which it is capable of maintaining on its surface is fully up to the measure of that capacity, both population and produce must come to a stop. Both will then remain stationary. But this does not invalidate the principle that they are capable of an increase up to this point. The period is very remote indeed at which they will have reached it, if rulers are wise enough to profit by the various resources which Nature places at their command for the benefit of those they govern. So distant indeed that we may not trouble ourselves about the consequences when that desirable consummation shall have been attained. The rate of increase, we must remember, is slow, when things are left to take their natural course.[91]

This is to deny that population growth need be feared, even as it approaches the subsistence limit.

The *Notes* conclude with comments on the Malthusian theory and a statement of Cardozo's quite different views. The relative strength of the preventive check and of the stimulus to increase, it is asserted, depends upon the nature of the society, and the stimulus to increase is not necessarily the stronger. Therefore, wrote Cardozo, "The error of Mr. Malthus consists, then, I think, in stating that *positively* as a *Law of Nature,* which, for what we know to the contrary, may be the result of an imperfect social organization."[92] It was, in fact, quite possible for Cardozo to imagine societies in which production, not reproduction, is more actively promoted.[93] In his words:

> Without indulging, therefore, in dreams of perfectibility, it is not venturing on visionary speculations of unattainable or impossible improvement to infer, that if the institution of primogeniture were abolished wherever it prevails, with every species of monopoly, supposing the security of person and property complete, and the public burthens moderate, the rate of increase in the production of food might greatly augment; whilst the more ample leisure for instruction permitted to the labouring

[90] *Ibid.,* pp. 40–42.   [91] *Ibid.,* pp. 51–52.
[92] *Ibid.,* p. 124.   [93] *Ibid.*

classes — by allowing them to receive sound and salutary lessons on the subject of population, or those maxims of prudence and foresight necessary to their comfort and respectability — might give much greater room than at present for the action of the check entitled by Mr. Malthus, *moral restraint.* It is impossible to foretell the precise effects of such an arrangement of the social elements, or to say what would be the relative ratio in the increase of food and population, on such a supposition; but that it would be very different from that which is generally exhibited in the present or any past condition of the species, I am satisfied.[94]

This was the concluding paragraph of Cardozo's *Notes,* and it summarizes his position on the population question.

Cooper · The year of publication of Cardozo's work saw the appearance of another political economy text in the United States, *Lectures on the Elements of Political Economy* (1826) by Thomas Cooper (1759–1839), president of South Carolina College and its professor of chemistry and political economy. This work consisted of lectures that had been delivered to the senior class, and included some discussion of population.

This was not Cooper's first statement of his views on population. Of British origin, he had followed his friend Joseph Priestley to the United States at the age of about thirty-five, had become active as a political pamphleteer, entered the legal profession, and then withdrawn from public life to devote himself to science and teaching. A brief presentation of his views on population is found in appendix notes he prepared for Priestley's *Memoires.*[95] There, with apparent reluctance, he acknowledged the probable truth of the Malthusian theory:

> . . . I am ready to acknowledge, it is possible that the melancholy theories of the present day, which judge of the future lot of mankind upon earth, from the history of past facts, may be too well founded; that war, pestilence and famine, and vice and misery in all its hideous forms, may be necessary to counteract the over increase of the human species, and make up for the difference between the arithmetical progression of subsistence, and the geometrical ratio of accumulating population.[96]

But he went on to express certain doubts he had about the Malthusian theory, seemingly reluctant as a social reformer to accept the implications of that theory for the future of mankind. He was, he wrote, ". . . well persuaded that much good may be brought about, without danger of too great population, by gradually putting in practice well founded theories of political reform."[97] It seemed to him quite possible that answers could

[94] *Ibid.,* pp. 124–125.
[95] *Memoires of Dr. Joseph Priestley, to the Year 1795 . . . including observations on his writings by Thomas Cooper . . . ,* 2 vol., Northumberland, 1806.
[96] *Ibid.,* Vol. II, Appendix 3, pp. 337–338.
[97] *Ibid.,* footnote, p. 338.

be found to Malthus' arguments. He doubted whether any country had ever been so fully peopled that it could not support more,[98] and he pointed out that "At present, the earth does not support above a tenth of the human creatures that might find subsistence by its cultivation, and yet we are daily victims of all the miseries. . . ."[99]

The *Lectures,* which came more than twenty years later, in the academic period of Cooper's life, were largely a restatement of Ricardo and others, with little new added, and they included a chapter on population that adhered quite closely to Malthus.[100] A second edition of the *Lectures* (1829) contained an added chapter on population that expanded some-what the treatment in the first edition.[101] A later work by Cooper, *A Manual of Political Economy* (1834), also included a few references to population.

The introductory chapter of the *Lectures* summarized the Malthusian doctrine of population and expressed Cooper's full agreement, with the words that the doctrine "may now be considered as settled," and that it is of "manifest truth."[102] But the chapter devoted to population departed from the Malthusian model to the extent of defending early marriage as being productive of a better state of society than late marriage, repressing selfish and vicious tendencies, and enhancing social responsibility.[103] Other reasons for preferring early marriage also were advanced:

> Obeying the urgency of the calls of nature common to the whole animal creation, men marry and beget children, and then strive to provide for them. Population therefore is the great stimulus to exertion, and the great check to parental extravagance and expensive indulgence. Marriage and its concomitant offspring, produce kind and social feelings; feelings of duty founded on natural associations, prompting to industry, regularity, and self denial.
>
> Moreover, early marriages are productive of a better state of society than late ones. This is manifest in our own country: and it must of course happen, that the earlier, vicious and selfish propensities and indulgencies are repressed and counteracted, the more virtuous will society be. Not merely more chaste, but more regular, more self denying, and social in its general tone and feeling. The earlier we are accustomed to give up our own wants and wishes for the sake of those we love, the sooner and more habitual will every social feeling be formed and become.
>
> The governing principle of voluntary celibacy, however prudent or even commendable it may be and sometimes is, rests upon an exclusive

[98] *Ibid.*, p. 339.
[99] *Ibid.*, p. 340.
[100] Thomas Cooper, *Lectures on the Elements of Political Economy,* Columbia, S.C., 1826, Ch. 24.
[101] Cooper, *Lectures,* 2nd ed., Ch. 25.
[102] Cooper, *Lectures,* 1st ed., p. 12 (2nd ed., p. 18).
[103] *Ibid.*, p. 235 (2nd ed., p. 276).

carefulness of a man's self, and a carelessness of the common good. Hence, although early marriages may produce poverty, and incessant exertion, it seems to me a less evil to society, that superfluous population should be gradually thinned by infantile diseases attendant on scanty subsistence, than that the first and most imperious precept of nature should be disobeyed, or subjected to every species of vicious substitute.[104]

Quite at variance with the rest of Cooper's treatment of population, this long defense of early marriage may have reflected strong American convictions; or perhaps the moral tone of the lecture was adapted to Cooper's student audience. With this one exception, the treatment of population was faithfully Malthusian: the means of subsistence are limited; population tends to grow more rapidly; and misery follows if the number of people presses on subsistence.

The population variable was assigned little role in Cooper's account of distribution except in wage determination, where a supply and demand explanation was given. Adopting Ricardo's concept of a natural wage level but preferring to think of wages in terms of the proportion of the total product that the laborers receive, Cooper explained that "This proportion will vary according to the prevailing ratio of demand and supply of labourers," and,

> When the demand and supply of labour and of the commodity produced by it, are regular and steady, the natural price of labour is every where what will enable him to live and maintain a wife and two children in the plainest manner. This plainest manner will depend on the custom of the country. . . .[105]

Further explanation made clear that the demand for labor depends upon the supply of capital:

> Labour can only be put in requisition by capital. If therefore there be not a regular annual addition to the aggregate amount of accumulated capital, there can be no regular addition to the quantity of labour in a nation. If labourers are propagated and there is no demand for them, the market becomes over stocked; they are competitors for employment; labour falls in price; poverty and diseases attendant upon it, appear; and the ranks are thinned till wages mount up by a lessened supply of working men, to the natural or necessary price of labour; to wit, adequate subsistence for a married couple and a child or two.[106]

This can be identified as a classical economic version of the iron law of wages, with the equilibrium point set at the wage level dictated by the customary mode of living of the workers. The primary importance of capital in determining the demand for labor and its price was even more emphatically stated in the conclusion of the chapter on population:

[104] *Ibid.*
[105] *Ibid.,* pp. 92, 93 (2nd ed., p. 104).
[106] *Ibid.,* p. 94 (2nd ed., p. 105).

. . . population may encrease momentarily, but it will be starved out of existence without a permanent and adequate demand to support it. That demand is the offspring of capital. I contend that capital gradually saved out of income, and set to work to produce profit, is the *only* source of regular demand for labour; the *only* basis of a permanently encreasing population, of national power, and of national prosperity. To capital quietly and gradually accumulated, rather than suddenly acquired, we owe all our comforts, all our improvements, and every useful scheme by which the condition of man in society has been or is likely to be ameliorated. Hence that government which being effective, is the least expensive, best answers these desirable ends.[107]

What Cooper says here is reminiscent of but goes beyond Ricardo and others, who stressed the importance of the ratio and relative rates of growth of capital and population, and who thought of capital as being the more fundamental economic variable.

The new chapter in the second edition of the *Lectures* did not depart from Malthusian orthodoxy except to note that "a dense population furnishes the means of gratifying most of the wants which it originates," that a dense population promotes national wealth by favoring the division of labor, and that along with their disadvantages, large cities contribute more discoveries and advances that add to national welfare.[108]

Cooper's late work, *A Manual of Political Economy* (1834), also was strongly Malthusian. It characterized overpopulation as ". . . the greatest of all misfortunes (which brings) in its train poverty, want, neglect of cleanliness, debility, disease, miserable lives, and premature death, from too much labor and too little food."[109] It also stated the tendency of population growth to maintain wages at a low level, and condemned poor laws, which add to the evil by enabling the poor to increase their numbers.[110]

From the writings reviewed here it can be seen that Cooper's position on the population question underwent change from one period of his varied life to another. Regarded in his early years as a dangerous radical, he later came to have firm respect for authority, at least in political economy. In this subject his writings are a faithful reflection of the English classical school, except for scattered traces of what may be American influence or his own early independence of thought.

Jennison · A small, elementary text, *An Outline of Political Economy*[111] was published in Philadelphia in 1828. Little is known of the author, William Jennison. The work itself was cast in the form of a series of questions and answers, and was said to be designed for use in seminaries.

[107] *Ibid.*, p. 240 (2nd ed., pp. 281–282).
[108] *Ibid.*, 2nd ed., pp. 295, 297–298.
[109] Cooper, *Manual of Political Economy*, Washington, D.C., 1834, p. 34.
[110] *Ibid.*, pp. 11, 13.
[111] William Jennison, *An Outline of Political Economy*, Philadelphia, printed for the author, 1828.

Only scattered references to population are found. Population size seems, on the whole, to have been regarded as a result of economic forces rather than an active economic variable itself. In a section on population and immigration it was stated that the population of the United States doubles in about twenty-three years, but in as little as ten years in specially favored districts.[112] Immigration was regarded as generally advantageous because of its contribution to population and capital.[113] Of population growth, the author wrote,

> Population has a natural tendency to increase, but this very increase carries with itself the power to supply its own wants. The extent of population regulates the amount of subsistence in the same manner, as it regulates the supply of clothing and housing . . . (because) the aggregate of subsistence raised, depends on the amount of labour bestowed on it.[114]

There was no mention of less optimistic views on the subject of population.

Phillips · Somewhat better known was another work on political economy that appeared in the same year, the *Manual of Political Economy* (1828) by Willard Phillips (1784–1873). Phillips was a prominent Boston lawyer and author, who wrote also on tariff policy and insurance law. His purpose in writing the *Manual,* according to the preface, was to state the principles of political economy applicable to the United States, and it is evident from the body of the work that he believed Old World economic doctrines did not necessarily apply in the New World.

The *Manual* gave no more than passing reference to population. There was mention of the "hackneyed" doctrine from Malthus that population increases up to the subsistence limit, but it was rejected with the comments that some nations export surplus food and that food is only one of the wants of civilized people.[115]

Population was only briefly mentioned in the chapters that dealt with distribution of the products of labor to landowner, laborer, and capitalist. The Ricardian rent theory was dismissed with the judgment that it is "somewhat metaphysical and now almost exploded."[116] It was suggested indirectly that population size might affect the level of rent,[117] but this was regarded as only one of a number of factors. The wage level was similarly described as determined by many things. One effect attributed to a greater density of people was a more rapid circulation of money.[118] For Phillips capital and natural resources especially were the important economic variables.

[112] *Ibid.,* pp. 31, 48.
[113] *Ibid.,* p. 49.
[114] *Ibid.,* p. 48.
[115] Willard Phillips, *Manual of Political Economy,* Boston, 1828, p. 75.
[116] *Ibid.,* p. 108.
[117] *Ibid.,* pp. 116, 118.
[118] *Ibid.,* p. 244.

2 · 1830–1839

Rae · John Rae (1796–1872), one of several writers of that name, was born near Aberdeen in Scotland, educated in the University there and at Edinburgh, moved to Canada in his middle twenties, and later went to Boston, where his *Statement of some New Principles on the Subject of Political Economy*[119] was published in 1834. Because of his education in Scotland it can be questioned whether Rae fairly belongs among the American economists; but he is included here because his work was published in America and because he had lived there for ten years by the time of its publication.

As the full title of the book suggests, Rae's work was directed against *The Wealth of Nations,* especially against free trade and Smith's emphasis on the role of capital in economic development. Rae argued in part that invention and the development of arts and manufactures are more effective than the accumulation of capital in increasing the supply of the means of subsistence.

This quite original work[120] was concerned with matters other than population, but some incidental notes on that topic were included. Rae's views, as far as they were revealed, were mildly Malthusian. It is incorrect, he stated, to assume that increase of population can insure the welfare of a nation.[121] Concerning the tendency of population to increase up to the subsistence limit, he wrote,

> The numbers of a state can never exceed, what its resources can support. When these resources are augmented, the principles which tend to the preservation and multiplication of the species are, in all well regulated communities, sufficiently active speedily to fill up their numbers to the amount of the increased supply.[122]

The endorsement of the Malthusian doctrine was then rounded out by the statement ". . . the fact is, that people, rather than live single, are inclined to marry at all risks, and hence population is kept down by misery, and premature death. . . ."[123] Rae put little faith in the practice of moral

---

[119] John Rae, *Statement of some New Principles on the Subject of Political Economy, exposing the fallacies of the system of free trade, and of some other doctrines maintained in the Wealth of Nations,* Boston, 1834.

[120] For example, Rae quite clearly anticipated Veblen in writing, "The things to which vanity seems most readily to apply itself are those of which the use or consumption is most apparent, and of which the effects are most difficult to discriminate. Articles of which the consumption is not conspicuous, are incapable of gratifying this passion" (Rae, *op. cit.,* p. 267).

[121] *Ibid.,* p. 28.

[122] *Ibid.*

[123] *Ibid.,* p. 29.

restraint. He did not deal with the possible effects of population numbers on distribution.

Newman · The next text on political economy to appear was *Elements of Political Economy* (1835) by Samuel Newman (1797–1842), for many years professor of classics and lecturer on political economy at Bowdoin College. Strongly influenced by Adam Smith, this work is judged to have contributed few really new ideas on political economy, although it was regarded as a leading text in its day.

The population variable received most attention in Newman's discussion of wages and wage determination, in which he dealt with the interrelations of labor supply, capital, "style of living," and the wage level. He approached wage determination in terms of the cost of production of labor, which was said to be set by the style of living of the laborers.[124] That the immediate mechanism of wage regulation is supply and demand, however, is indicated by Newman's remarks on Ireland, which he took as an example of a low style of living.

> The style of living is not only reduced to the lowest point possible, but many die of famine, or are compelled to emigrate to other countries. Here then the effect of the principle of supply and demand is most fully felt. The population is dense, and the amount of productive capital giving employment to laborers, is small. The supply of the commodity — labor, far exceeds the demand for it, and its price is reduced.[125]

Dealing with the case of a decline in the style of living, he explained further how population change enters into the natural regulation of the wage level:

> Look next at a community, in which from some cause the style of living is reduced. This reduction may also be attended with an increase of population, especially where the rate of wages continues the same. But generally, a reduction in the style of living is followed by a correspondent fall in the rate of wages. Hence, if the laboring population consent to a reduction in the style of living, it is usually followed by a lower rate of wages. But here it should be noticed that there is a limit, beyond which it ceases to be for the interest of the undertaker to effect a reduction in the price of labor. For unless the laborer is able to support himself, and to rear up a family, soon the numbers of the laboring population will be diminished, and then, the supply of labor becoming less than the demand, the price will rise.[126]

Newman evidently regarded the population variable as a dependent or adjustment factor, rather than an independent determiner of wages.

Later in the same chapter, however, Newman seems to assign a more

---

[124] Samuel P. Newman, *Elements of Political Economy,* New York, 1835, p. 242.
[125] *Ibid.,* pp. 245–246.
[126] *Ibid.,* pp. 247–248.

active role to population, and indicates two ways in which it may affect real wages:

> The tendency then of an excess of population must be to diminish the rate of wages, while at the same time, perhaps, from the great demand for the necessaries of life, the value of the small sum received by the laborer is also reduced. Hence poverty and suffering ensue, and population is said to press upon the means of subsistence.[127]

Noting that some political economists believe that population growth leads to disastrous results, and that others are confident production and capital advance with population numbers, Newman stated his own views in the form of two propositions:

> 1. The period when the surface of the earth shall be so covered with inhabitants, that population will equal the means of subsistence, is so distant, and all calculations and reasonings relating to this state of things so indefinite and shadowy, that the whole subject is one of no practical importance.
> 2. Most of the evils which are wont to be ascribed to an excess of population, may be traced to some existing abuses of civil institutions, or to some unwise neglect of nations to avail themselves of the productive resources within their power.[128]

In effect, Newman treated population size as a significant if not altogether independent economic variable, but denied that there is a "population problem."

Wayland · Francis Wayland (1796–1865), a clergyman, educator, and for many years president of Brown, was author of *Elements of Political Economy* (1837), of which at least four editions appeared between 1837 and 1857. Although it showed the influence of both European and American ideas in its treatment of political economy, the work did not incorporate distinctively American thought on population.

The influence of the population factor was dealt with most explicitly under the topic of wages. An account of the general principles governing wages stated that the minimum wage is set by the physiological requirements of the worker, who must be provided with the necessities of life; but in addition, wages must be sufficient for the worker to raise a family of at least two children and to support himself in his old age.[129]

Following European precedent, Wayland gave the following account of wage determination:

> . . . the average rate of wages, in any country, for a number of years taken together, must depend upon the ratio which the annual accumula-

[127] *Ibid.*, p. 253.
[128] *Ibid.*
[129] Francis Wayland, *The Elements of Political Economy*, New York, 1837, pp. 326–327.

tion of capital in any country, bears to the annual increase of human beings. If wages be high, and capital increase as fast as the human species increases, wages will, for any period that may be contemplated, continue as they are at present. If wages be low, and capital does not increase faster than the human race, they will continue low. If the increase of capital be more rapid than the natural increase of the human race, wages, however high, will rise, until they be so high that the production can yield no profit. The deficiency would then be supplied by foreigners, who would emigrate to the more favored country. If the increase of capital be less rapid than that of the human race, the price of wages will fall, distress in the working classes will ensue, and they must either emigrate or starve.[130]

The two production factors, capital and population, were not of equal weight in Wayland's eyes, however, for he explained further that

Population always follows capital. It increases, as capital increases; is stationary, when capital is stationary; and decreases, when capital decreases. And hence, there seems to be no need for any other means to prevent the too rapid increase of population, than to secure a corresponding increase of capital, by which that population may be supported.[131]

Population was thus viewed as a dependent variable, expanding or contracting with capital.

Rent was traced by Wayland to the necessity of using land of inferior fertility or location when population and the demand for food increase.[132]

Henry Carey · Henry C. Carey (1793–1879), son of Mathew Carey, followed in his father's footsteps as publisher, prolific writer on many subjects, and economist. As an economist he was an ardent protectionist, the most original and influential of the American economists of the period, and undoubtedly the one best known to political economists outside the United States.[133]

Carey's views on population are scattered throughout his many writings,

[130] *Ibid.*, pp. 338–339.
[131] *Ibid.*, p. 340.
[132] *Ibid.*, pp. 382–383.
[133] According to the testimony of his contemporaries, Carey was aggressively American in his sentiments and carried on his own private war of independence against British influence. The English economist T. E. C. Leslie, in his "Political economy in the United States," reported that, according to one of Carey's acquaintances, "he was an American and a patriot, and . . . his passionate hostility to the British system of foreign trade, and to the subsidiary British system of political economy, takes something of the temper and tone of national prejudice." He quoted the same informant as saying, "His father was an Irish patriot and a political exile from the land of his birth. Something hereditary may be detected running with much of the pristine force of blood through the life and character of his son." In a footnote Leslie added the interesting if unconfirmed remark of an unnamed English writer, who reported after visiting Carey that "He is a man of plain speech, and swears like a bargeman whenever Mill's name is mentioned" (Leslie, *op. cit.*, p. 502).

but especially in *The Harmony of Nature* (1836), *Principles of Political Economy* (1837), *The Past, the Present, and the Future* (1848), and *Principles of Social Science* (1858). Together these provide the fullest treatment of the subject by any of the American writers of the period. Although Carey himself did not make the separation when writing of population, it is helpful in summarizing his thought to follow the division made in other chapters and to consider separately his views on the relation of population to production, on the role of population in distribution, and on general theories of population.

Best known of Carey's contributions to economic thought is his assertion, presumably based on American experience, that cultivation does not necessarily start with the most fertile soils and progress to successively poorer soils. He wrote, "The soils first cultivated are very frequently not those of highest fertility."[134] Instead, the first choice depends on ease of clearing, on the location of roads, and on nearness to market; and since these considerations have nothing to do with fertility and may even favor poorer soils, the progression in cultivation is generally from poorer to better soils rather than the reverse. This was a central principle in Carey's economics, and it attacked the foundations of classical economics, for if true, it invalidated the law of diminishing returns, the Ricardian rent theory, and the corollary that population growth must be harmful in the long run.

Carey maintained the same position in his later works. In *The Past,* he explained that it is only with the growth of the labor supply and advances in agricultural techniques that the more fertile but less easily cleared and cultivated lands can be brought into use.[135] His still later *Social Science* contained a chapter, "On the occupation of the earth," which described how the light hilly soils are occupied first and how it is only with greater numbers and skill that population and agriculture can descend to the more fertile lowlands.[136]

The natural consequence of an advance from less fertile to more fertile soils would be an increase in the returns to agriculture, Carey pointed out, and he found other reasons for believing that returns do in fact increase. He was convinced that with the advance of population and cultivation there is an accelerated accumulation of capital and a rising ratio of capital to population.[137] In addition to the greater productivity due to the greater

---

[134] Henry C. Carey, *Principles of Political Economy,* Philadelphia, 1837, p. 38.
[135] Henry C. Carey, *The Past, the Present, and the Future,* Philadelphia, 1848, pp. 9–17.
[136] Henry C. Carey, *Principles of Social Science,* Philadelphia, 1858, Ch. 4.
[137] Carey, *Political Economy,* Part I, p. 99, Conclusion I: "That with the increase of capital and extension of cultivation, there is an increased facility of production"; and Conclusion II: "That with this increased facility of production there is increased ability to accumulate capital." Part III, p. 254, Conclusion XVII: "That every increase of population being, when not prevented by human interference,

abundance of capital, he reasoned, the growth of capital and population reduces the fraction of the national effort needed to insure security and to maintain the government.[138] This, of course, would add further to returns. In later works Carey described the progression toward greater and greater returns with advancing population:

> With the increase of population there arises a habit of union, tending to promote the growth of wealth and to facilitate the acquisition of machinery to be used in aid of labour; and with each step in this progress, man acquires increased power over the materials of which the earth is composed, and increased power to determine for himself which to select for cultivation, as being most likely to promote the object of maintaining and improving his condition; and with every increase of this power he is enabled to obtain a larger return to his labour, and to consume more, while accumulating with still increased rapidity the machinery required for further improvement.[139]

> Population and wealth tend to increase, and cultivation tends towards the more fertile soils, when man is allowed to obey those instincts of his nature which prompt him to seek association with his fellowmen. They tend to decrease as association declines, and then the fertile soils are everywhere abandoned; and with every step in that direction the difficulty of obtaining food is increased. Population it is that makes the food come from the rich soils of the earth; while depopulation drives the unhappy cultivator back to the poorer ones.[140]

At the time Carey wrote it was not surprising that an American should be convinced of the advantages of population growth.

Starting with assumptions about the relation of population growth to production that were quite different from those of the classical economists, Carey naturally came to quite different conclusions about the associated changes in distribution. Perhaps more influenced by American and other experience than by theoretical considerations, yet consistent with his belief in the accelerating advance of capital and production, Carey stated that the effect of increasing population and capital supply is to enlarge the proportion of the total product going to labor and to decrease the propor-

---

accompanied by an increase in the ratio of capital to population, there is a constant tendency to the improvement and equality of physical, moral, intellectual, and political condition, to the further growth of population and capital, and to the further improvement of condition." In his *Harmony of Nature* a year earlier Carey had written that capital increases faster than population in a society that enjoys security, freedom, and economy in government, and that the faster the population increases the more rapidly capital accumulates (*The Harmony of Nature, as exhibited in the laws which regulate the increase of population and of the means of subsistence . . . ,* Philadelphia, 1836, pp. 311–312).

[138] Carey, *Political Economy,* Part II, Ch. XVI, especially Conclusion VIII; and Part III, Ch. IX, Conclusion IX.

[139] Carey, *The Past,* pp. 56–57.

[140] Carey, *Social Science,* p. 139.

tions paid for the use of capital and land. The absolute amounts going to profits and rent increase, he thought, but the rate of return on capital and land decreases at the same time that per capita wages advance.[141] As evidence Carey cited experience in the American colonies and elsewhere. According to his summary of the effects of the increased facility of production and the greater supply of capital that were thought to accompany the growth of a nation,

> . . . with this increased facility of accumulation, there is a diminution of the power to demand rent or interest, and that the owner can claim, and the labourer will give, a diminished proportion of the product of labour, in return for the use of any species of capital.[142]

> . . . every increase in the ratio of capital to population, is attended with an increase in the ratio which the value of labour bears to that of capital and the labourer is consequently enabled to retain a constantly increasing proportion of the product of his labour, leaving to the owner of land or other capital a constantly diminished proportion.[143]

Carey did not explain what mechanism he thought controls distribution, but the passage quoted suggests he believed the strength of the claim of a given production factor for a share of the product depends upon the relative abundance or scarcity of the factor.[144]

In addition to dealing with the population factor in the economic context of production and distribution, Carey here and there expressed more general views about population. In his first major work in political economy, *Essay on the Rate of Wages* (1835), which foreshadowed a number of views that he developed more fully later, he asserted that the distress of the working classes is due to oppressive government, the burden of taxes, and other injustices; and he summarized his thought by saying, "The only disease under which mankind labours is oppression."[145]

In *The Harmony of Nature,* in which he attempted to refute the Malthusian doctrine, Carey asserted that if men are really free they exercise restraint in reproduction, and added that "The hope of bettering his condition prompts man to that action that is most advantageous to him."[146]

---

[141] Carey, *Harmony of Nature,* pp. 311–312; *Political Economy,* Part I, Ch. IV, pp. 27–35. See also *The Past,* p. 210.

[142] Carey, *Political Economy,* Part I, p. 99.

[143] *Ibid.,* Part III, p. 252.

[144] Concerning wages and profits, on the same point, see *Political Economy,* Part II, p. 286, and Part I, p. 86. Land value and rent determination were another case for Carey, however. In his *Harmony of Nature* he rejected the Ricardian rent theory as "too complex to be true" (p. 13), and asserted that value is given to land through the application of capital (p. 30). Later he stated explicitly that the ability of land to command rent is not because of its scarcity but because of capital investment (Carey, *Political Economy,* Part I, pp. 170, 191, 193 ff.)

[145] Carey, *Essay on the Rate of Wages,* Philadelphia, 1835, p. 244.

[146] Carey, *Harmony of Nature,* Ch. XXVI, and p. 313.

In *Social Science* he restated his earlier and optimistic views, but with an admixture of biological or pseudo-biological principles. In advance of Herbert Spencer, Carey stated as a natural law that man's "fecundity and development are in inverse ratio of each other."[147] He further explained that with the growth of numbers and wealth there is greater development of individuality and responsibility, and a consequently greater use of the preventive check.[148] Because of this natural principle, he believed, there is no reason to fear overpopulation: the advance of population is accompanied by a rising volume of production and standard of living which bring a more general exercise of the preventive check on numbers.[149]

Of less interest now is Carey's attempt to utilize advances in natural science in a new law of population. As more of the available matter on the earth takes on the form of man, he theorized, man's power to guide the forces of nature increases,[150] or as he explained:

> With increase in the numbers of mankind, the lower animals tend to diminish in their numbers, and gradually to disappear — vegetable products tending, as steadily, to increase in quantity. Were it otherwise, the earth would become less and less fitted for man's residence — carbonic acid being more and more produced, and the air declining in its powers for the maintenance of human life. Increase of vegetable life tends, on the contrary, to promote the decomposition of that acid — thereby increasing the supply of the oxygen required for maintenance of animal life, while diminution in the consumption of animal food is attended by decrease in the quantity of oxygen required for human purposes.
>
> To the equal balance of opposing forces is due, throughout nature, the maintenance of the perfect harmony that is every where observed, and such is here the case. The extension of cultivation is indispensable to increase in the supply of food. That extension involves, of course, a gradual extirpation of animal races that now consume so largely of the products of the earth, and were they not to be replaced by men, the production of carbonic acid would speedily diminish, with corresponding diminution in the reproductive powers of the vegetable world. The more numerous the men and women, the greater is the store of force required for the production of vegetable matter, the greater is the production of carbonic acid, and the greater the power for vegetable reproduction. The more complete the power of association, the more perfect becomes the cultivation — the greater is the development of the powers of the land — and the more admirably does the beauty of all natural arrangements exhibit itself, in the perfect adjustment of all the parts and portions of the wonderful system of which we are a part.[151]

[147] Carey, *Social Science*, p. 263.
[148] *Ibid.*, pp. 275–276.
[149] *Ibid.*
[150] *Ibid.*, Ch. 3.
[151] *Ibid.*, Ch. 46, section 4.

Like the other formulators of population theories from Malthus onward, Carey was a seeker after simple and fundamental principles that, he was convinced, govern human affairs in a way comparable to the natural laws being discovered for the physical world.

Vethake · Henry Vethake (1792–1866), then professor of mathematics and philosophy at the University of Pennsylvania, presented orthodox economic theory in his *Principles of Political Economy* (1838). The principle of diminishing returns in agriculture was accepted without question, wage and price levels were explained in supply and demand terms, rent was traced to different rates of yield on land, and population growth was said to divert a larger and larger share of the product to the landlord class.

Writing in more detail on the distribution effects of population growth, Vethake explained, with diminishing returns in mind, that

> . . . in the progress of society, from the very nature of the land, the whole amount of wealth produced will be proportionally diminished, that is proportionally to the amount of labour applied; the exchangeable value of agricultural products will rise in reference to all other products; and rents will be continually rising, and therefore continually inducing, by their rise, a corresponding rise in the value of the land; — also, that when wages are supposed to continue the same, profits will fall, there will be a less rapid accumulation of capital; and the rate at which population and wealth increase must, in consequence, be continually retarded.[152]

He recognized that invention and advances in the arts of production have the opposite effect, but by augmenting wealth they do at the same time stimulate population growth.[153] The latter effect was traced through wages, which were said to depend upon the ratio of capital to population.[154]

Further discussion of population followed Malthus with only minor differences. From the Malthusian principle of population, Vethake concluded that the rate of wages must remain constant while the marriage habits of the people remain constant, for if wages rise, the consequent population growth and use of inferior land return wages to their former level.[155]

Vethake then stated the important principle that "in every country, and in every period, the rate of wages is determined by the habits of the people."[156] By this he was led to conclude that a too rapid increase in population can be checked only by an increase in people's wants or by the exercise of greater foresight. Considering how man's desires can be raised, he believed the answer lay in a general diffusion of religion, morals, and

[152] Henry Vethake, *Principles of Political Economy*, Philadelphia, 1838, p. 93.
[153] *Ibid.*, pp. 94–97. [154] *Ibid.*, p. 100.
[155] *Ibid.*, pp. 110–111. [156] *Ibid.*, p. 112.

education.[157] However, he also noted that a rise in wages such as might follow an unusually high mortality could give people a taste for a higher level of living.[158]

3 · 1840–1849

Potter · The *Political Economy*[159] by Alonzo Potter (1800–1865), published in 1841, was "substantially a reprint" of the first ten chapters of Scrope's work of the same title, with an introduction and several chapters added by Potter. It omitted Scrope's chapter on population and subsistence, and did not take up the population question.

Ware · A more original work of a few years later was *Notes on Political Economy*[160] (1844), written by Nathaniel A. Ware (1780 or 1789–1854) and published under the pseudonym of "A Southern Planter." As the full title of the book indicates, a purposefully American point of view was taken. It was a long argument for tariff protection, and contained a separate chapter and scattered comments on the subject of population. Showing considerable independence of thought, it aligned itself with classical authority in condemning poor relief and taking a severe view of pauperism, but then took a most un-Malthusian position on the desirability of a large and dense population.

In a chapter on poor laws,[161] Ware stated firmly that no relief should be given to the able-bodied, and that poor relief creates pauperism. With even stronger emphasis, he wrote,

> Better, if it comes to the worst, let a few perish in the streets, than have one-twentieth part of mankind degraded, rendered worthless, and what is worse, eating the subsistence of the industrious and valuable portion of the community.[162]

In a later chapter Ware detailed the advantages of high population density, saying that "When mankind live more concentrated they act beneficially upon each other,"[163] and "A dense settlement has in its own bosom a thousand facilities for improvements, and the effectuating and carrying out any project or plan that promises well."[164] As he explained further,

> A certain density of population is necessary to a liberal consumption of a country, as well as improvements and a valuable production. Man-

157 *Ibid.*, Book 2, Ch. 7.
158 *Ibid.*, pp. 126–127.
159 Alonzo Potter, *Political Economy: its objects, uses, and principles: considered with reference to the condition of the American people*, New York, 1841.
160 (Nathaniel A. Ware), *Notes on political economy as applicable to the United States*, by a Southern Planter, New York, 1844.
161 *Ibid.*, Ch. 22. 162 *Ibid.*, p. 196.
163 *Ibid.*, p. 230. 164 *Ibid.*, p. 231.

kind act upon each other in reference to their wants, style, luxury, tastes, and the quality of the goods and food that they consume.[165]

Here Ware made quite clear that it is not a large but a concentrated population that most benefits a nation, in his opinion; and for this reason he opposed the addition of Texas and California to the United States.

A separate chapter on population rounded out Ware's treatment of the subject. In further support of the advantage of populousness, it was said that "It is important to have a full and efficient population in all countries, for the defence, wealth, and refinement, that ought to accompany every government or association of the human family."[166] Another reason, not fully explained, was that a full population leads to the formation of high consumption habits.

A final point was that there is no need to fear an excessive number of people, for there are natural checks to growth. As Ware explained,

> The natural check and limit to an increase of population is the capacity of the earth to support it and feed it. To this point it tends, and nothing in the end can prevent its reaching this maximum. Under certain circumstances and feelings this point will be reached sooner than under others; and in certain countries sooner than in certain other countries. This is owing to the habits of the people. If they are without any pride of style, and content with bare support of food, and that of the cheapest and most abundant sort, they will condense rapidly, and their natural increase, on the principles that pigs multiply, be great; but if they have this pride of style and comfort they will increase slower, for they will not then marry without a certainty of that style, and a great portion remain unmarried and will contribute nothing to our increase.[167]

Like Vethake, Henry Carey, and others of his predecessors, both European and American, Ware saw in a high standard of living and enlightenment the surest guarantee against excessive reproduction.

Seaman · A number of original ideas, some reasonable, others more questionable, were presented in the *Essays on the progress of nations* (1846) by Ezra Seaman (1805–1880), lawyer and government employee. With extensive census materials, mortality and immigration data, and other statistics, the author sought for the laws of nature that, as he said, determine the relations between man and his Maker, between man and other men, between man and the material world. In economic matters he was a strong protectionist and a believer that it is industry that gives strength to a nation; in population matters he was not so much anti-Malthusian as he was an independent thinker.

In a chapter on the laws that govern population, Seaman objected to the doctrine that population increases as food increases, with the reasonable

[165] *Ibid.,* p. 233.
[166] *Ibid.,* p. 246.
[167] *Ibid.,* p. 248.

argument that man has numerous other wants besides food. Searching for another law of population growth, he arrived at a curious geographical principle:

> The rule which governs the progress of population may be laid down as follows. When not affected by wars, population generally increases above the 40th degree of latitude about as fast as the comforts of life increase. The increase, however, can not exceed, or never has yet exceeded, about three per cent annually, or thirty-three per cent in ten years. It is very much increased by early marriages, which are promoted by the frugal and simple habits of an agricultural people, and particularly those settled in a new country. Population is influenced much more by climate, below the 40th degree of latitude, than it is above. Though good and comfortable dwellings, clothing and lodging adapted to the climate, together with a sufficient supply of fuel, have a very great influence upon health, longevity and the increase of population in warm countries; and the progress of population is in some extent in proportion to the increase of the comforts of life in the aggregate; yet no amount of comforts can guard against many of the diseases incident to the decay of vegetation in hot climates, and in the vicinity of marshy lands and stagnant waters.[168]

Mortality conditions in midnineteenth-century America may well have given some plausibility to this hypothesis. In a later chapter Seaman predicted a declining rate of population increase as a result of the growth of wealth and urbanization.[169]

Colton · The final work of the decade to be considered here is *Public economy for the United States* (1848) by Calvin Colton (1789–1857). Colton was a man of varied experience, trained for the ministry, author of a number of works on religious subjects, a resident of England for several years, more recently a political pamphleteer; and his *Public economy* contained a mixture of religion, political ideas, protectionism, and economic theory. On the subject of population it is enough to note that Colton condemned the Malthusian doctrine as a "libel on Providence" because it attributed to natural laws the evils produced by the defects of society.[170] He believed that American experience contradicted Malthus, and that European economic theory was not applicable to the United States.

4 · 1850–1869

Opdyke · A successful merchant and later office-holder, George Opdyke (1805–1880) wrote his *Treatise on political economy* (1851) not so much in criticism of Mill's *Principles* as to point out certain respects in which

---

[168] Ezra C. Seaman, *Essays on the progress of nations in productive industry, civilization, population, and wealth,* New York: Baker & Scribner, 1846, Ch. 14, p. 320.

[169] *Ibid.,* Ch. 17, p. 423.

[170] Calvin Colton, *Public economy for the United States,* New York, 1848, p. 159.

that work was not applicable to the United States. Without particular attention to the population variable, Opdyke assumed an automatic regulation of population numbers and wages, disagreed with Malthus on the basis of American experience, and stated as a law that "Capital has greater capacity of increase than population. . . ."[171]

Smith · *A Manual of Political Economy* by E. Peshine Smith (1814–1882) appeared in 1853, was translated into French in the following year and later into German, and reappeared in a second American edition in 1877. The author was a faithful follower of Henry Carey, to whose influence he attributed his interest in political economy. He was convinced of "the insufficiency and falseness of the system of the English Economists,"[172] and wrote the *Manual* to set forth "the American system of Political Economy."

The work is a restatement of Carey. With the same intermixture of natural science and economics Smith wrote:

> . . . Malthus's theory of the relations between population and subsistence is obviously founded upon the false notion, that man's consumption of food is its destruction — that having once served the purpose of supporting animal life, its capacity to contribute to that object is absolutely spent and exhausted. The failure to observe that, in the natural course of things it is returned to the earth, to be again formed into food, and resume its office of supporting animal life, is tantamount to this; and it is only in consequence of that failure, that the food-producing power of the soil can be regarded either as a fixed quantity, or as incapable of increasing in the same proportion as the food-consuming power of those who dwell upon it. It may account in part for the tacit adoption of so erroneous an opinion by an intelligent writer, that the discoveries in organic chemistry, which conclusively disprove it, have been made within the last twenty-five years, and are subsequent by an equal period, to the publication of Mr. Malthus.[173]

In his thinking, if soil fertility diminishes, it is because of "perverse arrangements, for which Nature has no responsibility,"[174] and

> . . . it is impossible to conjecture a limit to the increase of population, if man will but conform to the law which Nature exemplifies in all her processes, by which the soil regains whatever material of nutriment it has lent for the support of vegetable and animal life, and that with large interest, derived from the elements furnished by the atmosphere, and incorporated in the substance of the matter, which, on the extinction of its vitality returns to the bosom of the soil.[175]

[171] George Opdyke, *Treatise on political economy*, New York: Putnam, 1851, p. 132.
[172] E. Peshine Smith, *A Manual of Political Economy*, Philadelphia, 1853, p. 14.
[173] *Ibid.*, p. 35.
[174] *Ibid.*, p. 36.
[175] *Ibid.*, p. 37.

In other words, matter is indestructible and the fertility of the soil need never be exhausted.

Accepting Carey's theory of progression to better and better soils, Smith then traced the consequences in the following paraphrase:

> The theory of Mr. Carey reconciles all the facts, and explains them all. It is possible for food to increase more rapidly than population, when men begin with the inferior soils, and, as their numbers grow, pass to those of superior fertility. An increasing proportion of each community is thus released from direct employment in the raising of food, and enabled to apply its energies to the preparation of machinery and the improvement of processes. These give the ability to the husbandman to reap a larger return from his old soil, and to overcome more readily and effectually the difficulties which attend his subduing the new and richer lands. The result is necessarily a larger yield, in recompense of the same amount of labour, a further increase in the surplus of food, and the setting free of more labourers from the farm, to recruit the workshops and to undertake fresh branches of industry. Upon this theory we can comprehend the progress of civilization. . . .[176]

In further describing the accelerating upward trend of prosperity accompanying population growth, Smith stated that capital accumulates more rapidly than population, and that the rent of land decreases at the same time.[177]

Bowen · Another American writer who could not believe that population growth is harmful was Francis Bowen (1811–1890), a prolific writer, for a time editor of the *North American Review,* and for many years professor of natural religion, moral philosophy, and civil polity at Harvard. His *Principles of Political Economy*[178] (1856) included a chapter devoted to refuting the Malthusian theory and substituting what Bowen considered the true principles of population.

Bowen began his discussion of the Malthusian theory by stating the proposition that

> . . . the power of the earth to afford sustenance is now so far in advance of the actual numbers of mankind, that no probable, and in fact no possible, increase of those numbers, not even by a geometrical progression, can create a general and permanent scarcity for centuries to come.[179]

Among a number of arguments against Malthus, the two principal points made by Bowen were:

---

[176] *Ibid.,* p. 61.

[177] *Ibid.,* pp. 83, 89.

[178] Francis Bowen, *The Principles of Political Economy,* Boston, 1856. A fourth edition had appeared by 1865. The *American Political Economy,* published in 1870 and with at least two later editions (1877, 1890), appears to be essentially the same work under a new title.

[179] *Principles,* p. 141.

The first is, that the limit of population in any country whatever is, not the number of people which the soil of that country alone will supply with food, but the number which the surface of the whole earth is capable of feeding; and it is a matter of demonstration, that this limit cannot even be approached for many centuries. . . .

Then, secondly, I say that the practical or actual limit to the growth of population in every case is the limit to the increase and distribution, not of food, but of wealth. Among civilized men in modern times, a famine is created, not by any absolute deficiency in the supply of food, but because the poorer classes have no money to buy it with. As every human being is an implement for the production of wealth, a means of enlarging the aggregate national product, or the amount of exchangeable values belonging to a nation, the increase of population is not a cause of scarcity of food, but a preservative against it.[180]

That is to say, on the latter point, the actual problem is not production but distribution. The production problem is not a major one in Bowen's thinking, for reasons already noted above and because of his assurance that "More grain is raised because there are more men who need it, and not more men are raised because there is more grain to feed them with."[181]

To explain the existence of misery, having rejected the Malthusian explanation, Bowen stated, in agreement with the majority of his fellow American writers, "Turn the matter as we may, it is not the niggardliness of nature which is the source of misery, but the devices of man and the injustice of the laws."[182] A further effect was attributed to social injustice:

Whatever tends to keep men hopelessly poor is a direct encouragement, the strongest of all incentives, to an increase of population. Take away the causes of misery, remove the insurmountable barriers which now keep the various classes of European society apart, and educate the people, and there will be no fears of an excess of numbers.[183]

In other words, social injustices are a double cause of misery, first through inequitable distribution, and second by repressing the preventive check.

After presenting his arguments against the Malthusian theory, Bowen stated what he considered the true law regulating numbers in civilized society where considerations of self-interest that induce people to work and save also regulate marriage and population increase. In his words, "In a normal state, then, the inclination of people to marry is controlled by their opinion of the effect which marriage will have upon their position in life."[184] According to this principle, persons most assured of maintaining their present position would have the highest fertility, and Bowen realized

180 *Ibid.*, pp. 148–149.   181 *Ibid.*, p. 150.
182 *Ibid.*, p. 151.   183 *Ibid.*, p. 152.
184 *Ibid.*, p. 156.

that this would produce an inverse relation between socio-economic status and fertility such as already existed in many places.[185]

Some further ideas on population were expressed in a chapter on the growth of population, but the chapters on distribution attributed little significance to the number of people. Bowen rejected the Ricardian theory of rent and denied that population growth has forced the use of poorer land in England. Rent, he maintained, depends not upon the increase in population but upon its changes of distribution that create a local excess of demand over supply.[186] On the subject of wages he denied that the size or rate of growth of population affects the wage level, which in his opinion depends upon the relative number of employers and employees.[187]

Bascom · In contrast to the writers just discussed, John Bascom (1827–1911) gave a Malthusian account of population in his college text, *Political Economy* (1859). In particular he accepted the principle of diminishing returns in agriculture, the capacity for geometric increase of human populations, and their tendency to press on the means of subsistence. Concerning the checks, he wrote that the preventive check operates in some classes, the positive check in others, and that there is need to reduce the proportion in the latter category by means of education and a heightened sense of responsibility.[188]

In connection with the discussion of checks and in view of the apparently well-known inverse relation of fertility to socio-economic status, Bascom proposed the following natural law of population:

> If any class of animals is pressed with hunger, far from succumbing to the new enemy under the designed reaction of a natural force, they rush to the breach in increasing numbers; they swarm every avenue to life with the spawn of a prolific birth, struggling, by the multiplication of chances, to rescue the species from impending ruin. Judging by the number of births among the extreme poor, this law does not seem to have been suspended in the human constitution. . . .[189]

This is a theory more often associated with Doubleday and recently revived by de Castro.[190]

In the opposite case, advancing prosperity in a society, Bascom concluded that a rapid advance has a more permanent effect than a slow one, for in the latter case population may keep pace, but in the former men have an opportunity to attain a higher level of living and become motivated to retain it.[191]

[185] *Ibid.*, p. 158 ff.
[186] *Ibid.*, p. 180.
[187] *Ibid.*, Ch. XIV.
[188] John Bascom, *Political Economy*, Andover, 1859, pp. 138–139.
[189] *Ibid.*, p. 139.
[190] Josué de Castro, *The geography of hunger*, Boston: Little, Brown, 1952.
[191] Bascom, *op. cit.*, p. 141.

In his analysis of distribution Bascom gave an essentially Ricardian explanation of rent, according to which increased demand, as from population growth, would lead to the use of poorer land and add to the amount of rent.[192] The wage fund theory was accepted, but with the note that the size of the fund is affected by the productiveness of labor.[193] It was explained that the worker can also affect wages from the labor supply side:

> It is the ratio of population to capital, that is of chief interest to the working classes, and this ratio is largely at their own disposal. It is from the competition of their own numbers that they most suffer, and this competition they themselves create.[194]

Emphasizing further the significance of the ratio of population to capital, Bascom added that the division of the product between wages and profits depends upon the balance between the capital-created demand for labor and the labor supply.[195] Finally, linking three factors in the determination of the rate of return on capital, Bascom noted that continued increases in the supply of capital will depress profits, provided population growth is checked and the standard of living is maintained.[196] This assumed an inverse relation between wages and profits and an opposition of interests between capital and labor, a common idea in European classical economics that was less generally accepted by the American writers and vigorously attacked by Carey.[197]

Perry · The decade of the 1860's produced only two works that need mention here, the *Elements of Political Economy* (1866) by Arthur L. Perry (1830–1905), and the *Science of Wealth* by Amasa Walker.

Perry's *Elements* was a widely used text that, revised and retitled *Political Economy*, went through a total of twenty-two editions by 1895. The author, professor of history and political economy at Williams, dedicated his work to Bascom but did not hesitate to differ on some points. For the most part Perry was orthodox in his presentation of the principles of economics. In particular he gave a basic supply and demand explanation of wages, regarded capital as the creator of labor demand and the capital-labor ratio as the determiner of the wage level, accepted diminishing returns as a law of nature, and dismissed Carey's theory while only partially accepting the Ricardian rent theory.[198]

As quoted below, Perry questioned whether the population problem is properly a part of economics, and gave little attention to the subject except

[192] *Ibid.*, Part II, Ch. 2. [193] *Ibid.*, Part II, Ch. 3.
[194] *Ibid.*, p. 178. [195] *Ibid.*, p. 183.
[196] *Ibid.*, Part II, Ch. 5.
[197] Henry C. Carey, *Harmony of Nature*, p. 254.
[198] Perry later rejected the Ricardian explanation of rent more positively, saying that the theory was ingenious and plausible but "as full of fallacies as an egg is full of meat" (*Political Economy*, 18th ed., p. 291).

to state his reasons for rejecting the Malthusian theory. The reasons he summarized as follows:

In respect to the law of population and of human fecundity, I have only to say, that it is just that with which God saw best to endow the race; that experience has shown that it is not too strong for the purpose for which it was given; that under it, men are bound to act rationally and religiously, as accountable to God; that the same law of population which produces labourers, produces capitalists as well, and that the restraints on population, which economists have been at such pains to commend, are as likely to keep capitalists out of the world as labourers, which would be a disadvantage to the latter; that every human being is as much constituted by nature to receive services as to render them, and therefore, until it is demonstrated that the earth can no longer support the population that is in immediate prospect, no sound commercial reason can be given for artificial restraints on population; and finally, that Political Economy, as the science of exchange, presupposes the actual existence of men in society, and therefore, that it is without its province to discuss the laws under which they are born into society, and especially without its province to discuss the future possible contingency, nowise likely to happen in actuality, when the broad bosom of mother earth shall be unable any longer to nourish and support her children. In saying this, I would not be understood to deny that in certain states of society, in certain parts of the earth, population has pressed heavily upon food; or that poverty and improvidence do sometimes stimulate population, or that intelligence and self-respect are needful to order that marriages may be well and wisely contracted. What I affirm is, that, under freedom to receive and render services, to which freedom all men have a natural right, and under intelligence and morality, which all men are found to possess, this matter of population will perfectly regulate itself; that there is no prospective and calculable danger that population will ever outstrip the means of supporting it; that the population of the world, as a whole, was never so well fed and clothed and housed as it is to-day; that the alleged laws of nature in respect to the increase of population and of food, which are said to be in antagonism, have never yet been proved; and that, in any actual case of persistent pressure of numbers on the means of life, it is, to say the least of it, quite as reasonable to look for the causes in the miscalculations and maladministrations of men, as in alleged colliding laws of God.[199]

This is a good summary of American anti-Malthusian arguments, including the points that the Malthusian doctrine is inconsistent with belief in the divine order, that it is not consistent with observations, that population numbers will regulate themselves in a well-ordered society, and that if they do not do so there is reason to suspect human error as the cause. The

[199] Arthur L. Perry, *Elements of Political Economy*, New York: Scribners, 1866, pp. 126–127.

religious note found in Perry's writing was not uncommon in American political economy at the time.

In its revised form, under the title *Political Economy,* Perry's text was not fundamentally altered in its treatment of population. The Malthusian doctrine was said to be a topic of physiology rather than of political economy.[200] Confidence was expressed that human progress would bring increasingly effective population control:

> Experience has shown, that the strong impulse in mankind towards procreation is not too strong for the purpose intended; that as men under moral and religious training come more and more under the influence of reason and affection the preventive checks to population come silently and effectually into operation; and that, taking the world at large, food and comforts have more than kept pace with the stride of population, since its inhabitants as a whole were plainly never so well fed and clothed and housed as now.[201]

In his later, more elementary work, *An Introduction to Political Economy* (1877), Perry had very little to say about population except that although it is theoretically possible for population to increase geometrically it does not in fact do so, that the inhabitants of the earth were never as well fed and clothed as they are now, that the earth could support a thousand-fold increase of people, and that reason and affection may be trusted to keep population from increasing to the subsistence limit.[202]

Amasa Walker · *The Science of Wealth* (1867) by Amasa Walker (1799–1875) appeared the year after Perry's *Elements.* The author, identified on the title page as a lecturer in political economy at Amherst, was a businessman turned economist in his later years. In the preface of his work he especially praised the recent works by Bascom and Perry in the United States and of Bastiat and J. S. Mill abroad, and he acknowledged the assistance of his son, Francis Amasa Walker.

Walker, who gave particular attention to monetary questions and taxation, included a chapter on the Malthusian theory, but otherwise made only scattered references to population as an economic variable. The errors of the Malthusian theory were described at length. The three principal fallacies, Walker believed, were the assumptions that per capita production diminishes as population increases, that population necessarily increases when subsistence increases, and that these produce vice and misery. On the first point Walker denied the principle of diminishing returns and asserted that science and machinery add to productivity.[203] On the second point he

[200]Arthur L. Perry, *Political Economy,* 18th ed., New York: Scribners, 1883, p. 238.
[201] *Ibid.*
[202] Arthur L. Perry, *An Introduction to Political Economy,* New York, 1877, p. 82.
[203] Amasa Walker, *The Science of Wealth,* Boston, 1867, p. 453.

considered the geometric ratio of increase unrealistic and believed that the rate of growth in a society depends upon the conditions there.[204] On the final point he attributed the misery found in England to oppressive institutions, bad laws, and various causes other than overpopulation.[205] Furthermore, he was convinced that what he called social restraint really operates to check population growth.

Walker expressed the novel idea that an effect, but not a disadvantage, of manufactures, is that they repress population growth. This is even a "beneficient provision of Nature" in his opinion, because it means that city-dwellers are predominantly of rural origin and therefore healthier than if they were born in the city.[206] Another distinctive idea is found in his discussion of rent, in which it is said that among the several factors capable of affecting the rent level is an increase in population, which creates an excess demand and raises prices by requiring imports of food.[207]

5 · 1870 and Later

American political economy in the latter part of the nineteenth century was less distinctively national and less divergent from European economics, but its independent convictions on the subject of population were maintained. The population controversy was waning, it is true, and like their European colleagues, the political economists of the United States were becoming increasingly convinced that their proper concern was with other matters. But unlike their European colleagues, the majority of the American writers disapproved of the Malthusian doctrine of population. Accounts of the population thought of a few principal writers after 1870 will be enough to show the trend of thinking on population at that time.

Thompson · Robert Ellis Thompson (1844–1924) was born in Ireland but educated in the United States. He entered the ministry and then taught for many years at the University of Pennsylvania. A member of Carey's group in Philadelphia, he was a faithful follower of Carey in his economics, was a strong protectionist, believed in the progression from poorer to better soils, and saw in population growth a major stimulus to human advancement.

Population growth was described in his *Social Science and National Economy*[208] (1875) as a force for progress:

> At every step in this great past of man's industrial development, the growth of numbers and of wealth has gone on with equal strides. In the earlier stages the pressure of population upon the means of subsistence

204 *Ibid.,* pp. 453–454.   205 *Ibid.,* pp. 456–458.
206 *Ibid.,* p. 49.   207 *Ibid.,* Book IV, Ch. 7.
208 Robert E. Thompson, *Social Science and National Economy*, Philadelphia, 1875. The third edition (1882) was retitled *Elements of Political Economy*.

is marked and painful; yet beneficial, as thrusting men into closer and more helpful association, and forcing them to adopt wiser and better methods. But every advance has been richly rewarded, for with each acceleration in the rapidity of social movement, the resistance to be overcome has diminished.[209]

Therefore, he continued, it is good policy for a nation to facilitate the natural growth of its people, and the larger numbers give greater per capita production.[210]

On the Malthusian theory Thompson gave many of the common counter-arguments, such as that it is contrary to observations, that food shortage is greatest where population is most sparse, that much land remains unused, and that a more dense population would bring higher yields on land already in use. He also noted that the plant and animal species serving as food can multiply more rapidly than man, and that within the human race the more advanced peoples multiply more slowly than the less advanced. The true law of population, he concluded, is that ". . . population is self-regulative. Its multiplication brings the civilization, that is the one effectual and all-efficient check to undue multiplication."[211] Noting Doubleday's theory of a physiological mechanism affecting reproduction, Thompson expressed the commonsense idea that "cerebral development" is more apt to be the regulating mechanism.[212]

In the section of his work dealing with distribution Thompson rejected the Ricardian theory with its implications for the influence of population growth on rent, and also rejected the assumption that wages tend to be kept at a "natural" level by means of an upward or downward adjustment of population.

Francis A. Walker · Son of the author of *The Science of Wealth,* Francis Amasa Walker (1840–1897) had a varied career as brigadier-general, chief of the federal Bureau of Statistics, superintendent of the Censuses of 1870 and 1880, professor of political economy at Yale and during his last years president of Massachusetts Institute of Technology. Perhaps the leading American economist of his time and writer on a number of economic and statistical subjects, he is best known to students of population for his theory of the relation of immigration to the reproduction rate of the native-born population, which he presented in 1891.

Statements of Walker's views on population are found in his economic writings, of which the principal works are *The Wages Question* (1876), *Political Economy* (1883), and *Land and its Rent* (1891). In the first, Walker accepted Carey's belief in the progression to more fertile but more difficult soils in new settlements, but he was convinced that returns in

---

[209] *Ibid.,* p. 50.
[211] *Ibid.,* p. 66.

[210] *Ibid.,* pp. 50–51.
[212] *Ibid.*

agriculture diminish in the later stage of development.[213] He limited the diminishing of returns to agriculture, however, and noted that the cost of goods manufactured from raw materials may decline as population grows.[214] Along with the law of diminishing returns Walker accepted the Malthusian theory, with reservation only on the tendency of population to grow to excess. Walker's own opinion was that the urge to reproduction may be somewhat less strong and the motives for restraint somewhat stronger than Malthus believed; but he did not consider this an invalidation of the Malthusian theory.[215]

Walker's discussion of wage determination revolved about his concept of "necessary wages." In his explanation,

> The whole significance of the term necessary wages is that, in order to the supply of labor being maintained (sic), wages must be paid which will not only enable the laboring class to subsist according to the standard of comfort and decency, or discomfort and indecency it may be, which they set up for themselves as that below which they will not go, but will also dispose them to propagate sufficiently to make up the inevitable, incessant loss of labor from death and disability. If the standard of living referred to above varies among several communities or countries, then the term "necessary wages" must be interpreted in each community or country according to the habitual standard there maintained.[216]

More briefly he defined the necessary wage as "the wage that must be paid to keep the supply of labor good, if indeed, it is to be kept good,"[217] and recognized that it is affected by the habits of the people.[218]

Later in the same work Walker emphasized the desirability of mobility if the workers are to obtain the most advantageous employment and wages, and noted that early marriage and lack of sexual restraint may reduce labor mobility at a time of life when it is most desirable.[219] In conclusion he rejected the wage fund theory and the ratio of capital to population as wage determiners, and asserted that wages depend upon the productivity of the workers.[220]

Walker's *Political Economy*, which appeared seven years later, defended Malthus and accepted his theory in all essentials.[221] Concerning the influence of economic conditions it was said that

---

[213] Francis A. Walker, *The Wages Question*, New York: Holt, 1876, pp. 92–93.

[214] *Ibid.*, p. 99.   [215] *Ibid.*, p. 108.

[216] *Ibid.*, pp. 112–113.   [217] *Ibid.*, p. 116.

[218] Writing of the notorious case of the Spitalfields silk workers, Walker described the vicious circle of low wages, misery, and high fertility as follows: "Instead of its being true that their misery was a reason to them not to propagate, the more miserable they became, the more reckless, also, and the heavier grew their burdens" (*ibid.*, p. 85).

[219] *Ibid.*, pp. 354–356.

[220] *Ibid.*, p. 411.

[221] Francis A. Walker, *Political Economy*, New York: Holt, 1883, Part V, Ch. 1, section 340, and Ch. 2, section 348.

Any economic want may act in restraint of population in one or more of three ways: first, by diminishing the numbers of the marrying class, inducing celibacy among those who do not find the way to obtain an income adequate to the support of a family; secondly, by procrastinating the period of marriage; and, thirdly, by diminishing the birth-rate within the married state.[222]

However, Walker was well aware in fact of the higher fertility of the poor.[223] Perhaps with this in mind he wrote, concerning restraint in reproduction, of "the desire of decencies the greatest preventive check to population."[224]

On the subject of economic distribution Walker generally followed his previous work on wages. Rent was traced to population increase and diminishing returns in agriculture,[225] the interest rate was said to decline with the rise of population and the rent level,[226] and of wages it was written that

> The laboring class may do themselves an economic injury . . . through excessive reproduction, sexually, leading to overpopulation, involving the necessity of cultivating poorer and poorer soils, with the result of continually diminishing per-capita production. . . .[227]

There is no trace here of Carey and the early American opinion on population.

Land and its Rent, of interest for its treatment of wages and rent theory, added nothing to Walker's previously developed views on population. A Ricardian rent theory and a marginal explanation of commodity prices carried implications of the influence of population growth on distribution; and Carey's argument was said to be immaterial to the Ricardian theory, which dealt with "the lands under cultivation at the same time."[228]

Perhaps from his connection with the Bureau of Statistics, which was responsible for the official immigration statistics, Walker gave considerable attention to immigration in his writings. In one of his late works, a journal article published in 1891, he proposed what has come to be called the Walker theory.[229] Walker began by refuting the allegation that the white population of the United States would have become extinct if not replenished by continuing migration from Europe, pointing out the high rate of natural increase of the American population in the past and the

[222] *Ibid.,* p. 314.

[223] *Ibid.,* section 341; also Part V, Ch. 2, section 312.

[224] *Ibid.,* p. 317.   [225] *Ibid.,* Part IV, Ch. 2.

[226] *Ibid.,* Ch. 3. p. 234.   [227] *Ibid.,* p. 268.

[228] Francis A. Walker, *Land and its Rent,* Boston: Little, Brown, 1891, p. 91. Walker added that "Ricardo's doctrine can no more be impugned than the sun in heaven" (p. 108).

[229] Francis A. Walker, "Immigration and Degradation," *The Forum,* August 1891, Vol. XI, pp. 634–644.

unsubstantiated character of the opposing evidence. He then demonstrated with the available data that, quite the contrary, "as the foreigners began to come in large numbers, the native population more and more withheld their own increase."[230] This observation, Walker continued, can be accounted for in three different ways:

(1) It might be said that it was a mere coincidence, no relation of cause and effect existing between the two phenomena. (2) It might be said that the foreigners came because the native population was relatively declining, that is, failing to keep up its pristine rate of increase. (3) It might be said that the growth of the native population was checked by the incoming of the foreign elements in such large numbers.[231]

There was not enough evidence to permit a choice among the three alternatives, but pursuing a line of reasoning, Walker satisfied himself (but not later students of the subject) that the explanation lay in the third alternative, and theorized in terms of an excess of foreigners being "a shock to the principle of population among the native element."[232]

Sturtevant · Author of *Economics, or the Science of Wealth* (1877), Julian M. Sturtevant (1805–1886) was a student of theology but entered the teaching profession and taught mathematics, political economy, and other subjects at Illinois College for over fifty years.

A few passing references to population are found in his statement of the principles of political economy, especially in the account of distribution theory. Among the necessary conditions for the division of labor is a sufficient demand, it is said, and an increase in demand proceeds from growth of population and capital.[233] On the subject of wages Sturtevant denied that high density of population necessarily leads to low returns to the workers. The level of wages, he believed, depends in part upon the relation of labor supply to capital, and also upon the degree of comfort demanded by the workers.[234] Therefore, the price level of all commodities, not just necessities, affects the money level of wages. In rent theory Sturtevant followed neither Ricardo nor Carey. He reasoned that Ricardo mistook effect for cause in explaining how population growth causes a rise in commodity prices and rent. According to Sturtevant it is the greater demand that raises prices and rent, not the use of poorer land.[235]

Sturtevant's general views on the population question were given in a separate chapter. It was his opinion that the Malthusian law applies only

---

[230] *Ibid.,* p. 638. For Jarvis's earlier and similar observation see p. 505 above.
[231] *Ibid.,* pp. 638–639.
[232] *Ibid.,* p. 640.
[233] Julian M. Sturtevant, *Economics, or the Science of Wealth,* New York: Putnam, 1877, p. 44.
[234] *Ibid.,* pp. 172, 179.
[235] *Ibid.,* pp. 223–224.

when population has reached the subsistence limit, and that the "law of competition" can be trusted to take care of the human race as civilization advances.[236] According to Sturtevant's theory, there is a continuing selection from one generation to the next, with little contribution to the next generation from those unable to support themselves and their families.[237] The small wealthy class, because of self-indulgence, also has few descendants; and therefore the next generation is derived mostly from the third or intermediate class of the industrious and frugal.[238]

George · Henry George (1839–1897) ranks with Henry Carey as a rebel against the established principles of political economy, and like Carey he vigorously rejected the Malthusian theory, which he regarded as an integral part of the whole erroneous system of classical economics.

In *Progress and Poverty* (1880) George developed his own answers to the twin questions of the cause of economic depressions and the cause of increasing poverty in the midst of increasing wealth. At several points his work touched on the economic significance of population size or growth, and while attacking the Malthusian theory he presented an independent "law" of population. Pointing out the parallel between current wage theory, according to which an increase in labor supply reduces the supply of capital per worker, and the Malthusian theory, according to which an increase in population reduces the per capita means of subsistence, George stated emphatically that it is oppression rather than population growth that produces poverty and misery.[239] In his own forceful phrasing.

> . . . in any given state of civilization a greater number of people can collectively be better provided for than a smaller. I assert that the injustice of society, not the niggardliness of nature, is the cause of the want and misery which the current theory attributes to over-population. I assert that the new mouths which an increasing population calls into existence can in the natural order of things produce more. I assert that, other things being equal, the greater the population, the greater the comfort which an equitable distribution of wealth would give to each individual. I assert that in a state of equality the natural increase of population would constantly tend to make every individual richer instead of poorer.[240]

He explained further:

> . . . even if the increase of population does reduce the power of the natural factor of wealth, by compelling a resort to poorer soils, etc., it

[236] *Ibid.*, p. 262.
[237] *Ibid.*, pp. 268–269.
[238] *Ibid.*, p. 270.
[239] Henry George, *Progress and Poverty; an inquiry into the cause of industrial depressions, and of increase of want with increase of wealth,* New York, 1880, Book II, Ch. 1 and 2, especially pp. 86, 109.
[240] *Ibid.*, Book II, Ch. 4, p. 126.

yet so vastly increases the power of the human factor as to more than compensate. . . . The denser the population the more minute becomes the subdivision of labor, the greater the economies of production and distribution, and, hence, the very reverse of the Malthusian doctrine is true. . . .[241]

Also,

. . . increased population, of itself, and without any advance in the arts, implies an increase in the productive power of labor. The labor of 100 men, other things being equal, will produce much more than one hundred times as much as the labor of one man, and the labor of 1,000 men much more than ten times as much as the labor of 100 men; and, so, with every additional pair of hands which increasing population brings, there is a more than proportional addition to the productive power of labor.[242]

In short, the net effect of population growth is said to be a more than proportional increase in production.

As for the influence of population growth on distribution, George wrote that in the extreme case in which poorer land must be brought into use,

. . . increase of population, as it operates to extend production to lower natural levels, operates to increase rent and reduce wages as a proportion, and may or may not reduce wages as a quantity; while it seldom can, and probably never does, reduce the aggregate production of wealth as compared with the aggregate expenditure of labor, but on the contrary increases, and frequently largely increases it.[243]

Although the use of poorer soils may affect distribution, in others words, returns to labor do not diminish. And even if it does not lead to the use of poorer soils, according to George, population growth adds to the rental value of land by increasing the yield.[244]

George not only assumed a relation of population to production opposite that described by Malthus, but also advanced a general law of population to replace the Malthusian theory. What he considered the true law of population was:

. . . the tendency to increase, instead of being always uniform, is strong where a great population would give increased comfort, and where the perpetuity of the race is threatened by the mortality induced by adverse conditions; but weakens just as the higher development of the individual becomes possible and the perpetuity of the race is assured.[245]

This is a theory that population numbers tend toward and automatically stabilize at the most advantageous size; and in combination with George's

[241] *Ibid.*, p. 133.
[243] *Ibid.*, pp. 210–211.
[245] *Ibid.*, Book II, Ch. 3, p. 123.
[242] *Ibid.*, Book IV, Ch. 2, pp. 208–209.
[244] *Ibid.*, p. 211.

belief that population growth is a source of national well-being and high productivity it presents a highly optimistic estimate of the consequences of increase in the number of people.

Hawley · A work that achieved little recognition among economists but is of interest here because of its focus on economic aspects of population is *Capital and Population* (1882) by Frederick B. Hawley (1843–1929). A business man with an interest in economics, Hawley set himself the task of explaining the interrelations of capital and population, and although an admitted follower of the English school he formed his own independent conclusions, which differed at points from Ricardo and Mill.

One point of difference was the effect of high wages on population. Here Hawley reasoned that it is not a high but a low rate of wages relative to profits that stimulates population growth, for there will be fuller employment among the workers in the latter case than in the former.[246]

Throughout his work Hawley gave particular emphasis to the ratio of capital to population or labor supply, and, of the two, evidently regarded capital as the more dynamic and independent factor. There is, he believed, an optimum ratio of capital to population that maximizes the total amount paid in wages. An increase in capital above this amount would raise wages but lower the number employed, and a decrease in capital would lower wages while increasing employment; but according to the theory the total amount of wages would be less in either case.[247] Noting that capital growth may disturb the capital-population balance, Hawley doubted that a population increase automatically restores the balance, and believed that the means of restoring the balance is an increase in unproductive consumption that reduces the wage fund.[248]

Another matter Hawley considered especially important for the economic health of a society was the trend of net product per capita, or what is now called productivity. He wrote:

> The circumstance that seems to be important is the determination of the question whether the net produce of a nation bears an increasing, a decreasing, or a steady ratio to its population. If the income *per capita* of its people is growing larger, I should say it was enjoying an economic progress; if smaller, that it was going backward, irrespective of whether such advance or retrogression was accompanied by a growth or decline of the total wealth and population. It is, indeed, true that any increase in net income *per capita* is usually accompanied by an increase in the aggre-

[246] Frederick B. Hawley, *Capital and Population,* New York, 1882, pp. 16–17.
[247] *Ibid.,* p. 131.
[248] *Ibid.,* p. 17. Hawley had the somewhat Keynesian idea that individuals, by reducing their unproductive consumption and increasing their savings, reduce the employable capital and the amount of production in a society. As he said, "There is here a case where individual are opposed to social interests" (p. 55).

gate of accumulation, and of population; but the latter must be distinguished from the former as being its effect and counteractant. It is its effect, because any increase in net income is an additional stimulus to population; and its counteractant, because every increase of numbers lowers the margin of cultivation, and because every increase of capital beyond that of population decreases the capacity of the nation to produce by lessening the number of laborers employed. . . .[249]

It is evident that Hawley here treated population rather as a dependent variable; but he did believe that the growth of population stimulated by a rise in productivity tends in turn to check productivity.

Wilson · Among the last of the American political economists of this period to deserve special mention because of his population thought is William D. Wilson (1816–1900), clergyman and prolific writer on a number of subjects, and for many years professor of moral and intellectual philosophy at Cornell. His *First Principles of Political Economy* (1882), which for the most part followed Carey, has not been regarded as a very original contribution to economics but it contained some distinctive ideas on population.

In the discussion of rent, which adhered to Carey's teachings, two possible influences of population growth on rent were noted. First the greater demand adds to the value of produce and is reflected in a greater value and rental price of land. Second,

> In an advancing civilization, with a population increasing in density, something is done every year on the land or around it, to improve its value, to carry it towards a higher state of perfection, and to give it an increased intrinsic value, as a means of getting a living and supplying human wants.[250]

It is not clear in the latter case whether Wilson regarded the population increase or the advancing civilization as the active agent. However, in a later connection he described population growth as a social force that may urge a society to higher civilization. In a nation whose population is growing and from which emigration is not possible, he explained, the two alternatives are to check growth deliberately by infanticide or other means, or to increase production. The latter alternative leads to civilization.[251]

Additional advantages of a large or dense population were described in a chapter on the relation between population and wealth. A large number of people was said to be a prerequisite for differentiation of economic classes, such as producers, manufacturers, and traders.[252] A large volume

[249] *Ibid.,* p. 59.
[250] W. D. Wilson, *First Principles of Political Economy,* Philadelphia: Henry Carey Baird, 1882, p. 98.
[251] *Ibid.,* pp. 107–108.
[252] *Ibid.,* p. 109.

of demand was given as a condition for more specialized and efficient production, which reduces unit costs.[253] Advantages specifically attributed to a dense population included the promotion of division of labor, savings in cost of exchange, stimulation of new wants, the introduction of new commodities, and a larger proportion of the labor force in agriculture.[254]

A long final chapter dealt with overpopulation and presented a mixture of familiar and new ideas. Starting with the basic principle that the condition of human life depends upon the relative rates of growth of capital and population, Wilson pointed out that Malthus and Carey gave opposite theories of the relation of population and wealth. According to Malthus, wealth per capita must decrease after a certain stage of development; according to Carey, wealth increases progressively in all civilized states. Wilson agreed with Carey in the progression to better soils and in the advance of productiveness, but did not believe this invalidated the Malthusian theory. The amount of land on the earth is limited, he said, as is the productiveness of any given plot of land.[255] In effect, Wilson conceded that there must be a point of diminishing returns, and that population in the long run can increase faster than the means of subsistence.[256]

More optimistically, Wilson expressed the opinion that there are limits and limiting factors that the Malthusians had not considered. Specifically,

> Human beings . . . become generally less productive as they rise in the scale of culture. (and) As population becomes dense large cities arise and increase in number, and in the number of their citizens. But they are great consumers of human life.[257]

A city size of 30,000 inhabitants was taken as the critical point above which deaths come to exceed births. Expanding on the subject of the urban check, Wilson set forth the following principles:

> The tendency of population is to centralization.
> Great cities and large towns thus become pestiferous centers, absorbing the vigor and energy of the country and increasing at its expense.
> The causes tending to produce disease and death are more fatal and prevalent among a dense than among a scattered population.[258]

In essence, then, Wilson had a theory of a double check with advancing population and civilization, which consisted of low fertility with advanced culture and high mortality among the urban classes.

[253] *Ibid.*, pp. 115–116.
[254] *Ibid.*, pp. 117, 132–133. Wilson's explanation of how a larger proportion of the labor force can be employed in agriculture was that increased productivity in manufacturing releases workers for other employment.
[255] *Ibid.*, pp. 308–309.   [256] *Ibid.*, p. 310.
[257] *Ibid.*, p. 311.   [258] *Ibid.*, p. 312.

Wilson then turned to the question of whether these natural checks operate in time to prevent an economy going on to greatly diminished returns and general poverty. His answer was as follows:

> Taking then the two elements, (1) rate of increase of production, and (2) rate of increase of population, into consideration together, and considering the controlling causes that influence the nature of the rates, we find that there must come a time when the productions of the soil and the means of human subsistence shall have reached its highest limit, and can go no further; and a time, also, when the ratio of increase to the population will be reduced to unity; and then we shall have no further increase in the total or aggregate population of the earth.
>
> From the nature of the case, the two conditions, though *to some extent* independent of each other, are not, nevertheless, *so* independent but that they must occur at about the same time.[259]

Instances of poverty and assumed overpopulation, he decided, are the fault of man, not of the laws of nature.[260] Finally, he summed up his position on the population problem and the concept of overpopulation:

> ... instead of expecting any "over-population", in the sense in which the words are ordinarily used by Political Economists, I regard the thing as impossible. On the contrary, I look upon the increasing density of population in the world, as one of the indispensable conditions of an advancing civilization, and as one of the most efficient means towards a greater freedom and equality, a higher morality, and a more enlightened humanity, than the world has ever yet seen.[261]

These were the concluding words of Wilson's *First Principles*.

Patten · Finally there was Simon N. Patten (1852–1922), who was for many years teacher of political economy at the University of Pennsylvania and whose education in the United States was supplemented by study in Germany. His *Premises of Political Economy* (1885) was marked by originality at many points. It maintained that the law of diminishing returns applies only in the early development of a society, raised objections to the Ricardian rent theory, and was anti-Malthusian in its treatment of the population question.

A novel line of reasoning developed by Patten was that some products of nature are available in generous supply, others only in limited supply, and that complaints of the niggardliness of nature can be traced to a universal disposition of men to prefer the latter products.[262] He went on to say that:

[259] *Ibid.,* p. 317.
[260] *Ibid.,* p. 333.
[261] *Ibid.,* p. 341.
[262] Simon N. Patten, *The Premises of Political Economy,* Philadelphia: Lippincott, 1885, p. 14.

We have, then, two distinct types of civilization, — the one in which those things are desired of which nature is least productive, the other in which each individual conforms to those external conditions necessary for the greatest possible production. I desire to point out that the economic laws of these two different civilizations are not the same, and that the doctrines whose universality is asserted by the English school of economists are only true of a civilization where the mass of the people prefer those commodities which can be produced by nature only in relatively small quantities. It is only when the land is used to produce a very few articles of food that the Ricardian theory of rent is true, and it is only in those nations desiring but a small variety of food and having but few sources of pleasure where the tendency to increase of population is so great as to be injurious.[263]

The implication is that population growth, although it can be injurious, is in fact injurious only under very special conditions.

Concerning himself directly with the Malthusian theory, Patten reviewed the possible counter-arguments and asserted that population pressure on the food supply occurs only in a simple society in which there is no use of capital in the production process.[264] The accumulation of capital was said to occur only where there is concern for the future and prudence exercised in consumption. It is these qualities in a society that permit expansion of the number of people.[265] A final comment by Patten was that "The growth of population compels mankind either to progress or retrograde," but that advances in intellectual development and in education reduce the tendency to overpopulate.[266]

This by no means completes the list of American writers who dealt with the population question, but presents the principal contributions and indicates the range of thought among the political economists in the United States during this period.

6 · Some Features of American Population Theory[267]

Now that the separate writers and their theories have been reviewed, it may be useful to have a summary view of some of the common features in the population thought of the American political economists during the

---

[263] *Ibid.,* pp. 16–17.
[264] *Ibid.,* Ch. III, p. 83.
[265] *Ibid.,* pp. 84–85.
[266] *Ibid.,* p. 244.
[267] Especially useful surveys, for the most part concerned with economic theory, are: *The Ricardian Rent Theory in early Amercian Economics,* by John R. Turner, New York, 1921; "The early American reaction to the theory of Malthus," by George J. Cady, published in the *Journal of Political Economy,* October 1931, Vol. 39, pp. 601–632; and the article by Leslie that was cited earlier. See also J. J. Spengler, "Malthusianism in late eighteenth century America," *Amer. Economic Review,* 25:691–707, December 1935.

nineteenth century. A first impression is that they were a very diverse group, in background predominantly academic although there were many clergymen and businessmen among them, and even more varied in their economic theories and population thought.

In their population thought as well as in their economics, most of the wrtiers reviewed in this chapter fall into one of two fairly distinct categories. One is composed of the followers of English classical authorities such as Malthus, Ricardo, and John Stuart Mill. In the category of those who accepted the Malthusian view in whole or in large part are Baldwin, McVickar, Cooper, Rae, Vethake, Bascom, and Francis Walker; but of these some were perhaps more English than American in education and outlook, while others could not free themselves completely from the strong American conviction about population to which they were exposed. Most of the American writers, however, were firmly convinced that the Malthusian law was an alien doctrine whose fallacies were evident in both theory and experience; and the members of this category range from Raymond, Tucker, Everett, and Cardozo in the early decades of the century to Henry Carey, Bowen, George, and others in later years.

The system of classical economics, especially that of the English school, was the common core of the American work, for it provided either the framework of thought and analysis or the target for criticism and revision. To highlight what is distinctive or American in the population thought of these writers, however, we need to look especially at the writings of the dissenters from classical theory and at the occasional original interpolations or deviations from orthodoxy by the followers of classical precedent. The common conviction, of course, was that Malthus was in error and that a large and expanding population benefits rather than harms a nation. Criticism of Malthus followed much the same lines as the anti-Malthusian literature in Europe, and so is not reviewed here; but the advantages attributed to population are worth noting for they indicate the direction of American thought.

Generally the desirability of a large population was emphasized, but mention was also made of population growth, and the density factor was particularly emphasized by Tucker, Everett, Henry Carey, Ware, and George. It was also credited as a force for higher social organization and civilization, in particular by Everett, Carey, Thompson, and Wilson. Specific good effects noted by one or another writer included strengthened national defense, stimulation of manufactures, division of labor, greater industriousness and competition, habits of cooperation, the invention of machinery, the multiplication of wants, higher quality of goods, economies of production and distribution, and generally higher productivity or more efficient production.

Underlying this optimism in many instances was confidence that an increasing volume of production does not lead to diminishing per capita returns or increasing unit costs of production. For example, Raymond, Cardozo, Jennison, and Everett believed that returns remain at least proportional to labor, and Everett thought that returns increase with growing population density and more intensive use of land. Carey and his follower Smith believed in an accelerating rate of return, George took substantially the same position for other reasons, and Patten limited the condition of diminishing returns to the early stages of development in a society.

Consistent with rejection of the principle of diminishing returns was the attack on another fundamental principle of classical economics, the Ricardian rent theory, which to the American writers seemed completely at variance with experience in their own country and which they rejected for various reasons. Cardozo, the first, asserted that inferior soils are brought into use as advances in agricultural techniques increase the facility of production, and that population growth is the result rather than the cause of this process. Tucker reasoned that the cultivation of inferior soils is not the cause but the result of a rise in food prices. Phillips considered the Ricardian theory already discredited and not meriting serious attention. Henry Carey and his followers asserted that the progression is in fact from the more readily cultivated but less fertile soils to the more difficult but also more fertile soils. Bowen denied that the growth of the English population had forced poorer land into use. Sturtevant made much the same point as Tucker, that prices and rent are raised by increased demand, not by the use of poorer land; and Patten, finally, considered the Ricardian theory applicable only where there is little diversification of crops. But even though there was disagreement on specific reasons, the majority agreed in opposing the Ricardian explanation of rent.

Distribution theory on the whole seems to have been of less interest to the American than to the European political economists, perhaps because of the quite different economic environment in the United States; and the population factor did not play a very large part in American distribution theory. The role of capital was especially emphasized by a number of writers; it was recognized that a number of factors affect the pattern of distribution; and in some instances population was relegated to the position of a dependent variable responsive to changes in capital and food supply.

The population factor entered most prominently in the discussion of wages, but the American writers proceeded from a variety of assumptions about wage determination and came to diverse conclusions. A common-sense supply and demand wage mechanism was most often used, but the wage fund theory or an approximation to it was common, and a productivity theory of wages appeared in several places. And the variety of views on the trend of returns, whether increasing, constant, or decreasing led to further variety in wage theory. For example Tucker and Newman followed the classical economists in tracing a double effect of population growth on real wages, first through an increase in the labor supply, and second through growth of demand and an upward tendency of food prices. Raymond believed that the rate of payment of the workers, at least in agriculture, depends upon whether they own the land. Henry Carey, who carried his novel theories to their logical conclusions, maintained that population growth adds to the amount and proportion of the product taken by wages and decreases the proportion taken by rent and profits. In Bowen's opinion the important variable for wage determination is the ratio of employers to employees; and a suggestion of productivity theory can be found in discussions of wages by Francis Walker and others. Except among those who followed classical economic authority, there was no substantial agreement on wages among the American political economists. An inverse relation between population and wages was most commonly assumed, but for a variety of reasons, and population was not always considered a significant variable, or was sometimes treated as only one of several factors affecting wages.

Among the factors brought into the discussion of wage determination was a cultural variable. The concept of a natural level to which wages tend was adopted by some American writers, and a number of them accepted the idea from classical economics that the point of stabilization is not the subsistence level but the customary level of consumption of the workers. For example, Cooper wrote of the natural wage level as depending upon "the custom of the country." Newman believed "the style of living" of the people is an active factor affecting wage level and population. Vethake had the same concept in writing of "the habits of the people"; and Ware used the same term and attributed to it the same significance. What Francis Walker called "the standard of comfort and decency" entered into his concept of the necessary wage. And Sturtevant thought that wages depend upon "the degree of comfort demanded by the workers" as well as on the supply of capital. By no means distinctively American, this common feature in the treatment of wages was recognition of a non-economic factor in wage determination. A few writers recognized that the same non-economic factor might also in some measure determine the size of population attained with a given volume of production.

The rather general refusal to accept the Ricardian rent theory has been noted. As far as the relation of population to rent was concerned, however, those who rejected Ricardo's explanation often came to the same conclusion, that population growth tends to raise rent, arguing from a supply and demand basis, where population corresponds to the demand factor. Carey and his closest followers seem to have been alone in believing that a progressively smaller share of the product goes into rent as the number of people increases.

As a rule the population factor was considered to have little influence on the rate of profit on capital, except as it might act indirectly through wages and rent. As already noted, a number of the American writers, including some who did not follow classical doctrine, apparently looked upon capital as the more influential factor in the interaction of capital and population.

Outside the context of production and distribution, certain non-economic theories about population were expressed by the American political economists. Frequently accompanying the anti-Malthusian arguments was the assertion that poverty and misery are due to injustice and inequalities of distribution in societies rather than to any natural law. The opinion was expressed by Raymond, Newman, Henry Carey, Bowen, Perry, Amasa Walker, George, and Wilson, in the group considered here; and while it may reflect their satisfaction that their society was relatively free of the imperfections they saw in the Old World, their opinion also rested on the general conviction that populousness cannot of itself bring harm to a well-ordered society.

Another common theoretical ground for optimism about population was the belief that population growth is naturally and automatically checked before it goes too far. For example, Raymond wrote that the growth of artificial wants checks population growth before actual want or shortage appears. Tucker thought that the growth of cities, of civilization, and of artificial wants accompanying population increase are naural preventives of overpopulation. Henry Carey stated the theory that when men are really free, fecundity is inversely related to the degree of individual development. Ware wrote of the effect of pride of style and comfort. For Perry, reason and affection are the effective preventive checks. Amasa Walker ascribed the role of preventive check to manufactures, Thompson to civilization, and George to high development of the individual. Wilson named the same influences that Tucker had; and according to Patten education and intellectual development check population growth. These were all automatic checks that were thought to grow stronger as the number of people increases. Confidence in the ability of education to promote the prudential check was expressed by several writers, including Cardozo, Vethake, and Bascom; and this seems to have been a special case of the general American belief in education as a panacea for social problems.

In this connection it is of some interest to note that the inverse relation of fertility to socio-economic status was apparently well known and that various explanations were given. Raymond explained the phenomenon in terms of the different extent of artificial wants in different classes. Bowen's theory was that social injustice or maldistribution represses the preventive check, and that fertility varies with the degree of security of maintaining one's present position. Bascom believed, with Doubleday, that food shortage stimulates reproduction; and Francis Walker mentioned the phenomenon but gave no formal explanation of it.

A few more general theories of population can be noted. Tucker, who considered population growth a force for progress and civilization, held the theory that numbers tend toward the "golden mean" and stabilize there. Carey, as already mentioned, believed in the inverse relation of fertility and individual development, and had the further idea of an ecological and chemical balance in nature that assures provision for an increasing number of people. Bascom's theory that food shortage stimulates reproduction has been mentioned, and George believed that reproduction is stimulated by either adverse conditions or increasing returns, and that it is repressed by individual development and security in the perpetuation of the race.

For final comment there is the question of what can be called distinctive in the population thought of the American writers considered in this chapter. With the exception of a few particularly original thoughts, the bulk of the ideas had been expressed before. For example, those most independent of European doctrine used much the same arguments against Malthus and in favor of populousness as the anti-Malthusians in Europe. With exceptions already observed, what most distinguished the population thought of the American group as a whole, therefore, is the greater prevalence of certain convictions and viewpoints rather than the uniqueness of the ideas themselves. Noteworthy here is the strong majority opinion that a large, growing, and dense population is beneficial to the nation and the economy, and the quite common belief that a new system of economic and population thought is needed to fit the conditions of the New World. There was also a great diversity of economic and population thought, for although there were some orthodox writers and some of Carey's school, many did not accept any prior system consistently but quite independently expressed their own heterodox opinions. Especially in the early years, the American political economists seem to have had a somewhat less abstract or theoretical and a more observational approach to population and economics than their European counterparts. At the same time they were much less analytical. Political economy was still in its early stages in the United States and lagged far behind the European development, although the gap lessened as time went on.

As in Europe the population question receded from the forefront of discussion in political economy, but doubtless for quite different reasons.

Even when it was most active in Europe the Malthusian controversy was not a major issue in the American literature. With a rising immigration and a rapidly growing population the American political economists may well have felt that the population factor would take care of itself, and they turned their attention to other matters. For many of them, a high protective tariff seemed to be a far more important issue.

11

Other Population Theories of
the Nineteenth Century: General Theories

Only a part, although a central part, of nineteenth-century population theory was covered in the preceding chapters. The century following the publication of Malthus' *Essay* saw a great proliferation of writings on population; and in addition to the main body of systematic population theory developed in connection with production and distribution theory in classical economics, many other areas of population thought received attention. Nineteenth-century writers on the subject were not restricted to the confines of formal economics. Their interests ranged over all aspects of the population question, social and political as well as economic, and they had quite as much curiosity about the forces underlying population phenomena as about their socio-economic consequences.

Although very diverse, the non-economic literature on population displayed several common characteristics. As a whole, it was anti-Malthusian, actively or by implication. Many writers attacked the *Essay* and its author directly; others, without attempting to discredit Malthus and his work, felt that he had missed the true and underlying principle governing population and society and offered their own theories as substitutes. As noted before, there seemed to be a persistent belief at the time that the social world, like the physical, is governed by simple natural laws; and the success of the Malthusian theory also may have stimulated a swarm of rivals.

Another characteristic of the non-economic literature, especially in contrast to the economic writings, was that it did not form a unified and cumulative body of thought, but consisted largely of independent and isolated contributions. Each writer pursued his own train of thought and elaborated his own theoretical system, with a resulting lack of the theoretical continuity and the progression of ideas that distinguished the economic thought on population. And more than in the area of economic analysis, there was a tendency, also noted in other fields of inquiry, to have little regard for observers and empirical information and high esteem for the inventors of systems.[1]

[1] From M. Francois, a French physician of the mid-eighteenth century, quoted by Richard Shryock in *The development of modern medicine,* Philadelphia: University of Pennsylvania Press, 1936, p. 49.

Still, the varied writings on population outside the line of economic development merit attention; and in fact, an account of nineteenth-century population thought is not complete without them. Giving something of the flavor of the contemporary discussion, they illustrate the range and diversity of population thought in its period of greatest development, even though many of the more speculative and controversial writings are little more than curiosities today. And on the positive side, they helped to broaden the treatment of the population question and to give more recognition to non-economic forces affecting population. This chapter summarizes a selected group of the principal theories of population that appeared after Malthus, with the exception of the American theories described in the preceding chapter. The next chapter, which covers some lesser works as well as some already mentioned, traces certain recurrent ideas or themes that appeared in the nineteenth-century population literature. As in the preceding chapters, these two chapters are concerned primarily with the treatment of the socio-economic significance of population, but in this chapter especially each writer's work is outlined fully enough to reveal his distinctive ideas on population.

1 · The First Two Decades

Hall · Charles Hall[2] (1745?–1825?) was a doctor, thought to have been trained at Leyden, of whom little is known except that he had written on medical subjects before publishing two notable works in 1805, *The Effects of Civilization,* and the briefer supplement, *Observations on the Principal Conclusions in Mr. Malthus' Essay on Population.* An advocate of social reform somewhat after the fashion of Godwin, Hall diagnosed and prescribed for contemporary social problems in *The Effects of Civilization.* He did so with little reference to population and without evidence of knowing the Malthusian argument against egalitarian plans for social betterment of the sort he advocated. This work was soon followed, however, by the *Observations,* in which Hall dealt directly with the population factor.

Briefly, Hall's thesis was that there are two main classes in society, the poor who are the laborers and the rich who exploit them,[3] and that civilization, which he defined as consisting of "the study and knowledge of the sciences, and in the production and enjoyment of the conveniences, elegancies, and luxuries of life," is made possible by reducing the large

[2] One of the first of the nineteenth-century contributions to population literature was William Godwin's *Thoughts occasioned by the perusal of Dr. Parr's spital sermon* (1801), but this is considered later in connection with Godwin's more detailed reply to Malthus, *On population* (1820).

[3] Charles Hall, *The Effects of Civilization on the People in European States,* London, 1805, p. 4.

mass of the poor to their present condition.[4] According to Hall's explanation, the rich who command the labor of the poor direct too many laborers into manufactures to satisfy their own wants, and food shortages result because too few hands are employed on the land.[5] Manufactures, he continued, are a sign of national poverty, and together with civilization bring weakness by promoting an unequal division of property that leaves few who care to defend the nation.[6] In conclusion Hall recommended the abolition of primogeniture, the prohibition or heavy taxation of "refined" manufactures, and, above all, equal division of property.

In *The Effects of Civilization* Hall mentioned the population factor only as it related to his main thesis. He remarked on the slower growth of population in Europe than in America, which he attributed to a difference in infant mortality. He also noted that "It is remarkable, that poor living does not lessen the fertility of women, though it deprives them of the means of bringing up their children."[7] He either did not know of or took no notice of Malthus' contention that plans for social betterment through the equal distribution of property would be defeated by their stimulation of population growth; but perhaps he did not recognize any such problem, for he believed that the produce of land remains proportional to the amount of labor bestowed on it.[8] In the *Observations,* published later the same year, however, Hall asserted that the danger of overpopulation is remote and can be averted by wise measures, and that equal division of property is in fact the surest means of preventing undue population growth as well as of alleviating the ill effects of civilization.[9]

Jarrold · The population problem received more attention in a work published the following year, *Dissertations on Man* (1806) by Thomas Jarrold (1770–1853). Like Hall, Jarrold was a doctor by profession and had arrived at his own conclusions about contemporary social problems. Opposing Malthus on most points, he asserted that population growth is generally beneficial rather than harmful, and that increase in numbers is automatically checked before it can go to excess. He believed further that there is a direct relation between population size and civilization, and he did not share Hall's concern about the effects of the latter. According to Jarrold, population numbers vary directly with the degree of advancement of a people, for, as he wrote, ". . . I think it may be taken as a general fact, that a state increases in population in proportion as it becomes civilized. . . ."[10] But at the same time population growth was described as a civilizing force:

4 *Ibid.,* pp. 131–132. 5 *Ibid.,* p. 36.
6 *Ibid.,* sections XIX, XXI. 7 *Ibid.,* p. 16.
8 *Ibid.,* section XXXIX.
9 For further notes on Hall and the place of his writings in the Malthusian controversy, see Harold A. Boner, *Hungry Generations,* New York: King's Crown Press, 1955, pp. 50–53.
10 Thomas Jarrold, *Dissertations on Man,* London, 1806, p. 306.

A country thinly peopled is never civilized, because the service of
every individual is directed toward the means of subsistence and defense;
hence they have neither leisure, security, or emulation to devote much
time to study.[11]

Or, as he said in summary, ". . . it would seem that there exists a reciprocal connection between civilization and population; the one cannot
increase without the other, to a certain extent."[12] According to Jarrold,
therefore, an increase in the number of people is both a cause and a
consequence of national progress, not the obstacle Malthus had considered
it to be.

Jarrold gave particular attention to the question of what affects population growth. The increase in numbers that he believed accompanies
advancing civilization was presumably attributed to the removal of checks,
for he recognized the action of checks, and wrote that

Were the government of a country, in the state in which Europe now is,
to ameliorate the condition of the common people, the population would
increase in proportion as the hinderances were removed that had suppressed it.[13]

A worsening of the condition of the people would of course have the
opposite effect. According to a further theory of Jarrold's however, another principle operates to check increase as a nation advances in civilization and population. As he wrote, ". . . in every age the fullest peopled
states have increased the slowest, not because vice and misery have more
abounded, but because the principle of increase has lessened."[14] The explanation for the lessening of the principle of increase was that ". . . as
the man sinks down towards the animal, he is prolific; as he ascends above
them, his fruitfulness decreases."[15] That is to say, man's fertility varies
inversely with his condition.

Jarrold thus came to the seemingly contradictory conclusions that
population increases with national advancement but that improvement in
the condition of the people lowers their fertility. He partially resolved
the apparent contradiction, however, by adding that "There is a certain
rank which is most friendly to population, all above or below this lessen
the force of the principle of increase."[16] This optimum position for
population growth, one may infer, comes in the course of national advancement when the natural checks are reduced but fertility is still high.

In addition to the external influences of civilization and general well-
being, Jarrold also saw certain internal influences on reproduction and
population growth: "The relation of the mind to the body is intimate

[11] *Ibid.*, p. 201. [12] *Ibid.*, p. 312.
[13] *Ibid.*, p. 309. [14] *Ibid.*, p. 308.
[15] *Ibid.*, p. 250. [16] *Ibid.*, p. 310.

. . . (and) . . . the influence of the mind extends to the propagation of the species. . . ."[17] For example, he continued, savages who lead insecure lives are not prolific, but those who live tranquil lives have many offspring.[18] The greater fertility of the lower orders of society than of the upper classes was also explained in terms of mental influence, for exertion of the mind was said to lead to infertility.[19] Jarrold added that population growth in the United States would decline as the people there came to make more use of their mental faculties, and he concluded that fertility is regulated by more than the Malthusian checks, in such a way that no country will be overpeopled.[20]

Hazlitt · The following year saw the publication of *A Reply to the Essay on Population* (1807) by William Hazlitt (1778–1830). This work was largely negative in its theoretical content, for the most part an incisive statement of arguments against the Malthusian thesis and personal attacks on Malthus. Hazlitt had little interest in erecting a new population theory of his own, but did present some alternatives to the theory he attacked. Population was said to increase only with advances in "the state of cultivation and in the arts of life."[21] The great power of increase was acknowledged, but rational motives were thought to check population growth before it could go too far.[22] Concerning the operation of checks, it was said further that

. . . where the population begins to press on the means of subsistence . . . it naturally stops short of its own accord, the checks to it from vice, misery, and moral restraint taken all together becoming stronger as the excess becomes greater. It therefore produces it's (sic) own antidote and produces it in quantities exactly in proportion to it's own extent.[23]

With this confidence in the effectiveness of the preventive and positive checks, Hazlitt was convinced that the worst population growth can do is prevent the improvement in the general level of living that would otherwise follow advances in methods of production; and he was sure that population growth can never be the cause of deterioration in the material condition of the people.[24]

[17] *Ibid.,* pp. 254–255.　　　　[18] *Ibid.,* pp. 255–256.
[19] *Ibid.,* p. 269.　　　　[20] *Ibid.,* pp. 281, 288.
[21] William Hazlitt, *A Reply to the Essay on Population,* London, 1807, p. 102.
[22] *Ibid.,* p. 109 ff.
[23] *Ibid.,* p. 115.
[24] In his later writings in the Malthusian controversy, Hazlitt stated and restated his criticisms of the *Essay on Population,* questioned Malthus' originality and attributed priority to Wallace, but did not really add to population theory or analysis. See especially the several essays relating to the population question in *Political Essays* (1819), the sketch on Malthus included in *The Spirit of the Age* (anon., 1825), and a letter in *The London Magazine* (November 1823, pp. 459–460). For a useful account of Hazlitt and his work see William P. Albrecht, *William Hazlitt and the*

Ingram · Another of the many rebuttals to Malthus' *Essay* was *Disquisitions on Population* (1808) by Robert Ingram (1763–1809), an English clergyman and author of works on theological and economic subjects. Both Godwin and Malthus were criticized in an even-handed manner, the former for advocating dangerous tenets, the latter for promoting pernicious doctrines contrary to theology and national policy in spite of his good intentions and extensive research.[25]

Among the reasons Ingram gave for rejecting the thesis of the *Essay* were these: the assumption of geometric increase is not supported by experience; there is no constant growth of the food supply from year to year; human misery is attributable more to "a defect of virtue or intelligence, or other human imperfections" than to overpopulation; food shortages may be due to unequal distribution or to wasteful consumption; population has diminished in some nations instead of pressing continually on the means of subsistence; the greatest misery is found in the most thinly peopled areas; and finally, postponing marriage adds to the likelihood of immorality before marriage and of orphanhood of the children of late marriages.[26]

On the positive side Ingram was more optimistic than Malthus that a balance is maintained between population and food supply:

> Moral restraint, vice, and misery, are not the only efficient causes in adjusting population, and the means of subsistence. Virtue and intelligence have a very powerful influence in preventing, or alleviating, the misery, which originates in vice, or any causes connected with population, by other means, than, simply, as a restraint on the powers of generation.[27]

There are various ways in which population increase may be met and the advantages of a larger body of people enjoyed, he continued; and the increasing difficulty of supporting a family as the number of consumers grows, together with the "fear of misery," is probably sufficient to check further growth unless there is injudicious encouragement of marriage. But above all, Ingram was sure that Providence does not allow numbers to increase to a point at which misery is inevitable.[28]

Ingram was also impressed with the strength of the force of mortality, which he believed was not sufficiently appreciated by Malthus. Assuming the early twenties to be the usual age of marriage, he estimated that the

---

Malthusian Controversy, Albuquerque, N.M.: University of New Mexico Press, 1950; also Herschel Baker, *William Hazlitt*, Cambridge: Harvard University Press, 1962.

[25] Robert Ingram, *Disquisitions on Population, in which the Principles of the Essay on Population by the Rev. T. R. Malthus are examined and refuted*, London, 1808, pp. 1–2.

[26] *Ibid.*, pp. 15–19, 33.

[27] *Ibid.*, p. 8.

[28] *Ibid.*, pp. 38–39.

proportion surviving to that age was only about one person out of four in London, and a somewhat higher proportion in other towns.[29] This led to the conclusion that ". . . so far from being alarmed at the rapid increase of native population, we should rather find it difficult to account for that increase of our numbers, which is supposed to exist."[30] And if this is the case for the most prosperous parts of the nation, "surely all our dismal apprehensions of an unlimited increase, beyond the power of subsistence, are effectually dissipated."[31]

Ingram concluded with an inventory of the existing checks to population in the form of discouragements to marriage, luxury, high mortality in towns, and other causes. He urged that national policy seek to counteract these checks by means of subdivision of land, extra taxes on bachelors, diversion of people from manufacturing to agriculture, and so on. But with trust in Providence he added the warning, "We must not attempt to govern too much, nor derange the level of population by presumptuous efforts to raise or depress it."[32]

Simon Gray · The next considerable contributor to population literature and to the Malthusian controversy was Simon Gray, known only through his writings, *The Happiness of States* (1815), *All Classes productive of National Wealth* (1817), *Gray versus Malthus* (1818), and an open letter to Malthus that appeared in *The Pamphleteer* in 1820. Of these works, the second and third were published under the pseudonym George Purves.[33]

In *The Happiness of States* Gray dealt with population in two connections, first in answer to the question whether growth in the number of people adds to or diminishes the amount of happiness in a state, and second, on the relation between population and subsistence.[34] In both Gray showed himself quite as optimistic about the effects of populousness as his immediate predecessors,[35] for much the same reasons. In the first place, he described a number of ways in which population growth adds to national happiness. For one, "The increase of population is, directly as well as indirectly, the grand permanent source of the increase of wealth, both to individuals and to nations."[36] Here Gray noted a double stimulus to the economy, from increase of the number of consumers and from multiplication of their wants. A further effect, according to Gray, is to extend and improve agriculture.[37] "The increase of population tends equally to

[29] *Ibid.*, p. 63.   [30] *Ibid.*, p. 65.

[31] *Ibid.*, p. 67.   [32] *Ibid.*, p. 98.

[33] The *Dictionary of National Biography* does not include Gray, nor has his name been found in other biographical sources.

[34] Simon Gray, *The Happiness of States,* London, 1815, Books IV and VI.

[35] Writing later under the name of Purves, Gray reported that *The Happiness of States* was intended for publication in 1804, eleven years before it actually appeared (*Gray versus Malthus,* p. iv).

[36] Gray, *The Happiness of States,* p. 320.

[37] *Ibid.*, pp. 321–322.

cultivate and improve the mind of the population as the soil on which it dwells. It has as strong a natural civilizing as it has a fertilizing influence."[38] Particular emphasis was given this point by Gray, who went on to say that there is a close concomitance between population and civilization, the one rising or falling with the other.[39] Finally, it was stated that population growth sets in motion the development of commerce and its attendant advances, which also may be accompanied by greater luxury and other evils.[40]

Anticipating objections to his thesis of greater happiness with greater numbers of people, Gray admitted that population has a strong natural tendency to increase and that it has in fact increased greatly;[41] but he was confident it would not continue to increase indefinitely. This confidence rested on a general principle of population that he asserted as follows:

> . . . in proportion as the earth becomes more generally well peopled, there must be a gradual failure of the populating, and an increase of the depopulating forces. . . . Population thus naturally carries in its own increase a preventive against an over-increase.[42]

Eventually, he believed, a natural balance is attained and population growth stops.

In the section on population and subsistence Gray rejected the arithmetic ratios for the reason that no such progressions can be established, either for population or for food supply.[43] The truth of the matter as he saw it was that demand regulates the supply of food, and that an increase of population expands productive capacity in even greater proportion.[44] Conversely, the supply of the means of subsistence affects the rate of population increase but in an inverse direction, for the rate of increase is high at the subsistence level and diminishes as people enjoy greater abundance.[45]

Gray's two later works, appearing under an assumed name, praised and defended *The Happiness of States,* introduced no new ideas on population but explained and amplified the earlier work. In the first, *All Classes productive of National Wealth,*[46] Gray opposed the Physiocrat theory that agriculture is the source of national wealth and Adam Smith's division of the members of society into the productive and the nonproductive. Throughout the work he maintained the thesis expressed in the title, that all classes and all members of a society contribute to production.

[38] *Ibid.,* p. 323.
[40] *Ibid.,* p. 334.
[42] *Ibid.,* p. 351.
[44] *Ibid.,* pp. 439, 445.
[39] *Ibid.,* pp. 324, 328.
[41] *Ibid.,* Book IV, Ch. 6.
[43] *Ibid.,* Book VI, Ch. 1.
[45] *Ibid.,* Book VI, Ch. 4.
[46] George Purves (Simon Gray), *All Classes productive of National Wealth,* London, 1817. An appendix reprints several reviews, presumably by Gray, and a letter dated March 24, 1817, from Gray to the French economist Say, which contains comments on the Malthusian theory.

This thesis was called "the productive theory," and was said to have been formulated in *The Happiness of States*. It was supported by reasons and assertions given in the preceding work, and by many of the familiar optimistic arguments.[47]

The second work, *Gray versus Malthus*,[48] appeared the following year. It was both a restatement of the principal ideas in *The Happiness of States* and a detailed attempt to refute what Gray called the "subsistence theory," the theory that population tends to press on the limited supply of the means of subsistence. Sir James Steuart was named as the founder of this theory,[49] of which Malthus gave the fullest statement. Gray's rebuttal took the form of an examination of the Malthusian propositions each in turn, attempts to demonstrate that the propositions are self-contradictory and contrary to both reason and theory, citation of various observations inconsistent with the theory, and liberal quotations from Gray's earliest work, which was taken as unquestioned authority.

The essence of Gray's doctrine was said to be that with population growth man's wants are more fully supplied and his civilization advances; and the leading elements were summarized as follows:

1. The principle of population as connected with subsistence, climate, government, &c is, that, in all ordinary circumstances, population has a tendency to increase, but not to over-increase; for this increase carries in itself the power of fully supplying its various wants.

2. The natural progress of population, when compared with time, is according to no particular ratio, but depends upon the various circumstances in which it is placed. Compared with subsistence, in connected districts or countries, it uniformly renders the progress of the latter nearly the same with its own.

3. The amount of population thus regulates the amount of subsistence as completely as it regulates clothing, housing and all other species of circuland depending on the will.

4. Superabundance, or an excess of subsistence, has a defecundating and depopulating effect.

5. The increase of population tends uniformly to increase the average amount of employment divided among the circulators (i.e., workers and consumers), and, of course, to create an additional demand for hands.

6. The increase of population has, therefore, a uniform tendency to increase income and wealth; and not merely according to the old ratio,

[47] Among the points made by Gray was that population increase creates new wants, new employment, greater income and greater wealth; that it expands the amount of money in circulation; and that it tends to raise prices but lower the rate of profits.

[48] George Purves (Simon Gray), *Gray versus Malthus: The Principles of Population and Production*, London, 1818. Several essays are appended, including "On the Poor" by Gray.

[49] *Ibid.*, pp. iii, 329.

but according to a new and enlarged proportion, augmenting somewhat as the number of circulators increases.

7. The diseases and evils generated by the increase of population, are chiefly those which spring from luxury, or an excess of subsistence, and from riches.[50]

A central element in Gray's varied and wide-ranging theories about population and subsistence, as well as one source of his optimism, was his belief in the natural regulation and control of population growth. He denied the existence of any universal law or inevitable progression of growth, as stated in the second of the principles quoted above, and he believed instead that the trend of numbers is "entirely regulated by circumstances." A decisive factor, he wrote here, is the average age of women at marriage: if it is twenty-seven years or more, population falls; if it is around twenty-five years, population is stationary.[51] Being a populationist, to use his own term, he favored early marriage; and he recommended it because he thought it promoted morality, happiness, and wealth in a society.[52]

According to Gray's theory, early marriage insures population growth, but two different lines of reasoning assured him that this gave no cause for concern. In the first place, as already noted, he believed that greater numbers give proportionately greater wealth and production. "Every addition to population must necessarily create a corresponding addition to employment," he noted, and the number of producers increases as well as the number of consumers.[53] Also, subsistence has "a natural tendency to increase much faster than population, except as checked by lack of sufficient demand."[54] And, in the second place, Gray believed in natural and automatic checks on increase. He distinguished two classes of such checks, the "positively destroying," which raise mortality, and the "defecundating," which reduce fertility.[55] Of the former he wrote that population increase "does carry in itself the seeds of counter-action," in the growth of wealth and luxury, the development of cities and of "modes of business injurious to health."[56] Of the defecundating checks he theorized, somewhat as Spencer was to do later, that "It may be affirmed, generally, that labouring with the body has a fecundating virtue, and labouring with the mind, an influence of the opposite kind."[57] Also, ". . . population, far from increasing rapidly according to the abundance of subsistence, is checked by a superabundance of food, and increases faster in proportion as the style of living is more frugal. . . ."[58] In sum, Gray

[50] *Ibid.*, pp. 10–12.
[51] *Ibid.*, pp. 14, 17.
[52] *Ibid.*, Book IV, Ch. 2, 3, 4.
[53] *Ibid.*, p. 173.
[54] *Ibid.*, pp. 344–345.
[55] *Ibid.*, p. 18.
[56] *Ibid.*, p. 147.
[57] *Ibid.*, p. 19; also *Happiness of States*, p. 307.
[58] George Purves (Simon Gray), *Gray versus Malthus*, p. 165.

believed that population growth automatically provides for itself and that it is naturally self-limiting.

Gray's later article in *The Pamphleteer* reaffirmed his previously stated views on population, but added that the division of the people into rich and poor classes occurs when population is scanty, and that the inequality tends to disappear with increase in numbers.[59]

Weyland · Another reply to the *Essay on Population* appeared soon after Gray's *Happiness of States*. This was *The Principles of Population and Production*[60] (1816) by John Weyland (1774–1854), a lawyer who had written earlier on the poor laws.[61]

Weyland doubted whether there is a universal law of population increase. Instead, he believed, "The natural and spontaneous tendency of the principle of population in distinct states of society varies its rate with every difference in their political condition. . . ."[62] The relation of population numbers to subsistence he believed to be more uniform, and he asserted the principle that "Population has a *natural* tendency to keep *within the powers* of the soil to afford it subsistence in every gradation through which society passes."[63] As emphasized by his italics, Weyland meant the productive capacity, not the actual amount of produce of the soil. He recognized that population may well press on the supply of subsistence, and this pressure he considered to be the great force for human progress:

> During the alternate progress of population and subsistence in the earliest and most advanced stages of society, a *previous* increase of people is necessary to stimulate the community to a farther production of food; and consequently to the healthy advancement of a country in the career of strength and prosperity. It results from this proposition that the incipient pressure of population against the *actual* means of subsistence, or, more correctly speaking, the excess of population *just beyond the plentiful supply of the people's want,* instead of being the cause of most of the miseries of human life, is in fact the cause of all public happiness, industry, and prosperity.[64]

In the case of primitive peoples, according to this theory, the pressure of population urges them to a higher stage of economic organization, to the

[59] George Purves (Simon Gray), "Remarks on the Production of Wealth . . . in a letter to the Rev. T. R. Malthus . . . , *The Pamphleteer,* 1820, 17:385–416.

[60] John Weyland, *The Principles of Population and Production, as they are affected by the Progress of Society; with a view to Moral and Political Consequences,* London, 1816.

[61] Weyland, *A Short Enquiry into the Policy, Humanity, and Effect of the Poor Laws,* London, 1807; also, *Observations on Mr. Whitbread's Poor Bill and on the Population of England,* London, 1807.

[62] Weyland, *The Principles,* p. 17.

[63] *Ibid.,* p. 21.

[64] *Ibid.*

pastoral and later the agricultural form of economy. It seemed evident to Weyland that

> . . . this pressure is *necessary* to stimulate them to such exertions as would carry on the society to its next stage, and that any provision by which the pressure could be otherwise removed would be nothing less than a scheme for passing an eternal sentence of barbarism and ignorance against the unfortunate people, and for directly counteracting the ordination of Providence for the replenishment and happiness of the world.[65]

In the higher stages of society, he added, population increase raises the prices of some commodities and induces a shift of capital into other lines of production. This leads to the cultivation of lands formerly unused; and the improvements in the means of cultivation that accompany the investment of larger amounts of capital in agriculture release numbers of people whose labor is no longer needed and who then go to urban industry. As the urban fraction of the population increases in this manner, fertility rates fall and population growth is automatically checked.[66]

It was evident to Weyland that if this progression is followed, population eventually arrives at a "point of non-reproduction." He was sufficiently optimistic to believe that this point is reached well before the cultivation of land has been pushed to its limit and the per capita return to labor reduced to a low level. In his opinion this point of stabilization is attained when more than one-third of the total population resides in large cities. Malthus' twenty-five-year period of doubling might be applicable to a rural society, he added, but does not necessarily hold true under industrialization.[67]

The eventual stabilization of numbers depends upon the intelligence of the people and the type of government under which they live, according to Weyland. As he wrote,

> Where a moderately good government in its enlarged sense is found to prevail, there population will spontaneously restrain itself . . . but where the vices of bad government, and individual immorality and selfishness, are found to be predominant, there the production of food will be restrained while population will make efforts to extend itself, which will be checked by misery and famine till a better system be adopted.[68]

The positive checks that Malthus described as the eventual and inevitable results of population increase Weyland attributed to other social evils that interfere with the natural relation between man's numbers and his subsistence.

Grahame · The third of the trio of writers whose works appeared closely together in 1815 and 1816 is James Grahame (1790–1842), a Scottish

[65] *Ibid.*, p. 28.
[66] *Ibid.*, Ch. 6.
[67] *Ibid.*, Ch. 7.
[68] *Ibid.*, p. 162.

lawyer and writer, author of *An Inquiry into the Principle of Population*[69] (1816). Grahame's own ideas about population are of more permanent interest than his anti-Malthusian arguments, which received a reply from Malthus but which did not differ greatly from those of Gray and Weyland and have not been highly valued in accounts of the controversy.[70] Apparently trying to take a middle position, he expressed the opinion that there was overstatement and exaggeration of both the good effects and the dangers of population growth. For himself, he adopted the comfortable view that in the natural order of things population is automatically regulated to the best interests of society. Convinced that population growth does not lead to vice and misery, he also wrote that it is erroneous to regard population increase as the cause of a happy state, for expansion of the number of people is rather the result and symptom of that condition.[71] At the same time, he wrote, "it is always in the most crowded societies that the quantity and quality of subsistence obtained by individuals is the greatest and best,"[72] and it is especially advantageous to a society to have its lower ranks full.[73]

For a number of reasons, Grahame saw no danger in an excess of population. For one thing,

> Experience . . . has shown that . . . population (except when unnaturally forced by absurd laws against celibacy) always provides subsistence for its own wants; and that increase of the means of subsistence does not always precede, but generally follows increased population.[74]

Emigration is of course possible, although it encounters various obstacles;[75] and there are also effective natural checks on population growth. Human reproduction is under the control of prudence;[76] and in addition, Nature has placed a limit on improvident propagation "by rendering the power of supporting a family nearly coeval with the capacity of begetting it."[77] Grahame did not explain this last statement, which was at variance with other parts of his population theory, but he did emphasize the role of prudential restraint. The principal preventive of overpopulation according to Grahame, however, is another check provided by Nature, the "ordeal of childhood":

[69] James Grahame, *An Inquiry into the Principle of Population: including an exposition of the Causes and the Advantages of a Tendency to Exuberance of Numbers in Society, a Defence of Poor-laws and a critical and historical View of the Doctrines and Projects of the most celebrated Legislators and Writers, relative to Population, the Poor, and charitable Establishments*, Edinburgh, 1816.

[70] See James Bonar, *Malthus and his Work*, pp. 376–377; also Harold A. Boner, *Hungry Generations*, New York: King's Crown Press, 1955, p. 78.

[71] James Grahame, *An Inquiry*, p. 3.   [72] *Ibid.*, p. 167.

[73] *Ibid.*, p. 98.   [74] *Ibid.*, pp. 275–276.

[75] *Ibid.*, Ch. 3.   [76] *Ibid.*, pp. 89–90.

[77] *Ibid.*

There is established near the threshold of life, an ordeal, which can be passed only by those whose vigor is adapted to the exigencies of the afterpart of their career, and sufficient to sustain the peculiar difficulties which that career will present.[78]

This ordeal was considered by Grahame to have particularly beneficial effects, besides acting as a check on population growth. For one thing, he noted, it selects the strongest for survival and thereby affects the quality of the population.[79] Also, it partly counteracts the class difference in fertility, being most severe for the poor and milder for the well-to-do. Grahame recognized that the ordeal of childhood is somewhat reduced as a nation progresses in wealth and civilization, but assumed that there is a simultaneous trend toward greater concentration of wealth in a few hands, which maintains the force of mortality among the poor. For these reasons Grahame much preferred the ordeal of childhood to Malthus' postponement of marriage as a check on population growth, especially since he suspected the latter encourages the development of vice.

What is probably Grahame's most notable contribution to population thought lay in a quite different direction, in his account of the social class differential in fertility and its significance, which was intermingled with his discussion of the Malthusian problem. He was well aware that fertility and family size vary inversely with social and economic status. As he wrote, "It has long been observed, that poverty rather promotes than impedes propagation; that there are no beds so barren as those of the rich and luxurious, and none so fruitful as those of the poor."[80] The explanation he gave for the higher fertility of the poor was that they practice less restraint in reproduction for "They possess so little, that the odds are ten to one in favour of their transmitting every advantage they have enjoyed."[81] And in these terms the rich could not feel equally secure about their children.

Grahame then considered the implications of the class differential in fertility. One effect is that "The sterility of the rich, by leaving vacancies in the upper regions of society, encourages competition among the lower orders for translation to that envied sphere. . . ."[82] He theorized that this natural process of replacement of the upper classes from below is essential to the continued well-being of a society:

> The population of a great state is, and ought to be, mainly replenished by the marriages of the lowest ranks; and it is essential to the moral and

[78] *Ibid.,* p. 167.
[79] Grahame's theory is not known to have influenced Darwin, but the idea of selection and survival of the fittest is known to have been present well before Darwin incorporated it in his theory of evolution.
[80] Grahame, *An Inquiry,* p. 96.
[81] *Ibid.,* p. 94.
[82] *Ibid.,* p. 96.

political prosperity of a country that the lower ranks should be always full.[83]

It was recognized that the ordeal of childhood reduces the net difference of reproduction between rich and poor, even though the economic situation of the poor is somewhat relieved by charity and by the luxury of the rich; but according to Grahame the effect of luxury is to add to rather than reduce the fertility difference between the classes. As he explained,

> The operation of luxury appears to be inevitable, and the benefit with which it is attended is certainly great. While it enables the lower ranks to multiply their number, by conveying to them an additional share of the wealth of society; it thins the upper ranks by celibacy and sterility, and thus affords increased room to the others, and maintains that change and progression of condition so conducive to the happiness of society.[84]

In a later connection Grahame was led to conclude that artificial regulation may interfere with the natural class differential of fertility and upset the process of upward movement within a society. He stated with further emphasis that

> Whenever the upper ranks have been comparatively the most prolific, and have recruited from their overflowings the ranks below them, the society has been barbarous, poor, and unhappy. It is the opposite tendency that has universally been the parent of civilization, affluence, and enjoyment.[85]

In this theory of the replacement of the upper classes from below, Grahame qualifies as a predecessor of later theories of circulation of the elite and of social capillarity.

Ensor · Next to attempt to set forth the true principles of population, while pointing out the errors of Malthus, was George Ensor (1769–1843), Irish author of a number of political writings. His *Inquiry concerning the Population of Nations*[86] (1818) maintained that population growth is desirable and that the various ills of society are due to factors other than overpopulation. The *Inquiry* began by citing various authorities, both ancient and modern, who asserted the desirability of a large and growing number of people in a state. There followed an account of alleged contradictions in the *Essay on the Principle of Population* and attacks on its author, who was described as being of "no very commanding mind, with moderate learning, and . . . very limited knowledge."[87] And in addition

---

[83] *Ibid.;* elsewhere Grahame also noted that an abundance of workers results in low wages (p. 121 ff).

[84] *Ibid.*, p. 175.

[85] *Ibid.*, p. 278.

[86] George Ensor, *An Inquiry concerning the Population of Nations, containing a refutation of Mr. Malthus' Essay on Population,* London, 1818.

[87] *Ibid.*, p. 19.

to being criticized on religious grounds, Malthus was condemned for "his want of science; his infinite contradictions; his inhumanity; his loud abuse of the people," and much more.

Despite this polemic tone, Ensor's *Inquiry* contained some moderate and persuasive arguments to support its main thesis. One line of reasoning that ran throughout the work was that there are ample checks on population, among which are celibacy, late marriage, abortion, infanticide, war, and slavery.[88] Particular emphasis was given the preventive checks, of which there were said to be not one but several. For example, restraint might be employed for religious motives ("celestial check); marriages may be postponed because of taxes and other financial burdens ("fiscal check"); and producing the same effect on population are child marriages ("precocious check") and low productivity uses of land, such as for pasturage ("pastoral check").[89] Ensor believed some of these preventive checks are preferable to the postponement of marriage, and he noted that "Mr. Malthus, in ardour for his preventive check and late marriages, forgets that late children are early orphans."[90] This point had been made earlier by Ingram, and no doubt by others as well. Finally, there was mention of Jarrold's theory of an inverse relation between man's fertility and his degree of advancement ("intellectual check"). If this check operates, and Ensor believed it does, then the observed association of poverty and populousness can be explained in another way than by the Malthusian theory. In Ensor's own apt statement, "The people of Ireland are numerous and poor. On this association sages infer, either that they are poor because they are numerous, or that they are numerous because they are poor.[91] The latter interpretation of course appeared to him the more reasonable.

Ensor was firmly convinced that "the misery of the poor in England is not of their own making (or breeding, as Mr. Malthus would say)," and that widespread poverty is more properly attributable to bad government than to overpopulation. In this opinion the growing poverty in England was due to the expense of the monarchy, the church, and the government,[92] and this might also be true for Sweden and other nations.[93] As a rule, he believed, the number of people in a nation increases with good government and decreases with bad.[94]

A final theme that runs through the *Inquiry* is that the growth of population *per se* can only be beneficial. As Ensor reasoned,

[88] *Ibid.,* Part II, Ch. 3.   [89] *Ibid.,* pp. 88–89.
[90] *Ibid.,* p. 199.   [91] *Ibid.,* p. 260.
[92] *Ibid.,* Part III, Ch. 7. In a later work, *The Poor and their Relief* (London, 1823), Ensor defended the poor laws, denied they increase the number of poor or reduce their spirit of independence, and asserted that the poor have a right to assistance.
[93] Ensor, *An Inquiry,* p. 100, and Part II, Ch. 1.
[94] *Ibid.,* Part II, Ch. 6. Elsewhere Ensor stated that "Population is regulated by the habitual food of the people" (p. 312).

Without an increasing population, what would have induced savages to emancipate themselves from their immediate wants? . . . By their continued multiplication mankind have passed from hunters to shepherds; and thence, from shifting as the sward was cropped, and wandering over a waste world, they stopped, and of the rude earth made tilth.[95]

The growth of numbers and of population density, he added, has made feasible the division of labor, has brought greater security of life, and has enabled the nations "to effect a police among themselves." In short, he concluded, "Populousness is good, if the government be good."[96]

Sismondi · Several exceptions to the Malthusian theory were taken by the Swiss political economist, J. C. L. Simonde de Sismondi (1773–1842) in his two principal works, *Nouveaux principes d'économie politique* (1819)[97] and *Études sur l'économie politique* (1837).[98] In the former he pointed out that the limitation of population by the food supply cannot apply except for the world as a whole or for a completely closed economy, inasmuch as a nation may import food rather than be entirely dependent upon domestic production. Even if food cannot be imported, however, the subsistence limit is purely theoretical, for population has never reached the limit and probably never will.[99] The fact of the matter, as Sismondi saw it, is that population is checked at a much earlier stage of growth, for it adjusts itself to its income (revenue) rather than to the food supply, and the adjustment is a voluntary one.[100]

Elsewhere in the same work Sismondi gave an explanation for the inverse relation between economic states and fertility. As he pointed out, wealth is relative, for it is differently regarded by the different social classes; and those who are accustomed to little do not hesitate to have many children, for the children will be as well provided for as are the parents themselves.[101]

In his later work, the *Études,* Sismondi advanced further ideas on population and subsistence. It is uncertainty about the future, he believed, that prompts reckless propagation, for prudence is exercised if planning for the future is possible.[102] Whether prudence is exercised or not, however, the subsistence limit is still at an infinite distance, in par-

[95] *Ibid.,* p. 498.

[96] *Ibid.,* pp. 499, 500.

[97] The editions of the *Nouveaux principes* used here are the second and third, published in Paris, 1827, and Geneva, 1951.

[98] An earlier work by Sismondi, *De la richesse commerciale, ou principes d'économie politique* (2 vol., Geneva, 1803), did not deal specifically with questions of population.

[99] Sismondi, *Nouveaux principes d'économie politique,* 2nd ed., Paris, 1827, Book VII, Ch. 3.

[100] *Ibid.,* Book VII, Ch. 1.

[101] *Ibid.,* 3rd ed., Vol. II, Book 7, pp. 178–179.

[102] Sismondi, *Études sur l'économie politique,* Paris, 1837, p. 128.

ticular because the various plant and animal sources of food can be increased in a geometric progression exceeding that of man's numbers. A twenty-five-year period of population doubling is possible but unusual,[103] for populations seldom increase by more than one per cent a year.[104] Undue increase is furthermore unlikely, Sismondi concluded, because in every prosperous nation the prosperity itself is the best guarantee against any injurious growth of numbers.[105]

2 · 1820–1829: Godwin, Ravenstone, and Others

Godwin · In his first reply to Malthus, already noted in a preceding chapter,[106] Godwin mildly stressed his own conclusions while accepting some of the Malthusian premises; but his final and detailed reply, *On Population*[107] (1820) was of another tone. Here Godwin asserted the opposite of almost every proposition contained in the *Essay* and sought to overwhelm Malthus with arguments and evidence. Economic aspects of this work were mentioned earlier, but the general theory of population developed by Godwin remains to be described.

The effectiveness of Godwin's elaborate rebuttal is weakened for the modern reader by his personal attack on Malthus and by the quite general nature of much of the argument. Godwin's motives, it is true, may have risen above personal jealousy at another's success and his own declining recognition. Explaining his reference to Malthus by name and unable to foresee the ironical turn that time would give to his words, Godwin wrote that "I think it but fair, so far as it depends upon me, that his name should be preserved, whatever becomes of the volumes he has written."[108] He may have been motivated also by righteous indignation and a sense of duty to combat what he believed a false and harmful doctrine. Among other reasons Malthus was condemned because "He has made no allusion to Adam and Eve, and has written just as any speculator in political economy might have done, to whom the records of the Bible were unknown."[109] As for the immediate effects of the Malthusian doctrine, Godwin believed it "flattered the vices and corruption of the rich and great,"[110] and that

> For twenty years the heart of man in this island has been hardening through the theories of Mr. Malthus. What permanent effect this may

103 *Ibid.,* pp. 130–131.
104 *Ibid.,* p. 144.
105 *Ibid.,* p. 192.
106 See Chapter 6, section 4, above.
107 William Godwin, *On Population, An Inquiry concerning the Power of Increase in the Numbers of Mankind,* London, 1820.
108 *Ibid.,* p. 7.
109 *Ibid.,* p. 23.
110 *Ibid.,* Preface, p. v.

have upon the English character I know not: but it was high time that it should be stopped.[111]

To put a stop to the evil influence, Godwin assembled the widest range of arguments; but somewhat in the manner of Malthus he relied on appeals to common knowledge, dogmatic assertions, the citation of like-minded writers, and his own interpretations of past and present observations. His treatment of the population question was in the general terms of a social philosopher or an experienced observer of human affairs, without attempt to employ or attack the new analytical methods of the political economists who were developing theoretical support for the Malthusian population theory.

Underlying Godwin's long, diffuse treatment of the population question was the conviction that every worker in a civilized society can produce much more than he consumes, and that poverty, where it exists, is attributable to maldistribution rather than to overpopulation or unavoidable underproduction. There was agreement with Malthus that population numbers are held in check, but disagreement as to the nature and causes of the checks. Particular attention was given to Swedish evidence,[112] which was regarded as the only adequate information on population trends, and to the American data, which were said to provide the main substantive support for the Malthusian thesis. Regarding America,[113] Godwin maintained that the same forces act on population in the New World as in the Old, and pointed out that the Malthusian theory could not explain the large and almost uninhabited areas, such as the Missouri River country recently explored by Lewis and Clark. "May it not be," he wondered, "that races of men have a perpetual tendency to wear out?"[114] From United States census data Godwin drew the conclusion that the growth of population in that nation was due largely to immigration and the high fertility of the immigrants, who were in the prime of life. From rather dubious estimates based on the age distribution, he inferred that the American population was barely maintaining itself through its own reproduction and that numbers would have declined in the middle and southern states except for arrivals from abroad.[115]

Godwin was interested in the American population, he said, because un-

---

[111] *Ibid.*, p. 110.

[112] *Ibid.*, Book II, Ch. 4–7, inclusive.

[113] *Ibid.*, Book IV.

[114] *Ibid.*, p. 365. Compare Jarvis, pp. 259–260 above.

[115] Godwin noted that fertility was high in the rural areas, but also noted that in the cities it was probably much the same as in Europe and probably insufficient to balance the high mortality. Consumption, dysentery (or "summer complaint"), decay of teeth, and yellow fever were reported to be especially prevalent in the United States.

less proof can be given of man's ability to double in a generation, the Malthusian doctrine is no more than an abstraction like Price's calculation of how a penny at compound interest would grow in time to an astronomical sum; and if the reputed doubling of the American population is disproved, the whole Malthusian structure falls of its own weight.[116] Having thus pulled the foundation from under the Malthusian thesis to his satisfaction, Godwin gave as his own opinion that ample subsistence is provided, and that the only real checks are "ignorance, or the positive institutions of society."[117]

Ravenstone · A more closely reasoned criticism of the Malthusian population theory than Godwin's work, which it paralleled on several points, was Ravenstone's *A Few Doubts*[118] (1821) published the following year. Since Ravenstone's economic arguments were outlined under the topic of production theory,[119] only a few other aspects of his population thought remain to be described.

Ravenstone, of whom little is known except for this work and who may have been writing under a pseudonym, was evidently a very different sort of person from Godwin and most of the others who entered the population controversy. Less the social theorist and seeker after broad natural laws, he used an empirical, analytical approach resembling that preferred by modern students of population. Like Godwin, Ravenstone attacked what he considered a vulnerable point of the Malthusian theory by attempting to prove that the population of the United States had not multiplied as rapidly as supposed; and he too turned to the American census data for evidence, but made more skillful use of the material. Starting with what appeared to him the reasonable assumptions that eleven out of every twenty females born live to the usual age at marriage and that one of the survivors remains single, Ravenstone computed that an average of four children per family is needed to maintain a stationary population.[120] In tabular form, his estimates were as follows for different average family sizes:

4 children	stationary population	
4½ "	140-year period of doubling	
5 "	86 " " " "	
5¼ "	75 " " " "	

116 *Ibid.*, p. 479.

117 *Ibid.*, Book V, Ch. 4.

118 Piercy Ravenstone, *A Few Doubts as to the Correctness of some Opinions generally entertained on the Subjects of Population and Political Economy*, London, 1821.

119 Ch. 8, section 4, above.

120 That is, of the four children, two would be females on the average, and of them only one would survive and marry.

Allowance for adult mortality gave eleven years as the probable average duration of the childbearing period of life, and 5¼ as the maximum average number of children per family. From the latter figure Ravenstone computed that the shortest possible period of natural doubling was seventy-five years. From this he concluded the twenty-five years given for the United States must be impossible.[121]

With this a priori basis for doubling the high rate of natural increase attributed to the American population, Ravenstone turned to the empirical evidence provided by the censuses of 1790 and 1810. Subtracting the expected mortality of the 1790 population during the following two decades, he obtained an estimate of the number of survivors aged twenty and over in 1810. The number of such adults enumerated in the latter census exceeded the estimated survivals by 1,120,000. Adding to this number an estimated 280,000 deaths of immigrants who came after 1790 and died before 1810, gave the figure 1,400,000 immigrants during the twenty-year period, excluding those under age twenty in 1810. Other calculations no less rough but just as ingenious indicated that of the children born in the United States between the two censuses, no less than 1,250,000 were the offspring of foreign-born parents. Finally, subtracting the sum of this number and the number of surviving adult immigrants from the twenty-year increase in population gave a residual growth of 470,000 attributable to procreation of the native population. This last number, Ravenstone showed, indicated a natural increase corresponding to a population doubling in a little over 100 years, and he judged this to be about the rate of increase in Europe.[122]

Obviously these were tenuous calculations. Ravenstone's ingenuity could not take the place of reliable information on mortality and immigration; and his results must be judged as largely the product of assumptions favorable to his argument. In particular, his estimate of the fertility of the immigrants seems generous, and it is doubtful whether he was right in assuming that "among the immigrants of a breeding age, the proportion of young women will be greater than among the natives."[123] At the same time, however, he was undoubtedly justified in suspecting the extraordinary accounts given of the natural increase in the American population, as well as in surmising that immigration played a considerable part in the increase in numbers.

In more theoretical terms, as described in a preceding chapter, Ravenstone attacked the Malthusian theory on grounds that per capita returns to labor and the comforts of the people advance with their numbers. As he pointed out, "If population increased more rapidly than the means of subsistence, the state of the savage would be the only state of abun-

121 *Ibid.,* pp. 35–39.
122 *Ibid.,* pp. 130–131.
123 *Ibid.,* p. 133.

dance."[124] Much like Godwin, Ravenstone concluded that "human constitutions [not overpopulation] are the real cause of all the misery with which we are surrounded."[125] As a society grows, he explained elsewhere, rent, taxes, and accumulated capital come to take an increased share of the product of labor, and all of these are "the share of the idle in the earnings of the industrious."[126]

Ross · The economic writings of J. C. Ross[127] were summarized earlier, but there remain his theories of population as revealed in the 1825 and 1827 editions of his work. Taking a sharply anti-Malthusian position, he nevertheless accepted the three Malthusian propositions with some modification, but denied the conclusion that vice and misery are due to the principle of population. Rather, he said, they are due to ignorance and "defective human institutions."[128]

In the second volume of his work he offered his own substitute for the Malthusian principles:

1st. That, in every age, and every state in which mankind has existed, or can exist, while they and the earth retain their present nature, the increase of population is necessarily limited by the means of subsistence.

2nd. That the means of subsistence invariably increase with the increase of population which produce those means, and, therefore, population will naturally and regularly increase "unless (unnaturally accelerated, or) prevented by powerful and obvious checks."

3rd. That the check by which the means of subsistence and the population are regulated to each other, in an improved or improving state of society, is that of moral restraint, which moral restraint is the effect of just and enlightened government.

4th. That those checks (vice and misery) which destroy redundant population, and keep the savage and misgoverned people of any country in a scanty and wretched state, all are resolvable into ignorance and tyranny, as their primary causes.[129]

In conclusion, after presenting many of the usual optimistic arguments, Ross asserted that under a good government a population may approach the subsistence limit, but that no harmful consequences need follow, because as society advances, numbers are more firmly held within the subsistence limit. As he explained,

The higher men rank in the scale of intellect, the more refined are their notions; and the more multiplied their objects of comfort, the more

[124] *Ibid.,* p. 119.
[125] *Ibid.,* p. 120.
[126] *Ibid.,* p. 430.
[127] No information has been found on Ross, except what he revealed about himself — that he was Scottish, opposed to the English established church, and regarded the upper classes as idlers or worse.
[128] J. C. Ross, *An examination,* Vol. I, pp. 278–279.
[129] *Ibid.,* Vol. II, p. 18.

reason they will have to avoid and the less temptation to contract improvident marriages, and the greater will be their moral worth of character.[130]

In short, there is really no problem, for population takes care of itself in the natural order of society.

3 · 1830–1839: Sadler to Moreton

Sadler · A notable if somewhat controversial contribution to the population literature of the period was *The law of population* (1830)[131] by Michael T. Sadler (1780–1835), businessman and member of parliament with an avocation in social reform. Sadler had already given a preview of his ideas on population in a publication of two years before, *Ireland, its evils and their remedies*[132] (1828), described in the introduction as a supplement to the forthcoming work on population. With the purpose of attacking the Malthusian theory, the earlier work attacked the larger structure of political economy, of which the Malthusian theory was considered an integral part; and Ireland was used as the case with which to demonstrate the errors of economic theory.[133]

In the area of population theory Sadler by no means limited himself to arguments against the Malthusian law of population, but boldly advanced new theories of his own. In the work on Ireland he gave advance statement to two principles that were to be developed in his later work, concerning the relation of human fecundity to population density and to prosperity or well-being. He then went on in a broader vein to relate fecundity to social and economic progress:

> Excluding, of course, cases of extreme distress, a state of labour and privation is that most favourable to human fecundity. A dispersed and scanty population invariably implies that state; but as mankind advance from the hunting to the pastoral, and from thence to the agricultural stage of existence, and ultimately rise to the highest condition of civilization, labour becomes divided, and consequently diminished in its duration and intensity, and many are liberated from its drudgeries, so as to devote themselves to other and more intellectual pursuits, or are rendered independent of it altogether, while the means of subsistence become progressively augmented, and ease and luxury more generally diffused. At

130 *Ibid.*, pp. 429, 430.
131 Michael T. Sadler, *The law of population*, London, 1830.
132 Michael T. Sadler, *Ireland: its evils, and their remedies*, London, 1828.
133 Sadler expressed his opinion of political economy with a remark borrowed from a criticism of craniology: "Es ist viel darin was wahr ist, und viel was neu; aber das was wahr ist, ist nicht neu, und das was neu ist, ist nicht wahr" (Much of it is true and much is new, but what is true is not new, and what is new is not true), *ibid.*, p. 1 (Roman 50).

every step the principle of increase contracts, and, as I contend, would pause at that precise point where it had secured the utmost possible degree of happiness to the greatest possible number of human beings.[134]

Of the several different ideas expressed here, the last is essentially an optimum population theory, but a happiness rather than an economic optimum.

Sadler's *Law of Population* was a major effort of reasoning and argument, two volumes and over 1300 pages in length. It was divided into four books or parts, of which the first three attempted to demolish the Malthusian thesis, the fourth to present a new theory as a replacement. The anti-Malthusian argument of the first book took the form of contrary assertions, appeals to evidence, and references to various authorities. The second book sought to show that American population data did not support Malthus, since the increase was not in a geometric progression, and the admittedly rapid growth was attributed to immigration.

In the final part, Sadler presented what he considered the true law or laws of population, and he was a prolific inventor of theories. The fundamental law, in his opinion, is that

> The prolificness of human beings, otherwise similarly circumstanced, varies inversely as their numbers . . . (in such a way that) . . . prolificness shall be greatest where the numbers on an equal space are the fewest, and, on the contrary, the smallest where those numbers are the largest.[135]

Some qualifications were then attached to the law; for example:

> The prolificness of human beings, as thus regulated by the extent of the space they occupy, is furthermore influenced by the quality of that space, or otherwise by its potential produce; so that the same number of marriages in a population occupying an equal surface, will, all other circumstances remaining equal, be less productive in mountainous than in champaign countries, and less in the frigid than in the temperate regions.[136]

Corollary propositions were that prolificness varies with mortality: ". . . the prolificness of an equal number of individuals, other circumstances being similar, is greater where the mortality is greater, and, on the contrary, smaller where the mortality is less"[137]; and that emigration does not reduce the population of a nation.[138]

Sadler's theories were ingenious but they were essentially personal interpretations and after the fact explanations of selected observations.[139]

---

[134] *Ibid.*, p. viii.
[135] Sadler, *Law of population,* Book IV, Chapter 4, p. 352.
[136] *Ibid.*, Vol. II, p. 353.
[137] *Ibid.*, Vol. II, pp. 354–355.
[138] *Ireland,* p. 383.
[139] McCulloch's judgment of Sadler was that "His work consists principally of

In support of his law of population he cited, along with a number of other observations and statistics, the greater prolificness of marriage in rural areas than in cities, the comparative fertility of nations of different population densities, and class differences in family size. As further evidence he produced an alleged principle of human physiology, that "repletion is an enemy to generation."[140] It was his belief, of course, that food supplies become more ample as a society advances in population and economic development.[141]

Edmonds · Two years after Sadler's *Law* there appeared another major work on population, *An Inquiry into the Principle of Population* (1832) by Thomas R. Edmonds (1802–1889). An English social theorist and actuary, Edmonds was the author of an earlier work, *Practical Moral and Political Economy* (1828) in which he had outlined a planned society and given some attention to the problem of population growth. Here he stated as a law of nature that

> . . . the powers of reproduction in the different kinds (of animals) are proportionate to the abundance in which the food of each respective kind is supplied spontaneously by a given space of land or water. . . . a given space of land will produce, spontaneously, food for five times as many horses as monkeys, or men in the lowest state of barbarism . . . the powers of increase therefore in horses and men, are as the numbers five and one respectively.[142]

He added that man's power of increase rises with the healthfulness of his way of life but that this power is never fully exerted because it is restrained by fear of the consequences.[143] He also noted that if two nations have equal numbers of people, the one growing the more rapidly will be the weaker because it will have a larger proportion of younger members.[144]

---

declamatory abuse, and of lengthened statements to show that the fecundity of human beings is inversely as their numbers! A law which never had any existence except in his own distempered imagination. . . ."

[140] Sadler, *Law of Population,* Vol. II, p. 589.

[141] Entirely incidental to his law of population was Sadler's curious theory of a regulation of the sex ratio of births. It was a law of Providence, he stated, that:

> The proportion in which the sexes are born is governed and regulated by the difference in the ages of their parents, in such a manner, that on the average, among the total of the births, the sex of that parent shall exceed in number, whose age exceeds; and further, that excess shall conform to the mortality which would take place in a period equal in duration to the interval between the ages of the parents; preserving, therefore, the balance of the sexes at the usual ages at which they respectively marry (Vol. II, p. 333).

This law he discovered deductively, from the assumption that Providence would have so arranged matters that the numbers in each sex would be equal at their respective average ages at marriage.

[142] Thomas R. Edmonds, *Practical moral and political economy,* London, 1828, p. 40.

[143] *Ibid.,* pp. 42, 43.

[144] *Ibid.,* p. 49.

In his major contribution to population thought, *An Inquiry into the Principle of Population,* Edmonds dealt more fully with the subject he had touched on earlier. Taking an optimistic position on the population question, he maintained that numbers have never tended to exceed the means of subsistence in any stage of society from the barbarous to the most highly civilized,[145] that the application of capital and improved methods has prevented a diminishing of the returns to labor,[146] and that the powers of labor and the possibilities for invention are unlimited.[147] There is no reason to assume that land can yield only one crop of corn a year, he continued, for in the future it may yield as many as twenty a week.[148]

Quite distinctive was Edmonds' theory of the proper proportions of the various social classes in a society. The reason for widespread pauperism, in his opinion, is not a deficiency of arable land or soil fertility but a deficiency in the numbers of the middle class in proportion to the laboring class. The former are the employers of the latter, and since the fertility of the middle class is less than that of the workers, there is naturally a shortage of employment.[149]

Elsewhere in the *Inquiry* Edmonds expressed a number of well-considered thoughts on population, especially concerning moral restraint, which he favored in spite of his generally optimistic views. In a chapter on the checks on population growth, for example, he asserted that "To better the condition of the labouring classes, that is, to place more food and comforts before them, however paradoxical it may appear, is the wisest mode to check redundancy."[150] Separate chapters were devoted to a discussion of means of promoting prudential restraint in marriage and of strengthening feelings of self-respect among members of the most fertile section of the population.[151] Postponement of marriage was recommended as the preferred means of preventing overrapid growth of numbers, with age twenty-five for marriage suggested as perhaps most beneficial to society. And if population should become overabundant by reason of too little moral restraint, various measures of relief such as emigration and public works programs were recommended.

In the same year Edmonds published a work on life tables, largely technical in content.[152] However, the introduction contained some general comments on population, including the assertion that the control of fertility becomes increasingly effective as a society advances. It was further stated that the only advantage of population growth is that knowl-

[145] Thomas R. Edmonds, *An Inquiry into the Principle of Population,* London, 1832, Ch. 1, sections 2–4, inclusive.

[146] *Ibid.*, p. 45. In this connection he noted further that the free importation of foreign corn has forestalled the use of poorer soils in England.

[147] *Ibid.*, Ch. 2, section 3.   [148] *Ibid.*, p. 64.

[149] *Ibid.*, Ch. 2, section 1.   [150] *Ibid.*, p. 86.

[151] *Ibid.*, Ch. 7, 9.

[152] Thomas R. Edmonds, *Life tables, founded upon the discovery of a numerical law regulating the existence of every human being . . .* , London, 1832.

edge advances with increasing density of settlement, and that "In the moral, as in the physical world, the effect of each man's labour increases, as the number of individuals with whom he acts in concert increases."[153] With regard to mortality, the higher death rate in large cities and the lower death rate of females were noted.

Moreton · In 1836 there appeared a work entitled *Civilization, or a brief Analysis of the Natural Laws that Regulate the Numbers and Condition of Mankind,* the author of which was Augustus Moreton, a member of Parliament. Concerned with the interrelations between population numbers and human welfare, the work was a careful attempt to reconcile several apparent inconsistencies in the current theories about population.

One inconsistency involved the effect of advancing civilization on fertility and the regulation of numbers. Accepting the subsistence theory of wages of the political economists, Moreton saw that it followed from the theory that as a society progresses and increases the supply of subsistence, its numbers would necessarily expand. On the other hand, he found considerable evidence that as the progress of society brings lowered mortality it brings an even greater decrease of fertility. Seeking to explain the decrease of fertility, he suggested that progress provides greater comfort through improved quality and variety of products, and that ". . . in the ordinary progress of society, those improvements which tend to multiply the comforts of life increase more rapidly than those that merely tend to augment the population."[154] Also, he concluded, the dissemination of comfort lowers fertility. In explanation of this point he wrote that

> The occupations and prejudices engendered by wealth, and the complicated relations of civilized society induce many to marry late, or to remain in a single state. In all classes above those that depend upon their bodily labour for subsistence, it is not the difficulty of maintaining a family in the common necessaries of life that deters from marriage, but the fear of descending a grade in society. . . .[155]

Moreton then cited observations to support the supposition that an abundance of the means of subsistence lowers fertility, as for example, that plants in too rich soil grow vigorously but produce little seed. With regard to man he concluded that with advancing civilization numbers come to be regulated by the diffusion of wealth and comfort rather than by privation and disease,[156] and that the immediate mechanism for this regulation is an expansion of the unprolific classes to make up a larger part of the population.

At this point Moreton was faced with an inconsistency of theory and

[153] *Ibid.,* p. xxiii.
[154] Augustus Moreton, *Civilization,* London, 1836, p. 45.
[155] *Ibid.,* p. 138.
[156] *Ibid.,* p. 146.

observation, for while believing that the extent of the wealthy and un-prolific class was regulated by the stage of civilization, he was well aware that the balance between population numbers and the food supply is quickly restored by population growth following great mortalities or increases in the food supply. Evidently, some regulating mechanism operates in addition to the law of inverse proportion between fertility and social advancement.

His solution for the theoretical problem was that civilized society con-tains three classes with respect to reproduction. First, there are the wealthier members of the society who are unproductive because of a low birth rate. Second, there are those of the middle range whose numbers increase. Third, there are those who do not contribute to the growth of population because of misery and high infant mortality. With this formulation, Moreton was able to explain the previously inconsistent phenomena. As civilization advances, he reasoned, growth is more and more checked by the increased proportion in the first class; but because of unequal distribution a certain number remain in the third class despite the accumulation of wealth. This being the case, a sudden increase in the per capita supply of subsistence, for any reason, would temporarily elevate a number of people from the third to the second class, and a rapid natural increase would follow. As Moreton said, "Augment the comforts and supply of food to the poor, and the rapidity of their increase will be astonishing."[157]

In effect, Moreton's theory presents a double regulation of numbers, a long-run effect through growth of the unproductive class, a short-term adjustment through change in the condition of the lowest class. It is thus a combination of the Malthusian theory of positive and preventive checks with the observation of an inverse relation of fertility to status.

4 · 1840–1849: Alison, Doubleday, and Others

Alison · The Principles of Population[158] (1840) by Sir Archibald Alison (1792–1867), Scottish political writer and historian, was a lengthy, rambling, and religiously oriented discussion of population questions. Said by its author to have been first drafted in the years 1809 to 1810 and later rewritten, the work accepted the Malthusian principle of increase as a basic tendency of population, but in other respects was quite consistently anti-Malthusian. Population growth was seen as the stimulus that forces man on to higher stages of development and to civilization, enables man

---

[157] *Ibid.*, p. 152.
[158] Archibald Alison, *The principles of population and their connection with human happiness,* 2 vol., Edinburgh and London, 1840.

to overcome the obstacles of nature, and, by forcing shepherd tribes to migrate, has been "the means of peopling an uninhabited world."[159]

Affirming as a law of nature that the work of one man is more than adequate for his support, Alison was further confident that no problem of overpopulation can arise because as society advances certain checks on population growth automatically come into operation. The desire to acquire property, he believed, is a great deterrent to improvidence in reproduction.[160] But "the principal counterpoise which Nature has provided to the principle of population" is the growth of artificial wants and the desire to elevate one's level of comfort.[161] This is because "one of the strongest principles of our nature is the desire of bettering our condition."[162]

As a corollary Alison asserted that the poor laws encourage restraint in reproduction, and that Malthus was wrong in believing the opposite, because

> . . . nothing encourages a redundant and miserable population so powerfully as the existence of unrelieved suffering. . . . On the other hand, nothing tends to check an undue increase of mankind, so effectually, as those institutions which, by relieving distress, dry up the sources from which an indigent population invariably springs.[163]

Alison also saw other motives and forces opposing the tendency to increase, among them the progressive development of human reason, the distinction of rank which spurs ambition, and the growth of cities. Mentioned separately among other specific restraints on population growth, but related to his check of artificial wants, were what Alison referred to as habits of using costly foods:

> There can be no doubt, that if the food of the middling and lower orders were to be restricted to millet or rye-bread, as in Poland, or to potatoes, as in Ireland, at least double the population might be maintained from the same extent of land which is required under the costly system of subsistence which universally prevails in this country.[164]

This idea will be recognized as the same and the phrasing not very different from a previous quotation from Steuart.

Beyond these influences operating at the individual level, Alison saw a more general control mechanism affecting a whole society. It may be seen, he wrote, that there is a rapid increase of numbers in the early stages of a society, and that growth slows down with advancement and the accumulation of wealth.[165] From this he concluded that "empires,

---

[159] *Ibid.*, p. 20.
[161] *Ibid.*, Vol. I, p. 109.
[163] *Ibid.*, Vol. II, p. 208.
[165] *Ibid.*, Vol. II, p. 461.

[160] *Ibid.*, Vol. I, p. 122; Vol. II, p. 13.
[162] *Ibid.*, Vol. II, p. 15.
[164] *Ibid.*, Vol. I, p. 202.

like individuals, have a period of youth, maturity, and decay."[166] For all these reasons Alison was confident we can look forward to the future without fear.

Doubleday · In the following year a new theory of population was presented by Thomas Doubleday (1790–1870), a versatile author of poems, plays, and biographies who was also active in liberal political movements, *The True Law of Population*[167] (1841) began by stating that the increase of mankind obviously has been checked in such a way as to prevent the development of general misery and suffering, then asked what the check is. Doubleday's answer took the form of a law of population he believed he had discovered, a law that was at the same time an explanation of the well-known inverse relation between economic status and fertility, which was not readily explained by contemporary economic theory. The law was stated as follows:

> The *great general law* then, which, as it seems, really regulates the increase or decrease both of vegetable and of animal life, is this, that whenever a species or genus is endangered, a corresponding effort is invariably made by nature for its preservation and continuance, by an increase of fecundity or fertility; and that this especially takes place whenever such danger arises from a diminution of proper nourishment or food, so that consequently the state of depletion, or the deplethoric state, is favourable to fertility, and that on the other hand, the plethoric state, or state of repletion, is unfavourable to fertility, in the ratio of the intensity of each state, and this probably throughout nature universally, in the vegetable as well as the animal world. . . .[168]

In further explanation Doubleday assumed the existence in every society of three different classes with respect to reproduction. In his words,

> There is in all societies a constant increase going on amongst that portion of it which is the worst supplied with food; in short, amongst the poorest.
> Amongst those in the state of affluence, and well supplied with food and luxuries, a constant decrease goes on. Amongst those who for the mean or medium between these two opposite states; that is to say, amongst those who are tolerably well supplied with good food, and not overworked, nor yet idle, population is stationary. Hence it follows that it is upon the numerical proportion which these three states bear to each other in any society that increase or decrease upon the whole depends.[169]

[166] *Ibid.*, Vol. II, p. 472.
[167] Thomas Doubleday, *The true law of population*, London, 1841. References below are to the second edition, published in London in 1847; and the passages quoted are unchanged in the third edition (1853).
[168] *Ibid.*, pp. 5–6.
[169] *Ibid.*, p. 6.

This three-class schema suggests but differs from the one used by Moreton in his theory of regulation of numbers.

Doubleday supported his theory by citing numerous reproductive phenomena, some rather far-fetched from the viewpoint of a later reader, others at least consistent with his theory. The basic mechanism was presumed to be some physiological process whereby fertility varies inversely with the amount of food consumed.

Thornton · Unlike most of the preceding works on population, *Overpopulation and its Remedy* (1846) by William Thornton (1813–1880) was quite consistently Malthusian in its treatment of population. Thornton, a friend of John Stuart Mill and by career a civil servant, applied his concept of overpopulation to an interpretation of English economic history. By his definition, ". . . overpopulation is . . . that condition of a country in which part of the inhabitants, although able-bodied and capable of labour, are permanently unable to earn a sufficiency of the necessaries of life."[170] Alternatively, it could be identified as

> . . . a deficiency of employment for those who live by labour, or a redundancy of the labouring class above the number of persons that the fund applied to the remuneration of labour can maintain in comfort.[171]

The fund referred to here is of course the wage fund of economic theory. Thornton thought one underlying cause of overpopulation is an imbalance between labor supply and the wage fund; and the measures he recommended for relief of the overpopulation he thought existed in England and Wales were designed to restore the balance.

One departure from Malthusian orthodoxy was his treatment of the relation between misery and population numbers, for here he recognized a reciprocal relation: "Misery, the inevitable effect and symptom of overpopulation, thus seems to be likewise its principal promoter."[172] His further explanation of this reciprocal relation and of the inverse differential of fertility were especially well stated:

> It is only those who have never tasted the conveniences of life, that are ready to propagate their species, without any better prospect than that of ability to keep themselves alive. It is because the son of an Irish cottier has always considered a fill of potatoes to be the height of physical comfort, that he esteems a few square yards of ground a very competent marriage portion. The true cause of the overpopulation of Ireland must be looked for in the ancient and inveterate poverty of her people.[173]

Thornton continued in the same vein:

[170] William Thornton, *Over-population and its remedy*, London, 1846, p. 1.
[171] *Ibid.*, p. 3.
[172] *Ibid.*, p. 121.
[173] *Ibid.*, p. 263.

... misery renders men reckless in marriage, as in everything else; and, in order to make them provident, it is first necessary to make them comfortable, and to make the continuance of their comfort contingent on their own behavior. It has been asserted that indigence, the never-absent symptom of over-population, is likewise its principal upholder and promoter. If these opinions be correct, a permanent cure of over-population may be effected by any means that will raise the labouring classes from the poverty in which they are sunk, and provide them with adequate means of supporting themselves.[174]

This could serve as a definitive statement of mid-nineteenth-century English thought on the interrelation of misery and fertility.

5 · 1850–1859

Hickson · William Hickson (1803–1870) was a shoe manufacturer by family connection, writer on education and various contemporary social problems by predilection, and for a number of years owner and editor of the *Westminster Review*. He was also the author of a slender anti-Malthusian volume on population entitled *Malthus, an Essay on the Principles of Population in Refutation of the Theory of the Rev. T. R. Malthus* (1850?), in which he sought the "hidden cause of social disorganization."

Arguing against Malthus on every point at issue, Hickson's work is noteworthy especially on the positive side for its abundance of alleged laws or principles of population. Doubleday's inverse relation of fertility and dietary adequacy was accepted, but with the critical comment that Doubleday, like Malthus, generalizes too quickly, and that the ratio of population growth depends not on one but many factors.[175]

As for the Malthusian view that either moral restraint or vice and misery keeps population in balance with the means of subsistence, Hickson stated that these checks are not sufficient for the purpose, and vice and misery tend to stimulate rather than check reproduction. However, he was confident that nature provides other and stronger checks,[176] and he described them in terms of what he regarded as laws of population. For example, there was said to be a law of diminishing ratio of fecundity such that ". . . from the largest and longest-lived animals downwards to the insect tribes, we see a special adaptation of the prolific faculties to the quantity of food upon which each species is to live."[177] In the case of man, Hickson continued, he is most prolific under the lowest physical

[174] *Ibid.*, p. 271.
[175] William E. Hickson, *Malthus, an essay on the principles of population,* London, 1850(?), p. 64.
[176] *Ibid.*, p. 54.
[177] *Ibid.*, p. 56.

and moral conditions, as in city slums.[178] There is also a theory of a natural dying out of ruling classes and a replacement of them by new groups, a process described as necessary for progress toward civilization.[179]

Another law stated to prevail universally throughout the vegetable and animal kingdoms was that "the powers destined to attain the greatest longevity shall be the most slowly developed."[180] Still another principle, resembling Doubleday's, is that man tends to a higher rate of reproduction where mortality is greater, and, conversely, "luxurious habits" and intellectual occupations lower the birth rate. Other influences thought to lower fertility were family and class or racial intermarriage; while hard labor, sparse diet, and migratory habits were said to have the opposite effect.

After creating this structure of theory upon theory, however, Hickson implied that in the long run a quite different principle may operate, for he saw reason to believe that every species has its appointed term of existence upon the earth, after which it becomes extinct like the many fossil species. As he said, "We need not, therefore, afflict ourselves with the speculation of what will become of mankind when the world shall be fully peopled, since that period may never arrive."[181]

Spencer · In the April 1852 issue of the *Westminster Review,* after or near the end of Hickson's editorship, there appeared an unsigned article, "A theory of population, deduced from the general law of animal fertility."[182] Now known to have been written by Herbert Spencer, the article described population growth as a powerful force for human progress, and progress as a cause of reduced fertility. In Spencer's words, "It is clear that the wants of their redundant numbers constitute the only stimulus mankind have to a greater production of the necessaries of life. . . ."[183] But to increase production, it went on to say, there must be improvement in skills, intelligence, and self-control. And with advance in the ability to maintain a population there is a concomitant reduction of the power to multiply. Or, as further stated,

> . . . so long as population continues to increase, there must be pressure on the means of subsistence: and so long as there is pressure on the means of subsistence, further mental development must go on, and further diminution of fertility must result.[184]

At the end of this process a balance would be achieved, with reproduction at the replacement level and an end to population pressure.

[178] *Ibid.,* p. 57. [179] *Ibid.,* p. 76.
[180] *Ibid.,* p. 59. [181] *Ibid.,* p. 73.
[182] *Westminster Review,* New Series, Vol. I, pp. 468–501.
[183] *Ibid.,* p. 498.
[184] *Ibid.,* p. 500.

These words were paraphrased in Spencer's *Principles of Biology* (1864–67), in which it was stated that

> This constant increase of people beyond the means of subsistence, causes, then, a never-ceasing requirement for skill, intelligence, and self-control—involves, therefore, a constant exercise of these and gradual growth of them.[185]

and that

> . . . so long as there is pressure on the means of subsistence, further mental development must go on, and further diminution of fertility must result. Thus, the change can never cease until the rate of multiplication is just equal to the rate of mortality.[186]

Here Spencer stated his well-known law governing the multiplication of the human species, that individuation is inversely related to genesis: that is, reproduction varies inversely with the cultural development of the individual, a theory already approximated if not explicitly stated by earlier writers. Spencer's view was that beyond a certain point the future progress of civilization may proceed at increasing costs of individuation, and that this progression could be followed only until fertility fell and brought population growth to a stop.

Rickards · Some of the economic thought and the anti-Malthusian argument of Sir George Rickards (1812–1889) have already been described.[187] Further ideas on population in his *Population and Capital* (1854), a series of lectures given while he was professor of political economy at Oxford, remain to be described. Although these do not constitute a formal theory of population, they do reveal his thought more fully, especially on the status differential in fertility and on the relation between population and the "scale of living."

In his introduction Rickards acknowledged particular indebtedness to Sadler and Everett, and intimated that different laws of population may apply under different circumstances, for, as he said, the Malthusian theory is founded on observations of old nations and may not apply to the New World. Recognizing the relative nature of the standard of living, he wrote that

> The lowest scale of living in any community, being that which forms the practical limit of increase, is not measured by the minimum of the poorest sustenance adequate to sustain life; but it depends on the habits, manners, and conventional wants of the mass of the labouring population.[188]

[185] Spencer, *Principles of Biology*, New York: Appleton, 1897, Ch. 13, pp. 498–499.
[186] *Ibid.*, Ch. 13, p. 504.
[187] See Chapter 8 above.
[188] Sir George K. Rickards, *Population and capital*, London, 1854, p. 41.

Then noting the lower fertility of the middle and upper classes, he drew a distinction, made earlier by Destutt de Tracy, between the means of subsistence, a constant, and the means of existence, which is different for the rich and the poor.[189] In his final lecture, however, Rickards gave a somewhat different emphasis in explaining the status differential in fertility, saying that the self-imposed moral check operates strongly on the upper classes, less strongly but still to some extent on the lowest class.[190]

Elsewhere it was stated as a general principle that "As we descend in the scale of living, we find a gradually increasing fecundity."[191] In the same lecture Rickards presented the ecological concept of "mutually dependent links" or chains between species, and referred to Paley's belief in a "compensatory scheme," an equilibrium between numbers and food that corresponds to the modern concept of ecological balance.[192]

Guillard · A year after Rickards' publication, another work on population appeared, *Élements de statistique humaine ou demographie comparée* (1855) by Archille Guillard (1799–1876), French statistician and natural scientist. Here Guillard sought to demonstrate statistically two propositions, one called the law of inverse proportion, the other the law of subsistence. The former, adopted from Sadler, was that the annual rate of natural increase in a population is inversely proportional to its density,[193] and tables showing annual rates of increase were given as supporting evidence.

According to the second law, which had a quite Malthusian tone, population numbers are adjusted to the food supply,[194] and from this law several corollaries were drawn. One was the quite un-Malthusian conclusion that an overabundant population need not be feared, and the immediate basis for this optimism was an assumed organic equilibrium between production and consumption.[195] More Malthusian were the corollaries that an increase in the supply of subsistence does not raise the standard of living because population increases up to the new supply,[196] and that emigration is no cure for habitual misery because it only permits more multiplication.[197]

Garnier · Thoroughly Malthusian views were expressed several years later by Guillard's compatriot, Joseph Garnier (1813–1881), leading French political economist and for many years editor of the *Journal des économistes*. His *Éléments de l'économie politique* (1846) had included a chapter on population, entirely Malthusian in tone, in its first two editions; but, deciding that the subject called for fuller treatment, Garnier

189 *Ibid.*, Lecture II, p. 42–43.
190 *Ibid.*, Lecture X, pp. 247–248.
191 *Ibid.*, Lecture IV, p. 84.
192 *Ibid.*, p. 87.
193 Archille Guillard, *Éléments de statistique humaine,* Paris, 1855, Ch. 2.
194 *Ibid.*, Ch. 4, p. 55.   195 *Ibid.*, p. 83.
196 *Ibid.*, p. 95.   197 *Ibid.*, p. 97.

dealt with the population question in a separate work, *Du principe de population* (1857). This was not so much an original work as a condensed statement of the Malthusian principle, which Garnier believed too widely misunderstood, and a review of post-Malthusian thought; but the conclusions presumably represent Garnier's own views. These views differed little from Malthus. One somewhat optimistic note was that population growth can act as a stimulus to progress, but only if the growth does not exceed that of the means of subsistence, under the control of prudence.[198]

Perhaps most distinctive in a work that was a conscientious survey of contemporary population thought but that added few if any new ideas was a sentence that appears on the title page. This reads, "Il dépend de l'homme que l'accroissement de la population amène le Progrès ou la misère": it depends upon man himself whether growth of his numbers is a source of good or harm. Quite different in tone from the uniform Malthusianism of Garnier's work, this is a quite shrewd conclusion to draw from the conflicting theories on population.

Winkelblech (Marlo) · Most noted for a contribution to population thought described in a later chapter,[199] Karl Winkelblech (1810–1865), who wrote under the pen name of Marlo, was a chemist who became interested in social problems in Germany, took an active part in the liberal movement of 1848, and now ranks as a precursor of the German socialist economists.

The second volume of his economic work, *Untersuchungen über die Organisation der Arbeit* (1850–1859), published in 1857, contained a chapter on population that gave a systematic treatment of population theory and policy within an economic context. Here the author in spite of his socialist convictions accepted the Malthusian theory to the extent of believing that the number of people can affect the economic condition and general well-being of a nation, but his acceptance was qualified. As he said, there had been a diversity of opinion on the relation between population growth and the advance of national well-being, population growth being variously regarded as cause, effect, or symptom of the latter. He himself disagreed with such broad generalizations, for in his opinion population growth can have different effects under different conditions, sometimes raising and sometimes depressing the level of well-being.[200]

Winkelblech's thoughts on population were further revealed in his discussion of population policy for a planned state. The main objective here, he said, is to keep numbers in proportion to subsistence. The best

[198] Garnier, *Du principe de population,* Paris, 1857, p. 204.
[199] See Chapter 13, below.
[200] Marlo (Winkelblech), *Untersuchungen über die Organisation der Arbeit, oder System der Weltökonomie,* 3 vol. in 4, Kassel, 1850–1859, Vol. II, Ch. 8, p. 390; 2nd ed., Tubingen, 1884–1886, Vol. III, Ch. 25, p. 350.

means to prevent undue growth, in his opinion, is to secure for the worker the ability to better his condition.[201] If, on the other hand, a lack of people is indicated by a surplus of food, measures should be taken to encourage population growth.[202] Of the two, Winkelblech considered the former problem much more common, and present as a rule in all old-culture lands. In such cases an effort must be made both to increase production and to check population growth, for the former alone would only stimulate more population growth and worsen the condition of the people.[203]

6 · Later Theories of Population

Greg · William Greg (1809–1881), a businessman turned essayist on a great variety of social, political, and economic questions of the day, presented no distinctively new ideas on population in his *Enigmas of Life* (1872), but gave a thoughtful and reasonable discussion of the subject. Some twenty years earlier, in his *Essays on Political and Social Science* (1853), he had almost outdone Malthus in his criticism of the Poor Law.[204] By the time he wrote the *Enigmas,* however, Greg was definitely anti-Malthusian, although he admitted quite frankly he was less sure of his ground than he had once been.

On the basis of faith if not of proof, Greg expected

> . . . the future discovery and establishment of physiological influences or laws, of which Malthus was not cognizant, and the tendency of which is to counteract and control those which he perceived so clearly; but I recognize that at present these are not ascertained; and I must therefore confine myself to the task of pointing out a few persuasive indications of the existence of these undiscovered laws, the direction in which they may be looked for, and the vast expanse both of space and time left open wherein they may operate and have their perfect work.[205]

[201] *Ibid.,* 1st ed. Vol. I, p. 369.

[202] *Ibid.,* Vol. III, Ch. 2, pp. 72 ff.

[203] *Ibid.,* Vol. III, Ch. 2, pp. 75–122.

[204] Characterizing the Poor Law as based on "unsound social philosophy," he continued: "Nor, can it be said that, in contending that improvidence, idleness, dissipation, and early marriages should be allowed to encounter their point and salutary punishment among the poor, we are guilty of any partiality or special harshness. . . . Why should we enact that the poor alone should be idle and improvident, yet never come to want? — should be reckless and wasteful, and yet be fed at the cost of the sober and frugal? — why should they alone be allowed to marry without the smallest actual or prospective provision for a family, yet be guaranteed that their children shall never sink into lower poverty than themselves? . . . We contend only that the poor, like nearly all the middle classes — like the majority even of the higher classes — should not marry — have no right to marry — till they have made some provision for the maintenance of the expected family" (William R. Greg, *Essays on political and social science,* London, 1853, Vol. I, p. 230).

[205] William R. Greg, *Enigmas of Life,* Boston, 1873, p. 79.

Among indications of the undiscovered laws he was sure existed, Greg mentioned the observations that human fertility does not attain its maximum level,[206] that man can produce more food than he needs and is limited in numbers only by the land area available,[207] that food shortages occur more often in backward than civilized nations,[208] and that something must act to limit fertility among the rich and privileged.[209] For these and other reasons, as well as the "repellent character" of the Malthusian theory, he was sure that Malthus was wrong, and that there are ". . . natural laws, whose operation is to modify and diminish human fecundity in proportion as mankind advances in real civilization, in moral and intellectual development."[210] Especially mentioned was "the tendency of cerebral development to lessen fecundity," a principle Greg claimed to have formulated before Spencer did, although he did not publish it until later.[211]

Finally, in anticipation of later eugenic fears, Greg expressed his concern over the non-survival of the fittest, deplored the known inverse relation of fertility to socio-economic status, and noted that modern society interferes with natural selection.[212]

Kautsky · The German socialist writer, Karl Kautsky, friend and disciple of Karl Marx, dealt with the population question in several of his writings, especially in his early work, *Der Einfluss der Volksvermehrung auf den Fortschritt der Gesellschaft*[213] (1880), more a discussion of the Malthusian theory than of the subject indicated by its title, and again in a later work, *Vermehrung und Entwicklung in Natur und Gesellschaft*[214] (1910). Largely anti-Malthusian but selectively so, the earlier work did not attempt to develop a new and better theory, but it did advance certain positive ideas about population.

Although he accepted some Malthusian propositions, such as the assertions that any attempts to improve the condition of the poor will merely increase their numbers[215] and that overpopulation, while not the only cause of the distress of the lower classes, does inevitably lead to poverty, Kautsky was for the most part skeptical about accepted doctrines of population. For example, he doubted that control of numbers benefits the workers, for the decrease in labor supply is matched by decrease in

---

[206] *Ibid.*, pp. 80–82. [207] *Ibid.*, pp. 82–84.

[208] *Ibid.*, pp. 84–86. [209] *Ibid.*, pp. 86–89.

[210] *Ibid.*, p. 89. [211] *Ibid.*, p. 102.

[212] *Ibid.*, Part III.

[213] Published in Vienna in 1880. Elsewhere Kautsky states that the work was completed in 1878 but forbidden publication in Germany, along with other socialist literature. Finally published in Vienna, it was banned in Germany.

[214] Published in Stuttgart, 1910.

[215] A further reason noted by Kautsky was that improvement of the condition of the poorer classes adds to their intelligence, which in turn lowers their death rate.

demand for the products of labor.[216] He also doubted that advance to a higher stage of economy removes the danger of overpopulation more than temporarily.[217] And more generally he concluded that the many theories of automatic regulation of numbers are without foundation.[218]

Kautsky's *Vermehrung,* which falls outside the period covered here, can be noted insofar as it shows change in the author's later views on population. The incompatibility of Darwinism and Malthusianism was described at some length, with the assertion that the same force of population pressure cannot both raise mankind through evolution and depress man's condition.[219] Furthermore, it was asserted, the natural tendency of population is toward a balance of numbers rather than toward overpopulation and competition.[220]

Later in the same work Kautsky proposed what he regarded as a new law of population, that overpopulation is a result of misery, and conversely that the higher well-being and culture that come with social advancement lead to lower birth rates.[221] And in a more doctrinaire fashion he denied the old and telling argument that socialism will stimulate population growth, saying in part that each type of society has its own law of population, and it is not known what law applies to socialism.[222]

Leroy-Beaulieu · The population thought of the French economist and political scientist, Pierre Paul Leroy-Beaulieu (1843–1916), is found in a number of places throughout his writings, especially in *La question de la population* (1913), his last work, and to a lesser extent in his economic writings, *Essai sur la répartition des richesses* (1881), *Précis d'économie politique* (1888), and *Traité théorique et pratique d'économie politique* (1895).

Not a formulator of theories or "laws" of population in the style already becoming outmoded, Leroy-Beaulieu tended in the more modern fashion to look upon population questions more as questions of fact than of theory, and in his economic writings he gave no particular prominence to the population factor except in discussion of the Malthusian theory. In addition to the previously noted treatment of certain economic aspects of population in the economic writings, there is only a little more on population to be noted. Both the *Essai* and the *Précis* rejected the Malthusian theory as inapplicable either currently or in the recent past, but did concede that population growth can be too rapid and may have undesirable economic effects.[223] On the other hand, it was said, there is

---

216 Kautsky, *Der Einfluss,* p. 53.   217 *Ibid.,* Ch. 5.
218 *Ibid.,* p. 124.   219 Kautsky, *Vermehrung,* Ch. 3.
220 *Ibid.,* Ch. 4.   221 *Ibid.,* pp. 192–193.
222 *Ibid.,* p. 198.
223 Leroy-Beaulieu, *Essai sur la répartition des richesses et sur la tendence a une moindre inégalité des conditions,* Paris, 1881, p. 20, 385, and elsewhere; *Précis d'économie politique,* Paris, 1888, pp. 340, 342–343.

danger of too slow population growth in some nations, for it may weaken the nation relative to its neighbors, lower national prestige, interfere with the sending out of emigrants who provide bonds with other nations and spread the national culture. A nation not growing was also said to suffer from smaller families, more feminine characteristics in some respects, and less boldness of character.[224] All this may have been a reflection of contemporary concern over low fertility in the author's own country.

The *Traité* in the next decade added that the true law of population is that the development of civilization brings with it a check on the birth rate. In that event, population increase can be maintained only by lowering the death rate. And the real danger is not overpopulation but depopulation, a distinctively French view at the time.[225]

The same concern and much the same views on population in general were expressed in *La Question* a number of years later. Here Leroy-Beaulieu stated that "The general rule, without exception in civilized countries, is that in recent times fertility decreases with the development of well-being, of education, and of democratic and new ideas."[226] Particular attention was given to the causes and consequences of low fertility and a stationary population, with later chapters discussing the depopulation of France. In conclusion, Leroy-Beaulieu reiterated that the Malthusian theory does not apply to nations with old and advanced civilization and a high standard of living, and that for them the real danger is depopulation.[227]

Dumont · An important later theory of population was advanced by Arsène Dumont (1849–1902), French sociologist who was especially concerned at the low level of fertility in France. In his *Dépopulation et civilization* (1890) Dumont began by rejecting the Malthusian principle that man multiplies up to the full measure of the food supply. As he said, this principle may apply to man at a primitive level or at an early stage of social and economic development, but other principles must come into operation when man begins to be ruled by imagination and aspirations.[228]

Noting the relatively low fertility in contemporary society, Dumont attributed it to a voluntary limitation of the number of children, then inquired into the immediate reasons. These were, he realized, undoubtedly many and varied. In some instances it might be intellectual considerations; in other cases it might be moral or aesthetic considerations that predominated. But recognizing these divergent reasons, Dumont nevertheless

[224] Leroy-Beaulieu, *Précis*, pp. 344–346.
[225] Leroy-Beaulieu, *Traité théorique et pratique d'économie politique*, Paris, 1896 p. 613.
[226] Leroy-Beaulieu, *La question de la population*, Paris, 1915 edition, Ch. 4, p. 237.
[227] *Ibid.*, p. 493.
[228] Arsène Dumont, *Dépopulation et civilization, étude demographique*, Paris, 1890, pp. 40–41.

sought some common factor or principle underlying voluntary infertility, whatever its immediate motives. The common causal factor he found to be social capillarity, the upward movement of individuals to higher socio-economic status. As he explained his principle,

> Once its preservation is assured every social molecule, guided by an unfailing and fatal instinct and without considering its companions except in trying to surpass them, struggles with all its energy to climb toward a glowing ideal which attracts it. . . . The more brilliant the focus, the more active and consuming is this social capillarity.[229]

To some extent, he went on to say, the infertility accompanying social mobility may be due to the removal of the successful or partially successful individuals from their original social environment and the consequent reduction or postponement of their opportunity for marriage, but in the main the infertility was believed to be voluntary and deliberate. As Dumont said, in paraphrase of the familiar proverb, "He who starts from below and aims high must run fast and be unencumbered with baggage to succeed."[230]

In further elaboration of his theory he came close to Spencer's position, saying that "In a nation the development of numbers is inversely proportional to the effort made for individual development. . . ."[231] But as Dumont emphasized, it is not the degree of individual development in itself that is significant but rather the amount of effort expanded to this end. The effort itself may be either for the development of personal worth or for the increase of pleasure and self-indulgence, but the effect on fertility is the same in either case. In this connection it was Dumont's opinion that a democratic form of government does not necessarily lead to low fertility, but does favor social capillary and therefore low fertility to the extent that it removes obstacles to the social mobility of its citizens.[232] Conversely, a caste system by preventing capillarity would favor high fertility.[233]

Nitti · The last population theorist to be considered here is Francesco Nitti (1868–1953), distinguished Italian statesman, journalist, and professor of finance. His *Population and the Social System* (1894) was largely a survey of earlier population theories, but did achieve a synthesis that combined elements of the preceding formulations.

Believing that different principles of population operate at different stages of social development, Nitti considered that the Malthusian theory applies only to peoples at a relatively low stage of economic development, and that here population growth is an eventual force for progress rather

[229] *Ibid.,* pp. 106.
[231] *Ibid.,* p. 112.
[233] *Ibid.,* p. 117.

[230] *Ibid.,* p. 110.
[232] *Ibid.,* p. 127.

than a cause of misery. And at the higher stages of development, no population problem arises because numbers are automatically adjusted to the food supply.[234]

The next question was how this automatic regulation of numbers is effected. Nitti considered it obvious that prudence and forethought alone are insufficient, and that moral restraint could have little effect.[235] Rather, he believed in an economic determination, and wrote that "the birth rate is almost exclusively regulated by economic forms."[236] It was clear to him, too, that the economic influence operates in an inverse relation to the birth rate, for as he said, ". . . a great birth-rate always corresponds to a great depression of the working classes, to smallness of wages, to a bad distribution of wealth, to an absence of social capillarity."[237] This conclusion, it is seen, is quite the opposite of the classical theory, for it asserts that poverty coming from defects in the economic system causes population increase.

Nitti then proceeded to state as a new demographic law that ". . . the economic situation does not depend upon the increase of population, but, on the contrary, not only the number of those who live, but even the number of those who are born, depends upon the economic situation."[238] This law led in turn to the question of the mechanism of the economic influence on fertility. Convinced that a stronger motivation than foresight is needed to control fertility, Nitti believed it was supplied by a rise in the standard of living and the accompanying psychological factors unfavorable to large families. With this viewpoint, he drew two corollaries from his law, as follows:

1. The lower the economic situation and the moral feelings of the popular class, the more restricted are their pleasures to those of sense, and so much the more is their birth-rate abundant and disordered.

2. Every improvement of the general condition, every diffusion of wealth, every increase of wages, and of the standard of living exercise a useful influence on their birth-rate.[239]

In effect, Nitti gave in the two corollaries an explanation of the inverse socio-economic differential in fertility.

In later pages he suggested there may be some biological as well as psychological basis for the relation between individualism and low fertility, and he cited Doubleday, Darwin and Spencer in support. And as a final law or generalization he restated his position:

. . . in every society where individuality will be strongly developed, but where progress of socialization will not extinguish individual activity; in

[234] Nitti, *Population and the Social System,* London, 1894, pp. 111–112.
[235] *Ibid.,* pp. 161, 163.   [236] *Ibid.,* p. 161.
[237] *Ibid.,* p. 159.   [238] *Ibid.,* p. 162.
[239] *Ibid.,* p. 162.

every society where wealth will be largely subdivided and where the social cause of inequality will be eliminated by an elevated form of co-operation, the birth-rate will tend to become equal with the means of subsistence, and regular variations of demographic evolution will not have as in the past an element of fear and terror.[240]

In the last analysis, then, the regulation of population numbers to keep within the limits set by the food supply was believed to depend not only upon the development of a sufficient degree of civilization and economic advancement but also upon the nature of the economic, social, and political system. Given the appropriate environmental conditions, the inhabitants of a nation might be expected to regulate their numbers not so much through deliberate and purposeful action as in response to their immediate conditions of life and the influences to which they were exposed.

7 · Comment

The population theories included in this chapter have been described separately and for the most part without comment, but a few generalizations on this body of population theory as a whole can be added.

One feature of the works reviewed is the interest of the authors in the whole range of relations between population and society, not just in population as a cause of social problems. Their views of population, accordingly, were in the full context of contemporary national problems, public morals, human welfare, public policy, and religion; and their discussion of population questions provided an opportunity for them to express their views on the economy, the government, and the society as a whole.

A principal common characteristic of these writings was the strong, almost unanimous optimism running through them. At first cast in an anti-Malthusian frame and repeating the long-familiar arguments, this nineteenth-century optimism underwent changes of emphasis and even of substance as the century progressed. Although most of the writers lived in a time and country of rapidly growing population, the great majority were less impressed with the known increase in number of people than by the increase in production and level of living at the time. If anything, they gave more recognition to the economic progress of their day than did the political economists, who were long dominated by the pessimistically oriented early classical economists.

Optimism about the future, however, was not based solely on confidence in the continued growth of production but even more on confidence that various natural checks would prevent any undue growth of population.

[240] *Ibid.,* p. 191.

The number and variety of preventive checks on population perceived by these writers were large, for almost every one gave his own inventory of influences tending to limit population. Especially it was believed that advance in education, intelligence, standard of living, and civilization induces greater exercise of restraint in marriage and reproduction. Among those expressing some variant of this opinion were Jarrold, Gray, Spencer, and Leroy-Beaulieu. Also, this line of thought merged into belief in the operation of certain automatic checks with advances in population and civilization, as asserted for various reasons by Jarrold, Hazlitt, Gray, Weyland, Grahame, Greg, Nitti, and others.

Going hand in hand with the population optimism and its reliance on natural checks was a fundamental change of emphasis in the writings on population. Whereas the older generation of both optimists and pessimists had focused their attention particularly on the social and economic consequences of population size and growth, new inquiry was particularly directed toward discovering what influences affect population size and especially fertility. The emphasis was thus changed from population as a cause of socio-economic consequences to population as a consequence of certain prior causes.

In inquiring about the determinants of population size and change, the theorists advanced population theory by broadening the context in which population phenomena were considered. Advancing from the primarily economic framework in which the political economists had treated the subject, individual writers such as Jarrold, Weyland, and Ross emphasized the influence of political conditions; many pointed to various aspects of the social environment; mental and psychological influences were mentioned by Jarrold, Gray, Ensor, Ross, Hickson, Greg, and others; and a variety of other factors received attention. Specific conditions noted by one or another writer as determiners of population trend were age at marriage (Gray), degree of urbanization (Weyland, Alison), infant mortality rate (Grahame), artificial wants (Alison), class structure of the population (Moreton), and population density (Sadler, Guillard). Although too divergent to produce any united weight of opinion, the separate theories did serve to emphasize the complex character of population phenomena.

By far the most interesting phenomenon, and the most productive from a theoretical viewpoint, was the inverse relation of fertility to socio-economic status. Already known to Graunt and Petty, the founding fathers of English population study two centuries before, the inverse relation of fertility was mentioned by almost every population theorist of the nineteenth century, and many developed their own explanations for it. The phenomenon itself appeared inconsistent with, or at least was not readily explained by orthodox Malthusian and economic theory; and out of attempts to explain the apparently deviant phenomenon arose various results important in the development of population theory.

By its nature, it was evident that differential fertility involved more than a simple and direct economic mechanism, and the search for adequate explanations brought consideration of social and economic standards, customs, and motivations that broadened the treatment of the subject far beyond the narrow economic context. The same process of searching for reasonable explanations for the phenomenon further served to focus more on the causes than on the consequences of population phenomena, and contributed to the shift of emphasis toward regarding population more as a dependent variable, less as an independent variable.

With this came a reversal of the accepted view of the connection between populousness and human misery, a reversal that has already been seen within contemporary economic thought. As Alison, Thornton, Hickson, Kautsky, and others concluded, it is poverty that leads to high fertility rather than vice versa; and the converse influence of an ample food supply leading to a low birth rate was inferred by Gray, Edmonds, Moreton, and Doubleday. Again, this put the population phenomenon in the position of an effect to be explained rather than a cause of socio-economic consequences. In its own way, therefore, social thought during the nineteenth century came to a revised estimate of the significance of population, much as economic thought has been seen to have done during the same period.

12

Other Population Theories of the
Nineteenth Century: Some Common Themes

In addition to the general theories described in the preceding chapter, there were many lesser writings and briefer comments on various aspects of population outside the range of formal economics. Many of the political economists themselves noted certain non-economic considerations in their discussion of population questions, and countless other references ranging from "laws of population" to brief notes were included in the nineteenth-century population literature. Too numerous to be reviewed individually and for the most part expressing ideas already mentioned in earlier chapters, these lesser contributions nevertheless deserve mention, for they contain certain recurrent ideas or themes that, if not distinctively new or original, are an important part of nineteenth-century population thought.

1 · Another Viewpoint

Earlier thought, we have seen, viewed population largely in national political terms, and later shifted to a predominantly economic viewpoint. The strongly economic orientation given by the early nineteenth-century political economists waned gradually; and although there was some increase of emphasis on the influence of economic conditions on population, as for example, in Nitti's economic determinism, the trend was toward a broader, more eclectic viewpoint and a fuller appreciation of the complexity of population phenomena. As Blanqui wrote of the population controversy, Malthus had attributed all human troubles to one cause, overpopulation, but it is an error to take moral or social causes as unitary for they are as a rule complex.[1] And although individual writers mentioned below may have emphasized particular viewpoints and given unitary theories, as a group they testified to the complex nature of population phenomena.

In addition to the continuing treatment of population in economic and to some extent political terms, the religious approach to questions of

[1] Adolphe Blanqui, *Histoire de l'économie politique en Europe,* 2 vol., Paris, 1837, Vol. II, pp. 159–160.

population lingered. Already mentioned are Alison and Ingram who approached the population question with pious assurance that it had a place in the divine order. Or, as Sumner (1760–1862) stated,

> . . . a state of society, consisting of various ranks and conditions, is the state best suited to excite the industry and display the most valuable faculties of mankind. Taking, therefore, into consideration, the object of man's existence upon earth, it might naturally be expected that the Creator would devise a mean which would inevitably tend to bring the human race, for the most part, into such a situation.
>
> And this, in fact, I believe to be the final cause of that "principle of population," with whose powerful agency we have recently been made acquainted. . . .[2]

This conviction was no doubt appropriate for the future Lord Archbishop of Canterbury. On other religious grounds Atkinson, like Godwin before him, reproached Malthus for putting the blame for human misery on the Creator,[3] and numerous other writers expressed the same indignation. Lawson (1817–1887), in a work dedicated to Richard Whately, Archbishop of Dublin, was confident that the control of numbers could be left safely to Providence, but added cautiously that it is desirable to avoid direct encouragement of increase.[4] At about the same time, Rev. Henry Raikes in his lectures on population presented the matter as part of the divine plan for the advancement of mankind;[5] and many other expressions of the same assurance could be found.

The foregoing approaches to population questions continued older lines of thinking, but nineteenth-century population thought began to flow in new channels as new questions were raised and the range of inquiry was broadened. Concern over the consequences of population size and growth declined gradually during the century, as seen already, and attention turned more and more to questions of the background or determinants of population phenomena, for it was recognized that answers to these questions were needed to formulate effective policies for voluntary control of numbers. One series of considerations that appears with increasing frequency in the literature of the period concerns the role of psychological and intellectual factors. Most frequently mentioned as determinants of fertility, such factors are considered more particularly in the

---

[2] John Bird Sumner, *Treatise on the records of the creation and on the moral attributes of the Creator* . . ., London, 1816; reference here is to the 6th ed., London, 1850, Part II, p. 229.

[3] William Atkinson, *Principles of political economy, or the laws of the formation of national wealth*, London, 1840, p. 86; and *Principles of social and political economy, or the creation and diffusion of wealth*, London, 1858, Vol. I, p. 125.

[4] James A. Lawson, *Five lectures on political economy*, London and Dublin, 1844, pp. 76, 77.

[5] Henry Raikes, *Two lectures on population*, London, 1844.

next section, but it can be noted here that a related conclusion was that general education is an effective, almost necessary policy, if population numbers are to be brought under voluntary control. Thus Samuel Whitbread (1758–1815), whose bill on the poor laws in 1807 figured in the Malthusian controversy, was firmly convinced that the only lasting solution is to give the laborer a greater sense of pride in himself and a more active desire for advancement, and that the necessary first step is a national system of education.[6] The second step is to encourage the laborers to acquire property. In the same vein, if with a different order of priorities, was a paper published in 1820 concerning ways and means of inducing control of numbers. Here it was stated that "The first, and most essential step, therefore, towards establishing the required check to population, is to better the condition of the poor, and the second, is to give them a suitable education."[7] Some years later the *Familiar Letters* of John Burn recommended education and religion for the poor as deterrents to early and improvident marriage.[8] Belief in education as a sovereign remedy for the population problem was common at the time.

Search for explanation and understanding of population phenomena, particularly the socio-economic differential in fertility, pointed to the importance not only of psychological factors but of social influences, and the population literature of the nineteenth century shows a growing awareness of the interrelations of demographic and social phenomena. This appeared especially in theories of the determinants of fertility and population size and in explanations of the status differential, which are dealt with later in this chapter. Some additional references to social influences can be noted here. Attention was directed particularly toward the strength of the desire to maintain social position and the culturally dictated standard of living, as already seen. Among other writers who touched on one or another of these topics, the younger Laing (1812–1897) wrote of the force of public opinion:

> The great check on premature marriage in every class is the "public opinion" of that class, which requires a certain income and establishment in life before marrying. . . . When the standard prescribed by the "public opinion" of the class has sunk so low that . . . men commonly marry "without a home to go to" . . . it is evident that all moral check on population is at an end. . . .[9]

[6] Samuel Whitbread, *Substance of a speech on the poor laws: delivered in the House of Commons, Feb. 19, 1807,* London, 1807, pp. 21–22, 27.

[7] Anon., "On the means of retaining the population within any required limits," *The Pamphleteer,* Vol. 31 (1820), p. 416.

[8] John Burn, *Familiar Letters,* Letter XX, pp. 126–134.

[9] Samuel Laing, Jr., *National distress; its causes and remedies,* London, 1844, pp. 68–69.

The desire to maintain and the fear of losing one's position in society were mentioned by Lawson and Rogers, among others, and Moreton's similar statement has already been noted. In Lawson's words,

> The desire to maintain our position in society, and not sink below the level of those with whom we have been in the habit of associating, is so strong a principle in the mind of a member of a civilized community as to counterpoise the most powerful natural instincts: this leads to a postponement of the period of marriage, and so retards the increase of population.[10]

Rogers wrote in the same vein and continued with an explanation of the differential in fertility:

> In our own country, self-respect, the dread of falling from a higher to a lower social position, and perhaps the natural anxiety of parents that their children should occupy no worse a place and have no less advantages than they themselves enjoy, are powerful hindrances to rash and premature marriages among the middle classes of society. Such prudential motives, however, seldom operate on the very poor. Agricultural labourers marry early and improvidently; so do most artisans. . . .[11]

The stimulus of desire for personal advancement was mentioned by others, as for example Rossi (1789–1848), who noted the wish for greater well-being,[12] and of course Dumont emphasized the striving for social advancement.

Apart from differences in fertility, various writers noted social class or group differences in attitudes and behavior. For example, the German political economist Hermann noted the natural resistance of workers to a lower level of living, and stated that, if faced with declining wages, they may prefer making a greater productive effort to practicing restraint in marriage and reproduction.[13] Cauwès, for another, remarked that people differ in their pattern of using income, for some will limit reproduction in order to save while others prefer to have more children.[14]

Considerable attention was given to the way habits or customs, especially those regarding consumption, can affect population. In the eighteenth century, as we have seen, Steuart pointed out that population varies inversely with per capita consumption, other things remaining equal, which was also said by several nineteenth-century writers. The French economist, Carrion-Nisas, fils, made this point in his *Principes d'économie*

---

[10] James A. Lawson, *Five lectures on political economy*, pp. 72–73.

[11] James E. Thorold Rogers, *Manual of Political Economy*, p. 69.

[12] Pellegrino Rossi, *Cours d'économie politique*, 2nd ed., Paris, 1843, pp. 314–318 (1st ed., 1838).

[13] Frederich B. W. Hermann, *Staatswirthschaftliche Untersuchungen*, Munich, 1832, p. 245.

[14] Paul Cauwès, *Cours d'économie politique*, 3rd ed., 4 vol., Paris, 1893, pp. 22–23 (1st ed., 1878?).

politique (1825), for example;[15] and similar statements made by Alison and Rogers were quoted earlier.

Other references to the role of custom are scattered throughout the population literature. Jean-Batiste Say in the first edition of his *Traité* (1803) mentioned that the habits of the people affect what they consider necessary and, by implication, the level of their wages.[16] In Say's later work, the *Cours complet,* he wrote further that ". . . famines are much more deadly in countries where the mores, religion, and laws lead the people to an extreme frugality that produces an abundant population."[17] Many years later Bonamy Price wrote that the one sure defense against a tendency toward overpopulation is "a determinate standard of living, firmly established upon long habit."[18]

A quite early nineteenth-century statement of the by no means new idea that the customary level of living determines population size rather than vice versa was given by Thomas Attwood (1783–1856). He wrote, in his *Observations on currency, population, pauperism* . . . (1818), that a change in national production does not in the long run alter the situation of the lower classes, for per capita consumption soon stabilizes at a level

> . . . such as the nature and habits of the lower classes rendered them able and willing to exist upon, but it would not be better or worse, because, if it were either better or worse, they would again multiply or diminish their numbers, until it was brought to that level to which their nature and their habits had fitted them.[19]

There was a corollary proposition, already noted, that the workers by regulating their fertility and numbers can maintain a customary wage level. This was implied by Say and was fully stated by the German economist Schäffle, to name only one, in his *Nationalökonomie* (1861), in which he asserted that wages tend to stabilize not at the bare subsistence level but at the customary subsistence level of the workers.[20] In a later work he testified again to the influence of custom but in another connection, writing that a decline of the rate of natural increase is not a sign of national decay for it may be due to a change in custom or numbers approaching the limit set by the prevailing level of living.[21]

Among French writers, Bastiat recorded his agreement with Say's dis-

---

15 A. de Carrion-Nisas, fils, *Principes d'économie politique,* Paris, 1825, p. 31. His statement is that the population of a country, other things being equal, depends on what is the staple food.

16 Jean-Batiste Say, *Traité d'économie politique,* 2 vol., Paris, Vol. II, pp. 237–238.

17 Jean-Batiste Say, *Cours complet,* 1840, p. 145.

18 Bonamy Price, *Chapters on practical political economy,* London, 1878, p. 196.

19 Thomas Attwood, *Observations on currency, population, pauperism . . . in two letters to Arthur Young,* Birmingham, 1818, p. 5.

20 Albert E. F. Schäffle, *Die Nationalökonomie, oder allgemeine Wirthschaftslehre,* Leipzig, 1861, pp. 195–196.

21 Albert E. F. Schäffle, *Bau und Leben des socialen Körpers,* Tubingen, 1875; reference here to 2nd ed., Vol. II, Book 8, Part 2, p. 10.

tinction between the means of subsistence and the means of existence, of which the latter included the customary comforts of life.[22] The same distinction, we have seen, was made by Destutt de Tracy and Rickards. And Baudrillart described the necessary level of wages as being set by the cost of production of labor, which varies from country to country with the standard of living.[23]

Other references to the influence of social factors appear below, but those already noted indicate the increased awareness of social influences on population.

2 · Factors Affecting Fertility and Population Size

The earlier writers for the most part had thought of population as being checked and controlled by the positive checks, misery, war, famine, vice, and other evils, but most of the later nineteenth-century writers took a happier view. Whether or not they put any trust in moral restraint, they were generally confident that there are certain automatic controls inherent in man's nature, in the economic environment, or in the social system that prevent harmful growth of the number of people.

One group of such controlling factors, was made up of psychological and related influences. John Graunt, in seeking to explain the lower fertility of marriages in London, had said that "the minds of men in London are more thoughtful"; and much the same mechanism affecting fertility was presented in nineteenth-century population theory. Among the writers mentioned in the chapter above, Jarrold and Gray thought mental exertion and anxiety are checks on population growth; Ensor and Ross pointed to intellectual checks, and Hickson to intellectual occupations, while Spencer and Greg believed that fertility varies inversely with mental development. Bagehot, not previously cited, was of the opinion that fertility is reduced by "the nervous condition which luxury engenders."[24]

Many influences tending to affect fertility and check population growth were thought to exist within the conditions of daily life and employment, in the pattern of consumption and in the economic system generally; and various "laws" and theories stated these supposed fundamental relations.

A number of the economists, as seen, believed that capital is the major variable and that population rises or falls as changes in the amount of capital or its rate of formation bring higher or lower wages and affect the well-being of the workers; and they accepted the Malthusian proposition that fertility and population rise as the supply of the means of sub-

[22] Bastiat, *Harmonies économiques,* p. 441.
[23] Baudrillart, *Manuel d'économie politique,* p. 334.
[24] Walter Bagehot, *Economic studies,* 2nd ed., London, 1888, p. 141 (1st ed., 1879).

sistence rises. However, many others strongly suspected that the relation between fertility and the economic condition of the workers is inverse rather than direct. Among those mentioned in the chapter above, Sadler saw a state of labor and privation associated with high fertility, and repletion with a lower rate of reproduction. Similar views were expressed by Alison, Edmonds, Gray, Thornton, Doubleday, and Hickson. Rickards saw fertility varying inversely with what he called the scale of living. And according to Droz and Florez-Estrada, fertility is in inverse proportion to the degree of control exercised by those accustomed to the comforts of life.[25]

In the minds of these and other writers it became almost an axiom, directly the opposite of the Malthusian belief, that poverty promotes reckless reproduction and economic security induces restraint. This axiom was stated incisively by many nineteenth-century writers, including the anonymous author of an article in the *Pamphleteer* in 1820: "Is it not evident, therefore, that misery, far from preventing, is the principal cause by which the pressure of the population against the means of subsistence is produced? . . ." and

> I am most fully persuaded, that it is by promoting the comfort, the happiness and the virtue of the community at large, instead of having a large portion of our fellow-creatures in a state of misery and vice, that we can ever hope to obviate the evils said to arise from the principle of population.[26]

Parallel to the latter was the assertion by Francis Place (1771–1854) that improvement in the condition of the people encourages postponement of marriage,[27] and by William Thompson (1783?–1833) several years later that

> No truth of economy and morals is more certain, than that the increase of comforts amongst mankind engenders prudence, and arrests, instead of encouraging, the tendency to increase their numbers beyond the supply of those comforts.[28]

Later Sismondi wrote of prosperity as a preventive of excess increase in numbers.[29] And according to Samuel Laing, Sr., writing of the poor,

> It is their poverty that causes their over-multiplication, and their over-multiplication their poverty. Cure their poverty, give them property, inculcate the whole mass of society with the tastes, habits, and feelings of

[25] Droz, *Économie politique,* p. 216; Florez-Estrada, *Cours éclectique,* Vol. II, p. 103.

[26] Anon., "On the means of retaining the population within any required limits," *The Pamphleteer,* Vol. 31 (1820), pp. 414, 415.

[27] Francis Place, *The principle of population,* London, 1822, pp. 171–172.

[28] William Thompson, *An inquiry into the principles of the distribution of wealth,* London, 1824, p. 545.

[29] Sismondi, *Etudes,* p. 192.

prudence, which attend the possession of property . . . and over-multiplication is cured.[30]

Or, as put by the younger Laing, ". . . we may take as a demonstrated fact, that misery, up to the extreme point of famine and pestilence, instead of checking, tends to increase population."[31] The same thought was expressed by Émile Thomas,[32] by John Barton,[33] and many other writers of the time.

Still other factors or forces were presented as determinants of human fertility and population size. Urbanization, already mentioned by Weyland and Alison, was regarded by Bagehot as leading to lower fertility.[34] Earlier than Alison, Richard Jones regarded the development of "artificial wants" as tending to check population,[35] and a few years later Lawson wrote similarly that "The more highly a country is civilized, the more strongly will be felt the necessity of supplying those artificial wants which refinement has given birth to; and, therefore, the more powerfully will this restraint operate. . . ."[36] A quite different influence was mentioned by the French economist Passy:

> The sentiments aroused by land ownership have been overlooked. The man who owns, who has succeeded in acquiring land through his own labor, and who hopes to enlarge his holdings in the course of time, becomes accustomed to think of the future, and it is rare for him not to act with the thought and wisdom necessary for the continued improvement of his lot.[37]

He added that

> The facts are conclusive. They show that in France the freedom to subdivide land holdings has not urged the rural population to unbounded increase, but on the contrary has acted as a restraint on those tendencies . . . that might check or retard the development of general wellbeing.[38]

Like other French writers of the time, Passy was no doubt influenced in his thinking by the known low fertility of his native land.

In general, the thought underlying many of the particular theories cited above was that the progress of society and its increasing complexity generate forces that check fertility and population growth.

[30] Samuel Laing, Sr., *Notes of a Traveller on the Social and Political State of France, Prussia, Switzerland, Italy, and other parts of Europe*, London, 1842, p. 348.

[31] Samuel Laing, Jr., *National Distress*, p. 69.

[32] Émile Thomas, *Des conditions vraies de la science économique*, Paris, 1850, pp. 44, 54.

[33] John Barton, *An inquiry into the causes of the progressive depreciation of agricultural labour*, London, 1820, p. 40.

[34] Bagehot, *Economic Studies, Essay 4.*

[35] Richard Jones, *An Essay*, p. xxxvi.

[36] James A. Lawson, *op. cit.*, p. 72.

[37] Hippolyte Passy, *Des Systèmes de culture*, p. 212.

[38] *Ibid.*, p. 214.

An alternative idea leading to the same reassuring conclusion without assuming any specific controlling factors was that population numbers tend to come to a natural point of balance and then stop. For example, Proudhon in his *Système des contradictions économiques* (1846) described what he called the principle of population equilibrium.[39] Molinari believed there is an equilibrium between food and numbers in nature, although man may have disturbed it by substituting his own regulation.[40] And Kautsky, in his late work, devoted a chapter to "the balance of nature," in which he asserted that there is a natural tendency toward a balance of numbers rather than full competition and survival of the fittest.[41]

3 · Explanations of the Status Differential

Certain of the cultural and other factors thought to affect fertility, as described above, were brought into explanations of the status differential. The inverse relation between fertility and socio-economic status was a long-recognized phenomenon, and in the search for explanations a number of ingenious theories and hypotheses were developed. Those by Jarrold, Sismondi, Doubleday, Thornton, Rickards, and Nitti have already been seen, and many more may be found throughout the nineteenth-century population literature. Some of the more noteworthy ones are described below.

The author of a pamphlet published in 1803 saw the differential as quite simply due to moral restraint being practiced among civilized people except in the lowest classes.[42] Status considerations were emphasized by Say, who wrote that

> The continence that limits the number of children acts all the more strongly as families fear losing their position in society. The poor workman says, "My child will earn his living like his father", but a noble does not want to expose his descendants to the risk of having to work for he considers that a disgrace.[43]

To Richard Jones the differential in fertility indicated

> . . . the presence and influence, among communities of men, of causes which coming into action during the progress of plenty and refinement, serve to moderate the exercise of man's physical power of increase, and are not resolvable evidently into misery, and almost as evidently, not into unmixed vice, or into a faultless state of moral restraint.[44]

[39] P-J. Proudhon, *Système des contradictions économiques, ou philosophie de la misère,* 2 vol., Paris, 1846, Vol. II, pp. 408, 461.
[40] Gustav de Molinari, *La viriculture,* Paris, 1897.
[41] Kautsky, *Vermehrung,* Ch. 4.
[42] Anon., *Remarks on a late publication* . . . , London, 1803, p. 27.
[43] Jean-Baptiste Say, *Cours complet,* p. 139.
[44] Richard Jones, *op. cit.,* p. xvii.

For Proudhon it was not plenty and refinement that induce lower fertility but labor, and his explanation of the differential was original, if not persuasive. According to his theory, there is a natural antagonism between labor and reproduction, the one increasing at the expense of the other; and the poor have larger families because they are less industrious.[45]

A less original explanation was given by Burton:

> The further down we go in the scale of possessions, the more hopeless do lessons of celibacy become. The man who has nothing of his own in this world to divide, is the person who, with the most utter recklessness, is prepared to admit another to participate with him in living on the means of his neighbors.[46]

In a parallel line of thought, Cauwès stated that foresight diminishes with misery;[47] and conversely, the operation of prudential motives in direct proportion to economic status was cited by Rogers, quoted earlier in this chapter.

In summary of this group of writings, it can be seen that little if anything really new was added to the analysis and interpretation of the fertility differential beyond what was contained in the major theories of population (Chapter 11). However, there was a reenforcement of the prevailing diagnosis that fertility is affected by considerations of customary standards, social position and ambitions, and differing class viewpoints; and these social forces were shown to be capable of operating in a differential fashion to affect social classes differently and to produce the inverse relation of status and fertility.

4 · Progress and Population

As pointed out earlier, many theories described specific checks and controlling influences that presumably arise as a society progresses. Other theories dealt directly with progress itself, in one or another manifestation, as a powerful force in human affairs, and explored its relation to population. The idea of progress, political, economic, and social, was real and exciting, especially in the middle and late decades of the nineteenth century. In earlier centuries men had dreamed of a distant Utopia: now progress was present and visible, and the solutions to man's problems seemed to be within his grasp. The pessimistic prediction that population growth would bring the ideal society of the optimists to ruin was met by the confident belief that progress would solve that problem too. Nineteenth-century optimism was different from eighteenth-century optimism, but both assumed the population problem was nonexistent or would disappear.

---

[45] Proudhon, *op. cit.*, pp. 477–478.
[46] John Burton, *Political and social economy*, Edinburgh, 1849, p. 207.
[47] Cauwès, *op. cit.*, Vol. II, p. 32.

Among writers whose theories were described earlier, Jarrold saw an increase in control as man rises above an animal level of existence, Moreton saw the same effect produced by the diffusion of comfort, Spencer looked to development of the individual; and other variants of the same basic theme were advanced by Alison, Rickards, Wirth, and others. Hamilton wrote of a slowing down of the rate of population growth because

> . . . the difference of habits that accompany the change of the state of society . . . likely to operate still more powerfully as art and civilization are carried to a higher pitch, and without having recourse to harsh measures, may be expected to restrain the progress of population within the necessary limits.[48]

Jones, as previously quoted, believed the progress of plenty and refinement will lessen fertility.[49] And Lawson, also quoted above, spoke of civilization as leading to the same result.[50]

A distinctively different idea on fertility was expressed by Thomas, according to whom fertility is inversely related to longevity, but he linked this to progress: "As intellectual development and material well-being free man from manual labor and vulgar ignorance, his fecundity diminishes and his average longevity increases. . . ."[51] More conventionally, Schäffle saw higher levels of culture and well-being bringing a stronger exercise of restraint;[52] and Leslie wrote, in an essay on celibacy, that ". . . celibacy without vows or compulsion is a form of human existence which is commonly to be seen only in civilized society, and which becomes commoner as civilization goes forward and spreads."[53] For Cauwès it was development of the individual, with the accompanying increase of needs and desires and greater exercise of reason, that brings regulation of population size.[54] Later, in the final decade of the century, Nitti added to his demographic law that population depends upon the economic situation the corollary that for the "popular classes, . . . Every improvement of the general condition, every diffusion of wealth, every increase of wages, and of the standard of living exercises a useful influence on their birth-rate."[55] And in the same decade Leroy-Beaulieu stated as "the true law of population of civilized peoples" that the development of civilization brings a check on the birth rate.[56]

The relation between population and progress did not stop here, for it was seen as a reciprocal rather than a one-way relation. Population

[48] Robert Hamilton, *The progress of society,* London, 1830, p. 352.
[49] Richard Jones, *op. cit.,* p. xvii.
[50] James Lawson, *op. cit.,* p. 72.
[51] Émile Thomas, *op. cit.,* p. 43.
[52] Schäffle, *Die National okonomie,* Ch. XXI, p. 158.
[53] T. E. C. Leslie, *Essays,* Essay II, "The celibacy of the nation" (1863), p. 11.
[54] Cauwès, *op. cit.,* Vol. II, p. 8.
[55] Francesco Nitti, *Population and the social system,* p. 162.
[56] Leroy-Beaulieu, *Traité, théorique,* p. 613.

growth was thought in its turn to be a powerful force for progress. In this respect the nineteenth-century writers carried on and even added to the older optimistic belief in the beneficial effects of a growing number of people. Of writers mentioned earlier, Jarrold, Gray, Weyland, Sadler, Garnier, and others described population growth as a stimulus to mankind, a cause of change to higher levels of social organization, and a civilizing force. A few additional writers can be mentioned to illustrate this line of thought in more detail.

Sumner, for example, pursued his thesis that the wisdom of the Creator is displayed in the Malthusian principle of population, reasoning that the tendency of numbers to increase faster than the food supply is "the source of all effective industry," and leads to interchange among the various people of the earth with a civilizing effect.[57] With some reservations the economist Longfield also saw population growth as favorable to the diffusion of knowledge and civilization.[58] Lotz saw it as a necessary condition for economic progress.[59] In turn Thomas Smith, with a sort of *histoire raisonnée,* described how population gives impetus to economic development, and wrote that because of rapid increase in numbers in the early stages of a society,

> . . . the number of inhabitants becoming at last too great to be profitably employed in agricultural pursuits, a part of them turn to other objects. Those residing on the sea-shore become fishers and sailors. The materials for ship-building being generally in abundance and easily procured, some become ship-carpenters. Others take up the manufacturing of such articles as are of great bulk and little value, and therefore cannot be so easily or advantageously imported. As the population increases the number of manufacturers increase (sic) until at last they are greater than the agricultural produce of the country can support, and they become exporters of manufactures and importers of agricultural produce.[60]

This, according to Smith, is the natural course of development followed by all nations.

Another writer, Travers Twiss, reasoned that it may be undesirable for population to be so well restrained that there is no surplus of labor, for

> . . . it is the steady pressure of population against subsistence which stimulates the wit of man to new discoveries, which suggests the enterprise and enforces the necessity of perseverance in its execution.[61]

[57] John Bird Sumner, *op. cit.,* pp. 256, 260.

[58] Mountifort Longfield, *Lectures on political economy,* Dublin, 1834, p. 237.

[59] Johan F. E. Lotz, *Handbuch der Staatswissenschaftslehre,* 3 vol., Erlangen, 1821–1822, Vol. II, p. 43.

[60] Thomas Smith, *An attempt to define some of the first principles of political economy,* London, 1821, p. 65.

[61] Travers Twiss, *On certain tests of a thriving population,* London, 1845, pp. 93–94.

Stating another level at which the stimulus of population growth may operate, this may be recognized as one of the oldest of optimistic arguments. Soon after Twiss, the French economist Proudhon agreed, writing that without population pressure the need for subsistence is not enough to stimulate the development of human faculties.[62] Conventional statements of the spur of necessity engendered by population growth were given by Urquhart,[63] Macvicar,[64] and numerous others.

There was still another way in which nineteenth-century thought credited population pressure with contributing to human advancement. That was through organic evolution. As is well known, Charles Darwin expressed his indebtedness to Malthus:

> In October 1838, that is, fifteen months after I had begun my systematic enquiry, I happened to read for amusement "Malthus on Population", and being well prepared to appreciate the struggle for existence which everywhere goes on from long-continued observation of the habits of animals and plants, it at once struck me that under these circumstances favourable variations would tend to be preserved, and unfavourable ones to be destroyed. The result of this would be the formation of new species. Here then I had at last got a theory by which to work. . . .[65]

And significantly, A. R. Wallace, who arrived at the theory of evolution independent of Darwin, is also said to have been similarly influenced by reading Malthus' *Essay on population.*[66]

Actually, of course, the elements of the theory of evolution through competition, survival of the fittest, and natural selection were already widespread before the *Origin of Species,* just as Malthus himself had many precursors. In the population literature itself there is only a reference by Grahame in 1816 to the survival of the strongest.[67] In the scientific literature, however, the ideas of overpopulation and competition appeared earlier and were more prevalent. It has even been suggested that Malthus was indebted to the biologists for the germ of his theory, rather than they being indebted to him; and curiously, it is Charles Darwin's grandfather, Erasmus Darwin, who is mentioned here.[68] Although the pathway followed by an idea is difficult to trace with certainty, it would be strange if Malthus in his formative years did not pick up ideas that originated with the natural scientists whose successors he was to influence in turn.

[62] Proudhon, *op. cit.,* Vol. II, p. 411.
[63] William P. Urquhart, *Essays on subjects in political economy,* Aberdeen, 1850, Essay III, "On population."
[64] John G. Macvicar, *An inquiry into human nature,* Edinburgh, 1853, pp. 101–102.
[65] Charles Darwin, *Life and letters,* Francis Darwin, Ed., New York, 1889, Vol. I, p. 68.
[66] W. I. B. Beveridge, *The art of scientific investigation,* pp. 68–69.
[67] Grahame, *op. cit.,* Ch. VI.
[68] See previous reference to Erasmus Darwin, p. 126.

5 · Comment

The preceding sections on the secondary population literature in the nineteenth century point out certain recurrent themes but do not fully indicate the almost limitless number and diversity of these writings. Since the population question was regarded as a major social problem during at least a part of this period, those who expressed themselves on the subject represented a wide range of backgrounds and viewpoints. And the views they expressed, although for the most part paraphrases of the major treatises on population, ranged from shrewd observations to what now appear far-fetched theories and speculations.

Not yet mentioned are some contributions of interest in themselves, such as Canard's account, long before Veblen, of conspicuous and competitive consumption, which he linked with the low fertility of the wealthy,[69] and the law of population enunciated by the famous Belgian statistician Quetelet:

> The population tends to increase according to a geometric progression. The resistance, or the sum of the obstacles to its growth, is, other things being the same, equal to the square of the rate at which the population tends to increase.[70]

As a group, however, these writings had the weakness common to the non-economic literature on population, for they were made up of isolated and discrete theories rather than being a cumulative body of thought and analysis.

Another respect in which this body of population writings suffers in comparison with the economic treatment of population is its predominantly intuitive, non-analytic character. At best the various theories and opinions were founded on close observation and shrewd interpretation; at worst they were based on nothing more substantial than assumption and plausibility.

But as a group, these writings had a constructive side. They served to widen the context in which population questions were viewed and discussed, and especially to emphasize the social aspects of the subject. Also, they gave expression to certain current views on population on which there was some consensus. Perhaps the broadest consensus was in an optimistic view of population. The stronghold of pessimistic theory had come to lie within political economy; and outside political economy the literature leaned heavily toward the opposite opinion for reasons explained earlier in this chapter. These included a firm belief in progress, both

[69] N. F. Canard, *Principes d'économie politique,* Paris, 1801, pp. 85–86, 95, 101.
[70] Adolphe Quetelet, *Sur l'homme, et le développement de ses facultés, ou essai de physique sociale,* 2 vol., Paris, 1835, Vol. I, p. 277.

material and non-material, assurance that progress would prevent or help prevent excessive reproduction, and conviction that a developing society contains or generates natural and spontaneous controls on both fertility and population.

13

A Partial Solution

Public interest as well as the attention of the political economists turned away from the population question in the latter part of the nineteenth century. Fears of overpopulation tend to rise and fall with the alternation of hard times and good, and the difficult decades of the late eighteenth and early nineteenth centuries, which provided a climate favorable to the Malthusian pessimism, finally gave way to a more prosperous period. Population growth was rapid in many nations, but production and wealth advanced even more rapidly in the industrializing nations, and where needed elsewhere there were seemingly unlimited opportunities for emigration. The threat of overpopulation had receded visibly, and at least in the popular mind the Malthusian theory appeared to be disproved by the course of events.

The political economists did not dismiss the population problem, for, as more than one of them pointed out, the more rapid advance of invention and production than of population was no assurance that the same would be true in the future; but they turned their attention to other matters. They may have felt that the subject already had received more than enough attention, and that other topics more central to economic science remained to be explored. Some even questioned whether population was properly the concern of economics. There was indeed a growing awareness that population is strongly affected by non-economic factors and that, accordingly, it cannot be fully treated within a purely economic frame of reference.[1] Another development within economics during the latter part of the nineteenth century that had a similar effect was the device of static analysis, in which certain factors were assumed to remain constant while others varied. In application this mode of analysis generally assumed a constant population and removed population from the system of economic variables.

[1] The gradual replacement of the term "political economy" by economics was perhaps indicative of a growing specialization of the new science and a greater differentiation of separate disciplines within the social sciences as a whole.

1 · One Further Step

The ebbing away of interest in the population problem was not because agreement had been reached, for there were still wide differences of opinion on the economic and other significance of the number of people. Not all political economists were satisfied that the definitive formulation had been given by John Stuart Mill; and not even the cornerstone of classical theory, the principle of diminishing returns, was left unquestioned. Within and outside political economy there persisted the two opposite opinions on the population factor that had endured throughout the centuries of discussion of the subject: the old dilemma of whether population growth is a source of good or of evil to a society was still unresolved.

In spite of the waning of popular and technical interest, one further important contribution was made to population theory before the end of the nineteenth century. That was the concept of optimum population. What makes it especially noteworthy is that it was a partial synthesis and reconciliation of the optimistic and pessimistic theories of population, for it implied that growth of numbers up to the optimum size is beneficial, and beyond that size further growth is harmful.

The germ of the idea of optimum population has been detected in the work of many early writers, from Aristotle and Confucius to Wolff, Rousseau, Genovesi, Holbach, and others in the eighteenth century.[2] The idea that there may be an optimum number of inhabitants could have occurred naturally to anyone who recognized and reflected on the possibilities of either too many or too few in a given area, and in the general form of Tucker's "golden mean," the idea appeared in a number of places. But the modern concept was a more specific formulation, a logical development from theoretical foundations laid down quite early in nineteenth-century classical economics, for it set the optimum at the point of maximum productivity.

Seen in retrospect, the optimum population concept was a natural product of several developments in nineteenth-century population thought. It might have taken its origin from the principle of diminishing returns alone, for the growth of population and production was regarded as the active

[2] For accounts of the optimum population concept and the origins of the idea, see, for example, Lionel Robbins, "The optimum theory of population," in *London Essays in Economics: in honor of Edwin Cannan,* London: Routledge, 1927; A. B. Wolfe, "The theory of optimum population," *The Annals,* November 1936, pp. 243–249; Imre Ferenczi, *The Synthetic Optimum Population,* International Institute of Intellectual Cooperation, 1938; Edmund Whittaker, *A History of Economic Ideas,* New York: Longmans, Green, 1940, p. 348 ff; J. J. Spengler, "Population and per capita income," *The Annals,* January 1945, pp. 182–192; M. Gottlieb, "The theory of optimum population for a closed economy," *Journal of Political Economy,* December 1945, 53:289–316; and United Nations, *Determinants and Consequences of Population Trends,* 1953, pp. 21, 233–235.

factor affecting the trend of returns; and in that case, the optimum would have been set at a point just before the onset of lowered returns. However, the political economists quite specifically restricted application of the principle to agriculture or to the more general case of a limited agent of production, rather than applying it to all production; and they did not specify at what population level returns would begin to diminish, although they implied it would be at an early stage of development.

Instead it was the recognition of the opposite tendencies toward diminishing returns and increasing returns that most directly prepared the way for the optimum concept. An increase in returns with the increase of population and labor supply has been shown to be an old article of faith among the population optimists, who from Petty onward pointed out that larger numbers of consumers and workers permit greater division of labor and other efficiencies of production. The possibility of simultaneous upward and downward tendencies of returns within an economy was acknowledged from the first statement of the principle of diminishing returns; and the political economists went on to consider the relative strength and mode of operation of the opposed tendencies.

For example, West in his original statement of diminishing returns dealt with the opposite influences on returns and distinguished between their operation in manufacturing and agriculture:

> The division of labour and application of machinery render labour more and more productive in manufactures, in the progress of improvement; the same causes *tend* also to make labour more and more productive in agriculture in the progress of improvement. But another cause, namely, the necessity of having recourse to land inferior to that already in tillage, or of cultivating the same land more expensively, *tends* to make labour in agriculture less productive in the progress of improvement. And the latter cause more than counteracts the effects of machinery and the division of labour in agriculture. . . .[3]

Torrens, in the essay on the corn trade in which he stated the tendency toward diminishing returns in agriculture, noted the opposite price trends of "raw produce" and "wrought goods," and attributed the latter's behavior to "more accurate division of employment, and to the use of improved machinery." Ricardo, who linked prices to labor productivity, pointed out the same divergence of price trends and gave the same explanation except for the added factors of increasing skill in production.[4] McCulloch and others described the contrary tendencies toward increasing returns in manufacturing and decreasing returns in agriculture.

John Stuart Mill's treatment of the contrary tendencies and of the in-

[3] Edward West, *Application of Capital To Land*, pp. 23–24 (p. 25 of 1st ed.).
[4] Ricardo, *Principles*, Sraffa edition, pp. 93–94.

fluence on them of the population factor serves as a summary of classical economic opinion up to his time.[5] Approaching the subject most directly in his discussion of costs of production, Mill dealt with the variable factors capital, population, and advances in production methods. Costs of production are reduced (or conversely, returns are increased), he explained, by improvements in methods in both agriculture and manufacturing, and in the latter also by the greater efficiency of a larger scale of operation.[6] There is an opposite tendency for food and materials to rise in cost. The net change resulting from these opposite tendencies therefore depends in agriculture upon the relative rate of improvement and of diminishing returns, and in manufacturing upon the balance between changes in material costs and efficiency of production.

In Mill's analysis the population variable actively affects the trend of costs or returns. In agriculture the growth of population and production, which he regarded as inevitable, leads to diminishing returns and rising costs. As he wrote, "The cost of production of the fruits of the earth increases, *ceteris paribus,* with every increase of demand."[7] And whether the upward tendency is counterbalanced depends, Mill wrote, "on the conflict of the two antagonistic agencies, increase of population, and improvement in agricultural skill."[8] Noting temporary or local exceptions, he was nevertheless pessimistic about the ability of improvement to keep up with population, and asserted that "Population almost everywhere treads close on the heels of agricultural improvement, and effaces its effects as fast as they are produced."[9]

The trend of population was also believed to affect costs and returns in manufacturing. In Mill's explanation, the effect of population growth is to increase the cost of raw materials used in manufacturing but at the same time to permit the economies of large-scale production. It was his judgment that "the crude material generally forms so small a portion of the total cost" that it cannot counterbalance the efficiencies of greater production. In this connection Mill did not suggest population growth and expanding demand may stimulate advances in production methods and especially in the division of labor, but he may have believed that such effects were confined to a relatively early stage of development.[10]

[5] See especially Mill's *Principles,* Book IV, Ch. 2.

[6] According to Mill, "The larger the scale on which manufacturing operations are carried on, the more cheaply they can in general be performed" (*ibid.,* 5th ed., p. 281); but he added the qualification that this is probably and usually but not necessarily true.

[7] *Ibid.,* p. 281.

[8] *Ibid.,* p. 282.

[9] *Ibid.,* Book IV, Ch. 3, p. 304.

[10] Elsewhere Mill wrote that "The density of population necessary to enable mankind to obtain, in the greatest degree, all the advantages both of co-operation and

At this point the theoretical foundations for an optimum population concept were all or nearly all assembled: the tendency toward diminishing returns in some parts of the economy, the simultaneous influences toward increasing returns, and population change as one of several factors affecting the trend of returns. All that remained was to single out population as the active variable, consider how the separate movements towards increasing and diminishing returns might be related to the growth of population and demand in an economy, and designate as optimum the population size corresponding to the hypothetical maximum of returns.

This train of thought did not suggest itself to Mill, and it did not appear until afterwards. For one thing, Mill and his fellow economists were with few exceptions fully convinced of the overwhelming strength and inevitability of the trend toward diminishing returns. They regarded population growth as the dominant force pressing down returns, and attributed to it little influence in the advancement of production methods. The representatives of the opposite opinion, that population growth is a force for progress, were largely outside classical economics,[11] so that the two bodies of thought, one linking population growth with diminishing returns, the other linking it with increasing returns, were not in close contact. For their part, also, the economists were realistic enough to look on population change as only one of several factors affecting productivity, and they may have considered it unrealistic to deal with population change independent of other changes in the economy.[12] Although used on occasion by Mill, static analysis was not yet the developed instrument of economic theorists that it later became.

What have been called the general theories of population, the noneconomic and more intuitive or speculative theories reviewed in the two preceding chapters, cannot be dismissed altogether, but they made little recognizable contribution to the optimum concept that eventually emerged. With few exceptions, the authors of these theories were convinced that per capita production is advanced by an increase in the number of people, and this conviction did not lead naturally to the concept of an optimum beyond which further increase of the number of people is undesirable. Several of the writers of this group did acknowledge that there must be such a point, but for them this point was indefinitely remote, too remote to be a matter of more than theoretical concern; and there was confidence that the

---

of social intercourse, has, in all the most populous countries, been attained" (*ibid.*, Book IV, Ch. 6, p. 339). Here he went on to express the opinion that the earth would be a much less pleasant place to live if it were more crowded.

[11] See Chapters 11 and 12.

[12] As seen above, population was not treated as an altogether independent variable by the political economists, for some considered its increase dependent on the growth of capital and others linked it to the supply of the means of subsistence.

hand of Providence, the advance of civilization, or some other agency will bring a halt to man's multiplication before it goes too far.[13]

2 · An Early Formulation of the Optimum Concept

A further step in the direction of the optimum concept was the introduction of the term "underpopulation." The idea itself cannot have been new,[14] but the term achieved recognition when it was used by the eminent German economist, Wilhelm Roscher, by at least the thirteenth edition (1877) of his *System der Volkswirtschaft* (first edition, 1854). Here the first use of the term was credited to Gerstner, whose *Grundlehren der Staatsverwaltung* appeared in 1864. Concerning the two extremes of underpopulation and overpopulation, Roscher wrote that " 'Underpopulated' countries, which might easily support a large number of human beings, and which, notwithstanding, have, for a long period of time had only a few inhabitants, are on this account abodes of poverty. . . ." And,

> Overpopulation . . . exists whenever the disproportion between the population and the means of subsistence operates in such a way that the average portion of the latter which falls to the share of each is oppressively small, whether the effect produced thereby manifests itself in a surprisingly large mortality, or in the limitation of marriages and of the procreation of children carried to the point of hardship.[15]

The section that followed, on "The Ideal of Population," was not the statement of a population optimum that the title suggests, but rather was a review of the population thought of earlier times. But once the concepts of overpopulation and underpopulation were brought together, an optimum size lying somewhere between the two extremes became a logical necessity.

Apparently unknown to Roscher, a German writer had used the terms "overpopulation" and "underpopulation" a number of years earlier, and moreover had taken the logical step of assuming an intermediate optimum level of population. This was Karl Winkelblech (1810–1865), professor of chemistry at Kassel and socialist writer on economics, whose *Untersuchungen über die Organisation der Arbeit* (1850–1859) was published

---

[13] See, for example, the population theories of Jarrold, Hazlitt, Ingram, Gray, Sumner, Carey, and Bastiat, among many others. Such theories may have suggested the supplement sometimes attached to the optimum concept, that numbers tend to stabilize at the optimum.

[14] As early as 1823 or 1824, Pölitz wrote that a population either too large or too small relative to the productive power of an area is undesirable; and he added elsewhere, in words that suggest the optimum concept, "A population corresponding to the area and the activity of the people is necessary for the establishment, maintenance, and increase of the wellbeing of a people" (Karl Pölitz, *Die Staatswissenschaft im Lichte unsrer Zeit*, 5 vol., Leipzig: Hinrichs, 1823–1824, Vol. II, pp. 84, 121.

[15] Roscher, *Principles*, 1882 edition, Book I, Ch. 3, section 253, pp. 339, 340.

under the pseudonym Karl Marlo.[16] The second volume of the *Untersuchungen* (1857) included a chapter on population theory and policy. Here Winkelblech recognized three classes of nations with respect to population size.

First, there are the underpopulated nations, defined as those whose economic condition (*ökonomische Lage*) would be improved by an increase in number of people. It is explained that underpopulation hinders the development of large-scale, efficient production, leads to the production of some commodities with wasteful use of labor, causes inefficiencies because of the wider dispersion of customers, gives fewer social contacts, and does not provide enough competition to spur men to greater effort.[17]

Second, there are overpopulated nations, whose economic situation would be improved by a reduced number of people. Among the disadvantages of overpopulation are the limited consumption of products whose supply is difficult to increase, wasteful use of labor in production of the most important commodities,[18] possible undernourishment of the workers, and incomplete utilization of the labor supply.[19]

Last, there are nations with normal population (*normale Bevölkerung*), whose economic situation would be worsened by either increase or decrease of the number of people.[20] And what is especially noteworthy, Winkelblech was not thinking here in general terms of neither too many nor too few people, but had a quite specific concept of the "normal" population. Previously he had included among the disadvantages of both underpopulation and overpopulation the wasteful or inefficient expenditure of labor in production. Now, in describing the maximum of economic benefit to be derived from a normal population, he explained that "The economic situation of a people is at its most favorable if it is able to secure the greatest possible product through the least expenditure of labor.[21] What is described here is clearly a productivity maximum, and Winkelblech's normal population was of a size favorable to the greatest possible productivity. In all but name, this was the productivity optimum concept generally attributed to later writers.[22]

---

[16] Karl Marlo (Karl G. Winkelblech), *Untersuchungen über die Organisation der Arbeit, oder System der Weltökonomie*, 3 vol. in 4, Kassel: Appel, 1850–1859. The final volume stops in the middle of a sentence. A second edition, called revised but not changed significantly, except for the addition of a last chapter, appeared in 1884–1886. There are a number of references to Marlo in Roscher's *System,* but no mention of his concepts of underpopulation and optimum size.

[17] Winkelblech, *op. cit.,* Vol. II (1857), Ch. 8, pp. 377–379.

[18] This may be a reference to diminishing returns, but the term was not used.

[19] *Ibid.,* pp. 379–382.

[20] *Ibid.,* pp. 382–387.

[21] *Ibid.,* p. 382.

[22] Winkelblech appears to have been overlooked in accounts of the development of the optimum concept, and, as his biographer in the *Handwörterbuch der Staatswissenschaften* wrote, his contemporaries gave little attention to his work.

More light is shed on Winkelblech's concept of normal population size and its economic significance by comments elsewhere in the same chapter of the *Untersuchungen*. Acknowledging that a precise ratio cannot be set, he estimated that the normal or ideal population of a nation may be only half or less than half as great as the number that could be maintained at the subsistence level.[23] Exploring the possible relations of population size and economic well-being in some detail, he states in part that population growth can be a cause of greater well-being only in an underpopulated nation, and that it has the opposite economic effect if the nation has a normal or too great population. In the latter cases, however, an increase of numbers may be to the advantage of the landowning classes, and this may have led to the mistaken notion that population growth is beneficial.[24] Finally, with a rather Malthusian turn of thought, he asserts that the people of an overpopulated nation have little means of raising production through improvement of the productive machinery of their society, and therefore must impose a severe restraint on their fertility and reduce their numbers if they are to improve their condition.[25]

3 · Later Development of the Concept

The concept of an optimum size of population for productivity developed later in English political economy, as far as has been discovered uninfluenced by the earlier German work.[26] Sidgwick's *Principles of Political Economy* (1883) assembled the various elements of thought to focus on the trend of productivity as population increases. There, as previously quoted,[27] it was stated that beyond a certain density of population the productiveness of labor in agriculture and extractive industry decreases, the critical density varying with "the development of the industrial arts, and the accumulation of capital," and that at lower densities in agriculture and mining and at all densities in other industries, productiveness increases with population growth.[28]

Sidgwick further distinguished between the population level at which

[23] *Ibid.*, p. 385.
[24] *Ibid.*, p. 390.
[25] *Ibid.*, pp. 393–394.
[26] The development of an idea is difficult to trace; and in the present instance the evidence is only negative. Of the two English economists who contributed most to the development of the new concept, Sidgwick mentioned the German Socialists as a group, but in the chapter of the *Principles* containing the germ of the optimum population concept did not refer to Marlo-Winkelblech, nor was that author referred to in Cannan's *Theories of Production and Distribution, Elementary Political Economy*, or *Wealth*. A modern German writer on population theory refers to the concept as "the Anglo-Saxon optimum theory," saying that it originated with John Stuart Mill and was developed by Cannan.
[27] See Chapter 8, section 7, above.
[28] Sidgwick did add the qualification that sanitary considerations may put a limit to the density beyond which further growth brings increased productiveness.

returns began to diminish in agriculture and mining, and the level at which
returns begin to diminish on the average for all labor:

> . . . the Law of Diminishing Returns may be used both in a narrower
> and in a wider signification; and there is some danger of confounding the
> two. It may either mean (1) that the productiveness of agricultural and
> extractive labour tends, *ceteris paribus,* to diminish with every increase of
> population, even though capital increases proportionally; or (2) that,
> notwithstanding increased returns from the labour employed in manu-
> factures and internal trade, the productiveness of labour generally tends
> so to diminish. The degree of density at which the former tendency
> would begin to operate is of course lower than that which would introduce
> the latter.[29]

Sidgwick might have gone one step further, to point out that the degree
of density just before the onset of diminishing returns in the latter, more
general sense would be the point of maximum productivity, at what was
later to be called the optimum population. But without naming it he had
almost fully developed the concept of a productivity optimum population.[30]

Edwin Cannan went further in this direction and gave an explicit statement of the productivity optimum of population. His *Elementary Political
Economy* (1888), published five years after Sidwick's *Principles,* contained
a section[31] that described the extremes of overpopulation and underpopulation and asserted that there is an intermediate population size that permits a
maximum of productiveness. As explained in Cannan's careful style:

> Under certain circumstances the productiveness of industry in a coun-
> try or countries may be affected by an increase or decrease of the popula-
> tion of the country or countries in question. It is not true that an increase
> of population must always diminish the productiveness of industry, or
> that a decrease of population must always diminish it. The truth is that
> the productiveness of industry is sometimes promoted by an increase of
> population, and, sometimes by a decrease of population.
>
> The only real "Law of Population" is simply this: — At any given time
> the amount of labour which can be exerted on a given extent of land,
> consistently with the attainment of the greatest productiveness of industry

[29] Sidgwick, *op. cit.,* Book I, Ch. 6, p. 151. This is followed by the statement that
"Still the law, even in its wider signification, would seem to be applicable to the
present condition of England and of the European countries most advanced in
civilization. There can be little doubt that in these the growth of population has
passed the point at which the average efficiency of labour begins to be decreased by
any addition to its quantity, other things being the same. . . ."

[30] See Robbins for an appreciation of Sidgwick's contribution to the development
of the optimum concept. Although writing of Cannan as the real author of the
concept, Robbins acknowledges that "with a little judicious editing, a strong case
could be made out for the claim of Sidgwick to be the real parent of the modern
theory" (Robbins, p. 113).

[31] Edwin Cannan, *Elementary Political Economy,* Part I, section 7, pp. 21–25.
The edition used here is the third, published in 1903.

possible at that time, is definite. Assuming (what within short periods is almost exactly true) that the total amount of labour exerted on a given territory increases and diminishes according as the population of that territory increases or diminishes, we may word the law thus: — At any given time the population which can exist on a given extent of land, consistent with the attainment of the greatest productiveness of industry possible at that time, is definite. No one, probably, will deny that there might be too few people inhabiting a territory to allow of the attainment of the greatest productiveness of industry possible at the time. An increase of population is often one of the most essential requisites for increasing the productiveness of industry. A large population is necessary for the proper division of employments and for carrying out great works. Without a large population it is impossible to have such things as railways, large ships, and mills, to say nothing of art and literature. Hitherto in the world's history it is probable that increase of population has generally, if not almost always, increased, or rather assisted to increase, the productiveness of industry: that is to say, if the population had not increased, it would have been too small to allow of the attainment of the greatest productiveness of industry possible at the time — there would have been "under-population."[32]

Overpopulation, Cannan continued, exists where there are "too many inhabitants on a given area to allow of the attainment of the greatest productiveness of industry possible at the time." But, he added cautiously, it is not possible to prove the existence of overpopulation or under-population in a given case, nor would a decrease of numbers in an over-populated nation guarantee an improvement in productivity because "a mere reduction of population does not necessarily involve a diminution in the number of incompetent workers compared with the number of competent workers."

Cannan's next and principal work, *A History of the Theories of Production and Distribution in English Political Economy* (1894), dealt only with the period from Adam Smith's *Wealth of Nations* to John Stuart Mill's *Principles of Political Economy,* but the second edition in 1903 was supplemented by brief comment on developments since 1848. Here it was said to be generally recognized in the doctrine of population that there is a point of "maximum productiveness" at which the trend of returns changes from increase to decrease, and that the point is continually shifted by improvements, "generally in the direction of increasing the population which is consistent with the maximum productiveness possible at the time."[33]

[32] *Ibid.,* Part I, section 7, pp. 21–23.
[33] Cannan, *Theories of Production and Distribution,* 2nd ed., p. 397. Robbins comments on this passage that the existence of a point of maximum productiveness was less generally recognized than Cannan assumed.

In a later work, Cannan dealt most fully with what he now called the point of maximum return to all industries taken together.[34] Here he stated emphatically that Turgot's law of diminishing returns is "just as true of manufactures as of agriculture," and explained more fully:

> At any given time, or, which comes to the same thing, knowledge and circumstances remaining the same, there is what may be called a point of maximum return, when the amount of labour is such that both an increase and a decrease in it would diminish proportionate returns. It is a crude and barbarous idea of agriculture which represents it as almost entirely dependent upon original fertility of soil and footpounds of human muscular energy. . . The most we can say in contrasting agriculture and manufacture is that the advantages of producing a large aggregate quantity and therefore the advantages of a large population to produce and consume the large quantity are more obvious in manufacture than in agriculture. If we measure returns from the starting point of *nil* suggested by the historical progress of population and assumed by Malthus, West, and Ricardo in 1814, we can say that in both agriculture and manufacture returns increase up to a certain point, and beyond that point they decrease. If we can start from what I have called the point of maximum return, we can say of manufacture as well as of agriculture that returns diminish as we move in either direction from that point.[35]

This could be interpreted to refer only to a decrease of returns with change in labor supply, not change in population, but the next paragraph continued:

> If we suppose all difficulties about the measurement of the returns to all industries taken together to be somehow overcome, we can see that at any given time, or knowledge and circumstances remaining the same, just as there is a point of maximum return in each industry, so there must be in all industries taken together. If population is not large enough to bring all industry up to this point, returns will be less than they might be, and the remedy is increase of population; if, on the other hand, population is so great that the point has been passed, returns are again less than they might be, and the remedy is decrease of population.[36]

The rate of return, in other words, was definitely linked with population.

The term "optimum" was not used by Cannan until the third edition, which contained a section entitled "The optimum or best possible population."[37] Here with characteristic care he warned against possible misinterpretations or misapplications of the concept. The optimum population size, he explained, is not fixed but continually subject to change; the actual population can only slowly adjust itself to such change, and the

---

[34] Cannan, *Wealth,* London, 1914, Ch. IV, sec. 7, pp. 67–71.
[35] *Ibid.,* pp. 68–69 (3rd ed., pp. 57–58).
[36] *Ibid.,* p. 69 (3rd ed., p. 58).
[37] *Ibid.,* 3rd ed. (1928), Ch. 3, section 8.

concept itself is more readily applicable to a closed economy than to one affected by international exchange of men and goods.

4 · The Place of the Concept

Although the optimum concept rounded out an important segment of economic theory regarding population, it was not immediately accepted by Cannan's contemporaries. It is worth noting, for example, that Alfred Marshall, the leading English economist at the time, who devoted several chapters to population in his *Principles of Economics* (1890), dealt in detail with the opposite tendencies, increasing and decreasing returns, and suggested that if they balance there is in fact a "law of constant returns."[38] But although a number of later editions of the *Principles* appeared during his lifetime he did not include the optimum population concept under that or any other name.[39]

Another early exponent of the optimum population concept was the contemporary Swedish economist, Knut Wicksell (1851–1926), whose strong interest in the neo-Malthusian movement may have turned his thoughts in that direction. He is credited by Robbins with developing the the concept independent of Cannan, as far as is known, and with being the first to use the term "optimum population."[40] Wicksell's *Föreläsningar,*[41] (1901), designed as a university text in economics, began with a chapter on population that included sections on age and sex composition, fertility, mortality, and other demographic topics,[42] then discussed the Malthusian question,[43] and ended the chapter with a brief treatment of two population problems. One problem concerned national policy on the control of numbers; the other was stated as follows:

[38] Alfred Marshall, *Principles of Economics,* 2nd ed., 1891, Book IV, Ch. 13, section 2, p. 376; 8th ed., 1920, p. 318.

[39] The last edition of the *Principles* is the 8th (1920).

[40] Robbins, "The Optimum Theory of Population," footnote, p. 118. Actually Wicksell wrote of the optimum in the 1901 Swedish edition of his work on political economy rather than introducing the term in the 1913 German translation cited by Robbins.

[41] Knut Wicksell, *Föreläsningar i Nationalekonomi* (Lectures in Political Economy), Part I, Lund, 1901.

[42] Unfortunately this chapter was not included in the English edition of Wicksell's work, *Lectures in Political Economy,* translated from the third Swedish edition by E. Classen, London: Routledge and Kegan Paul, 1934.

[43] Wicksell's convictions were strongly Malthusian, or perhaps more strictly, neo-Malthusian. He concluded his treatment of Malthus by noting that the nineteenth century's experience of accelerated population growth with rising well-being in Europe might appear to be a conclusive rebuttal but did not in sober judgment weaken either the theoretical truth nor the practical value of the Malthusian theory; and he quoted with approval from the third edition of Adolf Wagner's *Grundlegung* that " 'Robert Malthus behält somit in allem wesentlichen Recht' " (Wicksell, *Föreläsningar,* pp. 47–48).

Under given conditions what population density is most advantageous to a nation? Is the actual population under the given conditions too large, the right amount, or too small; and on what criteria is the answer to be determined?[44]

In discussing the latter problem Wickell pointed out that the essential question concerns the optimum rather than the maximum size of population. To clarify the matter further he distinguished between several kinds of overpopulation. First, there is absolute overpopulation, defined as population in excess of what can be supported with the full use of all resources, which is unattainable. Second, there is relative overpopulation, when numbers are too great in relation to the actual supply of the means of subsistence; and this can occur only under exceptional circumstances, such as crop failure. Last, Wicksell recognized a third possibility of economic overpopulation, which he defined as

. . . overpopulation in social or economic sense, or in other words, the condition when the population is *larger than desirable,* such that a decrease would raise the general wellbeing and especially the condition of the worst situated classes.[45]

Here Wicksell referred to the example of Ireland, then left the subject without defining or explaining further what he meant by the optimum. Although he used the term, it does not appear that he used it in anything more than the most general sense of the population size most favorable to economic welfare, or that he visualized it in Cannan's terms of a point of maximum returns.

The idea of a population of optimum size for greatest returns gradually came to be quite generally accepted, especially through the work of Carr-Saunders. Later developments took the form of further elaboration and qualification of the optimum concept;[46] but hopes of determining in practice the optimal size for an actual population were not fulfilled. The real value of the concept proved to be not empirical but theoretical and conceptual, for within the framework of production theory it consolidated into a consistent body of theory what had previously been discordant views of the relation of population size to per capita production. Under the new conception of the relation between population and production, the uncritical optimism that regarded population growth as always beneficial was no longer tenable, nor was there justification for the equally uncritical pessimism according to which population growth must be harmful. Implicit in the new theory was the lesson that the significance of a given change in population does not depend only upon the direction of the

[44] *Ibid.,* p. 48.
[45] *Ibid.,* Ch. 1, section 8, pp. 49–50.
[46] For accounts of later discussion and critique of the optimum concept, see reference at the beginning of this chapter.

change, but also upon the conditions under which the change occurs, for an increase in numbers, for example, may be beneficial in some circumstances, detrimental in others. Thus the optimum theory, by showing that the optimistic position is justified in certain cases and the pessimistic in others, provided a theoretical resolution of the ancient debate on the relation of population to the welfare of societies.

Using criteria other than maximum productivity, other population optima could have been visualized; but it was the productivity optimum that evolved in the mainstream of theories of the socio-economic significance of population.

14

In Retrospect: Foundations of
Twentieth-Century Population Theory

This account of the history and development of theories about the socio-economic significance of population size and growth, one broad stream of population thought, stops with the optimum concept, or, in point of time, at about the beginning of the present century; and there are several reasons for stopping here. For one, the optimum concept was developed long enough ago to have received the testing of time and criticism, and now can be seen in some perspective. It is always the most recent developments that are most difficult to survey and evaluate. As Cannan wrote in 1903, looking back on the course of economic thought since Mill's *Principles* and deciding that it was too soon to deal with the past half-century in an historical spirit, "It must be left to be the next generation, or the next generation but one, to unravel the thread of progress."[1] Perhaps always applicable to the immediate past, this remark is particularly applicable to the recent course of population thought, which has moved further and further from the relatively simple and tidy system of classical economics.

Another reason for stopping here is that, as described in the chapters above, the optimum population concept was the end product of a long line of development, a theoretical resolution of the long debate that had persisted throughout the history of population thought. However indeterminate the productivity optimum was to prove in practice,[2] in terms of theory it made clear that the relation of population to production varies with the supply of other factors of production and with the stage of economic and demographic development, so that an increase in the number of people may increase productivity under some conditions, decrease productivity under others. Up to the present time, furthermore, it is still the last major contribution to the economic theory of population. It may be that new formulations eventually will come out of modern economic and

[1] Cannan, *Theories of Production and Distribution,* 2nd ed., 1903, p. 395.
[2] Robbins ("The Optimum Theory of Population," p. 124) was quite right in saying that the concept is useful in theory but a delusion to applying in practice.

demographic analysis, but present-day theories of population[3] are, with some modifications and refinements, still very much in the same form and still based on the foundations laid down or strengthened during the nineteenth century. The development of these theoretical foundations having been traced in the preceding chapters, each with its own summary, all that remains is to add a general appraisal of the position that had been reached on the population question by the turn of the century.

1 · The Economic Question of Production

As seen above, the fundamental belief was that continued population growth, other conditions remaining the same, is capable of lowering productivity. Based on the law of diminishing returns, this was one of the firmest beliefs in early classical population economics; and, if it stood the test of time and criticism, it was confirmation for Malthus and an end to the population debate. Its greatest acceptance was attained in the first half of the century, but thereafter the trend of thought was toward a less pessimistic appraisal and less certainty about the relation of population to productivity.

Some early limitations had been attached to the law of diminishing returns and its corollary in population theory. The application of the law had been restricted to agriculture and allied industries, the presence of an opposite trend of returns was recognized in other types of production, and in practice the point of diminishing returns was found to be indeterminate. However, another line of development led more directly to questioning of the influence of population on productivity. That was the realization on closer examination that total and per capita production do not depend on just one or a few but on several factors in the economic system. Under this broader and more realistic conception of the production process, the population variable was reduced from its pre-eminent role to the position of only one among several factors affecting production. It was also apparent that the influence of population on the trend of returns might be overbalanced by change in other variables, such as capital supply or technology.

This conception of the interaction of several factors affecting total and per capita production provided an opportunity for further exploration of the action of the population variable within the economic system. The concept itself can be represented in terms of the several principal factors of production as follows:

$$\text{Per capita production} = f\,(R, L, C, T)/P$$

[3] For an authoritative and conservative summary of present-day views on the socio-economic aspects of population, see the United Nations publication, *Determinants and consequences of population trends* (New York, 1953), especially Ch. 13.

where per capita production is directly a function of the supply of land and other resources (R), the labor supply (L), capital (C), and technology (T), and inversely related to the number of people (P). The population variable was seen to enter the relation directly through its dual role of both consumer and producer, as divisor of the total product and again through the labor supply factor. It was the former role that had been more emphasized by the Malthusians, the latter role that was given more weight by the optimists. Not much attention was given the ratio of workers to total population, the producer-consumer ratio, in the nineteenth-century treatment, for population was generally taken loosely as equivalent to labor supply. True, there was some mention of the quality of the workers in terms of skill or strength as a variable affecting productivity, and a distinction was sometimes made between producers and nonproducers in the total population. But very few of the many who believed in the "iron law" of wages or some modification of it, and who therefore believed that population automatically adjusts its numbers of labor demand and wage level, stopped to reflect that there must be a lag of a number of years before an increased number of births, for example, adds to the labor supply, and that meanwhile the additional births reduce the ratio of producers to consumers, and thus increase the imbalance between labor supply and demand.

The direct influence of the population variable on the producer-consumer or supply-demand balance was difficult enough to estimate, but the problem was further complicated because population might also interact with the capital and technology factors in the productivity equation. These possible interactions, however, were little explored during the nineteenth century. It might have been reasoned under classical production theory that population growth, by leading to diminishing returns, depresses the rate of return on capital and the rate of capital formation. From classical distribution theory, on the other hand, it might have been reasoned that population growth tends to have the opposite effect, capital and labor being presumably rival claimants for a share of the product. Actually, however, distribution theory came to hold instead that capital and labor lose together in relation to the landowner as the rate of returns diminishes; and there was also some tendency in classical economics to regard capital as a prior variable that influences population size and growth, rather than the reverse. The net effect of population change on the return to capital and on capital formation was uncertain, in any event; and on the whole the subject of capital formation did not receive the attention then that it was to attract later.

With regard to the possible influence of population on the progress of technology, there were some conjectures and differences of opinion about the direction of the influence. It was an old article of faith among the optimists that the pressure of numbers on the means of subsistence stimulates technological progress; but the newer economic thought suggested the opposite conclusion that overabundant population, plentiful labor supply, and low wages favor the continued use of outmoded machinery and processes, and that labor shortage and high wages give the most effective stimulus to labor-saving improvements.

Although nineteenth-century population theory recognized the various direct and indirect relations between population and production, it did not attempt on this basis to estimate the net influence of population on productivity. Another and simpler solution suggested itself, to form a judgment of the relative strength of the opposite tendencies toward increasing and diminishing returns at different levels of population size. Opinions differed, of course, and the judgments that were formed depended on the training and temperament of the observers; but for most of the economists in the classical tradition the tendency toward diminishing returns was the stronger and consequently dictated the long-run effect of population growth on productivity.

Another development that still further undermined belief in the relation of population to productivity was a growing doubt whether returns do in fact decrease in the long run. As described elsewhere, from John Stuart Mill's time onward it became more and more apparent that population and productivity were increasing together. This observation encouraged growing optimism that advances in capital and technology may counteract whatever tendency there is to lower returns in the production of food and raw materials, and that returns do not necessarily fall but may even increase as a nation advances in population and economic development. Since the theory of population and productivity was based on the law of returns, the revised opinion on the latter naturally led to changed views on the role of population. In Marshall's work, for example, in the last decade of the nineteenth century, little mention was made of population in the discussion of production.

It is well to note that the nineteenth century did not end with a complete denial of the influence of population on productivity. Most of the political economists recognized that population may have such an influence per se, but that others, stronger influences may act in the opposite direction under ordinary circumstances. In the extreme case of excessive population, it is true, returns might be depressed; but in the generally prosperous and optimistic climate of the latter part of the century, this effect appeared to be an eventuality of a remote and rather hypothetical future or of distant parts of the world, not a present reality.

One further step, described in Chapter 13 above, was the development of a concept of an optimum population size at which per capita production is maximized. It was a disappointment that the optimum size proved impossible to locate empirically, but the new concept made an important theoretical contribution by showing that up to a certain point population growth may be beneficial and beyond that point harmful in its effect on per capita production. It thus resolved the theoretical debate by taking a middle position between the old optimistic and pessimistic views and showing that population growth is intrinsically neither good nor bad but that its consequences depend on the circumstances.

2 · The Economic Question of Distribution

The second range of economic effects that the early nineteenth-century political economists traced was the relation of population to distribution. Classical distribution theory, described in Chapter 9, concerned itself with the division of the total product between the principal agents of production, in the form of wages to labor, rent for land, and profits on capital. Here also, just as in production theory, the population variable presented difficulties for analysis. In the early stage of distribution theory the explanation for the pattern of distribution was most generally in supply and demand terms, according to which, for example, the wage level depends on the relation of labor supply to the demand for labor, and the price of a commodity is the result of the balance between the amount available and the demand for it. In these terms population was not a simple factor to deal with for it could affect both production and consumption. An increase in the number of people, for instance, would add to the demand for commodities but at the same time provide labor for more production; and in the same way both labor supply and demand would be affected. Furthermore, if the population increase had a direct influence on one share, such as wages, it would also have a referred effect by changing the amount available for the other claimants and thus alter the entire pattern of distribution.

Several different paths were therefore open for distribution theory to follow in exploring the effects of population on distribution. If an increase in the number of people was treated as an increase of consumers alone, the indicated consequence would be rising prices for necessities as a result of the increased demand, but with a still stronger rise of prices if the greater population and demand brought on diminishing returns in production. Rising food prices in turn would add to the value and rent of land, and profits and wages would be affected. An opposite trend in prices of manufactured goods might occur at the same time, however, if economies of scale and increasing returns in manufacturing followed the growth of population. If the increased number of people was treated as increased labor supply, on the other hand, a quite different sequence of events could be traced: in the first place, wages would drop, with secondary effects on profits and rent. Each of the two lines of reasoning, however, dealt with only one side of the dual population variable, and the problem was to find a solution that took into account both consumption and production, both labor supply and labor demand.

The nineteenth-century solution to this problem of population and distribution resembled the treatment of the rather similar problem in production theory, in that it by-passed the insoluble theoretical complexities and based final judgment on what were considered the dominant forces or elements affecting distribution. Again the law of diminishing returns weighed heavily, and in distribution theory it had its corollary in the Ricardian rent theory. Also prominent was a supply and demand explanation for the determination of prices, wages, and other elements of distribution; and carried forward from earlier thought was the lingering belief in the "iron law" of wages. Subsequent modifications raised the assumed level of wage stabilization from the "iron law" subsistence level to a labor replacement level, sufficient to enable the worker to support his family and maintain the size of the next generation, and finally to a customary level that provided certain habitual comforts. But whatever the level at which wages were assumed to stabilize, there remained the quite Malthusian assumption that whenever the share available to the wage-earner increases for any reason, there is an automatic and immediate growth of population that prevents wages ever rising far or remaining long above the appointed level.

Other wage theories based on other mechanisms were developed during the nineteenth century, but, as described earlier, all such theories led to the same conclusion, that increase in population and labor supply exerts a downward pressure on wages. As regards the other shares of the product, Ricardian rent theory taught that the effect of continued growth of numbers and progressive diminishing of returns is to transfer a larger and larger share of the total product to the landowner at the expense of both laborer and capitalist. Classical distribution theory thus reenforced and went beyond the pessimistic conclusions of production theory, for it traced in some detail how population growth leads to the progressive worsening of the condition of the great majority of people by raising the price of necessities, forcing down or keeping down wages, and enriching the landowner at the expense of all other classes.

As in the parallel case of production theory, the strength of pessimistic distribution theory reached its maximum in the first half of the century; and the final judgment on the relation of population to distribution became more optimistic in the latter part of the century. As the process of distribution was analyzed in more detail and found to be more and more complex, the population variable was forced to take a more subordinate place in wage theory and in other topics of distribution theory; and as has been seen, this was in keeping with the decreasing emphasis given to population in economics as a whole. Nevertheless, economic opinion in the latter part of the century still held that an increase in the number of people is *in the long run* a threat to the level of living, and that wages cannot long remain above a minimum level unless the general population controls its fertility. But this thinking was rather in terms of a very long run, a much more remote or hypothetical possibility than the very present reality seen by Malthus and Mill.

There remains the question of the soundness of the nineteenth-century analysis of the relation of population to the pattern of distribution, and of the appropriateness of the assumptions upon which the body of distribution theory was based. Once the assumptions were selected, the conclusions followed according to the logic of distribution theory; and in some of the assumptions there lingered the influence of the economic conservatism and the Malthusian pessimism that were current when distribution theory was young. Population and distribution theory was further limited by its apparent inability to deal with both consumer and producer aspects of population at the same time, and so to arrive at a net effect on supply relative to demand. When wage determination was discussed, for example, population growth was treated as growth of labor supply without allowance for its effect on the demand for labor; and conversely, when price determination was considered, it was the demand side of population growth rather than the producer side that received more attention. It is understandable that different aspects of the population variable suggested themselves in different connections, but the result was an incomplete view of the impact of population change on the pattern of distribution.

Other assumptions underlying or built into distribution theory may have limited its applicability. From the "iron law" onward, nineteenth-century distribution theory incorporated the belief that the socio-economic system, like other systems then being discovered in nature, is a self-regulating system that, if not interfered with, returns to its own stable equilibrium. If appropriate at the time it was made, the assumption of an unregulated, laissez-faire economy in which supply and demand and other economic forces operate freely to determine the pattern of distribution is no longer realistic. Also obsolete is the old view that wages are the residual category in distribution, at least above the subsistence level, and that the laborer is the weakest claimant who receives what is left after the landowner and capitalist have taken their portions. For whatever the reasons, nineteenth-century distribution theory relating to population has not retained its influence on modern thought to the same extent as its companion, production theory;[4] and modern theories of wage, rent, and profits determination are

---

[4] For example, the United Nations report, *Determinants and consequences of population trends,* devotes a separate chapter to the consequences of population trends for per capita production, but does not deal with possible consequences for wages, prices, etc.

quite far removed from what now seem the relatively simple formulations of the previous century.[5]

3 · The Habits of the People

The trend of late nineteenth-century thought, as already seen, was to postpone the danger of overpopulation from a present or nearby threat to one that might arise at some indefinite future time if population continued to increase. The obvious next question was whether population would in fact continue to increase to a point of overpopulation, one of the long-standing issues in the population debate and much older than the Malthusian controversy. It was a Malthusian and pre-Malthusian premise of pessimistic doctrine that numbers inevitably continue to grow through their own internal dynamics until stopped by the positive checks of misery and mortality brought on by overpopulation. On the other side, many of the optimists were willing to concede that there is some limit to population size, however remote and theoretical, beyond which further increase is undesirable; but they were confident that increase stops naturally through the operation of preventive checks before overpopulation is reached. Some trusted in the hand of Providence, others in man's own good sense or the operation of various automatic checks; and social philosophers such as Condorcet and Godwin believed that the advance of civilization, of enlightenment, and of man's taste for the comforts of life prevents unwise growth of numbers.

These optimistic beliefs in the effectiveness of preventive checks were for the most part outside the field of political economy, and probably they had little influence on economic thought. In fact, the early nineteenth-century economists tended to react against such "airy" theories and to take a gloomy view of the long-range outlook for population growth and per capita production. Gradually, however, population and economic thought relaxed on this point. If the reasoning of the optimists did not convince their opponents, the well-known inverse relation of fertility or family size to socio-economic status indicated that voluntary controls may be exercised independent of the pressure of necessity, and economic theory itself moved toward a more optimistic appraisal of the population question. In any event, whether from observation or theory, the possibility that a population may voluntarily check its growth short of the subsistence limit came to be more widely accepted by the political economists and population theorists as the nineteenth century progressed. As already described, wage theory moved from the "iron law" assumption that population

[5] It is possible that the earlier theories of distribution retain some relevance, but that the reaction to economic forces takes a different form in a more regulated or differently regulated economy. The law of supply and demand has not been repealed, in spite of attempts to do so; and if prices and wages are not free to fluctuate naturally, the adjustment may take other forms such as unemployment, wider business cycles, and inflation.

tends toward the maximum and wages toward the subsistence minimum to the more hopeful belief that wages and per capita consumption are protected from falling below a customary level[6] by the willingness of the workers to limit their reproduction if their customary mode of living is threatened. The latter conception of the relation between population size and consumption retained the older belief that the per capita share of the means of subsistence can be regulated by population controls, but it added the newer idea that once a given level of consumption has become customary it sets an upper limit on population size at a given volume of production. At this point the relation between population and consumption is reversed, for it is now the level of consumption that regulates population size, not vice versa.[7]

In the diagram the theoretical relation between population and the level of consumption that emerged from the nineteenth-century analysis can be represented as below. Other factors such as capital and technology being

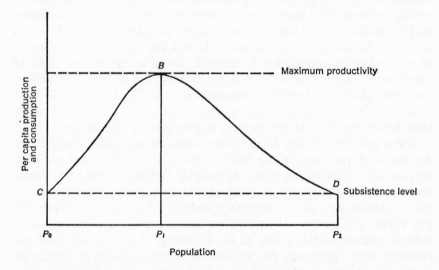

assumed to remain constant, the curve of per capita production and consumption (CBD) rises as population grows from P_0 to P_1, with maximum productivity reached at point B when population is at its productivity optimum, P_1. If population continues to increase, per capita production

---

[6] The idea of a customary level of living capable of affecting reproduction was expressed in various terms by many writers. Adam Ferguson wrote of the habits of living, Paley of habitual superfluities, Ricardo and McCulloch of the taste for comforts and enjoyments, Torrens of the habits of the country, Malthus of the habits of the people, Florez-Estrada of the mode of life, Bastiat of custom or "habitude," Marshall of the standard of comfort, etc.

[7] The two-way relation between population and consumption was of course no new discovery. Steuart in his *Principles* (1767), for example, stated both sides of the relation in emphatic terms, as quoted earlier.

and consumption fall until the subsistence level at point D and the maximum population, P_2, are reached. In these terms, the alternatives faced by a society past its early stage of development are maximum productivity at the optimum size of population, subsistence level of living at the population maximum, or some intermediate level of productivity, consumption, and populousness.

Population theory did not attempt to predict the levels of size and productivity at which a society would stabilize, for these were seen to vary from one society to another. Some writers were hopeful that numbers would tend to stabilize at or near the optimum, while some of the political scientists who discussed the subject, such as John Stuart Mill, were doubtful whether standards of living could in the long run hold firm against the force of reproduction. The population size at which a society stabilizes evidently depends on social rather than on purely economic and demographic factors. A society setting high value on personal consumption presumably would stabilize somewhere near the optimum, while another society, with a strong familistic orientation and a weakly defended standard of living, would tend to grow to maximum size and a subsistence level of living. This conception led ultimately to the conclusion that the population variable is in some respects a dependent variable, influenced by social factors outside a strictly economic context; and in fact, some political economists of the late nineteenth century questioned whether population, so central to early classical economic theory, was properly a concern of economics.

From a later viewpoint, the above line of thought on the relation of population and consumption carries several further implications. One is that there are two polar types of societies in the world and at least two different laws of population, one where effective control of numbers is exercised, the other where numbers are allowed to approach the Malthusian limit. In the former case, which may be called a neo-Malthusian society, population is a dependent variable; and in the latter or Malthusian[8] type of society population is more nearly an independent variable relative to the standard of living.[9]

Another implication to be drawn is that an at least moderately high level of productivity is a necessary condition for a standard of living high enough to motivate effective voluntary control; and that the higher the level of productivity the greater the probability that customary standards will motivate the effective control. A further conclusion to be drawn is that the exercise of effective control may depend quite as much on the pattern of

[8] It is not really fair to use the term Malthusian for the society that does not control its fertility, for the other alternative, voluntary control, is equally Malthusian.
[9] All existing societies presumably contain classes or strata that tend more to one or the other type, and on the average fall somewhere between the two extremes.

distribution as on the level of productivity within a society, for high productivity would not be effective in itself unless the abundant product is distributed widely enough for the majority of the people to attain a sufficiently high level of consumption and living standards.

4 · Final Appraisal

The nineteenth century was the period of greatest advance in population theory, and it arrived at a final judgment on the population question much different from the opinions current at the beginning of the century. Perhaps the principal accomplishment was to advance the treatment of the subject from the level of commonsense or intuitive but isolated theories to a systematic analysis of economic if not social aspects of the problem, that traced the wide-ranging influence of the population variable on per capita production and on the pattern of distribution. But in addition to such changes in the specific economic role ascribed to population, there were equally fundamental changes in the general estimation of the population question; for even though systematic theory in the hands of the political economists concentrated on selected economic aspects of the subject and left other topics to the social philosophers and other writers on population,[10] a much broader and more balanced appraisal arose from the new work. The latter part of the nineteenth century was no doubt a favorable time for such a reappraisal, for the population controversy and its contentiousness had receded, and economic progress in many nations had brought higher productivity and greater prosperity along with rapid population increase. Under these conditions and with the aid of new analytical approaches, the population question could be viewed in better perspective than before. Several interrelated aspects of this revised appraisal of the population question can be noted:

1. There was a considerable deflation of the claims that had been made for population as a socio-economic force. From being cast in the role of a uniquely powerful cause of human misery according to one body of theory, or of human advancement according to another, population came to be assigned a more modest and more plausible role. Out of the developing theory and analysis of the economics of population came a conservative estimate of the demographic influence, a de-emphasis where there had been overemphasis, and the conclusion that population is not the dominant and determining factor but only one of a complex of variables that affect production, distribution, and other human affairs.

2. Another product of the same development in population thought was a fuller recognition of the dimensions and complexities of the population

[10] See Chapters 11 and 12 for a review of non-economic theories of population after Malthus.

question. Much of the earlier theory on the significance of population size stated quite simple, direct relations between the number of people and the supposed effects, for there was a persistent belief that societies are governed by simple natural laws and unitary causes similar to those being discovered in the natural sciences. An anonymous critic of Malthus made the remark, which applied equally well to many another writer on population, that he had been drawn into ". . . the great error of all system-formers; and by confining his attention to one object solely, he has neglected the operation of all the other wheels in the great machine of society."[11] The belief that human phenomena can be explained in terms of simple laws and forces has not yet disappeared completely, but population theory during the nineteenth century advanced toward more analytical and detailed treatment that more adequately recognized the complexity of the subject. One of the most distinguished of Mill's successors was reproached for the "curious obsession that nothing simple can ever be true," but Mill and those who followed him were moving in the right direction when they elaborated population theory in recognition that socio-economic phenomena in general and the influence of the population variable in particular are far from simple.

3. A related effect of fuller recognition of the complex nature of the population problem was a more conditional and qualified statement of the principles of population. Many of the early nineteenth-century theorists and their predecessors had seen population as an absolute and irresistible force whose effects could be clearly predicted. Toward mid-century, when Mill wrote, the related principles of population and diminishing returns were central to the apparently completed theoretical structure of political economy, and the place of population in the structure appeared well established. During the remainder of the century, however, the appraisal of the socio-economic role of population grew more and more cautious and an increasing number of qualifications and limitations were attached to population theory. Population growth was believed capable of affecting per capita production, for example, but it was evident that the actual course of productivity could also be affected by simultaneous changes in the other factors of production, that a given increase in numbers might have different effects at different stages of economic and demographic development, and that the tendency toward diminishing returns was not as inevitable as had been thought.

4. Another by-product of the new development was a resolution of the old theoretical debate, whether the socio-economic consequences of a large and growing population are beneficial or harmful. According to the new optimum theory, the problem does not really exist, for population growth may be desirable under some conditions, undesirable under

---

[11] Anon., *Remarks on a late publication entitled "An Essay on the Principle of Population . . .,"* London, 1803, p. 4.

others. Whereas previous theory had regarded population and its growth as forces having an inherent and constant influence, now it appeared that the significance of population varies with time and place. As was said, "Il dépend de l'homme que l'accroissement de la population amène le progrès ou la misère"[12]: it depends on man himself whether population growth brings progress or misery. The optimum theory was a step toward a fuller appreciation of the population problem but it left unanswered the question of the conditions in which population growth is beneficial and in which it is harmful. From Marshall and others, however, it may be inferred that population growth was regarded as not harmful and perhaps even rather beneficial in a vigorously growing economy enjoying technological progress and a rate of capital formation exceeding the rate of population growth. Conversely, population growth presumably had quite the opposite effects in a stationary or slowly growing economy.

5. A final point to be noted is that inquiry into the influence of non-demographic factors on population raised reasonable doubt whether population is really a primary force or an ultimate variable in social and economic affairs. Early nineteenth-century theorists treated population as an independent variable, a cause of various consequences, good and bad. In the course of time, however, it became increasingly clear that population is not an ultimate cause, but is itself affected in size and trend by many factors in the social and economic environment. In this respect it is a dependent variable, a product of prior influences, a link in rather than the origin of a chain of cause and effect.

The increasingly optimistic appraisal of the population question during the latter part of the nineteenth century reflected the spirit of the times, but in spite of the generally less influential position assigned to the population variable and the belief that growth of the number of people may be desirable under some conditions, late nineteenth-century thought did not altogether dismiss the Malthusian bogey of overpopulation. It is true, some hope was expressed that numbers may tend to stabilize near the optimum

[12] From the title page of Joseph Garnier, *Du principe de population* (Paris, 1857). Of the relatively few present-day writers who have expressed a firm opinion on the subject, the majority have attributed various economic effects to population growth. According to a recent dissenting opinion, however, "I would argue, and not alone on the basis of the data presented, that *there is no effective relationship between population growth and economic development*. Population growth *can* be either a deterrent or a stimulant to economic growth, but it *is* neither consistently. That is, between population growth and economic development there are a number of important intervening variables whose net effect is to produce no consistent relationship between the two variables in question. Between population growth and human productivity there is a vast array of social structures — family, community, firm, market, government, etc. . . . I submit that there are neither logical nor empirical grounds for postulating that all these structures will react in the same direction to changes in population size" (Gayl D. Ness, "Population growth and economic development," *American Sociological Review,* 27:552–553, August 1962).

size, but the majority opinion among the theorists still held population growth to be a threat to productivity and to economic well-being. The difference was that it had become a much more remote and theoretical threat: the timetable had been revised, and the threat was postponed to a somewhat indefinite future. With this revision of terms, a hard core of Malthusian thought persisted to the end of the century and was passed on to the next; and the two alternatives stated by Malthus still appeared inescapable, either control of numbers on a voluntary or involuntary basis or the consequences of overpopulation.

Whether nineteenth-century population thought finally arrived at a well balanced judgment, striking a middle position between Malthusian pessimism and anti-Malthusian optimism, neither exaggerating nor underestimating the influence of the population variable in human affairs, is not a question that can be answered once and for all. As Marshall wrote many years ago and as has been demonstrated again in the comparatively short space of the past several decades, there is an ebb and flow of concern about population; and the late nineteenth-century views would be judged quite differently at a time of alarm over prospective decline than at a time of active fear of overpopulation. But even if what passes for true population doctrine varies from one time to another, it can be seen that, as the nineteenth century progressed, population thought moved away from the extreme views prevalent in the early years toward a more comprehensive and sounder if not necessarily definitive appraisal of the socio-economic significance of population.

The twentieth century, which falls outside the limits of this account, has shown no lack of interest in the subject of population, for revivals of Malthusian fears have alternated with temporary alarms over depopulation. The debate on overpopulation versus underproduction and maldistribution has continued, sometimes personified in terms of Malthus versus Marx. The population factor is still brought into general theories, introduced as a sort of *deus ex machina* to explain a variety of events, for it seems no less self-evident than ever that the numbers of people and their change must be major forces affecting the course of human affairs.[13] At the level of formal theory, however, there has been a turning away from the population question, perhaps because of an understandable feeling of inconclusiveness in the theoretical approach or of inapplicability of the older formulations to the present-day world. With a few exceptions modern economists have left the subject to the new specialists in popula-

---

[13] For example, population change has been linked with such diverse occurrences as the rise and fall of secularization (Josiah Russell, "Late medieval population patterns," *Speculum*, April 1945), the transformation of medieval society in Europe (Henri Pirenne, *Economic and social history of medieval Europe*, circ. p. 68) and the Russian revolution (J. M. Keynes, *The economic consequences of the peace*, pp. 14–15).

tion, the demographers; and the latter, less theoretically inclined than their predecessors, have preferred an empirical and descriptive approach to questions of population. If empirical evidence on the socio-economic significance of population is rather limited and inconclusive as yet, it is nevertheless more in accord with the twentieth-century turn of thought; and a working partnership of tested theory with empirical evidence eventually may permit firmer generalizations about the influence of population than have yet come from either theory or observation alone. In that case, however, not just one but at least two sets of generalizations would be needed, one concerned with the influence of population in the neo-Malthusian setting of high productivity and controlled fertility to which late nineteenth-century theory is most applicable, the second concerned with other parts of the world where the Malthusian dynamics of population may still operate.

Biographical Notes

Abbreviations of source references

•

AB	Dictionary of American Biography
ADB	Allgemeine Deutsche Biographie
App.	Appleton's Cyclopaedia of American Biography
Aubrey	John Aubrey, Brief Lives, University of Michigan Press, 1962
BU	Michaud, Biographie Universelle
Chal.	Alex Chalmers, General Biographical Dictionary
Daire	Eugene Daire, Économistes financièrs du XVIII siècle
DNB	Dictionary of National Biography
EB	Encyclopedia Britannica
MacL	H. D. MacLeod, Dictionary of Political Economy
NBG	Nouvelle Biographie Generale
Pal.	Palgrave, Dictionary of Political Economy
SBL	Svenskt Biografiskt Lexikon
SS	Encyclopedia of the Social Sciences

Achenwall, Gottfried (1719–1772)   ADB

German statistician and university professor. Studied at Jena, Halle, and other German universities. Was appointed privat docent in history, statistics, and law at Marburg, then was called to the chair of philosophy at Göttingen in 1748. Recipient of many academic and official honors, author of works on statistics, history, politics, and law; credited with being the father of statistics in Germany. His *Staatsklugheit nach ihren ersten Grundsätzen* was published at Göttingen, 1761.

Adelung, Johann Christoph (1732–1806)   EB
Principally known as a grammarian and philologist. Educated at University of Halle; from 1787 to the end of his life was librarian of the elector of Saxony, Dresden. The anonymously published *Versuch einer Geschitchte der Cultur des menschlichen Geschlechts* (Leipzig, 1782) is attributed to him.

Alison, Archibald (1792–1867)   DNB
Educated at the University of Edinburgh, after which he studied law and became a member of the bar. Was appointed judge of the small debts and criminal jury courts in Glasgow in 1835, and retained the judgeship until the end of his life; was made a baronet in 1852, and for a time held the academic post of lord rector of Marischal College, Aberdeen; is reported to have been deeply conservative in politics, and to have shown anti-liberal attitudes in his judicial capacity and in his writings. Author of a ten-volume history of Europe (1833–1842), works on law and political economy, the two-volume *Principles of population and their connection with human happiness* (Edinburgh and London, 1840), and lesser writings. The work on population is said to have developed from an anti-Malthusian paper, written as early as 1808 and completed by 1828, although it was not published until twelve years later.

Anderson, James (1739–1808)   DNB
Scottish economist with a particular interest in agriculture. Graduated from Aberdeen in 1780; later was given the L.L.D. degree in recognition of his writings on agriculture. Father of a large family, a practicing farmer as well as a writer on agriculture, editor for several years (1790–1794) of a weekly paper that he founded, friend of Bentham, and author of a number of tracts. He is credited with stating the theory of rent determination later called Ricardian in two tracts, *Observations on the means of exciting a spirit of national industry,* and *An inquiry into the nature of the Corn Laws, with a view to the Corn Bill proposed for Scotland,* both published in 1777.

Arnberg, J. W. (1832–1900)   SBL
Swedish political economist. Graduated from Uppsala, then traveled abroad to study political economy. Was appointed docent in political science in 1856. Active in numerous official and committee positions; had a lifelong interest in questions of economics and national policy; business experience as a bank director. The study of political economy in the Freedom Period was his principal work.

Asp, Pehr Olof von (1745–1808)   SBL
Swedish diplomat and civil servant. Educated at Uppsala; then spent many years in the diplomatic service. Member of many official commissions; minister to Turkey, 1791–1795; then was stationed in England until 1802. Widely traveled; writer on a variety of subjects but with particular interest in economic affairs.

Attwood, Thomas (1783–1856)   DNB, SS
English liberal, writer on currency and other economic topics. Took an active part in politics, supporting various reform · movements including the

Chartist movement. Was elected a member of Parliament for Birmingham in 1832 but withdrew from public life in 1839. Author of several works, including *Observations on currency, population, and pauperism, in two letters to Arthur Young* (London, 1818).

Auxiron, Claude-Francois-Joseph d' (*1728–1778*)   NBG, BU
French engineer and economist. First engaged in a military career, he later resigned his captaincy in the artillery and went to Paris to pursue his interests in engineering and other applied fields. Author of the two-volume work, *Principes de tout gouvernement, ou examen des causes de la faiblesse ou de la splendeur de tout état, considéré en lui même et independamment des moeurs* (Paris, 1766).

Baldwin, Loammi (*1780–1838*)   AB
American civil engineer and writer. Born in North Woburn, Massachusetts, son of the engineer of the same name, who while surveying for the Middlesex Canal discovered the wild apple that was named after him and became for many years the staple of the apple industry. Graduated from Harvard in 1800, studied law and was admitted to the bar in 1804. Practiced law for several years in Cambridge, then turned to civil engineering in 1807 and traveled widely in Europe to extend his knowledge of current engineering practice. Thereafter had a distinguished career as engineer on many projects, including canals, dry docks, dams, and the Bunker Hill Monument. Credited by his biographer with ranking as the father of civil engineering in the United States. Author of several works on engineering in addition to *Thoughts on political economy in connection with the population, industry and paper currency of the United States* (Cambridge, Mass., 1809).
Biog. George L. Vose, *Sketch of the life and works of Loammi Baldwin, civil engineer* (1885).

Barbon, Nicholas (*1640?–1698*)   SS, DNB
English physician and businessman. Born in London, studied medicine at Leyden, received a medical degree at Utrecht in 1661, and became an honorary fellow of the College of Physicians in 1664. Established the first fire insurance office in London after the great fire of 1666, was active in the rebuilding of the city, was a member of Parliament in 1690 and 1695. Author of *A discourse of trade* (1690).
Biog. introductory notes by Jacob H. Hollander, editor of a reprinted edition of the *Discourse* (Baltimore: Johns Hopkins Press, 1905).

Barton, John (*1789–1852*)   Pal.
Born of Quaker parents, but left the Society in 1827 because of doctrinal differences. Author of various economic writings, correspondent of Ricardo, fellow of the Royal Statistical Society. His works show considerable independence of classical economic authority, and perhaps for this reason were not as highly regarded in his day as they now seem to have deserved.
Biog. introductory notes by George Sotiroff, editor of *John Barton, Economic writings* (2 vol., Regina, Saskatchewan, 1962).

Bascom, John (1827–1911)   AB
   American philosopher and educator. Graduated from Williams in 1849.
Studied law but found it not to his taste and turned to theological studies and
philosophy. Taught rhetoric and oratory at Williams from 1852 until he was
appointed president of the University of Wisconsin in 1874. Resigned the
presidency in 1887 after some conflict with the Board of Regents, among other
reasons, it is said, because of his advocacy of prohibition. Returned to Williams
where he first lectured in sociology, then was appointed professor of political
science in 1891. Resigned in 1903 to devote his remaining years to "writing
and public service." Author of works on religion, psychology, and philosophy,
in addition to his major work, *Political economy* (1859).

Bastiat, Frederic (1801–1850)   MacL., SS
   French political economist. Orphaned at an early age, he was trained for
a family business but was attracted to a life of study and writing. After
a period in political office he became a crusader for a free-trade policy in
France, and as a result of his publications was offered the editorship of the
influential *Journal des économistes* in 1845. He refused, preferring a more
quiet life, but after a visit to England in 1845, was increasingly drawn into the
free-trade movement and into politics. Finally persuaded to go to Paris, his
health was undermined by the burden of editorial duties and his political activities. The *Harmonies économiques* (1850) remained incomplete at his death.

Baudreau, Nicholas (1730–1792)
   Not included in the usual biographical sources, and not much is known of
his life. According to Dubois, he was an abbé, calling himself a disciple of
L'âme des hommes. From an early interest in economics, he became one of
the Économistes (Physiocrats) in 1762 or earlier. In 1775 he had founded the
journal, *Éphémerides du citoyen,* and made it a physiocrat organ.
   Biog. introductory notes by Auguste Dubois, editor of the *Collection des
économistes et des reformateurs de la France,* in which was reprinted *Première
introduction à la philosophie économique* (Paris: Geuthner, 1910).

Baudrillart, Henri Joseph Leon (1821–1892)   EB, SS
   French political economist. Little is known of his early life. Professor of
economic history at the University of Paris from 1866 onward, then professor
of political economy at the École des Ponts et Chausées. Published on Turgot
and Bodin as well as two works on political economy.

Becher, Johann Joachim   Pal., ADB
   Birth variously reported 1625 to 1635, death 1682 to 1685. German scientist and political economist. Of Protestant origin, was converted to Catholicism in his youth. Learned in the sciences, he was medical professor and court
physician in Mainz, later moved to Wurzburg, then to Vienna, where he was
active in the Commerz-Collegium, the founding of foreign trading companies,
and other financial activities. Late in life he fled to Holland to avoid his
debtors, then to England in 1680. Principal publications were the *Moral
Discurs* (Frankfurt, 1669) and *Politischer Discurs* (Frankfort, 1667?).

Bell, William (1731–1816) DNB

English clergyman. Graduated from Magdalen College, Cambridge, with distinction in 1753, received M.A. degree in 1756. Also in 1756 he received a Lord Townshend prize for his dissertation on the causes and effects of populousness. His later career was in the church, and his later writings were on religious subjects.

Bellers, John (c. 1654–1725) DNB, SS

English social reformer. A Quaker philanthropist with numerous social concerns, including the education of the poor, hospitals, and the treatment of prisoners. Author of numerous works on humanitarian and religious subjects.

Berch, Anders (1711–1774) SBL

Swedish political economist. Educated at Uppsala. Was appointed to the first Swedish professorship of economics at the age of thirty. Had an active professional career, with many published works. His economics were for the most part in the contemporary mercantilist pattern, with belief in state control of the economy.

Bertrand, Jean (1708–1777) NBG

Swiss agronomist. Studied at Lausanne and Geneva, then in the Netherlands. A member of the clergy, but he also devoted himself to agronomy. Member and secretary of the Société économique of Bern.

Besold, Christopher (1577–1638) ADB, SS

German jurist. Born in Tubingen, received a law degree, then was professor of law at several universities. Was for a time court counsellor in Austria, then moved to a professorship at Ingolstadt, where he remained for the rest of his life. Author of works on a wide variety of subjects, including law, theology, and history.

Bielfeld, Jakob Friedrich von (1717–1770) Pal., ADB

German political scientist and litterateur. Came from a family of Hamburg merchants; traveled and studied abroad. Well regarded by Frederick the Great, he entered the king's service and spent some time in the diplomatic service in London. In 1747 was appointed curator of all Prussian universities, and was raised to the nobility in 1748. He retired to his estates in 1758 to devote himself to literary pursuits.

Blanqui, Jerome Adolph (1798–1854) NBG

French economist. Acquainted with and influenced by Say to become a political economist. In 1833 he succeeded to Say's professorship at the Conservatoire des arts et métiers. Member of the chamber of deputies, 1846–1848. Author of many articles, a history of political economy, and numerous other works on economics.

Blodget, Samuel (1757–1814) AB

American merchant, economist, architect. After service in the Revolutionary War, he entered business in his home state of New Hampshire. Being unsuccessful there, he went to Boston and entered the East India trade, in which he made a fortune; then went to Philadelphia in 1789, where he engaged in insurance and designed the building of the first Bank of the United States, a building of classical design that is still preserved. Had an active interest in real estate development in the new national capital, which brought him to financial ruin and debtor's prison. Besides the *Economica,* he wrote *Thoughts on the increasing wealth and national economy of the U.S.* (1801).

Böcler, Johann Heinrich (1611–1672)   **ADB**
German historian and teacher. Educated at Heilbron and Nuremberg, later at Tubingen and Strassburg. Taught Latin, was appointed "professor of eloquence" at Strassburg at age twenty. In 1648 was brought by Queen Christina of Sweden to be professor of eloquence at Uppsala, and was made historiographer of Sweden the following year, but later retired with pension for reasons of health. Was appointed counsellor by Emperor Ferdinand III; later received an offer from Louis XIV of France, but preferred to remain at the court of Vienna, where he was highly honored. Regarded as one of the most learned men of Germany in his day; proficient in Latin, Greek, and Hebrew, philosophy, history, politics, and law.

Bodin, Jean (c. 1530–1596)   **SS**
French lawyer, political writer. Educated at Toulouse, practiced law in Paris for a time, then turned to literary pursuits. Enjoyed favor of Henri III at first, then fell from favor and had to leave Paris. Deputy to the states-general of Blois in 1576, where he supported the rights of the people against the royal authority. Died of the plague at Laon. Apparently adaptable in religion, he was alleged at one time or another to have been Protestant, Catholic, Jew, deist, and atheist. Author of a number of works on government, law, etc., his fame now rests largely on his *Six livres de la republique.*

Booth, David (1766–1845 or 1846)   **DNB**
English lexicographer and writer. Said to have been almost entirely self-taught, he was for a time in business, then left to become a school master and later settled in London to pursue a literary career. Connected with the Society for the Diffusion of Useful Knowledge, he wrote on a wide variety of subjects. Principal publications include his *Analytical Dictionary of the English Language* (1833), and *Principles of English Composition* (1831) in addition to the *Letter to Malthus* (1823). Godwin, in his *On Population* (1820), acknowledged his indebtedness to Booth. Described by Robert Blakey in his *Memoires* as "not, I believe, five feet high, of very dark visage, eyes very red and watery, and presenting altogether an impish and fiendish look. He was, however, very kind."

Bornitz, Jacob   **ADB, Pal.**
German economist and lawyer. Little is known of his life except that he was born in the late sixteenth century, studied law, was for a time an imperial councillor with considerable influence at court, and probably traveled widely in Europe. He is reported to have suffered considerable personal hardship and loss during the Thirty Years War. Credited with being the first systematic

economist in Germany, comparable to his contemporary Montchrétien in France.

Botero, Giovanni (1540?–1617)   SS, Pal., NBG
Italian statesman and writer on politics and economics. Member of the Jesuit order, he later became secretary to the Cardinals Borromeo, then entered the service of Charles Emanuel I of Savoy, where he held various official positions of high responsibility.

Bowen, Francis (1811–1890)   AB
American philosopher and college professor. Born in Charlestown, Massachusetts, he was educated at Boston, Phillips Exeter and Harvard while working to help support himself. After a few years of teaching and then of travel and study abroad, he became editor of the *North American Review* (1843). In 1851 he was appointed professor of history at Harvard but then denied the position, because of the unpopularity of his views on imperialism and the liberation movement in Hungary. Two years later, however, he became professor of "natural religion, moral philosophy and civil polity" at Harvard, a position he held until his retirement at the age of 74. In addition to works on political economy, he wrote *Modern philosophy, from Descartes to Schopenhauer and Hartmann* (1877).

Browallius, Johan (1707–1755)   SBL
Swedish theologian and educator. Graduated from Uppsala in 1731 and entered the priesthood the same year. After several years of travel, he accepted a professorship at Åbo in Finland (1737), first in physics and then in theology (1741). Member of the Swedish Riksdag 1746–1747, 1751–1752. Became bishop of Åbo in 1749.

Bruckner, John (1726–1804)
Lutheran minister, migrant from Netherlands to England. Little is known of his early life except that he was educated for the ministry at Leyden. Proficient in a number of languages and able to preach in four of them (Latin, Dutch, French, English). Pastor at Leyden, he moved in 1753 to a church in Norwich, England, where he continued to serve to the end of his life, a half-century later.

Brydges, Sir Samuel Egerton (1762–1837)   DNB
English poet, novelist, political economist. Studied law and was admitted to the bar but never practiced, in spite of litigiousness in his later years. Having adequate means, he gave up a professional career at the bar for literary pursuits, in which he received less than the recognition he felt he deserved. Member of Parliament, 1812–1818, where he took a particular interest in the Poor Law; and it is in this period that his economic writings, including *The population and riches of nations* (1819), are concentrated. An expatriate from the end of his term in Parliament.

Buffon, George Louis Le Clere, Comte de (1707–1788)   SS, Chal.
French naturalist. Intended for the law, he turned to science, in which he showed an early aptitude. At the age of 21 he became independently wealthy

through inheritance, and was able to devote his time to literary pursuits and science and to travel. Appointed superintendent of the Jardin du Roi and of the natural history museum in 1739, he became one of the most widely famed scientists of his day. It is related that during the war of 1755–1762 packages from all parts of the world addressed to Buffon on vessels captured by British privateers were duly forwarded to him as a mark of respect. In the eyes of his contemporaries he was not altogether unjustified in the remark attributed to him, that "I know of but five great geniuses — Newton, Bacon, Leibnitz, Montesquieu, and myself."

Burn, John Ilderton (c. 1840)
No information.

Burton, John Hill (1809–1881)   DNB
Scottish historiographer and biographer. Educated at Aberdeen, then studied law, but later was forced to turn to writing to support himself. Successful as biographer of Hume and other Scotsmen, editor of Bentham's works and of the *Scottish Registers,* author of *History of Scotland* and *Treatise on the law of bankruptcy in Scotland,* as well as the *Manual of political and social economy.*

Cairnes, John Elliott (1823–1875)   DNB
English economist. Considered a dull boy by his tutor, he nevertheless succeeded in persuading his father to send him to Trinity College, Dublin, where he received his B.A. in 1848, his M.A. in 1854. Later becoming interested in political economy, he succeeded in securing by competitive examination the professorship of political economy at Dublin (1856–1861). Later held professorships at Queen's College, Galway, and University College, London. Friend of John Stuart Mill, author of numerous works on political economy, and a strong defender of the anti-slavery position of the Northern States during the American Civil War. His last years were spent in declining health, but with growing reputation as a leading economist.

Campanella, Tommaso (1568–1639)   EB, SS
Italian philosopher. From early years was interested in classical studies, member of the Dominican order, imprisoned in 1699 by the civil authorities and the inquisition for his independence of thought. Released in 1626, it is said, through the influence of Pope Urban VIII, who protected and pensioned him. For greater security his last years were spent in a Dominican monastery in Paris, where he enjoyed the favor of Cardinal Richelieu.

Cannan, Edwin (1861–1935)   DNB
English economist. Educated at Oxford, was appointed lecturer in economics at the newly founded London School of Economics in 1895, became professor there in 1907. Member and president of the Royal Economic Society, and recipient of various academic honors. Of his numerous writings, the principal work is the *History of the theories of production and distribution in English political economy from 1776 to 1848* (1894), which displays the capacity for analysis of others' theories for which he was characterized, unfairly it would seem, as "critical rather than constructive."

For more favorable estimates of his contribution to economics, see *London essays in economics: In honour of Edwin Cannan,* a collection of essays by his students.

Cantillon, Richard (? *-1734*)   DNB
English economist. Born in Ireland late in the seventeenth century. Was a merchant in London for a time; then moved to Paris, where he founded a banking house and acquired a large fortune. Later moved to the Netherlands and then to England. Was murdered in London, allegedly by his cook, in 1734. His *Essai sur la nature du commerce en general* (1755) is presented as a translation from the English, but no prior English edition is known.

Cardozo, Jacob Newton (*1786–1873*)   AB, SS
American economist and educator. A businessman in Charleston, S.C., he became interested in writing, assumed the acting editorship of the newspaper *Southern Patriot* in that city in 1817, later became its owner and editor until 1845. He continued in one or another newspaper enterprise, including editorships in Mobile and Atlanta during the Civil War. His *Notes on political economy* (1826) was written to refute Ricardo and McVickar.

Carey, Henry C. (*1739–1879*)   AB
American economist and publisher. Eldest of nine sons of the Philadelphia publisher, Mathew Carey (see below). Without formal schooling, he became widely read while a partner in the family business. In middle life he developed an interest in political economy and came to be a rebel against European economic authority, especially the English, and an ardent protectionist. Probably more widely read abroad than any other American economist of the nineteenth century, and in his own country the leader of an aggressively American school of economic thought. See also footnote, p. 286 above.

Carey, Mathew (*1760–1839*)   AB
Irish-American publisher and writer. Born in Dublin, an avid reader, although with little formal education. Forced to leave Ireland because of writings considered treasonable by the British government, he went to Paris where he became acquainted with Franklin and Lafayette. On return to Dublin in 1783 he published a journal with strongly Irish sentiments, for which he was imprisoned briefly, then fled in disguise to America (1784). With the aid of a loan from Lafayette he established a journal of his own in Philadelphia, then engaged in other publishing ventures. Active thereafter in public affairs in Philadelphia, a founder of the Hibernian Society and supporter of other Irish causes, prolific writer on a variety of subjects. Strongly protectionist in his economic thinking.

Carleson, Carl (*1703–1761*)   SBL
Swedish official and writer. Orphaned at an early age, educated at Uppsala and then in government service. Held many official positions during his career; long service in the Riksdag and as head of parliamentary committees. From 1730 to 1731 published the weekly *Sedo-lärande Mercurius,* in the style of and the greater part of it a translation of the English models by Addison and Steele.

Active in the Swedish Academy of Science (Vetenskapsakademien). Name originally was Carlson, changed when he was raised to nobility.

Carleson, Edvard (1704–1767)   SBL
   Swedish official and diplomat. Younger brother of Carl, also educated at Uppsala. Travel abroad 1726–1730, followed by many official positions and service in the Riksdag. Envoy to Turkey in 1738. Chairman of the Statistical Commission (Tabellcommissionen) in 1756. It is reported that his interest in economics developed while he was in college and that he was instrumental in interesting his fellow student, Anders Berch (see above), in the subject.

Cary, John (d. 1720?)   DNB, SS
   English merchant, author of works on trade. Nothing is known of his early life. Holder of various official positions, active in commercial ventures and public affairs, author of numerous works on business and trade in the 1690's and early 1700's.

Chalmers, George (1742–1825)   DNB
   Scottish antiquary and historian. Educated at Aberdeen, then studied law at Edinburgh. Practiced law for a time in Baltimore but returned to England before the colonies declared their independence. A prolific writer, his first works concerned with the American colonies; later published biographies of Daniel Defoe, Thomas Paine, and others, the three volume *Caledonia,* a history of Scotland, and many other writings.

Chalmers, Thomas (1780–1847)   DNB
   Scottish clergyman and scholar. The sixth in a family of fourteen children, he attended the University of St. Andrews, studied for the ministry, but also found himself attracted to scientific studies. Career as a pastor, but also lecturer in chemistry for a time; developed evangelical convictions in his early 30's, and became deeply concerned with the condition of the laboring class and questions of social reform. Writings on theology, natural science, political economy, and social problems.

Chastelleux, François Jean, Marquis de (1734–1788)   BU, Pal.
   French soldier and writer. A professional soldier with considerable wartime experience who devoted to literature the time not taken by military service. An associate of the leaders in literature and learning, including Buffon. Spent three years in America as one of Rochambeau's officers and became acquainted with Washington. One of the first in France to be inoculated against smallpox, he actively promoted its adoption. Elected to the Académie Française in 1755; author of many works, including accounts of his travels in America, and contributor to the *Encyclopédie.*

Child, Sir Josiah (1630–1699)   DNB, SS
   English businessman, mercantilist writer. A career of rapid success in business, first in Portsmouth where he became mayor. Later life was spent in London, where he rose to be director, then governor, in the East India Company, which he is said to have ruled with absolute authority. Perhaps the leading representative of the rising merchant class of his day, it was reported

with some awe at the time that he had amassed a fortune estimated at £200,000. At various times member of Parliament; received a baronetcy in 1678.

Christiernin, Pehr Niclas (1725–1799) SBL

Swedish educator and clergyman. Educated at Uppsala, studied abroad, was appointed docent in jurisprudence, economics and commerce at his university (1770), then professor of logic and metaphysics (1771), and finally became a member of the clergy (1777). Together with a religious turn of mind, he had a pragmatic preference for observation and experience, and held a life-long interest in economic matters.

Chydenius, Anders (1729–1803) SBL

Swedish clergyman and writer on social problems. Born in Finland, then a Swedish province, of well-to-do and educated parents. Studied at Åbo and Stockholm, entered the church in 1753. Career as pastor and church official, member of the Swedish Riksdag for a number of sessions. His writings were characterized by highly original and incisive opinions on social and economic questions of the day.

Coke, Roger (d. 1696) DNB

English political and economic writer. Born sometime after 1626 of a dis-tinguished family. Educated at Cambridge but did not take a degree. Little is known of his later life except for his writings on trade, but it is reported that he was unsuccessful in business and that his last years were spent in straitened circumstances.

Colton, Calvin (1789–1857) AB

American clergyman, writer, and educator. After graduation from Yale, he attended a theological seminary, then served as missionary and later pastor in western New York. Spent four years in England as correspondent for a New York newspaper, and after his return was active as editor and political writer. After publication of his *Public Economy* he was given the chair of the same name at Trinity College, Hartford, where he remained for the last years of his life (1852–1857).

Condillac, Etienne Bonnot de (1714–1780) SS, BU

French abbé and philosopher. No information on his early life. Abbé of Muraux, preceptor to the young Prince of Parma, a grandson of Louis XV. Elected to the Academy in 1768. Major works: *Traité des sensations* (1754) and *Le commerce et le gouvernement* (1776).

Condorcet, Marie Jean Antoine Nicolas, marquis de (1743–1794) MacL., SS

French mathematician, economist, and philosopher. Brought up by an over-protective mother, he eventually entered the College de Navarre in Paris, where he took up the study of mathematics and showed great aptitude. Under the guardianship of the Duc de Rochefoucauld he was introduced to the highest circles in Paris. Achieving recognition for his mathematical ability, he was offered membership in the Academy of Sciences in 1764, refused at first be-cause of family opposition, but later accepted it in 1769. Friend of Turgot, member of the Legislative Assembly in 1791, and its president in 1792. Stayed in hiding after the fall of the Girondins but was discovered and arrested; and he took his own life in prison.

Conring, Hermann (1606–1681)   Pal.
German physician and scholar. Studied philosophy and medicine at Helmstadt, was professor there for some years, then court physician to Queen Christina of Sweden. Later served the Duke of Brunswick and Louis XIV of France, the latter of whom gave him a pension. Numerous publications on law, politics, and political economy.

Cooper, Thomas (1759–1839)   AB
English-American scientist, political propagandist, and teacher. Studied at Oxford without receiving a degree. Was attracted to the study of medicine, but studied law instead at the insistence of his father. Varied activities in the practice of law, science, and philosophy; active also in various unpopular political causes, following which he went to America with his friend Joseph Priestley in 1794. Settled in Pennsylvania and became active there in politics and political controversy. A friend of Jefferson, he finally became disillusioned with democracy in practice, and devoted the remainder of his life to science and teaching. Professor of chemistry at Carlisle (now Dickinson) College until 1815, then occupied the same position at the University of Pennsylvania. Later professor and then president at South Carolina College.

Coxe, Tench (1755–1824)   AB
American businessman, economic writer. Educated at the College of Philadelphia (now the University of Pennsylvania) but is not known to have received a degree. Studied law, then entered his father's countinghouse. According to some accounts had royalist sympathies at the time of the American Revolution, but was a delegate at the Annapolis Convention of 1786 and at the Continental Congress in 1788. Regarded as a predecessor of Henry Carey in the Americanism of his economic views.

Cunningham, J. (fl. 1770)
No information.

Dahlbom, Herman (fl. 1761)
No information.

Darjes, Joachim (1714–1791)   NBG
German philosopher. Born in Mecklenburg, studied philosophy and theology, then jurisprudence. A famous professor of philosophy at Jena, later on the faculty at Frankfort. Writings in political economy as well as in law and philosophy.

Davenant, Charles (1656–1714)   DNB
English mercantilist writer. Studied at Oxford without obtaining a degree, but later received the L.L.D. degree through "favour and money." Member of Parliament, holder of various official positions, including that of inspector-

general of the exports and imports. Author of numerous political tracts in addition to his major works on trade and national policy.

Dawson, William (fl. 1814)
No information.

De Bow, James Dunwoody Brownson (1820–1867) AB
American editor and statistician. Orphaned at an early age, but by hard work and economy succeeded in getting a college education. Unsuccessful in law, he turned to journalism, became contributor and editor of the *Southern Quarterly Review* in Charlestown, S.C., then moved to New Orleans and engaged in journalistic projects. Professor of political economy for a time at the University of Louisiana, head of the state Bureau of Statistics. Appointed superintendent of the federal census of 1850. Thereafter published *De Bow's Review,* an influential, ardently southern and pro-slavery journal.

Decker, Sir Matthew (1679–1749) DNB
English merchant and writer on trade. Born in Amsterdam of a family that later fled as refugees to London. Became a prosperous merchant, then director and for a time governor of the East India Company. Member of Parliament, sheriff of Surrey, made a baronet by George I. Wrote on trade and tax policy.

Defoe, Daniel (1661?–1731) DNB
English writer. Member of a dissenting sect, prepared for the ministry but turned to a business career in London. Writer on political questions and a supporter of King William, after whose death he was fined and imprisoned for publication of his dissenting views. Imprisoned again for debt following losses in business, released in 1704, thereafter was actively engaged in writing and involved in controversies. Principal writings on religious subjects, political tracts, some verse, social and economic works, and fiction (Robinson Crusoe, 1719; Moll Flanders, 1722; Journal of a Plague Year, 1722).

De Quincey, Thomas (1785–1859) DNB
English author, political economist. Younger son of a family of some distinction, experienced a disturbed childhood but showed marked scholarly promise in spite of interruptions in his education. Studied for a time at Oxford; admirer and later friend of Coleridge. Had a continuing addiction to opium as described in his *Confessions,* with alternating periods of greater addiction and of literary productivity. A reading of Ricardo's *Principles* in 1819 gave him the ambition to undertake a work in political economy, but because of various obstacles it was not until 1844 that he completed and published *The Logic of Political Economy.* He is said to have been quite incapable of managing his own finances, and to have shown increasing eccentricity in his later years.

Derham, William (1657–1735) DNB
English clergyman. Entered the church after graduation from Oxford, progressing from chaplain to deacon and then to priest in 1682. Interested in science, especially natural history and mechanics; elected fellow of the Royal Society in 1702, he contributed a number of papers to its *Transactions.* Chap-

lain to the Prince of Wales during the reign of George I, and canon of Windsor. His *Physico-Theology, or a demonstration of the being and attributes of God from His works of creation* had gone through twelve editions by 1754. Author of religious works and others on natural history.

Destutt de Tracy, Count Antoine Louis (1754–1836) BU, EB

French soldier, philosopher. Of a noble French family of Scottish origin, he followed the military career of his father after study at Strassbourg. During the Revolution he supported the revolutionary cause and was a commander of cavalry, but came under suspicion during the Terror, was imprisoned, and escaped execution only by the timely death of Robespierre. Thereafter he devoted himself to philosophy and literature. Elected to the Academie in 1808.

Dillon, William (fl. 1882)

No information.

Doubleday, Thomas (1790–1870) DNB

English author, reformer, political economist. Entered the family business but took little interest in it, devoting himself to politics and reform movements. His literary production included plays, poems, and songs; and was author of numerous tracts. Some time after publication of his *True law of population,* late in his life, he was registrar of births, marriages, and deaths.

Droz, Francois Xavier Joseph (1771 or 1773–1850) BU, EB

French philosopher, historian, political economist. Received a good education and especially pursued the study of philosophy until interrupted by the Revolution. Engaged in a period of active military service but continued his scholarly interests, and after the Restoration devoted himself to a literary career. Contributor to various journals, elected to the Academie in 1824, author of a three-volume history of the reign of Louis XVI and of works on philsophy, political economy, and, late in life, religion.

Du Buat-Nançay, Count Louis-Gabriel (1752–1787) BU

French historian. Of noble family in poor circumstances. Received a good education, after which he was employed in several minor diplomatic posts abroad. Experiencing some frustrations, he left public service for a life of study and writing. Wrote on political science and history, especially ancient history.

Dugard, Samuel (1645?–1697) DNB

English clergyman. Graduate of Oxford with B.A. in 1661, M.A. in 1664. Author of *The true nature of the divine law, and of disobedience thereunto* (1687) as well as *A discourse concerning the having many children, etc.* (1695). Was survived by five sons and five daughters.

Duhre, Anders Gabriel (c. 1680–1739) SBL

Swedish mathematician. Studied at Uppsala without receiving a degree. Career as mathematician but with interest also in economics. His writings were in both fields. According to Schaumann, was an agronomist as well as a prominent mathematician.

Dumont, Arsène (1849–1902) SS
French sociologist, demographer. Studied at the École d'Anthropologie at Paris, then devoted himself to a life of study and writing, with particular attention to the decline of the birth rate in his country. As told by G. F. McLeary (*Peopling the British Commonwealth,* London: Faber & Faber, 1955, pp. 55–56), "Dumont's researches left him no time for paid employment, and in order to live he had to draw upon his capital. In 1892 it was necessary for him to make a decision of vital importance. His slender resources, husbanded with the most rigorous economy, could be made to last only another ten years. What then? He could try to find paid employment. But that would have seriously curtailed the precious time he required for his researches, in which he had found the only life he cared to live. His decision was soon made. He would continue to live his life of strenuous research and *réflexion solitaire.* [then in 1902] He arranged his papers in a way most likely to be useful to other students, bequeathed his publications to the School of Anthropology, and wrote his farewell letters. On the 31st of May 1902, the last day for which he had sufficient money to pay his hotel bill, he put an end to his life."

Dutens, Joseph Michel (1765–1848) BU, Pal.
French engineer. Inspector-general of roads and bridges from 1830 to the end of his life. Held various other engineering posts; at one time was sent by the government to inspect public works in England. Member of various learned societies, interested in political economy, and author of several works on that subject.

Eden, William, first baron of Aukland (1744–1814) DNB
English statesman and diplomat. Graduate of Oxford (B.A., 1765, M.A., 1768). Entered the legal profession, where showed great promise. Became undersecretary of state in 1772 and gave up his legal career. Entered Parliament in 1774 and came to be respected for his knowledge of law and economics. Was sent to America in 1778 as member of a commission seeking a settlement of the "disturbances" there. Continued a distinguished career in government service, including diplomatic missions abroad; member of several ministries, ambassador to the Netherlands during the French Revolution.

Edmonds, Thomas Rowe (1803–1889) SS
English social theorist and actuary. Graduate of Cambridge. Wrote on political economy and population, then in 1832, because he was actuary of an insurance company in London, published his *Life tables,* and thereafter devoted himself largely to actuarial and related studies.

Ehrenström, Olof (1713–1750) SBL
Swedish surveyor, writer on economic subjects. Showed early promise as a student, studied at Uppsala, was trained as a surveyor and held various positions in that capacity. His *Anmärkningar* contributed to a controversy on the relative advantages of agriculture and manufactures for the nation. Principal writings were related to surveying.

Eisdell, Joseph Salaway (fl. 1839)
No information.

Ensor, George (*1769–1843*)   DNB
   Irish political writer. Of English ancestry, educated at Trinity College. Wrote in a characteristically incisive style on contemporary social and political problems, including poor relief, population, and the distribution of property.

Estenberg, Carl E. (*1728–1815*)   SBL
   Swedish official. Participated in the discussion of the question of Swedish underpopulation and the extension of cultivation to new land. Member of the court of appeals (*hovrättsrådet*); incurred royal disfavor by raising the question of freedom of publication.

Everett, Alexander Hill (*1790–1847*)   AB
   American editor and diplomat. Graduated as the youngest member of his class at Harvard in 1806; then studied law in the office of John Quincy Adams. When Adams became Minister to Russia in 1809, Everett served as his private secretary. Later held diplomatic posts at The Hague, 1815–1824, and served as Minister to Spain. Controlled the *North American Review* for a time, but it was not a financially successful venture. Left Massachusetts after disappointments in politics. Was briefly president of Jefferson College in Louisiana but resigned because of ill health. Sent on governmental missions to Cuba and, in 1845, to China, where he died.

Expilly, Jean Joseph (*1719–1795*)   BU, Chal.
   French clergyman, traveler, geographer. Educated for the church, career as official of church and state; member of many learned societies in France and abroad. Widely traveled and highly regarded as a geographer. Author of numerous works on geography, population, and politics, based on observations made during his travels.

Faggot, Jacob (*1699–1777*)   SBL
   Swedish official. Educated at Uppsala. A career in governmental service, head of the commission on weights and measures, member or head of many other commissions, including the Statistical Commission (1754–1777). Secretary of the Royal Academy of Science, 1741–1744, and its president in 1747 and 1760.

Fawcett, Henry (*1833–1884*)   DNB
   English political economist, member of Parliament. Educated at Cambridge, then began the study of law. Blinded in a hunting accident at the age of 25, he continued his activities and interests with great determination in spite of his handicap. Returned to Cambridge to pursue his earlier interest in political economy, became professor of political economy in 1863, and remained there to the end of his life. Elected in 1865 to Parliament, where he had a long and distinguished service and was a supporter of liberal legislation. A fellow of the Royal Society and recipient of many academic honors.

Fénelon (*François de Salignac de la Motte; 1651–1715*)   BU, Chal.
   French churchman and author. Of a distinguished family, educated at Cahors and Paris, where he was noted for his ability and learning. Took holy orders at the age of 24, was well received at court, and was appointed tutor

to the Dukes of Burgundy, Anjou, and Berri. Elected to the Academie in 1693, appointed Archbishop of Cambrai in 1695. Later involved in religious controversy, he fell out of favor at court and retired to his diocese. The *Telemachus* was composed for his royal pupil, but reportedly was not well received because of some of the ideas it expressed.

Ferguson, Adam (1723–1816)   DNB
   Scottish philosopher and teacher. Received M.A. degree at St. Andrews in 1742, after which took divinity studies there and at Edinburgh. Pursued clerical career until his early thirties; then became professor of natural philosophy at Edinburgh in 1759, of moral philosophy from 1764 to his retirement in 1785. Friend of David Hume. Traveled on the Continent, 1774–1776; in 1778 went to Philadelphia accompanying the British Commissioners being sent to negotiate a settlement with the colonists. Principal works on government, philosophy, and Roman history.

Florez-Estrada, Alvaro (1765–1853)   Pal., SS
   Spanish official, political economist. A finance officer in Spain, active in resistance to Napoleon. A refugee in England on two occasions, at which time he studied political economy and became a follower of the English classical school. Later a member of the Spanish Senate and of learned societies.

Fontenoy, Roger de (fl. 1854)
   No information.

Forbonnais, François Veron de (1722–1800)   Chal., BU
   French official and economist. After a period in the family textile business and foreign travel, he settled in Paris, where he wrote on public finance and urged fiscal reform. Was appointed inspector-general of the mint, later assistant to the comptroller-general. Retired before the Revolution, but continued to write and to play some part in public affairs.

Fortrey, Samuel (1622–1681)   DNB
   English mercantilist writer. Born of a merchant family, became a "gentleman of his majesties . . . privy chamber." Little is known of him except for his tract, "England's Interest and Improvement," 1663.

Ganilh, Charles (1758–1836)   EB
   French economist. Trained for the law and practiced for a time, active in public affairs during the Revolution, a public official during the Napoleonic period. Author of works on political economy and finance.

Gardner, Edward (fl. 1800)
   No information.

Garnier, Joseph Clement (1813–1881)   SS
   French political economist. Educated and later taught at the École Supérieure de Commerce in Paris. Professor of political economy at several schools; one of the founders of the Société d'Économie Politique in 1842. In 1845 became editor of the influential *Journal des économistes* and continued in this position except for brief intervals until his death in 1881.

George, Henry (1839–1897)   AB
American economist and reformer. Born in Philadelphia, the second of ten children, he left school by the age of fourteen but educated himself by reading. After experiencing failure and poverty he became established as a newspaper editor in California. Struck by the apparent paradox of advancing wealth and advancing poverty, he devoted himself from that time on to politics and writing to advance his ideas for economic and tax reform.

Godwin, William (1756–1836)   DNB
English writer by profession. The seventh of thirteen children, he showed early promise as a student. At first entered the ministry, but after several years he came into disagreement with his congregation and turned to a writing career in London in his late 20's. A prolific writer of essays and pamphlets, he then achieved both professional and financial success in 1793 with his *Political Justice,* a work regarded by the authorities as dangerously liberal in thought. Author also of works of fiction, history, social philosophy, and verse, and considered to be one of the leading writers of his time. In spite of his philosophical views on marriage, Godwin reacted more as the outraged parent than the philosopher when his daughter Mary eloped with the already married Shelley, but became more reconciled when Shelley later married Mary and her father envisaged the possibility of borrowing from his well-to-do son-in-law. His later life was made less happy by declining reputation, financial troubles, and difficulties in his complicated personal life.

Gottmarck, Johan (fl. 1795)
No information.

Goudar, Ange (1720–1791)   NBG
French economist and writer on varied subjects. Son of an inspector-general of commerce, and student of political economy and ethics. Lived for a time in England (c. 1760) and later in Italy; exiled from Naples because of writings held to be subversive and returned to England. Author of numerous works.

Grahame, James (1790–1842)
English advocate, pamphleteer, historian. Educated at home, then attended Glasgow University and, briefly, Cambridge. Admitted to the bar in 1812 but turned increasingly to a career of writing. Involved in controversy with Malthus. Later years were devoted to his *History of the United States,* which was not well received when the first volumes were published in 1827 or the revised edition in 1836, but with further revision (1839), Grahame was honored by the Royal Academy of Nantes and by Harvard College. From biographical notes by Josiah Quincey in the Lea and Blanchard (Philadelphia, 1845) edition of the *History.*

Graunt, John (1620–1674)   DNB
English shopkeeper and statistician. Apprenticed to a "haberdasher of small wares," he followed his trade but also held ward and city offices in London. His *Observations* brought him quick recognition and membership in what became the Royal Society. Long-time friend and later business agent of Sir

William Petty, to whom the *Observations* has been attributed. In a biographical sketch his friend John Aubrey wrote that "he had his Hint from his intimate and familiar friend Sir William Petty"; but the weight of later scholarly opinion attributes authorship to Graunt. The most detailed account we have of Graunt is given by D. V. Glass, "John Graunt and his 'Natural and political observations,' " *Proceedings of the Royal Society* 159:2–37, 1963.

Gray, John (1799–1852?)   SS
   English reformer. Little biographical information. Was regarded as radical, for the times, in his social reform ideas and his anti-capitalist opinions.

Gray, Robert (fl. 1609)
   No information.

Gray, Simon (fl. 1815–1820)
   Used the pseudonym George Purves for some of his works. No biographical information.

Greg, William Rathbone (1809–1881)   DNB
   English businessman, writer. Educated at the University of Edinburgh, entered the family business, then went into business on his own account. Was not successful, and left that business in 1850 to pursue a literary career. Numerous works on economics, politics, religion, and other subjects. On the merits of his work he was appointed to public office, as commissioner of the board of customs (1856) and later as comptroller of the stationery office (1864–1877).

Guillard, Archille (1799–1876)   Pal.
   French statistician and scientist. In addition to statistics, was interested in natural science, especially botany. Also author of a work on population.

Guyot, Yves (1843–1928)   EB, SS
   French official and economist. After completion of his education, became a journalist and settled in Paris. Editor of a journal and writer for other publications, members of the chamber of deputies in 1885, minister of public works, 1889–1892. Anti-socialist in his economics and politics; author of works on economics and social problems.

Hakluyt, Richard (1552?–1616)   DNB
   English geographer. Graduate of Oxford, where he received both the B.A. and M.A.; took holy orders. Displayed an avid interest in geography from boyhood, and had opportunity to pursue his researches both at Oxford and Paris. Holder of various appointments in the church, while he continued study and writing in his chosen field. One of the promoters of the South Virginia Company (1606). His *Virginia* was a translation of a Portugese account of the travels of de Soto. Was buried in Westminster Abbey.

Hale, Matthew (1609–1676)   DNB
   English jurist. Orphaned at an early age, educated at Oxford where he acquired a liking for the theater and fencing and a distaste for lawyers. Later, however, was attracted to the law, his father's profession, and entered Lincoln's Inn (1628). During the troubled mid-century he pursued a neutral course,

serving both Stuarts and the Commonwealth. Was elected to Parliament, and served also as justice of common pleas under Cromwell; returned to Parliament for the University of Oxford after Cromwell's death, and was active in the Stuart restoration. Was appointed chief justice of the king's bench in 1671, and regarded as one of the great English jurists. In addition to many legal treatises, he wrote on a wide range of other subjects.

Hales, John (? -1571)   DNB
    English writer. Member of Parliament, an opponent of enclosures, appointed land commissioner in 1548. Experienced various vicissitudes of fortune after the death of Henry VIII; was forced to flee from England, and his property was confiscated on the accession of Mary, but he returned to England when Elizabeth came to the throne. Later was imprisoned in the Tower for a time because of his opinions on the succession.

Hall, Charles (1745?–1825?)   DNB
    English physician, writer on social issues. Is thought to have studied at Leyden in 1765. Wrote on medicine, social problems, and economics. Imprisoned for debt, he refused to be released by friends who offered to pay his debts, and died in prison at the age of about 80.

Hamilton, Robert (1743–1829)   DNB
    English economist, mathematician. Educated at the University of Edinburgh. Was in business for a time and active in literary circles in Edinburgh, then devoted himself entirely to literary pursuits. Appointed to the chair of natural philosophy, then to the chair of mathematics at Aberdeen, where he taught for fifty years. See also biographical notes attached to his posthumously published Progress of society.

Harrington, James (1611–1677)   DNB, Aubrey
    English political theorist. Studied at Oxford but left before completing his studies. Traveled abroad, then returned to England and continued his studies; did not become actively involved in the civil war in spite of acquaintance with and some attachment to Charles. Following the publication of his Oceana (1656) he took an active part in discussing what form of government was most desirable; after Cromwell's death was confined to the Tower for his political views.

Harris, Joseph (1702–1764)   DNB
    English writer and official. Reportedly employed for a time as a blacksmith in his youth, he went to London, was employed in the mint, and became assay master there in 1748. His writings include works on navigation, coinage, and optics.

Hawley, Frederick B. (1843–1929)   SS
    American merchant and economist. Graduate of Williams College, then employed as cotton broker in New York City. Author of two works, Capital and population (1882) and Enterprise and the productive process (1907).

Hazlitt, William (1778–1830) EB
   English essayist. After attending a theological college was slow to find his career. Portrait painter for a time, then turned to a literary career. Acquainted with Coleridge, Wordsworth, Lamb, and other writers of the time, he became a literary figure in his own right, known for incisiveness of style and strongly liberal views. Works include a four-volume life of Napoleon, writings on English drama, and numerous essays on a variety of subjects. For a recent biography of Hazlitt and an account of his intellectual environment, see Herschel Baker, *William Hazlitt* (1962).

Hermelin, Samuel Gustav (1744–1820) SBL
   Swedish industrialist and cartographer. Educated at Uppsala. From 1782 to 1784 traveled in America on an official visit to study industry and to look into the question of establishing diplomatic relations between Sweden and the newly formed United States. Held mining interests, especially in northern Sweden; a pioneer in the mapping of Sweden. Recipient of various public honors, head of the Academy of Science.

Helvétius, Claude Adrien (1715–1771) SS
   French philosopher. Wealthy, widely traveled, holder of various official positions, but eventually resigned to devote himself to philosophy. Leader of an intellectual salon in Paris. His one work, *De l'homme,* was publicly condemned and ordered burned because of the anticipated harmful influence of its utilitarian philosophy.

Herbert, Claude Jacques (1700–1758) Pal.
   No information on his life is given by Palgrave except that he was farmer-general of the royal mail coaches. He was a physiocrat in his views on the importance of agriculture, and a believer in free trade.

Herrenschwand, Jean F. de (1715–1796) BU
   Swiss economist. Born at Morat, moved to London, where he published works in French, then passed the remainder of his life in Paris. Author of works on political economy, the credit of nations, and the distribution of agricultural land.

Hickson, William Edward (1803–1870) DNB
   English philanthropist and writer. Early engaged in the family shoe business, but retired from that in 1840 to devote himself to philanthropic works and writing. Associated with Senior in an investigation of unemployment of handicraft workers, he became an active promoter of elementary education and repeal of the corn laws. Owned and edited the *Westminster Review* from 1840 to 1852.

Hobbes, Thomas (1588–1679) DNB, Aubrey
   English political theorist and philosopher. Received a varied education, leading to a B.A. from Magdalen Hall. Thereafter served for many years as tutor in the Cavendish household, during which time he traveled widely on the Continent. Lived in Paris in self-imposed exile after 1637 for fear of persecu-

tion because of his political and religious views. Returned to England in 1651, the year of publication of his principal work, *Leviathan*.

Holbach, Paul Heinrich (1723–1789)   SS
French scholar and philosopher. Educated in Paris, then at the University of Leyden. Of independent means, he was well known in learned circles in Paris, friend of Rousseau and Diderot, and led a life of study, writing and intellectual society. Works on natural philosophy, politics, and the social system.

Holinshed, Raphaell (? –1580)   DNB
English historian. Little is known of his life. Said to have attended Cambridge and entered the ministry. Later was employed as a translator in a printing office. Here he was set to work on a projected compendium of information on "history and cosmography." After the death of his employer, Holinshed carried on the work in abbreviated scope, published in 1578 as his *Chronicles*.

Holmen, Bengt (fl. 1765)
No information.

Ibn Khaldun (1332–1406)   EB, SS
Arab scholar and historian. Born in Tunis of a family said to be from Seville, driven out by the Christian reconquest. Received a liberal education and distinguished himself as a scholar. Served various rulers of Moslem North Africa and Spain. The greater part of his later life, from about 1382 on, was spent in Cairo, where he taught law and served as judge. His lifetime of public service was interrupted by many alternations of favor and disfavor, and he presumably developed a first-hand knowledge of politics and skill as a courtier in the midst of court intrigue. See also: Charles Issawi, *An Arab philosophy of history; selections from the Prolegomena of Ibn Khaldun* (London: Murray, 1950), and Muhsin Mahdi, *Ibn Khaldun's philosophy of history* (London: Allen & Unwin, 1957).

Ingram, Robert Acklom (1736–1809)   DNB
English political economist. Graduate of Cambridge, where he continued as fellow and tutor. Entered the church and served as curate and rector to the end of his life. Author of works on theology, social problems, and political economy.

Jarrold, Thomas (1770–1853)   DNB
English physician, essayist. Educated at Edinburgh, where he may have taken a medical degree. Practiced medicine for many years in Manchester, was a member there of the Literary and Philosophical Society. In addition to several contributions to the literature of the Malthusian controversy, he wrote essays on the poor laws, anthropology, national character, and a medical treatise on curvature of the spine.

Jarvis, Edward
American statistician. No further information.

Jennison, William (fl. 1828)
No information.

Jevons, William Stanley (1835–1882) DNB
English economist. Graduate of the University of London, after interruption of his studies to earn money, working as assayer of the mint in Australia. Taught for a time at Manchester, then returned to London as professor of political economy. Fellow of the Royal Society and recipient of other professional honors. In addition to political economy, he wrote on logic with particular emphasis on Boolian logic.

Jones, Richard (1790–1855) DNB
English political economist. Studied for the clergy at Cambridge, where he received the B.A. and M.A. degrees. Served as curate for a time, then in 1833 was appointed professor at King's College, London. Resigned two years later to succeed Malthus at Haileybury as professor of political economy and history.

Joplin, Thomas (1790–1847) DNB
English banker and political economist. Active in the establishment and direction of several banks, writer on political economy, the principles of banking, and the monetary system.

Justi, Johannes Heinrich Gottlieb von (1717–1771) SS
German mineralogist, cameralist. Studied at Jena, where he acquired a wide knowledge of mineralogy. Served Frederick the Great as administrator of mines, later was professor of political economy and natural history at Göttingen. Died in prison, but accounts differ on whether his offense was the views expressed in his treatise on money or financial difficulties connected with his administration of mines.

Kautsky, Karl (1845–1938) EB
German Marxist. A friend and disciple of Marx, founder of a socialist paper, *Die Neue Zeit,* published first in London, then in Stuttgart. Politically active in Germany, he fled from the Nazi regime in 1934 to Czechoslovakia and Vienna, from there at the Anschluss to the Sudetenland, and from there to Amsterdam, where he died in poverty. He was not a follower of Lenin or Trotsky.

King, Gregory (1648–1712) DNB
English statistician. Son of a mathematician, he was a genealogist, herald, and engraver as well as statistician, and engaged in a wide range of other activities at one time or another — map-making, city planning, etc. His best known work the *Natural and political observations.*

König, Christian (1678–1762) SBL
Swedish official. Studied at Uppsala, followed by many years of study abroad. After holding several lesser positions, he was named secretary of the chancellery.

Kryger, Johan Frederick (*1707–1777*)   SBL
   Swedish official and mercantilist writer. From a poor family, he rose through various employments to a series of official positions. Head of the Academy of Science in 1755, and of the Statistical Commission (Tabellverket) in 1771. A leading writer on economic subjects, a mercantilist in his convictions, but with some liberal ideas. Publisher of the periodicals *Den Wälmenande Patrioten* (1751) and *Den Förnunftige Fritänkaren* (1767–1769), and others.

Laing, Samuel (*1780–1868*)   DNB
   Scottish traveler and writer. Educated at Edinburgh, followed by a period of study at Kiel. Saw action in the Peninsular campaign, after which he was employed in Scotland. Inherited the family estate in the Orkneys in 1818, but being forced to add to his income, he traveled widely in Europe and published his observations in a series of travelogue volumes (1836–1852) that included accounts of social and political conditions in the principal countries of Europe.

Laing, Samuel, Jr. (*1812–1897*)   DNB
   English railroad official, member of Parliament. Son of Samuel Laing, Sr., born in Scotland, received B.A. at Cambridge in 1831. Entered Lincoln's Inn to study law, was called to the bar in 1837. Rose to be managing director and an authority on railroads; served a number of terms in Parliament. In 1860 was appointed minister in India. Major works on India and China.

Lau, Theodor (*1670–1740*)
   No information.

Lawson, James (*1817–1887*)   DNB
   Irish political economist, jurist. Graduate of Oxford and recipient of advanced degrees (LL.B. in 1841, LL.D. in 1850). Professor of political economy, 1840 to 1845, meanwhile a member of the Irish bar and maintained a law practice. His later career was entirely in the law, as legal advisor to the crown in Ireland, solicitor-general, and then attorney-general for Ireland, justice of common pleas, and other appointments.

Leroy-Beaulieu, Pierre Paul (*1843–1916*)   EB, SS
   French economist and political scientist. Studied law in Paris, followed by further studies in Germany and England. One of the outstanding French economists of his time, editor of the *Journal des débats,* professor at the École Libre des Sciences Politiques, then at the College de France (from 1880).

Leslie, Thomas Edward Cliffe (*1827?–1882*)   DNB
   English political economist. B.A. from Trinity College, Dublin, with honors in 1847, LL.B. in 1851, honorary LL.D. later. Held the chair of jurisprudence and political economy at Queen's College, Belfast, and meanwhile studied law. Friend of J. S. Mill, author of numerous journal articles on economics and land tenure.

Leuhusen, Carl (*fl. 1761*)
   No information.

Liljencrantz, Johan (born Westerman; 1730–1815)   SBL
   Swedish nobleman, statesman. Studied at Uppsala under Wargentin and
Berch, from whom he developed an interest in economic affairs. But perhaps
was influenced more by several years of travel abroad, 1757–1760. Holder of
numerous official positions from 1750 onward. In 1768 was chairman of the
Academy of Science; in 1773 was appointed secretary of trade and finance.
He held this position until 1786, during which time he worked ably to
strengthen the Swedish economy.

List, Friedrich (1789–1846)   EB, SS
   German political economist. Little is known of his early life. He is known
to have entered the civil service as a clerk, and to have risen rapidly. In 1817
was appointed professor of administration and politics at Tübingen but was
forced to resign soon after. Member of the Württemburg chamber of deputies
but was expelled through political pressure and forced to emigrate to America,
where he remained from 1825 to 1832. There he worked as a journalist, became financially successful, and in 1832 was appointed United States consul at
Leipzig. Author of a work on American political economy (1827) in addition
to his major work, *Das Nationale System* (1841).

Machiavelli, Niccolo (1469–1527)   EB
   Italian political theorist and historian. Little is known of his early life, but
he evidently received a liberal education. Advanced through various public
positions in his native Florence to become second chancellor and secretary, a
position he held for fourteen years. In 1502 was sent as envoy to Caesar
Borgia, thought to have been the prototype of The Prince. Actively served the
Florentine state at home and on many diplomatic missions, and acquired first-
hand experience of political intrigue. His political career ended with the return
of the Medici to Florence in 1512, and although he gradually gained favor
with the new rulers of the city, it was during the enforced leisure after 1512
that he wrote the works on which his fame now rests. For a recent biography,
see Roberto Ridolfi, *Life of Niccolo Machiavelli* (University of Chicago Press,
1963).

Malynes (or Malines), Gerard (fl. 1586–1641)   DNB
   English merchant and writer on economic matters. Born in Antwerp of
English parents who later returned to England. No information on education
and early life. Regarded as expert on mercantile matters during the reigns of
Elizabeth and James I, assaymaster of the mint and an authority on coinage.
Author of works on trade, and a contributor to the development of economics.

Mandeville, Bernard (c. 1670–1733)   DNB
   Dutch-English writer. Educated in the Netherlands, received a medical
degree frm Leyden. Settled in England and is thought to have practiced medicine there, but turned his hand especially to writing. Wrote works on diverse
subjects; *The Fable of the Bees* (1814) now his chief claim to fame.

Mangoldt, Hans von (1824–1868)   ADB
   German economist. Entered Leipzig University in 1842, studied law and
government. Expelled for association with a forbidden student group, so con-

tinued studies at Geneva. Returned to Tübingen, obtained doctorate in 1847. Edited a journal in Weimar, but then pursued an academic career. Docent in political economy at Göttingen, 1855.

Mann, Theodore-Augustin (1735–1809)   NBG
   Belgian monk and writer. Born in York but of Belgian nationality. Went to Paris in 1854, then spent some time in Spain, where he attended a military academy in Barcelona. He soon left the military life to enter a monastery, and eventually became a prior. Left the monastery in 1777 to reside in Brussels, where he became secretary of the Academy. Prolific writer on diverse subjects, including history and metaphysics.

Marshall, Alfred (1842–1924)   DNB
   English economist. Son of a Bank of England employee, educated at Oxford. Influenced by Sidgwick to study economics. In 1868 received a lectureship at Oxford. In 1885 succeeded Fawcett as professor of political economy at Cambridge, where he remained until he retired in 1908. Probably the most influential English economist from Mill to Keynes.

McCulloch, John Ramsay (1789–1864)   SS
   Scottish economist. Born in Scotland, studied law but turned to economics. Went to London in 1820, where he became acquainted with the members of the English school of political economy, and was appointed professor of political economy in the University of London (1828–1832). Active contributor to journals, especially the *Edinburgh Review;* more an editor and compiler than a contributor of new ideas to economics.

McVicar, John (1787–1868)   AB
   American economist. Born in New York City of Irish parentage, graduated in 1804 from Columbia at the head of his class. After graduation, he traveled abroad, then studied theology and was ordained in 1811. Served as rector until 1817, when he was appointed to the chair of moral philosophy at Columbia. As one of the five members of the faculty there he also taught history and rhetoric. He was one of the first in the United States to teach political economy, treating it as a part of moral philosophy.

Melish, John (1771–1882)
   American geographer. Born in Scotland, he came to the United States and settled in Philadelphia. Traveled widely in the United States and in the British and Spanish possessions in the Western Hemisphere; became interested in geography, cartography, and population. Author of numerous geographical works, compilations of statistics of the United States, and accounts of his travels. See Marvin Wolfgang, "John Melish, an early American demographer," *Pennsylvania Magazine of History and Biography,* 82(1):65–81, January 1958.

Melon, Jean François (1675 or 1680–1738)   EB, Daire
   French economist, official. No information on his early life. One of the founders of the academy of Bordeaux, of which he was the secretary. According to Daire, he was educated in law and began to practice in Bordeaux, but gave up his legal career at his interests turned to literature and political econ-

omy. See also Franz Megnet, *Jean-François Melon* (dissertation), Zurich: Keller-Winterthur, 1955. Here Melon is described as a forerunner of the physiocrats rather than being considered a late mercantilist.

Mennander, Carl Fredrik (1712–1786) SBL

Swedish archbishop and scientist. Studied at Åbo, then Uppsala. Professor of physics at Åbo, 1746–1752; entered the priesthood in 1746. Received the degree of doctor of theology at Åbo in 1752, and was professor of theology there, 1752–1757. Bishop of Åbo, 1757–1775, archbishop of Uppsala, 1775–1786. Head of the Academy of Science in 1744.

Messance Pal.

French statistician. Held various official positions; in 1759 was undersecretary to the intendant of Auvergne, where he pursued statistical investigations designed to disprove Mirabeau's theory that the population of France was declining. Wrote two works on population, and also is said to have prepared a mortality table.

Mill, James (1773–1836) DNB

British economist and utilitarian philosopher. Entered the University of Edinburgh in 1790, took up divinity studies in 1794. Was admitted to the ministry but had little success. During the following years he supported himself and his family by tutoring, editing a journal, and writing for various periodicals. Financial success came with his *History of India* (1817) and a subsequent position in which he employed his knowledge of India. A long-time friend of Ricardo and Bentham, with an active interest in politics and in utilitarianism. According to the DNB, "He ultimately became the father of nine children, an oversight for which his eldest son apologizes."

Mill, John Stuart (1806–1873) SS

English logician, political economist, and liberal. Son of James Mill, he was educated at home and quite strictly. Worked in the India Office and became its chief, 1856–1858, and served a term in Parliament (1865–1868). Actively participated in intellectual and political movements of his time, wrote for the *Westminster Review* and other publications. Principal works on logic, political economy, and on government.

Mirabeau, Victor Riqueti, marquis de (1715–1789) EB, SS

French intellectual. Little is known of his early life. Saw military service, from which he returned with honors in 1743. His reputation was established by *L'Ami des hommes* (1756). Later came under the influence of Quesnay and became an ardent promoter of physiocrat doctrine. Was imprisoned and then exiled to his estates for a work on taxation (1760), but he continued to support the physiocrats to the end of his life.

Misselden, Edward (fl. 1608–1654) DNB

English merchant and writer on economic matters. Little information on his life. Was deputy governor of the Merchant Adventurers' Company at Delft for ten years, and was employed in various capacities by the East India Company. Writer on economic policy, and opponent of Malynes' views on free trade.

Moheau, M. (*1733–1820*)   SS, Pal.
French statistician and writer on population. Little is known of his life. Was secretary to Montyon, and some sources attribute the *Recherches* to the latter. For a recent review of the question of authorship, see the article by Esmonin in *Population*, Vol. 13, No. 2, April–June 1958.

Molinari, Gustave de (*1819–1912*)   SS
Belgian-French economist. A journalist for a time in Paris, he was appointed professor of political economy at Brussels in 1852 and later taught at Antwerp. Returned to Paris and became editor of the *Journal des débats* (1871–1876), and then the *Journal des économistes* (1881–1909). Author of several works on political economy.

Montchrétien, Antoine de (*1575 or 1576–1621*)   EB
French dramatist and economist. No information on his early life. Fled to England after killing an opponent in a duel, but was enabled to return through the intercession of James I. Established a steel foundry on his return, joined the Huguenot side during the religious wars, and was killed in action in 1621. Author of dramatic works in addition to his treatise on political economy (1615).

Montyon, Antoine Jean Baptiste Robert Auget, baron de (*1773–1820*)   EB
French lawyer and official. No information on his early life. A successful lawyer and holder of public office. A philanthropist and donor of many academic prizes. Apart from the work of questioned authorship, the *Recherches et considerations sur la population de la France* (see Moheau), he wrote a later work on the impact of taxation.

More, Thomas (*1478–1535*)   DNB
English scholar, jurist, statesman. Received a sound classical education, studied at Oxford for two years, then went to London to study law with marked success. His interest in literature and liberal arts continued, however, and brought him a lifelong friendship with Erasmus. He came to favor with Henry VIII, became member of the privy council, was knighted in 1521, and succeeded Wolsey as chancellor in 1529. But opposed the king on the issue of religion, and was sent to the Tower and executed. Author of numerous works in Latin and English, besides the *Utopia*.

Moreton, Augustus H. (*fl. 1836*)
No information.

Möser, Justus (*1720–1794*)   EB, SS
German statesman. No information on his early life except that he was son of a high official in Osnabruck. Spent some time in London following the Seven Years War; later served at Osnabruck as state attorney and in other official positions. Author of miscellaneous literary works and a history of Osnabruck in addition to his *Patriotische Phantasien* (1775–1786).

Mun, Thomas (1571–1641) DNB

English merchant and mercantilist. Is believed to have engaged in trade in Italy and the Levant early in his career. In 1615 elected to a position with the East India Company, and continued with the Company to the end of his life. His *Discourse of Trade* (1621) involved him in controversy with Malynes, but he was supported by Misselden. He attained great wealth and was a prominent representative of the rising merchant class.

Necker, Jacques (1732–1804) BU

Swiss-French financier. Born in Geneva. Was intended for a business career but showed a liking for literature and philosophy in his studies. Went to Paris for experience in banking, in which he showed great aptitude and made a considerable fortune. Was appointed representative to the French court by the republic of Geneva. In the period of troubled French finances he showed ability as director of finances, and proposed reforms in taxation and administration. Resigned abruptly in 1781 when refused the position of minister. Was recalled to power briefly in 1788. An anti-physiocrat, author of works on fiscal policy and economics.

Newman, Samuel Phillips (1797–1842) AB

American author, teacher. Born in Andover, Massachusetts, graduated from Harvard with honors in 1816. Studied theology, was made professor of Greek and Latin at Bowdoin College in 1819, professor of rhetoric and oratory in 1824. Also taught political economy and was for a time acting president. Author of a text on rhetoric and style in addition to his political economy.

Nitti, Francesco Saverio (1869–1953) EB

Italian statesman. Trained in the law, professor of financial science at the University of Naples. Member of the Italian parliament, and cabinet minister 1911–1914. Premier for several brief periods after 1919. Left Italy during the Fascist period, returning only after World War II to serve in the national assembly and as senator.

Nordencrantz, Anders (born Bachmansson; 1697–1772) SBL

Swedish economist. Received a limited education before entering his father's business. Traveled abroad 1721–1724 for study and observation, and began preparation of a work on political economy, the *Arcana*. Member of parliament in 1726; consul at Lisbon in 1728. On return to Sweden took a prominent part in the discussion of national economic policy, on the side of the Cap party. Probably the most influential Swedish economist of his generation.

Opdyke, George (1815–1880) AB

American merchant and reformer. Born in New Jersey, went to work at an early age, became successful in merchandising, manufacturing, and importing. Then turned to banking. Active in politics, was mayor of New York City at the time of the draft riots in 1863. His *Treatise on political economy* (1851) was directed against John Stuart Mill's *Principles*.

Ortes, Giammaria (1713–1790) SS
Italian monk and economist. Member of a monastic order until the age of 30. Thereafter he devoted himself to studies and travel, the latter to the principal cities of Europe. In addition to the work on population he wrote a text on political economy (1774).

Paley, William (1743–1805) DNB
English clergyman and teacher. Received B.A. from Cambridge in 1762, then continued his studies and entered the ministry. Was lecturer on moral philosophy and then tutor at Cambridge. Rose in the church to become archdeacon in 1782. An admirer of Malthus, author of several works on moral philosophy, of which the major ones are the *Principles* (1785), *A view of the evidences of Christianity* (1794), and *Natural theology* (1802).

Passy, Hippolyte (1793–1880) NBG
French cabinet minister, economist. Began a military career and took part in Napoleon's last campaigns. Left France after 1814 because of lack of sympathy with the royalist government, and visited Louisiana and the Antilles. On the voyage he read *The wealth of nations* and became interested in political economy. On returning to France he entered politics, held various official posts and became finance minister briefly in 1834. Raised to the peerage in 1843. One of the founders of the Societé d'économie politique, in 1848.

Patrizzi, Francesco (1412–1492) Pal.
Italian churchman and political scientist. Born at Siena, became bishop of Gaeta and pursued studies of politics. A close follower of Aristotle in his writings.

Patten, Samuel N. (1852–1922) AB
American economist. Born in Illinois, prepared for the law, entered Northwestern University, then studied in Germany, at Halle. Received Ph.D. there in 1878. After an unsuccessful period he achieved some reputation with the publication of his *Premises of political economy* (1885) and was appointed professor of political economy at the University of Pennsylvania in 1888. Remained there until his retirement; was regarded as a gifted teacher.

Perry, Arthur Latham (1830–1905) AB
American economist. Brought up in extreme poverty, but was able to attend Williams College and graduated with honors. Was tutor and then professor of political economy and history at Williams. Publications on political economy and on Massachusetts history.

Petty, William (1623–1687) DNB, Aubrey
English self-made man of many abilities. Went to sea in his youth and was put ashore in France with a broken leg, but supported himself by giving English and navigation lessons. Received education in a Jesuit school in Caen. Served for a time in the English navy, then studied at Utrecht and Amsterdam, and followed a medical course first at Leyden, later at Oxford. After holding several academic positions at Oxford, he became professor of anatomy and achieved renown for his revival of a woman hanged for murder. Was physician-

general to the army in Ireland, then was put in charge of the survey of Ireland, which he administered with great ability and through which he acquired great estates in Ireland. Made the adjustment to the Stuart restoration easily, and at this time became one of the founders of the Royal Society. Inventor of many devices, including a double-keeled boat. Aubrey relates that being challenged to a duel by a professional soldier, Petty, who was "extremely short sighted, and being the chalengee it belonged to him to nominate place and weapons. He nominates, for the place, a darke Cellar, and the weapon to be a great Carpenter's Axe. This turned the knight's challenge into Ridicule, and so it came to nought." Much occupied with lawsuits over his Irish estates, but also a prolific writer on taxation, "political arithmetick," surveying, etc.

Petyt, William (c. 1641–1707)   DNB
   English archivist, writer on trade. Studied at Cambridge then at the Middle Temple, and entered the legal profession. Custodian of records at the Tower of London, author of historical and bibliographical works; the anonymous *Britannia languens* is attributed to him.

Philips (or Philipps), Erasmus (d. 1743)   DNB
   English writer on economic matters. Educated at Oxford but did not complete work for a degree. Member of Parliament from 1728 to his death; author of numerous works on economic questions.

Phillips, Willard (1784–1873)   AB
   American lawyer and writer on economics. Was a teacher for a time, then entered Harvard and graduated in 1810. Continued there for several years as tutor, meanwhile studied law. Did editorial work with several periodicals, began law practice in Boston in 1818. Was probate judge for Suffolk County, then became president of an insurance company, where he remained until retirement. Author of works on insurance, political economy, and the free-trade question.

Place, Francis (1771–1854)   DNB
   English labor reformer. Apprenticed at early age to a leather-breeches maker and advanced to be independent journeyman in that trade. But was forced to turn to other work by decline of the trade and because he was blacklisted for his activity in a strike (1793). Turned to study, which he pursued avidly, became active in labor organizations. Achieved financial success by 1800 in a tailoring business, went into politics, and came to know and be known by the leading liberals of the early nineteenth century—Robert Owen, Godwin, Bentham, and others. His one major work was the *Principles of Population* (1822), but he also wrote numerous essays, tracts, and journal articles.

Plomgren, Thomas (1702–1754)   SBL
   Swedish businessman and politician. Trained in business abroad, then settled in Stockholm, employed by an exporter of iron. Active in politics, and head of the Academy of Science in 1739.

Plumard de Dangeul (fl. 1754)
   No information. May be a pseudonym.

Pölitz, Karl (1772–1838)   **ADB**
German scholar and writer. Educated in philosophy, history, and theology at the University of Leipzig. Professor of ethics and history at Dresden, then of philosophy at Leipzig, followed by other professorships. A prolific writer on a wide variety of subjects, but especially history.

Polhem, Christopher (born Polhammar; 1661–1751)   **SBL**
Swedish industrialist. Came to Stockholm at the age of 10, after the death of his father and remarriage of his mother, to live with an uncle. After various employments, established a watch and tool workshop and sought technical training. In recognition of his ability he was recommended for a professorship at Uppsala, where he studied mathematics, 1687–1690. A period of travel followed, during which he became acquainted with foreign scientists. Took an active interest in industrial and mechanical developments, and on his recommendation a technical laboratory for experimental work was established in Sweden. Was called the father of Swedish mechanics, and was highly respected in the economic field. A recent biography is available in English translation, W. A. Johnson, *Christopher Polhem,* Hartford; Trinity College, 1964.

Pollexfen, John (fl. 1697)   **DNB**
English merchant and economic writer. Born about 1632, settled in London and there became a leading member of a "committee of trade and plantations" in 1675 and of the board of trade, 1696–1705. Engaged in controversy with Davenant over the East India Company. His principal work is *A discourse of trade, coyn, and paper credit, and of ways and means to gain and retain riches.* . . (1697).

Postlethwayt, Malachy (c. 1707–1767)   **DNB**
English economic writer. Not a great deal is known of him. Was elected fellow of the Royal Society in 1734. Is said to have spent some twenty years preparing *The universal dictionary of trade and commerce* (1751), translated from a French original but with considerable revision. A prolific writer, especially on trade. According to DNB, "He died suddenly 'as he had often wished.' "

Potter, Alonzo (1800–1865)   **AB**
American clergyman and political economist. Born in New York State, and graduated with distinction from Union College. Lived for a time in Philadelphia, became attracted to the Protestant Episcopal Church, studied for the ministry, and was ordained in 1824. Served as rector for five years in Boston, then became professor of moral and intellectual philosophy at Union, where he remained for fifteen years. In 1845 was elected bishop of Pennsylvania. Active in the establishment of church institutions, author of a *Political economy* (1840).

Price, Bonomy (1807–1888)   **DNB**
English economist. Educated at Oxford, received B.A. with honors in 1829, M.A. in 1832. Taught mathematics and classics at Rugby, 1830–1850. In London, 1850–1868, was occupied with business and various appointments.

Professor of political economy at Oxford, 1868–1888, where he followed and in turn was followed by Rogers. Principal writings on currency, banking, and political economy.

Proudhon, Pierre Joseph (1809–1865)   SS
   French socialist economist. Of working class origin, he became active in the socialist political movement. Essentially conservative in his social views, he represented a moderate socialist rather than communist position in economics. Served a term in the chamber of deputies following the revolution of 1848.

Pufendorf, Samuel (1631 or 1632–1694)   ES, Chal.
   German jurist. Son of a Lutheran minister who wanted his son to prepare for the ministry, but he preferred public law as offering greater opportunity. Was employed for a time as tutor in the household of the Swedish ambassador to Denmark, and was imprisoned with his employer when war broke out between the two countries. During the imprisonment he drafted a treatise of law, whose later publication (1660) brought his recognition and a professorship of law at Heidelberg. Then went to Lund University in Sweden at the invitation of Karl XI of that country; was later royal historian and counsellor to the King. Held similar positions later in Berlin.

Quesnay, François (1694–1774)   Chal., Pal.
   French economist. With no formal education in his youth, he took up the study of medicine and achieved considerable reputation as a doctor. Later turned to the study of mathematics and economics; in the latter field he became influential, the center of the physiocrat school. He collaborated with Mirabeau. It is said that Adam Smith might have dedicated *The Wealth of Nations* to Quesnay if the latter had not died before publication of the work.

Quetelet, Adolphe (1796–1874)   SS
   Belgian astronomer and statistician. Became professor of mathematics, then went to Paris to study astronomy and there also studied probability under Laplace. On his return to Belgium his interest turned more toward statistics. Had a distinguished career in official and professional positions, and contributed to the development of census methods.

Rae, John (1796–1872)   AB
   Scottish-American economist and teacher. Born in Scotland, studied at Aberdeen, where he took the M.A. degree in 1815. Studied medicine at Edinburgh but was denied the degree because of unaccepted views expressed in his dissertation. Emigrated to Canada in 1821 at the age of 25; established a private school, and subsequently moved to Quebec, then Montreal and Boston. His work on political economy was published in Boston in 1834. Went back to Canada for a time, then returned to the United States, then went to California at the time of the gold rush and to Hawaii in 1851, where he remained for twenty years. A biographical sketch is contained in *The sociological theory of capital* (New York, 1905), an edition of his *New Principles*.

Ralegh (or Raleigh), Walter (1552?–1618)   DNB
English courtier, soldier and author. Educated at various schools, including a period at Oxford. Served for a time in France as a volunteer in the Huguenot army. Leader of military and naval expeditions to Ireland and the New World, was a court favorite during the reign of Elizabeth, served in Parliament. Fell into disfavor with James I and was executed in 1618. Author of *History of the World* (1614) and of essays and narratives.

Ramsey, George (1800–1871)   DNB
English philosopher. Educated at Harrow and Cambridge, succeeded his brother as baron in 1859. Prolific writer on philosophy in addition to the *Essay on distribution*.

Rau, Karl Heinrich (1792–1870)   EB
German political economist. Educated at Erlangen and became professor there. Then took the chair of political economy at Heidelberg, where he remained for the rest of his life. Also took some part in public affairs. His major work was the three-volume *Lehrbuch* (1826–1837).

Ravenstone, Piercy   SS, Pal.
English writer on economics. Little or nothing is known of him except from his writings, and the name may be a pseudonym. Whoever he was, his writings reveal an exceptionally acute and empirically oriented mind that should have made the author well known in his day. Harold Boner (*Hungry generations,* pp. 209–210) mentions a conjecture that Ravenstone was really Hazlitt, but as far as known this is only a conjecture.

Raymond, Daniel (1786–1849?)   AB
American lawyer and political economist. Born in Connecticut, studied law, and admitted to the bar in Baltimore (1814). Several works on current issues, in addition to his principal work, *Thoughts on political economy* (1820), which favored a protectionist policy.

Read, Samuel (fl. 1829)   Pal.
British political economist. No information about his life. In addition to his *Political economy* (Edinburgh, 1829), he wrote *Money and the bank restriction laws* (1816) and *Exposure of certain plagiarisms of J. R. McCulloch* (1819).

Ricardo, David (1772–1823)   AB
English businessman and economist. Son of a prosperous member of the London stock exchange, Ricardo entered his father's business at the age of fourteen. Later he established his own business and was highly successful. A reading of *The wealth of nations* in 1799 is said to have turned his attention to economics, and after a period of study he became an authority in the subject. Member of Parliament, and a long-time friend and correspondent of Malthus. Author of several other economic works in addition to the *Principles* (1817).

Ricci, Lodovici (1742–1799) Pal.
Italian scholar and official. Born near Modena, where he spent the greater part of his life. Studied with the Jesuits, then held various civic positions. In 1787 he was elected counsellor, with responsibility for the archives, food supplies, the census, the police, and other civic matters. His *Riforma* was published in the same year (1787).

Rickards, George Kittilby (1812–1889) DNB
English economist. B.A. from Oxford in 1833, M.A. in 1836. Member of the bar, counsel to the speaker of the House of Commons (1851–1882). Professor of political economy at Oxford (1851–1857). Author of works on economics and other subjects.

Roberts, Lewes (Lewis) (1596–1640) DNB
English writer on economic subjects. No information on his early life. Employed by the East India Company, of which he later became a director. His best known work the *Treasure of trafficke, or a discourse of forraign trade* (1641).

Rodbertus, Johann Karl (1805–1875) EB, ADB
German economist. Received legal education but turned to economics, a decision said to have been influenced by political events at the time. Studied economics, history, and philosophy at German universities; in 1835 bought an estate in Pommerania and retired there to a life of study and writing, interrupted only briefly by public office after the revolution of 1848.

Rogers, James Edwin Thorold (1823–1890) DNB
English political economist. An eleventh son, he attended King's College, London, then Oxford where he received the B.A. and M.A. degrees. Was ordained soon after and became curate in Oxford, but later resigned from the clergy (1870). In 1859 became professor of statistics and economic science at King's College, a position he retained for life. Also chosen professor of political economy at Oxford in 1862, was replaced by Bonamy Price, but resumed the position after Price's death. Active in economic research on prices and wages; author of a *History of agriculture and prices* (1866) and *The economic interpretation of history* (1888), in addition to the *Manual of political economy* (1868).

Rooke, John (1780–1856) DNB
English writer on economics. Had no advanced education but was self-taught. Acquired knowledge of political economy and of geology. Author of works on money, the national debt, and economic principles. Credited by some with having stated the principle of rent at about the same time as Malthus and others.

Roscher, Wilhelm (1817–1894) SS, Pal.
German economist. Born in Hanover, studied history and political science at Göttingen and Berlin, then taught these subjects at Göttingen (1840). Promoted to professor of political economy in 1843. Went to the University of Leipzig in 1848, where he remained. One of the leading economists of his

generation, his economic works were published in many editions and in translation.

Ross, J. C.

No biographical information. Also wrote under the pseudonym John McIniscon. In his work, *An examination of opinions. . . ,* he identified himself as Scottish, opposed to the English established church, and no respecter of the upper classes, whom he called "idlers and worse."

Rossi, Pellegrino Luigi Edoardo, Count (1789–1848) EB

Italian statesman and political economist. Educated at Pavia and Bologna. In exile for a time in Switzerland and in France, where he was professor of political economy at the Collége de France. Then professor of constitutional law. Was sent to Italy as French ambassador. After the revolution of 1848 he remained in Rome to become minister of the interior. Assassinated late that year at the House of Assembly. Author of several works on political economy and penal law.

Rudbeck, Olof (1630–1702) SBL

Swedish physician and writer. Educated at Uppsala where he was later professor of theoretical medicine, which also included some physics, botany, anatomy, and chemistry. Rector of the University, 1661–1662 and 1679–1680. The first part of his Utopian work, *Atland,* was published in 1679, the second part in 1689, and the third part in 1698. The fourth part was in press in 1702 but was destroyed by fire except for a few copies; and the work remained incomplete at the author's death.

Runeberg, Edvard Frederik (1721–1802) SBL

Swedish economist and author. Studied at Uppsala in 1733. Was made inspector of weights and measures in Stockholm in 1747; and held various other public offices. Head of the Academy of Science in 1757. An opponent of mercantilism.

Runeberg, Ephraim Otto (1722–1770) SBL

Swedish political economist. Younger brother of the preceding. Educated at Uppsala, then employed for a time on the construction of fortifications. Head of the Academy of Science in 1759, chief of the Finnish survey. His economic writings mark the transition from mercantilism to a greater freedom of the economy.

Sadler, Michael Thomas (1780–1835) DNB

English political economist and liberal. Went into business but turned to public affairs. Active writer and speaker on economic matters. Went to Parliament in 1829, where he identified himself with social reform, especially child labor legislation and improvement of the condition of the workers.

Sahlstedt, Abraham Magni (1716–1776) SBL

Swedish political economist and critic. Studied a number of years at Uppsala, then entered the civil service, in the national archives and other positions. Author of tracts on economic questions, and some literary works.

Saint-Pierre, abbé de (Charles Castel; 1658–1743)   BU
   French abbé and scholar. Of a distinguished family, educated at Caen, then
entered the church at the wish of his parents. Studied ethics and politics in
Paris, was elected to the French Academy in 1695 but excluded in 1718 because of writings critical of the reign of Louis XIV. Works on politics and
social institutions, directed toward improvement and reform.

Salander, Eric (1699–1764)   SBL
   Swedish industrialist and political economist. Little is known of his early
life. Active in various industries and well known in leading political circles.
Holder of official positions, and author of economic works.

Salvius, Lars (1706–1773)   SBL
   Swedish publisher, with interest in economics. Studied at Åbo, then Uppsala.
Thereafter entered public service, including the board of trade (Kommerskol-
legium). Lacked a theoretical approach but had a large practical interest in
economics, and was regarded as a spokesman for reform mercantilism. Chosen
archivist of the Academy of Science in 1739. Married into a publishing family
and himself became a prominent publisher; obtained the privilege of importing
books, and established the first real bookstore in Sweden.

Sartorius von Waltershausen, Georg F. C. (1765–1828)   SS, Pal.
   German scholar and teacher. Born at Kassel, student of theology at Göttingen, but turned to history. From 1792 was privat docent in eighteenth-
century history and in politics. Then professor of philosophy. Ennobled in
1827 by the king of Bavaria, as Baron Waltershausen. As an economist, introduced Adam Smith's doctrines to Germany. Principal works in history and
economics.

Saxe, Maurice de (1696–1750)   Chal.
   Polish-born soldier. According to D'Auvergne, he was "the eldest of three
hundred and fifty-four illegitimate sons of a king," Frederick Augustus II of
Poland. With no talent for learning and reportedly never able to spell, he
early showed great aptitude for the military life. Famed for his military ex-
ploits and at the same time somewhat notorious for his private life. In 1744
was appointed marshal of France, and in the following year defeated the
English at Fontenoy. With the ending of hostilities by the peace of Aix-la-
Chappelle (1748), he retired to the estate of Chambord, given him for his
services. His striking career has attracted biographers, most recently E. B.
D'Auvergne (*The prodigious marshal*, New York: Dodd, Mead, 1931) and
J. M. White (*Marshal of France*, New York: Rand McNally, 1962).

Say, Jean Baptiste (1767–1832)   SS, Pal.
   French economist. No information on his early life. Took no active part in
the French revolution. Appointed to office by Napoleon but incurred disfavor
through his liberalism and his *Traité d'économie politique* (1803). Lectured
on political economy after the fall of Napoleon, and late in life held the chair
in this subject at the Collége de France. Leading French economist of his time.

Schäffle, Albert Eberhard Friedrich (1831–1903)   EB, SS
   German statesman and economist. Student at Tübingen, and after 1860 was professor there of political economy. Later was at the University of Vienna. Holder of various political offices, he spent his last years in retirement and writing. Numerous writings, mainly on economic subjects.

Scheffer, Carl Fredrik (1715–1786)   SBL
   Swedish diplomat. Studied at Uppsala, then entered government service in the war department. Several years of travel and study abroad, after which he entered the foreign office. Holder of various diplomatic and other official posts, minister in Paris for about ten years. Not an ardent mercantilist, and was influenced by the physiocrats in his economic thought. Head of the Academy of Science in 1753.

Schönberg, Anders (1737–1811)   SBL
   Swedish politician and author. Educated at Uppsala, and went on to study law. Held various official positions, but because of ill health gave up his position and turned to politics and science. Member of parliament, of the Hat party.

Schröderheim, Elias (born Schröder; 1747–1795)   SBL
   Swedish official and author. Educated at Uppsala, then held various governmental positions. Raised to the nobility in 1759; enjoyed royal favor and acted as contact between king and parliament. Head of the Academy of Science in 1786.

Scrope, George Julius Poulett (1797–1876)   DNB
   English geologist and economist. Educated at Oxford and Cambridge (B.A., 1821). While on a visit to Italy, the sight of Vesuvius in an active stage gave him a deep interest in geology. Through his study of volcanic areas and his publications he achieved reputation as a geologist and became a secretary of the Geological Society. Member of Parliament, 1833–1868, where he supported free trade and social reforms. His *Principles of political economy* (1833) was his only major work in that field, but he was author of many pamphlets and came to be called "Pamphlet Scrope." Also author of many scientific papers.

Seaman, Ezra Champion (1805–1880)   App.
   American lawyer and official. Member of the bar in New York State. Was chief clerk to the comptroller of the United States Treasury (1849–1853), and later became inspector of prisons in Michigan. Editor of the *Ann Arbor Journal* (1858–1863), author of *Essays on the progress of nations* (1846).

Seckendorf, Veit Ludwig von (1626–1692)   EB, ADB
   German statesman and scholar. His father was in the Swedish service during the Thirty Years War and executed by opponents. The family was aided by Queen Christina. He studied philosophy, jurisprudence, and history at Strasbourg with support from Swedish officer companions of his father. Served the Duke of Gotha, and came into correspondence with the learned people of his time. Later retired to devote himself to a life of study and writing, but his

retirement was interrupted by various appointments, including that as chancellor of the University of Halle. Works on law and politics.

Senior, Nassau William (1790–1864)   DNB
English economist. Eldest of ten children, educated at Eton and Oxford (B.A. in 1812, M.A. in 1815). Entered the legal profession, but his interest turned toward economics and economic problems such as the poor law. Member of the Political Economy Club in 1823, was appointed Oxford's first professor of political economy (1825–1830), 1847–1852). Member of the poor law commission and was offered a knighthood for his services but declined. Master of chancery, 1836–1855, member of various commissions. His principal works were on political economy.

Seybert, Adam (1773–1825)   AB
American scientist and author. Born in Philadelphia, educated at the University of Pennsylvania, where he studied medicine. Then studied abroad, at London, Edinburgh, and other cities. After return to Philadelphia, he became member of Congress (1809–1815, 1817–1819). Had a reputation as a scientist, and was author of several learned works. Last years were spent in travel abroad, then he settled in Paris where he spent the final year of his life.

Short, Thomas (1690?–1772)   DNB
British physician, and statistician. Received medical education, and practiced in Sheffield. Is said to have made a study of water supplies in England, and wrote *A rational discourse on the inward uses of water* (1725). Major works: *New observations on the bills of mortality* (1750) and *A comparative history of the increase and decrease of mankind* (1767).

Sidgwick, Henry (1838–1900)   DNB
English philosopher and economist. A precocious student, he was educated at Rugby and Cambridge, where he won academic honors. From the classics he turned to moral philosophy and political economy, the latter under the influence of John Stuart Mill. A career of teaching and study, with major works in ethics and political economy.

Sismondi, Jean Charles Leonard Simonde de (1773–1842)   SS
Swiss historian and economist. Born of a family of French Protestant refugees in Switzerland. Educated at Geneva and entered business for a time. Went to England at the time of the French Revolution, then to Italy, where he began a long period of independent study and writing. From this period of his life came a history of the Italian republics and the incomplete *History of France*. Returned to Geneva by 1811 to continue his scholarly activities, with some involvement in politics late in life. Author of works on political economy in addition to history. See also Paul Chanson, *Simonde de Sismondi, précurseur de l'économie sociale* (1944).

Smith, Adam (1725–1790)   DNB
Scottish economist. Educated at Glasgow and Oxford. Returned to Edinburgh to continue his studies. Was elected professor of logic at Glasgow in 1751, then to the chair of moral philosophy. Travel abroad as tutor to the

young Duke of Buccleuch, and met Quesnay, Turgot, and others of the physiocrats. Appointed commissioner of custom for Scotland, rector of the University of Glasgow (1787).

Smith, Erasmus Peshine (1814–1882)   App., Pal.

American official and economist. Born in New York City, graduated from Columbia in 1832 and from Harvard Law School in 1833. Practiced law, served as newspaper editor, and briefly was professor of mathematics at the University of Rochester. Held numerous later positions: state superintendent of schools in New York, commissioner of immigration in Washington (1864), sent to Japan as advisor to the Japanese government, etc. His principal work the *Manual of political economy* (1853). He is said to have coined the word "telegram."

Smith, Thomas (fl. 1820)

No information. May be the Thomas Smith, London accountant, who wrote *An essay on the theory of money and exchange* (1807).

Soden, Julius von (1754–1831)   ADB

German official and political economist. Studied law at Erlangen, followed by Jena and Altdorf. Rose rapidly in the civil service of Brandenburg, then in the Prussian service. In 1796 resigned office and turned to a scholarly life. Had earlier produced various literary works, and after government service received academic honors, was a patron of the theater, and a prolific publisher of economic studies.

Sonnenfels, Joseph von (1735–1817)   ADB

Austrian scholar and official. His father of Jewish origin, converted to Catholicism, and given the name Sonnelfels when raised to the nobility. The son entered military service at a time of reduced family circumstances, but when the family's finances improved he studied law at Vienna. In 1763 was made professor of policy and cameral science at the University of Vienna. He retained an interest in literature and founded one or more journals that were not successful. Was in favor at court and used his influence to promote certain social causes, especially penal reform.

Steuart, James (1712–1780)   DNB

Scottish political economist. Only son of Sir James Steuart who was at one time solicitor-general of Scotland. Educated at Edinburgh, studied law, then traveled widely on the Continent as part of his education. Met and became attached to the Stuarts in exile. Returned to Scotland in 1740 but was compelled in 1745 to go into exile with the failure of the Stuart cause. Remained in exile until 1763, during which time he developed his knowledge of and views on political economy.

Stiles, Ezra (1727–1795)   AB

American scholar and clergyman. Educated at Yale, then remained in New Haven to study theology and was admitted to the Congregational ministry in 1749. Was admitted to the bar in 1753. Served in churches in Newport and Boston; in 1777 was elected president of Yale, where he served during the difficult wartime years and taught Hebrew, church history, science, and other subjects. Principal published works are collected sermons.

Storch, Heinrich Friedrich von (1766–1835)   Pal.
German-Russian economist. Born at Riga, studied at Jena and Heidelberg. After travel returned to Russia where he became professor of literature and secretary to the chancellery. Charged with instructing the grand dukes Nicolas (later tsar) and Michael in political economy. His *Cours* (1815) was based on lessons prepared for his tutees.

Sturtevant, Julain Monson (1805–1886)   AB
American teacher and clergyman. Born in Ohio, graduated from Yale in 1826, then studied theology there. In 1830 he joined the faculty of newly founded Illinois College, where he remained until 1885, teaching mathematics, natural philosophy, and astronomy, among other subjects. Served as president 1844–1876.

Sumner, John Bird (1780–1862)   DNB
English clergyman. Educated at Eton and Cambridge (B.A., 1803, M.A., 1807). Ordained in 1803 and rose through various church offices to be bishop of Chester (1828) and then archbishop of Canterbury (1848). An energetic administrator, also served as poor-law commissioner in 1834. Author of many theological works, the best known *A treatise on the records of the creation and the moral attributes of the Creator* (1816).

Süssmilch, Johann Peter (1708–1767)   Pal., ADB
Prussian army chaplain. Studied law, medicine, and theology at Halle and Jena, and served for a number of years as pastor in Berlin. His *Göttliche ordnung* (1741) brought him recognition and membership in the Prussian academy of science. For other biographical notes and an appreciation of his work, see Robert Horvath, " 'L'ordre divin' de Süssmilch," *Population*, 17(2):267–288, April–June 1962.

Temple, William (1628–1695)   DNB
English statesman. Studied at Cambridge (1644–1648) without receiving a degree. Employed in diplomatic missions after the Restoration, to Holland, then Brussels. Created baron in 1666, appointed ambassador to the Hague in 1668 and again in 1674 when he is said to have favored the marriage of William of Orange to Mary. Between diplomatic missions returned to his estates for study and writing. In 1689 he added to his household an amanuensis, Jonathan Swift, at £ 20 per year. Major works on government, the Netherlands, and English history.

Thiers, Louis Adolphe (1797–1877)   EB
French statesman and historian. Trained in law but turned toward literature. To Paris in 1821 to live the life of a writer, and at this time began his first historical works. Came to take an active part in politics, elected to the chamber of deputies, then in the finance ministry. In other ministries and became foreign minister in 1836, again in 1840. Active in the reestablishment of civil govern-

ment after the Franco-Prussian War, and chosen president of the Republic. Member of the Academy since 1834.

Thomas, Pierre Émile (1822–1880)   Pal.
French engineer. Author of *Des conditions,* in which he advocated free trade, and an earlier work, a report on a mission to the French Antilles, concerned with the development of a system of free labor following the abolition of slavery.

Thompson, Robert Ellis (1844–1924)   AB
Irish-American clergyman and economist. Born in Ireland. His family migrated to Philadelphia in 1857. Received A.B. with honors from the University of Pennsylvania in 1865. Ordained to the Presbyterian ministry in 1874. Served in various parishes, then returned to his University to teach Latin and mathematics. Was appointed professor in 1874 and given the responsibility for a new social science course; made professor of history and English literature in 1883, also served at times as librarian and chaplain. Associate of Henry Carey and his circle in Philadelphia. In 1892 he left the University with some dissension and became head of a local high school for the remainder of his active life. Principal works are textbooks on political economy and social science.

Thompson, William (c. 1783–1833)
Irish writer on economics. Born and died in County Cork, Ireland, where he lived on the income from his estate. A friend and guest of Bentham, an acquaintance of John Stuart Mill. Willed his estate for the setting up of co-operative communities, his bones to an anatomical museum. From biographical notes in Esther Lowenthal, *The Ricardian socialists,* Studies in History, Economics and Public Law, Vol. 46, No. 1, Columbia University, 1912, pp. 15–17.

Thornton, William Thomas (1813–1880)   DNB
English office-holder and writer. Born in England, lived for a time in Malta, then in Constantinople. In 1836 became a clerk in the East India House, later was in charge of public works department, and in 1858 became first secretary for public works in the India office. Had an avocation in literary work and economics. Friend of John Stuart Mill. Principal works on contemporary questions, including overpopulation.

Thünen, Johann Heinrich von (1783–1850)   Pal., ADB
German economist. Son of a landowner, he was well trained in agriculture. Became owner of an estate in Mecklenburg-Schwerin and grew famous for his management of the estate. Given honorary Ph.D. degree by the University of Rostock in 1830.

Torrens, Robert (1780–1864)   DNB
English political economist. Served with distinction in the army, including the Peninsular Campaign, and was promoted to colonel. Member of Parliament, member of various official commissions, elected fellow of the Royal Society in 1818. Principal works on political economy and on the colonization of Australia. See also Lionel Robbins, *Robert Torrens and the evolution of classical economics* (London: Macmillan, 1958).

Townsend, Joseph (*1739–1816*) DNB
English clergyman and writer. Received B.A. from Cambridge in 1762, M.A. in 1765, after which he studied medicine at Edinburgh. Then turned to theology and entered the church. Was a chaplain and rector, but is best known for his accounts of his travels. He visited many of the countries of Europe, met notable men of science, and published his observations and comments.

Tucker, George (*1775–1861*) SS
American economist. Born in Bermuda and came to the United States at about age twelve. Attended William and Mary College, later studied law and practiced in Richmond. Served in the Virginia legislature and in Congress. Was appointed to the chair of moral philosophy and political economy at the University of Virginia at the recommendation of President Madison. Retired in 1845 at the age of seventy. Author of works on political economy and a compendium of data on the United States. A recent biography: Robert McLean, *George Tucker, moral philosopher and man of letters* (Chapel Hill: University of North Carolina Press, 1961).

Tucker, Josiah (*1712–1799*) DNB
British clergyman and economist. Born in Wales, B.A. at Oxford in 1736, M.A. in 1739, D.D. in 1750. Rose through various church positions to become dean of Gloucester. While in Bristol he took the unpopular position of favoring the naturalization of foreign Protestants and Jews, but later came to be highly regarded in his parish. Principal works on economic subjects.

Turgot, Anne Robert Jacques, Baron de Laune (*1727–1791*) EB, SS
French statesman, economist. Prepared for a career in the church, and entered the Sorbonne in 1749, but soon decided to turn from theology to public affairs. Held various official posts; became acquainted with Quesnay and Voltaire, wrote for the *Encyclopedia,* and developed a great interest in economic questions. From 1761–1774 was intendant of a district of France, after which he was in succession minister of marine and comptroller-general. In the latter position he had some success in improving the national finances, but was removed from office in 1776, probably through court intrigue. The remainder of his life was passed largely in Paris in literary and scholarly pursuits. Major works on economic subjects.

Twiss, Travers (*1809–1897*) DNB
English jurist and teacher. Received B.A. from Oxford in 1830, M.A. in 1832, and other degrees in later years. In various academic posts at Oxford, studied law and became member of the bar in 1840, professor of political economy at Oxford, 1842–1847. Then held the chair of international law at King's College in London (1852–1855), followed by professorship of civil law at Oxford (1855–1870). Writings were mainly legal, with only limited attention to economics.

Ungern-Sternberg, Matthies Alexander von (*1693–1763*) SBL
Swedish officer and legislator. Service in the army, member of the Swedish parliament. Appointed general in 1751, field marshal in 1753, and enjoyed royal favor. Head of the Academy of Science in 1747.

Uztariz, Jeronimo (1670–1732)   SS
Spanish economist. No information on his early life. Known to have traveled widely in Europe, and to have held various positions at the Spanish court. In 1724 was in charge of the War and Finance offices; and received other appointments and honors.

Vauban, Sebastien Le Prestre de (1633–1707)   EB
French military engineer. Born in poverty and orphaned at an early age, he chose a military career, served with distinction, and was appointed royal engineer in 1655. Became an expert in fortifications, both in constructing and besieging them. The most famed military engineer of his day, but his prestige and his favor at court declined as one after another of his fortresses was captured during the War of the Spanish Succession. From military matters, he became interested in the related topics of finance, agriculture, and population. Is said to have taken the initiative for the first census of France in 1694. His *Dixme royale,* a proposal for taxation, was written in 1698, published in 1707, and was suppressed quite promptly with the king's disfavor, which may or may not have hastened its author's death in the same year.

Vethake, Henry (1792–1866)   AB
American economist. Born in British Guiana, brought to the United States at age four. Graduated from Columbia in 1808, then taught mathematics and geography there and studied law. Later taught at Queen's College (now Rutgers), and a number of other schools. At the University of Pennsylvania as professor of mathematics and philosophy, 1836–1855, and also served as provost. Writings on political economy.

Walker, Amasa (1799–1875)   AB
American businessman and economist. Born in Connecticut, taught school for a time and prepared for Amherst College but was prevented from entering by poor health. Went into business but maintained his academic interests, and lectured on political economy at several colleges. Also had active interest in politics, served in the Massachusetts legislature and in Congress from 1862–1863. *The Science of wealth* (1866) was his principal work.

Walker, Francis Amasa (1840–1897)   AB
American economist and statistician. Received A.B. from Amherst in 1860, then studied law before entering the Union army. Had a distinguished military career, in which he rose from private to brigadier-general, but was left with ill health after wounds and imprisonment. Became chief of the Bureau of Statistics in 1869, and superintendent of the censuses of 1870 and 1880. Professor of political economy and history at Yale, 1873–1881, thereafter president of the Massachusetts Institute of Technology. Principal publications on economics.

Wallace, Robert (1694 or 1697–1771)   DNB, SS
English clergyman. Year of birth variously reported as 1694 and 1697. To University of Edinburgh in 1711, later assistant to the professor of mathematics there. As a clergyman he held various parishes, was appointed royal chaplain for Scotland in 1744, and given an honorary D.D. by the University of Edinburgh in 1759. His two major works relate to population.

Wappäus, Johan Eduard (1812–1878)   DNB
German geographer and statistician. Handicapped by ill health all his life but studied sciences at Göttingen and Berlin. Privat docent in geography at Göttingen (1838), where he remained for forty-one years. Made professor of geography and statistics in 1845, and in his lectures included material on population. A prolific writer on geography, and through his efforts he raised the academic standing of the subject. In addition to his geographical writings, his principal work was the *Vorlesungen über allgemeine Bevölkerungsstatistik.*

Ware, Nathaniel A. (1780 or 1789–1854)   AB
American official and writer. Taught school and practiced law, settled in Natchez about 1815, and in that year was appointed secretary of the Territory of Mississippi. Acting territorial governor, 1815–1816. Advocated a plan to use cotton as basis for currency. His major work the *Notes on political economy* (1844).

Wargentin, Pehr Wilhelm (1717–1783)   SBL
Swedish astronomer and scientist. Son of a refugee from Åland, and may have acquired his interest in science from his father. Entered Uppsala in 1735 and studied mathematics and astronomy. Became widely known as an astronomer, was chosen chairman of the Academy of Science in 1748, and its secretary in 1749. Active in science, with wide correspondence abroad, but continued work in astronomy and with population statistics. His early life table was widely known outside Sweden.

Wayland, Francis (1796–1865)   AB
American clergyman and teacher. Graduated from Union College in 1813, studied medicine, then went to Andover Theological Seminary. In 1821 accepted a pastorate in Boston, in 1826 went to Union College as professor of mathematics and natural philosophy. The following year was chosen president of Brown University, a position he held for twenty-eight years of effective service to the University. Major works on political economy, "moral science," the slavery question, philosophy, and education.

West, Edward (1782–1828)   DNB
English economist and official. Graduate of Oxford (B.A. in 1800, M.A. in 1804). Member of the bar, recorder of Bombay and then chief justice there from 1823. Was knighted in 1822. Principal works on political economy.

Weyland, John (1774–1854)   DNB
English writer on population and the poor law. Educated at Oxford, then entered the legal profession. Member of Parliament, 1830–1832. Author of tracts and a larger work on the poor laws, and of *The principle of population* (1816).

Whately, Richard (1787–1863)   DNB
English clergyman and teacher. Student at Oxford (B.A. in 1808, M.A. in 1812). Entered the church and served in a parish in Suffolk for a time, then returned to Oxford in 1825 as principal of St. Albans Hall. Was Senior's tutor

and developed his interest in political economy. Was highly respected for his intellectuality; followed Senior as professor of political economy in 1829. Was appointed archbishop of Dublin in 1831, and his interests were largely clerical and theological thereafter. Principal works on logic, rhetoric, political economy, and religion.

Wicksell, Johan Gustaf Knut (1851–1926) SBL

Swedish economist and reformer. Trained in mathematics at Uppsala but took an increasing interest in social questions, and became involved in controversy on a number of issues (population, military service, teachings of the church, etc.). Was appointed docent at Uppsala, but objections were raised to his being promoted to professor because of his controversial views. The faculty, however, felt that his private opinions should not affect his appointment, and he was made professor in 1901. *Political economy* was his principal work, regarded as the first Swedish theoretical work in economics. He retired from the University in 1916 but continued his active interest in public affairs and his writing of articles for newspapers.

Williams, Edward (fl. 1650) DNB

English writer. Known only for his *Virginia truly valued* (1650).

Wilson, William Dexter, (1816–1900) AB

American clergyman and teacher. Born in New Hampshire, graduated from Harvard Divinity School in 1838. Served as minister for a time, taught moral and intellectual philosophy at Geneva divinity school (later Hobart), then was made professor of the same subjects at Cornell (1868). Works on logic, psychology, and political economy.

Winkelblech, Karl Georg (Karl Marlo; 1810–1865)

German chemist and socialist. Born near Mainz. Was not at first interested in his studies and so was put to work with a druggist. From this he developed an interest in chemistry; studied chemistry with Leibig and physics at Giessen. Became privat docent at Marburg in 1837, professor of chemistry at Kassel in 1843. Doing industrial consulting work in northern Europe as a chemist, he became deeply concerned with the condition of the workers, and from 1844 on gave increasing attention to economics and related matters. Spent five years in study of economics and political science. The first volume of his *Untersuchungen*, published under the pseudonym of Karl Marlo, appeared in 1848. In 1850 he was arrested as a revolutionist but freed. Delayed by his illness, the second volume did not appear until 1852, the third in 1856, and the fourth was incomplete at his death. In his late years was much saddened and depressed by the scant attention paid to his work. Biographical sketch given in *Handworterbuch der Staatswissenschaft* (Vol. 6, pp. 710–712). For an extended biography, see W. E. Biermann, *Karl Georg Winkelblech: Sein Leben und sein Werk*, 2 vol., Leipzig, 1909. Two doctoral dissertations on his economic thought that also gave biographical information are Erich Schirmeister, *Marlo-Winkelblech und sein Zukunftsstaat* (University of Greifswald, 1904); and Stanislaus Grabski, *Karl Marlo, Socialtheoretiker* (University of Bern, 1898).

Wirth, Max (1822–1900)
No information.

Wolff, Christian (1697–1754)   EB
German philosopher and mathematician. Educated at Jena, then taught at Leipzig, after which he was appointed professor of mathematics and natural philosophy at Halle. Political and religious pressure forced him to leave for a time, but later he was recalled, when Frederick the Great came to the throne of Prussia. Was raised to chancellor at Halle.

Wood, William (1679—1765)
No information.

Wrede, Hindric Jakob (1696–1758)   SBL
Swedish officer and statesman. Entered the army as a volunteer. Became active in politics, and served in parliament, 1738–1739. Governor of a province, 1747–1753. Had a continuing interest in economic affairs and served on various economic committees in parliament. Chairman of the Academy of Science in 1741, its president in 1742.

Yarranton, Andrew (1616–1684?)   DNB
English engineer, Apprenticed but ran away from his master. Served in the parliamentary army during the civil war, and rose to be captain. Retired from the army in 1652 and interested himself in certain canal projects. Aroused suspicion and was arrested several times in the early Restoration years, but finally was acquitted. In his later years he acted as consulting engineer for various canal and other construction projects.

Young, Arthur (1741–1820)   DNB
English agronomist and author. Left school at the age of seventeen; was apprenticed to a business firm and at the same time wrote political pamphlets and novels. In 1761 went to London and launched a monthly magazine, against the advice of Dr. Johnson. It failed. After this he made several attempts at farming, also unsuccessful, but he had more success in his *Farmer's letters to the people of England* (1767), the *Annals of agriculture* (1784–1809), a monthly journal, and accounts of his travels (*Tour of Ireland,* 1780, *Travels in France,* 1792), the latter in part an eye-witness account of the French Revolution. He has been called "the greatest of English writers on agriculture."

Author Index

Achenwall, Gottfried, 96, 409
Adelung, J. C., 103, 410
Albrecht, William, 324–325
Alcock, Thomas, 133
Alison, Archibald, 347–349, 363, 364, 365, 369, 371, 372, 375, 410
Almgren, Hans, 79
Ander, O. Fritiof, 260
Anderson, James, 147, 149–150, 204, 210, 410
Andrews, Charles M., 40
Anon., *Britannia Languens*, 59, 68, 100, 101, 140, 146, 147, 148
Anon., *England's great happiness*, 58–59
Anon., *An essay on trade and commerce*, 142
Anon., *An humble address . . .*, 58
Anon., *On the means of retaining the population*, 367
Anon., *The Planter's Plea*, 39
Anon., *The Politician's Dictionary*, 97, 105, 106
Anon., *Remarks on a late publication*, 157, 405
Arco, Gherado d', 112
Aristotle, 9, 11, 13, 16, 18, 20, 26, 27, 90, 381, 438
Arnberg, J. W., 69, 77, 410
Asp, Pehr von, 83, 85, 88, 92, 410
Atkinson, William, 366
Attwood, Thomas, 369, 410–411
Auld, J. B., 258–259
Auxiron, Claude, 119, 159, 411

Bacon, Francis, 25, 34, 40, 67, 104, 115
Bagehot, Walter, 370, 372
Baker, Herschel, 167, 325, 429
Baldwin, Loammi, 261–262, 314, 411
Barbon, Nicholas, 60, 411
Barton, John, 226, 372, 411
Bascom, John, 298–299, 301, 314, 317, 318, 412
Bastiat, Frederic, 187–188, 301, 369–370, 385, 402, 412
Baudeau, Nicholas, 98, 106, 412
Baudrillart, Henri, 247, 370, 412
Bauer, Etienne, 119
Becher, Johann, 31–32, 115, 412
Beer, George L., 3
Bell, William, 102, 116, 149, 413
Bellers, John, 65, 413
Beloch, Julius, 11
Berch, Anders, 72, 76, 79, 80, 82, 84, 90, 413, 418, 433
Bergues, Helene, 40
Berkeley, George, 99
Besold, Christophe, 31, 115, 413
Beveridge, W. L. B., 377
Bielfeld, Jacob von, 99, 103, 104, 413
Biermann, W. E., 454

Blakey, Robert, 414
Blanqui, Adolphe, 365, 413
Blodget, Samuel, 261, 413–414
Böcler, Johann, 32, 67, 414
Bodin, Jean, 17–18, 27, 29, 414
Bonar, James, 5, 41, 111, 136, 154, 225, 332
Boner, Harold, 322, 332, 442
Booth, David, 414
Bornitz, Jakob, 30–31, 33, 414–415
Botero, 17, 18–20, 111, 115, 136, 415
Bouthoul, Gaston, 10
Bowen, Francis, 296–298, 314, 315, 316, 415
Browallius, Johan, 80, 415
Breckenridge, 142
Brückner, John, 115, 124–125, 126, 128–129, 137, 138, 415
Brulons, Jacques des, 96
Brydges, Egerton, 216, 415
Buffon, 124, 126, 127, 415–416
Burgdörfer, Friedrich, 2
Burn, John, 182–183, 199, 200, 367, 416
Burns, Arthur, 242
Burton, John, 374, 416
Butel-Dumont, 100, 106

Cady, George, 313
Cairnes, John, 192–193, 201, 248–249, 257, 416
Caldwell, James, 104
Campanella, Tommaso, 41, 416
Campbell, Anna, 20
Campbell, Mildred, 3
Canard, N. F., 378
Cannan, Edwin, 4, 5, 158, 159, 160, 162, 164, 177, 223, 387, 388–391, 392, 394, 416–417
Cantillon, Richard, 114, 118, 127, 149, 417
Cardozo, J. N., 275–278, 314, 315, 317, 417
Carey, Henry, 171, 195, 286–291, 295, 296, 299, 302, 303, 305, 307, 310, 311, 314, 315, 316, 317, 318, 385, 417, 450
Carey, Mathew, 265–266, 417
Carleson, Carl, 83, 417–418
Carleson, Edvard, 71, 90, 418
Carr-Saunders, A. M., 392
Carrion-Nisas, fils, 368–369
Cary, John, 62–63, 68, 105, 418
Castro, Josue de, 298
Cauwès, Paul, 368, 374, 375
Chalmers, George, 111, 121, 418
Chalmers, Thomas, 177–178, 199, 200, 212, 418
Chanson, Paul, 447
Charles, Enid, 2
Chastelleux, François de, 119–120, 129, 418

Child, Josiah, 45, 51–52, 53, 68, 140, 418–419
Christiernin, P. N., 77, 78, 79, 419
Chydenius, Anders, 70, 75, 419
Clibborne, 259
Cock, Charls G., 26, 43, 67, 123
Coke, Roger, 52–54, 68, 419
Colton, Calvin, 294, 419
Condillac, Etienne de, 120, 150, 419
Condorcet, 134, 154, 401, 419–420
Confucius, 381
Conring, Hermann, 32, 420
Cooper, Thomas, 278–281, 314, 316, 420
Courcelle-Seneuil, Jean, 189–190, 200, 257
Coxe, Tench, 260, 420
Creighton, Charles, 20

Dahlbom, Herman, 86, 420
Darjes, Joachim, 96, 97, 103, 420
Darwin, Charles, 126, 193, 333, 361, 377
Darwin, Erasmus, 126, 377
Daugherty, Carroll, 223
D'Auvergne, E. B., 445
Davenant, Charles, 63–65, 67, 68, 72, 76, 96, 99, 101, 420–421, 440
Dawson, William, 205, 224, 421
DeBow, J. D. B., 259, 261, 421
Decker, Matthew, 141, 146, 147, 148, 421
Defoe, Daniel, 97, 101, 144–145, 146, 147, 418, 421
De Quincey, Thomas, 214, 219, 241, 421
Derham, William, 115, 126, 421–422
Destutt de Tracy, Antoine, 165–166, 354, 370, 422
Dillon, William, 249–250, 422
Dinarchus, 9
Dittmer, C. G., 122
Dobb, Maurice, 223
Doubleday, Thomas, 298, 317, 349–350, 351, 361, 364, 371, 373, 422
Douglas, Paul, 210, 223
Droz, Joseph, 175, 212, 371, 422
Dubois, Auguste, 412
Du Buat-Nançay, Louis G., 107, 422
Dugard, Samuel, 61–62, 68, 99, 422
Duhre, Anders, 78, 79, 87, 422–423
Dumont, Arsène, 359–360, 368, 423
Dunlop, John, 223
Dutens, J., 158, 213, 218, 223–224, 423

East, E. M., 2
Eden, William, 125, 423
Edmonds, Thomas, 178, 200, 344–346, 364, 371, 423
Ehrenström, Olaf, 82, 86, 423
Eisdell, Joseph, 183, 423
Ensor, George, 9, 171–172, 175, 334–336, 363, 370, 424
Estenberg, Carl, 77, 424

Everett, Alexander, 272–274, 314, 315, 353, 424
Expilly, J. J. d', 141, 148, 424

Fage, Anita, 94
Faggot, Jacob, 73, 83, 84, 85, 424
Fawcett, Henry, 247, 424, 434
Fénelon, 29–30, 68, 98, 99, 424–425
Ferenczi, Imre, 381
Ferguson, Adam, 104, 108, 116, 150, 402, 425
Florez-Estrada, Alvaro, 133–134, 179–180, 239–240, 371, 402, 425
Fontenoy, Roger de, 188, 246, 425
Forbonnais, François de, 96, 119, 160, 425
Forsman, Karl, 69, 86
Fortrey, Samuel, 50, 425
Franklin, Benjamin, 112, 116, 117, 126, 134, 141

Gardner, Edward, 132, 425
Garnier, Joseph, 354–355, 376, 406, 425
Gasquet, Francis, 20
Genovesi, 381
George, Henry, 307–309, 314, 315, 317, 318, 426
Gerstner, 385
Gide, Charles, 5
Glass, D. V., 427
Glotz, Gustav, 10
Godwin, William, 98–99, 154, 166–167, 200, 321, 325, 337–339, 341, 366, 401, 414, 426
Goldsmith, Oliver, 106
Gonnard, Rene, 5, 16, 28, 112, 118
Gottlieb, M., 381
Gottmarck, Johan, 88, 426
Goudar, Ange, 97, 98, 115, 426
Grabski, Stanislaus, 454
Grahame, James, 331–334, 363, 377, 426
Graunt, John, 45–46, 50, 55, 66, 72, 111, 363, 370, 426–427
Gray, Robert, 36–37, 44, 67, 427
Gray, Simon, 164–165, 199, 200, 326–330, 363, 364, 370, 371, 376, 385, 427
Greenwood, 45
Greg, William, 356–357, 363, 370, 427
Guillard, Archille, 354, 363, 427
Guyot, Yves, 194, 199, 249, 427

Hakluyt, Richard, 24–25, 27, 127, 427
Hale, Matthew, 49, 55–58, 66, 67, 111, 123, 124, 126, 127, 137, 427–428
Hales, John, 22, 428
Hall, Charles, 321–322, 428
Hamilton, Robert, 375, 428
Haney, Lewis H., 5
Harrington, James, 41–42, 68, 428
Harris, Joseph, 105, 428
Hawley, Frederick, 309–310, 428
Hazlitt, William, 324, 363, 385, 429, 442
Hecker, J. F. C., 20
Heckscher, Eli, 69, 92

Helvétius, Claude, 129, 142, 429
Herbert, Claude, 122, 123, 429
Hermann, Frederich, 368
Hermelin, Samuel, 79, 429
Herodotus, 8
Herrenschwand, Jean de, 120, 122, 131, 143, 429
Hertzler, J. C., 2
Hess, Ludwig von, 103
Hickson, William, 351–352, 363, 364, 370, 371, 429
Himes, Norman E., 2
Hjelt, August, 74, 76
Higgs, Henry, 119
Hobbes, Thomas, 41, 67, 115, 123, 127, 429–430
Holbach, 129, 381, 430
Holinshed, Raphaell, 23–24, 430
Holmén, Bengt, 79, 430
Hollander, Jacob H., 411
Horvath, Robert, 449
Hull, C. H., 45, 46, 47
Hume, David, 107, 112, 269, 425
Husum, Hermann von, 31
Hutchinson, E. P., 69, 260
Hutten, Ulrich von, 17

Ibn Khaldun, 15–16, 26, 27, 430
Ingram, Robert, 325–326, 365, 385, 430
Issawi, Charles, 15, 430

Jarrold, Thomas, 322–324, 363, 370, 373, 375, 376, 385, 430
Jarvis, Edward, 259–260, 430
Jennison, William, 281–282, 315, 431
Jevons, W. Stanley, 193, 248, 431
Johnson, E. A. J., 5, 94
Jones, Richard, 177, 212, 372, 373, 375, 431
Joplin, Thomas, 232, 431
Jung, Heinrich, 107
Justi, J. H. G. von, 103, 431

Kapp, Frederic, 260
Kautsky, Karl, 154, 193–194, 357–358, 364, 373, 431
Keynes, J. M., 208, 309, 407, 434
King, Gregory, 111, 431
Knibbs, G. H., 2
König, Christian, 71, 75, 431
Kryger, Johan, 73, 76–77, 82, 83, 85, 86, 87–88, 432

Laing, Samuel, Jr., 367, 372, 432
Laing, Samuel, Sr., 371–372, 432
Lansdowne, Marquis de, 45
Lau, Theodor, 94–95, 96, 101, 432
Lawson, James, 366, 368, 372, 375, 432
Lecky, W. E. H., 15
Lerner, Max, 154
Leroy-Beaulieu, Paul, 184, 194, 249, 255, 358–359, 363, 375, 432
Leslie, T. E. C., 206, 258, 286, 313, 375, 432
Lester, Richard, 223

Leuhusen, Carl, 74, 83, 432
Levett, Ada E., 20
Liljencrantz, Johan, 84, 433
List, Friedrich, 183–184, 199, 433
Locke, John, 60–61
Longfield, Mountifort, 376
Lotz, Johan, 376

Machiavelli, Niccolo, 16–17, 22, 27, 34, 127, 433
Macvicar, John, 377
Mahdi, Muhsin, 15, 430
Malthus, Thomas R., 3, 12, 19, 27, 56, 67, 92, 103, 109, 119, 131, 136, 160–161, 163–164, 167–168, 169, 177, 179, 188, 198, 205, 206, 208–209, 210, 212, 214, 215, 216, 220–221, 225, 227–231, 233, 238, 253, 254, 256–257, 262, 264, 273, 275, 279, 291, 311, 314, 325, 328, 335, 337, 365, 366, 377, 390, 391, 395, 402, 404, 407, 438, 442
Malynes, Gerard, 37–38, 67, 68, 123, 433, 437
Mandeville, Bernard de, 114, 123, 145, 433
Mangoldt, Hans von, 190–191, 247, 433–434
Mann, Theodore, 115, 120, 130, 139, 143, 434
Marlo, pseudonym; see Winkelblech
Marshall, Alfred, 3, 196–197, 202, 251–252, 254, 391, 402, 406, 407, 434
Marx, Karl, 190, 407
McCulloch, John R., 50, 59, 105, 112, 136, 172–174, 180, 199, 216–218, 219, 221, 232–235, 255, 256, 274, 343–344, 381, 402, 434, 442
McLean, Robert, 451
McLeary, G. F., 423
McVickar, John, 274–275, 314, 417, 434
Megnet, Franz, 435
Melish, John, 261, 434
Melon, Jean-François, 101, 118, 434–435
Mennander, Carl, 75, 80, 84, 87, 435
Messance, 124, 125, 127, 148, 209, 435
Mill, James, 170, 172, 210, 231–232, 435
Mill, John Stuart, 164, 196, 199, 200, 201, 204, 238, 242–245, 249, 252, 253, 255, 256, 286, 301, 309, 314, 350, 381, 382–384, 387, 389, 394, 403, 405, 432, 434, 435, 447
Mirabeau, Marquis de, 96, 106, 115, 118, 119, 139, 141, 149, 435, 441
Misselden, Edward, 38, 435–436, 437
Mitford, William, 10
Moheau, 98, 100, 117, 436
Mohl, Robert von, 5, 103
Molinari, Gustav de, 373, 436
Montchrétien, Antoine de, 29, 67, 105, 436
Montyon, 436
Moore, Adam, 43
More, Thomas, 18, 22, 27, 34, 436

Moreton, Augustus, 346–347, 363, 364, 368, 375, 436
Möser, Justus, 130, 142–143, 436
Mullett, Charles, 20, 28
Mun, Thomas, 50–51, 437
Myrdal, 2

Necker, Jacques, 96, 107, 129–130, 142, 437
Negley, Glenn, 40
Ness, Gayl D., 406
Newman, Samuel, 284–285, 316, 437
Nitti, Francesco, 5, 360–362, 363, 365, 373, 375, 437
Nordencrantz, Anders, 71, 81, 88, 437

Oncken, August, 119
Opdyke, George, 294–295, 437
Orrelius, Magnus, 81
Ortès, Giammaria, 113–114, 134, 138, 139, 438
Osborn, Fairfield, 2

Paley, William, 107, 113, 121, 150–151, 255, 402, 438
Parr, Samuel, 167
Passy, Hippolyte, 184, 199, 372, 438
Patrizzi, Francesco, 16, 438
Patten, Simon, 212, 312–313, 315, 317, 438
Perry, Arthur, 299–301, 317, 438
Petander, Karl, 69, 82
Petty, William, 45, 46–50, 55, 66, 68, 72, 84, 100, 111, 127, 146, 363, 382, 427, 438–439
Petyt, William, 59, 439
Philips, Erasmus, 96, 439
Phillips, Willard, 282, 315, 439
Pirenne, Henri, 407
Place, Francis, 371, 439
Plato, 11–13, 16, 18, 26, 27
Plomgren, Thomas, 83, 439
Plumard de Dangeul, 96, 127, 141, 439
Plutarch, 9
Pölitz, Karl, 174–175, 385, 440
Polhem, Christopher, 70, 71, 83, 84, 87, 90, 440
Pollexfen, John, 65–66, 68, 440
Postlethwayt, Malachy, 96, 106, 440
Potter, Alonzo, 292, 440
Power, Eileen, 21
Price, Bonamy, 369, 440–441, 443
Priestley, Joseph, 278, 420
Proudhon, P-J., 373, 374, 377, 441
Pufendorf, Samuel von, 32, 441
Purves, George, pseudonym; see Gray, Simon

Quesnay, François, 119, 127, 435, 441, 448, 451
Quetelet, Adolphe, 378, 441

Rae, John, 283–284, 314, 441
Raikes, Henry, 366

Raleigh, Walter, 25, 34–35, 67, 115, 123, 442
Ramsay, George, 181–182, 200, 213–214, 241, 442
Rau, Karl, 211, 236–237, 442
Ravenstone, Piercy, 171, 199, 200, 339–341, 442
Raymond, Daniel, 262–265, 314, 315, 317, 442
Read, Conyers, 22
Read, Samuel, 211, 238–239, 442
Ricardo, David, 160, 161–162, 165, 166, 168, 169, 170, 172, 177, 188, 196, 200, 205–206, 207–208, 209, 210, 212, 215, 216, 224–226, 227, 238, 242, 253, 275, 279, 281, 309, 314, 382, 390, 402, 417, 421, 435, 442
Ricci, Lodovico, 133–134, 139, 443
Rickards, George, 188, 353–354, 370, 371, 373, 375, 443
Ridolfi, Roberto, 433
Robbins, Lionel, 198, 381, 388, 389, 391, 394, 450
Roberts, Lewes, 38, 443
Rodbertus, Johan, 246, 443
Rogers, James E., 191–192, 247–248, 256, 368, 369, 374, 443
Rooke, John, 210, 443
Roscher, Wilhelm, 3, 5, 17, 31, 103, 186–187, 246, 385, 386, 443–444
Ross, E. A., 2
Ross, J. C., 209–210, 218, 221–222, 235–236, 341–342, 363, 370, 444
Rossi, Pellegrino, 368, 444
Rothschild, K. W., 223
Rousseau, 381
Rudbeck, Olaf, 80, 86, 444
Runeberg, Edvard, 74–75, 77, 78, 79, 80, 83, 84, 85, 89, 444
Runeberg, E. O., 74, 77–78, 79, 84, 86, 89, 444
Russell, Josiah, 20, 407
Ruyer, Raymond, 40

Sadler, Thomas, 176, 183, 200, 342–344, 353, 363, 371, 376, 444
Sahlstedt, Abraham, 91, 444
Saint-Pierre, Abbé de, 95, 96, 102, 445
Salander, Erik, 72, 77, 86, 445
Salvius, Lars, 90, 445
Sartorius von Waltershausen, Georg, 215, 445
Sauvy, A., 94
Saxe, Maurice de, 95, 111, 445
Say, Jean-Baptiste, 158, 175–176, 199, 216, 223, 256, 369, 373, 445
Schade, Louis, 259–260
Schäffle, Albert, 247, 369, 375, 446
Schauman, Georg, 69, 72, 422
Scheffer, C. F., 91, 446
Schirmeister, Erich, 454
Schönberg, Anders, 83, 84, 446
Schröderheim, Elias, 81, 446
Scrope, G. P., 179, 200, 292, 446

Seaman, Ezra, 293–294, 446
Seckendorf, Ludwig von, 32–33, 67, 103, 446–447
Seligman, 210
Senior, William Nassau, 180–181, 200, 218–219, 240, 255, 429, 447
Seybert, Adam, 261, 447
Shah, Khushal, 9
Short, Thomas, 112, 447
Shryock, Richard, 320
Sidgwick, Henry, 194–196, 199, 200, 201, 250–251, 253, 387–388, 447
Sismondi, 336–337, 371, 373, 447
Smith, Adam, 110, 112, 117, 120, 130, 143, 145, 154, 167, 177, 179, 228, 233, 283, 284, 327, 389, 441, 447–448
Smith, E. P., 295–296, 315, 448
Smith, Thomas, 376, 448
Soden, Julius von, 158, 448
Sonnenfels, Joseph von, 95, 96, 98, 102, 104, 116, 448
Sotiroff, George, 411
Spann, Othmar, 5, 184
Spencer, Herbert, 290, 352–353, 361, 363, 370, 375
Spengler, J. J., 3, 5, 15, 94, 160, 313, 381
Stangeland, Charles E., 3, 5, 12, 16, 17, 31, 32, 107, 115, 130, 131
Steuart, James, 99–100, 116–117, 120, 121, 126, 127–128, 136, 137–138, 142, 150, 160, 256, 328, 348, 368, 402, 448
Stiles, Ezra, 113, 448–449
Storch, Henri, 172, 449
Strauss, E., 45
Sturtevant, Julian, 306–307, 315, 316, 449
Sumner, John, 366, 376, 385, 449
Süssmilch, Johann, 104, 112, 123, 449
Swift, Jonathan, 54, 133, 449

Tawney, R. H., 21
Temple, William, 45, 54–55, 67, 68, 76, 84, 97, 99, 100, 102, 147, 449
Thiers, Louis, 186, 449–450
Thomas, Émile, 372, 375, 450
Thompson, Robert, 302–303, 314, 317, 450
Thompson, William, 371, 450
Thornton, William, 350–351, 364, 371, 373, 450
Thünen, Johann von, 174, 210, 221, 236, 237–238, 450
Torrens, Robert, 160, 163, 168–169, 200, 205, 206–207, 209, 212, 215, 220, 224, 225, 227, 255, 256, 382, 402, 450
Townsend, Joseph, 112, 114, 121, 131, 133, 135, 138, 139, 451
Trevelyan, G. M., 24
Tucker, George, 261, 266–272, 314, 315, 316, 317, 318, 381, 451
Tucker, Josiah, 97, 100, 147, 451
Turgot, 141, 147, 159, 419, 448, 451

Turner, John, 313
Twiss, Travers, 376–377, 451

Ungern Sternberg, Mathias von, 82–83, 91, 451
United Nations, 381, 395, 400
Urquhart, William, 377
Utterström, Gustav, 92
Uztariz, Geronimo, 95, 452

Vauban, 29, 30, 452
Veblen, Thorsten, 378
Vethake, Henry, 291–292, 314, 316, 317, 452
Vogt, William, 2
Voltaire, 108, 451
Vose, George L., 411

Wadström, C. B., 91–92
Wagner, Adolf, 391
Walker, Amasa, 301–302, 317, 452
Walker, Francis A., 301, 303–306, 314, 316, 318, 452
Wallace, A. R., 377
Wallace, Robert, 112, 135, 137, 324, 452
Walras, Antoine, 245–246
Wappäus, Johann E., 5, 453
Ware, Nathaniel, 292–293, 314, 316, 317, 453
Wargentin, Pehr, 73–74, 78, 84, 87, 88–89, 433, 453
Wayland, Francis, 285–286, 453
Wermel, Michael, 160, 223
West, Edward, 160, 162–163, 200, 206, 210, 215, 382, 390, 453
Weulersse, Georges, 119
Weyland, John, 165, 330–331, 363, 372, 376, 453
Whately, Richard, 176–177, 199, 366, 453–454
Whitbread, Samuel, 367
White, Frederic R., 40
White, J. M., 445
Whittaker, Edmund, 210, 381
Wicksell, Knut, 210, 391–392, 454
Wicksteed, 181
Willcox, W. F., 45
Williams, Edward, 39–40, 68, 454
Wilson, William, 310–312, 314, 317, 454
Winkelblech, Karl, 355–356, 385–387, 454
Wirth, Max, 189, 200, 375, 455
Wohlin, Nils, 92
Wolfe, A. B., 381
Wolff, Christian, 103, 106, 381, 455
Wolfgang, Marvin, 261, 434
Wood, William, 99, 455
Wrede, Hindric, 78–79, 455
Wörd, Sebastian von, 17

Yarranton, Andrew, 58, 68, 455
Young, Arthur, 105–106, 125, 131, 133, 142, 145, 455

Subject Index

Age structure, 191
Agriculture, and population growth, 162–163; productiveness, 162, 184, 185, 188
American population, 112, 113, 155, 171, 188, 266–267, 273, 282, 338–339, 340, 343
American viewpoint, 258, 262, 282, 286, 292, 294, 295, 313–319

Balance, of population and subsistence, 179, 192, 201, 216, 325, 327, 358, 373; of production and consumption, 167–168, 198, 354, 396; of trade, 38, 59, 70, 82, 84, 85, 144, 232; see also Ecological balance

Cameralist doctrine, 33
Capital, in American political economy, 315; circulating, 226, 229, 241; and labor demand, 161, 166, 280–281, 299; productiveness of, 163, 220; relative to population, 169, 170, 171, 172, 197, 220, 221, 222, 231, 236, 239, 254, 286, 288–289, 295, 299, 309, 370; and rent, 211; trend of, 225; and trend of returns, 170, 178, 188, 195, 196, 220, 313, 345, 395–396; and wage level, 143–144, 166, 228, 229–230, 231, 236, 239, 241, 244, 286, 309
Capital accumulation, conditions for, 313, 396; effects of, 206, 228, 229, 237, 247, 249, 264, 281, 283, 287, 291, 309–310, 370, 406; profits and, 240; relative to population 296, 406
Capital punishment, 47, 65, 103
Celibacy, 122, 123, 124, 127, 134, 179, 305, 334, 335, 375
Census recommended, 18, 43, 262
Checks, 17, 19, 27, 35, 37, 38, 44, 57, 67, 114, 122–125, 126, 130, 137, 155, 156, 176, 180, 182, 273, 278, 293, 298, 313, 326, 329, 335, 336, 338, 339, 341, 345, 351, 352–353, 370, 401; artificial wants, 372; see also Wants; automatic, 173, 317, 322, 324, 332, 358, 361, 363, 370, 401; childhood mortality, 332–333; cities, 122, 125, 156, 269, 311, 317, 326, 331, 348, 363; civilization, 303, 317, 323, 359, 385, 401; disease, 16, 17, 34, 37, 39, 43, 44, 57, 122, 123, 125, 126, 156, 270; education, 278, 298, 317; famine, 34, 37, 39, 43, 44, 57, 123, 125, 129, 168, 173; high standard of living, 178, 194, 256–257, 264–265, 271, 293, 345; individual development, 290, 317, 318; intellectual development, 303, 317, 370; manufactures, 302; positive, 16, 155, 156, 157, 194, 244; poverty, 16, 171; preventive, 155, 156, 157, 189,

194, 244, 256, 277, 355; prosperity, 337; struggle for existence, 137; war, 17, 27, 37, 38, 39, 43, 44, 57, 123, 125, 126, 129; see also Prudential restraint
Cities, as check, see Checks; growth of, 45; growth of demographic consequences of, 122, 125, 156, 269, 311, 317, 326, 331. 348, 363; growth of, economic consequences of, 48–49, 85; progress aided by, 281; rural origin of dwellers, 302
Civilization, 1, 54, 269, 296, 310, 313, 321–322, 334, 338, 352, 353, 359, 375, 376, 385; cause of population growth, 322–323; and growth of wants, 246; from population growth, 47, 102, 179, 267, 303, 310, 312, 314, 318, 322–323, 327, 328, 346–347, 357; and preventive check, 189, 317, 346, 362, 363, 368, 372, 401
Class structure, 321–322, 327, 330, 333–334, 345, 346–347, 349–350, 363, 365; behavior differences and, 368
Clergy, members of, 139, 151
Colonies, 10, 11, 19, 22, 25, 30, 35, 36, 37, 38, 39–40, 44, 45, 51–53, 64, 66, 91, 101–102, 169, 183, 186, 192
Consumption level, see Level of living
Cost of living, 85, 248; affected by population, 54; greater in cities, 134; influence on population, 243–244; influence on wages, 141; stimulus from, 54
Crime, check to population, 19; result of population growth, 1, 25, 27, 37, 44, 67, 127, 129, 130; result of prudential restraint, 179
Customs, influence of, 255, 368–370, 401–404; influence of, on level of living, 228, 348, 353, 369; influence of, on population size, 149–150, 223, 236, 256, 265, 293, 368–369, 375; influence of, on wage level, 223, 224, 231, 233, 237, 243–244, 245, 247, 249, 291, 316, 369; marital, 291; see also Social variables

Defense, see Military aspect
Density of population, advantages of high, 46–47, 48–49, 55, 67, 75–77, 97, 98, 108, 183, 185, 186–187, 195, 263, 265–266, 267, 268, 281, 282, 292–293, 308, 310–311, 312, 314, 336, 346; disadvantages of high, 268, 387; disadvantages of low, 100; effects on agriculture, 162, 273, 303, 387; and happiness, 268–269; influence on population, 343–344, 354, 363; stimulus of high, 54, 63, 89, 267; and value of land, 49, 55, 146, 211, 264, 310; and wages, 306

Depopulation, 2–3, 51, 80–81, 107, 111, 118, 186, 288, 359; economic effects of, 275
Diet, and population size, 150, 270, 271, 348, 368–369
Dilemma of population theory, 6–7, 11, 19, 93, 381
Disease, 124; as checks, *see* Checks; from overpopulation, 34, 37, 137
Division of labor, 48–49, 68, 85, 163, 168, 171, 175, 179, 183, 186, 190, 267, 273, 274, 281, 306, 308, 311, 314, 336, 382
Doubling, period of, 46, 49, 89, 111–114, 137, 172, 180, 266–267, 331, 337, 340

Ecological balance concept, 56–57, 115, 124, 126, 137, 139, 290, 318, 354
Economic development, stimulus to, 38, 42, 47, 52–53, 55, 59, 62, 68, 75, 77, 83, 100, 102, 109, 273; *see also* Stimulus
Education, as check, *see* Checks; as preventive of overpopulation, 297, 313; and prudential restraint, 278, 298, 317, 363, 367; and rise of wants, 291–292
Emigration, 75, 90, 92, 101, 125, 183, 186, 191–192, 205, 310, 332, 359; check to population growth, 19; does not reduce population, 176, 343, 354; economic effects of, 60; other causes for, 58, 80, 106, 141; policy, 99; population pressure and, 10, 11, 12, 17, 32, 34, 35, 36, 41, 43, 67, 118, 126, 131, 169, 345, 348; right to, 32
Enclosures, 20–24
Eugenic views, 41, 333, 357
Euthanasia, 125
Evolution, 377

Fertility, influences on, 318, 323–324, 342–343, 344, 357, 361, 364, 370–375; comfort, 346; cultural advancement, 311, 323, 351–353, 357, 359; economic situation of people, 361, 371; education, 359, 367; food supply, 183, 298, 318, 327–328, 344, 346, 349, 351, 364; individual development, 290, 317, 318, 353, 361–362, 368, 375; longevity, 375; mental, 46, 303, 323–324, 329, 335, 352–353, 357, 366, 370; physical labor, 329, 342, 352, 371, 374; social factors, 367–370, 372; uncertainty, 336; urbanization, 331, 372
Fertility differential, inverse, 305, 317–318, 333, 334, 344, 347, 354, 357, 363–364, 367, 401; consequences of, 333–334, 345; explanations for, 265, 297, 298, 318, 324, 333, 335, 336, 349, 350–351, 354, 361, 363–364, 368, 373–374

Food prices, 18, 63, 147, 148, 168, 207, 209, 210, 213, 237, 244, 247, 248–249, 291; *see also* Prices
Food supply and population, 90, 104, 121, 164, 176, 183, 298, 327, 344, 349–350, 354, 361, 364, 376; *see also* Subsistence limit

Geometric increase, 56, 57, 67, 103, 111, 113–114, 137, 138, 175, 180, 182, 194, 278, 296, 298, 301, 302, 325, 337, 343
Greek thought, 4, 8–13, 245
Growth of population, 73, 75, 77, 85, 86, 94, 96–97, 100, 184, 186, 188, 191, 245, 261, 274, 282, 314, 322–323, 335, 368, 375; conditions favoring, 277, 294, 297, 309; consequences of, 129, 159, 168, 178, 179, 246, 255, 267, 273, 274, 275, 281, 287–288, 303, 313, 322–323, 326–330, 332, 335–336, 347–348, 355, 358–359, 383, 387, 389, 406; consequences of, for distribution, 101, 148, 206, 209, 211, 214, 217, 230, 231, 236, 237–238, 244–245, 247, 248–249, 250, 270, 291, 308, 341; dietary change and, 270, 271; with growth of food supply, 91, 118, 120, 121, 137, 155, 223, 232, 246, 276, 301; with growth of capital, 166, 206–207, 208, 222, 224, 225, 230, 231–232, 244–245, 276; population density and, 354; undesirable, 91

Happiness, 30, 73, 75, 78, 79, 86, 104, 106, 107, 108, 134, 135, 165, 261, 267, 268, 326–327, 332, 334, 343

Immigration, 31, 32, 51, 53–54, 58–59, 61, 64, 83, 116, 260, 265, 267, 273, 282, 286, 319, 338, 340; influence on native population, 142; influence on wages, 142, 247; Walker theory, 303, 305–306
Indian thought, 9
Individual vs. national interest, 14, 33, 106, 144, 151
Infant mortality, as check, 130; increased by overpopulation, 130
Infanticide, 124, 127
Invention, 40, 55, 63, 68, 75, 84, 174, 178, 184, 188, 189, 193, 195, 199, 200, 218, 248, 283, 291, 314, 345
Ireland, 63, 266, 284, 335, 342, 350
Iron law of wages, *see* Wages, subsistence theory

Labor supply, lag in adjustment, 226–227, 233–234, 396
Land, value of, 40, 49, 53, 59, 61, 63, 68, 146, 148, 186, 205, 291; *see* Rent
Laws of population, 257, 290, 293–294, 297–298, 303, 307, 308, 327–329, 330–331, 332, 341, 343, 346, 348, 351–352, 358, 361–362, 378, 408; civilization, 307, 323, 358, 359, 375;

existence of laws doubted, 190, 330, 358; density factor, 343, 354; food supply and fertility, 183, 298, 327, 344, 346, 351; government, type of, 331; individual development, 308, 353, 360; security of position, 297–298; social capillarity, 360, 361; species endangered, 349

Level of living, 165–166, 249, 254, 293, 298, 324, 362; affected by population size, 16, 149, 157, 227, 249, 293, 400; affects population size, 116, 118, 120, 149–150, 152, 190, 240, 256, 348, 350, 368–369, 402–403; change of, 233–234, 284, 369; custom and, 84, 149–151, 223, 224, 228, 233, 237, 353, 369; e-fects of, 82, 369; group differences in, 116; inverse relation to fertility, 183, 354, 361, 370, 371; resistance to change of, 368; and wage level, 227–228, 284, 292, 316; *see also* Standard of living

Life cycle of nations, 16, 113, 338, 348–349, 352

Limitation of numbers, by land supply, 91, 118, 128, 176; by subsistence, 8, 19, 32, 35, 41, 44, 66, 67, 104, 115–117, 121, 172, 176, 336, 341; motives for, 61; need for, 166; *see also* Checks, Prudential restraint, Food supply

Luxury, 81, 92, 122, 125, 134, 151, 156, 235, 269, 326, 327, 334, 352, 370

Malthus, precursors of, 89, 92, 109, 111, 115, 118, 122, 133, 136–139, 149

Malthusian theory, 4, 89, 92, 151, 154–158, 194–195, 196, 198, 199, 248, 252, 259–260, 306–307, 360; acceptance of, 165, 180, 182, 183–184, 189, 192, 247, 274, 278–280, 291, 304, 314, 355, 391; rejection of, 164, 175, 176, 179, 182, 183, 188, 190, 191, 193, 239, 241, 247, 249–250, 258, 264, 269, 289, 294, 295, 296, 300, 301, 302, 303, 307, 312, 314, 320, 322, 324, 325, 328, 334–335, 337–338, 339–340, 341, 342–343, 351, 357, 358, 359

Marginal analysis, 174, 210, 213, 216, 218, 219, 220, 221, 237

Marriage, age of, 43, 114, 279–280, 304, 305, 325, 329, 335, 345, 363, 368, 371; evils of postponement, 325, 333, 335; right of poor to, 356

Maximum population, 150, 403

Mercantilism, 3, 17, 28, 33, 38, 50, 55, 58, 59, 61, 63–64, 65, 67, 71, 72, 77, 78, 82, 92, 95, 106, 110, 140, 144, 145–146, 150, 151, 261

Middle class, role of, 18

Migration, internal, 262

Military aspect, 4, 8, 9, 14, 16, 26, 32, 48, 66, 70, 95, 97, 108, 261; defense, 11, 12, 21, 23, 31, 48, 63–64, 70, 72, 74, 76–78, 84, 93, 95, 97, 104, 288, 293

Money, purchasing power of, 85

Moral restraint, 156, 157, 173, 181, 186, 196, 278, 283–284, 341, 345, 351, 361, 373

National strength, 1, 7, 8, 14, 17, 25, 26, 28, 29, 30, 31, 33, 38, 50, 51, 52, 54, 58, 59, 60, 61, 63, 64, 67, 70, 72, 73, 74, 75, 76–77, 78, 79, 89, 90, 94, 95, 96, 97, 98, 105, 108, 179, 186, 261, 265; economic, 94; *see also* Natural strength

National wealth or prosperity, 13, 16, 18, 29, 38, 46, 47, 50, 51, 53, 54, 58, 59, 61, 63, 64, 65, 67, 71–72, 73, 75, 78, 86, 95, 96, 101, 105, 108, 146, 165, 173, 176, 183, 184, 186, 189, 246, 261, 267, 281; promotes populousness, 96, 119, 175, 189, 245; promotes pruden-tial restraint, 180

Natural resources, 22, 31, 70, 83, 86, 87, 88, 89, 90, 98, 103, 108, 121, 132, 179, 193, 200, 261

Natural strength, 76, 77, 78

Needs, *see* Wants

Netherlands, 54, 58, 63

Optimum population, 11, 104, 268, 342–343, 381–393, 394, 397–398, 405–406; exceeded, 181, 195, 199; stabilization at, 308–309, 318, 343, 403

Overpopulation, 127, 136, 290, 350, 358, 365, 385, 388, 389, 392, 401; causes of, 185–186, 239, 331, 358; conse-quences of, 17, 24–25, 27, 34, 36, 37, 39, 67, 90–91, 123, 125–132, 138, 186, 193, 229–230, 266, 281, 285, 334, 357, 385, 386; fear of, 1–3, 16, 17, 24–25, 27, 32, 33–34, 67, 90, 91, 125–132, 135, 184, 187, 201, 274, 302, 311, 313, 325, 380, 406–407; prevented by checks, 129, 173, 348; prevented by higher standard of living, 178, 369, 371; remote or improbable, 174, 194, 202, 239, 254, 293, 312, 322, 332, 354, 397

Physiocrat theory, 80, 106, 119, 327

Policy, 355–356; for control of numbers, 11, 13, 22, 26, 41; and wages, 86; populationist, *see* Populationist policy

Political arithmetick, 28, 45, 66

Political stability, 13, 18, 24, 27, 36, 37, 39, 44, 66, 67

Political viewpoint, 9, 13, 15, 17, 18, 27

Poor relief, 10, 25, 92, 133, 134, 135, 136, 146, 169, 215, 216, 292, 356; cause of population growth, 281; en-courages prudential restraint, 348; pre-vents action of checks, 139

Populationist policy, 6, 9, 14, 18, 29, 30–31, 32, 33, 42, 50, 54, 65, 70, 94, 95, 98, 99, 102, 103, 106, 107, 110, 326

Populousness, 107; advocated, 96, 293; causes of, 102, 106, 335, 363; effects of, 84, 90, 100, 102, 335, 363; *see also* Stimulus

Poverty, 122, 179, 335; manufactures sign of, 322; not from overpopulation, 18, 167; from overpopulation, 13, 16, 17, 24, 27, 36–37, 44, 55–56, 58, 67, 73, 90–91, 110, 119, 127, 129, 130, 131, 132, 136, 138, 152, 163, 180; from underpopulation, 51, 58, 63; from unequal distribution, 264, 307; of workers, advantages of, 81, 132, 144

Power of increase, 56, 67, 111–115, 124, 131, 136, 137, 138, 170–171, 172, 175, 180

Price, 18, 60, 76, 82, 85, 101, 145, 174, 211, 214–219, 237, 244, 270–271; of commodities, 58, 63, 68, 82, 84, 85, 147, 148, 306, 331; of food, *see* Food; natural and market, 216; of necessities, 54, 68, 85, 275; opposite influences on, 215, 217–218, 219; of raw materials, 169, 217–218

Price theory, cost of production, 160, 214, 215, 218, 219; marginal, 216, 218, 219, 305; population growth, 214; supply and demand, 60, 152, 160, 214, 216–217, 263, 291, 398, 399

Production, advances in methods of, 177–178, 191, 194, 200, 221, 245, 247, 249, 254, 283, 287, 383, 395–396; counteract diminishing returns, 163, 174, 178, 185, 186, 193, 199, 218, 291; and population growth, 266, 276; and prices, 213; and profits, 221, 245; and rent, 209, 245; and wages, 236, 245, 270; *see also* Progress

Productive element, 65, 77, 105, 175, 191, 198

Productivity, 163, 197, 198, 199, 200, 202, 246, 270, 273, 301, 309–310, 386, 394, 395–396, 397, 402–403, 405, 407; capital and, 178, 240, 299; falls as population grows, 155, 195, 221, 251; and production costs, 85; rises as population grows, 85, 89, 197, 274, 303, 308, 314, 340, 384; and wages, 249, 270; *see also* Returns

Profits, and capital accumulation, 240, 288–289; marginal analysis of, 220, 221, 237; rate of, 85, 168, 174, 205, 206, 209, 219–222, 240, 243, 244, 245, 246, 291, 299, 317, 396; and wage level, 220, 230

Progress, 176, 352, 374–377, 378–379; and checks to population, 125, 137; influence of population on, 165, 173, 183, 315, 330; technological, 396–397, 406; *see also* Production, advances in methods of; *see also* Stimulus to progress

Providence, trust in, 87, 88, 99, 110, 173, 183, 300–301, 325, 344, 366, 384–385, 401; *see also* Religion, viewpoint of

Prudential or voluntary restraint, 32, 133–135, 136, 138, 152, 171, 173, 179, 189, 192, 212, 239, 243, 270, 290, 301, 302, 304, 317, 324, 325, 332, 335, 336, 341–342, 354, 359, 363; alternatives to, 368; education and, 278, 298, 317, 363; inverse relation to status, 178, 257, 290, 293, 346, 371–372; motivation for, 289, 305, 335, 341–342, 345, 348, 351, 367–368, 372, 373–374, 375; public opinion and, 367, 403–404; skepticism about, 179, 272, 283

Quality of population, 35, 38, 51–52, 67, 77, 78, 79, 104–105, 109

Ratios, the Malthusian, 155, 157, 158

Religion, viewpoint of, 4–5, 15, 27, 365–366

Rent, 49, 68, 86, 101, 141, 145–147, 152, 177, 204–214, 244, 245, 246, 291, 296, 302, 305, 308, 310; and consumer preferences, 214; and density of population, 146, 310; *see also* Land, value of

Rent theory, density of population, 211, 214, 264, 275; food prices, 213; marginal analysis, 210, 213, 243; net return on land, 209, 211, 212, 213, 246, 247, 275–276; Ricardian, 147, 177, 205, 207–208, 209–210, 214, 218, 247, 252, 253, 286, 299, 305, 313, 399; Ricardian, rejected, 191, 204, 211–213, 246, 247, 248, 249–250, 258, 272, 275–276, 282, 287–288, 298, 299, 303, 306, 312, 315, 316–317; supply and demand, 214, 271–272, 306, 310, 317

Returns, 88, 89, 109, 121, 176, 177–178, 200, 316; constant, 30, 89, 109, 121, 176, 177–178, 200, 316, 322, 391; diminishing, 158–164, 165, 166, 170, 172, 173–174, 175, 178, 180, 182, 185, 186, 188–189, 193, 194, 195, 196–197, 199, 200, 203, 205, 206, 207, 208, 209, 210, 211, 212, 213, 215, 217–218, 220, 221, 224, 225, 230, 231, 238, 241, 242, 244, 250, 251, 252, 253, 263, 291, 298, 299, 303–304, 305, 311, 345, 381, 388, 390, 395, 396, 398, 399, 405; diminishing denial of, 167, 177, 178, 179, 188–189, 212, 246, 254, 275, 287, 301, 312, 315; increasing, 68, 77, 85, 89, 99, 168, 171, 195, 196, 252, 273, 287, 288, 296, 308; maximum, 390; opposite influences on, 163, 168, 169, 174, 181, 184, 187–188, 189, 195, 196–197, 200–201, 215, 248, 291, 382–384, 395, 397

Ricardian rent theory, *see* Rent theory

Roman thought, 6, 13–14

Science, ideas from, 290–291, 295, 377
Self-sufficiency, national, 96
Sex ratio, 45, 344
Slavery, 80, 271, 335
Social mobility, upward, 333–334, 352, 360, 361; and form of government, 360
Social variables, and fertility, 367–370; *see also* Fertility; and population size or trend, 149–151, 368, 403; and wage level, 223, 224, 228, 236; *see also* Checks, Customs, Prudential restraint
Social viewpoint, 106, 109, 110, 145
Society, nature of, and population growth, 277; population a condition for, 31, 42, 78, 85; types of, 313; Malthusian, neo-Malthusian, 257, 408
Standard of living, 84, 194, 241, 244, 249, 257, 271, 299, 353, 354, 359; affects wage level, 250, 256, 304, 370; effects of high, 178, 257, 290, 293, 346, 359; and prudential restraint, 178, 244, 363, 367–368; and overpopulation, 178, 369, 403
Stationary population, 4, 10, 12, 13, 22; disadvantages of, 186; economic effect of, 275, 406; family size for, 239–240
Stimulus given by population, to economic development, 38, 42, 48, 52, 53, 54–55, 59, 83, 95, 96, 97, 100, 101, 102, 118, 121–122, 129, 146, 165, 200, 262, 274, 293, 310–311, 314, 326–327; to effort, 54–55, 58, 59, 62, 63, 68, 75, 76, 77, 82, 84, 85, 89, 99–101, 102, 109, 116, 121, 133, 176, 187, 188, 234–235, 246, 267, 279, 314, 330–331, 376, 377; to progress, 173, 177–178, 187, 189, 267, 270, 273, 302, 330–331, 347, 352, 355, 360–361, 376; *see also* Economic development, Populousness
Subsistence limit, 117, 122, 128, 130, 131, 135, 136, 150, 154, 155, 156, 158, 263, 268, 271, 277, 312, 341; remote or nonexistent, 87, 121, 134, 179, 186, 277, 285, 295, 296, 300, 336–337, 345; tendency of population to approach, 117–122, 137, 138, 175, 188, 239, 283, 298; *see also* Food supply

Taxation, 48, 122, 341; per capita, 47, 68, 84, 96
Technological progress, *see* Invention, Production, Progress

Underpopulation, 2–3, 20, 70, 79, 81, 88, 89, 187, 388; consequences of, 64, 74, 76, 80, 83, 94, 100, 385, 386
Unemployment, 122, 182, 183; from overpopulation, 131
Urban-rural differentials, cost of living, 134; fertility and mortality, 19, 45–46; growth rate, 45; natural increase, 134
Urbanization, *see* Cities, Checks
Utopias, 22, 40–42, 66, 80, 374; and population control, 12, 20, 135

Volksvermehrung, 33, 47, 103, 104

Wage theory, capital-population ratio, *see* Wage theory, supply and demand; marginal productivity, 237, 241; production cost of labor supply, 231, 253–254, 276, 284, 285, 370; productivity, 225, 238, 241, 248, 250, 270, 291, 304, 315–316; residual, 248, 250; subsistence or "iron law," 61, 138, 140, 141, 143, 144, 152, 203, 223, 233, 238, 240, 247, 249, 271, 346, 396, 399–402; subsistence or "iron law," amended customary comforts included, 246, 254, 280, 316, 369, 399; supply and demand, 52, 65–66, 85, 140, 141, 142, 143, 144, 145, 152, 224–225, 226, 228, 231, 232, 236, 237, 238, 240, 241, 243, 246, 263, 270, 271, 280, 284, 291, 298, 299, 315, 398, 399; wage fund, 143, 144, 226, 228, 229, 231–232, 239, 240, 241, 243, 246, 249, 250, 285–286, 299, 304, 309, 315, 350
Wages, 52, 59–60, 65–66, 68, 76, 82, 85, 86, 129, 170, 205, 222–242, 244–245, 246, 247, 249, 251–252, 253, 263, 266, 273, 276, 295, 298, 308, 315–316; affect labor supply, 140, 142, 143, 144, 240; affected by cost of living, 141, 148, 223–224, 225, 236, 237, 239, 241, 243, 247, 306; and capital accumulation, 206–207, 223, 225, 229–230, 237; and capital supply, 237, 240, 241, 306; cost of production and, 85, 221; high, advantages of, 144–145, 212, 234–235, 237; high, stimulus to population, 237, 251; influence of customs on, 236, 245, 256, 280, 291, 304, 306; influence on population, 142, 143, 145, 148, 240, 309; influence on prices, 141, 147, 216; and level of living, 224, 228, 231, 237, 250; natural and market level of, 223, 224, 225–226, 227–228, 232–233, 235–236, 239, 256, 280, 303, 316; and profits, 220, 240; proportion of total product, 235, 250, 280; real, 88, 221, 225, 226, 229, 230, 232, 244, 245, 246, 270, 277, 285, 304, 316; subsistence or minimum level of, 236–237, 263
Wants, 60, 264, 294, 314, 328, 352, 369, 375; changeability of, 187, 228, 233–234, 235; in civilized society, 189, 246; conditions favoring growth of, 291–292, 311; effects of growth of, 245, 247; imaginary or artificial, 149, 265, 269, 317, 318, 348, 363, 372; natural, 150; and population size, 150; pre-

Wants (*cont'd*)
  ventive of excessive population, 291; relative nature of, 150, 151, 353; unlimited extent of, 222
War, justification for, 22, 34, 57; preventive of overpopulation, 34, 36, 38, 43, 44, 57, 90, 114, 156; result of overpopulation, 1, 19, 27, 34, 41, 44, 49, 57, 67, 118, 135, 137; *see also* Checks

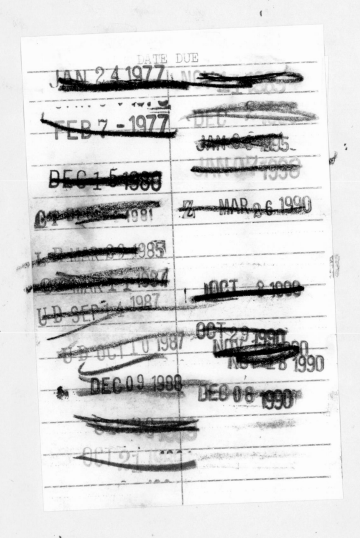